S0-AJX-929

A TREASURY OF
MISSISSIPPI RIVER
FOLKLORE

A TREASURY OF
MISSISSIPPI RIVER
FOLKLORE

Stories, Ballads & Traditions
of the Mid-American River Country

EDITED BY B. A. BOTKIN

Foreword by Carl Carmer

AMERICAN LEGACY PRESS • NEW YORK

Copyright © MCMLV by B. A. Botkin

All rights reserved.

This edition published by American Legacy Press, distributed
by Crown Publishers, Inc., 225 Park Avenue South, New York,
New York 10003.

Manufactured in the United States of America

LIBRARY OF CONGRESS CATALOGING IN PUBLICATION DATA
Main entry under title:

A Treasury of Mississippi River folklore.

   Reprint. Originally published: New York : Crown, 1955.
   Includes index.
   1. Folklore—Mississippi River Valley.   2. Mississippi River Valley
—Social life and customs.   3. Mississippi River—Folklore.
I. Botkin, Benjamin Albert, 1901–   .
GR109.T74   1984   398.2'0977   84-19133
ISBN 0-517-641372

h g f e d c b a

COPYRIGHT ACKNOWLEDGMENTS

The editor and publishers wish to thank the following authors or their representatives, folklore and historical societies, publishers and publications for their kind permission to use material in this book. Full copyright notices are given on the pages on which the material appears.

The American Folklore Society, Inc.; The American Name Society; Appleton-Century-Crofts, Inc.; Badger State Folklore Society; Robert O. Ballou; Ruth Bass; Carleton Beals; Mrs. Roark Bradford; Burton Publishing Company; Cincinnati *Times-Star;* The Arthur H. Clark Company; William E. Clement; Columbia University Press; Robert L. Crager & Company; Capt. Joe Curtis; The John Day Company, Inc.; Dodd, Mead & Company; Dorrance & Company, Inc.; Doubleday & Company, Inc.; Duell, Sloan & Pearce, Inc.; E. P. Dutton & Co., Inc.; The Filson Club; H. T. Fitz-Simons Company; Paul Flowers; Funk & Wagnalls Company; Lee Furman; Joe Glaser (for Louis Armstrong); S. G. Grandjean (for Leon H. Grandjean); Greenberg, Publisher; Harcourt, Brace and Company, Inc.; Harper & Brothers; Harvard University Press; Hastings House; Henry Holt and Company, Inc.; Houghton Mifflin Company; The Illinois State Historical Society; Indiana Historical Bureau; The Iowa State Department of History and Archives; Arthur S. Johnson (for Clifton Johnson); Philip D. Jordan; Arthur A. Knopf, Inc.; George W. Lee; Library of Congress (Folklore Section); Little, Brown & Company; Mrs. Ruby Terrill Lomax; Louisiana State University Press; A. C. McClurg & Co.; McGraw-Hill Book Company, Inc.; The Macmillan Company; The McQuiddy Press; Harold Matson (for James H. Street); Memphis *Commercial Appeal;* Missouri Historical Society; William Morrow & Company, Inc.; *The New York Times;* The Ohio Historical Society; Outlet Book Company; E. Dudley Parsons, Jr. (for E. Dudley Parsons); Pelican Publishing Company; Ross Phares; Press of Tribune Publishing Company; G. P. Putnam's Sons; Julian Lee Rayford; Rinehart & Company, Inc.; Jay Sanford (for Ben Lucien Burman); Murray Schumach; Charles Scribner's Sons; Mrs. Clarence R. Skinner (for estate of Mrs. Ada B. Skinner); Southeastern Folklore Society; Stanford University Press; State Historical Society of Iowa; State Historical Society of Missouri; State Historical Society of Wisconsin; Charles D. Stewart; Tiptonville Lions Club; Jean Thomas; Twin City Printing Company; University of Alabama Press; University of Chicago Press; University of Illinois Press; University of Minnesota Press; University of Texas Press; D. Van Nostrand Company, Inc.; The Viking Press Inc.; Mrs. Leonard H. Wells (for Leonard H. Wells); Isabel H. Williams (for Watauga Press); Yale University Press.

CREDITS FOR ILLUSTRATIONS APPEARING ON: p. 1, "The Way They Travel in the West," from *Davy Crockett, American Comic Legend,* edited by Richard M. Dorson (New York, Rockland Editions, 1939); p. 51, "And the pilot has got to know all about it," from *Partners of Providence,* by Charles D. Stewart (New York, The Century Co., 1907); p. 195, from *Forty Years a Gambler on the Mississippi,* by George H. Devol (New York, George H. Devol, 1887); p. 263, "Flood at Cairo," from *Midwest Heritage,* by John Drury (New York, A. A. Wyn, 1948); p. 299, "The Keelboat," from *Underground,* by Thomas W. Knox (Hartford, J. B. Burr, 1876); p. 381, "The Mississippi at High Water," from *Travels at Home,* by Mark Twain (New York, Harper, 1910); p. 453, "Smoke and Gossip," from *Life on the Mississippi,* by Mark Twain; p. 493, "The Run of the *Robert E. Lee," ibid.;* p. 555, "The Parting Chorus," *ibid.*

An exhaustive effort has been made to locate all persons having any rights or interests in material, and to clear reprint permissions. If any required acknowledgments have been omitted or any rights overlooked, it is by accident and forgiveness is desired.

Down the Yellowstone, the Milk, the White and Cheyenne;
The Cannonball, the Musselshell, the James and the Sioux;
Down the Judith, the Grand, the Osage, and the Platte,
The Skunk, the Salt, the Black, and Minnesota;
Down the Rock, the Illinois, and the Kankakee
The Allegheny, the Monongahela, Kanawha, and Muskingum;
Down the Miami, the Wabash, the Licking and the Green
The Cumberland, the Kentucky, and the Tennessee;
Down the Ouachita, the Wichita, the Red, and Yazoo—
Down the Missouri, three thousand miles from the Rockies;
 Down the Ohio, a thousand miles from the Alleghenies;
Down the Arkansas, fifteen hundred miles from the Great Divide;
 Down the Red, a thousand miles from Texas;
Down the great Valley, twenty-five hundred miles from Minnesota,
 Carrying every rivulet and brook, creek and rill,
Carrying all the rivers that run down two-thirds the continent—
 The Mississippi runs to the Gulf.
        —PARE LORENTZ, *The River*

Foreword

Ben Botkin was one of the most indefatigable researchers in the field of Americana and in this volume of Mississippi River lore he has made use of his gifts to the top of their bent. It takes more than plodding scholarship to arrive triumphantly at the end of so comprehensive a collection as is here presented. It takes an imaginative skill equal to that of a truly great detective and, added to that, a kind of special intuition to run down so vast and entertaining a group of tales, anecdotes, descriptive passages, songs, little-known bits of history, as Mr. Botkin put together in the laudable effort to give his readers ample evidence from which to draw their own conclusions about the social history of the big river which flows through the heart of our Midwest.

Mr. Botkin tried for more than size and more than entertainment, however, in this remarkably contrived composite photograph of a great watershed. His anthology will be welcomed by thoughtful American readers who have sought time and again for adequate explanations of the mental processes current in the age of roar and gusto that succeeded the periods of discovery and settlement. Historians have been inclined to accept the period of brawl and boast at its literal or face value or to regard it with disdain as neither funny nor significant. The precise and precious among interpreters of our literary and social progress have deplored our admiration of the "sublimated roughneck" as it has appeared in our writings from the days of Leatherstocking to contemporary times. By placing selections from the works of the early nineteenth century creators of this school, such as Davy Crockett, side by side with paragraphs by such eminent adherents of it as Mark Twain and such contemporary exponents as Ben Lucien Burman, Richard Bissell, Harnett Kane and others, Mr. Botkin proved the vitality of the succession and the right of the tradition to a serious critical consideration which American aesthetes sometimes try to deny it. Botkin provides such a mass of first-rate materials for consideration that reappraisals based upon them may confidently be made and should be encouraged.

I would add a final note to these comments and hope that I will not be accused of chauvinism when I suggest that it be that of a bugle. The reading of this hefty tome made up of narratives from the uninhibited pens of hundreds of independent Americans aroused in me a swelling pride of country. From early times the inhabitants of the Mississippi valley have found hardship the material of humor, have exercised their fancies by straight-faced recountals of impossible adventures, have felt a jubilant and healthy consciousness that to them, by right of environment, has befallen the especial duty of carrying on American tradition and protecting a hearty untrammeled way of life which in other sections of the country might be hampered by the effete, the regimented, the dissatisfied. Such sentiments exist as well in other areas of this vast nation but few of our citizens would deny these river-dwellers the gift Mr. Botkin presented them—"their night to howl."

CARL CARMER

Acknowledgments

In the preparation of this book I have been indebted to many persons, some of whom I have corresponded with, but most of whom I have consulted and interviewed personally, especially during a month's field trip in May, 1955, in Illinois, Missouri, Tennessee, Louisiana, Alabama and Ohio. In addition to advising and assisting me in research, many of them have suggested, loaned or contributed material. For their kindness and helpfulness, I am particularly grateful to the following:

John Allen, Southern Illinois University, Carbondale; Paul Angle, Chicago Historical Society; Capt. Roy L. Barkhau, Mid-West Navigation, Inc., St. Louis, Mo.; Elizabeth Baughman, Chicago Historical Society Library; Arna Bontemps, Fisk University Library, Nashville, Tenn.; Mrs. Roark Bradford, Santa Fe, N. M.; Lester B. Bridaham, Louisiana State Historical Museum, New Orleans, La; Harold E. Briggs, Southern Illinois University; Dee Brown, University of Illinois Library, Urbana, Ill.; Gerald H. and Lettie Gay Carson, Millerton, N. Y.; Jack Conroy, Chicago, Ill.; Capt. Dave Cook, U.S. Steamer *Mississippi*, Memphis, Tenn.; Capt. Joe Curtis, *The Commercial Appeal*, Memphis, Tenn.; Peter Decker, New York City; Howard Duncan, Corps of Engineers, U.S. Army, Mississippi River Commission, Memphis District, West Memphis, Ark.; Evan Esar, New York City; John T. Flanagan, University of Illinois; Margaret A. Flint, Illinois State Historical Society Library; Paul Flowers, *The Commercial Appeal*, Memphis, Tenn.; Katharine Q. Griffith, East St. Louis, Mo.; W. C. Handy, New York City; Jesse W. Harris, Southern Illinois University; Barnard Hewitt, University of Illinois; Stewart H. Holbrook, Portland, Ore.; Alice P. Hook, The Historical and Philosophical Society of Ohio, Cincinnati; Donald D. Jackson, University of Illinois Press; Moritz Jagendorf, New York City; Dr. S. Charles Kendeigh, University of Illinois; Benjamin F. Klein, The Picture Marine Publishing Co., Cincinnati; George and Rae Korson, Washington, D.C.; Edith S. Krappe, Southern Illinois University; George W. Lee, Memphis, Tenn.; William McDaniel, Nashville, Tenn.; Franklin J. Meine, Chicago, Ill.; Capt. J. W. Menke, *Goldenrod Showboat*, St. Louis, Mo.; Mamie Meredith, University of Nebraska, Lincoln, Neb.; Carey Moore, Cossitt Library, Memphis, Tenn.; Ralph Henry Newman, Abraham Lincoln Bookshop, Chicago, Ill.; Pageant Book Co., N. Y. C.; Cyrus E. Palmer, University of Illinois; Julian Lee Rayford, Mobile, Ala.; Gene Rose, Ossining, N. Y.; Margaret Ruckert, New Orleans Public Library; Marilyn Satterlee, University of Illinois Library; Margaret Scriven, Chicago Historical Society Library; Dr. V. F. Shelford, University of Illinois; Dr. Hurst Hugh Shoemaker, University of

Illinois; Charles Edward Smith, New York City; Grace Partridge Smith, Carbondale, Ill.; Charles van Ravenswaay, Missouri Historical Society, St. Louis; Sylvester L. Vigilante, New York Historical Society, New York City; Warren S. Walker, Blackburn College, Carlinville, Ill.; Helen M. Welch, University of Illinois Library; Martha G. Westfeldt, New Orleans Public Library; Capt. Donald T. Wright, *The Waterways Journal*, St. Louis, Mo.

Special thanks are due to the staffs of the following libraries:

Chicago Historical Society; Cincinnati Public Library; Columbia University Library; Cossitt Library, Memphis, Tenn.; Croton Free Library; Field Library, Peekskill, N. Y.; The Historical and Philosophical Society of Ohio; Library of Congress, especially the Archive of American Folk Song; Louisiana State Historical Museum; Missouri Historical Society; New Orleans Public Library; New York Historical Society; New York Public Library, especially the American History, Local History and Genealogy, and Music Divisions, and the 58th Street Music Library; Ossining Public Library; St. Louis Public Library; University of Illinois Library (where I was the first outside scholar to consult the newly purchased Franklin J. Meine American Humor and Folklore Collection); White Plains Public Library.

The staffs of *The Commercial Appeal*, Memphis, Tenn., and *The Waterways Journal*, St. Louis, Mo., were most hospitable and accommodating, as were the officers of the Illinois Folklore Society and the Corps of Engineers, U.S. Army, Mississippi River Commission, Memphis District.

Portions of my interview with Capt. Joe Curtis were published in the Summer, 1955, issue of *Manuscripts*, the quarterly publication of the Manuscript Society.

For assistance in preparing the manuscript and seeing it through the press, I am indebted to my wife, Gertrude F. Botkin, to Kathryn Pinney, Carolyn Wood, and members of the editorial and production staffs of Crown Publishers, Inc.

Contents

II. RIVER CONQUERORS, FIGHTERS AND TRICKSTERS

III. STAR PERFORMANCES

PART THREE: PIRATES, OUTLAWS AND SHARPERS

PART FOUR: OLD DEVIL RIVER

PART FIVE: RIVER BOATS AND RIVERMEN

Introduction

At the heart of America's myth of the Great Open Spaces lies the mid-American legend of the Great Waters. To Western distance, scale and magnitude the many waters have added movement, flow, rhythm—the natural rhythm, in Constance Lindsay Skinner's words, "moving the pioneer life of America forward." Not inappropriately, then, were the rivers flowing into the Gulf of Mexico christened the "Western rivers," in the days when Midwest was West, and the rivers we now know as Western had not yet become a part of the United States. "One more river to cross"—the Allegheny, the Cumberland, the Ohio, the Mississippi, the Missouri—each has marked a successive stage of the frontier.

To those who decided to go on, the Missouri became the dividing line between East and West. Beyond were mountains and Indian country, furs and gold, the Oregon, Santa Fé and California trails. But for those who stayed, who built homes and towns by the river and refused to leave even when flooded and drowned out, the Great Central Valley became the valley of democracy—the crossroads and forcing ground of North, East, South and West.

As such—as a way of life rather than a mere highway—the river country has had its greatest impact on the American character and folk imagination.

The result of the mixture has been diversity rather than unity. The river country feels no such regional solidarity and loyalty as, say, the South or the Southwest. With the people of the Upper Mississippi, the people of the Lower Mississippi have little in common save the river. By reason of history and tradition, St. Louis considers itself a Missouri river town. The Delta country of southeastern Missouri is quite different from the Delta country of Mississippi and Louisiana. And Bayou country is distinct from Delta country. The Delta plantation heritage of cotton and slavery is a world apart from the pioneer homestead pattern. Southern Indiana and Illinois are Southern in culture as well as in name. The Hoosier is a blend of Northern and Southern.

Diversity is the keynote of the river country—the ethnic diversity of Anglo-Saxon, French, Indian, Negro, German, Scandinavian and other elements; the economic diversity of Furs, Lumber, Wheat, Corn, Hogs, Cattle, Cotton, Tobacco, Sugar, Oil; the diversity of transportation, with the Fur Trader, the Voyageur, the Raftsman, the Keelboatman, the Captain and the Pilot taking their place in the galaxy of American heroes beside the Miner, the Logger, the Cowboy and the Sodbuster. From frigid Lakes and North Woods to semi-tropical Gulf, the river country has also been a region of extremes and sharp contrasts and violent changes.

In all this diversity the shifting, meandering rivers have played a dual role, as protagonist and antagonist of man, as "Father of Waters" and "Old Devil River," as fertile "American Bottom" and dirty "Great Sewer." In their battle with the river, men became like the enemy they fought, now deceptively calm and quiet, now rebellious, rampaging and roaring. This dualism is inherent in the river. wilderness, in clearing which men conquered the rivers but not always themselves.

Fortunately for folklore, the river country liberated the imagination and loosened the tongues of men so that good (as well as tall) talk and stories flowed like water.

If the Lower Mississippi region has been richer in what is commonly known and accepted as folklore—folk belief, folk speech, folk song, folk tale—that is because folklore has always been at home in the South, where it is close to the soil and rooted in tradition. At the same time the Upper Mississippi and Missouri country has been rich in another kind of lore, the epic of the fur trade and the Indian Wars, whose heroic spirit is the "outcome of a society cut loose from its roots, of a time of migrations, of the shifting of populations."

But there are subtler and more complex sub-regional variations—in tradition and folkways. Though the Yankee cult of thrift and hard work, love of comfort and improvements, has dominated a "Yankee state" like Ohio, the rivers themselves encouraged a kind of easy-going shiftlessness close to the subsistence level, which fitted naturally into the Southern pattern of taking things as they come but, above all, taking them easy. And for this sort of existence, the drifting, floating life of the river was admirably suited, from the days of the raftsmen and flatboatmen, with their floating homes, shops and "towns," to the latter-day shantyboat people, river rats and swamp angels.

At the beginning of the nineteenth century, the Mississippi was for Americans what Timothy Flint called an "ultima Thule—a limit almost to the range of thought." By the end of the century it had quickened the American Dream with the Golden Age of Steamboating. Today, when the giant rivers are pretty well tamed and harnessed, there are fewer and fewer old-time captains and pilots left to remind us of the river giants of yesterday and the day before yesterday as they recall the dreams that never die in the stories that never die. In the fabulous empire of the river country as seen in the Mississippi panorama of this book, folk story is close to folk life and folk history, and the ways of the river folk are never very far from the ways of the river.

B. A. BOTKIN

Croton-on-Hudson, N. Y.

PART ONE

With a Touch of the Snapping Turtle

Introduction

A Creole gentleman of New Orleans once challenged a French savant to a duel in order to vindicate the honor of the Mississippi. The Chevalier Tomasi had published a dogmatic and dictatorial article on the hydraulics of the river, and when the Creole suggested that what was applicable to the smaller European rivers could not apply to so mighty a stream, the Frenchman said with a sneer: "How little you Americans know of the world! Know that there are rivers in Europe so large that the Mississippi is a mere rill, figuratively speaking." "Sir," replied the Creole in anger, "I will never allow the Mississippi to be insulted or disparaged in my presence by an arrogant pretender to knowledge."

With equal ardor and considerable humor the superiority of one river over another has been upheld by the defenders of the Ohio, the Missouri and the Mississippi—*La Belle Rivière*, Big Muddy, and Father of Waters (the last from a Frenchman's mistranslation of the Indian name, *Mis-ipi*, as *vieux Père des Rivières*). Thus adherents of the Missouri argue that their river (which should be called the "Missourissippi") is not only longer than the Mississippi but the longest in the world; that the Mississippi empties into the Missouri instead of vice versa; and that after their confluence the Missouri refuses to associate with the Mississippi. "But of course after a while it gets used to it and mixes up. It makes it all muddy, and is satisfied." In *Life on the Mississippi* Mark Twain similarly maintains that the Ohio doesn't like to mix with the Mississippi, and even after the two meet, the Ohio keeps a wide band of clear water all the way down the east side for a hundred miles or more.

The very mud of the Mississippi is nutritious, according to the "Child of Calamity," and a man that drinks it could grow corn in his stomach if he wanted to. The health- and life-giving properties of Ohio, Mississippi and Missouri river water have been the subject of numerous jokes and yarns. So have the crookedness and trickiness of the Mississippi, with its bends making it crookeder and longer and its cut-offs straightening and shortening it. To many, the Missouri is the trickiest and cussedest of rivers—so cussed that Missouri mules are said to get their cussedness from drinking its water.

The Missouri river steamboats have also learned a few tricks from the river, being so light in draft that they can run on a heavy dew. Like the rivers and the boats, the men of the river country have had to be tricky and tough to survive—half horse, half alligator, with a touch of the snapping turtle, a crossing of the wildcat, and a sprinkling of the steamboat, the earthquake, and crooked snags. So, in the lexicon of the West (Bartlett's *Dictionary of Americanisms*, 1859), a "hoss" was a "man remarkable for strength and courage, etc.," was akin to a "steamboat," "a dashing, go-ahead character." Musing on the big-fish-eat-little-fish law of survival on the river, Mike Fink observes, "I've seen trout swallow a perch, and a cat would come along and swallow the trout, and perhaps, on the Mississippi, the alligators use up the cat, and so on to the end of the row."

But all rivalry, competition and conflict are forgotten in times of "hell and high water," which create a bond of unity not only among flood victims, because they are all in the same boat, but also between men and wildlife, as in the case of the shrimp fishermen who prefer hunger to eating fish trapped in a half-submerged shed because "them fish are fighting for their lives, same as us." Even the widely assorted crew of a dirty little Monongahela coal boat like the *Coal Queen* learn to get along with one another and with the river in the group adjustment necessitated by a "stretch on the river."

Yankees and Southerners together settled the Mississippi Valley; and in their combined heritage Yankee grit, thrift and ingenuity have met and merged with Southern neighborliness, hospitality and ability to "make do or do without." The result has been a dynamic democracy of social energy and adaptability, folk fantasy and humor, the like of which has never been known and probably never will be known again.

B. A. B.

The Saltless Mississippi

The Mississippi! the great big rollin', tumblin', bilin', endless and almost shoreless Mississippi! There's a river for you! I don't care what John Bull may say, or any other ruffle-shirt feller, about their old castles with their bloody-murder legends. I tell you the United States is a great country! There ain't nobody but Uncle Sam as could afford such a river as that! Where *in* airth so much water comes from I can't think! Why, it might set in and jest rain from January tu July and it couldn't make a mud-puddle half as big at wun eend. I'll tell you what I guess about it: you see the jography books tell about the almighty grate Gulf-stream as runs up along the coast, and is lost near where they catch mackerel!—wal, it strikes me it just sinks down there in a hole and biles up agin on this side the mountains, where it's pushed thro' sich a tight place as squeezes all the salt out. . . .

From "A Blow-up on the Mississippi!" by Yankee Doodle, Esq. *The Spirit of the Times,* a Chronicle of the Turf, Agriculture, Field Sports, Literature and the Stage, edited by William T. Porter, Vol. XIV (August 24, 1844), No. 26, p. 302. New York.

Consolidated Aggregation of Rivers

There is a heap more goes down the Mississippi than ever goes up it again, and that sets you a-thinking. On some rivers you think a good deal about the scenery, but when you're floating down this river you don't think of nothing but the Mississippi. Some ways I hain't treated this river quite fair. But I guess I give it just as much credit as most people do right at the first. I'll tell you how it is. You see there is the Missouri coming in above St. Louis, and it is more rivers put together than you would take time to count up; and it joins the Upper Mississippi, which brings along a lot of pretty fair rivers; and they take in the Ohio, which is made up of the Monongahela and the Allegheny and takes in the Muskingum and the Little Kanawha and the Great Kanawha and the Big Sandy and the Scioto and the Kentucky and the Wabash and the Cumberland and the Tennessee and others; and there comes in the Arkansas, which is two thousand miles long itself and is only second to the Missouri and takes in more streams than anybody would have patience with; and there comes the Red River, in partners with the Wichita—there ain't no use to tell about the St. Francis and the rest, because when I looked on the map it had me beat. Besides them main ones there is a lot of second-class rivers that go right into the lower Mississippi for themselves, like the Obion and the Hatchie and the Yazoo and the Big Black—the map is wormy with them.

Well, the Mississippi is all them put together. It gets deeper and swifter and widens out sometimes and gets narrower sometimes; and when you see it you just give it a look and think it is a pretty fair wide river. It does it so easy it fools you. But when you have lived on it and laid around on it with nothing else to do, and when you have seen how it can swallow up a river and not notice it, and when you begin to see how many solid square miles of water is going past every hour, it gets worked into your head and soaked right down into you that this here is the Mississippi . . . the Consolidated Aggregation of Rivers.

That Remarkable River Water

I [1]

. . . Captain Barney . . . every evening before supper lowers a tin bucket into the muddy river, and, when it is filled, drinks the thick brown fluid

From *Partners of Providence*, by Charles D. Stewart, pp. 258–259. Copyright, 1907, by The Century Co. New York.

[1] From *Big River to Cross,* Mississippi Life Today, by Ben Lucien Burman, p. 24. Copyright, 1938, 1939, 1940, by Ben Lucien Burman. New York: The John Day Company.

until every drop has vanished. "Keeps my health a-going good," he drawls lazily. "It's this here filtering and all these fancy fixings they do to the water that causes all the sickness there is nowadays. Just takes all the strength out of it."

II [2]

"Talk about filters," said a Cincinnatian; "just drink a quart of Ohio river water, and stand in the sun for five minutes, and you will find the water coming out of every pore, beautifully filtered, while your stomach becomes converted into a sand bag, and you can hear the gravel rattle as you walk."

III [3]

. . . Visitors, particularly foreign ones, were impressed by the decidedly muddy color of the water [of the Missouri and Mississippi Rivers] and also by the apparent relish with which the natives drank it. Some of them, such as Francis Pulszky who accompanied Louis Kossuth to St. Louis in 1851, were tactless enough to ask why the water wasn't filtered before using it for drinking purposes. He was told that "We are such *go-ahead people* that we have no time to filter our water." Less polite was the answer given a woman traveler on a Missouri River steamboat who asked the Captain why the water—so charged with sand and mud—was supposed to be healthful. Poised with paper and pencil to record his answer, she was probably silenced by the Captain's glare and "Because it scours out your bowels, Ma'am."

Burdette on the Missouri River

The dust blows out of the Missouri River. It is the only river in the world where the dust blows in great columns out of the river bed. The

[2] From *Pat Rooney's Quaint Conundrums and Funny Gags,* p. 65. Copyright, 1879, by Clinton T. DeWitt. New York.

[3] From "Notes of a Missouri Rambler," by Charles van Ravenswaay, *Bulletin of the Missouri Historical Society,* Vol. III (October, 1946), No. 1, p. 8. St. Louis: The Missouri Historical Society.

If one believes what he reads, the river water *was* of remarkable purity. T. M. Easterly, the distinguished St. Louis daguerreotypist, said that the captain of the packet ship *Mississippi,* on which he was traveling from New York to New Orleans in 1844, told him that the water they were using was Mississippi River water which had been taken on at New Orleans on a previous trip, carried to Liverpool, and now, on the return voyage, was still fresh. The Captain also told Easterly that Mississippi River water would keep longer at sea than any other water known to seafaring men. This so intrigued Easterly that he made a number of tests in St. Louis. One sample he kept more than 17 years and reported it "still clear, pure and sweet."—C.V.R.

By Robert J. Burdette. From *Gems of Modern Wit and Humor,* with Stories and an Introduction by Robert J. Burdette, Containing All that is Best in the Literature

catfish come up to the surface to sneeze. From the great wide-stretching sandbars on the Kansas shore great columns of dust and sand, about two thousand feet high, come whirling and sweeping across the river and hide the town, and sweep through the train and make everything so dry and gritty that a man can light a match on the roof of his mouth. The Missouri River is composed of six parts of sand and mud and four parts of water. When the wind blows very hard it dries the surface of the river and blows it away in clouds of dust. It is just dreadful. The natural color of the river is seal-brown, but when it rains for two or three days at a time, and gets the river pretty wet, it changes to a heavy iron-gray. A long rain will make the river so thin it can easily be poured from one vessel into another, like a cocktail. When it is ordinarily dry, however, it has to be stirred with a stick before you can pour it out of anything. It has a current of about twenty-nine miles an hour, and perhaps the largest acreage of sandbars to the square inch that was ever planted. Steamboats run down the Missouri River. So do newspaper correspondents. But if the river is not fair to look upon, there is some of the grandest country on either side of it the sun ever shone upon. How such a river came to run through such a paradise is more than I can understand.

Why the Missouri Is the Longest River in the World

The Missouri is the longest river in the world, and the Mississippi is only a branch of it. The Mississippi River joins its current with that of the Missouri about two hundred miles above the mouth of the Ohio; consequently, as we are now to allow the largest stream [the Missouri] to bear its name from its source all the way to the Gulf of Mexico, it follows that the Ohio flows into the Missouri and not into the Mississippi River. The Missouri, and *not* the Mississippi, is the main stream of what has been called the Mississippi Basin. The Missouri, when taken from its fountain-heads of the Gallatin, Madison, and Red Rock lakes, or, if we take the Jefferson Fork as the principal tributary, has a length, from its source to its union with the Mississippi, of above three thousand miles. The United States Topographical Engineers have credited it with a length of two thousand nine hundred and eight miles, when divested of some of these tributary extensions. The same good authority gives the Mississippi a length of thirteen hundred and thirty miles from its source to its junction with the Missouri.

of Laughter of All Nations, pp. 367–368. Copyright, 1903, by L. G. Stahl. [No publisher or place.]

From *Four Months in a Sneak-Box*, A Boat Voyage of 2600 Miles down the Ohio and Mississippi Rivers, and along the Gulf of Mexico, by Nathaniel H. Bishop, pp. 119–121. Copyright, 1879, by Nathaniel H. Bishop. Boston: Lee and Shepard, Publishers.

At this junction of the two rivers, the Missouri has a mean discharge of one hundred and twenty thousand cubic feet of water per second, or one-seventh greater than that of the Mississippi, which has a mean discharge of one hundred and five thousand cubic feet per second. The Missouri drains five hundred and eighteen thousand square miles of territory, while the Mississippi drains only one hundred and sixty-nine thousand square miles. While the latter river has by far the greatest rainfall, the Missouri discharges the largest amount of water, and at the point of union of the two streams is from fifteen to seventeen hundred miles the longer of the two. Therefore, according to natural laws, the Missouri is the main stream, and the smaller and shorter Mississippi is only a branch of it. From the junction of the two rivers the current, increased by numerous tributaries, follows a crooked channel some thirteen hundred and fifty-five miles to the Gulf of Mexico. The Missouri, therefore, has a total length of four thousand three hundred and sixty-three miles, without counting some of its highest sources.

The learned Professor A. Guyot, in a treatise on physical geography written for *A. J. Johnson's New Illustrated Family Atlas of the World*, informs us that the Amazon River, the great drainer of the Eastern Andes, is three thousand five hundred and fifty miles long, and is the longest river in the world.

According to the figures used by me in reference to the Missouri and the Mississippi, which are the results of actual observations made by competent engineers, the reader will find, notwithstanding the statements made by our best geographers in regard to the length of the Amazon, that there is one river within the confines of our country [the Missouri] which is eight hundred and thirteen miles longer than the Amazon, and is the longest though not the widest river in the world. . . .

River Towns

. . . Steamboating is an incurable disease. . . .

After you have been on the river long enough to get the disease, everything looks different. Chicago is a town 200 miles east of the river. South Dakota is some place west of Minneiska and of no interest as it hasn't even a mile of Mississippi River in the whole state. Lake Superior is an inferior watery deposit of some kind, in a general northeasterly direction from Grey Cloud Landing. And as for St. Louis, Quincy, Davenport, Moline, Rock Island, Dubuque, La Crosse, Winona—what are they? River towns, of course. Not towns—*river towns*. And what a difference that makes.

From *A Stretch on the River*, by Richard Bissell, pp. 111–114. Copyright, 1950, by Richard P. Bissell. Boston: Little, Brown and Company. An Atlantic Monthly Press Book.

What possible charm can we attach to any of these towns other than
that the Mississippi River flows past them, touches them? What is John
Deere at Moline? French and Hecht at Davenport? Standard Lumber Co.
at Dubuque? Ah, we love and cherish these mammoth enterprises because
they are by the river. What is left of glamor at Reads Landing? A store
with Rice Krispies—and the river. McGregor, Iowa, is all tired out but
the river keeps it on the map. Lansing, Iowa, would be worse than South
Dakota—but it's on the river, and in the evening it's better than Lake
Louise.

* * * * *

There isn't anything in any of these towns, but they are the most
romantic and wonderful in the world because they are old Upper Mississippi River towns. Of course there's a bird in La Crosse who made a scale
model of St. Patrick's Cathedral out of match sticks, a girl down in
Muscatine born without any arms who can knit with her feet, and a fellow
at Winona named Trask who made two holes in one, one Sunday in
1928, but those towns would be worse than Prairie City, S. Dakota, in
spite of these local attractions, except for the big Mississippi River rolling
past the door day and night.

Over at Indianapolis, Ind., they advertise they are the biggest city in
the U.S.A. not on a navigable body of water. They don't need to advertise
it—you can tell there's something wrong the minute you get there. And
I'll take the Pfister in Milwaukee or the Spalding in Duluth or the Stod-
dard in La Crosse anyway—that Claypool Hotel in Indianapolis has a
colorful name but no body of water except the municipal pool within
several miles. When you get someplace where they commence to boast they
got no water around it's time to buy transportation and move on.

Nimrod Wildfire: Half Horse, Half Alligator

I. HIS LETTER TO HIS UNCLE

Uncle Peter—Washington, July 1st. Here I am, only two days' journey
from New York! The very day I got your coaxing letter I packed up my
shirts and some other plunder and set right off a-horseback under high
steam. On my way I took a squint at my wild lands along by the Big

From *The Lion of the West,* Retitled "The Kentuckian, or A Trip to New York,"
A Farce in Two Acts, by James Kirke Paulding, revised by John Augustus Stone and
William Bayle Bernard, edited and with an introduction by James N. Tidwell, pp.
21, 24–25, 35–36, 54–55. Written in 1830 and revised in 1831 and 1833. First dramatic
production, April, 1831. First published, December, 1954. Copyright, 1954, by the
Board of Trustees of the Leland Stanford Junior University. Stanford, California:
Stanford University Press. All dramatic production rights reserved.
The story of Tidwell's discovery of the manuscript in the British Museum consti-
tutes a dramatic chapter in the history of "probably the most famous 'lost' play of
the nineteenth-century American stage." For further history and discussion, see

Muddy and Little Muddy to Bear Grass Creek, had what I call a real, roundabout catawampus, clean through the deestrict. If I hadn't I wish I may be *te-to-taciously ex-flunctified.* But, uncle, don't forget to tell Aunt Polly that I'm a full team going it on the big figure! And let all the fellers in New York know—I'm half horse, half alligator, a touch of the airth-quake, with a sprinkling of the steamboat. "If I an't, I wish I may be shot. Heigh! Wake, snakes, June bugs are coming." Good bye. Yours to the backbone. Nim Wildfire.

II. Fishing for Lawyers

. . . I was chuckle head enough to go down the Mississippi fishing for lawyers one day. . . . Why, look here. I call catfish lawyers—'case you see they're all head and [their] head all mouth. . . . I was fishing for lawyers, and knowing what whappers some on um are, I tied my line in a hard knot right around my middle—for fear the devils might twitch it out of my hands afore I know'd it. . . . Well, what do you think if a varmint as big as an alligator didn't lay hold and jerk me plump head foremost into the river—I wish I may be stuck into a split log for a wedge! There was I twisted about like a chip in a whirlpool! Well, how to get away from the varmint I was sort of "jubus," when all of a sudden, I grabb'd him by the gills and we had a fight—he pulled and flounced—I held fast and swore at him! Aha, says I, you may be a screamer, but perhaps I'm a horse! The catfish roll'd his eyes clean round till he squinted—when snap went the line, crack went his gills, and off he bounced like a wild Ingen.

III. In No-bottom Swamp

. . . Old Kaintuck's the spot. There the world's made upon a large scale. . . . The gals! Oh, they go to it on the big figure too—no mistake in them. There's my late sweetheart, Patty Snaggs. At nine year old she shot a bear, and now she can whip her weight in wild cats. There's the skin of one of 'em. (*Takes off his cap.*) . . . The soil—oh, the soil's so rich you may travel under it . . . particularly after the spring rains. Look you here now, tother day I was a-horseback paddling away pretty comfortably through No-bottom swamp, when suddenly—I wish I may be curry-comb'd to death by 50,000 tom cats, if I didn't see a white hat getting along in mighty considerable style all alone by itself on top of the mud—so up I rid, and being a bit jubus, I lifted it with the butt end of my whip

---

Francis Hodge, "Biography of a Lost Play: *Lion of the West,*" *The Theatre Annual,* Vol. XII, 1954, pp. 48–61.

A report of the speech, "A Fight on the Mississippi," as originally published in the *Daily Louisville Advertiser,* October 17, 1831, is given in *A Treasury of American Folklore* (1944), pp. 13–14, together with the Crockett version and a discussion of Nimrod Wildfire and the backwoods "screamer" tradition (pp. 3–5).

A preliminary sketch of the encounter with a raftsman is to be found in the contest between a wagoner and a Shenandoah River batteauxman in Paulding's *Letters from the South, Written during an Excursion in the Summer of 1816* (New York, 1817), Vol. II, pp. 89–92.

when a feller sung out from under it, "Hallo, stranger, who told you to knock my hat off?" "Why," says I, "what sort of a sample of a white man are you? What's come of the rest of you?" "Oh," says he, "I'm not far off—only in the next county. I'm doing beautifully—got one of the best horses under me that ever burrowed—claws like a mole—no stop in him—but here's a wagon and horses right under me in a mighty bad fix, I reckon, for I heard the driver say a spell ago one of the team was getting a leetel tired."

IV. A FIGHT ON THE MISSISSIPPI

. . . I was riding along the Mississippi one day when I came across a fellow floating down the stream sitting cock'd up in the starn of his boat fast asleep. Well, I hadn't had a fight for as much as ten days—felt as though I must kiver myself up in a salt bin to keep—"so wolfy" about the head and shoulders. So, says I, hullo, stranger, if you don't take keer your boat will run away wi' you. So he looked up at me "slantindickular" and I looked down on him "slanchwise." He took out a chaw of tobacco from his mouth and, says he, I don't value you tantamount to that, and then he flopp'd his wings and crowed like a cock. I ris up, shook my mane, crooked my neck, and neighed like a horse. Well, he run his boat foremost ashore. I stopped my wagon and set my triggers. Mister, says he, I'm the best man—if I ain't, I wish I may be tetotaciously exflunctified! I can whip my weight in wild cats and ride strait through a crab apple orchard on a flash of lightning—clear meat axe disposition! And what's more, I once back'd a bull off a bridge. Poh, says I, what do I keer for that? I can tote a steam boat up the Mississippi and over the Alleghany mountains. My father can whip the best man in old Kaintuck and I can whip my father. When I'm good-natured I weigh about a hundred and seventy, but when I'm mad, I weigh a *ton*. With that I fetched him the regular Ingen war-whoop. Out he jumped from his boat and down I tumbled from my wagon—and, I say, we came together like two steam boats going sixty miles an hour. He was a pretty severe colt, but no part of a priming to such a feller as me. I put it to him mighty droll—tickled the varmint till he squealed like a young colt, bellowed "enough" and swore I was a "rip staver." Says I, *ain't* I a horse? Says he, stranger, you're a *beauty*, any-how, and if you'd stand for Congress I'd vote for you next *lection*. Says I, would you? My name's Nimrod Wildfire. Why, I'm the yaller flower of the forest. I'm all *brimstone but* the *head,* and that's *aky fortis.*

Floating Towns

In the spring one hundred boats have been numbered that landed in one day at the mouth of the Bayan, at New Madrid. I have strolled to the point on a spring evening, and seen them arriving in fleets. The boisterous gaiety of the hands, the congratulations, the moving picture of life on board the boats, in the numerous animals, large and small, which they carry, their different loads, the evidence of the increasing agriculture of the country above, and more than all, the immense distances which they have already come, and those which they have still to go, afforded to me copious sources of meditation. You can name no point from the numerous rivers of the Ohio and the Mississippi from which some of these boats have not come. In one place there are boats loaded with planks, from the pine forests of the southwest of New York. In another quarter there are the Yankee notions of Ohio. From Kentucky, pork, flour, whisky, hemp, tobacco, bagging, and bale-rope. From Tennessee there are the same articles, together with great quantities of cotton. From Missouri and Illinois, cattle and horses, the same articles generally as from Ohio, together with peltry and lead from Missouri. Some boats are loaded with corn in the ear and in bulk; others with barrels of apples and potatoes. Some have loads of cider, and what they call "cider royal" or cider that has been strengthened by boiling or freezing. There are dried fruits, every kind of spirits manufactured in these regions and, in short, the products of the ingenuity and agriculture of the whole upper country of the West. They have come from regions thousands of miles apart. They have floated to a common point of union. The surfaces of the boats cover some acres. Dung-hill fowls are fluttering over the roofs as an invariable appendage. The chanticleer raises his piercing note. The swine utter their cries. The cattle low. The horses trample, as in their stables. There are boats fitted on purpose and loaded entirely with turkeys, that, having little else to do, gobble most furiously. The hands travel about from boat to boat, make inquiries and acquaintances, and form alliances to yield mutual assistance to each other on their descent from this to New Orleans. After an hour or two passed in this way, they spring on shore to raise the wind in town. It is well for the people of the village if they do not become riotous in the course of the evening; in which case I have often seen the most summary and strong measures taken. About midnight the uproar is all hushed. The fleet unites once more at the Natchez or New Orleans and, although they live on the same river, they may perhaps never meet each other again on the earth.

From *Recollections of the Last Ten Years,* Passed in Occasional Residences and Journeyings in the Valley of the Mississippi, from Pittsburgh and the Missouri to the Gulf of Mexico and from Florida to the Spanish Frontier; in a Series of Letters to the Rev. James Flint, of Salem, Massachusetts, by Timothy Flint, pp. 103–105. Boston: Cummings, Hillard and Company. 1826.

Next morning at the first dawn, the bugles sound. Everything in and about the boats that has life is in motion. The boats in half an hour are all under way. In a little while they have all disappeared, and nothing is seen, as before they came, but the regular current of the river. In passing down the Mississippi, we often see a number of boats lashed and floating together. I was once on board a fleet of eight that were in this way moving on together. It was a considerable walk to travel over the roofs of this floating town. On board of one boat they were killing swine. In another they had apples, cider, nuts, and dried fruit. One of the boats was a retail or dram shop. It seems that the object of lashing so many boats had been to barter and obtain supplies. These confederacies often commence in a frolic and end in a quarrel, in which case the aggrieved party dissolves the partnership by unlashing and managing his own boat in his own way. While this fleet of boats is floating separately, but each carried by the same current, nearly at the same rate, visits take place from boat to boat in skiffs.

While I was at New Madrid, a large tinner's establishment floated there in a boat. In it all the different articles of tinware were manufactured and sold by wholesale and retail. There were three large apartments, where the different branches of the art were carried on in this floating manufactory. When they had mended all the tin and vended all that they could sell in one place, they floated on to another. A still more extraordinary manufactory, we were told, was floating down the Ohio and shortly expected at New Madrid. Aboard this were manufactured axes, scythes, and all other iron tools of this description, and in it horses were shod. In short it was a complete blacksmith's shop of a higher order, and it is said that they jestingly talked of having a trip-hammer worked by a horse power on board. I have frequently seen in this region a dry goods shop in a boat, with its articles very handsomely arranged on shelves. Nor would the delicate hands of the vender have disgraced the spruce clerk behind our city counters. It is now common to see flat boats worked by a bucket wheel and a horse power, after the fashion of steamboat movement. Indeed, every spring brings forth new contrivances of this sort, the result of the farmer's meditations over his winter's fire.

Ferryman's Logic

A traveler from across the ridge came up late one evening [to the ferry on the Leaf River, Mississippi], like the chieftain to the highlands bound

From *The Greenhouse*, Cuttings from Another Year's Crop in the *Commercial Appeal*, by Paul Flowers, Vol. VII (December 1, 1950), p. 32. Memphis, Tennessee.

Ben Hilbun, who hails from Sullivan's Hollow [Mississippi], and functions as elder statesman at Mississippi State College, is authority for the story of a ferryboat operator on the Leaf River back in the early days of this century.—P.F.

who cried, "Boatman, do not tarry and I'll give thee a silver pound to row us o'er the ferry." The river was on a rampage, what with a spring freshet and all; driftwood threatened to swamp any craft that ventured out, and the ferryman was reluctant to set forth.

The traveler was so insistent, however, that the ferryman finally consented. "All right," he said, "I'll carry you over, but I ain't a-goin' to resk my life an' limb an' my boat for th' reg'lar fare. It's goin' to cost you a quarter to get acrost."

"But I ain't got but fifteen cents," explained the traveler. "You got to take me for that. Your reg'lar fare's only ten cents."

"I ain't a-goin'," ruled the ferryman. "That's all. Anybody that ain't got but fifteen cents, it don't make no dif'rence which side o' the river he's on anyhow."

The Steamboat

The Steamboat is an engine on a raft, with $11,000 worth of jig-saw work around it.

Steamships are built of steel and are severely plain except on the inside where the millionaire tourist is confined. Steamboats are built of wood, tin, shingles, canvas, and twine, and look like a bride of Babylon. If a steamboat should go to sea, the ocean would take one playful slap at it and people would be picking up kindling on the beach for the next eleven years.

However, the steamboat does not go to sea. Its home is on the river, which does not rise up and stand on end in a storm. It is necessary that a steamboat shall be light and airy because if it were heavy it would stick to the bottom of the river several feet and become an island instead of a means of transportation.

The steamboat is from a hundred to three hundred feet long and from thirty to fifty feet wide. It is from forty to seventy feet high above water, but does not extend more than three feet into the water. This is because that is all the water there is. A steamboat must be so built that when the river is low and the sandbars come out for air, the first mate can tap a keg of beer and run the boat four miles on the suds.

Steamboats were once the beasts of burden for the great Middle West and the city which could not be reached at low water by a steamboat with two large, hot stacks, twenty-five Negro roustabouts on the bow end and a gambler in the cabin, withered away in infancy. But the railroad, which runs in high water or low and does not stab itself in a vital spot with a snag, came along and cleared the steamboat out of business. There are

By George Fitch. Cited in *The Log of the Betsy Ann,* by Frederick Way, Jr., pp. 26–27. Copyright, 1933, by Frederick Way, Jr. New York: Robert M. McBride & Company.

only a few left now, which is a great pity, for the most decorative part of a river is a tall, white steamboat with a chime whistle and a flashing wheel in the far foreground.

Light-draft Vessels and Heavy Dew

. . . Rivers were then navigated regularly that seem now no more than meadow creeks. Steamboats traversed the Des Moines clear to the forks of the Raccoon, where a trading-post had been established on the site of what is now the capital city of Des Moines. They traveled by schedule on streams like the Iowa, the Cedar, and even the Maquoketa. This seems incredible now, because you would not think that anything heavier than a dead oak leaf could navigate the Maquoketa, but it is a fact of record, nevertheless. . . .

Steamboats went 150 miles up the Rock River. I once remarked this to a resident of Dixon, Illinois, and he inquired in an insulting manner if the steamboats of my prehistoric era customarily moved upon skids. Steamboats ran on the Black, the Wisconsin, and the Chippewa. The St. Croix was a main traveled road as far as Taylor's Falls. Navigators then used to do things that seemed inexplicable except as legerdermain. . . .

All these rivers were physically alike. They were shallow, they had soft alluvial bottoms, they shifted and twisted about, they had more different moods and tempers than any woman. The difficulties of navigating them were great and complicated. Because they were so shallow, steamboats built for use on them (after builders had passed out of the imitative stage) must be flat-bottomed and constructed with a care that pondered every ounce of weight. Considering their burden, they were in their prime the lightest-draft steam vessels that ever floated. The hackneyed old phrase about the Western steamboat that could run over a field after a heavy dew was not so wild an exaggeration after all. The packet *Iowa City*, on which I once traveled, drew but twenty inches, and the *Chippewa Falls*, when light, but twelve. If I remember correctly, the largest steamers ever constructed for use on the upper Mississippi had no more than five feet of hold; most of them had three and a half feet or four.

The hull was only a platform on which to place machinery and freight. Seldom was anything carried in it; everything was carried upon it. Necessarily the upper works, cabin, and structure for state-rooms and the like must be of the flimsiest construction. And yet, with all these limitations, many a Mississippi River steamer was beautifully designed, beautifully built, and adorned into a floating palace. Often the skill and sometimes the good taste of the builders went beyond praise.

* * * * *

From *A-Rafting on the Mississip'*, by Charles Edward Russell, pp. 22–25, 28. Copyright, 1928, by Charles Edward Russell. New York and London: The Century Company.

The Chippewa was another shallow stream that required light-draft vessels. One of the most successful that ever stemmed its fidgety current was called the *Monitor*. One day in 1863 while bound up she ran into the bank above Rumsey's Landing and went aground broadside on. In a few moments she was observed to be floating again and proceeding upon her way. The accepted version of the incident was that she grounded on the starboard side while the pilot was on that side of the wheel. He moved over to the other side and the boat floated free. He himself stated that all he shifted was his quid of tobacco, but this seems improbable. I have heard it said in pilot-houses that when the *Monitor* struck a bar head-on, two deck hands would get out, seize her one on each side, walk over the bar with her, and deposit her on the other side; whereupon she would resume the journey. This may be deemed doubtful, because it appears from the registry list that she was of nearly twelve tons burden, and it seems unlikely that two deck-hands could carry so heavy a weight unless they were persons of unusual muscular development.

Shallow Water

When we started up toward Fort Peck, Montana, with the two diesel towboats, the *John Ordway* and the *Patrick Gass,* in 1934, we ran into a drouth. The upper Missouri was just about dried up and, if we had not had two motorboats with 19 horsepower Johnson Sea Horse outboard motors and plenty of cable, we could not have gone much farther than Omaha.

Captain W. I. ("Tobe") Maulding was in charge of these boats. When up near Chamberlain, South Dakota, we were pulling and washing the *John Ordway* up over a shallow place near shore, we had out two thousand feet of cable and the two motorboats were lashed in front of the towboat. It was wash and pull over less than two feet of water, and the *Ordway* was drawing three feet strong. A big Indian came down from his tepee on the hill and scooped up a bucket of water.

Captain Maulding hollered at him and said, "John, throw that water back in the river. We need every drop of it."

The Indian paid no mind but walked back up the hill, saying, "Squaw, she having baby, need um water too."

From *Steamboating*, Sixty-Five Years on Missouri's Rivers, The Historical Story of Developing the Waterway Traffic on the Rivers of the Middlewest, by Captain William L. Heckman, "Steamboat Bill," pp. 201–202. Copyright, 1950, by Burton Publishing Company. Kansas City.

Cursing on the River

Cursing is an art that bears cultivation, and the Allegheny River came in for its share. One youngster started in as a raft hand and it was said of him that he "was the most awkward swearer on the river." But he persevered, and one day became proficient. An old lady was sitting on the steamboat's boiler deck one summer afternoon while this gentleman was urging an unruly cow down the stageplank. Nothing went right. The cow sat down. The bull rails slipped and went into the river. An offshore breeze blew the boat around and the heel of the gangplank nearly fell over the edge of the forecastle. The situation became intolerable. Unmindful of the dear old lady's presence, the irate riverman started in softly, gained in volume, erupted and exploded, came to crescendo, and faded away like a retreating thunderstorm. The cow, hypnotized by this spell of music, got up and walked aboard as placidly as could be. The wind died down. The old lady removed her hand from her heart, blushed to the roots of her hair. Waveringly she arose, leaned over the rail and called, "You, down there!" The riverman looked aloft. He stammered, "I'm sorry, ma'am."

The old lady could only repeat, "What language! What language! Saints protect us, what language!"

In the evening this riverman had a strange request. The little lady asked him, oh! so secretly, would he mind writing down those blasphemous words! She confided that her heart was touched. What she had heard that afternoon was the most honest poetry "told in the liveliest way" she had run onto in her lifetime, she said.

What was said will never be known, for, try as he could, this riverman could not remember the formula. One of the crying shames of literature is that all such honest expression of provocation is deleted. Actually (when expertly done, of course) it easily ranks with the works of the immortals. And the Allegheny River brand would fill Volume One.

A Christian Captain

"Then we had some moral men on the river, too," continued the man at the wheel, after refreshing himself with a drink brought from the bar below. "There was old Captain Jerry Flumkins that used to run the *Jim Crank* in the lower Ohio trade. You see, the boat used to make a trip a

From *The Allegheny*, by Frederick Way, Jr., pp. 168–169. Copyright, 1942, by Frederick Way, Jr. *The Rivers of America*, edited by Stephen Vincent Benét and Carl Carmer. New York and Toronto: Farrar & Rinehart, Inc.

From *The Man at the Wheel*, by John Henton Carter (Commodore Rollingpin), pp. 25–29. Copyright, 1898, by John Henton Carter. St. Louis: E. B. Carter.

week, and Captain Jerry was always particular to have her get back home before twelve o'clock on Saturday night, because he had conscientious scruples against working on Sunday, and if he got caught out on account of fog or low water, and didn't make his time, he'd just tie right up in the woods and wouldn't budge till Monday morning. He used to say that he built all his boats according to Scripture, and run them according to Scripture, and when he had to trespass on the Lord's day to make a living, he'd just quit boating and go to preaching. Moral! Don't talk. He wouldn't carry a barrel of whisky for his dearest friend, and you couldn't buy a drop of liquor on the *Crank* for love or money. Of course, she wasn't ever bothered with gamblers, for they always gave her a wide berth; but white horses and preachers the old man just honed for, and would land anywhere, day or night, to take them aboard. Said he didn't see how it could be bad luck to carry men or beasts that were in the service of the Lord, and if it was, he just wanted some of the bad luck, and wanted it bad.

"That's the kind of a man old Cap'n Jerry Flumkins was, and they all knew him. They used to talk about him a good deal, and make fun of him, but I take notice he went right on just the same, and always had a good boat under him and money to pay off the crew. And accommodating! Why, he thought nothing of landing just to leave a woman a drawing of tea or a roast of fresh meat when she happened to have company; and on Mondays, when everybody was at the river washing, he just had the steward stand on the forecastle with bundles of soap and starch done up ready to toss to everybody that asked for them. Well, of course, there couldn't anybody run a man like that out of the trade, and they didn't try to. There wasn't anything that the people could do for Jerry that they wouldn't do, especially the moral, church-going community, for they knew his record.

"For a long time everything went well with the old man, but one day the *Crank* took a sheer on the pilot and run out on the bank till her bow was about twenty feet out of the water. She was in an awful fix, and no mistake! The crew sparred and heaved at her for three days, but couldn't get her back into the river, and it began to look like she'd have to stay where she was until the water rose unless they could get about a hundred tons of something to put her stern down so that the bow would swing clear. Old Captain Jerry knew that this weight was all he needed to put him afloat again, but where to find it was what troubled him.

"At last, an idea strikes him. The boys said it was a vision, because he used to see visions and dream dreams, as the Bible says that good old men sometimes do, and so he lights out and slips up to where the Methodists were holding a camp-meeting about a mile off, made a speech, and tells everybody about his troubles. Of course, they all wanted to help old Captain Jerry out, because he was a member of that denomination and they knew him. So the leaders came together and wanted to know what they could do for him.

" 'Well,' said Capt. Jerry, 'if it wouldn't be asking too much, I would like to have you adjourn this meeting to the *Jim Crank*. She is lying down there awful hard aground, and as nothing we can do has any effect on her I have concluded, as a last resort, to try the power of prayer. It seems to me that a camp-meeting of this size ought to have some weight with Providence.'

"The motion was put and unanimously carried to adjourn to the boat. When they arrived old Captain Jerry marched them all on board and told them to go aft. 'Go aft, my brothers and sisters,' he said, 'go aft.'

"When everything was ready to begin the meeting, he ordered the fireman to get up a good head of steam, the men to heave hard on the capstan and get a strain on the spars. Then he goes aft himself and asks one of the deacons to lead in prayer. The old man waited till the meeting got well warmed up and the deacons began to respond with their fervent 'amens,' and then he whispered to the engineer, 'Back her hard,' and, sure enough, away she slipped into the river like she was greased.

"Now Captain Jerry Flumkins was what I call a practical Christian. Whenever he got in a close place, he always used judgment and fixed things so as to make it as easy on Providence as he could, and you could just win more money on old Captain Jerry Flumkins getting an answer to prayer than any man that ever followed the business; do you hear me?"

The Wreck of the *Rosa May*

Old Hamp, the veteran bear hunter, had belonged to Colonel Damascus Woodville before the Civil War, and still made headquarters at Ruthven where he and Colonel Rye were close friends. The Colonel let him keep his cabin, and Hamp occasionally came back to it. Then the two old cronies would sit on the front porch and reminisce, the planter in a rocking chair while Hamp squatted on the top step and leaned against the broad white column.

"Cunnel," the tall brown Negro remarked, " 'pears to me dere's a heap mo' water nowadays dan what yo' pa used to git."

"No, we don't get any more water, but it rushes down on us all at once, because forests have been cut away at the north and fields cleared. Instead of seeping through grass and woods, it runs off now like rain from a roof."

"Is dat de way of it? Anyway in 1882 de *Rosa May* got sucked through a crevasse at de same place where yo' levee busted las' spring, an' went whirlin' 'cross dat field where yo' plows is workin' at. Hit dat sycamore. Cunnel, I come down from Memphis on dat trip o' de *Rosa May*, an'

From *The Story of King Cotton,* by Harris Dickson, pp. 126–130. Copyright, 1937, by Funk & Wagnalls Company. New York and London.

since den I ain't been no han' to prank wid ole Miss'ip when she's fixin'
to bust loose."

"You were on that boat? When she got wrecked?"

"Sho was," came the prompt response. "I'd been huntin' in Arkansas
but de whole country went under water an' I was tryin' to git home.

"Anyhow I kotched de *Rosa May* at Memphis. Whalin' big boat, stout
as a flock o' bulls. It was her first trip down de river an' she had one o'
dese smart-aleck cap'ns. De pilot steered close inshore so her passengers
could see de big water. Huh! I jest couldn't keep my mouf shut. Here
we come, bulgin' downstream, puffin' an' blowin', actin' biggety. So I sidles
up alongside de cap'n an' says, 'Dat water's powerful deceivin'. Us better
steer away from dem crevasses.'

" 'Where's yo' pilot license?' de cap'n asked me. '*I'm* runnin' dis boat.'

"Sho nuff, Cunnel, him an' de pilot was runnin' it. Atter while dey run
her smack jam in a crevasse. De *Rosa May* quivered, den went slidin'
'long, same as if she was slippin' down hill. Lordee, how dem bells jangled
an' dem firemen throwed wood in de furnace. Passengers run ev'y which
way. De pilot spins round an' round on his wheel, whilst de *Rosa May*
backed an' splashed an' kicked, but 'twarn't no use. Ole Miss had done
reached up an' grabbed her. Atter a turrible scufflin' she straightened out
an' tuk a shoot through de crevasse. 'Don't jump! Don't jump!' Cap'n
rushed around like a crazy man, beggin' his passengers to stay on de boat.
Now we went through dat crevasse, crashin' amongst dem willers. Wim-
men was screamin', an' 'peared like nobody knowed what to do.

"Curyus, ain't it, Cunnel," old Hamp chuckled, "de things which a man
cornsiders in dem times. All de way from Memphis I'd been wonderin'
how I was goin' to git home. 'Twarn't nary place to land on neither side
de river. Ef a levee warn't already broke, white men wid shotguns was
guardin' it, warnin' us to keep off. 'Peared like I'd go plum to Vicksburg
befo' de *Rosa May* could drap a stageplank. Shucks!

"All of a sudden us went tearin' through a new crevasse an' headed fer
dis plantation. So I grins to myself an' say, 'Ef I does git spilt, I'll git
spilt at home.'

"Next thing I cornsidered was a lady which was huddlin' two little boys
an' awful skeered. I goes up to her wid my hat in my han' and says, 'Scuse
me, ma'am, lemme have dese chillun an' I'll git 'em out, no matter ef dis
boat do sink.'

"Some white folks is got sense. Dat lady tuk one squint at me an' say,
'I'll trust you wid my sons.' Dat was all.

"I cut me a piece o' rope an' tied dem youngsters' wrists together, 'bout
two yards apart, so dey couldn't git loose from me. Ef us was flung in de
water I could drag 'em ontil I kotch a limb.

"Bless yo' soul, Cunnel, it didn't take no time for de *Rosa May* to reach
dis plantation, tearin' through briar patches an' bumpin' 'mongst de woods.
Den us struck de open field, dat very field out yonder, an' hit de sycamore. 'Co'se, de swiftest current run through yo' slough, an' I figgered it

would throw us ag'inst de ridge at Bullhorn. So I says, 'Cap'n, we'se 'proachin' some high ground. Gimme a line an' I'll pass it round a tree. Maybe you kin hold her.'

" 'Twarn't no trick, Cunnel. I knowed where de shallers was, an' when dem roustabouts seen me jump wid a line in water less'n knee-deep, dey follered wid mo' lines. Huh! Dem passengers helt deir breff whilst dem lines drawed tight. Den de *Rosa May* stopped an' de passengers could be took off in skiffs.

"Atter de water went down it sho did look comercal to see a steamboat perched on Bullhorn Ridge twenty miles from de river. But de white man what owned her didn't see nothin' funny, an' never said nothin' funny neither. Lord, Lord, Cunnel, when I tuk him dere to look at his boat, dat white man cussed a blue streak, cussed de pilot, cussed de cap'n, called 'em ev'ything except a child o' God. Den he kinder snickered an' 'spressed hisself, 'Good-by, *Rosa May*. Dere you lays; dere you stays.'

"For de longest kind o' time whenever dese plantation hands needed a cabin door, or a lock or most anything, dey tuk it from de wreck, ontil de *Rosa May* was ontirely toted off."

The Coolest Feller

Jim Smith was fur sartin the coolest feller in the country. He had a little one-room cabin on the banks of the Mississip', an' one night as he sot cleanin' his rifle, one side o' the fire, an' Matty, his wife, on the other, knittin', the' cum a terrible explosion out on the river, an' the next minute somethin' cum plum through the roof an' dropped at their feet, right between 'em, without disturbin' either. Jim went on a-cleanin' his gun an' Matty, she kep' knittin'. The stranger—fur it was a man—was a little dazed at fust, but gittin' up, he squinted at the hole in the roof an', says he, "Well, my man, what's the damage?" Jim put down his rifle, took a careful look at the hole, figured a while an', says he, "Ten dollars." "You be hanged," said the traveler. "Last week I was blown up in another steamboat, opposite St. Louis, and fell through three floors of a new house, and they only charged me five dollars. No, no, my man, I know what the usual figure is in such cases. Here's two dollars; if that won't do, sue me as quick as you please!"

From *The Lance, Cross and Canoe;* The Flatboat, Rifle and Plough in the Valley of the Mississippi; The Backwoods Hunter and Settler, The Flatboatman, The Saddle-Bags Parson, The Stump Orator and Lawyer, as the Pioneers of Its Civilization; Its Great Leaders, Wit and Humor, Remarkable Extent and Wealth of Resource, Its Past Achievements and Glorious Future, by W. H. Milburn, p. 474. Entered . . . 1892, by William Henry Milburn. . . . New York and St. Louis: N. D. Thompson Publishing Company.

Up among the Splinters

I was going up to Maysville, Kentucky, to take a "sit" on the *Bulletin,* and of course I took the steamer *Magnolia,* after reaching Cincinnati, in preference to all others. She was a tidy-looking boat, and her head clerk wore a diamond pin. He was the first steamboat clerk I had ever seen fastened to a $600 diamond, and I was determined to go on that boat if it killed me.

A runner for a rival boat assured me that the *Magnolia* would blow up, while his boat would slide up the river like grease, but the diamond pin decided me.

"Good-bye, my white-haired rural friend!" sorrowfully exclaimed the rival runner as he turned away, and I never saw him again. Our paths diverged right there. Mine went skyward, and he went off and fell down a hatchway and was killed.

After the steamer left the wharf-boat I sat down in the cabin and listened, with others, while a fat man from Illinois read four or five columns of the impeachment trial of Andy Johnson. Throwing the paper down, he said: "Gentlemen, it seems to me—"

He stopped right there. He couldn't go on. The boilers exploded just then, and we had business aloft. I don't exactly remember who went up first, or how we got through the roof. I am a little absent-minded sometimes, and this was one of the times.

The boilers made a great deal more noise than there seemed any occasion for. The explosion would have been A 1 with half the whizzing, grinding, and tearing. One of the men who came up behind me seemed to think something or other was out of order, and he yelled to me:

"Say! what's all this?"

I pointed to the fat man, who was about five feet ahead of me, and then I began to practice gymnastics. I went up a few feet right end up, then a few feet more wrong end up, and then I wasn't particular which way I went up. The golden eagle off the pilot-house sailed around our heads, and it was a fine chance for the fat man to get off a handsome eulogy on the proud bird of freedom. He didn't do it, however. One of his ears had been torn off, a leg broken, and flying timbers kept pegging him every minute. I wanted to ask him to finish the remark he commenced in the cabin, but he seemed so cast-down and discouraged that I hadn't the heart to speak.

We finally arrived there. It was a good ways up, and the route had sev-

---

From *"Quad's Odds";* by "M. Quad, The Detroit Free Press Man," Anecdote, Humor and Pathos and Other Things [by Charles B. Lewis], pp. 17–22. Entered . . . 1875, by Charles B. Lewis. Detroit: R. D. S. Tyler & Co., Publishers.

For an account of the explosion of the *Magnolia,* a tri-weekly boat which plied between Cincinnati and Maysville, Ky., on March 18, 1868, at California, Ohio (now part of Cincinnati), and for further comment by "Quad," see *The Thrills of the Historic Ohio,* by Frank Y. Grayson, pp. 101–103 (Cincinnati, no date).

eral little inconveniences. It was a grand location from which to view the surrounding country, but we didn't stop to view it. We had business below, and our motto was business before pleasure.

Somehow I got mixed up with the fat man, and we couldn't hardly tell which was which. He made no complaints and I didn't care, and so we got along very well together until we struck the water. When we went down to look for bottom we let go of each other. He stayed down there and I came up. A number of others also came up about that time. One man got hold of a door and warned us that he was a member of the Legislature, and must therefore be saved, but we held a mass convention and decided that the Constitution of the United States guaranteed equal rights to all men, and we crowded him along.

As the door wouldn't float over ten or twelve, a half-dozen of us got hold of brooms, foot-stools, dusters, and so forth, and compared notes. A six-footer from Missouri was rushing around with a boot-jack in one hand, a tablecloth in the other, and a look of anxiety on his face. As he floated near me, he called out:

"Young man, where are we going?"

I called back that I was a stranger in that locality, and couldn't say whether we'd bring up in New Orleans or Fort Leavenworth.

I finally got hold of the dining table, to which a red-headed woman from St. Louis was clinging. As I caught the table, she exclaimed:

"Go away, young man—go away!"

I replied that the state of her toilet needn't confuse her in the least. Her dress-skirt had been blown off, her hair singed, and part of her hoop-skirt was over her head, but I warned her that it was about an even thing. The band of my shirt was still buttoned around my neck, and I had one boot on, and it was no time to be captious. I remarked to her that her nose was broken and several of her teeth were gone, but she fired up and said I'd better "look to home," as I had one eye ruined, a hole in my head, and was cooked in a dozen places.

Before I could learn much of her history we were drawn to the bank and taken off. I called out for a breadth of rag carpet to make me a toga of, but no one would bring it, and I had to faint away to avoid hearing any criticisms from the crowd.

When I came to, a dozen of us were piled up together, and the captain of the boat was making a speech. He said it wasn't his fault, and that we mustn't feel hard toward him. He had lost a fine dog by the accident, and he couldn't bear any further burden just then. He said that boats often blew up without apparent reason, but if he could ever ascertain the reason of this blow-up he would send us the particulars. He seemed like an honest-hearted man, and we felt sorry over the loss of his dog.

When we got down to Cincinnati a policeman asked me if it made any difference to me where I was buried, and they sent me to the hospital until I could make up my mind. The hole in my head got to aching about that time, and the last I remember was hearing a man with a coarse voice call out:

"Tell Jim to get a box ready for this corpse!"

Sixteen days after that I got my senses back, and for the succeeding six weeks had a very easy time. The coroner dropped in once a day to see if I still persisted in living; six daily reporters included me in their round; the doctors worked at the hole in my head, and at my burns by turns, and after three months they came to the conclusion that I would live. Such little side issues as pneumonia, blindness, proud flesh, and fever were not supposed to have any bearing on the main question.

It isn't good to be blown up. There are better ways of ascending and descending. Such things interrupt traveling programs and are often the foundation of funeral processions. I met the red-headed woman about a year ago, and she was quite friendly, but the fat man hasn't been heard of since. I fear that some of the machinery of the boat got into his pockets and held him down.

Rival Steamboats Stopping for Wood

. . . There are occasions when "stopping to wood" is an event of positive interest and excitement. Passed over be the fine sun-shiney morning when, jogging along—nothing behind—nothing before, the passengers lounging about—heels up, or heads down—the unnoticed bell gives the signal for "wood," and the boat draws listlessly alongside of the "pile." Equally unregarded be the rainy day, when, mud to the knees and drenched to the skin, the steaming throng, slipping and plashing, drop their backloads, with a *"Whew!"* and fail to find, even in the whisky barrel, a laugh or a "break down." But *not* so the star-lit evening in June, when, the water at a "good stage," and out for a "long trip," with a rival boat behind, and the furnaces roaring for "more" the more they are fed, the signal is given and a faint flicker on the distant bank beacons the hungry monster towards its further supply of fuel. From New Orleans thus far on the trip up, the two boats, of nearly equal speed, have alternately passed each other during the stop to "wood," showing no gain of consequence on the part of either, and the grand struggle has been as it as present is, to "rush" the operation so as to get a start before being overtaken. The bank is reached—the boat made fast—gangways are formed—"Lively, men, lively!" cries the mate, and while the upper cabins pour out their crowds upon the boiler deck, the "hands" and the swarms of wild-looking passengers below (obliged by contract) dash ashore among the brush. Now ensues a scene that tasks description! The fire, augmented by piles of the driest wood,

From *The Drama in Pokerville*, The Bench and Bar of Jurytown, and Other Stories, by "Everpoint," (J. M. Field, Esq., of the *St. Louis Reveille*), pp. 173–176. Entered . . . 1850, by A. Hart. Philadelphia: T. B. Peterson and Brothers. In *Colonel Thorpe's Scenes in Arkansaw*, Philadelphia: T. B. Peterson & Brothers, 1858.

crimsons the tangled forest! Black and white, many of them stripped to their waist, though others, more careful, protect their skins by ripping and forming cowls of empty saltsacks, attack the lengthened pile, and amid laugh, shout, curse, and the scarcely intermitting scream of the iron chimneys (tortured by the still making steam) remove it to the boat.

"Lively, men, lively!" rings the cry, and lively, lively is the impulse inspired by it! See that swart, gigantic Negro, his huge shoulder hidden beneath a pyramid of wood, hurl to the deck his load, cut a caper along the plank, and, leaping back, seize a flaming brand to whirl it round his head in downright enjoyment! "Lively! lively!" Laugh, shout, whoop, and the pile is rapidly disappearing, when a cry is heard from the "hurricane deck"—

"Here she comes, round the point!"

'Tis the rival steamer, sure enough; and once more she will pass during this detention. Now dash both mate and captain ashore to "rush" the matter. The bell is struck for starting, as if to compel impossibility; the accumulated steam is let off in brief, impatient screams, and the passengers, sharing the wild excitement, add to their cries.

"Passed again, by thunder!" "We've got enough wood." "Leave the rest!" Etc. In the mean time, round the point below, sweeps the up-comer —all lights and sparks—moving over the water like a rushing fire-palace! Now her "blow" is heard, like a suppressed curse of struggle and defiance, and, now, nearing the bank where lies her rival, a sort of frenzy seizes on the latter—

"Tumble it in!" "Rush her!" "D—n the rest!" "You've got enough!" *Ra-a-a-sh!* goes the steam; the engine, "working off," thunders below; again, the bell rings, and the hurly burly on shore is almost savage. At length, as the coming boat is hard on astern, the signal tap is given, "all hands aboard!" The lines are let go, the planks are shoved in by the Negroes who are themselves drawn from the water with them, and amid a chaos of timber, a whirl of steam, and a crash of machinery, once more she is under weigh. The struggle is to leave the bank before she can be passed, and fuel, flame, and frenzy, seemingly unite to secure the object; barrels of combustibles are thrust into the furnaces, while, before the doors, the "firemen," naked and screaming, urge their wild efforts!

"Here she is, alongside!" and now the struggle indeed is startling; the one endeavoring to shoot out from the bank across the bows of the other, and *she,* authorized by river custom, holding her way, the consequences of collision resting alone on her imprudent competitor. Roar for roar—scream for scream—huzza for huzza—but now, the inner boat apparently gaining, a turn of her antagonist's wheel leaves her no option but to be *run into* or turn again towards the bank! A hundred oaths and screams reply to this maneuver, but *on she comes*—on, on—a moment more and she strikes! With a shout of rage the defeated pilot turns her head—at the same moment snatching down his rifle and discharging it into the pilot-house of his opponent! Fury has now seized the thoughts of all, and the iron

throats of the steamers are less hideous than the human ones beneath
them. The wheel for a moment neglected, the thwarted monster has now
"taken a sheer in the wild current," and, beyond the possibility of prevention, is driving into the bank! A cry of terror rises aloft—the throng
rushes aft—the steam, every valve set free—makes the whole forest shiver,
and, amid the fright, the tall chimneys, caught by the giant trees, are
wrenched and torn out like tusks from a recoiling mastodon.

"That's a stretcher," will cry out some readers, and such a scene is not
likely to be witnessed *now*, but the writer will not soon forget that such
he bore a part in, some ten years ago, and that the captain, when asked
what he thought of it, replied, "Well, I think we've got h—l, anyhow!"

Dayton Randolph's *Hurronico*

Dayton Randolph came aboard the *General Crowder* at Pittsburgh. I
looked upon this fellow as a very learned man, for he had a pilot license
468 miles long, and could tell you all about the Ohio River from Pittsburgh to Cincinnati. He had guided all the big boats rivermen talked
about: was habitually selected to "take out" the Mardi Gras trips on the
Queen City, Ohio, and the *Joe Fowler,* and had the distinction of never
splitting a timber in a steamboat's hull by reason of running on a rock or
a snag. He knew the bottom of the river and he knew the top of it; he
could call off the names of the counties which bordered it; and he knew
the people in the counties, and who they married, and all about them. He
was a wonderful fellow who had a cargo of data warehoused in his head
which would stagger a college professor—and all of it was in reach all of
the time and he could use it with dexterity.

Dayton looked learned. It oozed out of every pore of him. He had a
hawk-like nose shaded by heavy, shaggy eyebrows, and a noble forehead.
He habitually stood around with the thumb and forefinger of one hand
supporting his elbow. He stood with heels together, and toes spread wide
apart, and bent slightly forward as though piercing his gaze intently into
whatever object met his attention. This came from his long service in a
pilothouse. Singularly, he is the only pilot I ever saw who never, on any
occasion, sat down on a stool or a chair while on duty. He stood up to it—
even though he was on duty for ten or twelve hours—he still stood up and
showed no sign of tiring.

* * * * *

"So you're the pur-suer [1] on this boat?" inquired Dayton when I had
introduced myself.

From *Pilotin' Comes Natural,* by Frederick Way, Jr., pp. 133–137. Copyright, 1943,
by Frederick Way, Jr. New York and Toronto: Farrar & Rinehart, Inc.

[1] All through the palmy days of Mississippi steamboating the man in charge of the
office was termed "head clerk," or "chief clerk," or "first clerk." The term "purser"

"Yes, sir; and it certainly feels fine to be head clerk on such a big steamboat as this one!" I was still drunk with that.

"Big boat?" inquired Dayton, with a slight rise of his eyebrows. His huge, brawny hands shook the eight-foot pilotwheel until it nearly pulled loose from the roots. "This wheel ain't what you'd call overly well put together," he commented.

He steered along, saying nothing for a time, and finally he whisked off his black slouch hat, scratched the top of his head, and said, "Ever hear of the *Hurronico?*" [2]

No, I never had.

"She was the biggest thing that ever floated up this way—well, she was up this way a few times. Too big for regular trade, but they come to Pittsburgh with her once or twice. I helped bring her up—too big a job for one pilot—had thirteen partners; we all stood watch together. Worked in daytime only, because she'd got to wherever she was going by time night came, so there wasn't any use in having a double crew—always run single crew."

"I thought the *Sprague* was the biggest—"

"Pshaw!" ejaculated Dayton. "*Sprague* wasn't in it. They laid the *Sprague* up in a creek when the *Hurronico* went by so's not to let her get sunk in the suck. Ever notice how the water on the shore will draw away when a packet comes along?"

"Yes—but—"

"Well, that was the chief trouble about the *Hurronico* up in this end of the river. Even running slow bell she'd suck up all the river ahead of her, and leave the catfish standing on their heads to keep their gills wet, and all the shantyboats would come racing out on the suck to meet her, and she never landed for coal, because the coal flats would come right out to her. She'd draw a power of stuff out from the shores, and make kindling and drift out of it all in a hurry, too. They used to send telegraph warnings ahead, and farmers would take their johnboats up in a field, and get ready hours ahead for the *Hurronico* to pass by."

"I never heard of that boat," I mused.

"She didn't last long. Too big," Dayton commented.

"My!" I exclaimed. "She must have been powerful!"

"Biggest stroke engines I ever saw in my life, and I've seen a few big ones," Dayton went on. He leaned on the frail pilot-wheel and peered away ahead. "I forget her stroke, never was good on figures, but her piston went out in the morning and came back in the afternoon. The twenty-second assistant engineer lived in a shanty built on the end of the pitman so's he could keep pouring oil on the bearings. I think she had eighteen boilers."

---

appeared in the twentieth century. Dayton Randolph toyed with the new word when he said "pur-suer."—F.W., Jr.

[2] Dayton variously pronounced this *Hur-ron-i-co* and *Hugh-ron-i-co,* mostly the former.—F.W., Jr.

"Eighteen! Why the *Crowder* only has two!"

"Well, eighteen on the steamboat, I mean," he recollected with a little frown. "They carried two extras alongside in a fuel flat to blow the whistle with. Dang it, boy, you ought to have heard that whistle on the *Hurronico!* It was made out of an eighteen-foot length of oil well casing and it would strip leaves off trees for a half mile around when you bore down on it. They passed ordinances in Wheeling and Martin's Ferry and a lot of places, and fined the captain five hundred dollars if he so much as tooted the littlest toot anywhere near those places—broke all the store fronts out —plate glass windows and the like."

"How do you suppose I ever missed seeing or hearing about—"

"Oh," said Dayton easily, "she only lasted about a year. They opened her wide up down in Racehorse Reach and the friction caught her hull afire and burned her up."

My slow wits were commencing to function. "How long was the *Hurronico?*" I asked suspiciously.

"Mile and a half, not counting the wheel. Her hull was jointed—had hinges in it—so she'd get around bends; she didn't always make it at that."

Dayton turned around and eyed me. "How do you figure islands were formed?"

"I never thought about it."

"Well, you ain't busy right now. Think about it."

For a few moments my brain worked in a whirl and I said, "I suppose the river came along to a wide, flat place and couldn't make up its mind which way to take, so it compromised, and reached out two ways and finally met later on, and formed islands."

Dayton took a big chew of tobacco. "Nope," he said, "—the *Hurronico* done it. She was too long to get around the sharp bends, so she took over the sharp points and wore a groove until the river run through, and left islands sticking around."

He looked at me in triumph, and gave a loud, merry chuckle which went on for minutes. Dayton Randolph and his *Hurronico!* He continually stood there at the wheel and invented tales about that boat of his own devising. The *Hurronico* was the super-impossible steamboat; the Paul Bunyan of the Ohio River with a hull under her.

Alligator Boats

I had never felt so like a passenger before. I thanked [the pilot], with emotion, for each new fact, and wrote it down in my notebook. The pilot

From *Life on the Mississippi,* by Samuel L. Clemens, pp. 192–195. Copyright, 1874 and 1875, by H. O. Houghton & Company; 1883, 1899, 1903, by Samuel L. Clemens; 1911, by Clara Gabrilowitsch. New York and London: Harper & Brothers, Publishers.

warmed to his opportunity and proceeded to load me up in the good old-fashioned way. At times I was afraid he was going to rupture his invention; but it always stood the strain, and he pulled through all right. He drifted, by easy stages, into revealments of the river's marvelous eccentricities of one sort or another, and backed them up with some pretty gigantic illustrations. For instance:

"Do you see that little boulder sticking out of the water yonder? Well, when I first came on the river, that was a solid ridge of rock, over sixty feet high and two miles long. All washed away but that." [This with a sigh.]

I had a mighty impulse to destroy him, but it seemed to me that killing, in any ordinary way, would be too good for him.

Once, when an odd-looking craft, with a vast coal-scuttle slanting aloft on the end of a beam, was steaming by in the distance, he indifferently drew attention to it, as one might to an object grown wearisome through familiarity, and observed that it was an "alligator boat."

"An alligator boat? What's it for?"

"To dredge out alligators with."

"Are they so thick as to be troublesome?"

"Well, not now, because the government keeps them down. But they used to be. Not everywhere; but in favorite places, here and there, where the river is wide and shoal—like Plum Point, and Stack Island, and so on —places they call alligator beds."

"Did they actually impede navigation?"

"Years ago, yes, in very low water; there was hardly a trip, then, that we didn't get aground on alligators."

It seemed to me that I should certainly have to get out my tomahawk. However, I restrained myself and said:

"It must have been dreadful."

"Yes, it was one of the main difficulties about piloting. It was so hard to tell anything about the water; the d——d things shift around so— never lie still five minutes at a time. You can tell a wind-reef, straight off, by the look of it; you can tell a break; you can tell a sand-reef—that's all easy; but an alligator reef doesn't show up, worth anything. Nine times in ten you can't tell where the water is; and when you *do* see where it is, like as not it ain't there when *you* get there, the devils have swapped around so, meantime. Of course there were some few pilots that could judge of alligator water nearly as well as they could of any other kind, but they had to have natural talent for it; it wasn't a thing a body could *learn*, you had to be born with it. Let me see: There was Ben Thornburg, and Beck Jolly, and Squire Bell, and Horace Bixby, and Major Downing, and John Stevenson, and Billy Gordon, and Jim Brady, and George Ealer, and Billy Youngblood—all A 1 alligator pilots. *They* could tell alligator water as far as another Christian could tell whisky. Read it? Ah, couldn't they, though! I only wish I had as many dollars as they could read alligator water a mile and a half off. Yes, and it paid them to do it, too. A good alligator pilot could always get fifteen hundred dollars a month. Nights, other people had to lay up for alligators, but those fellows never laid up for alligators; they never laid up for anything but fog. They could *smell* the best alligator water—so it was said. I don't know whether it was so or not, and I think a body's got his hands full enough if he sticks to just what he knows himself, without going around backing up other people's say-so's, though there's a plenty that ain't backward about doing it, as long as they can roust out something wonderful to tell. Which is not the style of Robert Styles, by as much as three fathom—maybe quarter-*less*."

[My! Was this Rob Styles? This mustached and stately figure? A slim enough cub, in my time. How he has improved in comeliness in five-and-twenty years—and in the noble art of inflating his facts.] After these musings, I said aloud:

"I should think that dredging out the alligators wouldn't have done much good, because they could come back again right away."

"If you had had as much experience of alligators as I have, you wouldn't talk like that. You dredge an alligator once, and he's *convinced*. It's the last you hear of *him*. He wouldn't come back for pie. If there's one thing that an alligator is more down on than another, it's being dredged. Besides, they were not simply shoved out of the way; the most of the scoopful were scooped aboard; they emptied them into the hold; and when they had got a trip, they took them to New Orleans to the government works."

"What for?"

"Why, to make soldier-shoes out of their hides. All the government shoes are made of alligator hide. It makes the best shoes in the world. They last five years, and they won't absorb water. The alligator fishery is a government monopoly. All the alligators are government property—just like the live-oaks. You cut down a live-oak, and government fines you fifty dollars; you kill an alligator and up you go for misprision of treason—lucky duck if they don't hang you, too. And they will, if you're a Democrat. The buzzard is the sacred bird of the South, and you can't touch him; the alligator is the sacred bird of the government, and you've got to let him alone."

"Do you ever get aground on the alligators now?"

"Oh, no! it hasn't happened for years."

"Well, then, why do they still keep the alligator boats in service?"

"Just for police duty—nothing more. They merely go up and down now and then. The present generation of alligators know them as easy as a burglar knows a roundsman; when they see one coming, they break camp and go for the woods."

Steamboats and Church

On Sunday evening about the middle of June, [1854], the *John B. Gordon* made a third arrival [at Fort Des Moines] at "early candle lighting." It is probable that this arrival gave rise to the story that the worshippers of the various churches slipped out at the sound of the whistle far down the river, and headed for the landing, sexton and all, without waiting for the benediction, leaving the ministers to put out the lights and follow in a more dignified manner if they wished. It was once said by a humorous pioneer that he supposed if at a wedding the minister had gotten so far along in the ceremony as the question, "Will you have this woman—" and a steamboat whistle should be heard in the distance, he would by force of circumstances be compelled to say, "The remainder of the service will be completed at the steamboat landing."

Signal Fires

... We ... amused ourselves in watching the woodmen's lights on the shore—large fires built at the points where wood for steamers was to be found. ... The pilot related to the colonel a very remarkable use which he once made of these lights on the shore.

"We were coming up from Orleans in a thick fog," said he. "The night was dark as pitch. We could not land in safety, as it blew hard. Our only chance was to keep in the middle of the stream and run for it. These woodmen at that time did not light their signal fires till they heard a boat ring her bell, as a token that it wanted wood. You would then see a score of fires kindled along a stretch of four miles or so. We could discern no fires to guide us or tell us where either shore was; so I rang the bell as a signal for wooding. The next minute a fire blazed up through the fog on the left bank, quarter of a mile ahead; and a half a mile above upon the other shore shone another like a star in the dog-days. By these we were enabled to steer; and every quarter of an hour I tolled my bell, as I ascended the river, and fire after fire would blaze up, one on this shore, one on that. In this way we ran all night, full a hundred miles, lighted by these signal fires, which we made these poor fellows kindle, supposing we were coming in to take in wood; but the rogues ought to have done us this service, as they live and get rich by steamboats."

From "History of Steamboating on the Des Moines River, from 1837 to 1862," by Tacitus Hussey, *Annals of Iowa,* 3d Series, Vol. IV (April, 1900), No. 5, p. 359. Des Moines: Published by the Historical Department of Iowa.

From *The Sunny South;* or, The Southerner at Home, Embracing Five Years' Experience of a Northern Governess, in the Land of the Sugar and the Cotton, edited by J. H. Ingraham, pp. 255–256. Entered ... 1860, by G. G. Evans. Philadelphia.

A Gambler's Close Call

Charlie Clark and I left New Orleans one night on the steamer *Duke of Orleans*. There were ten or twelve rough-looking fellows on board who did their drinking out of private bottles. Charlie opened up shop in the cabin, and soon had a great crowd around him. I saw that the devils had been drinking too much, so I gave Charlie the wink and he soon closed up, claiming to be broke. Then we arranged that I should do the playing, and he would be on the lookout. I soon got about all the money and some watches out of the roughs, besides I beat seven or eight of the other passengers. They all appeared to take it good-naturedly at the time; but it was not long before their loss, and the bad whisky, began to work on them. I saw there was going to be trouble, so I made a sneak for my room, changed my clothes, and then slipped down the back stairs into the kitchen. I sent word for Clark to come down. I then blackened my face and hands, and made myself look like a deck-hand. I had hardly finished my disguise when a terrible rumpus up stairs warned me that the ball was open.

The whisky was beginning to do its work. They searched everywhere; kicked in the state-room doors, turned everything upside down, and raised h——l generally. If they could have caught me then, it would have been good bye George. They came down on deck, walked past, and inquired of a roustabout who stood by me if he had seen a well-dressed man on deck. He told them "he had not seen any gemman down on deck afore they came down." They had their guns out, and were swearing vengeance. The boat was plowing her way along up the river; the stevedores were hurrying the darkies to get up some freight, as a landing was soon to be made. The whistle blew, and the boat was headed for shore. Those devils knew I would attempt to leave the boat, so as soon as the plank was put out they ran over on the bank, and closely scanned the face of every one who got off. There was a lot of plows to be discharged, so I watched my chance, shouldered a plow, followed a long line of coons, and I fairly flew past the mob. I kept on up the high bank and threw my plow on to the pile, and then I made for the cotton fields. I lay down on my back until the boat was out of sight, and then I came out, washed myself white, and took a boat for Vicksburg, where I met Clark the next day, and we divided the boodle that he had brought with him. He told me that after I had left the

From *Forty Years a Gambler on the Mississippi*, A Cabin Boy in 1839; Could Steal Cards and Cheat the Boys at Eleven; Stack a Deck at Fourteen; Bested Soldiers on the Rio Grande during the Mexican War; Won Hundreds of Thousands from Paymasters, Cotton Buyers, Defaulters and Thieves; Fought More Rough-and-Tumble Fights than Any Man in America and Was the Most Daring Gambler in the World, by George H. Devol, pp. 53–55. Entered . . . 1887, by George H. Devol. New York.

boat they got lights and went down into the hold, looking for me, as they were sure I was still on the boat. It was a pretty close call, but they were looking for a well-dressed man and not a black deck-hand.

The Grateful Alligators

The passenger who was going down the Mississippi River for the first time in his life secured permission to climb up beside the pilot, a grim old grayback, who never told a lie in his life.

"Many alligators in the river?" inquired the stranger, after a look around.

"Not so many now, since they got to shootin' 'em for their hides and taller," was the reply.

"Used to be lots, eh?"

"I don't want to tell you about 'em, stranger," replied the pilot, sighing heavily.

"Why?"

" 'Cause you'd think I was a-lying to you, and that's sumthin' I never do. I kin cheat at kards, drink whisky or chaw poor terbacker, but I can't lie."

"Then there used to be lots of 'em?" inquired the passenger.

"I'm 'most afraid to tell ye, mister, but I've counted 'leven hundred allygaters to the mile from Vicksburg clear down to Orleans! That was years ago, before a shot was ever fired at 'em."

"Well, I don't doubt it," replied the stranger.

"And I've counted 3,459 of 'em on one sandbar!" continued the pilot. "It looks big to tell, but a government surveyor was aboard, and he checked 'em off as I called out."

"I haven't the least doubt of it," said the passenger as he heaved a sigh.

"I'm glad o' that, stranger. Some fellows would think I was a liar when I'm telling the solemn truth. This used to be a paradise for alligators, and they were so thick that the wheels of the boat killed an average of forty-nine to the mile!"

"Is that so?"

"True as a Gospel, Mister; I used to almost feel sorry for the cussed brutes, 'cause they'd cry out e'enamost like a human being. We killed lots of 'em, as I said, and we hurt a pile more. I sailed with one captain who allus carried 1,000 bottles of liniment to throw over to the wounded ones!"

"He did?"

From *Wit and Humor of the Age,* Comprising Wit, Humor, Pathos, Ridicule, Satires, Dialects, Puns, Conundrums, Riddles, Charades, Jokes and Magic, by Mark Twain, Josh Billings, Robt. J. Burdette, Alex. Sweet, Eli Perkins, with the Philosophy of Wit and Humor, by Melville D. Landon, pp. 190–192. Copyright, 1883, by L. W. Yaggy; 1901, by R. W. Patton. Chicago: Star Publishing Company.

"True as you live, he did. I don't 'spect I'll ever see another such a Christian man. And the allygaters got to know the *Nancy Jane,* and to know Captain Tom, and they'd swim and rub their tails against the boat, and purr like cats, and look up and try to smile!"

"They would?"

"Solemn truth, stranger. And once, when we grounded on a bar, with an opposition boat right behind, the allygaters gathered around, got under the stern, and humped her clean over the bar by a grand push. It looks like a big story, but I never told a lie yet, and never shall. I wouldn't lie for all the money you could put aboard this boat."

There was a painful pause, and after a while the pilot continued:

"Our injines gin out once, and a crowd of allygaters took a tow line and hauled us forty-five miles up stream to Vicksburg."

"They did?"

"And when the news got along the river that Captain Tom was dead every allygater in the river daubed his left ear with black mud as a badge of mournin', and lots of 'em pined away and died."

The passenger left the pilot house with the remark that he didn't doubt the statement, but the old man gave the wheel a turn and replied:

"There's one thing I won't do for love nor money, and that's make a liar out of myself. I was brung up by a good mother, and I'm going to stick to the truth if this boat doesn't make a cent."

"You Never See a River Man with Less Than Two Ears"

A veritable river Scheherazade is George Heckman, brother of the legendary "Steamboat Bill" Heckman. George, who was a river-boat engineer, is a specialist in animal stories, with an emphasis on hunting and fishing, that have a strong appeal for river men. He told two of his favorites . . . in the galley of the *Mama Lere,* while she was tied up beneath the cliffs of St. Paul.

One day, said George, he had been having no luck at all fishing. He recalled having heard that frogs made irresistible bait for catfish. After a fruitless search for frogs, he was about to give up when he saw a moccasin trying to swallow a frog. He tried to pull the frog away from the snake, but the reptile hung on to its meal. Finally, said George, he reached into his boot, pulled out a bottle of whisky, and poured some liquor down the snake's mouth. It let go of the frog and slipped giddily away. A few minutes later, while George was preparing to fish again, he felt a tap on his boot. He looked down. The snake was back with another frog in its mouth, looking for a drink.

* * * * *

From "New Life on the Mississippi," by Murray Schumach, *The New York Times Magazine,* April 18, 1954, p. 67. Copyright, 1954, by The New York Times Company.

Another of George's tales concerns a hunting dog that was the best retriever he'd ever known. Once, George said, another man matched his dog against George's. At first, each dog had to retrieve a frankfurter without marring the skin. Each dog succeeded. Then the dogs brought back a mouthful of raw hamburger without swallowing any. It looked like a deadlock, said George, until he suggested that his competitor's dog retrieve some Jello. The other said this was impossible. Whereupon, George vowed, he dropped a handkerchief near the Jello. His dog gently nudged it onto the handkerchief, snatched it up by the four corners, and returned with the dessert shaking but intact.

Captain Avis Trosclair, skipper of the *Gona* and himself a skilful weaver of tall stories, is fond of an old river saying. "They say," he likes to remark during a story session, "that every time a river man tells the truth one of his ears falls off. You never see a river man with less than two ears, did you?"

Audubon's Fish Story

. . . Audubon, it seems, was at that time [of Rafinesque's visit to him in Henderson, Kentucky, in 1818] a good deal of a wag, and whether to vent his dislike of species-mongers, to avenge the loss of his violin [which his guest had battered to pieces in attempting to kill bats in his room], or to gratify some spirit of mischief, he played upon the credulity of his guest, in a way that could be deemed hardly creditable, in giving him detailed descriptions and even supplying him with drawings of sundry impossible fishes and mollusks. Rafinesque took the bait eagerly, duly noted down everything on the spot, and, what was more unfortunate for American zoology, a year later began to publish the results. The fictitious species of fish, to the number of ten, "communicated by Mr. Audubon," first appeared as a series of articles in a short-lived and long forgotten Western magazine [*The Western Review and Miscellaneous Magazine*, Lexington, 1819–20], but in 1820 they were gathered into a little volume now considered so quaint and rare that it has been reproduced in its entirety. In this pioneer work on the ichthyology of the Ohio River and the great Middle West, 111 kinds of American fresh-water fishes are briefly described. Those ten "new species," representing apparently a number of new genera, "so like and yet so unlike to anything yet known," long remained a stumbling block to American zoologists; naturally they tended to discredit the work of Rafinesque.

As a specimen of these spurious fish stories, which were previously published in both America and Europe, we reproduce a part of Rafinesque's

From *Audubon the Naturalist*, A History of His Life and Time, by Francis Hobart Herrick, pp. 291–293. Copyright, 1938, by D. Appleton-Century Company, Inc. New York and London.

description of the "91st Species. Devil Jack Diamond-Fish. Litholepis adamantinus":

> This may be reckoned the wonder of the Ohio. It is only found as far up as the falls, and probably lives also in the Mississippi. I have seen it, but only at a distance, and have been shown some of its singular scales. Wonderful stories are related concerning this fish, but I have principally relied upon the description and figure given me by Mr. Audubon. Its length is from 4 to 10 feet. One was caught which weighed four hundred pounds. It lies sometimes asleep or motionless on the surface of the water, and may be mistaken for a log or a snag. It is impossible to take it in any other way than with the seine or a very strong hook; the prongs of the gig cannot pierce the scales which are as hard as flint, and even proof against lead balls! Its flesh is not good to eat. It is a voracious fish. Its vulgar names are Diamond fish (owing to its scales being cut like diamonds). Devil fish, Jack fish, Garjack, etc. . . . The whole body covered with large stone scales laying in oblique rows, they are conical, pentagonal, and pentahedral with equal sides, from half an inch to one inch in diameter, brown at first, but becoming of the color of turtle shell when dry; they strike fire with steel! and are ball proof!

The Story of Annie Christmas

First, let me say that Lyle [Saxon] and Brad [Roark Bradford] went to work on the [New Orleans] *Times-Picayune* at practically the same time. Both men had a sly sardonic attitude toward the silly and pretentious "traditions" of New Orleans. They were fed to the teeth on such things as the descendants of the *filles à la cassette*. True, there were a few girls who were indeed sent over from France to marry the colonists and they did indeed carry with them small caskets filled with money and jewels given as a *dot* by the King of France. But Lyle said that each girl would have to have at least 100 children to take care of the descendants (*soi-disant*) who claim them as ancestors. These two inventive brains, Lyle and Brad, made up out of whole cloth the goddamdest funniest stories in the early '20s which have since crept into the folklore of New Orleans.

One night Brad and Lyle were walking in Decatur Street, that dark, dangerous four-block-long skidrow between Chartres and the docks. Thirty years ago Decatur was full of speaks, dives, clip joints, whore houses, greasy spoons, etc., and it was worth your life to go into most of them. Together B. and L. made up a story of a large, Tug-boat-Annie type of woman who ran one of the dives. She had seven huge sons who were

---

From letter to the editor by Mrs. Roark Bradford, Santa Fé, New Mexico, December 29, 1954.

For "Annie Christmas," see *Gumbo Ya-Ya*, by Lyle Saxon, pp. 376–377 (Boston, 1945); *The Hurricane's Children*, by Carl Carmer, pp. 103–109 (New York, 1937), reprinted in *A Treasury of Southern Folklore*, pp. 228–230 (New York, 1949).

bouncers for the joint. God knows how many poor seafaring men on their first night in town were rolled and dumped into the Mississippi by these seven giants. "Let's call her Mary Christmas," said Lyle. "You go too far," said Brad. "Nobody would believe *that*. Call her Annie Christmas." Result: folklore.

Brad was Sunday editor of the *T-P* and had $15 per Sunday to spend on features. This generous sum he passed around among Lyle, Bill Faulkner, Sherwood Anderson, and other Ganymedes of the French Quarter. Lyle wrote the Annie Christmas story as if he'd just come across her in some old manuscripts; it was a Sunday feature; and it gave Lyle a week's supply of bootleg as dispensed by Bussey at the "Press Club"—a euphemism for the speak that the *T-P* gang patronized. (I arrived first in N.O. in July, 1931, in time to make several visits to the Press Club before dat ole debbil Repeal closed it up. Bussey went to bartending at what is now called the Gay '90s on the corner of Royal and Toulouse. Bussey had been a member in the early 1900's of the first band to be called a "jazz" band. It was called "The Razzy, Dazzy, Jazzy Spasm Band.")

Shantyboat Fishing Lore

It is a lazy life, the life of the shantyboat fisherman. There is much time to talk. And there are few who are better conversationalists, with their mellow philosophy and vast store of information, so much of it inaccurate. I know of nothing more delightful than to sit in a flatboat while Catfish Johnny runs his lines, and listen to him tell of the lore of the river: how if you take a fish out of the Red River or Black River and drop it in Mississippi water it will die as quickly as though you had pierced it with a bullet; how fish will spoil quicker in the moonlight than under the sun. He will tell you how it is useless to fish after a night of bright moonlight, because fish will gorge themselves feeding in the light of the moon, and so the next day will bite at nothing; or how a fish cannot be kept with its head down stream or it will drown like a human. He will explain how if you wish to catch an alligator, you must put a piece of garlic on a stick, and when you poke this into the alligator's hole, the smell will drive him out in panic; he will describe how the fish travel on great highways through the water, just as if they were on roads marked out by Government men.

From *Big River to Cross,* Mississippi Life Today, by Ben Lucien Burman, p. 82. Copyright, 1938, 1939, 1940, by Ben Lucien Burman. New York: The John Day Company.

In the Same Boat

An overflow of the great Mississippi is a massive, elemental thing. It is not easily described so that an uplander can sense its vastness and power. If the people of the Delta lowlands are different from people elsewhere; if their "culture" is distinctive and therefore interesting, that is at least partly because the waters of the Mississippi and of the lesser streams coming down out of the Ozark hills have spread over so much of the lowlands so often in the past, and in some large areas still do so or threaten to do so during the winter and spring of each year.

* * * * *

Do you know that when you have to do it, you can make a boat out of practically anything? There was a saying in the bottoms that you can make a boat out of a picket fence, if that is all you've got. I should say there were about fifteen hundred families living then in the bottoms of my country that were overflowed [in 1937]. Most of them, after the break, had twenty-four hours to do what they could before the river filled in the lowest land and rose to their houses and barns. I venture to say that every household had its boat completed in that time. No two were alike. A little later on when the country was covered and everybody had done all he could and saved what he could, there was lots of visiting around, and people made humorous, uncomplimentary remarks about each other's boats.

Most barns had hay lofts that would be above water. So everything that could be got to a hay loft went there, often including mules, cows, hogs, chickens, with the family setting up housekeeping in a fenced-off corner. . . .

* * * * *

If you had a two-story house you just carried everything upstairs and stacked it up the best you could and set up housekeeping with your boat tied to an upstairs window. A few one-story houses were built up on high blocks so the river had room under them. There was no moving out of such houses that I know of, and where the boat could be tied at the front door, or maybe to the front porch, it made living convenient, not to say luxurious. There was no water problem; you just let down a bucket and filled it. Maybe at first you let it settle before you drank it, because it was very muddy, but you soon stopped such nonsense. There was no sewage disposal problem, either. You just dumped it out.

As I remember it, the river stayed up two months in 1912. I would say that more than half the families who lived in the bottoms stayed on clear through, either in their own houses or in somebody else's houses or barns.

From *From Missouri,* by Thad Snow, pp. 97–103. Copyright, 1954, by Thad Snow. Boston: Houghton Mifflin Company.

Many had to scaffold up their belongings the best they could and get out as soon as the river filled up the country enough to make it good boating. But the overflowed bottoms remained quite well peopled throughout.

Were the water-bound people downhearted and dispirited? Not on your life! I never saw people happier. They made it a grand jamboree. Everybody was good-humored. I knew two families that had been at outs a long time, and they made it all up, and it lasted after the river went down. There was nothing to do but have a good time, and it was easy to get around, and interesting too, if only to see how the other fellow made out. . . .

*   *   *   *   *

I have sometimes wondered why it was that the people who stayed it out in the water were so cheerful and happy all the time. It wasn't because they were accustomed to floods and inured to their hardships, for the bottoms had not been flooded for many years, and weren't expected ever to be flooded over again. Most, like myself, had only hazy notions what a flood would be like; but they took it in high spirits. I think it may have been because everyone had similar problems and discomforts, which gave them a fine sense of unity, which people appear to enjoy whenever they attain it. They were all in the same boat, so to speak, although their sure-enough boats were ludicrously variegated.

"Same As Us"

A friend of mine was engaged in rescue work among some of [the Barataria Bay] shrimp fishermen during the great hurricane that struck the region in 1947. For a number of days the rescue workers had been trying to reach one group completely isolated by the huge tidal seas, and certain that all their food had been washed away, were greatly concerned that they might be starving.

After a tremendous struggle, the rescuers at last reached the battered dock, with its buildings still under two feet of water. As they feared, they found the fishermen gathered in a half-submerged shed, exhausted and suffering acutely from hunger. As the rescuers hastened to distribute their supplies, my friend noticed half a dozen great fish swimming about in the water that covered the floor, washed into the building at the height of the storm, and trapped in some fashion so they could not escape. So helpless they could have been caught by a child, they would have provided an excellent meal for all those marooned in the shed's narrow quarters.

From *Children of Noah*, Glimpses of Unknown America, by Ben Lucien Burman, p. 146. Copyright, 1951, by Ben Lucien Burman. New York: Julian Messner, Inc.

My friend, wondering, asked why the shrimpers didn't eat the fish, instead of almost starving.

The fisherman he addressed, a gaunt Mississippian, looked at him in shocked surprise. "We couldn't eat them fish," he answered. "Them fish were fighting for their lives, same as us."

The Long Way Round

A story is told of a young Indian boy whose dignity and wholesomeness delighted a vacation visitor to the north country. The white man, being childless, but having an abstract taste for paternity, decided in a night of inspiration to make the great gesture and adopt the boy. Agleam with benignity, he announced to the young guide the next day: "I'm going to take you back with me to Chicago. You're to be my son."

The Indian considered the suggestion coolly. What would he do in Chicago, he wanted to know. Well, he would go to school until he was old enough to enter the business. And after that what? Well, he would work his way up through the various departments of the factory. He would be a foreman, then a department head, then general manager. The boy was beginning to look puzzled, and the man who wished to be a foster-father felt his whole scheme of life to be under critical examination. He wanted deeply to justify it. "Finally," he went on in a great burst of generosity, "when I die, you will inherit all that I have, my business, my house, everything." The boy still looked aloof and unpersuaded. "And then what?" he asked once more. "Why, then you'll be a rich man. You can do what you like, you can retire and come up here and spend all your time fishing." The boy's eyes widened in complete despair at being asked to follow such whimsical nonsense. "But I can do that now," he said.

"It's All Changed Now"—Steamboat *vs.* Railroad

The locomotive is in sight from the deck of the steamboat almost the whole way from St. Louis to St. Paul—eight hundred miles. These railroads have made havoc with the steamboat commerce. The clerk of our boat was a steamboat clerk before these roads were built. In that day the influx of population was so great, and the freight business so heavy, that

From *Pine Stream & Prairie,* Wisconsin and Minnesota in Profile, by James Gray, pp. 37–38. Copyright, 1945, by James Gray. New York: Alfred A. Knopf, Inc.

From *Life on the Mississippi,* by Samuel L. Clemens, pp. 432–434. Copyright, 1874 and 1875, by H. O. Houghton & Company; 1883, 1899, 1903, by Samuel L. Clemens; 1911, by Clara Gabrilowitsch. New York and London: Harper & Brothers, Publishers.

the boats were not able to keep up with the demands made upon their carrying capacity; consequently the captains were very independent and airy—pretty "biggity," as Uncle Remus would say. The clerk nutshelled the contrast between the former time and the present, thus:

"Boat used to land—captain on hurricane roof—mighty stiff and straight—iron ramrod for a spine—kid gloves, plug tile, hair parted behind—man on shore takes off hat and says:

" 'Got twenty-eight tons of wheat, cap'n—be great favor if you can take them.'

"Captain says:

" 'I'll take two of them'—and don't even condescend to look at him.

"But nowadays the captain takes off his old slouch, and smiles all the way around to the back of his ears, and gets off a bow which he hasn't got any ramrod to interfere with, and says:

" 'Glad to see you, Smith, glad to see you—you're looking well—haven't seen you looking so well for years—what you got for us?'

" 'Nuth'n,' says Smith; and keeps his hat on, and just turns his back and goes to talking with somebody else.

"Oh, yes! eight years ago the captain was on top; but it's Smith's turn now. Eight years ago a boat used to go up the river with every stateroom full, and people piled five and six deep on the cabin floor; and a solid deckload of immigrants and harvesters down below, into the bargain. To get a first-class stateroom, you'd got to prove sixteen quarterings of nobility and four hundred years of descent, or be personally acquainted with the Negro that blacked the captain's boots. But it's all changed now; plenty staterooms above, no harvesters below—there's a patent self-binder now, and they don't have harvesters any more; they've gone where the woodbine twineth—and they didn't go by steamboat, either; went by the train."

The *Coal Queen*

I plugged up and down the Illinois River for a couple of years as deckhand on the towboats, hauling coal from Havana up to Joliet, and then in the drainage canal up to Chicago, and the draft board took the second mate, so Captain Bloodworth called me up to the pilothouse and said, "You're the new second mate." I took my paper suitcase out of the pigpen and up to the mates' room, and one thing sure, that mates' room smelled better than the deckhands' bunkroom, and even had a light in the bunk to read by, and a clean blanket with no fuel oil or coal ground into it. You go out and carry ratchets and chains and those 100-foot lock lines for a

From *The Monongahela*, by Richard Bissell, pp. 5–23. *The Rivers of America*, edited by Carl Carmer. Copyright, 1949, 1952, by Richard Pike Bissell. New York and Toronto: Rinehart & Co., Inc.

while and you will understand what I felt like to be a mate. I couldn't have felt any better if they'd made me governor of the state.

I was mate for over a year. We brought up a lot of coal from down below, and if summer nights in the canal weren't much of a treat to the nose, and winter nights pulling ice cakes out of the lock gates weren't very romantic, still it was $145 a month and all you could eat, and ten days off with pay every forty, a good tavern near the dock at Joliet, and the boat was a home.

One afternoon a week or so before Thanksgiving when the wind from Lake Michigan was slicing down through the frame houses and factories, we had just tied off six loads at the Joliet landing and the shore watchman came hunting me up where I was having coffee in the galley.

"Ole Murphy he wants to see you up in the office," he said. "My, I wisht I was a big mate so's I could set in the galley drinkin' coffee."

"You wanna make this trip downriver and back for me?" I said.

"I gotta get back," he said.

I went up to the office and Helen, the new office girl with the glasses, told me to go right in, that Captain Murphy was waiting for me.

"Not that I think you'll ever amount to a damn," says Murphy looking out the window at the canal with a sour look, "but the pilot on the *Coal Queen* fell off a barge last night and got himself drownded like a jackass and the boat is tied up. Now you go and pack up and take the train for Morgantown—you can be there tomorrow afternoon."

"Okay," I said, feeling a little dizzy. "But I'm no pilot, and where in hell is Morgantown? I never heard of it."

"West Virginia," he said. "Monongahela River. You stand a few watches and you'll either be a pilot or in the nuthouse. Now get goin'. Expense money from Miss Rundel."

"I never knew the company had boats way over there," I said.

"There's a lot of other things you don't know," he said, "but don't let the strain injure your brains."

A couple of days later, after missing a train in Pittsburgh and other incidents, I got off a crummy old day coach and there I was in Morgantown, and a guy comes up and says, "Are you Bissell?"

"Yes, I am, and where is the boat?"

He loaded me in his car and said we would go out to the landing and I could go to work right away, they had only been doing day work since the pilot drowned—the captain was working days and they tied up nights.

We came down across some tracks toward the Monongahela and I noticed a little old dirty boat with a telescoping pilothouse and a single stack, a piece of marine junk overdue for the scrap yard.

"Who owns that palatial yacht?" I said.

"Why, that's the *Coal Queen*," he said. "That's the boat."

"Uh-huh," I said. "Well, let's you and me go right down to the depot again. I can probably still get a train out this afternoon."

"Why," says the shore boss, looking hurt, "what's the matter?"

"Why, man oh man, I just came off the *Inland Coal,* 1,350 horsepower Atlas Imperial. What makes you think I'm gonna live in this old converted oil drum?" I said. "Look at the stack, tied up there with baling wire. Look at that deck—looks like Blum's junk yard. Look at them tow knees all bunged over. And what are them two dwarfs standin' there all over coal dust? Deckhands, I suppose, or is that the captain and chief engineer?"

Well, I went aboard. What the hell, it was awfully cold back on the Illinois. I pretty near changed my mind again once I got aboard though. What a layout. First place, all the officers, the deckhands, and the cook slept in one bunkroom in a great pile of bunks, suitcases, pillows with no pillowcases, shoes, overalls, comic books, oily blankets, newspapers, shaving cream, oilskins, dirty socks, orange peel, cigarette butts, coffee cups, underwear, rubber boots, foot powder, razors, *Western Stories,* and cough syrup. And in order to get the most benefit out of all this, the system was to keep all the windows sealed tight and get an oil-soaked engineer and a couple of ripe deckhands in there, get the cook to fire up his pipe with some Plough Boy, turn the stove up high, and leave the whole thing to simmer for six hours at a time.

I opened the door and went in the bunkroom. A slim, swarthy-looking bird with curly hair and sheik mustache was lying on a bunk reading *Blue Beetle Comics* and smoking cigarettes; he had his shirt off and his shoes off and his feet resting politely on the pillow of the next bunk.

"Ain't this here *Blue Beetle* the goddamnedest?" he said to me as I set down my case and lit a Revelation to kill some of the smell.

"They sent me over here to go pilot," I said. "Where's the captain at?"

"What a shame," he answered. "Now we got to go to work again. My, it's been peaceful here since Happy drownded."

"You the captain?" I asked.

"I'm it," he said. "Ain't it the berries? What boat you come off of?"

"The *Inland Coal,*" I said.

"Finding it kind of a shock so far, hey, buddy?" he said. He got up and stretched, and reached over and poked some old boy asleep in a bunk across from him and hollered, "Gas! Get the hell outa here. Here's the new pilot aboard and that's his bunk from now on. Come on, Gas, you'll hafta double up with National."

This deckhand was in between the sheets in his work clothes—an old pair of greasy pants and check wool shirt—and even had his shoes on. You can imagine what a deckhand's shoes have to put up with in the way of oil, coal, dust, water, mud, grease, and paint in a six-hour watch, so you can picture the sheets easily enough. He rolled out and fell on another bunk about four feet away.

"Where'd that guy get a name like Gas?" I said.

"Come on up to the pilothouse," says the captain. "Why, that's because he comes from Edna Gas."

"Maybe I better go home," I said. "What's Edna Gas?"

"Why, man, it's one of these here coal mines upriver a ways. That's his home. His ole man is blacksmith at the mine."

We got up to the pilothouse. There was just barely room for the two of us, quite a change from the big roomy pilothouses I was used to, with benches, chairs, stoves, water coolers, and so on.

"Hey, National," the captain hollered, sliding the windows back. "Get up off yer dead ass and turn that line loose. Come on, buddy, let's go!" And one of the dwarfs, who had been sitting on the bank looking at his shoelaces, got up and commenced to turn her loose.

"Where's he come from?" I asked.

"National Consolidated, up by Lock 14."

"Why don't you call him Consolidated, then?"

"Sometimes we do." He gave the engineer a backing bell, and the old Fairbanks-Morse shot a bushel basket of soot and rust out of the stack, which was right behind the pilothouse, and the boat commenced backing away from the bank into the stream.

"Hey, National!" he hollered down to the deck, "bring us up a couple of coffees, okay?"

"Where we goin'?" I said.

"We're goin' over to the Dupont landing and pick up an empty and take off for Kingmount. You watch me make the pickup and this first lock and then you can take her."

"Okay, but understand this is all new to me. I never piloted anything bigger'n a Illinois River duckboat."

"Didn't you never steer on the *Inland* and them other boats?"

"Why, sure, but any damn fool can steer out in the river. It's these here locks and landings makes it hard."

"Aw, have some coffee. It ain't bad."

We got across the river and there was a fleet of about ten or fifteen barges, empties and loads, and a big coalyard behind them. And then piled up on the hill behind the heaps of coal was the damnedest-looking plant you ever saw, a monster—big buildings and towers, chimneys and trestles, cranes and sheds, smoke, flame, cinders. I don't know what they made there but they called it the Morgantown Ordnance and we expected to see the whole works blow up most any time and move Monongalia County down around Pittsburgh someplace.

We came up on the barge fleet and the captain rang a slow bell and then a stopping bell and we drifted up easy to an empty barge.

"What's your name?" the captain asked me.

"Bissell," I said.

"Okay, Beedle, now watch how we face up to this here empty," and he never called me anything else again as long as I knew him except when he wanted to borrow money, and then he used my first name.

The deckhand got up on the deck of the empty and grabbed the face wires and dumped them in place on the timberheads. Then he trotted out to the other end of the barge and turned it loose, and before we even had the wires tightened up the captain gave a full ahead bell and we bounced alongside a couple of empties, cleared them, and sailed off up the river. The whole thing didn't take more than three or four minutes.

"My God, do you make all your landings that fast?" I asked.

"Beedle, we make 'em as fast as we can, boy," he said.

"How much coal do we deliver there?"

"All we can tow," he said. "We gave 'em 68,000 tons last month. Here, get the feel of this here thing," and he got up off the pilot's chair. "Set down, Beedle, and make yourself at home. I'm goin' down and get me a slice of salami. Just hold her off this point easy and the lock is around the bend."

"If you say so," I said.

"Call me Duke," and he climbed down the ladder to the deck.

It was a dreary day for sure, with a greasy sky, and a yellowish foggy smoke hanging in the air, and the whole world looked sick and sad. The damned old barge in front of me was a cheerless, banged-up derelict, I was 900 miles from home and still had a hangover from my stop-over in Pittsburgh, and I was very lonesome for Joliet and those familiar locks and landings—Dresden Island, Starved Rock, Brandon Road, and the canal into Chicago. I couldn't see myself sleeping down there in that rat's nest, even to be a pilot. However, the sensation of being at last a pilot, even on this tin can, grew increasingly pleasant, and I lit a cigarette, leaned back on the pilot's stool, and steered with my feet.

The door opened and National stuck his head in. "Say, cap, you want some more coffee?"

That was the first time anybody ever called me "cap," and it sounded pretty fair after I had been crawling around on deck so long with my ears full of soft coal.

"No, no more coffee now," I said. "Say, where's that lock at?"

"You'll see it in a minute. You can blow for it any time now."

Sure enough, out of the yellow winter fog I saw the lock and I found the whistle and blew a long and a short. Duke showed up with a pile of crackers with salami in between them.

"Now, I'll take you in, Beedle, and show you how we do it over here. Want some salami?" He gave me a handful.

Man, I never saw anything like the way we went into that lock. We slammed into her like a taxicab on Wabash Avenue about 5:00 P.M. And when they had raised the water and opened the upper gate we came charging out with the barge alongside, turned it loose, picked it up again on the fly, knocked some concrete off the lock wall with our stern, and away we flew like a wild mustang.

"National," Duke shouted down to the deck, "bring up a couple more coffees."

So I took her again and Duke went down and tackled *Blue Beetle*. This was the toughest, dreariest, most god-forsaken-looking country I ever saw—the hills looked as though a battle had just been fought among the barren trees; they were desolate, dirty, scarred, and under the dull winter sky looked like there was not much hope left anyplace.

The mines, with their coal tipples and lines of coal cars, and the clusters of unpainted frame company houses, and slate piles and muddy streets and Royal Crown Cola signs, made you sick just to look at them. How a man could put in his time whacking away underground and come out into a mess like this and raise up a family in one of these terrible-looking shanties was more than I could understand. It was just homesickness working on me, I suppose—God knows there are some awful places along the drainage canal and in South Chicago, places that would give you the blues even on a spring morning.

Later on I got used to the burnt-over look to things, and it seemed natural and right to me that the world should consist of coal mines, coal trains, coal houses, coal taverns, coal trees, coal streets, coal children, coal everything.

This was bad enough on this dismal afternoon, but night came and I had some pot roast and apple pie in the galley messroom, a little hole aft of the engine room, and Duke said, "You lay down and I'll call you at midnight. Get some sleep, Beedle."

I lay down and tossed around for a couple of hours, dozed, woke up, heard shouts on deck, dozed, woke, listened to National snoring, smoked a cigarette, finally fell asleep. Seemed like about ten minutes later the deck-hand came and woke me. "Hey, cap," he said. "Midnight."

The most dismal words in the world, the call for night watch. Getting up at midnight is bad enough if you're just a deckhand with no responsibilities, but to stagger up to a strange pilothouse on a strange river—well, no, thanks.

"She's rough and she's tough, Beedle boy, but oh how we love it," Duke said. "Well, call me if you get in trouble." And with this sad farewell he was gone.

My first night watch was a humdinger. I bounced off the bank; I wound up in the trees and backed out. I couldn't see and didn't know what to look for anyway—the mountains towered above me on both sides and cast shadows that looked like islands, and the lights from the coal mines we passed made it even worse. I crawled in and out of a couple of locks, making them the slow old way instead of Duke's flying switch style, and finally, running on a slow bell in an intermittent fog, ran my barge head on into a riverside farmyard and practically into the barn.

I tooted the whistle for a deckhand and National stuck his head in the door, eating a sandwich.

"It's three A.M.," I said, "and I've had enough of this. You get out on the head and I'll hunt up a tree and we'll tie her off."

"Oughta be easy to find a tree, cap," he said. "You found a good many already tonight."

After that I stood day watch until I found out what this Monongahela looked like, and in a couple of weeks I was running up through fog, smoke, and the black night, smoking cigarettes, hollering for more coffee, and paying no more attention to the river than High Street after midnight back home.

Oh, we had some hair-raisers—it wouldn't be towboating otherwise. One night I was shoving my empty out of Lock 15 and I turned the boat loose and rang a backing bell to get behind the barge so I could face up to shove again. When I rang the come-ahead bell I got no answer and kept right on going back. I rang some more bells but nothing happened and then I opened the door and looked back to see how hard we would hit the lock gates.

The engineer had run out of compressed air to start the Diesel engine and was so mad he was picking Stillson wrenches off the wall and bouncing them off the deck plates. I never heard such a noise or such loud cussing, even in Illinois. That man went clear off his nut he was so mad.

He finally built up some air and we got the engines started again.

After we got hooked up I told National to ask the engineer to come to the pilothouse. He showed up after a while eating a fried egg sandwich.

"You got kind of a hot temper, ain't you?" I said.

"Well, look here," he said. "I see those indicator lights, and I hear those bells a-ringin' and I know sure to God I'm all out of air and nothin' to do. Still, you kep' a-ringin' them bells. Cap, that just made me so dang mad I had to do somethin', and I started with the old 8-inch Stillson wrench and I pulled her off the wall and slammed her on the deck. Then I slammed the rest of them and I felt some better."

"Well," I said, "it's a lucky thing there's a film of ice up here above the lock. While you were down there slammin' wrenches on the deck, our barge ran out and stuck in the ice; otherwise she would of gone over the dam."

"How about an egg sandwidge?" he said.

"Okay, thanks," I said. "But don't put no salt on it." And he ducked out into the bitter cold again and fried me up an egg sandwich and we were the best of friends.

A couple of nights later he and the deckhand on watch fell asleep on the galley table, and if I hadn't jumped out of the pilothouse and gone down and yanked them off onto the floor, we would have taken the lock and all right on down to Pittsburgh.

Then we got into high water. These locks have an open dam beside them, with the water going right over the top like a waterfall.

"There's some bad currents around these here locks in high water, Beedle," Duke told me. "Watch it close when you're comin' down with loads."

I got all messed up at Lock 12 one afternoon and the barge, with 800 tons of coal in it, and the boat commenced drifting crosswise right onto the dam. The cook was making an upside down cake and he happened to look out and saw us right on top of the dam and he came hell-bent for the pilothouse and got up on the roof. I pulled the general alarm signal and Duke came up to the pilothouse in his underwear.

I rang the engineer for an overload—for once he wasn't asleep or dreaming—and he really poured it to that old tired-out engine. We hung there with our stern right on the crest of the dam, and finally she began to shove up out of it.

"Well, I ain't gettin' no sleep up here," Duke said, and he went back to bed.

When we got back down to Morgantown that trip, the cook went up the bank and back to home and mother, and then we lived on cheese and crackers for a couple of days until the shore boss sent us a new cook.

This old man was all in from forty-five years in the mines and thought he would make a good steamboat cook. He couldn't cook anything but fried eggs and pork chops, and used the same dishwater for breakfast, lunch, and dinner until it looked like the Chicago drainage canal, so Duke fired him and he went uptown and got a job sweeping out the courthouse on Sundays.

The next cook was out of the mines but he was so dumb they couldn't make a miner out of him, so he came aboard and all he could do was roast. We had roast this and roast that and roast everything but roast eggs. He would throw a chunk of meat and some potatoes and carrots in the roaster and then sit out on the deck all day watching the mountains and the coal mines go past or reading *Western Detective*.

"Listen, Roast," I said one morning when he was sitting on the floor of the pilothouse carving his fingernails with the paring knife, "why don't you just get down there and make a couple of pies for dinner? Them canned peaches are getting terrible tiresome."

"Cap, if I could cook a pie, what would I be doin' on this here boat? I could easier be boss of the Arkwright mine than I could make a pie." And he went down and stuck a fork in the pork roast and turned over the potatoes.

The Monongahela runs almost straight north to Pittsburgh, where it joins the Allegheny to form the mighty Ohio. We were about a hundred miles from Pittsburgh, at the headwaters up in the mountains, and the river flowed in sharp bends and twists, past coal mines, wild timberland, villages, the B. & O. railroad yards, and two towns, Morgantown and Fairmont.

We ran into ice and bucked it, and froze in, and broke loose, and finally tied off our load of coal on a smoky Christmas Eve and took the boat down to the Morgantown landing and tied up for Christmas. There was no snow on the ground, and a damp smoky fog hung in the streets as we climbed up the old brick sidewalk to celebrate in a joint called the Imperial.

Seated in a booth and trampled by coal miners with their dome hats on, we drank Kinsey blended whisky with the Tube City beer for chasers, and I thought of home.

That was the worst Christmas I ever put in—everybody had on overalls or $25 blue serge suits, and by midnight they were rolling on the floor and fighting and the girls were drunk and bawling, with their hair coming down, and there were pools of beer and spilled drinks every place. A couple of booths away there was a kid about ten years old who should have been home in bed dreaming of sugar plums—instead he was stealing drinks of beer and was the life of the party.

"How old are you, honey?" I said to my girl Emma, who was smoking cigarettes like her life depended on it.

"How old you think?" she said, draining another shot and chasing it with orangepop.

"Oh, about nineteen," I said, giving her the benefit of the doubt.

"Well, I ain't," she said. "I'm only sixteen. Wahoo! Frank! How's about some service over here?"

So about 2:30, while St. Nick was still busy filling stockings, I went back to my crummy hotel and turned in. Some Christmas Eve.

The winter slowly dragged away, and we had a succession of cooks, and it rained, snowed, sleeted, froze in, thawed, fogged up; and where the sun had gone to nobody seemed to be able to say, but I swear I never saw it for four months at least.

When spring came we opened the bunkroom door a little bit and let some of the fumes escape, tossed some odd shoes in the river, and we were even going to air out the blankets but Duke thought that would fade them. The smoke and fog cleared up for a while, and the sun came out, and I began to get a look at the country, and it was really something to look at. There were trees in bloom in the hills, and mountain laurel with big blossoms on it like I'd never seen before, and the meadows were the greenest green, and the air all through the valley commenced to smell of leaves and flowers instead of soft-coal smoke. With a few trees in leaf around them, these beat-up frame company houses at the mines looked a little better, and the people even seemed less like lost souls; you would see a little girl with a spring hat sitting in the slate piles and it was a big change from winter.

For me to be drawing wages for piloting a towboat under these conditions, why, that's just like paying a kid to watch the circus. The rest of the world was punching the time clock or shooting holes in each other, but here I was all full of roast and Jello, up in a little glass box with nothing to do but steer this cute little boat up and down the river and study the cloud effects over the mountains.

It was kind of a tie which was the most useless, the cook or the second engineer. This engineer I had on my watch was about twenty years old and one of these guys that can't stand to watch you pick your teeth without giving a few pointers.

I was coming downriver one afternoon and he came up to the pilothouse to chew the rag for a while, and we talked about how to make seine nets and whether a horsehair would turn into a snake if you put it in rain water, and a raft of other nonsensical topics, and after a while he said, "It ain't none of my business but you ain't in the channel here. You'll find deeper water over yonder."

"That's funny," I said. "Duke told me to run this stretch by holding her right about down the middle."

"It ain't up to me to make no suggestions," he said, "but all the other pilots run close down the left bank until they get down there to the powerhouse."

"All right," I said, and pulled her over toward that deep water he was raving about. In about four minutes the barge began to plow up mud and the engine commenced to labor.

"All of them other pilots must of been dreaming," I said. "In another minute we'll be hard aground."

"Well, I didn't mean quite so far over. Now you got her in too close."

"Okay," I said. "In the meantime would you mind stepping down into the engine room and giving me a backing bell and I'll see if I can work her out of here."

"There used to be plenty of water in here," he said as he left for the engine room.

"I guess it all went for a trip down to Pittsburgh to see a ball game," I said.

And so the spring turned toward summer and it was nearly as hot as Illinois sometimes, and then in midsummer it was all over between me and the Monongahela; they had transferred me again, back to the canal, just in time for the hot weather. I shook hands all around and Duke said, "I'll be seein' you over there, kid. I ain't gonna stay here in these West Virginia wilderness forever," and I packed up my old suitcase and got on the two-car steam train for Connellsville, Pa., where the express for Chicago came through.

The train followed right along the riverbank, and pretty soon I saw the boat coming up from Rosedale with a load, with that old stack kind of pushed back and a cloud of blue exhaust trailing behind, and as we passed abreast of her I saw Duke up in the glass box, and National out coiling down a line on the barge, and Roast was lying down on the deck sound asleep. I wanted to holler at Duke and say, "So long, Duke, meet me up at the Imperial" and "So long, Roast, don't forget them canned peaches," and I wanted to tell the guy sitting beside me here in the train, "That's Duke Harmison up in the pilothouse, he's the captain. And that's the cook asleep there. He's a no-good bum. They must have about eight hundred tons in that barge—looks like Rosedale coal. That deckhand's name is Clarence Adams but we call him National. And I'm the pilot."

Then in a second we had passed them, and they faded in the distance, and that was the end of me and the towboat *Coal Queen* and the Monongahela River, Duke Harmison, and the coal mines.

"See that old boat?" said the fellow in the overalls beside me on the green plush. "Ain't it a miracle what some fools will do to earn a living? Can you imagine living on a thing like that?"

"Yeh," I said, "I can imagine it."

PART TWO

Kings of the River and the River Country

Introduction

"I like grit, wherever I see it," said Mr. Symmes to Eliza Harris as he pulled her out of the Ohio after her miraculous crossing of the ice. The trials of the river and the river country have called for many types of heroism, including Eliza's, and many heroic traits besides pure grit. In a region dominated by water the river is the chief antagonist, and anyone who can match or master it in strength and trickiness is a hero. By the same token, the epic feats of the river country's legendary heroes generally involve knowledge of the river, and the skill, presence of mind and adaptability necessary to meet its emergencies.

First of the giant breed to pit their strength and cunning against river hazards and tricks were the voyageurs, keelboatmen and fur-traders. Then, with the coming of the steamboat and two-way traffic to the Western waters, the captains and pilots were kings of the river. Curiously enough, like the Kentucky flatboatmen who made the name "Kaintuck" synonymous with "American" among the Creoles of New Orleans, the great triumvirate of captains—Russell, Leathers and Cannon—were all Kentucky born, and bore the Kentucky Colonel stamp.

The early captains continued the rip-roaring tradition of the keelboatmen and flatboatmen because rugged individualism, bluster and bravado were good showmanship if not good business. Bluff, swagger and swearing were the prerogative as well as the prerequisites of these "lords of creation." "What's the use of being a steamboat captain," said Tom Leathers, "if you can't tell people to go to hell?"

As steamboats became "floating hotels" and social and neighborhood institutions (government inspected and licensed since 1852), captains, being smart operators, began to compete with one another in courtesy and hospitality. They prided themselves as much on setting a good table as on setting a new speed record. "Roaring Jack" Russell may have been the "best scrapper aboard a steamboat," but he was also a ladies' man and an ardent dancer, and in his encounter with river desperadoes at Natchez-under-the-Hill, he was a firm adherent of fair play. In the same way, Tom Leathers may have been the "best curser on the Mississippi," but in the grand manner he was devoted to the exquisite architecture of his Natchez home, "Myrtle Terrace," and to the ornate Indian decorations of his *Natchez* boats. And the fighting knight-errant of the steamboats, Jim Bowie—rough-and-tumble scion of a distinguished Maryland family—made a chivalrous hobby of rescuing suckers from river sharpers.

In spiritual, civic and even aesthetic spheres, the Mississippi has inspired men to do big things and noble things, but only by dint of the riverman's courage and prowess. Even the noted pioneer preacher, Peter

52

Cartwright, was a "fighting preacher," who could make the devil pray. And John Banvard, aspiring to make his Mississippi panorama the largest painting in the world, traveled thousands of miles in an open skiff and endured incredible hardships and dangers in the interest of artistic accuracy. Lincoln's knowledge of the river, acquired during his flatboating days, stood him in good stead when, in the Rock Island Bridge case, he became the author of the American doctrine of bridges by arguing that "one man had as good a right to cross a river as another had to sail up or down it."

Some of the more foolhardy feats of the river supermen, like Commodore David D. Porter's Yazoo River expedition, were doomed to failure. But even he succeeded in bringing his gunboats out safely after having taken them on a quixotic cruise through thickly wooded bayous. From Johnny Appleseed, floating down French Creek asleep in his canoe on a cake of ice, to Paul Boynton, floating down the Ohio from Pittsburgh to Cairo in an inflated rubber suit (in 1881), the line between daring and daredeviltry on the river was a thin and shifting one.

Whether a Confederate mail carrier running the Vicksburg blockade, or a slave ferrying fellow slaves to freedom, the star performer of the river country has had to prove himself master of the river in order to serve his fellow man on or through the river. Perhaps none of the kings of the river has ever experienced a greater reward than Mark Twain, when traveling down the Mississippi from St. Paul with his family in the summer of 1886. Hearing the leadsman call "Mark Twain, Mark Twain," his little daughter Clara ran up to him with the reproach: "Papa, I have hunted all over the boat for you. Don't you know they are calling for you?"

B. A. B.

I. STEAMBOAT MASTERS AND PILOTS

Roaring Jack Russell

I. "THE BEST SCRAPPER ABOARD A STEAMBOAT" [1]

River navigation was not a new thing to the people of the Kentucky valley. For nearly half a century they were hearing about river navigation.

[1] From *The Kentucky*, by Thomas D. Clark, pp. 73–80. Copyright, 1942, by Thomas D. Clark. *The Rivers of America*, edited by Hervey Allen and Carl Carmer. New York and Toronto: Rinehart & Co., Inc.

Some of the yarns of those hardy men who had floated down to New Orleans and walked back rivaled the favorite tales of the old pioneers who had driven the Indians beyond the Ohio. Among these early navigators was the apt scholar, Jack Russell. Young Jack had back of him the best of Kentucky pioneer tradition. He and his folks had been the first of his line to cross the great Appalachian wall, mark out a land claim and plant a home upon it. He had heard the bloodcurdling screams of the Indian warrior. Too, the Russells had undergone all the hardships of a raw frontier country. When their fields produced more grain and hemp than the family could use, the menfolks put off to New Orleans with the surplus loaded on flatboats.

"Roaring Jack," as the boy was soon called, drifted to market past snags and bandits and sold his family's goods, sewed the money securely in the pockets of his grimy pantaloons, and walked home. The river was the boy's school. Floating leisurely down the Kentucky, the Ohio, and the Mississippi, the bright-eyed Kentuckian was always conscious of his surroundings. Sand bars, snags, points, bends, and eddies were daily assignments in his process of education. He rubbed shoulders with hard-fisted men, and with boys who acted like men. They all knew about the pirates' dens, the wiles of the river cheats, and the dives which held on under the bluffs of the low country like half-drowned dogs to driftwood.

Physically, the Kentuckian was all that legend has made out his fellows of the state to be. He was tall, with a muscular system as tough and flexible as steel cables. Jack was without fear, and at the same time possessed the rugged sense of fairness and courtesy which was to mark the men of his community. When later he became one of the most famous steamboat captains between New Orleans and Frankfort, all these qualities were to stand out in his dealing with passengers and shippers.

The real career of Roaring Jack Russell was to begin soon after 1811. In that year . . . Nicholas Roosevelt took the famous old *New Orleans* for its trial run downstream from Pittsburgh to New Orleans. . . .

. . . [But] Jack Russell was caught up in [the 1812] war hysteria. He volunteered for militia service to avenge the disgraceful treatment of his fellow Kentuckians at the horrible River Raisin slaughter. Old raftsmen drilled up and down streets of Kentucky towns while their rafts rotted at river landings. Soon they marched away to war, and very soon the Americans were victorious. The war was over. Victory at the Thames was a great matter of Kentucky pride.

Tramping back through the woods of Michigan and Ohio, many a Kentucky raftsmen dreamed of taking up where he had left off in the river trade. Among these was Jack Russell. Jack was anxious to get back to his pike pole and the river's hazards. The boy was grown, and he was rugged and tough. Campaigning with Shelby and Harrison had matured him. He was of man's estate and the river held nothing but hope for him. Soon he was to win his spurs as the long-horned fighter of the bends. Down at New Orleans a crawfish-eating snapping turtle had proved especially irksome to the Kentucky boys. He had, in good frontier river vernacular, "put the bee on them." There were few things which could match a half-horse, half-alligator Kentucky boatman, and the low-country bully was one of them. It had now become a matter of saving state pride that a Kentuckian be found who could whip the rascal. A scrapper, or at least he said he was one, was taken down on one of the runs to win back the glory of Ol' Kaintuck. All the way down the big bruiser recited menacingly what he was going to do. His threats were awful, and his backers were overjoyed, but as is true with all shadow fighters, the big Kentuckian ran when he was confronted by the snorting Louisiana gouger. Kentucky pride was at stake. Roaring Jack Russell stepped into the breach. He snatched off his coat, rolled up his sleeves, and tangled with the puffing "crawfish eater." It was a fine frontier battle. Fists swung through the air as though they were miniature cannonballs on tough steel cables. Ribs were gouged, and knees and feet whirled into action. Never had the Kentucky boys, in all their days of conflict, seen such a fight. Russell teetered, stumbled, sagged back and forth until it seemed that he most certainly would fall under the crushing onslaught of his opponent. He remained, however, and the big bully was soundly thrashed, and limped from battle a humiliated and deflated braggart. In his place stood the young Kentuckian. His fame spread fast, and soon people were whispering behind his back, "There is Jack Russell, the best scrapper aboard a steamboat."

Truly Kentuckian, Jack Russell was fond of feminine company and of dancing. When on his boat he led many a fancy figure with the fairest maid aboard for a partner, and in New Orleans he was always an ardent patron of the dance halls. There was something in his Kentucky courtliness, however, which antagonized other men. On one occasion he was throwing himself into a dance with whole soul and body when he was tripped. At first he thought it was an accident, but in the crowd he spied a swarthy, thick-set man, distinctly of the Latin dandy type. On the dandy's breast was pinned a huge diamond brooch, his fingers were loaded with glittering rings, and his ear lobes drawn with gaudy bangles. Decorative chains hung in profusion from his clothing, and over this gear were strapped bowie knives and pistols. On a second swing around he tripped Jack Russell again. This was too much. The Kentuckian hit the dandy squarely between the eyes and landed him flat on his back. The crowd gasped. Did Jack Russell know that he had just hit the pirate Jean Lafitte? No man in all New Orleans would have dared touch the brigand, let alone knock him down.

Lafitte was said to be a brave man, but he had never exactly encountered a determined Kentuckian before. He rushed from the dance hall and assembled his henchmen for an assault on the place. Doors and windows were barred, and the occupants prepared themselves to stand off the siege. Battering rams were thrust against the doors, flails pounded at the windows, and blunderbuss pistols were fired through the building. New Orleans policemen rushed to the scene, but they were driven back by the pirates. They hurried back to headquarters to report a second battle of New Orleans in process, and it was not until militiamen were marched to the scene of conflict that the pirates were beaten back and quiet once again established.

Among the excited defendants of the dance hall was hardy old Captain Holton, of Kentucky, who had been under heavy fire at the battle of the Thames. The old captain came out frightened, and he told bystanders in a quavering voice that Roaring Jack Russell's fight with the pirates was the worst experience of his life.

Jack Russell now was regarded as the chieftain of rivermen. He had proved his bravery by knocking Lafitte down, and he was again to prove his strength in a less belligerent manner. It is said that Cap'n Jack had lifted a 1,647-pound weight and on another occasion had carried a burden of 1,245 pounds all the way across the deck of a large steamboat. He literally was the personification of the famous Paul Bunyan.

* * * * *

Scores of legends survive this Kentucky riverman. They have to do with his iron courage in the face of river trials. Fires, snags, explosions, and racing make up vigorous chapters in the Russell story. There was the heroic account of the explosion of the *General Brown* just opposite Helena. The *General Brown* was loaded with passengers, livestock, and gunpowder. Its captain was one of those vainglorious creatures who proved a constant threat to the general peace of mind. He couldn't bear for another boat to pass him, and disregarding responsibility for his cargo, he would take a chance in order to win a race. The *General Brown* was "holding its steam" for a race with Russell's boat when its stay bolts let go. Roaring Jack became a hero when he helped rescue the injured passengers and crew, and prevented the fire from spreading to the shipment of gunpowder.

Later Captain Jack Russell quit the river trade and retired to his farm at Frankfort to become a Whig candidate for the state legislature. For four years he was a successful legislator, and then went back to the soil to live out his life as a Kentucky gentleman.

II. OUTWITTING THE ROBBERS AT NATCHEZ-UNDER-THE-HILL [2]

. . . Captain Russell . . . commanded the old *Constellation* in the palmy days of boating.

Russell was a man of great strength—one of those minor Samsons that are occasionally encountered in this degenerate age—and his courage was in proportion to his muscular power. The boat which he commanded had stopped at Natchez, "under-the-hill," for the night, and many of the passengers had gone on shore to see the fun going on among the various drinking, gambling, and dancing houses that made up the town, such as

---

[2] From *A Stray Yankee in Texas*, by Philip Paxton (Samuel A. Hammett), pp. 407–408. Entered . . . 1853, by J. S. Redfield. New York.

it was. Now the said fun was never very decorous, seldom over safe, and one of the said passengers made both discoveries at his cost. He was robbed of his pocketbook, which contained the proceeds of the sale of his flatboat and cargo.

Early the next morning Russell was informed of the robbery, and sending for the loser, requested all the particulars.

Having satisfied himself that the money was really lost, and that, too, in a notorious house, immediately opposite the boat, on shore he went, and, marching bold as a lion into the den of thieves, demanded the pocketbook and contents of the proprietor. Of course the theft was denied, and the denial accompanied with many a threat of vengeance upon Russell, whose prowess, however, they were too well acquainted with to make any overt demonstration.

"I'll give you," said Russell, "until I get my boat ready to go to hand over the money, and then if *they* don't come, the house shall." True to his word, just before the boat started, on shore he went, accompanied by a gang of deck hands, bearing the largest cable the steamer possessed.

This was passed around the house and in and out some of the windows, and when all was ready Russell again demanded the pocketbook.

No answer but curses being returned, he jumped on board the boat, sung out to the pilot to "go ahead" and to the engineer "to work her slow," and off the boat moved very moderately.

The rope began to tighten, and the house to creak. Two minutes more would have done the business for building and people, when the latter signified their surrender, and pitched pocketbook and money out of the window.

Tom Leathers

I. "THE BEST CURSER ON THE MISSISSIPPI" [1]

Tom Leathers was probably the steamboat captain of all steamboat captains. He adopted Natchez as his own, loving her with all the fervor of his explosive soul; after her he named a succession of seven majestic barks. Tom Leathers was a man of height, with girth and bulk to match. He stood nearly six feet four in his big bare feet, and he weighed two hundred and seventy pounds. His locks and curling, flowing white mustache stayed in place to the last hair; his costume, sheer flawless whites with white hat or dark, expensive black with black hat, was practically a uniform. He carried a cigar almost as if it were a baton, and his blue eyes changed from smiling agreement to raging command. A man of extremes, he ranged between overflowing generosity and Jovian fury. It is only fair to add that the

---

[1] From *Natchez on the Mississippi*, by Harnett T. Kane, pp. 299–304, 310–311. Copyright, 1947, by Harnett T. Kane. New York: William Morrow & Company.

river people varied similarly in their attitude toward him; they either admired him extravagantly or they wouldn't set foot on one of his boats.

Captain Tom had a manner with ladies and his big planter friends that was so heavy and courtly it seemed almost a caricature. Among roustabouts and crew members, he was hailed as the "best curser on the Mississippi." His mastery of invective had a phenomenal breadth and versatility. In five minutes, it was said, he could shrivel any man, without repeating a single oath. . . .

* * * * *

The Captain was a Kentuckian of Kenton County, born in 1816. He had an elder brother, Jim, who lacked Tom's gusto, being merely a colorful individual. As a schoolboy Tom yearned after a life on the river; at twenty he was on it, riding between New Orleans and Natchez, shifting from one vessel to the next, learning to know the Mississippi as he did the palm of his hand. To be Captain of a big boat, one had to be a business man, a shrewd and efficient one; the Captain was "making his contacts," acquiring connections and capital. By the 1840's he was erecting the first of his series of boats called *Natchez;* with his first wife he was beginning to build up his family. She died, and the widower went to the Natchez country for a second bride, one of the high-placed Claibornes, the same family that gave Mississippi its early territorial governor.

. . . She was as gentle as he was imperious, and she had rare tact. Tom Leathers presided at home in the same grand style, almost as grand anyway, as he showed on the water. He wished every one at home at a certain hour, to the dot. (He was that way with his steamboat departures.) The children were expected to eat every item of food, or tell the Captain why. (On his boats, sometimes, the Captain grew miffed if his guests did not show the proper delight over his delicacies.) He saw that the cuisine at home matched that on his vessels, in quality and bulk. And every day that strawberries were in season, the Captain liked them before him in heaping bowls. Before he signaled to the butler to pass them he went through a rite. Over each bowl he sliced and squeezed the biggest lemon that he could get; and not once did he omit his remark: "This brings out the flavor, you know." A guest who did not enjoy a lemon taste did not eat Leathers' strawberries. Every once in a while the Captain began to roar at home; only then did the serene little wife intervene. She said only two words: "Now, Tom," but they had more decision in them than even the Captain's flow. He became silent immediately.

The Captain could unbend, and the Natchezians tell dozens of stories of his generosity. A widow in difficulty found him ready to help, with hardly a question in advance. Let a sick child or an injured man appear, and he would drop everything to assist. One case among many tells how a woman approached him at the Natchez landing. Her husband was very ill in a little Ohio town; she had only a dollar or two. The Captain bowed and removed a male passenger from a room to make space for her; when they arrived upriver, he paid her transportation from Cincinnati to the inland point and back to the river, where he picked her up with the husband and saw that they arrived home. More than that, the Captain was known to be, if properly approached, the softest of touches.

He built so many vessels called *Natchez* that, half affectionately, half derisively, the river experts nicknamed him Pushmataha, after the Indian chief who was a friend of Andy Jackson. (People still remembered Natchez' Indian origin.) On the wheelhouse of his vessels he painted a figure of a mighty Indian in war-paint and feathers. Whenever he was in a race, it is claimed, the Captain would have an artist do a little extra work, so that Pushmataha-on-the-wheelhouse had his tomahawk lifted!

The Captain seemed always in a fight, trying to cut a rival's time, dropping rates, or bankrupting his opposition. Part of it was sheer bravado, or truculence; the rest, horse-sense. The public wanted steamboat captains that way; it wanted fireworks, and Tom Leathers could provide them. He liked to crowd other boats, using a trick to take an advantage—the sudden dropping of a tub of lard into the boilers for an unexpected spurt, the crossing of another's path by a sharp maneuver at a river bend. He was known to fire his cannon across the bow of another, for no reason except to irk a competitor and put on a show for the gallery. There was little, then, in the way of established rules of courtesy, safety or fair trade practices. Tom Leathers enjoyed delaying his departure, deliberately, to let another leave ahead of him. Then he would catch up, pass it and hear the crowd cry its appreciation. The trade went to the man who made the big splash.

On went the line of Leathers' *Natchezes*, each more richly embellished than its predecessor. No. 3 was in commission less than six weeks when it burned at New Orleans in a fire that took a dozen vessels; Tom Leathers' brother Jim, asleep in his room, was killed. The fourth *Natchez* came a few years later; then in 1859 arrived the fifth, perhaps the most heavily ornate of all. His vessels always pictured Indian life but this one went to unusual lengths for its effects. In rich reds, yellows and blues, the cabin skylights showed a series of panoramas, "The War Dance," "Smoking the Pipe of Peace," "The Hunter Returns to His Family," and many more. Wall panelings, draperies, even some of the gilt work was supposed to look Indian. It all had a sad fate. Ever a rigid Confederate, Tom Leathers was in New Orleans as the city was about to fall to the Unionists. To save his *Natchez* from capture, he took her upriver near Yazoo City and tied her up, then helped the Confederates take her expensive machinery and use it for war purposes. The Federals learned of his attitude, and ultimately they were accused of smashing his proud boat almost to nothing. For years after the war, the Captain waged a warm legal fight with the government; now and then he received a favorable verdict, but collected little. The situation hardly improved his feeling for the North.

During the war, when matters quieted a bit, Mrs. Leathers decided that she wished to live in New Orleans. The great captain, ever devoted to Natchez and his Myrtle Terrace, said No. He would never move; he was settled there for all time! And so the quiet Mrs. Leathers soon had him packing his things, and he sold Myrtle Terrace in favor of a more extensive establishment in the Creole City. But the Captain returned to Natchez at every chance, to survey the field and swap yarns with his friends.

War's end brought a temporary upsurge for the steamboats. Tom Leathers stepped forward as before, inspecting the trade from beneath his shaggy brows. Somewhat older, he grew hardly more mellow. It was the Leathers of this day who drew the description: "the Eagle of his Tribe, with war paint in his words if not on his face, and a tomahawk in his logic." For years he had been proclaiming himself cock of the rur between New Orleans and Natchez. In 1855 he had made the distance upriver in seventeen hours and thirty minutes. At his Natchez wharfboat he nailed up a great pair of buckhorns, painted the time below them, and challenged the world: "Take Them If You Can."

Now, suddenly, there was tension. Captain John W. Cannon, like Tom Leathers, was a Kentuckian. Several times he had been the victim of Leathers' contemptuous tactics. His boat, the *Robert E. Lee,* was launched in 1866. Three years later the newest *Natchez* came along and everybody said the two were rather evenly matched. Most people felt that the *Lee,* though slightly smaller, was not a delicate, graceful boat; she appeared to thrust her bow deep in the water, struggling and straining, with a great swell. The *Natchez* cut through the river like a sharp finger, with hardly a ripple. But now here was the *Lee,* making new, ever-quicker runs. Tom Leathers made several disparaging gestures toward John Cannon. The newspapers, scenting excitement, carried tales back and forth, touching the captains' pride by provocative items. Then the die was cast. There'd be a race. By God, said each man, he'd show 'im! On June 30, 1870, the two vessels were scheduled to leave New Orleans for St. Louis. That would be it.

*   *   *   *   *

[After the race], Tom Leathers insisted he had not lost. Deducting the hours he had laid up in the fog and other delays, he figured that his time was better than Cannon's. Generally in America the bets were paid in Cannon's favor; but thousands asserted that the victory could not be termed a clear-cut one. In Europe most wagers were called off on the grounds that the stripping of the *Lee* and the use of the *Pargaud* in loading violated the normal standards. Today, among a dwindling few in Natchez, you can still get up a strong argument on the score. Tom Leathers has never lost his supporters.

The Captain carried on, building more vessels with the name of *Natchez,* enjoying a lion's life, drawing bows and cheers whenever he stepped ashore in his favorite town. There were more races, and these won, but none ever took the attention of the one in which, for once, he dropped behind.

On his eightieth birthday Tom Leathers died at New Orleans in an ironic accident; a hit-and-run bicyclist struck him, leaving the Captain lying on the street. In modern Natchez tokens of him are to be found—decorations from his steamers, mementos of trips made under the eye of the white-haired tyrant. A rural church is proud of a chandelier from one of his wrecked boats. His Myrtle Terrace, for which he cared as earnestly as he did his steamers, looks prim and proper behind its iron fence in its neat landsman's setting, . . . and there appear scant hints of the booming Tom Leathers. But wherever there are older Natchezians and memories, the Captain remains.

II. THE CAPTAIN'S PREROGATIVE [2]

Captain Tom Leathers was in the habit of refusing to take freight on the Natchez if he didn't like the shipper or the consignee. For some reason or other he had it in for the firm of Lamkin & Eggleston, wholesale grocers here in Vicksburg, and declined their freight. They sued him in the Circuit Court and got judgment. Leathers carried the case to the Supreme Court, but the verdict was sustained and he had to pay $2500 damages. He was furious.

"What's the use," he said, "of being a steamboat captain if you can't tell people to go to hell?"

Old Joe La Barge and the Englishmen

On one of [Captain Joseph La Barge's] trips up the [Missouri] River in the earlier part of his career there were several Englishmen aboard. They had a map and applied themselves industriously for the first day or two in trying to identify the various places upon it with those along their route. They were in the pilot-house a good deal, and one of them questioned La Barge rather officiously about the geography of the country.

"What place is this that we are approaching, Mr. Pilot?" he asked.

"St. Charles, sir," La Barge replied.

"You are mistaken, sir; according to the map it is ———."

La Barge made no reply. He stopped as usual at St. Charles and then went on his way. Presently they came to another village.

"What place, Captain?" inquired the Englishmen.

"Washington, Missouri, sir."

---

[2] From *American Adventures,* A Second Trip "Abroad at Home," by Julian Street, p. 513. Copyright, 1917, by the Century Co.; 1916 and 1917, by P. F. Collier & Son, Inc. New York.

From *History of Early Steamboat Navigation on the Missouri River,* Life and Adventures of Joseph La Barge . . . , by Hiram Martin Chittenden, Vol. II, pp. 344–345. Copyright, 1903, by Francis P. Harper. New York.

"Wrong again. The map gives this place as ———."

This experience was gone through several times, the Captain's temper becoming more ruffled with each repetition, though no one would have suspected it from his unruffled exterior. Presently a flock of wild geese passed over the river and drew the attention of the passengers and crew. The Englishmen were standing on the hurricane roof immediately in front of the pilot-house.

"What kind of birds are those, Captain?" asked one of them in eager haste.

The Captain, whose language still smacked somewhat of the French idiom, replied: "Look at your map; he tell you."

"——or Blow Her to Hell!"

... In 1857 Captain George H. Wilson of Onalaska, Wisconsin, brought out the powerful sternwheel towboat, *G. H. Wilson*. Built at Brownsville, Pennsylvania, this 159-ton craft was capable of showing a foaming wake to most of the race horses on the Upper Mississippi. After running somewhat irregularly in the St. Paul trade during the year 1857, Captain Wilson entered her in the Des Moines River trade. . . .

It appears that the Des Moines River was obstructed with numerous dams thrown across its course by mill owners. It was the practice of steamboatmen to take a run at these makeshift obstructions and force the boat through or over them. Sometimes a boat was hung up on the crest of the dam without being able to run either forward or back.

. . . The *G. H. Wilson* stuck several times in attempting to pass the dam [at Keosaugua] and had to fall back and try it over again. "Getting desperate," eyewitnesses relate, "the captain ordered the engineer to get up a big pressure of steam, open the throttle valves wide, and shouted his commands so that they could be heard half a mile: 'Send her over—or blow her to hell!' The boat went over amid the cheers of the spectators. The engineer said afterwards that he rather expected the other alternative."

From *Steamboating on the Upper Mississippi, The Water Way to Iowa*, Some River History, by Wm. J. Petersen, pp. 443–444. Copyright, 1937, by the State Historical Society of Iowa. Iowa City.

Captain Heerman Delivers a Raft

Captain E. E. Heerman . . . in July, 1874 . . . had his own most satisfying experience with the fitful climate of the great golden Northwest. With his steamboat, *Minnietta*, he was towing a log raft from Beef Slough to Burlington [Iowa]. Thirteen strings he had; so of course when he reached Clinton bridge, that seven times accursed place, he had to split the tow, drop a half between two piers, and then with the *Minnietta* take the other half through the draw.

Just as they caught up with the floating half and were busy renewing the fastenings, somebody looked up, and there was a cyclone bearing straight down upon them, the veritable cyclone, black funnel, whirling cloud, torn edges, and the rest.

Captain Heerman ordered the two parts of the raft to be lashed together as hard as possible, and then thought about his little son, nine years old, who was making the trip with him.

Every raft now carried what were called the "snubbing works" or "checking works." . . . These made a kind of platform of logs securely fastened and bore the huge cleats with which the raft was moored. Captain Heerman told his son to run for the snubbing works, lie down, clasp a cleat with both hands, and hold on. He might be wet, but that part of the raft would hold together and he would be safe if he did not move. Heerman then darted for the pilot-house.

On the stairs he met the cub pilot running so fast he seemed to be falling bolt upright with his heels playing a tune on the steps. "I'm going for the raft!" he yelled as he shot past; "the old boat can't live in this storm!"

Heerman got to the deserted pilot-house.

When the storm had struck, the *Minnietta* heeled far over to larboard, so that he could hardly stand. The pilot-house door was stuck fast. He forced a window open, straddled the sill, and getting to the speaking-tube, asked the engineer if he purposed to stand at his post.

"I'll stick all right," shouted the engineer, "but this boat's done for. The water's up to the sheet iron on the boiler and covers the ash pan."

"Well," said Heerman, coolly, "you hearten the fireman, if you have one, and if you two will stand by, I will save the boat."

Meantime, the raft had gone to pieces—literally to pieces, as if it had been to a cyclops' mill and ground. A fragment of about forty logs was

From *A-Rafting on the Mississip'*, by Charles Edward Russell, pp. 296–299. Copyright, 1928, by Charles Edward Russell. New York and London: The Century Company.

E. E. Heerman was one of the pilot kings of my time, equally good at handling rafts or packets, and celebrated from Sauk Rapids to St. Louis. He was another of the tribe of lightning pilots and as competent a master, for he could operate as either.—C. E. R., *ibid.*, p. 261.

left intact where the snubbing works were, and on this frail refuge all the crew was gathered except the three brave men on the boat. By skilful manipulation and backing hard, Heerman got the stern around until it pointed into the wind, and so eased the pressure on the side, but even thus the boat and the checking works were driven headlong upon the shore. The little boy obeyed his father and, clinging desperately to the cleat, came through unhurt.

But the raft was now destroyed, and when the storm had passed, the crew, demoralized, disgusted, and wet to the skin, refused to go out to chase the logs, which were scattered over all that part of Illinois. A raft commander must have tact as well as courage. Captain Heerman did not urge the point, but ordered the cook to get the men a first-class dinner: chicken with gravy, and pie. When they had eaten they forgot the mutiny and went to work.

Eight days they spent hunting those logs. Some were in corn-fields, some were hidden in creeks, some were on islands, some were sailing serenely down the river and must be pursued in skiffs. Hundreds had been carried into the thickets along the river bank. To dislodge them it was necessary to work in the brush with cant-hooks and levers, and before the task was done captain and crew were naked. Not by way of metaphor: I mean literally clad for the most part in their innocence, if any, and not otherwise. Thorns, briars, and branches had torn their clothes to tatters. In the whole entourage was not the clothing to make for one man a complete suit.

It was a log raft, a rafting steamer. There were but five barrels on board, all in use. The traditional recourse in such cases was out of the question. They put together enough shreds and patches to enable one of the crew to go into town without being arrested, and Heerman went with him through the woods until they came to the outskirts of an Illinois hamlet. There, wrapped in a sheet, the captain hid while his emissary went to buy clothes. It was not a large store; the stock was limited and allowed no choice. When he returned, the trousers for the captain were so small he could not button them around his waist.

They went back to the boat, got the skiff, and pulled to Cordova, and again the captain hid while his deckhand went into town. This time he brought out a pair of trousers the legs of which were so short there was a space of five inches between the bottom of the trousers and the tops of the captain's shoes. In this fantastic garb he went himself into the town, and by diligent inquiry came by a suit of clothes he could wear, got a supply for the crew, and went upon his way rejoicing.

He delivered that raft at Burlington with only three logs missing, a feat in rafting comparable to beating an army of veterans with a company of recruits.

Running a Steamboat through a Sandbar

Captain [Grant] Marsh had at different times commanded all the boats of the Benton Packet Company, but in the early autumn of 1905, while in charge of the *Weston,* he had a steamboating experience at Bismarck [North Dakota], which was unique even in his varied career. One day, through some freak of the current, a sandbar suddenly began forming along the eastern bank of the Missouri, just below the Northern Pacific Railroad bridge. As is always the case on the Big Muddy, the bar built up rapidly; and almost before its presence had been noticed, it had attained a height of eighteen inches above the surface of the water and a length of two hundred feet along the bank, completely choking the intake pipe of the Bismarck water-works, which entered the river at this point. The water famine thus produced seriously affected not only the city but also the railroad, which depended upon the same source for the supply of its engines. Vigorous measures to reopen the intake pipe became imperative.

It happened that Mr. Nickerson, a constructing engineer of the Northern Pacific, was in Bismarck at the time, in charge of a large force of men who were remodeling the railroad bridge. He made an examination of the bar and then went to Captain Baker and asked him for his best captain and his best boat. Captain Baker instantly designated Grant Marsh as the navigator most thoroughly qualified for any difficult work to be done, and Mr. Nickerson chartered the *Weston* and sent for Captain Marsh. His instructions were brief.

"Captain," said he, "that bar has got to be cleared away at once so that the water-works can operate. I think you can do it with your boat. Ask for what you want, spare no cost, but *open the intake pipe!"*

"Well, I'll tell you, Mr. Nickerson," replied the Captain, doubtfully, "I never tried to run a steamboat through a 200-foot sandbar before, but I'll do my best if you will be responsible in case the boat is damaged or lost."

"I'll take the responsibility and help you all I can, too," answered the engineer. "You can do it and it must be done."

The next day was Sunday. At eleven o'clock in the morning, Captain Marsh backed the *Weston* down on the head of the bar, close in by the main bank, with her stern wheel resting against the sand. From the bow capstans he ran two long hawsers back past the stern, one on either side of the boat, and fastened the end of each to a large log, or "dead man," buried some distance out on the bar. Then he started the wheel, which, as it revolved, dug out the sand and pushed it toward the bow, while the

From *The Conquest of the Missouri,* Being the Story of the Life and Exploits of Captain Grant Marsh, by Joseph Mills Hanson, pp. 428–431. Copyright, 1909, by A. C. McClurg Co.; renewed, 1937; 1946, by Rinehart & Company, Inc. New York and Toronto: Murray Hill Books, Inc., a division of Rinehart & Company, Inc.

capstans slowly wound up the hawsers, keeping them taut and pulling the boat back as the wheel cut into the bar. No current from the river, only slack water, followed the boat into the pocket she was making and presently the sand which was being thrown toward the bow began to settle in front of her, leaving her isolated in a small pool. It began to look as though she were going to imprison herself effectually in the heart of the bar, but her captain kept on with his work doggedly. Back on the bluffs, nearly the entire population of Bismarck had assembled to watch the interesting experiment, though not until afterward did the captain know how many intent observers he had on that Sabbath afternoon. Mr. Nickerson had suspended operations on the bridge and put his entire force to work carrying coal to the *Weston* to keep her boilers going.

By mid-afternoon the boat had eaten halfway through the bar and it became evident that, unless an accident occurred, her effort was going to be successful. Fortunately all went well and at half-past nine that night the pounding wheel broke through the last ridge of sand, and the steamer backed triumphantly out into the main channel. Once the way was cleared, the river current surged into the passage and by the following morning the bar had entirely disappeared, the intake pipe was clear, and the water famine ended. Twelve hours after he had cut it through, Captain Marsh ran his boat down over the course she had followed on Sunday and, by sounding, found not less than eight feet of water at any point. The undertaking had come out even more satisfactorily than Mr. Nickerson had hoped, while both Captain Marsh and Captain Baker were gratified at its result.

Lords of Creation

With the coming of peace, the elegance of the steamboat blossomed anew for the brief season before that steamboat on wheels, the railroad, replaced the river queens. The ladies' cabin with its carpets and mirrors, the dining salon with a menu the envy of Lucullus, the passengers that can only be described with the nostalgia of a vanished romance—all saw a brief return to glory. Over all ranked the captain, a king of men in whose presence ordinary mortals trod lightly and spoke softly.

There is a little story to illustrate the proper attitude before these Lords of Creation. A lanky countryman astride a mule hailed a steamboat tied up at a small landing. He insisted on seeing the captain, although every man on board tried to learn his business without disturbing that august personage. Finally the irascible captain strode out on the deck and demanded what was wanted. This was the request: "Just wanted to know, can my mule take a drink out of your river?"

From "Rivers That Meet in Egypt," by Barbara Burr Hubbs, *Papers in Illinois History for the Year 1940*, pp. 18–19. Springfield, Illinois: The Illinois State Historical Society. 1941.

"The Best Pilot on the Missouri River"

My first acquaintance with Captain Hal [Henry N. Dodd] was as cub pilot on his favorite boat, the old *General Meade*, in the early eighties. He said to me: "They tell me you are Bill Heckman's boy. I'll take you along uptown when we get to St. Louis, but you will have to excuse my bashfulness with the ladies. I took three bottles of Dr. Pierce's Favorite Prescription for Women by mistake several years ago and I have steered shy of the critters ever since. It is like being poisoned by mushrooms."

Captain Hal was a giant of a man whom all feared yet worshipped. He was a diamond in the rough, a Kentucky Colonel, only more rawboned and larger in every way. . . .

Captain Hal Dodd was born on Dodd's Island at the mouth of the Osage River in the year 1846. Captain James Dodd, his father, owned this island, the largest in the lower Missouri River. His father was a boat owner, having operated the *Maid of Orleans* and several other boats before the Civil War.

*   *   *   *   *

When Captain Hal was working for Contractor Farney on the Missouri River, he came in late one day. Farney wanted to know what the trouble was and Dodd replied: "This crazy river is too thick to navigate and not thick enough to cultivate."

Another time Mr. Farney was standing on the edge of a barge. Dodd was coming up a big eddy with a gasoline boat and he found he could not stop her. He pulled out in the river, turned clean around and came up the second time. Again he failed to find the pilot-house combination to stop her. Farney cried, "Hal, I want you to land that boat right here."

Farney had a habit of standing with his legs spread apart like a sailor. Dodd sang back: "Send an engineer up here and show me how to stop this thing and I'll land her right between your legs."

*   *   *   *   *

About this time one winter, a Missouri Pacific freight train ran in the river about a quarter of a mile below New Haven [Missouri]. It was a cold, dark night pouring down rain. The river was high and full of drift. Nobody was willing to risk going down to the wreck on shore. But Dodd said to his friend Henry Zebilin: "We will go down there by the water." They owned a large skiff, but Zebilin refused to go along. Dodd went up to town but could find no one willing to go with him.

Finally he started out alone. He first got some bums out of the boxcars

From *Steamboating*, Sixty-Five Years on Missouri's Rivers, The Historical Story of Developing the Waterway Traffic on the Rivers of the Middlewest, by Captain William L. Heckman, "Steamboat Bill," pp. 83–84, 91–92, 93–94. Copyright, 1950, by Burton Publishing Company. Kansas City.

and put them ashore. He then went down to the engine and released the fireman who was too badly hurt to help him. He worked all night and at daylight was back up at the wharf with a badly injured fireman and the dead engineer, lying in the skiff which was half full of water.

A well-dressed man came down the bank and said: "You go up to the livery stable and have a rig sent down to get these men hauled to the depot."

Dodd looked him over and asked: "Who in the hell are you?"

The gentleman replied: "Perhaps you do not know me. I am superintendent of the Missouri Pacific Railroad."

Dodd answered: "Well, you do not know me, either. I am superintendent of this skiff. And if you do not get up this bank and go and get your own rig, I will throw you in the river and that dead engineer on top of you." The super got the rig.

Mr. Bixby Takes a Cub

Mark Twain tells us in *Life on the Mississippi* that he "ran away," vowing never to return until he could come home a pilot, shedding glory. This is a literary statement. The pilot ambition had never entirely died; but it was coca and the Amazon that were uppermost in his mind when he engaged passage on the *Paul Jones* for New Orleans, and so conferred immortality on that ancient little craft. He bade good-by to Macfarlane [his Scotch boarding-house friend in Cincinnati], put his traps aboard, the bell rang, the whistle blew, the gang-plank was hauled in, and he had set out on a voyage that was to continue not for a week or a fortnight, but for four years—four marvelous, sunlit years, the glory of which would color all that followed them.

In the Mississippi book the author conveys the impression of being then a boy of perhaps seventeen. Writing from that standpoint he records incidents that were more or less inventions or that happened to others. He was, in reality, considerably more than twenty-one years old, for it was in April, 1857, that he went aboard the *Paul Jones;* and he was fairly familiar with steamboats and the general requirements of piloting. He had been brought up in a town that turned out pilots; he had heard the talk of their trade. One at least of the Bowen boys was already on the river while Sam Clemens was still a boy in Hannibal, and had often been home to air his grandeur and dilate on the marvel of his work. That learning the river was no light task Sam Clemens very well knew. Never-

From *Mark Twain, A Biography,* The Personal and Literary Life of Samuel Langhorne Clemens, by Albert Bigelow Paine, Vol. I, pp. 116–120. Copyright, 1912, by Harper & Brothers. New York and London.

theless, as the little boat made its drowsy way down the river into lands
that grew ever pleasanter with advancing spring, the old "permanent
ambition" of boyhood stirred again, and the call of the faraway Amazon,
with its coca and its variegated zoology, grew faint.

Horace Bixby, pilot of the *Paul Jones,* then a man of thirty-two, still
living (1910) and at the wheel,[1] was looking out over the bow at the
head of Island No. 35 when he heard a slow, pleasant voice say:

"Good morning."

Bixby was a clean-cut, direct, courteous man.

"Good morning, sir," he said, briskly, without looking around.

As a rule, Mr. Bixby did not care for visitors in the pilot-house. This
one presently came up and stood a little behind him.

"How would you like a young man to learn the river?"

The pilot glanced over his shoulder and saw a rather slender, loose-
limbed young fellow with a fair, girlish complexion and a great tangle
of auburn hair.

"I wouldn't like it. Cub pilots are more trouble than they're worth.
A great deal more trouble than profit."

The applicant was not discouraged.

"I am a printer by trade," he went on, in his easy, deliberate way.
"It doesn't agree with me. I thought I'd like to go to South America."

Bixby kept his eye on the river; but a note of interest crept into his
voice.

"What makes you pull your words that way?" ("pulling" being the
river term for drawling), he asked.

The young men had taken a seat on the visitor's bench.

"You'll have to ask my mother," he said, more slowly than ever. "She
pulls hers, too."

Pilot Bixby woke up and laughed; he had a keen sense of humor,
and the manner of the reply amused him. His guest made another advance.

"Do you know the Bowen boys?" he asked—"pilots in the St. Louis and
New Orleans trade?"

"I know them well—all three of them. William Bowen did his first
steering for me; a mighty good boy, too. Had a Testament in his pocket
when he came aboard; in a week's time he had swapped it for a pack of
cards. I know Sam, too, and Bart."

"Old schoolmates of mine in Hannibal. Sam and Will especially were
my chums."

"Come over and stand by the side of me," he said. "What is your
name?"

The applicant told him, and the two stood looking at the sunlit water.

"Do you drink?"

---

[1] The writer of this memoir interviewed Mr. Bixby personally and has followed his
phrasing throughout.—A.B.P.

"No."

"Do you gamble?"

"No, sir."

"Do you swear?"

"Not for amusement; only under pressure."

"Do you chew?"

"No, sir, never; but *I must smoke*."

"Did you ever do any steering?" was Bixby's next question.

"I have steered everything on the river but a steamboat, I guess."

"Very well; take the wheel and see what you can do with a steamboat. Keep her as she is—toward that lower cottonwood snag."

Bixby had a sore foot and was glad of a little relief. He sat down on the bench and kept a careful eye on the course. By and by he said:

"There is just one way that I would take a young man to learn the river: that is, for money."

"What do you charge?"

"Five hundred dollars, and I to be at no expense whatever."

In those days pilots were allowed to carry a learner, or "cub," board free. Mr. Bixby meant that he was to be at no expense in port or for incidentals. His terms looked rather discouraging.

"I haven't got five hundred dollars in money," Sam said; "I've got a lot of Tennessee land worth twenty-five cents an acre; I'll give you two thousand acres of that."

Bixby dissented.

"No; I don't want any unimproved real estate. I have too much already."

Sam reflected upon the amount he could probably borrow from [his sister] Pamela's husband without straining his credit.

"Well, then, I'll give you one hundred dollars cash and the rest when I earn it."

Something about this young man had won Horace Bixby's heart. His slow, pleasant speech; his unhurried, quiet manner with the wheel; his evident sincerity of purpose—these were externals, but beneath them the pilot felt something of the quality of mind or heart which later made the world love Mark Twain. The terms proposed were agreed upon. The deferred payments were to begin when the pupil had learned the river and was receiving pilot's wages. During Mr. Bixby's daylight watches his pupil was often at the wheel, that trip, while the pilot sat directing him and nursing his sore foot. Any literary ambitions that Samuel Clemens may have had grew dim; by the time they had reached New Orleans he had almost forgotten he had been a printer; and when he learned that no ship would be sailing to the Amazon for an indefinite period the feeling grew that a directing hand had taken charge of his affairs.

From New Orleans his chief did not return to Cincinnati, but went to St. Louis, taking with him his new cub, who thought it fine, indeed, to come steaming up to that great city with its thronging waterfront; its levee fairly packed with trucks, drays, and piles of freight, the whole flanked with a solid mile of steamboats lying side by side, bow a little upstream, their belching stacks reared high against the blue—a towering front of trade. It was glorious to nose one's way to a place in that stately line, to become a unit, however small, of that imposing fleet.

At St. Louis Sam borrowed from Mr. Moffett the funds necessary to make up his first payment, and so concluded his contract. Then, when he suddenly found himself on a fine big boat, in a pilot-house so far above the water that he seemed perched on a mountain—a "sumptuous temple" —his happiness seemed complete.

Mark Twain Learns the Shape of the River

At the end of what seemed a tedious while, I had managed to pack my head full of islands, towns, bars, "points," and bends; and a curiously inanimate mass of lumber it was, too. However, inasmuch as I could shut my eyes and reel off a good long string of these names without leaving out more than ten miles of river in every fifty, I began to feel that I could take a boat down to New Orleans if I could make her skip those little gaps. But of course my complacency could hardly get started enough to lift my nose a trifle into the air, before Mr. Bixby would think of something to fetch it down again. One day he turned on me suddenly with this settler:

"What is the shape of Walnut Bend?"

He might as well have asked me my grandmother's opinion of protoplasm. I reflected respectfully, and then said I didn't know it had any particular shape. My gun-powdery chief went off with a bang, of course, and then went on loading and firing until he was out of adjectives.

I had learned long ago that he only carried just so many rounds of ammunition, and was sure to subside into a very placable and even remorseful old smooth-bore as soon as they were all gone. That word "old" is merely affectionate; he was not more than thirty-four. I waited. By and by he said:

"My boy, you've got to know the *shape* of the river perfectly. It is all there is left to steer by on a very dark night. Everything else is blotted out and gone. But mind you, it hasn't the same shape in the night that it has in the daytime."

"How on earth am I ever going to learn it, then?"

"How do you follow a hall at home in the dark? Because you know the shape of it. You can't see it."

"Do you mean to say that I've got to know all the million trifling

From *Life on the Mississippi*, by Samuel L. Clemens, pp. 70–77. Copyright, 1874, 1875, by H. O. Houghton & Company; 1883, 1899, 1903, by Samuel L. Clemens; 1911, by Clara Gabrilowitsch. New York and London: Harper & Brothers.

variations of shape in the banks of this interminable river as well as I know the shape of the front hall at home?"

"On my honor, you've got to know them *better* than any man ever did know the shapes of the halls in his own house."

"I wish I was dead!"

"Now I don't want to discourage you, but—"

"Well, pile it on me; I might as well have it now as another time."

"You see, this has got to be learned; there isn't any getting around it. A clear starlight night throws such heavy shadows that, if you didn't know the shape of a shore perfectly, you would claw away from every bunch of timber, because you would take the black shadow of it for a solid cape; and you see you would be getting scared to death every fifteen minutes by the watch. You would be fifty yards from shore all the time when you ought to be within fifty feet of it. You can't see a snag in one of those shadows, but you know exactly where it is, and the shape of the river tells you when you are coming to it. Then there's your pitch-dark night; the river is a very different shape on a pitch-dark night from what it is on a starlight night. All shores seem to be straight lines, then, and mighty dim ones, too; and you'd *run* them for straight lines, only you know better. You boldly drive your boat right into what seems to be a solid, straight wall (you knowing very well that in reality there is a curve there), and that wall falls back and makes way for you. Then there's your gray mist. You take a night when there's one of these grisly, drizzly, gray mists, and then there isn't *any* particular shape to a shore. A gray mist would tangle the head of the oldest man that ever lived. Well, then, different kinds of *moonlight* change the shape of the river in different ways. You see—"

"Oh, don't say any more, please! Have I got to learn the shape of the river according to all these five hundred thousand different ways? If I tried to carry all that cargo in my head it would make me stoop-shouldered."

"*No!* you only learn *the* shape of the river; and you learn it with such absolute certainty that you can always steer by the shape that's *in your head,* and never mind the one that's before your eyes."

"Very well, I'll try it; but, after I have learned it, can I depend on it? Will it keep the same form and not go fooling around?"

Before Mr. Bixby could answer, Mr. W. Came in to take the watch, and he said:

"Bixby, you'll have to look out for President's Island, and all that country clear away up above the Old Hen and Chickens. The banks are caving and the shape of the shores changing like everything. Why, you wouldn't know the point above 40. You can go up inside the old sycamore snag, now." [1]

---

[1] It may not be necessary, but still it can do no harm to explain that "inside" means between the snag and the shore.—M.T.

So that question was answered. Here were leagues of shore changing shape. My spirits were down in the mud again. Two things seemed pretty apparent to me. One was, that in order to be a pilot a man has got to learn more than any one man ought to be allowed to know; and the other was, that he must learn it all over again in a different way every twenty-four hours.

That night we had the watch until twelve. Now it was an ancient river custom for the two pilots to chat a bit when the watch changed. While the relieving pilot put on his gloves and lit his cigar, his partner, the retiring pilot, would say something like this:

"I judge the upper bar is making down a little at Hale's Point; had quarter twain with the lower lead and mark twain [2] with the other."

"Yes, I thought it was making down a little, last trip. Meet any boats?"

"Met one abreast the head of 21, but she was away over hugging the bar, and I couldn't make her out entirely. I took her for the *Sunny South* —hadn't any skylights forward of the chimneys."

And so on. And as the relieving pilot took the wheel his partner [3] would mention that we were in such-and-such a bend, and say we were abreast of such and such a man's woodyard or plantation. This was courtesy; I supposed it was *necessity*. But Mr. W. came on watch full twelve minutes late on this particular night—a tremendous breach of etiquette; in fact, it is the unpardonable sin among pilots. So Mr. Bixby gave him no greeting whatever, but simply surrendered the wheel and marched out of the pilot-house without a word. I was appalled; it was a villainous night for blackness, we were in a particularly wide and blind part of the river, where there was no shape or substance to anything, and it seemed incredible that Mr. Bixby should have left that poor fellow to kill the boat, trying to find out where he was. But I resolved that I would stand by him anyway. He should find that he was not wholly friendless. So I stood around, and waited to be asked where we were. But Mr. W. plunged on serenely through the solid firmament of black cats that stood for an atmosphere, and never opened his mouth. "Here is a proud devil!" thought I; "here is a limb of Satan that would rather send us all to destruction than put himself under obligations to me, because I am not yet one of the salt of the earth and privileged to snub captains and lord it over everything dead and alive in a steamboat." I presently climbed up on the bench; I did not think it was safe to go to sleep while this lunatic was on watch.

However, I must have gone to sleep in the course of time, because the next thing I was aware of was the fact that day was breaking, Mr. W. gone, and Mr. Bixby at the wheel again. So it was four o'clock and all well—but me; I felt like a skinful of dry bones, and all of them trying to ache at once.

---

[2] Two fathoms. Quarter twain is 2¼ fathoms, 13½ feet. Mark three is three fathoms.—M.T.

[3] "Partner" is technical for "the other pilot."—M. T.

Mr. Bixby asked me what I had stayed up there for. I confessed that it was to do Mr. W. a benevolence—tell him where he was. It took five minutes for the entire preposterousness of the thing to filter into Mr. Bixby's system, and then I judge it filled him nearly up to the chin; because he paid me a compliment—and not much of a one either. He said:

"Well, taking you by and large, you do seem to be more different kinds of an ass than any creature I ever saw before. What did you suppose he wanted to know for?"

I said I thought it might be a convenience to him.

"Convenience! D——nation! Didn't I tell you that a man's got to know the river in the night the same as he'd know his own front hall?"

"Well, I can follow the front hall in the dark if I know it *is* the front hall; but suppose you set me down in the middle of it in the dark, and not tell me which hall it is; how am *I* to know?"

"Well, you've *got* to, on the river!"

"All right. Then I'm glad I never said anything to Mr. W."

"I should say so! Why, he'd have slammed you through the window and utterly ruined a hundred dollars' worth of window-sash and stuff."

I was glad this damage had been saved, for it would have made me unpopular with the owners. They always hated anybody who had the name of being careless and injuring things.

I went to work now to learn the shape of the river; and of all the eluding and ungraspable objects that ever I tried to get mind or hands on, that was the chief. I would fasten my eyes upon a sharp, wooded point that projected far into the river some miles ahead of me, and go to laboriously photographing its shape upon my brain; and just as I was beginning to succeed to my satisfaction, we would draw up toward it and the exasperating thing would begin to melt away and fold back into the bank! If there had been a conspicuous dead tree standing upon the very point of the cape, I would find that tree inconspicuously merged into the general forest, and occupying the middle of a straight shore, when I got abreast of it! No prominent hill would stick to its shape long enough for me to make up my mind what its form really was, but it was as dissolving and changeful as if it had been a mountain of butter in the hottest corner of the tropics. Nothing ever had the same shape when I was coming downstream that it had borne when I went up. I mentioned these little difficulties to Mr. Bixby. He said:

"That's the very main virtue of the thing. If the shapes didn't change every three seconds they wouldn't be of any use. Take this place where we are now, for instance. As long as that hill over yonder is only one hill, I can boom right along the way I'm going; but the moment it splits at the top and forms a V, I know I've got to scratch to starboard in a hurry, or I'll bang this boat's brains out against a rock; and then the moment one of the prongs of the V swings behind the other, I've got to waltz to larboard again, or I'll have a misunderstanding with a snag that would snatch the keelson out of this steamboat as neatly as if it were a sliver in your hand. If that hill didn't change its shape on bad nights there would be an awful steamboat graveyard around here inside of a year."

It was plain that I had got to learn the shape of the river in all the different ways that could be thought of,—upside down, wrong end first, inside out, fore-and-aft, and "thort-ships,"—and then know what to do on gray nights when it hadn't any shape at all. So I set about it. In the course of time I began to get the best of this knotty lesson, and my self-complacency moved to the front once more. Mr. Bixby was all fixed, and ready to start it to the rear again. He opened on me after this fashion:

"How much water did we have in the middle crossing at Hole-in-the-Wall, trip before last?"

I considered this an outrage. I said:

"Every trip, down and up, the leadsmen are singing through that tangled place for three-quarters of an hour on a stretch. How do you reckon I can remember such a mess as that?"

"My boy, you've got to remember it. You've got to remember the exact spot and the exact marks the boat lay in when we had the shoalest water, in every one of the five hundred shoal places between St. Louis and New Orleans; and you musn't get the shoal soundings and marks of one trip mixed up with the shoal soundings and marks of another, either, for they're not often twice alike. You must keep them separate."

When I came to myself again, I said:

"When I get so that I can do that, I'll be able to raise the dead, and then I won't have to pilot a steamboat to make a living. I want to retire from this business. I want a slush-bucket and a brush; I'm only fit for a roustabout. I haven't got brains enough to be a pilot; and if I had I wouldn't have strength enough to carry them around, unless I went on crutches."

"Now drop that! When I say I'll learn [4] a man the river, I mean it. And you can depend on it, I'll learn him or kill him."

Captain Charlie's First Trip as a Pilot

"Captain," I said, "when did you really get to be a pilot?"

He didn't need much prodding. "I really didn't do much towboat work," he said, "until after I had received my first issue of license. Anyhow, I served an apprenticeship of about three years—about a year on deck as a deckhand and roustabout and one thing and another; and two years as a cub pilot and roof watchman in the pilot house. I took an examination for a pilot's license in St. Louis. My first issue of license was from St. Louis

---

[4] "Teach" is not in the river vocabulary.—M.T.

From *Towboat River*, by Edwin and Louise Rosskam, pp. 113–118. Copyright, 1948, by Edwin and Louise Rosskam. New York: Duell, Sloan and Pearce.

to Cairo, and they were issued on the eleventh day of August in 1913, about eleven o'clock in the morning.

"And after I got those license and come out of the ol' custom house here in St. Louis, why, I pushed my derby over on one side of my head and said, 'Okay, I'm now a pilot.' And I been tryin' to pilot boats ever since. I was roof watchman at the time on the *St. Louis*. It was the largest stern-wheel packet boat in the St. Louis to Tennessee packet trade. And I was settin' down on the boiler deck, a-wonderin' what I was gonna do. I had those license in my pocket. No job, of course, and very few dollars. They didn't anybody know whether I could do the work of a pilot. . . . And then I heard somebody ask the porter if Charlie was aboard. The porter said yes. It was a friend of mine, a pilot that I'd steered with during one of the winter cruises in the lower river here. He liked to bet on the horses and he was known as Racehorse Jim. He says, 'Well, I hear you got your license this mornin'.' I says, 'Yessir.' He says, 'Well, they's a boat layin' down here and she's been given a permit to go to the Mound City ways for repairs.' That's just above Cairo on the Ohio River. And he says, 'You're the only available man at St. Louis at this time, which is posted on the river, with license to Cairo.' He says, 'You want the job? I'll take you down there and introduce you to the captain.' And I says, 'Okay,' and I went down there with him. . . . Well, I was introduced to the captain, and then Racehorse Jim he left. And after he'd gone, why, the captain of that boat, he asked me how much I'd charge to take him to the Mound City ways. And I told him, well, the customary price at that time. It was twenty-five dollars and my expenses back to St. Louis.

"And he says, 'Well,' he says, 'you just got your license today and you have never piloted a boat.' He says, 'We don't feel like we have to pay you that much.'

"I says, 'Well, I feel that way about it.' He says, 'Well, we can't do that.' I says, 'Well, all right,' I says, 'I'll just leave.' So I reached down to pick up my little derby and my grip that had this celluloid collar in it, to go back to my boat before I lost that other job.

"Then he stops me and says, 'Well, you sit down there and think about it a minute. See if you can't take the job for twenty dollars.' So I just reached over and grabbed ahold of that captain's hand, and shook hands with him. And I says, 'Well, it'd just be a waste of my time and of your time, too, for me to sit down and think about it, because the longer I think, the scareder I'm gonna get, and the price'll go up, I imagine.'

. . . "So when I started to walk out of that captain's office . . . he stops me and tells me it's all right and that he'll pay me the money. At one o'clock that day I backed that boat out of St. Louis, a very, very scared pilot. . . . She was just goin' out with a single crew and I was the only pilot on her. There was a hundred and eighty miles between St. Louis and Cairo. We run to dark and tied up for the night and then left out the next day and went into Cairo. . . . The boat, you see, she was condemned, crossed out of business, and she was only operatin' on a permit to go to the ways. We got to Waters Point that afternoon. It was a close channel and as I went into Waters Point to pull her down to go around the reef, why, there was a pronounced list to the boat. She rolled considerably. And I tooted the whistle and one of the roustabouts come up on the roof and I asked him, I says, 'What's makin' this boat list like she is? Is there water in her hold?' And he says, 'Yessir, there's a little water.' I says, 'How much water?' He says, 'Two feet.' Well, I like to died then. 'Cause I had a picture of what would happen if somethin' went wrong with that boat on my first trip out. I woulda been ruined as a pilot then. . . .

"But we got safely by that place and tied up that night. And then the next morning we left out before breakfast. And when breakfast time come, a gentleman on the boat, who was watchman, come up to the pilot house and said the captain had sent him up there to relieve me while I eat breakfast. An' bein' quite a youngster, I asked him a few questions, and it seemed as though he knew as much or more about the river than I did. And I thought it'd be perfectly all right to let him hold her.

"So I went down to breakfast and left him up there. And I was just settin' down to breakfast, and I could feel the boat listin'. And I looked out forward and I seen her swingin' toward the bluff. And I run to the pilot house and I got up there and rung the stoppin' bell and set the boat to backin'. I just backed her in time. She just cleared the rocks. . . .

"And I'm satisfied that they felt that it would be more to their advantage to collect the insurance on the boat than it would be to repair her. At that time, it was just about the time of the death of the packet boats on the river. That boat, when we did finally get her safely to the marine ways where she was repaired, never left port. She was sold by the United States marshal for five hundred dollars. And was bought and converted into a towboat. . . .

"And so my first trip as pilot come out all right. When I got off that boat I went to Nashville, Tennessee, to stand another examination, as pilot from Cairo, Illinois, to Paducah, Kentucky, on the Ohio River, and from Paducah, Kentucky, to Waterloo, Alabama, on the Tennessee River. And I've had many an issue of license after that. I have license for all the tributaries south of Memphis with the exception of the St. Francis River and the Arkansas. Yessir, I've towed logs from all the tributaries: the Little River, the Ouachita River, Bayou Mason, Black River, the Red River, the Kenesaw, the Yazoo River, the Sunflower, the Little Sunflower, White River, and all those old rivers and lakes in the lower-river country down there."

The Best Handler

Next to *Grey Eagle*, the old *Key City* was the grandest steamboat that ever climbed a bar, and there were eminent authorities that held her to have shaded the favorite. For years in the good old times she traveled up and down the upper Mississippi, never was beaten in a race, and never declined the chance of one, either. Incidentally, she was known as the best handler that ever went afloat.

"You could thread the eye of a needle with that boat," said one of the old-timers.

"You bet you could," said West Rambo. "Why, you could move that wheel with your eyelash."

*　*　*　*　*

She has also a certain though unacknowledged place in literature.

Readers of Mark Twain may recall the story he tells in Chapter XXIV of *Life on the Mississippi*, about Bob Styles and the *Cyclone*. Mr. Styles has been condemning an untruthful man with whom he piously declined to associate. Then he says:

"That *Cyclone* was a rattler to go, and the sweetest thing to steer that ever walked the waters. Set her amidships in a big river, and just let her go; it was all you had to do. She would hold herself on a star all night, if you let her alone. You couldn't ever feel her rudder. It wasn't any more labor to steer her than it is to count the Republican vote in a South Carolina election. One morning, just at daybreak, the last trip she ever made, they took her rudder aboard to mend it; I didn't know anything about it; I backed her out from the woodyard and went a-weaving down the river all serene. When I had gone about twenty-three miles and made four horribly crooked crossings—"

"Without any rudder?"

"Yes—old Captain Tom appeared on the roof and began to find fault with me for running such a dark night—"

"Such a dark night? Why, you said—"

And so on. To a landsman the notion of running a steamboat twenty-three miles without a rudder would seem to be grotesque enough to constitute excellent humor, but to a riverman there is nothing preposterous about it; it has been done more than once, conspicuously by Bill Tibbals and the old *Key City*.

One day she was coming down above Trempealeau in a fog and hit something that tore off the rudder. They stopped and fished it up and got it aboard but could not hang it again, because some of the irons had been broken out. Bill Tibbals was chief pilot. The Old Man (captain) said to him:

From *A-Rafting on the Mississip'*, by Charles Edward Russell, pp. 253–256. Copyright, 1928, by Charles Edward Russell. New York and London: The Century Company.

"Can you run without a rudder?"

"You bet I can," said Tibbals. "Start her right out."

They backed her out of Trempealeau, straightened her down the river, and before long they saw the chimneys of the *Northern Belle,* another crack boat of the packet class. So they took after her and passed her at her best clip. Next they sighted La Crosse, where they had a landing to make, and it was one of the worst on the Mississippi, but the *Key City* negotiated it with ease. When they were through handling their freight at La Crosse, they backed out again and went on as far as Brownsville, forty miles from Trempealeau, where they stopped and put the rudder on her and went ahead.

On this occasion the *Key City* ran forty miles, passed a rival steamboat, threaded two crooked sloughs, made several nasty crossings and two landings, without any more rudder on her than there is on a church.

As she was going downstream, part of each landing consisted of the delicate maneuver of rounding-to. That is to say, she came down below the landing, swept around in a semicircle, and landed, bow up—without a rudder.

At this landsmen will gape as at something impossible, but it actually happened. The feat was wonderful enough to be talked of for many years, and is still, I think, wherever old pilots get together. . . . Landsmen overlook the fact that the two wheels of the *Key City* had independent engines. Tibbals steered her with the wheels, and Bob Styles could have steered the *Cyclone* the same way, if there had been such a steamboat. Instead of engine bells Tibbals used the speaking-tube.

"More on your labboard! Stop the stabboard! Go ahead on it! Ease off that labboard!" and the thing was done. It was not just as easy as it is for a city council to grant a franchise, but it could be done by a smart pilot.

I have always believed that Twain got his humor story of Bob Styles and the *Cyclone* from the true story of Bill Tibbals and the *Key City*. One reason for that notion is that the two stories begin in the same way. "The old *Key City* was the sweetest thing to steer that ever was," said the old-timer whenever he warmed up to the Tibbals incident, and in that shape it went the whole length of the Mississippi, St. Anthony to the jetties.

The Pilot's Test

Captain Jerry Webb, when a Mississippi river pilot, was once being examined by the U.S. Steamboat Inspectors for a license. In the course of his examination he was asked the following question: —"Captain, what

From *Old Man River,* Upper Mississippi River Steamboating Days Stories, Tales of the Old Time Steamboats and Steamboatmen, by Charles E. Brown, p. 19. Madison, Wisconsin: Wisconsin Folklore Society. 1940.

would you do if your boat was moving along and you suddenly saw a big rock sticking up out of the water right in front of your boat? You could not go back."

"By———," said Captain Webber without a moment's hesitation, "I'd bust into it." No one could have done otherwise, the examining officer agreed.

The Rival Pilots

The *Uncle Sam* was the largest boat of her day, and had two of the best pilots on the river. Between these two men, whom we will call for the nonce, Smith and Brown, there existed a bitter feeling of rivalry. The first engineer sided with Smith, the first pilot; and the second engineer with Brown. One day when the boat was leaving Natchez, Brown, who was steering, ran her a short distance down stream in order to pass the town under a full head of steam. Just as he was abreast of it, the first engineer, who was working the boat, shut the steam nearly off; nor would he put it on again until they finally and very slowly passed the town.

Brown saw the finger of Smith in this maneuver, and determined to be revenged in kind. He was. On the next down trip a heavy fog arose at sunset, and Smith, who at that time abandoned the wheel to Brown, ordered him to run the boat until nine o'clock and then to tie her up; to have steam kept up all night; and, if the fog should lift, to call him.

"Tie the boat up!" exclaimed Brown. "I can run her in any such fog as there is tonight. I'll run her till twelve, and then tie up, as you are afraid."

"I can run her any night, and anywhere that you can," replied Smith; "and if you *do* move her till twelve, call me then, that's all."

Brown kept on for a time, but the fog came on heavier and heavier, and having made sure that his coadjutor was fast asleep, he rounded the boat to a woodyard and tied up. His friend, the second engineer, was on duty, and according to Brown's directions, the wheel was unshipped and the steam kept up. At twelve, Brown went to the wheel again, and sent a waiter to call Smith, who soon made his appearance, rubbing his eyes and anything but pleased at the prospect before him—although, strictly speaking, prospect there was none, for he could not fairly discern the top of his nose for the fog.

"Hallo!" said Brown, "are you there? I've called you according to orders, and now I think you'd better tie up and turn in again, or you'll make a smash-up before morning."

Smith growled out that he was able to steer any boat in any fog, and took the wheel. Brown went below.

From *A Stray Yankee in Texas*, by Philip Paxton [Samuel A. Hammett], pp. 409–411. Entered . . . 1853, by J. S. Redfield. New York.

The boat was fast to the bank, but neither bank nor anything else could poor Smith see. The wheel, which was ungeared, turned around and round with the swift current, and the splashes reached his ear; the hissing of the steam in her low pressure boilers sounded all right to him; so cursing his bad luck, Brown's obstinacy, and his own stupidity in accepting the banter, he turned his wheel now this way and now that, expecting every moment to hear and feel the boat crash against something. A thousand times, during his dreary watch, did he determine to give up his desperate undertaking, and as often did pride step in and prevent him; and so, finally, having made up his mind to let the worst come, he gave a tubular order to the engineer to work her very slow, and keep on—as he supposed.

About sunrise, Brown, accompanied by the Captain and other officers, ascended the hurricane deck.

"Hallo! Smith," said Brown, "is that you?"

"Yes, it is," replied Smith, crossly enough.

"You haven't been running all night, I reckon?" continued Brown.

"Can't you see I have?" answered Smith. "Don't you know where you are? If you don't, you better get your eyes scrubbed out."

"No," returned Brown, "I can't say I do. Where are we?"

"Just above Natchez," was the reply.

"There's matey," said Brown. "You *have* done it this time, and I wouldn't be in your boots for a hogshead of niggers."

"What have I done, and what do you mean?" demanded Smith, ferociously.

"Done! Done enough!" roared Brown. "I left the boat tied up to old Jones's plantation, and if you have gone and towed *that* down to Natchez, they'll have you up for abduction, and sea-duction, and nigger stealing, and putting obstructions in the channel of the river, and the Law a marcy on ye."

A very moist ray of the sun peeping through the mist, at this moment, partially disclosed the situation of the boat and shore to the astonished and discomfited Smith, and darting below, he remained there until the boat *did* reach Natchez. And from that time ever after, neither the *Uncle Sam* nor the Mississippi River knew him more.

II. RIVER CONQUERORS, FIGHTERS AND TRICKSTERS

The First Voyage of the First Steamboat on the Western Waters

Mr. Nicholas J. Roosevelt ... married my eldest sister in the year 1809; and she made the voyage with her husband in 1811. Its events were the stories I listened to in my childhood. The impressions then made have never been effaced. They were deepened, when my father removed his family to Pittsburgh, in 1813, having become interested with Livingston and Fulton in the steam navigation of the Ohio. Here he superintended the building of the *Buffalo,* the fourth of the steamboats launched at Pittsburgh. The second and third were the *Vesuvius* and *Aetna,* already in course of construction when the *Buffalo* was commenced, and completed before it. My playmates were the boys who had seen the *New Orleans* leave for the lower Mississippi, only two years before. Our playground, on Saturday afternoons, was often the shipyard where she had been built, at the foot of Boyd's Hill, on the banks of the Monongahela. Steam navigation was the one engrossing thought of Pittsburgh in those days. Even children were interested in the discussion of it. My memory, therefore, supplies me with some of the matter of my story. I am in possession, besides, of my father's letter books of that date. His correspondence with Mr. Fulton was voluminous, and abounded in minute detail. No name is mentioned in it much more frequently than Roosevelt's—no experience is oftener referred to. Mrs. Roosevelt, too, is still alive, in a green old age; and, in view of the present paper, I have refreshed my memory of the stories I listened to at her knee, by comparing it with hers. It is in this way I have come to venture on the present narrative. I, at one time, thought of hunting up the newspapers of the day; but a busy professional life has not permitted me to take the time necessary for the search. I am satisfied, however, that, should they be consulted, nothing will be found inconsistent with what I now set down.

From *The First Steamboat Voyage on the Western Waters,* by J. H. B. Latrobe, pp. 3–32. Fund Publication No. 6. Maryland Historical Society. Baltimore. October, 1871.

When reading to the Maryland Historical Society, on a former occasion, "A Lost Chapter in the History of the Steamboat," I had occasion to refer to the first voyage of a vessel of that description on the Western waters, calling it a Romance in itself. The desire of the members present seemed to be to hear it told. I now propose to tell it. And, first, a word or two to explain how I come to be the narrator.—J.H.B.L.

Before coming to the voyage itself, it may not be uninteresting to state some matters germane to the subject, by way of preface.

Prior to the introduction of steamboats on the Western waters, the means of transportation thereon consisted of keelboats, barges and flatboats. Keelboats and barges ascended, as well as descended, the stream. The flatboat was an unwieldy box, and was broken up, for the lumber it contained, on its arrival at the place of destination. The keelboat was long and slender, sharp fore and aft, with a narrow gangway just within the gunwale, for the boatmen as they poled or warped up the stream, when not aided by the eddies that made their oars available. When the keelboat was covered with a low house, lengthwise, between the gangways, it was dignified with the name of "barge." The only claim of the flatboat, or "broad horn," to rank as a vessel was due to the fact that it floated upon water and was used as a vehicle for transportation. Keelboats, barges, and flatboats had prodigious steering oars, and oars of the same dimensions were hung on fixed pivots on the sides of the last named, by which the shapeless and cumbrous contrivance was, in some sort, managed. Ignorant of anything better, the people of the West were satisfied with these appliances of trade in 1810.

Whether steam could be employed on the Western rivers was a question that its success between New York and Albany was not regarded as having entirely solved; and after the idea had been suggested of building a boat at Pittsburgh, to ply between Natchez and New Orleans, it was considered necessary that investigations should be made, as to the currents of the rivers to be navigated, in regard to the new system. These investigations Mr. Roosevelt undertook with the understanding, that if his report were favorable, Chancellor Livingston, Mr. Fulton, and himself, were to be equally interested in the undertaking. The Chancellor and Fulton were to supply the capital, and Roosevelt was to superintend the building of the boat and engine. For this duty . . . the latter was peculiarly qualified. He accordingly repaired to Pittsburgh, in May, 1809, accompanied by his wife, to whom he had been but recently married. The only means of conveyance to New Orleans, where his investigations were to terminate, were the keelboats, barges, and flatboats already described. None of those then in use were suited to Mr. Roosevelt's purpose; and as the accuracy of his examination, rather than the speed of the voyage, was important, he determined to build a flatboat which should contain all necessary comforts for himself and wife, and float with the current of the Ohio and Mississippi from Pittsburgh to New Orleans. This he accordingly did; and, with the exception of some three weeks passed on shore at Louisville and some nine or ten days in a row boat between Natchez and New Orleans, the flatboat was the home of Mr. and Mrs. Roosevelt for the next six months. Cincinnati, Louisville, and Natchez, were then the only places of even the smallest note between Pittsburgh and New Orleans. Furnished with letters of introduction to their leading men, the travellers were kindly received and most hospitably entertained. Mr. Roosevelt's explanations were listened to respectfully, as he stated his purpose in visiting the West, and narrated what steam had accomplished on the Eastern rivers. But he was evidently regarded as a sanguine enthusiast, engaged in an impracticable undertaking. From no one individual did he receive a word of encouragement. Nor was this incredulity confined to the gentlemen he met in society; it extended to the pilots and boatmen, who, passing their lives on the Ohio and Mississippi, possessed the practical information that he wanted. They heard what he had to say of the experience of Fulton and Livingston, and then pointed to the turbid and whirling waters of the great river as a conclusive answer to all his reasoning. That steam would ever be able to resist them they could not be made to understand. Nothing, however, shook the confidence of Mr. Roosevelt. He had made up his mind that steam was to do the work of the Western world, and his present visit was but for the purpose of ascertaining how best the work could be done upon its streams. The Ohio and Mississippi were problems that he had undertaken to study; nor did he leave them until he had mastered them in all their bearings. He gauged them: he measured their velocity at different seasons; he obtained all the statistical information within his reach, and formed a judgment with respect to the future development of the country West of the Alleghenies that has since been amply corroborated. Not only did he do this, but finding coal on the banks of the Ohio, he purchased and opened mines of the mineral; and so confident was he of the success of the project on hand that he caused supplies of the fuel to be heaped upon the shore, in anticipation of the wants of a steamboat whose keel had yet to be laid, and whose very existence was to depend upon the impression that his report might make upon the capitalists, without whose aid the plan would, for the present at least, have to be abandoned.

Arriving in New York in the middle of January, 1810, Mr. Roosevelt's report, bearing on its face evidence of the thoroughness of his examination, impressed Fulton and Livingston with his own convictions; and in the spring of that year he returned to Pittsburgh to superintend the building of the first steamboat that was launched on the Western waters.

I am not aware that this preliminary exploration has ever been noticed in any of the published histories of steam navigation. It has seemed to me to be of sufficient importance to have a place in the present communication. It appears to us now, with our present knowledge of the Ohio and Mississippi, to have been a work of supererogation; but with the information then possessed geographically, and, as far as steam was in question, scientifically, it would have been most imprudent to have dispensed with it.

Pittsburgh, when Mr. Roosevelt took up his residence there in 1811, had but recently commenced the career which has now entitled it to the name of the Birmingham of America. The main body of the town was built on the right bank of the Monongahela, and extended from the point where the junction with the Allegheny takes place, for perhaps three-quarters of a mile up the former stream, to within a short distance of the mouth of a small creek, with low grounds on either side, that here debouched into the river. On the Allegheny side, which was liable to overflow, there were but few buildings in 1811. Close by the creek and immediately under a lofty bluff, called Boyd's hill, was an iron foundry, known as Beelen's foundry; and in immediate proximity to this was the keel of Mr. Roosevelt's vessel laid. The future antiquarian may, perhaps, find satisfaction in knowing that the Depot of the Pittsburgh and Connellsville Railroad now occupies the ground I am speaking of.

The size and plan of the first steamboat had been determined on in New York, and had been furnished by Mr. Fulton. It was to be 116 feet in length, with twenty feet beam. The engine was to have a 34-inch cylinder, and the boiler and other parts of the machine were to be in proportion.

The first thing to be done was to obtain the timber to build the boat; and for this purpose men were sent into the forest, there to find the necessary ribs, and knees, and beams—transport them to the Monongahela, and raft them to the shipyard. White pine was the only material for planking that could be obtained without a delay that was inadmissible. The sawing that was required was done in the old-fashioned and now long forgotten saw pits of 1811. Boat builders, accustomed to construct the barges of that day, could be obtained in Pittsburgh; but a shipbuilder and the mechanics required in the machinery department had to be brought from New York. Under these circumstances, Mr. Roosevelt began the work. One of the first troubles that annoyed him was a rise in the Monongahela, when the waters backed into his shipyard and set all his materials that were buoyant afloat. This occurred again and again; and on one occasion it seemed not improbable that the steamboat would be lifted from its ways and launched before its time. With my own recollection of the remnants of the rude shops in which Mr. Roosevelt had the engine built, some four years after they had been abandoned, the wonder to this day is how he could have accomplished what he did. At length, however, all difficulties were overcome by steady perseverance, and the boat was launched —and called, from the place of her ultimate destination, the *New Orleans*. It cost in the neighborhood of $38,000.

As the *New Orleans* approached completion, and when it came to be known that Mrs. Roosevelt intended to accompany her husband on the voyage, the numerous friends she had made in Pittsburgh united in endeavoring to dissuade her from what they regarded as utter folly, if not absolute madness. Her husband was appealed to. The criticisms that had been freely applied to the boat by the crowds of visitors to the shipyard were now transferred to the conduct of the builder. He was told that he had no right to peril his wife's life, however reckless he might be of his own. Mrs. Roosevelt, too, expected before long to become a mother; and this was held to enhance the offense which the good people of Pittsburgh fancied he was committing. But the wife believed in her husband; and, in the latter part of September, 1811, the *New Orleans*, after a short experimental trip up the Monongahela, commenced her voyage.

There were two cabins, one aft, for ladies, and a larger one forward for gentlemen. In the former there were four berths. It was comfortably furnished. Of this, Mrs. Roosevelt took possession. Mr. Roosevelt and herself were the only passengers. There was a captain, an engineer named Baker, Andrew Jack, the pilot, six hands, two female servants, a man waiter, a cook, and an immense Newfoundland dog, named Tiger. Thus equipped, the *New Orleans* began the voyage which changed the relations of the West—which may almost be said to have changed its destiny.

The people of Pittsburgh turned out in mass and lined the banks of the Monongahela to witness the departure of the steamboat; and shout after shout rent the air, and handkerchiefs were waved and hats thrown up by way of "God speed" to the voyagers, as the anchor was raised, and heading up stream for a short distance, a wide circuit brought the *New Orleans* on her proper course, and, steam and current aiding, she disappeared behind the first headlands on the right bank of the Ohio.

Too much excited to sleep, Mr. Roosevelt and his wife passed the greater part of the first night on deck, and watched the shore, covered then with an almost unbroken forest, as reach after reach, and bend after bend, were passed at a speed of from eight to ten miles an hour. The regular working of the engine, the ample supply of steam, the uniformity of the speed, inspired at last a confidence that quieted the nervous apprehension of the travellers. Mr. Jack, the pilot, delighted with the facility with which the vessel was steered, and at a speed to which he was so little accustomed, ceased to express misgivings and became as sanguine as Mr. Roosevelt himself in regard to the success of the voyage. The very crew of unimaginative men were excited with the novelty of the situation; and when the following morning assembled all hands on deck to return the cheers of a village whose inhabitants had seen the boat approaching down a long reach in the river and turned out to greet her as she sped by— it probably shone upon as jolly a set as ever floated on the Ohio.

On the second day after leaving Pittsburgh, the *New Orleans* rounded to opposite Cincinnati, and cast anchor in the stream. Levees and wharf boats were things unknown in 1811. Here, as at Pittsburgh, the whole town seemed to have assembled on the bank, and many of the acquaintances of the former visit came off in small boats. "Well, you are as good as your word; you have visited us in a steamboat," they said; "but we see you for the last time. Your boat may go *down* the river; but, as to coming up it, the very idea is an absurd one." This was one of those occasions on which seeing was not believing. The keelboatmen, whose shoulders had hardened as they pressed their poles for many a weary mile against the current, shook their heads, as they crowded around the strange visitor, and bandied river wit with the crew that had been selected from their own calling for the first voyage. Some flatboatmen, whose ungainly arks the steamboat had passed a short distance above the town, and who now floated by with the current, seemed to have a better opinion of the newcomer, and proposed a tow in case they were again overtaken. But as to the boat's returning, all agreed that *that* could never be.

The stay at Cincinnati was brief, only long enough to take in a supply of wood for the voyage to Louisville, which was reached on the night of the fourth day after leaving Pittsburgh. It was midnight on the first of October, 1811, that the *New Orleans* dropped anchor opposite the town. There was a brilliant moon. It was as light as day almost, and no one on board had retired. The roar of the escaping steam, then heard for the first time at the place where now its echoes are unceasing, roused the population, and, late as it was, crowds came rushing to the bank of the river to learn the cause of the unwonted uproar. A letter now before me, written by one of those on board at the time, records the fact—that there were those who insisted that the comet of 1811 had fallen into the Ohio and had produced the hubbub!

The morning after the arrival of the vessel at Louisville, Mr. Roosevelt's acquaintances and others came on board, and here the same things were said that had been said at Cincinnati. Congratulations at having descended the river were, without exception, accompanied by regrets that it was the first and last time a steamboat would be seen above the falls of the Ohio. Still, so far, certainly, Mr. Roosevelt's promise had been fulfilled; and there was a public dinner given to him a few days after his arrival. Here any number of complimentary toasts were drunk, and the usual amount of good feeling on such occasions was manifested. *Sed revocare gradum*, however, was still the burden of the song.

Not to be outdone in hospitality, Mr. Roosevelt invited his hosts to dine on board the *New Orleans,* which still lay anchored opposite the town. The company met in the forward or gentlemen's cabin, and the feast was at its height, when suddenly there were heard unwonted rumblings, accompanied by a very perceptible motion in the vessel. The company had but one idea. The *New Orleans* had escaped from her anchor, and was drifting towards the Falls, to the certain destruction of all on board. There was an instant and simultaneous rush to the upper deck, when the company found that, instead of drifting towards the Falls of the Ohio, the *New Orleans* was making good headway up the river and would soon leave Louisville in the distance downstream. As the engine warmed to its work, and the steam blew off at the safety valve, the speed increased. Mr. Roosevelt, of course, had provided this mode of convincing his incredulous guests, and their surprise and delight may readily be imagined. After going up the river for a few miles, the *New Orleans* returned to her anchorage.

It had been intended, on leaving Pittsburgh, to proceed as rapidly as possible to New Orleans, to place the boat on the route for which it was designed, between that city and Natchez. It was found, however, on reaching Louisville, that there was not a sufficient depth of water on the Falls of the Ohio to permit the vessel to pass over them in safety. Nothing was to be done, therefore, but to wait, as patiently as possible, for a rise in the river. That this delay might, as far as practicable, be utilized to the extent, at least, of convincing incredulous Cincinnatians, the *New Orleans* returned to that city, where she was greeted with an enthusiasm that exceeded even what was displayed on her descent from Pittsburgh. No one doubted now. In 1832, I was detained for several days in Cincinnati, on my return from a visit to the South. There were numbers, then alive, who remembered the first advent of steam, and from some of these I learned what is here stated in regard to the public feeling at the time—the universal incredulity of the first visit—the unbounded confidence inspired by the second.

Returning to Louisville, the great interest of all on board the *New Orleans* centered in watching the rise in the Ohio. Rain in the upper country was what was wanted, and of this there seemed small promise. There was nothing in the aspect of the heavens that indicated it. On the contrary, there was a dull misty sky without a cloud—a leaden atmosphere that weighed upon the spirits, and the meaning of which would have been better understood at Naples under the shadow of Vesuvius than on the banks of the Ohio. The sun, when it rose, looked like a globe of red hot iron, whose color brightened at noon, to resume the same look when it sank below the horizon. All day long, one might have gazed on it with unflinching eyes. The air was still and heated; and a sense of weariness was the characteristic of the hours as they wore slowly by. At last, and when a nervous impatience affected every one on board, it was announced one morning that there had been a rise in the river during the night. There was another announcement of a very different character. Mrs. Roosevelt had, for the second time, become a mother. The events of the voyage were certainly multiplying. Fortunately, this addition to the passengers happened when the *New Orleans* was necessarily detained in port.

Morning after morning, the rise in the river during the night was reported; and finally, in the last week in November, it was ascertained that the depth of water in the shallowest portion of the Falls exceeded by five inches the draught of the boat. It was a narrow margin. But the rise had ceased; there was no telegraph in those days to tell hourly what was the weather in the country drained by the Ohio; and Mr. Roosevelt, assuring himself personally of the condition of the Falls, determined to take the responsibility and go over them if he could. It was an anxious time. All hands were on deck. Mrs. Roosevelt, whom her husband would willingly have left behind to join him below the Falls, refused to remain on shore, and stood near the stern. The two pilots, for an extra one had been engaged for the passage through the rapids, took their places in the bow. The anchor was weighed. To get into the Indiana channel, which was the best, a wide circuit had to be made bringing her head downstream, completing which the *New Orleans* began the descent. Steerage way depended upon her speed exceeding that of the current. The faster she could be made to go, the easier it would be to guide her. All the steam the boiler

would bear was put upon her. The safety valve shrieked; the wheels revolved faster than they had ever done before; and the vessel, speaking
figuratively, fairly flew away from the crowds collected to witness her
departure from Louisville.

Instinctively, each one on board now grasped the nearest object, and
with bated breath awaited the result. Black ledges of rock appeared only
to disappear as the *New Orleans* flashed by them. The waters whirled and
eddied and threw their spray upon the deck, as a more rapid descent
caused the vessel to pitch forward to what at times seemed inevitable
destruction. Not a word was spoken. The pilots directed the men at the
helm by motions of their hands. Even the great Newfoundland dog seemed
affected by the apprehension of danger, and came and crouched at Mrs.
Roosevelt's feet. The tension on the nervous system was too great to be
long sustained. Fortunately, the passage was soon made; and, with feelings of profound gratitude to the Almighty at the successful issue of the
adventure, on the part of both Mr. Roosevelt and his wife, the *New
Orleans* rounded to in safety below the Falls. There was still the same
leaden sky—the same dim sun during the day—the same starless night;
but the great difficulty had been overcome, and it was believed that there
would now be nothing but plain sailing to the port of destination. It was
yet to be seen how far the expectations of those on board, in this respect,
would be realized.

Hitherto the voyage had been one of pleasure. Nothing had marred the
enjoyment of the travelers. The receptions at Louisville and Cincinnati
had been great events. But now were to come, to use the words of the
letter already referred to, "those days of horror." The comet of 1811 had
disappeared, and was followed by the earthquake of that year, of which
the atmospheric phenomena just mentioned were prognostics; and the
earthquake accompanied the *New Orleans* far on her way down the
Mississippi.

The first shock that was observed was felt on board the *New Orleans*
while she lay at anchor after passing the Falls. The effect was as though
the vessel had been in motion and had suddenly grounded. The cable
shook and trembled, and many on board experienced for the moment a
nausea resembling sea sickness. It was a little while before they could
realize the presence of the dread visitor. It was wholly unexpected. The
shocks succeeded each other during the night. When morning came, the
voyage was resumed; and while under way, the jar of the machinery, the
monotonous beating of the wheels and the steady progress of the vessel
prevented the disturbance from being noticed.

It has already been mentioned that, in his voyage of exploration, Mr.
Roosevelt had found coal on the Ohio and that he had caused mines to be
opened in anticipation. Their value was now realized; and, when he
reached them on his way down the river, he took on board as much coal
as he could find room for.

Some miles above the mouth of the Ohio, the diminished speed of the current indicated a rise in the Mississippi. This was found to be the case. The bottom lands on either shore were under water, and there was every sign of an unwonted flood. Canoes came and went among the boles of the trees. Sometimes the Indians attempted to approach the steamboat; and, again, fled on its approach. The Chickasaws still occupied that part of the State of Tennessee lying below the mouth of the Ohio. On one occasion, a large canoe, fully manned, came out of the woods abreast of the steamboat. The Indians, outnumbering the crew of the vessel, paddled after it. There was at once a race, and for a time the contest was equal. The result, however, was what might have been anticipated. Steam had the advantage of endurance; and the Indians with wild shouts, which might have been shouts of defiance, gave up the pursuit, and turned into the forest from whence they had emerged.

While the crew of the *New Orleans* were more amused than alarmed at this incident of the voyage, Mr. Roosevelt . . . was not sorry . . . when he lost sight of the canoe. That he bestowed a second thought upon the matter illustrates the nervous excitement that prevailed on board. Mrs. Roosevelt and himself were still discussing the adventure when they retired to rest. They had scarcely fallen asleep when they were aroused by shouts on deck and the trampling of many feet. With the idea of Indians still predominant, Mr. Roosevelt sprang from his bed and seizing a sword— the only weapon at hand—hurried from the cabin to join battle, as he thought, with the Chickasaws. It was a more alarming enemy that he encountered. The *New Orleans* was on fire; and flame and smoke issued from the forward cabin. The servant who attended there had placed some green wood too close to the stove in anticipation of the next day's wants; and, lying down beside it, had fallen sound asleep. The stove becoming over-heated, this wood had taken fire; the joiners work close by had caught, and the entire cabin would have been in flames had not the servant, half suffocated, rushed on deck and given the alarm. By dint of great exertion, the fire, which by this time was making rapid headway, was extinguished; but not until the interior woodwork had either been destroyed or grievously defaced. Few eyes were closed for the remainder of the night; nor did the accident tend to tranquilize the nerves of the travelers.

A supply of provisions had been taken on board the *New Orleans* at Louisville, amply sufficient for the voyage to Natchez, and this was occasionally supplemented by purchases at settlements along the river. These, however, were few and far between, and not at all to be relied on. The crew, accustomed to the simple fare of boatmen on the Mississippi, were easily provided for. The commissariat of the voyage therefore—longer than a voyage to Europe now—gave no trouble.

Early in the afternoon of each day, the steamer was rounded to and fastened to the bank, the crew going ashore to cut the wood required, after the coal was exhausted, for the next day's consumption. On some of these occasions, squatters came on board with tales of their experiences upon the land, which they insisted shook and trembled under their feet.

At New Madrid, a great portion of which had been engulfed, as the earth opened in vast chasms and swallowed up houses and their inhabitants, terror-stricken people had begged to be taken on board, while others, dreading the steamboat even more than the earthquake, hid themselves as she approached. To receive the former was impossible. The would-be refugees had no homes to go to; and ample as was the supply of provisions for Mr. Roosevelt and his wife, it would have been altogether insufficient for any large increase of passengers; and as to obtaining provisions on the way, the *New Orleans* might as well have been upon the open sea. Painful as it was, there was no choice but to turn a deaf ear to the cries of the terrified inhabitants of the doomed town.

One of the peculiar characteristics of the voyage was the silence that prevailed on board. No one seemed disposed to talk; and when there was any conversation, it was carried on in whispers, almost. Tiger, who appeared alone to be aware of the earthquake while the vessel was in motion, prowled about, moaning and growling; and when he came and placed his head on Mrs. Roosevelt's lap, it was a sure sign of a commotion of more than usual violence. Orders were given in low tones; and the usual cheerful "aye, aye, sir" of the sailors was almost inaudible. Sleeplessness was another characteristic. Sound, continuous sleep was apparently unknown. Going ashore for wood was the event of each twenty-four hours, and was looked forward to by the crew with satisfaction, notwithstanding the labor that it involved. And yet the men, if not sullenly, toiled silently; and if the earth shook, as it often did, while they were at work, the uplifted ax was suspended, or placed quietly on the log, and the men stared at each other until it ceased. Nor was this depression confined to the steamer. Flatboats and barges were passed, whose crews, instead of bandying river wit, as they had done when met on the voyage from Pittsburgh to Louisville, uttered no word as the *New Orleans* went by. Before the travelers had been many days on the Mississippi, they fancied, as they looked at each other, that they had become haggard. Mrs. Roosevelt records "that she lived in a constant fright, unable to sleep or sew or read."

Sometimes Indians would join the wood choppers; and occasionally one would be able to converse in English with the men. From these it was learned that the steamboat was called the "Penelore" or "Fire Canoe" and was supposed to have some affinity with the Comet that had preceeded the earthquake—the sparks from the chimney of the boat being likened to the train of the celestial visitant. Again they would attribute the smoky atmosphere to the steamer, and the rumbling of the earth to the beating of the waters by the fast revolving paddles. To the native inhabitants of the boundless forest that lined the river banks, the coming of the first steamboat was an omen of evil; and as it was the precursor of their own expulsion from their ancient homes, no wonder they continued for years to regard all steamboats with awe. As late as 1834, when the emigration of the Chickasaws to their new homes, west of the river, took place, hundreds refused to trust themselves in such conveyances but preferred making their long and weary pilgrimage on foot.

One of the most uncomfortable incidents of the voyage was the confusion of the pilot, who became alarmed and declared that he was lost; so great had been the changes in the channel caused by the earthquake. Where he had expected to find deep water, roots and stumps projected above the surface. Tall trees that had been guides had disappeared. Islands had changed their shapes. Cut-offs had been made through what was forest land when he saw it last. Still, there was no choice but to keep on. There was no place to stop at. There was no possibility of turning back.

In the first part of the voyage when the steamboat rounded to at night, she was made fast to the river bank; but when it was seen that trees would occasionally topple and fall over, as the ground beneath them was shaken or gave way, it was thought safer to stop at the foot of an island, which might serve as a breakwater, taking care the trees were far enough from the boat to obviate apprehension from them. Once, however, when such a fastening had been made and a plank carried ashore and the wood chopping had been finished at an earlier hour than usual, a new experience was had. No shock had been felt during the day, and Mrs. Roosevelt anticipated a quiet rest. In this, however, she was disappointed. All night long she was disturbed by the jar and noise produced by hard objects grating against the planking outside the boat. At times severe blows were struck that caused the vessel to tremble through its entire length. Then there would follow a continuous scratching mingled with the gurgling sound of water. Driftwood had caused sounds of the same sort before, and it was thought that driftwood was again busy in producing them. With morning, however, came the true explanation. The island had disappeared; and it was the disintegrated fragments sweeping down the river that had struck the vessel from time to time and caused the noises that Mrs. Roosevelt had been disturbed by. At first, it was supposed that the *New Orleans* had been borne along by the current; but the pilot pointed to landmarks on the banks which proved that it was the island that had disappeared while the steamboat had kept its place. Where the island had been, there was now a broad reach of the river; and when the hawser was cut, for it was found impossible otherwise to free the vessel, the pilot was utterly at a loss which way to steer. Some flatboats were hailed, but they, too, were lost. Their main effort was, by dint of their long oars, to keep where the current was the strongest. This was evidently the best plan for the *New Orleans*. It was not without its peculiar risks, however. In the bends, where the rushing waters struck the shore, to whirl around the curve and glance off to form a bend in an opposite direction, the deepest water was immediately under the bank; and here the trees, undermined by the current, would be seen at times to sink into the stream, often erect until the waters covered their topmost twigs—sometimes falling against each other, interlacing their great arms, as strong men might do, struggling for life when drowning. Sometimes they fell outward into the water; and then, woe to the vessel that happened to be near them in the bend. This danger, however, steam enabled the *New Orleans* to avoid. Referring to it all, it is not wonderful that the survivor of the voyage still speaks of it as "one of anxiety and terror."

As the *New Orleans* descended the river it passed out of the region of the earthquake, and the principal inconvenience was the number of shoals and snags and sawyers. These were all safely passed, however, and the vessel came in sight of Natchez, and rounded to opposite the landing place. Expecting to remain here for a day or two, the engineer had allowed his fires to go down, so that when the boat turned its head up stream it lost headway altogether and was being carried down by the current far below the intended landing. Thousands were assembled on the bluff and at the foot of it; and for a moment it would have seemed that the *New Orleans* had achieved what she had done, so far, only that she might be overcome at last. Fresh fuel, however, was added—the engine was stopped that steam might accumulate, presently the safety valve lifted—a few turns of the wheels steadied the boat—a few more gave her headway; and, overcoming even the Mississippi, she gained the shore amid shouts of exultation and applause.

The romance [1] of the voyage ended at Natchez, where the same hospitalities were extended to Mr. and Mrs. Roosevelt that had been enjoyed at Louisville. From thence to New Orleans, there was no occurrence worthy of note. The *Vesuvius* and the *Aetna* followed the *New Orleans,* and they in their turn were followed by others and again by others until now the traveller on the Mississippi is never or rarely, if ever, out of sight of the white and feathery plumes that accompany the boats of the Western waters as their high pressure engines urge them on their way.

And this is the story of the "First Voyage of the First Steamboat on the Western Waters"—another link in the chain that should have connected the name of Roosevelt with the names of Fulton and Livingston among the benefactors of mankind.

Shreve's Snag-Boat

After [Henry Shreve] began the construction of the snag-boat at New Albany, Indiana, a few miles above Louisville, opposition to it sprang up

---

[1] Although forming no part of the story of the voyage proper, yet, as this has been called a romance, and all romances end, or should end, in a marriage, the incident was not wanting here; for the Captain of the boat, falling in love with Mrs. Roosevelt's maid, prosecuted his suit so successfully as to find himself an accepted lover when the *New Orleans* reached Natchez; and a clergyman being sent for, a wedding marked the arrival of the boat at the chief city of the Mississippi.—J.H.B.L.

From *Master of the Mississippi,* Henry Shreve and the Conquest of the Mississippi, by Florence L. Dorsey, pp. 148–154. Copyright, 1941, by Florence L. Dorsey. Boston: Houghton Mifflin Company.

from some of the Valley folk themselves. As soon as rumors of the new
device drifted about, indignant protests began to assail the already dubious
Washington officials. One letter insultingly declared:

It is said the present Superintendent [of Western River Improvements] has
in contemplation to construct a large and powerful steamboat for the purpose of
cutting out the snags and pulling them down by force of steam. Now, those
projects are only calculated to get through the appropriation, without anything
like the object contemplated. All machinery, whatsoever, whether used by level
or steam power, is considered by persons who are well acquainted with the Mississippi River navigation, as a useless expenditure of time and money.

So gusty were these critics that it looked for a while as though Shreve
might be retired and the cause of the rivers lost. But there were a few
steamboat men anxious to have any means tried to make the rivers safer,
and these petitioned the Government to let Shreve go on with his project.

It had taken him a year and a half to gain the War Department's
consent to have the snag-boat built—permission had been sent him June
27, 1828—and it would take almost another year to complete the vessel.
Meanwhile, Shreve further improved the hand-run boats and worked them
in the Ohio and in cleaning off some of the island and sandbar edges in the
Mississippi. Even with the stoutest efforts the hand-boats could not be
made to lift any of the large trees planted in the Mississippi's bed.

*   *   *   *   *

The snag-boat, which Shreve had named the *Heliopolis,* was finished in
April of 1829. Although it had a draft of only five feet and one inch, the
boat could not then come down the Ohio. That river was at its lowest
stage for many years; the sandbars stretched high above it and glistened
in the spring sun.

Throughout the summer the sandbars baked. Shreve, busy with hand-
machine boats on the Ohio, waited impatiently for a freshet. It looked
as if it would never rain again. Then August brought a deluge. The Ohio
surged about the parched islands and over the sun-cracked bars. Shreve
hastened to get the snag-boat, which now seemed almost mythical to the
Washington office, across the river to Louisville.

A crowd gathered on the New Albany shore to watch the peculiar craft
pull out. Some men were indignant about the absurd thing; others shook
their heads. At Louisville, townsmen and traders who had ridden the
freshet down from the East, gaped at the snag-boat as it drew into port.
It was more startling than Shreve's radical river boats.

The snag-boat had twin hulls placed side by side about eleven feet
apart, and connected abaft midships. The bows were connected at the
waterline by a heavy wedge-shaped beam. This stout protruding beam
was to be the main weapon against the giant trees embedded in the Mississippi. Besides the warlike beam, there were ingenious windlass, lever,
and roller devices.

On the whole, though, the boat was trim and innocent-looking. It could never, the spectators agreed, dislodge the massive drift-timbers in the Mississippi. Its first blow against one of them would jar its machinery to pieces. As the rumors from New Albany had insisted, this craft was a waste of government money. Louisville people regretted it. They liked Henry Shreve. He was a strange, deep man, with long silences and sudden enthusiasms. He was enthusiastic about this twin-hulled boat, but he would soon be disillusioned. The trees would still stand half-buried in the Mississippi. Boats would still crash against them and sink.

Perhaps Shreve took in the grave faces of these men and heard their prophecies and warnings, but he was too anxious about hiring a good crew for the *Heliopolis* to be concerned over anything else. It was getting harder all the time to persuade men to work at river clearance. There was no adventure in it; the government pay was small; and lately malignant fevers had followed the streams. When he finally had the boat manned, he sent it to Trinity, Illinois, at the Grand Chain of Rocks, where the hand-machine boats were working. He followed a few days later, bringing for the *Heliopolis* a missing iron shaft of 7354 pounds' weight, which belonged "to the machine for rasing snags." The shaft, difficult to cast and turn on account of its weight, had not yet arrived from Cincinnati.

On an August day Shreve sailed the snag-boat out of Trinity and down the hot, glassy Mississippi. He was buoyant over the coming test, although no one but himself believed in the *Heliopolis*. He had chosen Plum Point, halfway down the Tennessee state shore, for this trial. Here was the worst timber-clogged passage on the whole river, the terror of boatmen. As the unusual double boat made its way downstream, men on steamboats, keels, broadhorns, and barges shouted questions at it. The answers that were shouted back were taken as a joke. A steam snag-boat to pull the deep-planted trees out of the Plum Point channel! Ha, ha, that was a good one!

Some of the boats fell in behind. When Shreve stopped at Plum Point he had for an audience the crews of a short line of craft. Jeering quips were bandied from boat to boat. Raucous laughter came in gusts on the breeze.

Shreve knew that if his test failed, a cheer of cynical elation would ring from these very men who would benefit by its success. Not only this small group, but his countrymen up and down the Valley, would feel a bitter exultation. Even the officials at Washington would find a certain satisfaction in a failure that they had persistently foretold; the cause of a cleared Mississippi might suffer a severe setback. He poised the *Heliopolis* for its first onslaught.

The twin boat drove head-on at a massive planter. There was a booming impact and crash. It seemed to the onlookers that the boat must shatter to pieces. But there is was, still intact, and the huge tree toppling into the water. A spontaneous cheer went up from the audience. The boat chains caught the tree, the windlass pulled it up until it lay on a series of fore and aft rollers. It was dismembered, cut into lengths, and pushed into the channel to float off.

In this headlong encounter there had not been a quiver in the boat's machinery, so perfectly was the shock distributed over the whole vessel. Repeatedly the boat attacked the thicket of large trees, vanquishing it. Of those who witnessed this battle, only Shreve was not disappointed. He wrote simply to the Brigadier-General Charles Gratiot, Chief of Engineers, of the War Department:

Mouth White River, Arkansaw Tery,
23 August 1829

Sir

I have the honor to inform you that I have made some successful experiments with the U States Steam Boat Heliopolis. I got underway from Trinity, Ill, on the 19th instant at 9 A.M. and proceeded down to Plum Point (the Most dangerous place on the Mississippi River) where I arrived at 12 M. There I made the first attempt to remove snags with the boat & am proud to say that the performance far exceeded my most sanguine expectations. In eleven hours that whole forrest of formidable snags, so long the terror of the Boatman (many of which were six feet in diameter) were effectually removed. All of them were broken off several feet below the surface of the sand at the bottom of the river. . . .

From Plum Point Shreve had sailed to another danger spot, Islands Number 62 and 63, below Helena, Arkansas. Here many of the planted trees were completely under water and could not be struck by the bow beam. For such as these Shreve had provided a method which he described in a report:

When snags are invisible except by the breakers made by them, they are removed by a large chain, the two ends of which are made fast to the two bows of the boats, the middle bite of it is taken thirty feet abaft the main beam, where it is fastened by a line to the gunwale of each boat. In this manner the boat passes over the breaker in such a position as to bring the breaker between the two boats; when the snag or breaker is a few feet abaft the bows of the boats, the lines are let go, the bite of the chain falls below the surface of the water, and either breaks the snag off in the mud or sand, or throws the end of it above the water, where it is held by the headway of the boat, being kept between the wheels, until the chain from the main windlass is fastened to it; it is then thrown on deck and disposed of as before described. . . . I have no longer a doubt of being able to carry every snag out of the river—should the Government continue the work.

Eads' Diving-Bell

For five years [James B. Eads] was a clerk in [a] dry-goods house [in St. Louis]. At the end of that time, probably, because he was in poor

---

From *James B. Eads*, by Louis How, pp. 5-6, 8-13. Copyright, 1900, by Louis How. Boston: Houghton, Mifflin and Company.

health, he left that position for one that would take him more into the open air. Though his health was not strong, he was by no means an invalid; for at nineteen his muscles were solid and his fund of nervous energy was inexhaustible. So, with the natural taste of a boy for a more exciting life, he took a position as clerk on a Mississippi River steamboat. While he had nothing to do with actually running the boat, he certainly kept his eyes open to everything going on both on board and in the river; and began then to make an acquaintance with the stream which was later to be the scene of his greatest labors . . . [and] the opportunity for three of his chief works [the Union gunboats, the St. Louis bridge, and the jetties at the mouth of the Mississippi]. . . .

* * * * *

. . . In 1839, when steamboats were the only means of rapid transit in the West, when there were more of them in the harbor of St. Louis than today when it is a great city, [the] class of pilots [so learned and so alert as to have the shifting bars and courses always in their minds] was a large and a very respectable one. Much of their knowledge of the river was what young Eads learned while he was a clerk among them; and as time went on, he came to realize that although the Mississippi seems so capricious in its terrible games that one would think them the result of chance, yet in truth they "are controlled by laws as immutable as the Creator."

Despite all care that could be used, steamboats were every week sunk and wrecked, and with their valuable engines, boilers, and cargoes were often left where they lay in the ceaseless brown current. After he had been for three years on the river, Eads gave up his clerkship to go into the business of raising these boats, their machinery, and their freight. In 1842, at the age of twenty-two, he formed a partnership with Case & Nelson, boat-builders. His first appearance in the new business was an experience that well shows his quick inventive genius, his persistency, and his courage. While his diving-bell boat was building, a barge loaded with pig-lead sank in the rapids at Keokuk, 212 miles from St. Louis. A contract having been made with its owners, Eads hurried up there to rescue the freight from fifteen feet of water. He had no knowledge himself of diving-armor; but he had engaged a skilled diver from the Great Lakes, who brought his own apparatus. They set out in a barge and anchored over the wreck; but, once there, they soon discovered that the current was so exceedingly rapid that the diver could do nothing in it. Eads at once returned to Keokuk, and, buying a forty-gallon whisky hogshead, took it out to the wreck; and having knocked out one head, he slung pigs of lead round his improvised diving-bell, made a seat inside it, rigged it to his derrick and air-pumps, and then asked the diver to go down in it. The diver having very naturally refused, Eads on the spot set himself a precedent which, during his after life, he never broke—saying that he would not ask an employee to go where he would not trust himself, he got inside his hogshead and was lowered into the river. His assistants were unused to managing diving-bells, and, when they came to haul him up, the derrick got out of order. By main force they were able to raise the hogshead to the surface, but not above it. As the air-pump continued to work all the while, Eads, though wondering what was amiss, sat patiently in his place till finally he saw a hand appear under the rim of the hogshead. Seizing this, he ducked under and got out. Although the rough diving-bell worked thus awkwardly at first, it served well enough, and finally all of the lost freight was saved.

* * * * *

The insurance companies were willing to give the wreckers a large interest, sometimes as much as half, of the rescued cargoes; and there was a law by which a vessel or freight that had been wrecked five times belonged to whoever could get it up. Eads and his partners worked up and down the river for hundreds of miles. The first diving-bell boat was followed by a larger one, provided with machinery for pumping out sand and for raising whole hulls. While in this hazardous business, Eads invented many new appliances for use in its various branches. Because he was in charge of a boat people began to call the young wrecker Captain Eads, and that was the only reason for a title which clung to him always. He grew now to know the river as few have ever known it—his operations extended from Galena, Illinois, to the Balize at the river's very mouth, and even into the tributaries of the Mississippi—and he used to say that there was not a stretch of fifty miles in the twelve hundred between St. Louis and New Orleans in which he had not stood on the bottom under his diving-bell.

Commodore Porter's Cruise in the Forests

I [1]

All imaginable plans were tried to get the army below the city [of Vicksburg]; for Grant's command had come down from Cairo and were at the northern and most impregnable side of the enemy's works. As at Island No. 10, a sharp bend in the river made a long peninsula right under the Confederates' guns. Grant, remembering the plan adopted before, set to work to cut a canal through the peninsula, so that the gunboats and transports might get below the forts. Twelve hundred Negroes worked with a will upon this ditch for weeks. Then came a terrible rain-storm: the swollen, muddy torrent of the river broke in upon the unfinished canal, and that work was wasted. Then a new plan was suggested, this time by

---

[1]From *Blue Jackets of '61*, A History of the Navy in the War of Secession, by Willis J. Abbot, pp. 255–257. Copyright, 1886, by Dodd, Mead and Company. New York.

Commodore David Porter, who all through the war showed the greatest delight in taking his big gunboats into ditches where nothing larger than a frog or muskrat could hope to navigate, and then bringing them out again safe after all.

The country back of Vicksburg was fairly honeycombed with shallow lakes, creeks, and those sluggish black streams called in the South bayous. Porter had been looking over this aqueous territory for some time, and had sent one of his lieutenants off in a steam-launch to see what could be done in that network of ditches. When the explorer returned, he brought cheering news. He was confident that, with tugs and gangs of axmen clearing the way, the gunboats could be taken up the Yazoo River, then into a wide bayou, and finally through a maze of small waterways, until they should reach the Mississippi again below the Vicksburg batteries. Then the transports could follow, the troops could march down the other side of the river, be met by the transports, ferried across, and take Vicksburg on the flank. It was a beautiful plan; and Porter went to Grant with it, full of enthusiasm.

General Grant considered the matter for some time, but finally gave his consent, and detailed a number of blue-coated soldiers to aid Porter's blue-jackets in the work. They first cut the levees, and let the mighty tide of the Mississippi sweep in, filling the bayous to the brim, and flooding all the country round about. Then the gunboats plunged in, and were borne along on the rushing tide until they brought up, all standing, against the trunks of trees, or had their smokestacks caught by overhanging branches.

Then came the tug of war; and the axmen were called to the front, and set to work. They chopped their way along for some distance; the rapid current from the river banging the vessels against the trees and stumps, until all the standing rigging and light cabins were swept away. After a good deal of work they saw before them a broad river, wide enough for two vessels to steam abreast. Soon they drifted out into it, and the commanding officer sang out cheerily, "On to Vicksburg, boys, and no more trees to saw." And so they steamed on, thinking how neatly they should take the "gray-coats" in the rear, when suddenly a bend in the river showed them, just ahead, a fort in the middle of the river, with the channel blocked on either side. That was a surprise. The works were new, and the water was still muddy about the sunken steamers. Clearly the wily Pemberton had heard of this inland naval expedition, and was determined to check it effectually.

The gunboats backed water, and crowded in confused groups. The gunners in the fort took hurried aim, and pulled the lanyards of their cannon, forgetting that those pieces were not loaded. It was hard to tell which party was the more excited at the unexpected meeting. This gave the blue-jackets a chance to collect their thoughts, and in a minute or two the gunboats opened fire; but they were soon convinced that the fort was too much for them, and they turned and crawled back through the woods to the fleet above Vicksburg. Pemberton scored one point for successful strategy.

But, even while this expedition was working its way back to the station of the vessels on the Mississippi, Porter was starting another through a second chain of watercourses that he had discovered. This time he was so sure of getting into the rear of Vicksburg that he took four of his big iron-clads and two light mortar-boats built especially for work in the woods. General Sherman, with a strong army-force, marched overland, keeping up with the gunboats. . . .

II [2]

This was one of the most remarkable military and naval expeditions ever sent out in any country, and will be so ranked by those who read of it in future times. Here was a dense forest, deeply inundated, so that large steamers could ply about among the trees with perfect impunity. They were as much at home there as the wild denizens of the forest would be in dry times. The animals of all kinds had taken to the trees as the only ark of safety. Coons, rats, mice, and wildcats were in the branches; and, if they were not a happy family, it was because, when they lay down together, the smaller animals reposed within the larger ones.

It was a curious sight to see a line of iron-clads and mortar-boats, tugs and transports, pushing their way through the long wide lane in the woods without touching on either side, though sometimes a rude tree would throw Briarean arms around the smokestack of the tin-clad *Forest Rose* or the transport *Molly Miller*, and knock their bonnets sideways.

It looked as though the world had suddenly gone topsy-turvy, or that there was a great camp-meeting in the woods on board iron-clads and transports.

* * * * *

We ran on in line of battle eight or ten miles through the open way in the trees, carrying fifteen feet of water in the lead-line. Let the nautical reader imagine an old quarter-master in the "chains" of an iron-clad, steaming through the woods and singing out, "Quarter less three!" Truth is stranger than fiction.

At last we came to a point where the forest was close and composed of very large trees—old monarchs of the woods, which had spread their arms for centuries over those silent solitudes; Titans, like those in the old fables, that dominate over all around them. In the distance, between the trees, would spring into sight gray, sunless glens, in which the dim, soft ripple of day seemed to glimmer a second, so fancifully, indeed, that it required but a slight stretch of imagination to see the wood-nymphs disporting in their baths. The sun seldom reached these woody glades; and,

---

[2] From *Incidents and Anecdotes of the Civil War*, by Admiral [David D.] Porter, pp. 145–158, 161, 168–172. Copyright, 1885, by D. Appleton and Company. New York.

if it did, it was but to linger for a moment and disappear, like the bright star of eve, behind a silver cloud.

It all looked like some infinite world in which we were adrift, where the sky, soft and serene (which we had been accustomed to see), had been furled in anticipation of a squall. Every turn of the wheels sent an echo through the woods that would frighten the birds of prey from their perches, whence they were looking down upon the waste of waters, wondering (no doubt) what it all might mean, and who these mighty buzzards, skimming over the waters and carrying everything before them, could possibly be.

Our line of battle was broken on approaching the large trees; then we had to go more cautiously. What, thought I, if the trees should become so dense that we could not pass between them; what would we do then? I solved the difficulty at once. "Ram that large tree there," I said to the captain of the *Cincinnati;* "let us see what effect the old turtle will have on it." It was an unnecessary act of vandalism to injure the old Titan; but it would shorten our road, and we would not be obliged to go meandering about to find a channel. We struck the tree while going at the rate of three knots an hour, and bounded off, but started it about twenty degrees from the perpendicular. The light soil about its roots had become softened by the water, and the tree had not much staying power. I backed again, and gave it another ram; and the weight of eight hundred tons, with a three-knot velocity, sent it out of all propriety. I hailed the iron-clad astern of me, and ordered her to bend a heavy chain to it, and pull it down, which was accomplished in half an hour.

I wanted to see what we could do at ramming and pulling at big trees, and our experience so gained came into play before we got through the expedition. It was all very pleasant at first, skimming along over summer seas, under the shade of stalwart oaks; but we had no conception of what we had before us.

We had to knock down six or eight of these large trees before we could reach the point where Sherman was disembarking part of his troops. When I came up, he was on a piece of high ground, on an old white horse some of his "boys" had captured.

"Halloo, old fellow!" he sang out, "what do you call this? This must be traverse sailing. You think it's all very fine just now, don't you; but, before you fellows get through, you won't have a smokestack or a boat among you."

"So much the better," I said. "It will look like business, and we will get new ones. All I want is an engine, guns, and a hull to float them. As to boats, they are very much in the way."

At this point we ran up alongside higher land, which looked like a levee.

"Is this the last of it?" I asked Sherman.

"No," he said. "Steam on about twenty yards to the west, and you will find a hole through a kind of levee, wide enough, I think, for your widest vessel. That is Cypress Bayou; it leads into Sunflower, about seventy-five miles distant; and a devil of a time you'll have of it. Look out those fellows don't catch you. I'll be after you."

Sherman knew every bayou and stream in that part of the country better than the oldest inhabitants knew them.

I pushed on, my fleet following, and soon found myself inside the bayou. It was exactly forty-six feet wide. My vessel was forty-two feet wide, and that was the average width of the others. The place seemed to have been a bayou with high levees bordering, reaching, indeed, above the vessel's guns. It had been made, I suppose, into a kind of canal to connect the waters of the Sunflower by a short cut with those of the Yazoo, near Haines's Bluff. All on the left of the levee was deep water in the woods. On the other side were cornfields. The levee had stopped the further encroachment of the flood. This bayou had not been used for many years for the purposes of navigation. It had almost closed up, and the middle of it was filled with little willows, which promised to be great impediments to us; but, as there was nine feet of water in the ditch, I pushed on.

*   *   *   *   *

We supposed we were doing all this very secretly, and were going to surprise the natives. No doubt we did surprise those who dwelt on or along the Cypress Bayou; but our movement was probably no surprise to the Confederates in Vicksburg. I am quite satisfied in my own mind that while we were steaming along, and performing naval evolutions in the woods, the president of the Southern Confederacy was reading something like the following dispatch to his cabinet:

Sherman and Porter pirouetting through the woods in steamers and iron-clads. Are keeping a lookout on them. Hope to bag them all before tomorrow.

We had not entered the bayou more than half a mile before we saw the greatest excitement prevailing. Men on horseback were flying in all directions. Cattle, instead of being driven in, were driven off to parts unknown. Pigs were driven by droves to the far woods; and five hundred Negroes were engaged in driving into the fields all the chickens, turkeys, ducks, and geese; and what were a few moments before smiling barnyards were now as bare of poultry as your hand. I had issued an order against capturing anything on shore; but the difficulty was to find out where the shore was, as apparently the Cypress Bayou ran right through the middle of a stable-yard.

I informed the sailors that loot naturally belonged to the army, but that prize in the shape of cotton marked "C.S.A." belonged to them. A mile from the entrance to the bayou there were two piles of cotton, containing six thousand bales, and placed opposite each other on the banks of the stream in which we were then just holding our way against its two-knot current. Suddenly I saw two men rush up from each side of the bayou and apply a lighted pine-knot to each pile. "What fools these mortals be!" I said to an officer; "but I suppose those men have a right to burn their own cotton, especially as we have no way of preventing them."

"I can send a howitzer shell at them, sir," he said, "and drive them away."

"No," I replied, "that might kill them, and we don't want to do that except in battle."

So the two men went on with their work of destruction. They applied the torches to every part of the two piles; and in twenty minutes there was a column of smoke ascending to the skies, and the passage between the piles became very much obscured.

"How long will it take that cotton to burn up?" I inquired of a Negro who was asking permission to come on board.

"Two day, Massa," the Negro answered, "sometime t'ree."

By this time all the outside of the cotton was blazing. "Ring the bell to go ahead fast," I ordered, "and tell those astern to follow after me." I was on board the *Cincinnati*. "Go ahead fast the tug and mortar-boat," and away we all went, darting through between the burning bales.

All the ports were shut in, and the crews called to fire-quarters, standing ready with buckets to meet the enemy's *fire*. It reminded me a little of the fire-raft at Fort Jackson, but we soon got used to it. The fellows on the tug wet themselves and the boat all over very thoroughly, and as they darted through, being below the bank, they did not suffer very much; but the paint was blistered on the boat, and the fire scorched the men.

Myself, captain, and wheelman were the only ones on deck when the *Cincinnati* passed through; but the heat was so intense that I had to jump inside a small house on deck, covered with iron, the captain following me. The helmsman covered himself up with an old flag that lay in the wheel-house. The hose was pointed up the hatch to the upper deck, and everything drenched with water; but it did not render the heat less intolerable. The boats escaped with some blistering. The smoke was even worse than the heat, and I have often since imagined how a brave fireman feels when he is looking through a burning house in search of helpless people.

Just after we passed through the fire, there was a dreadful crash which some thought was an earthquake. We had run into and quite through a span of bridge about fifty feet long and demolished the whole fabric, having failed to see it in the smoke.

There was a yell from the Negroes on the bank, who looked on with amazement at the doings of "Mas' Linkum's gunboats."

"What dey gwine ter do nex'?" said an old patriarch.

* * * * *

A burly overseer, weighing over two hundred pounds, sat at the door of a log-hut with a pipe in his mouth. He was a white man, half bull-dog, half blood-hound, and his face expressed everything that was bad in human nature, but he smoked away as if nothing was the matter—as Nero fiddled while Rome was burning.

He looked on us with perfect indifference; our presence didn't seem to disturb him at all. Doubtless he felt quite secure; that we didn't want anything so bad as he was.

I called to him, and he came down in his shirt-sleeves, bareheaded and looked stolidly at me as if to say, "Well, what do you want?"

"Why did those fools set fire to that cotton?" I inquired.

"Because they didn't want you fools to have it," he replied. "It's ourn, and I guess things ain't come to such a pass that we can't do as we please with our own."

"Tell them we won't trouble it," I said. "It is wicked to see such material going off like smoke."

In five minutes he had a dozen Negroes at his side, and they were all sent up the bayou on a full run to stop the burning of the cotton. He believed our word, and we did not disappoint him.

"And who are you?" I inquired of the man.

"I am in charge of this plantation," he replied. "This is the mother of my children"—pointing to a fat, thick-lipped Negress, who stood, with her bosom all bare and arms akimbo, about ten yards away—"and these fine fellows are my children," he continued, pointing to some light-colored boys who had followed him down.

"I suppose you are Union, of course? You are all so when it suits you," I said.

"No, by G——, I'm not, and never will be; and as to the others, I know nothing about them. Find out for yourself. I'm for Jeff Davis first, last, and all the time. Do you want any more of me," he inquired, "for I am not a loquacious man at any time."

"No, I want nothing more with you," I replied. "But I am going to steam into that bridge of yours across the stream and knock it down. Is it strongly built?"

"You may knock it down, and be d——d," he said. "It don't belong to me; and, if you want to find out how strong it is, pitch into it. You'll find a hard nut to crack; it ain't made of candy."

"You are a Yankee by birth, are you not?" I asked.

"Yes, d——n it, I am," he replied. "That's no reason I should like the institution. I cut it long ago," and he turned on his heel and walked off.

"Ring 'Go ahead fast,'" I said to the captain. "We will let that fellow see what bridge-smashers we are."

In three minutes we were going four knots through the water, and in one more we went smashing through the bridge as if it was paper. I looked toward the overseer to see how he would take it, but he did not even turn his head as he sat at his door smoking.

This man was but one remove from a brute, but there were hundreds more like him.

We came to one more bridge; down it went like ninepins; and we steamed slowly on, forcing our way through small, lithe willows that seemed to hold us in a grip of iron. This lasted for an hour, during which we made but half a mile. But that was the last of the willows for a time. Had they continued, we would have been obliged to give it up. The small sprouts, no larger than my little finger, caught in the rough plates of the overhang, and held us as the threads of the Lilliputians held Gulliver.

Now we came to extensive woods again on either side, the large trees towering in the air, while underneath they looked as if their lower branches had been trimmed to give them a uniform appearance; but they had only been trimmed by the hand of Nature, whose fair impression fell on all about us. Man only marred the prospect there.

The banks of the bayou were high, with large, overhanging trees upon them; and the long branches of the latter stretched out into the stream, endangering our pipes and boats. The channel was here exactly the width of the iron-clads—forty-two feet—and we had to cut our way, with the overhang, through the soft soil and the twining roots. It was hard and slow work. The brutal overseer felt quite sure that we would be bagged before night. He didn't know that Sherman was right behind us with an army, and an army, too, that was no respecter of ducks, chickens, pigs, or turkeys; for they used to say of one particular regiment in Sherman's corps that it could catch, scrape, and skin a hog without a soldier leaving the ranks. I was in hopes that they would pay the apostate Yankee a visit, if only to teach him good manners.

The gunboats, at this stage of the cruise, were following each other about a quarter of a mile apart. The only idea I can give of Cypress Bayou is to *fake* a string up and down a paper two hundred or more times. We did nothing but turn upon our course about every twenty minutes. At one time the vessels would all be steaming on different courses. One would be standing north, another south, another east, and yet another west through the woods. One minute an ironclad would apparently be leading ahead, and the next minute would as apparently be steering the other way. The tugs and mortar-boats seemed to be mixed up in the most marvelous manner.

There was a fair road on the right of the bayou, along which Sherman's troops would have to march; and all that was required to make the situation look confusing and confounding was to have the soldiers marching beside the gunboats.

I was in the leading vessel, and necessarily had to clear the way for the others. The bayou was full of logs that had been there for years. They had grown soggy and heavy; and sometimes one end, being heavier than the other, would sink to the bottom, while the other end would remain pointing upward, presenting the appearance of *chevaux-de-frise*, over which we could no more pass than we could fly. We had to have working-parties in the road, with tackles and hook-ropes, to haul these logs out on the banks before we could pass on.

Again we would come to a "Red River raft" that had been imbedded in the mud for ages. All these had to be torn asunder and hauled out, with a labor that no one who had not tried it could conceive of. Then, again, we would get jammed between two large, overhanging trees. We could not ram them down as we did in the woods, with plenty of "sea-room" around us. We had to chop away the sides of the trees with axes.

A great many of these large trees had decayed branches; and, when the heavy iron-clad would touch the trunk of one (though going only at the rate of half a mile an hour, which was the most we could make at any time in the ditch), the shock would be so great, and the resultant vibration of the tree so violent, that the branches would come crashing on deck, smashing the boats and skylights and all the framework that they reached.

An hour after entering the very narrow part of the ditch, where we really had not a foot to spare, we had parted with everything like a boat, and cut them away as useless appendages. Indeed, they were of no use to us, and only in the way. When we got rid of them, we got along better.

* * * * *

We stopped that evening about seven o'clock, and about an hour later we heard the chopping of wood in the forest. We had seen no one along the stream since we had left that burly overseer. The truthful and intelligent contrabands, in whom I was wont to repose confidence, were nowhere to be seen; whereat I marveled much, knowing their social disposition and the lofty aspirations they felt with regard to the liberty of their race. They were so faithful in adherence to their protectors that they would come in crowds with wild inventions of moves on the part of the enemy if they could not find something real to tell.

I missed these ingenious creatures, and wondered what had become of them. . . . I was always of an inquiring mind, and determined to find out what the wood-chopping meant. It seemed to me that there were a dozen axes at work. I put a twelve-pound howitzer on the tug, and sent her ahead to see what was going on. In twenty minutes I heard the report of the howitzer, and then another and another. Then a steam whistle was blown from the tug, and all was silent. No more axes heard cutting wood.

In a very short time the tug returned, snorting as if carrying a very heavy pressure of steam and every now and then giving some playful screams with the whistle. The forest fairly reverberated with the sound. The officer in charge reported that he had suddenly come upon a large body of Negroes, under the charge of some white men carrying lanterns, cutting trees on the banks of the stream we were in; that they had felled a tree three feet in diameter, and this had fallen right across the bayou, closing the stream completely against our advance. There was the secret of our not meeting the truthful contraband. He was employed in hemming us in. . . .

There was but one thing to do—move ahead and clear the channel. . . . It was not a matter of great labor. Two large snatch-blocks were strapped to standing trees as leaders. The largest hawser was passed through the snatch-blocks, one end made fast to the fallen tree, and the other end taken to a steamer. "Back the iron-clad hard," and the obstruction began to move slowly over the water. In less than ten minutes it was landed clear across the road, so that Sherman's soldiers wouldn't have to march around it.

A second application of this improvised "power gear" and the route was again free. The Confederates didn't think of all that when they tried to bag us in that way. They forgot the ingenuity of American seamen.

"Now," I said to the officer in charge of the tug, "go ahead with all the speed you have, and see that no more trees are cut down tonight; and, though I shall be sorry to harm that faithful friend and brother, the contraband, if he continues to chop at any one's dictation you must give him shrapnel," and off the tug started.

We could already hear the faint strokes of the axes in advance of us; and no doubt the managers, having cut one tree down, and supposing that they had blocked the game on us for the night, and not knowing our facilities for removing trees, had, as soon as they imagined themselves out of reach of the howitzer, set to work cutting other trees, with the intention that we should never see the Sunflower, nor get in the rear of Vicksburg. The Confederates were energetic; and it was wonderful how soon they got their machinery to work.

Some twenty minutes after the tug left us, we heard the howitzer firing rapidly; and then all was quiet, excepting three steam whistles, which meant *all well*. At one o'clock that night the tug's small boat returned to us, with the report that the choppers had commenced cutting about twenty of the largest trees, but that none had been completely felled; that they had captured two truthful contrabands, who informed them that the parties directing the cutting of trees were officers from Vicksburg; that they had pressed three hundred Negroes into the work and made them use their axes, with pistols to their heads, and gave them plenty of whisky.

"The officers are from Vicksburg!" I said; "and we thought ourselves so smart. No doubt they started before we did, and got their instructions from Richmond. What next?"

"The officer [Lieutenant Murphy] says, sir, he will continue on all night, and thinks no more trees will be cut down at present."

I didn't care about the trees. I was just then thinking how I would feel if they should block up the head of the pass with cotton bales and earth and leave me and mine sticking in the mud at the bottom of the bayou.

* * * * *

It were vain to tell all the hardships of the third day. The plot seemed to thicken as we advanced; and old logs, small Red River rafts, and rotten trees overhanging the banks seemed to accumulate.

The dead trees were full of vermin of all sorts. Insects of every kind and shape, such as are seen only in Southern climes, infested these trees. Rats and mice, driven from the fields by the high water, had taken up their abode in the hollow trunks and rotten branches. Snakes of every kind and description had followed the rats and mice to these old arks of safety. These innocent creatures knew nothing of the insecurity of their adopted homes in presence of the butting ironclads. Small wonder. Who would have dreamed of such things in these regions? A canoe might have been seen, perhaps, of late years, winding its way down these tortuous channels, of a moonlight night, manned by a couple of dissipated Negroes out on a coon hunt; but navigation by anything larger in these waters was unknown.

Sometimes, when we would strike against one of these trees, a multitude of vermin would be shaken out on the deck—among them rats, mice, cockroaches, snakes, and lizards, which would be swept overboard by the sailors standing ready with their brooms. Once an old coon landed on deck, with the life half knocked out of him; but he came to in a short time, and fought his way on shore. Even the coons were prejudiced against us, and refused to be comforted on board; though, I am sorry to say, we found more Union feeling among the bugs of all kinds, which took kindly to the iron-clads and would have remained with us indefinitely had they been permitted to do so.

* * * * *

I noticed right at the head of the pass a large green patch extending all the way across. It looked like the green scum on ponds.

"What is that?" I asked of one of the truthful contrabands.

"It's nuffin but willers, sah," he replied. "When de water's out ob de bayou—which it mos' allers is—den we cuts de willers to make baskits wid. You kin go troo dat like a eel."

I thought I would try it while the vessels were "coming into port." I sent the tug on ahead with the mortar-boat and followed on after.

The tug went into it about thirty yards, began to go slower and slower, and finally stuck so fast that she could move neither ahead nor astern. I hailed her and told them that I would come along and push them through. We started with a full head of steam, and did not even reach the tug. The little withes caught in the rough iron ends of the overhang and held us as if in a vice. I tried to back out, but 'twas no use. We could not move an inch, no matter how much steam we put on. Ah, I thought, this is only a temporary delay.

We got large hooks out and led the hook-ropes aft, and tried to break off the lithe twigs, but it was no use; we could not move. We got saws, knives, cutlasses, and chisels over the side, with the men handling them sitting on planks, and cut them off, steamed ahead, and only moved three feet. Other withes sprang up from under the water and took a fresher grip on us, so we were worse off than ever.

* * * * *

. . . I set to work again to overcome the willows.

"What a dodge this was of the Confederacy," I said to the captain, "to plant these willows instead of a fort! We can take their forts, but we can't, I fear, take their willows."

I stepped out to the bank (where the Negroes had assembled . . .) to see if I could learn anything about willows from these innocent people.

All I could find out from them was that "dey was mo' tougher'n ropes."

"Why don't Sherman come on?" I said aloud to myself. "I'd give ten dollars to get a telegram to him."

"I'm a telegram-wire, Massa," said a stubby-looking Negro, coming up to me. "I'll take him for half a dollar, sah. I'm de county telegraph, sah. I does all dat bizness."

"Where's your office, Sambo?" I inquired.

"My name ain't Sambo, sah. My name's Tub, an' I run yer line fer yer fer half a dollar."

"Do you know where to find General Sherman?" I said.

"No, sah, I don' know him. Ef he's in Vicksburg, I kin find him."

"Can you carry a note for me without betraying it to the Confederates?"

"I don't understan' one of dem words, sah; but I'll take a note to Kingdom Kum if yer pay me half a dollar."

Then I told him who General Sherman was, and where to find him. "Go along the road," I said, "and you can't miss him."

"I know nuff better 'an dat manner when I carry telegraph, sah. I don' go de road; I take de ditches. It's nuff shorter an' mo' safer. On de lef' han' comin' up, dar's all marsh an' wata, an' a kenoe kin allers git 'long dar. I'll go de way we takes when we go chicken-huntin'."

"Where will you carry the dispatch?" I inquired.

"In my calabash-kiver, Massa," he answered, pointing to his thick, woolly head.

I wrote the dispatch and handed it to him. He stowed it away in a pocket in his hair, where it was as safe as a telegram traveling on a wire. I wrote:

DEAR SHERMAN—Hurry up, for Heaven's sake, I never knew how helpless an iron-clad could be steaming around through the woods, without an army to back her.

*   *   *   *   *

. . . "Old Tecumseh" came riding up, about half an hour after the last mishaps, on the old horse he had captured. He had received my county telegraph man, who explained to him pretty well how we were situated, and he had pushed on at night, by the aid of pine torches, through swamps and canebrakes, having undertaken a short cut recommended by the telegraph "operator," Mr. Tub, and found the traveling almost as bad as that experienced by the gunboats.

"Halloo, Porter," said the general when he saw me, "what did you get into such an ugly scrape for? So much for you navy fellows getting out of your element; better send for the soldiers always. My boys will put

you through. Here's your little [Negro]; he came through all right, and
I started at once. This is the most infernal expedition I was ever on; who
in thunder proposed such a mad scheme? But I'm all ready to go on with
you again. Your gunboats are enough to scare the crows; they look as if
you had got a terrible hammering. However, I'll start at once, and go back
with you; my boys will clean those fellows out."

"Thank you, no," I said, "I have had enough of this adventure. It is
too late now; the enemy are forewarned, and all the energies of the Confederacy will be put forth to stop us; they will fill all the rivers with
torpedoes, and every hill will be turned into a heavy fort. They have the
laugh on us this time, but we must put this down in the log-book as 'One
of the Episodes of the War.' We will take Vicksburg yet, when it is more
worth taking."

"You are satisfied, then," said Sherman, "with what my boys have done
for you and can do?"

"Yes, perfectly so," I answered, "and I never knew what helpless things
ironclads could become when they got in a ditch and had no soldiers about.
Won't you come aboard?"

"No," said he, "I must call in my men; they could not catch those
fellows if they chased them a week. Good morning," and "Old Tecumseh"
rode off on his ancient horse, with a rope bridle, accompanied only by one
or two aids.

* * * * *

The game was up, and we bumped on homeward. The current was running very rapidly now, and the vessels were so helpless, dropping down
stern foremost, that we could not protect them in any way. There was no
knowing what part of them would strike the trees, or when huge dead
branches would fall upon the decks. Every one remained between decks
except those who were absolutely required above. There was still a chance
of the enemy playing us a bad trick by blocking the head of the pass at
Rolling Fork; there was plenty of cotton along the road to do it with,
if they only should think of it. Twelve hundred bales of cotton would
turn the water from the bayou, and in an hour after we would be on the
bottom. With these unpleasant possibilities before me, I continued on
homeward, and protracted my run until eight o'clock that night, when
I came up with the main body of Sherman's army, which was encamped
along on the road near the edge of the pass.

Encamped! They had no tents, but a plentiful supply of fence-rails
and bonfires of pine-knots. The whole route for miles was all in a blaze.

It was great fun for the soldiers to see our dilapidated condition.

"Halloo, Jack," one fellow would sing out, "how do you like playing
mud-turtle? Better stick to the briny."

Another would say, "You've been into dry-dock, ain't you, and left
your boats behind?"

"Don't go bushwhacking again, Jack," said another, "unless you have

Sherman's boys close aboard of you. You look as if your mothers didn't know you were out."

"Where's all your sails and masts, Jack?" said a tough-looking fellow, who was sailor all over, though he had a soldier's uniform.

"By the Widow Perkins!" cried another, "if Johnny Reb hasn't taken their rudders away and sent them adrift!"

"Dry up," sang out an old forecastleman, "we wa'n't half as much used up as you was at Chickasaw Bayou"; for which the old tar got three cheers.

* * * * *

I am quite satisfied that no one who went on that party desired to try it again. It was the hardest cruise that any Jack Tar ever made, and we all determined to cultivate the army more than we had done, in case we should go on a horse-marine excursion.

It was with the greatest delight that we got out of that ditch and into the open woods again, with plenty of "sea room" and no lee shores. We took our time, went squirrel-hunting in the few boats we had left, and got a fine mess of turkey-buzzards out of the old oaks which surrounded us.

In ten days more we anchored again in the mouth of the Yazoo River and commenced to repair damages.

* * * * *

This was one of the many expedients adopted to bring about the reduction of Vicksburg, and, of all of them, never one more hazardous or more laborious. . . .

Colter's Run

[John Colter] came to St. Louis in May, 1810, in a small canoe from the head waters of the Missouri, a distance of three thousand miles, which he traversed in thirty days. I saw him on his arrival, and received from him an account of his adventures after he had separated from Lewis and Clarke's party: one of these, from its singularity, I shall relate.

On the arrival of the party on the head waters of the Missouri, Colter, observing an appearance of abundance of beaver being there, he got permission to remain and hunt for some time, which he did in company with a man of the name of Dixon, who had traversed the immense tract of country from St. Louis to the head waters of the Missouri alone. Soon after

From *Travels in the Interior of America*, in the Years 1809, 1810, and 1811; including a Description of Upper Louisiana, together with the States of Ohio, Kentucky, Indiana, and Tennessee, with the Illinois and Western Territories, and Containing Remarks and Observations Useful to Persons Emigrating to those Countries, by John Bradbury, pp. 25–29n. Second edition. London: Sherwood, Neely, and Jones. 1819.

he had separated from Dixon, and trapped in company with a hunter named Potts; and aware of the hostility of the Blackfeet Indians, one of whom had been killed by Lewis, they set their traps at night, and took them up early in the morning, remaining concealed during the day. They were examining their traps early one morning, in a creek about six miles from that branch of the Missouri called Jefferson's Fork, and were ascending in a canoe, when they suddenly heard a great noise, resembling the trampling of animals; but they could not ascertain the fact as the high perpendicular banks on each side of the river impeded their view. Colter immediately pronounced it to be occasioned by Indians, and advised an instant retreat; but was accused of cowardice by Potts, who insisted that the noise was caused by buffaloes, and they proceeded on. In a few minutes afterwards their doubts were removed by a party of Indians making their appearance on both sides of the creek, to the amount of five or six hundred, who beckoned them to come ashore. As retreat was now impossible, Colter turned the head of the canoe to the shore; and at the moment of its touching, an Indian seized the rifle belonging to Potts; but Colter, who is a remarkably strong man, immediately retook it, and handed it to Potts, who remained in the canoe, and on receiving it pushed off into the river. He had scarcely quitted the shore when an arrow was shot at him, and he cried out, "Colter, I am wounded." Colter remonstrated with him on the folly of attempting to escape, and urged him to come ashore. Instead of complying, he instantly leveled his rifle at an Indian, and shot him dead on the spot. This conduct, situated as he was, may appear to have been an act of madness; but it was doubtless the effect of sudden but sound reasoning; for if taken alive, he must have expected to be tortured to death, according to their custom. He was instantly pierced with arrows so numerous that, to use the language of Colter, "he was made a riddle of."

They now seized Colter, stripped him entirely naked, and began to consult on the manner in which he should be put to death. They were first inclined to set him up as a mark to shoot at; but the chief interfered, and seizing him by the shoulder, asked him if he could run fast. Colter, who had been some time amongst the Kee-kat-sa, or Crow Indians, had in a considerable degree acquired the Blackfoot language, and was also well acquainted with Indian customs. He knew that he had now to run for his life, with the dreadful odds of five or six hundred against him, and those armed Indians; therefore cunningly replied that he was a very bad runner, although he was considered by the hunters as remarkably swift. The chief now commanded the party to remain stationary, and led Colter out on the prairie three or four hundred yards, and released him, bidding him to save himself if he could. At that instant the horrid war whoop sounded in the ears of poor Colter, who, urged with the hope of preserving life, ran with a speed at which he was himself surprised. He proceeded towards the Jefferson Fork, having to traverse a plain six miles in breadth, abounding with the prickly pear, on which he was every instant treading with his naked feet. He ran nearly half way across the plain before he ventured to look over his shoulder, when he perceived that the Indians were very much scattered, and that he had gained ground to a considerable distance from the main body; but one Indian, who carried a spear, was much before all the rest, and not more than a hundred yards from him. A faint gleam of hope now cheered the heart of Colter; he derived confidence from the belief that escape was within the bounds of possibility; but that confidence was nearly being fatal to him, for he exerted himself to such a degree that the blood gushed from his nostrils, and soon almost covered the fore part of his body. He had now arrived within a mile of the river, when he distinctly heard the appalling sounds of footsteps behind him, and every instant expected to feel the spear of his pursuer. Again he turned his head, and saw the savage not twenty yards from him. Determined, if possible, to avoid the expected blow, he suddenly stopped, turned round, and spread out his arms. The Indian, surprised by the suddenness of the action, and perhaps at the bloody appearance of Colter, also attempted to stop; but exhausted with running, he fell whilst endeavoring to throw his spear, which stuck in the ground and broke in his hand. Colter instantly snatched up the pointed part, with which he pinned him to the earth and then continued his flight.

The foremost of the Indians, on arriving at the place, stopped till others came up to join them, when they set up a hideous yell. Every moment of this time was improved by Colter, who, although fainting and exhausted, succeeded in gaining the skirting of the cottonwood trees, on the borders of the fork, through which he ran, and plunged into the river. Fortunately for him, a little below this place there was an island, against the upper point of which a raft of drift timber had lodged. He dived under the raft, and after several efforts, got his head above water amongst the trunks of trees, covered over with smaller wood to the depth of several feet. Scarcely had he secured himself when the Indians arrived on the river, screeching and yelling, as Colter expressed it, "like so many devils." They were frequently on the raft during the day and were seen through the chinks by Colter, who was congratulating himself on his escape, until the idea arose that they might set the raft on fire. In horrible suspense he remained until night, when hearing no more of the Indians, he dived from under the raft, and swam silently down the river to a considerable distance, when he landed, and traveled all night. Although happy in having escaped from the Indians, his situation was still dreadful; he was completely naked, under a burning sun; the soles of his feet were entirely filled with the thorns of the prickly pear; he was hungry, and had no means of killing game, although he saw abundance around him, and was at least seven days' journey from Lisa's Fort, on the Bighorn branch of the Roche Jaune [Yellowstone] River. These were circumstances under which almost any man but an American hunter would have despaired. He arrived at the fort in seven days, having subsisted on a root much esteemed by the Indians of Missouri, now known by naturalists as *psoralea esculentu.*

Old Robidoux

Decatur told me a good joke that old [Joseph] Robidoux played, many years ago, on a competitor of his in these parts, Manuel Lisa. Both were traders with the Pawnee. Each of them tried to acquire by trade as many pelts as possible for himself without being at all squeamish as to the means he employed, and, for that reason, they often quarreled. In order to prevent such wrangles and under the conviction that neither had the power to ruin the other, they pledged reciprocally to be "loyal," i.e., if a band of Indians arrived at their trading posts for the purpose of exchange and barter, neither would attempt to take advantage of the other. Manuel Lisa, however, had no intention of trading on honorable terms for any length of time; accordingly, upon an occasion when both of them expected a band of Pawnee he tried to circumvent Robidoux. While he ordered his post supplied in secret with commodities to barter to the Pawnee, he went over to see Robidoux by way of putting him off his guard, by his own presence there to hinder preparations, and to see what was really going on in the other storehouse. Robidoux played the part of unsuspecting host just as well as his opponent played his role; acted just as though he had allowed himself to be really duped. He invited Lisa to drink a glass of champagne to the success of prospective trade; but regretted that on account of his gout he was not able to stoop down, and therefore would have to ask Lisa to fetch the flask from the cellar himself. The latter obligingly raised the trapdoor in the room and went down the steps. Joe let fall the door, rolled a cask upon it, and with mocking words left his opponent imprisoned, in order that he might trade alone with the Pawnee.

On this same occasion I related to Decatur another story I had often heard in St. Joseph about old Robidoux. By his first marriage he had a son, Joe, who inherited from his deceased mother so many building lots in St. Louis that, according to current prices of city property, he was worth about $90,000. Now, Joe, Jr., was a confirmed drunkard and, on account of his bibulous habits, gave his father a great deal of trouble. Some years ago he went into the Catholic Church dressed like an Indian, i.e., practically naked, to the amazement of the assembled worshippers. The old man, being in rather poor circumstances financially on account of his great number of children and his unfortunate addiction to cards, took advantage of this opportunity to confine his drunken son, as a punishment, for several weeks in his cellar and refused to release him until Joe, Jr., put in a favorable mood by receiving a glass of whisky after a long fast, signed a deed, already prepared, transferring the property to his father.

From *Journal of Rudolph Friederich Kurz*, An Account of His Experiences among Fur Traders and American Indians on the Mississippi and the Upper Missouri Rivers during the Years 1846 to 1852, translated by Myrtis Jarrell, edited by J. N. B. Hewitt, pp. 66–67. Smithsonian Institution, Bureau of American Ethnology, Bulletin 115. Washington: United States Printing Office. 1937.
Journal entry of June 14, 1851.

Father De Smet, Rain-Maker

Although the spring of 1851 had been very backward and wet in the lower country, it was not so higher up, and when the *St. Ange* arrived at the Aricara villages the corn crop of those Indians was found to be actually suffering from drought. The Aricara chief, White Shield, came on board and said to La Barge, who understood his language well:

"I am glad to see you, and I hear the Black Robe is on board."

La Barge replied that that was so. The chief then continued:

"I want to ask him a favor. It is very late in the season and no rain. Corn ought to be up now. We want the Black Robe to send us rain."

La Barge took the Indian back to De Smet's room and said to the priest. "Father, here is the White Shield, who wants you to make it rain, for the corn is not up yet."

De Smet, who knew the White Shield well, laughed heartily, and said he would do all he could. He then asked La Barge if the boat was going to remain there all day, and being informed that it was, he said to the White Shield: "Go to your village and put your lodge in order, and call in some of the chiefs. I will come and offer prayer to the Almighty and ask him to be merciful and grant your requests; and I am satisfied that, if you deserve it, the Great Spirit will look down and favor you."

Captain La Barge and several of the passengers went along with the father, and the interpreter translated the prayer to the Indians. They left the Indians satisfied, and at noon had them on the boat for a feast, after which they returned to their village. As good fortune would have it, along about three or four o'clock in the afternoon, there came up a heavy thunder shower which fairly deluged the place. Father De Smet laughed and said:

"They will think I did it. They will give me all the credit for it."

Some time after the shower Pierre Garreau, a French Canadian, who had spent all his life among the Indians, and had become almost an Indian himself, came to the boat and said to La Barge:

"I want you to help me. I want to find out how Father De Smet did that."

"Did what?" asked La Barge.

"Made it rain. I will pay a good price if he will tell me. I will give him ten horses."

La Barge took him back to De Smet, where he presented his request himself. De Smet told him to be a good Christian, and pray when he wanted it to rain, and if he deserved it, it would come. Garreau went away

From *History of Early Steamboat Navigation on the Missouri River,* Life and Adventures of Joseph La Barge, Pioneer Navigator and Indian Trader for Fifty Years with the Commerce of Missouri Valley, by Hiram Martin Chittenden, Vol. I, pp. 196–198. Copyright, 1903, by Francis P. Harper. New York.

disappointed, for he fully believed that the father had some secret art by which he produced so signal a result. After he had gone, De Smet laughed and said: "Did I not tell you they would say I did it?"

John Banvard and the "Largest Painting in the World"

There was a young lad of fifteen, a fatherless, moneyless youth, to whom there came a very extraordinary idea, as he was floating for the first time down the noble Mississippi. He had read in some foreign journal that America could boast the most picturesque and magnificent scenery in the world, but that she had not yet produced an artist capable of delineating it. On this thought he pondered and pondered till his brain began to whirl; and as he glided along on the smooth surface of the river, gazing with wonder and delight upon the ever varied and beautiful shores, the boy resolved within himself that he would take away the reproach from his country—that *he* would paint the beauties and sublimities of his native land.

Some years passed away, and still John Banvard—for that was his name—dreamed of being a painter. What he was in his waking, working moments, we do not know; but, at all events he found time to turn over and over again the great thought that haunted him, till at length, ere he had attained the age of manhood, it assumed a distinct and tangible shape in his mind, and he devoted himself to its realization. There mingled no idea of profit with his ambition, and, indeed, strange to say, we can learn nothing of any aspirations he may have felt after artistical excellence. His grand object, as he himself informs us, was to produce for his country *the largest painting in the world*. He determined to paint a picture of the beautiful scenery of the Mississippi which should be as superior to all others, in point of *size*, as that prodigious river is superior to the streamlets

From *Description of Banvard's Panorama of the Mississippi River*, Painted on Three Miles of Canvas, Exhibiting a View of Country 1200 Miles in Length, Extending from the Mouth of the Missouri River to the City of New Orleans, being by far the Largest Picture Ever Executed by Man, pp. 7–20. Boston: John Putnam, Printer. 1847.

What became of the panorama is a question always asked. Because of its enormity, it was impossible to preserve properly, so it was cut up into sections and used in part for scenery in theaters, the rest stored away in the cellars of relatives. Time and neglect did the rest. John Banvard died in 1891, in the home of his son at Watertown, South Dakota, leaving a considerable body of poems, many of which still exist in various historical museums, as well as numerous paintings, such as "The Sea of Galilee," which hangs in the Public Library of St. Paul, Minnesota.—Adele Banvard, "The First Moving Picture," *Manuscripts*, Vol. VII (Spring, 1955), No. 3, pp. 175–176.

For an account of Banvard's pamphlets and his moving panorama (unwound from one roller and wound on to another, to the accompaniment of a lecture and sometimes pianoforte selections), see John Francis McDermott, "Banvard's Mississippi Panorama Pamphlets," *The Papers of the Bibliographical Society of America*, Vol. 43 (First quarter, 1949), pp. 48–62. Banvard's panorama, which Longfellow saw in Boston in 1846 (see his journal for December 19) was one of the sources of his description of the Mississippi in *Evangeline*.

of Europe—a gigantic idea!—which seems truly kindred to the illimitable forests and vast extent of his native land.

* * * * *

When Banvard was about fifteen years of age, his family met with a severe reverse of fortune. His father lived just long enough to see his property, collected by frugal industry and perseverance, swept away from him by the mismanagement of an indiscreet partner, and his family turned houseless upon a pitiless world. John then went to the West, poor and friendless, and far away from his mother, brother and sisters, and those he held dear. He arrived at Louisville, Kentucky, sought employment, and procured a situation in a drug store; but this did not suit his taste. Instead of making pills, his employer would often find him with a piece of chalk or coal, sketching the likenesses of his fellow clerks upon the walls of the rooms, where they were putting up medicines. His employer told him he thought he could make better likenesses than he could pills. John thought so too, and so "threw physic to the dogs," and left the druggist.

We next find him engaged in his favorite employment of painting—he having made an engagement to ornament and decorate a public garden. But this concern soon failed and left him without money or employment. At this time he was about sixteen years old. Our hero, nothing daunted, by persevering labor obtained a little money, engaged a room, and pursued the business of painting for himself. The day had not arrived for success in his chosen pursuit; so being fond of adventure, he started down the river with some young men of his acquaintance, to seek anew his fortune.

When they had reached the mouth of the Saline River, they met with a disaster which had well nigh proved fatal to the young artist. The river was lashed by a terrific storm; the night was dark; the boat broke loose from its moorings. By great exertions of all hands on board, in pumping and bailing all night, they succeeded in keeping the craft afloat, and made a safe landing. During this perilous night, our young adventurer, at the hazard of his own life, saved the life of one of his comrades who fell overboard. When day broke they discovered a stock boat but a few yards below them, whose proximity they had not discovered during the night, from the noise of the storm. It was an ill-fated night for the stock boat. It was sunk, all the stock was drowned, and the men were found sitting on the bank nearly frozen, whom the more fortunate party generously relieved. A large number of boats met with a similar fate with the stock boat on that fatal night.

The next we find of Banvard, he is in the village of New Harmony, on the Wabash River, where, in company with three or four other young men, he "got up" some dioramic paintings, fitted them up for public exhibition, in a flatboat which they built for the purpose, and started off down the Wabash with the intention of "coasting" that river into the Ohio and so down the Mississippi to New Orleans, thus exhibiting to the sparse population of the wilderness specimens of the fine arts, at the same time replenishing their exhausted funds. This proved to be a very unfortunate speculation. The capital of the company gave out before they were able to complete their plans, and they left port with their boat in an unfinished condition, calculating to finish it with their first proceeds, they having invested their last few dimes in a supply of bacon, corn, meal, and potatoes. But fate conspired against them. The river was low, and none of them had ever descended the Wabash; consequently they were ignorant of the channel, lodged on the sand bars, and hung on the snags until they exhausted their scanty supply of provisions. They at length found themselves fast on a sand bar, and down to their last peck of potatoes at the same time. They labored hard all day to get out of this predicament, but without success; and having roasted their last potatoes, they went to bed, or rather to bench, for their money gave out before they had procured bedding, and they had to content themselves with the softest plank of their seats for their slumbers.

Next morning they were up before the sun, with their spirits refreshed by a night's repose; but without any breakfast they jumped into the water and with their rails went stoutly to work again to force their boat over the bar. Overexertion, together with being in the water too long without food, brought a severe fit of ague upon Banvard. The bar upon which they were fast was called the "Bone Bank" bar, as, immediately opposite on the shore, the bank was full of organic remains. Some of the large bones were then protruding out of the side of the bank in full view. As Banvard lay on the soft sand of the bar, as it was more comfortable than the hard plank of the boat, his head burning with the fever and his limbs racked with pain, he looked at these gloomy relics of an antediluvian race and felt as though his bones would soon be laid with them.

But at sunset the rest of the company got the boat over the bar, took Banvard aboard, and landed in the woods, all nearly exhausted. Food was as scarce here as it was upon the bar, and all hands went supperless to bed. Next morning they started early, not intent on exhibiting specimens of the fine arts, but on obtaining something to eat, as by this time they were nearly half starved. But the contrary winds landed their luckless craft on Wabash Island, which was uninhabited. Here, fortunately, they found some pawpaws, and they all feasted voraciously on them except Banvard, who was too sick to eat anything, and who lay upon one of the benches burning with a violent fever. Next day they sent their handbills down to the village of Shawneetown, which was in sight, about seven miles ahead, informing the inhabitants that something would be "exhibited" in the dioramic line that evening, at their wharf; and so there was; for as the company approached the wharf with their boat, no doubt with high expectations of a good supper, they observed a large audience awaiting their arrival. But the exhibition turned out different from what was expected. The boat lodged on a ledge of rocks about half a cable's length from the shore. The men from the boat got out a line to the people on the wharf, who pulled with the same eagerness that the half starved company on board pushed and pried with their poles. But fate, regardless of the philosophy of action and reaction, as well as of the interests of the fine arts at Shawneetown, held the boat fast, and the audience went away without a sight of the paintings, and the artists to sleep again without a supper. That night the swells from a passing steamer lifted the boat from the rocks, and set it afloat down the river; and when those on board awoke in the morning, they found themselves hard aground again on the Cincinnati bar, about eight miles below Shawneetown. The boat was got off with but little trouble, and they landed in a settlement. Here they were very liberal in their terms, as money was scarce, and they wanted to make sure of something to eat. A bushel of potatoes, a fowl, or a dozen of eggs, were good for an admission to their interesting exhibition. That night, after they got through exhibiting their paintings, they had a luxurious supper. Fasting so long appeared to have done Banvard some good, for it starved the fever out of him; he found, as we often do, that adversity has its blessings, and in a few days he was entirely well.

The adventurers continued on with their boat, stopping at the settlements along the shore, and "astonishing the natives" with their dioramas. The boat was not very large, and if the audience collected too much on one side, the water would intrude over the gunwales into the exhibition room. This kept the company, by turns, in the un-artist-like employment of pumping, to keep the boat from sinking. Sometimes the swells from a passing steamer would cause the water to rush through the cracks of the weather-boarding, and give the audience a bathing. Banvard says they made no extra charge for this part of the exhibition, although it was not mentioned in the programme.

Money being scarce, they were compelled to receive "truck and trade" for admissions, such as onions, potatoes, eggs, et cetera. It was no unusual thing to see a family coming to witness the "show boat," the father with a bushel of potatoes, the mother with a fowl, and the children with a pumpkin a-piece, for their admission fees. On a certain night, while they were exhibiting, some rogue let the boat loose, and it drifted off several miles down the stream with the unconscious spectators, who were landed in a thick cane brake, about two miles below. They were obliged to make their way home as best they could.

At Plumb Point the boat was attacked by a party of the Murrell robbers, a large organized banditti, who infested the country for miles around; and here our hero came near losing his life. Several pistol shots were fired at him, but being in the dark, none of them took effect, although several lodged in the deck of the boat within a few inches of him. After a desperate resistance, during which one of the robbers was shot, the boat was rescued. During the encounter, one of the company received a severe wound in the arm from a bowie knife, but the rest escaped unhurt. Mr. Banvard continued with the boat until it arrived at the Grand Gulf, where he obtained a commission to paint some views. He had found the receipts of the floating expedition to be more potatoes than dimes, more eggs than dollars;

so he sold out his interest and left. We know nothing further of this expedition, but Banvard seems to have been satisfied with the floating dioramas.

After this, he engaged in painting at New Orleans, Natchez, and subsequently at Cincinnati and Louisville, and was liberally rewarded. Not content, however, he executed a very fine panorama of the city of Venice, and exhibited it in the West with considerable success. He finally lost this painting by the sinking of a steamer upon which it was being transported to the city of Nashville. Having accumulated, by his art, a little capital, we next find him at St. Louis, as the proprietor of the St. Louis museum, which he had purchased. But here fate frowned again upon his efforts. He remained in St. Louis just long enough to lose all he had previously earned, and then left for Cincinnati, where he fared little better. He then procured a small boat and started down the Ohio river without a dime, and living several days upon nuts which he collected from the woods. His next stopping place was a small town where he did some painting, and sold a revolving pistol for which he had given twelve dollars in St. Louis, for twenty-five dollars. With this capital be bought a larger boat, got some produce aboard, which he retailed out along shore; then sold his concern for fifty dollars. Having now a little capital, the young artist made several very successful speculations, and managed to make during this Quixotic expedition several thousand dollars. With the capital thus accumulated, he commenced his grand project of painting the Panorama of the Mississippi.

For this purpose, he procured a small skiff, and descended the river to make the necessary drawings, in the spring of 1840, and the first sketch was made just before he became of age. Had he been aware, when he commenced the undertaking, of the vast amount of labor it required, he would have shrunk from the task in dismay; but having commenced the work, he was determined to proceed, being spurred on to its completion, perhaps, by the doubts of some of his friends to whom he communicated his project, as to its practicability, and by the assertions of some foreign writers, that "America had no artists commensurate with the grandeur and extent of her scenery." The idea of gain never entered his mind when he commenced the undertaking, but he was actuated by a patriotic and honorable ambition, that America should produce the *largest painting* in the world.

One of the greatest difficulties he encountered was the preparatory labor he had to undergo in making the necessary drawings. For this purpose he had to travel thousands of miles alone in an open skiff, crossing and re-crossing the rapid stream, in many places over two miles in breadth, to select proper points of sight from which to take his sketch; his hands became hardened with constantly plying the oar, and his skin as tawney as an Indian's, from exposure to the rays of the sun and the vicissitudes of the weather. He would be weeks together without speaking to a human being, having no other company than his rifle, which furnished him with his meat from the game of the woods or the fowls of the river. When the sun began to sink behind the lofty bluffs, and evening to approach, he would select some secluded sandy cove, overshadowed by the lofty cottonwood, draw out his skiff from the water, and repair to the woods to hunt his supper. Having killed his game he would return, dress, cook, and from some fallen log would eat it with his biscuit, with no other beverage than the wholesome water of the noble river that glided by him. Having finished his lonely meal, he would roll himself in his blanket, creep under his frail skiff, which he turned over to shield him from the night dews, and with his portfolio of drawings for his pillow, and the sand of the bar for his bed, would sleep soundly till the morning; when he would arise from his lowly couch, eat his breakfast before the rays of the rising sun had dispersed the humid mist from the surface of the river—then would start fresh to his task again. In this way he spent over four hundred days, making the preparatory drawings. Several nights during the time, he was compelled to creep from under his skiff where he slept, and sit all night on a log, and breast the pelting storm, through fear that the banks of the river would cave upon him, and to escape the falling trees. During this time, he pulled his little skiff more than two thousand miles. In the latter part of the summer he reached New Orleans. The yellow fever was raging in the city, but unmindful of that, he made his drawing of the place. The sun the while was so intensely hot that his skin became so burnt that it peeled from off the back of his hands, and from his face. His eyes became inflamed by such constant and extraordinary efforts, from which unhappy effects he has not recovered to this day. His drawings completed, he erected a building at Louisville, Kentucky, to transfer them to the canvas. His object in painting his picture in the West was to exhibit it to, and procure testimonials from, those who were best calculated to judge of its fidelity,—the practical river men; and he has procured the names of nearly all the principal captains and pilots navigating the Mississippi, freely testifying to the correctness of the scenery.

*　*　*　*　*

During the times this undaunted young man was transferring his drawings to the canvas, he had to practice the most rigid economy, lest his money should give out before the picture was completed. He could not afford to hire a menial assistant to do the ordinary labor about his paintroom; and when the light of day would recede from the canvas upon which he was at work, instead of taking relaxation when the night came, he would be found grinding his colors or splitting his wood for the ensuing day. Still, with all these self denials and privations, his last cent was expended long before his last sketch was transferred to his last piece of canvas. He then endeavored to get credit for a few pieces of this material from the merchant of whom he had purchased the principal part for his painting, and with whom he had expended hundreds of dollars while speculating on the river, but in vain. Still, not discouraged, he laid his favorite project aside for a time, and sought other work. Fortunately, he obtained a small job to decorate regalia for a lodge of Odd Fellows, and with a light heart went cheerfully to work to earn the money which would purchase the material to complete his picture. With the avails he procured the needed canvas.

At last his great project is finished! Mississippi is painted! and his country now boasts the largest painting in the world! But the trials of our persevering artist were not all passed. The history of the first exhibition of this wonderful production is curious, and furnishes another illustration of the necessity there is, never to despair. The gas company of Louisville, before they would put up fixtures for him, compelled him to deposit *double* the price of such fixtures in the bank. To raise this amount, he *gave* a piece of philosophical apparatus to a society in the city, provided they bought fifty tickets in advance. They agreed to this, as they desired the apparatus very much, as it was worth twice the amount they gave for the tickets. The city authorities also ordered him to pay a tax for exhibiting his work,—a work of which they ought to have been proud, and which would not only reflect honor upon the city, but make it noted throughout the civilized world.

The first night he opened his great picture for exhibition in Louisville, not a single person thought it worth while to visit it. He received not a cent,—the night was rainy. The artist returned to his room with a sorrowful heart,—he sat down upon a box and looked upon the blank wall, where but a few days before, with high spirits and cheerful heart, he had put the finishing touch to his task of long years of toil and hope. His heart almost sank within him; but he did not despair. The next day he sallied out among the boatmen by the river, and gave them tickets; telling them they must see it; that it was their river he had painted. At night the boatmen came, and with them a few of their friends. When they saw the accuracy of the painting they were delighted, and their wild enthusiasm was raised as one well known object after another passed by them. The boatmen told the citizens it was a grand affair; that it was correctly delineated, and its accuracy could be relied upon. Finally the public became convinced that the picture was really worth looking at, and then they rushed to see it by hundreds.

Peter Cartwright and the Ferryman

There is an old friend of mine, my first presiding elder, yet living in Illinois—Peter Cartwright—who was one of those old preachers in the West, and has many of their peculiarities. I may give you one incident of this man's life, as a specimen of their physical courage and prowess;

From *The Pioneers, Preachers and People of the Mississippi Valley*, by William Henry Milburn, pp. 374–376. Entered . . . 1860, by William Henry Milburn. . . . New York: Derby & Jackson.

A similar story is told of Mike Fink. See Walter Blair and Franklin J. Meine, *Mike Fink* (New York, 1933), pp. 113–117.

for it was sometimes necessary for them to fight with carnal weapons, and many of them had obstinate combats with the rough pioneer people—and commonly came off victorious.

Cartwright, in common with most of those early old preachers, was a strong opponent of slavery. Now the question was being canvassed in Illinois, between 1818 and 1823, whether this institution should be engrafted upon the Constitution, when the State was applying for admission into the Union. The old gentleman resolved to remove to Illinois, and take a hand in the quarrel. He had been living in Kentucky and Tennessee, and had preached there for a quarter of a century, when he was appointed to Illinois as presiding elder, and had a circuit from Galena on the northwest to Shawneetown on the south—a district nearly as great as the entire· country of England.

Around this he was to travel once in three months, at a time when there were no roads, scarcely a bridge or ferry—and keep his regular appointments to preach, Sunday after Sunday, besides attending love-feasts and administering the sacrament. Then, after preaching on the Sunday, he would generally announce a stump speech for the Monday and call upon his fellow-citizens to come and hear the question discussed, whether slavery should be admitted or not. Of course, taking a political side, he was regarded as a politician, and there was a good deal of angry feeling about the old preacher.

On one occasion he rode to a ferry upon the Sangamon River; the country about was rather thickly populated, and he found a crowd of people about the ferry, which seemed to be a sort of gathering place for discussing politics. The ferryman, a great herculean fellow, was holding forth at the top of his voice about an old renegade, one Peter Cartwright, prefixing a good many adjectives to his name, and declaring that if ever he came that way he would drown him in the river.

Cartwright, who was unknown to any one there, now coming up, said: "I want you to put me across."

"You can wait till I am ready," said the ferryman.

Cartwright knew it was of no use to complain; and the ferryman, when he had got through with his speech, signified his readiness to take him over. The preacher rode his horse into the boat, and the ferryman commenced to row across. All Cartwright wanted was fair play; he wished to make a public exhibition of this man, and, moreover, was glad of an opportunity to state his principles. About half way over, therefore, throwing his bridle over the stake on one side of the boat, he told the ferryman to lay down his pole.

"What's the matter?" asked the man.

"Well," said he, "you have just been using my name improper, and saying that if ever I came this way, you would drown me in the river. I'm going to give you a chance."

"Are you Peter Cartwright?"

"Yes."

And the ferryman, nothing loth, pulls in his pole, and at it they go. They grapple in a minute, and Cartwright, being very agile as well as athletic, succeeds in catching him by the nape of the neck and the slack of the breeches, and whirls him over. He souses him down under the tide, while the companions of the vanquished ferryman look on, the distance ensuring fair play. Cartwright souses him under again, and raising him, says, "I baptize thee in the name of the Devil, whose child thou art." He thus immerses him thrice, and then drawing him up again, inquires, "Did you ever pray?"

"No," answered the ferryman, strangling and choking and dripping in a pitiful manner.

"Then it's time you did," says Cartwright. "I'll teach you. Say 'Our Father who art in Heaven.' "

"I won't," says the ferryman.

Down he goes under water again for quite a time. Then lifting him out, "Will you pray now?"

The poor ferryman, nearly strangled to death, wanted to gain time and to consider the terrors. "Let me breathe and think," he said.

"No," answers the relentless preacher, "I won't. I'll make you." And he immerses him again. At length he draws him out, and asks a third time, "Will you pray now?"

"I will do anything," was the subservient answer.

So Cartwright made him repeat the Lord's prayer.

"Now, let me up," demanded this unwilling convert.

"No," says Cartwright, "not yet. Make me three promises: that you will repeat that prayer every morning and night; that you will put every Methodist preacher across this ferry free of expense; and that you will go to hear every one that preaches within five miles, henceforth."

The ferryman, all helpless, barely alive and thoroughly cowed, promised; and Cartwright went on his way.

That ferryman joined the church afterward, and became quite an eminent and useful member.

Davy Crockett on the River

I. Crockett Goes Down the Mississippi With His Lumber [1]

Having now closed my hunting for that winter, I returned to my hands, who were engaged about my boats and staves, and made ready for a trip

---

[1] From *The Life of David Crockett,* The Original Humorist and Irrepressible Backwoodsman, Comprising His Early History; His Bear Hunting and Other Adventures, His Services in the Creek War; His Electioneering Speeches and Career in Congress; with His Triumphal Tour Through the Northern States, and Services in the Texan War, to which is added An Account of His Glorious Death at the Alamo While Fighting in Defence of Texan Independence, pp. 158–162. Entered . . . 1869, by John E. Potter and Company. Philadelphia.

down the river. I had two boats and about thirty thousand staves, and so I loaded with them, and set out for New Orleans. I got out of the Obion river, in which I had loaded my boats, very well; but when I got into the Mississippi, I found all my hands were bad scared, and in fact I believe I was scared a little the worst of any; for I had never been down the river, and I soon discovered that my pilot was as ignorant of the business as myself. I hadn't gone far before I determined to lash the two boats together; we did so, but it made them so heavy and obstinate that it was next akin to impossible to do anything at all with them, or to guide them right in the river.

That evening we fell in company with some Ohio boats; and about night we tried to land, but we could not. The Ohio men hollered to us to go on and run all night. We took their advice, though we had a good deal rather not; but we couldn't do any other way. In a short distance we got into what is called the "Devil's Elbow"; and if any place in the wide creation has its own proper name, I thought it was this. Here we had about the hardest work that I ever was engaged in, in my life, to keep out of danger; and even then we were in it all the while. We twice attempted to land at Wood-yards, which we could see but couldn't reach.

The people would run out with lights, and try to instruct us how to get to shore; but all in vain. Our boats were so heavy that we couldn't take them much any way, except the way they wanted to go, and just the way the current would carry them. At last we quit trying to land, and concluded just to go ahead as well as we could, for we found we couldn't do any better. Some time in the night I was down in the cabin of one of the boats, sitting by the fire, thinking on what a hobble we had got into; and how much better bear-hunting was on hard land than floating along on the water, when a fellow had to go ahead whether he was exactly willing or not.

The hatchway into the cabin came slap down, right through the top of the boat; and it was the only way out except a small hole in the side, which we had used for putting our arms through to dip up water before we lashed the boats together.

We were now floating sideways, and the boat I was in was the hindmost as we went. All at once I heard the hands begin to run over the top of the boat in great confusion, and pull with all their might; and the first thing I know'd after this we went broadside full tilt against the head of an island where a large raft of drift timber had lodged. The nature of such a place would be, as everybody knows, to suck the boats down, and turn them right under this raft; and the uppermost boat would, of course, be suck'd down and go under first. As soon as we struck, I bulged for my hatchway, as the boat was turning under sure enough. But when I got to it, the water was pouring through in a current as large as the hole would let it, and as strong as the weight of the river would force it. I found I couldn't get out here, for the boat was now turned down in such a way that it was steeper than a house-top. I now thought of the hole in the side, and made my way in a hurry for that. With difficulty I got to it, and when I got there, I found it was too small for me to get out by my own power, and I began to think that I was in a worse box than ever. But I put my arms through and hollered as loud as I could roar, as the boat I was in hadn't yet quite filled with water up to my head, and the hands who were next to the raft, seeing my arms out, and hearing me holler, seized them, and began to pull. I told them I was sinking, and to pull my arms off, or force me through, for now I know'd well enough it was neck or nothing, come out or sink.

By a violent effort they jerked me through; but I was in a pretty pickle when I got through. I had been sitting without any clothing over my shirt; this was torn off, and I was literally skin'd like a rabbit. I was, however, well pleased to get out in any way, even without shirt or hide; as before I could straighten myself on the boat next to the raft, the one they pull'd me out of went entirely under, and I have never seen it any more to this day. We all escaped on to the raft, where we were compelled to sit all night about a mile from land on either side. Four of my company were bareheaded, and three barefooted; and of that number I was one. I reckon I looked like a pretty cracklin ever to get to Congress!!!

We had now lost all our loading; and every particle of our clothing, except what little we had on; but over all this, while I was setting there, in the night, floating about on the drift, I felt happier and better off than I ever had in my life before, for I had just made such a marvelous escape that I had forgot almost everything else in that; and so I felt prime.

In the morning about sunrise, we saw a boat coming down, and we hailed her. They sent a large skiff, and took us all on board, and carried us down as far as Memphis. Here I met with a friend, that I never can forget as long as I am able to go ahead at anything; it was a Major Winchester, a merchant of that place: he let us all have hats, and shoes, and some little money to go upon, and so we all parted.

A young man and myself concluded to go on down to Natchez, to see if we could hear anything of our boats; for we supposed they would float out from the raft, and keep on down the river. We got a boat at Memphis, that was going down, and so cut out. Our largest boat, we were informed, had been seen about fifty miles below where we stove, and an attempt had been made to land her, but without success, as she was as hard headed as ever.

This was the last of my boats, and of my boating; for it went so badly with me, along at the first, that I had not much mind to try it any more. I now returned home again, and as the next August was the Congressional election, I began to turn my attention a little to that matter, as it was beginning to be talked of a good deal among the people.[2]

---

[2] Everything of the speculative or business sort seems to have turned out badly with the Colonel. He had no talent for that sort of thing. His real forte in the way of exertion was war and bear-hunting. Politics was rather an amusement; and yet on the whole he was successful in this line. His stump speeches, made off hand, pleased

II. How Crockett and Ben Hardin Won a Race With a Steamer [3]

You see, as how I war cradled by the Mississippi, schooled among her holler log canoes, an' tharefore I'm a hull double bilered steamboat at a row or paddle; an' my old Salt-water friend, Ben Hardin, is nearly half equal to me. Ben an' me went to take passage down the Big Muddy on a late 'kashion, in one o' them locomotive river towns called a western steamer, but we war refused a berth bekase we had a barr in our company, an' I wanted a berth for him along with myself. Takin' this anti-republican refusal as an insult to my Congressional dignity, as well as to my well-bred pet Death Hug, Ben an' me detarmined to revenge our insulted respectability on 'em by beatin' thar double-breasted steamer down the river by an independent private conveyance, built on our own hook entirely; so we walked out to the woods, cut down a very ancient holler gum tree, cut it open one side, corked up both eends, cut a pair o' ten feet paddles, an' launched her into the Mississippy, jest as the great steamer got out o' sight. I took old Death Hug aboard, put him at the starn, an' made him sit thar, an' hold up the pole o' Uncle Sam's flag, an' steer with his tail. Ben an' I lit our great bowl pipes, took our paddles near the bow, an' the way we made 'em walk in an' out the water made the fish stare, an' the banks o' Old Muddy fly behind us as fast as if etarnity war comin' all at once, an' we made the smoke roll up from our pipes thick enough to choak a common steambiler. Death Hug held up our flag, grinned, an' steered us with his sweepin' tail as straight as a chalk line, an' take my paws for steamer paddle wheels if in two hours we didn't pass the tarnal aristycratical steamer in sassy triumph; while Ben puffed his smoke at 'em, an' I waved my Crockett flag an' grinned victory.

Well, you see, arter beatin' thar steamer with our holler gum tree into teetotal disgrace, I took a notion to build a regular independent steamer o' my own, to avoid all insults to my pet Bruin an' myself, for like the poet George Byron, I never say Lord when talkin' o' men. I always have my bear with me for company, so I jest went an' caught a ninety feet alligator, split him apart, an' hollered him out, arter which I sewed his two halves together, then dried it for about six months in our old smoke house, enlarged for that purpose, seasoned it with snappin' turtle taller, till it war as hard as the hinges on eternity. I then put a five hundred horse power steam engine into it, flattened its back into a deck, shod it with oak plank, hoisted Uncle Sam's flag, took Death Hug for helmsman, an' have used it ever since as a steam packet up and down the Big Muddy.

the people more than the elaborate performances of highly educated orators, and his course in Congress gained him the respect of the first statesmen of his time, as we shall see in the sequel of his narrative.—Ed., *The Life of David Crockett.*

[3] From *Mince Pie for the Million* [unpaged]. Philadelphia and New York: Turner & Fisher. [1846.]

An' if ever war breaks out between Uncle Sam an' any other nation, I mean to cut port holes in her sides, ship about fifty cannon, an' set up man o' war on my own hook.

Mike Fink Yarns

I. A New Coat for Mike Fink's Stomach [1]

A story is told of a clergyman from the east travelling down the Ohio River, some years ago, who was anxious to learn something about Mike Fink. Somebody told him that the pilot of the boat on which he was travelling had been acquainted with Mike. The clergyman approached him, and said,—

"Do you know anything about Mike Fink?"

"Yes," said the pilot; "knew him like a brother."

"Can you tell me some peculiar incident of his life?" asked the clergyman.

"Well, I don't know," replied the pilot, hesitatingly. "Yes, I can. He ate a buffalo robe once."

"Ate a buffalo robe!" said the clergyman, astonished.

"Certainly, a buffalo robe, with the hair on," replied the pilot.

"Well, what did he do that for?"

"Why, you see," said the pilot, resting a moment, to shift his quid of tobacco, "you see, Mike drank so much whiskey that he destroyed the coating of his stomach, and the doctor told him that before he could get well, he would need a new coat for it. Mike thought the thing over, and said, when he had a new coat for his stomach, he would have one that would stand the whiskey; and he made up his mind that a buffalo robe with the hair on it was just the thing, and so he sat down, and swallowed it. He could drink any amount of whiskey after that, and never so much as wink. Fact, now, as true as you are standing there."

The clergyman turned away, satisfied.

---

[1] From *Underground, or Life Below the Surface,* Incidents and Accidents Beyond the Light of Day; Startling Adventures in All Parts of the World; Mines and the Mode of Working Them; Under-Currents of Society; Gambling and Its Horrors; Caverns and Their Mysteries; The Dark Ways of Wickedness; Prisons and Their Secrets; Down in the Depths of the Sea; Strange Stories of the Detection of Crime, by Thomas W. Knox, pp. 683–684. Entered . . . 1873, by J. B. Burr & Hyde. Hartford and Chicago.

Cf. "Lige Shattuck's Reminiscence of Mike Fink," *The Spirit of the Times,* Vol. XVIII (April 15, 1848), No. 8, p. 89.

II. Mike Fink's Still [2]

. . . Mike had had charge of many keelboats, with valuable cargoes; and a friend of mine, one of the oldest and most respected of the commanders of steamboats in the Nashville trade, related to me, within the last four days, that in 1819 he was employed to leave Pittsburgh, and go down the Ohio in hunt of Mike and his cargo, which had been detained by some unaccountable delay. At some distance above Wheeling he found the loiterer lying to, in company with another keel, apparently in no hurry to finish the trip. Mike did not greet our envoy in very pleasant style, but kept the fair weather side out, knowing that my friend was able to hoe his own row. Mike was determined not to leave good quarters that night, and all went to bed wherever they could.

In the night my friend was awakened by some noise or other, and before falling asleep again, he heard Mike say in a low voice, "Well, boys, who's going to still tonight?"

This question drew his attention, as it was something he did not understand. Watching for some time, he saw Mike take a tin bucket, that had apparently been fixed for the purpose, with a small pipe inserted in its bottom, about the size of a common gimlet. This was taken to a cask of wine or brandy, and a hole made in either cask, the pipe put in, and then a couple of quarts of water turned into the bucket. Then the "still" began to operate, as they drew from the head of the cask until the water in the bucket disappeared.

Thus they obtained the liquor, and the cause of their long detention [was] ascertained. The very casks of wine that Mike drew from were returned to the merchant in Pittsburgh, more than a year afterwards, having soured.

Thus you see Mike *did* have charge of merchandise, and to considerable extent.

III. Mike Fink and the Kicking Sheriff [3]

[A] tale apparently circulated orally for years—for it did not find its way into print until 1895—told how Mike was quieted at the hands—or rather the feet—of the sheriff of the tiny town of Westport [Indiana], opposite Louisville on the Ohio.

Mike was telling jokes one day in the grocery (grog shop), and all of the drinkers laughed heartily, uproariously, at his yarns—all save one

[2] From "Mike Fink," by "K.," Cincinnati, February 11, 1845, letter to the editor, *The Cincinnati Miscellany,* or Antiquities of the West; and Pioneer History and General and Local Statistics, compiled from the *Western General Advertiser,* from October 1st, 1844, to April 1st, 1845, by Charles Cist, Vol. I, January, 1845, pp. 156–157. Cincinnati: Caleb Clark, Printer. 1845.

[3] From *Mike Fink,* King of Mississippi Keelboatmen, by Walter Blair and Franklin J. Meine, pp. 111–113. Copyright, 1933, by Henry Holt and Company, Inc. New York.

man, a little dried up fellow, whose pensive face suggested that he was contemplating death and eternity.

Mike at last walked over to him.

"See here, Mister," he said, "these yarns I been tellin' is funny, and you stand there as glum as a dead catfish on a sandbar. I tell snorters for folk to laugh at in a good humored way, an' by God, I don't let no man make light of 'em."

"Is that so?" the little man asked, negligently, and he sank back into his gloomy contemplation.

Mike, at the bar, told another yarn, and the company dutifully howled. But the little man, sternly watched by Mike, looked positively tearful. Mike stamped across the floor.

"Whoop!" yelled Mike. "Calamity's a-comin'! I'm a Salt River roarer, an' I'm chockful o' fight. I'm——"

But in the middle of his boast, Mike was surprised. For the wizened mourner suddenly leaped into the air and as his body swooped downward, his fist smacked Mike below the ear, and the keeler fell sprawling.

"Is that so?" said his opponent, and he lay down as if to rest.

Mike staggered to his feet, blood in his eye, roaring with anger. But as he came forward, the little man doubled into a tangle of flaying feet and clawing fists. Mike went into a whirl of flying arms and legs, and emerged with a scratched face and a sinking in his stomach where a swift kick had landed. Angrier than ever, he flopped on the man again; and again, against the torrent of claws and leaping boots, he was able to do nothing. Four times more he tried in vain to seize or to strike his rival, and each time, Mike looked more as if calamity and desolation had struck him.

"Stranger," panted Mike at last, "I'm free to own I can't do nothin' with you. You're tougher to chaw nor buckskin."

"Is that so?" dreamily asked the visitor. "Listen to me. I'm Ned Taylor, sheriff of this county; and if you and your crew don't get the hell out of here in ten minutes, I'll arrest the mess of ye!"

"Five's enough," said Mike, according to the tale. "You're a snag, a riffle, and a sawyer all in one."

And the people who handed down the tale maintain that the sheriff said, "Is that so?" and resumed his gloomy contemplation.

James Bowie to the Rescue

The river sharpers often went to great trouble and expense in setting the stage of their operations, and usually their elaborate and well-planned schemes were successful. Sometimes, however, the gamblers came to grief at the last moment, either by the quarry becoming suspicious or through

From *Sucker's Progress,* An Informal History of Gambling in America from the Colonies to Canfield, by Herbert Asbury, pp. 206–209. Copyright, 1938, by Dodd, Mead and Company, Inc. New York.

interference on the part of chivalrous passengers. One of the busiest of these knights-errant of the steamboats was no less a personage than the redoubtable James Bowie, inventor of the Bowie-knife, once an associate of the pirate Jean Lafitte, and the most noted duelist of his time. This noble-minded killer, who died with Davy Crockett in the defense of the Alamo in 1836, was a menace to the river gamblers for several years; he spent considerable time on the lower Mississippi, and seems to have made a practice of ferreting out crooked gamblers, beating them at their own game, and restoring to suckers the money of which they had been fleeced. But he always required the sucker to swear a solemn oath that he would gamble no more.

Bowie's most celebrated exploit of this character was performed on the steamer *New Orleans* in the fall of 1832, when he saved a young gentleman of Natchez from dishonor and a suicide's grave. In the summer of that year this young gentleman, who fancied himself as a card player and a man of the world, went to New York on his honeymoon, and while there collected about $50,000 on behalf of various merchants and planters of Natchez. A syndicate of gamblers was formed to despoil him, and one of the sharpers was sent to New York, where he made the young gentleman's acquaintance and learned that the latter intended to go home by way of Pittsburgh and Louisville, with a stopover of several days in Louisville to visit relatives. When the young gentleman took a boat at Pittsburgh the sharper was on board, and so were two "Louisiana planters," who made themselves very agreeable. Twenty-card poker was introduced, and the young man from Natchez was permitted to win several hundred dollars. By the time the boat reached Louisville the four men had become such friends that the "planters" and the sharper, who posed as a New Orleans merchant, agreed to wait and go down the river on the *New Orleans,* on which the young gentleman had booked passage for himself and his bride.

The gamblers went after the young gentleman in earnest when the *New Orleans* left the wharf at Louisville. In a few sessions they had cheated him out of $45,000, and he was betting frantically in a desperate effort to retrieve his losses. Bowie, wearing a black, broad-brimmed slouch hat and black broadcloth clothing of clerical cut, boarded the boat at Vicksburg and became an interested spectator of the game, which he saw immediately was crooked. After a few more hours' play the young man's last dollar vanished into the capacious pockets of the gamblers, and crazed by remorse he rushed to the rail and attempted to throw himself into the river. He was restrained by Bowie and his wife and taken to his cabin, where Bowie instructed that he be closely watched.

Bowie then went to the bar, casually displayed a bulging wallet, and asked for change for a hundred dollar bill. One of the gamblers, who were opening wine to celebrate the success of their *coup,* obliged, and after a few moments of conversation suggested a card game, to which Bowie agreed. On the first few hands Bowie won, and then the sharpers began to forge ahead. At length one of the "planters" dealt Bowie a hand which any poker player would bet as long as he could see, and which Bowie recognized as being intended for the big cleanup. The "planters" dropped out after a few bets, but Bowie and the "merchant" continued to raise each other until $70,000 was piled on the table between them. Finally Bowie saw what he had been watching for—the gambler's hand flicking quickly into his sleeve. Like lightning Bowie seized the sharper's wrist, at the same time drawing from his shirt-bosom a wicked-looking knife.

"Show your hand!" he commanded. "If it contains more than five cards I shall kill you!"

The gambler attempted to break loose, but Bowie twisted his wrist and his cards fell to the table—four aces, a queen and a jack.

"I shall take the pot," said Bowie, "with a legitimate poker hand, four kings and a ten."

"Who the devil are you, anyway?" cried the discomfited gambler.

"I," said the famous duelist, "am James Bowie!"

"The voice was like velvet," says an account of the affair, "but it cut like steel into the hearts of the chief gambler's confederates and deterred them from any purpose or impulse they might have had to interfere. They, with the crowd, shrank back from the table, smitten with terror by the name. Bowie softly swept the banknotes into his large slouch hat and lightly clapped it on his head."

There are two versions of what happened next. One is that Bowie let the gambler go with a lecture, but kept the pot. The other is that the sharper insisted on a duel, and that Bowie borrowed a pistol and shot him off the wheelhouse "just as the great round face of the sun, like a golden cannon ball," appeared over a neighboring cliff. This trifling matter disposed of, Bowie gave the young gentleman of Natchez two-thirds of the contents of the hat, and kept the remainder as spoils of war. With tears in his eyes the young gentleman swore never to touch another card, and both he and his bride prayed that Heaven might bless their benefactor.

Lincoln and the River

I. Loading Hogs [1]

While [Lincoln was] a laboring man, Lincoln, Hanks & Johnston on one occasion contracted to build a boat on Sangamon River, at Sangamon Town, about seven miles northwest of Springfield. For this work they were to receive twelve dollars a month each. When the boat was finished (and every plank of it was sawed by hand with a whip-saw), it was launched on the Sangamon, and floated to a point below New Salem, in Menard

---

[1] From *Anecdotes of Abraham Lincoln and Lincoln's Stories,* including Early Life Stories, Professional Life Stories, White House Stories, War Stories, Miscellaneous Stories, edited by J. B. McClure, pp. 23–24. Entered . . . 1879, by J. B. McClure and R. S. Rhodes. Chicago: Rhodes & McClure.

(then Sangamon) County, where a drove of hogs was to be taken on board. At this time, the hogs of the region ran wild, as they do now in portions of the border states. Some of them were savage, and all, after the manner of swine, were difficult to manage. They had, however, been gathered and penned, but not an inch could they be made to move toward the boat. All the ordinary resources were exhausted in the attempts to get them on board. There was but one alternative, and this Abraham adopted. He actually carried them on board, one by one. His long arms and great strength enabled him to grasp them as in a vise, and to transfer them rapidly from the shore to the boat. They then took the boat to New Orleans, according to contract.

II. Piloting A Flatboat Over A Mill Dam [2]

Governor Yates of Illinois, in a speech at Springfield, quoted one of Mr. Lincoln's early friends—W. T. Greene—as having said that the first time he ever saw Mr. Lincoln, he was in the Sangamon River with his trousers rolled up five feet, more or less, trying to pilot a flatboat over a mill dam. The boat was so full of water that it was hard to manage. Lincoln got the prow over, and then, instead of waiting to bail the water out, bored a hole through the projecting part and let it run out; affording a forcible illustration of the ready ingenuity of the future President in the quick invention of moral expedients.

III. At A New Orleans Slave Auction [3]

In New Orleans, for the first time [on his flatboat trip], Lincoln beheld the true horrors of human slavery. No doubt, as one of his companions has said, "slavery ran the iron into him then and there."

One morning in their rambles over the city the trio passed a slave auction. A vigorous and comely mulatto girl was being sold. She underwent a thorough examination at the hands of the bidders: they pinched her flesh and made her trot up and down the room like a horse, to show how she moved and in order, as the auctioneer said, that "bidders might satisfy themselves" whether the article they were offering to buy was sound or not.

The whole thing was so revolting that Lincoln moved away from the scene with a deep feeling of "unconquerable hate." Bidding his companions follow him, he said, "Boys, let's get away from this. If ever I get a chance to hit that thing, I'll hit it hard!"

IV. Young Lincoln And The Ferryman [4]

One of the picturesque figures of early steamboat days on the Ohio was Abraham Lincoln, who, in 1827, lived near Posey's Landing, Indiana. At

---

[2] *Ibid.*, p. 34.

[3] As told by John Hanks. From *Lincoln Talks*, A Biography in Anecdote, Collected, Collated, and Edited by Emanuel Hertz, p. 15. Copyright, 1939, by the Viking Press, Inc. New York.

[4] From *The Romance of the Rivers*, by John T. Faris, pp. 163–164. Copyright, 1927, by Harper & Brothers. New York and London.

that time a ferry was operated across the river by John T. Dill, who had a license from the State of Kentucky, which has jurisdiction over the river to low-water mark on the Ohio bank. Young Lincoln owned a rowboat, which he sometimes used in taking passengers out to a passing steamer.

William E. Barton, in his *Life of Abraham Lincoln*, tells an interesting story of a contest between the two ferrymen:

One day, when Lincoln was in his boat, Dill hailed him from the Kentucky side, and Lincoln rowed to the shore; when he was seized by Dill and his brother, the brother having hidden till Lincoln was within reach. They accused him of taking their business away from them, and threatened to duck him in the river. Perhaps they felt some misgivings as to whether even the two of them were safe in an undertaking of this character. For whatever reason, they offered to modify the plan if Lincoln would go with them to the house of a magistrate and have the matter settled according to law. Lincoln readily consented, and the three went together to the home of Squire Samuel Pate, only a few hundred yards away. There the Dills entered complaint, and swore out a warrant. This was issued and served upon the defendant, present in court, and the case of the Commonwealth of Kentucky against Abraham Lincoln was called. Both parties owned themselves ready for trial. The complaining witnesses introduced their evidence. The defendant had transported passengers from the Indiana shore to steamboats on the Ohio River, though having no license to operate a ferry on that stream. The defendant admitted the facts as alleged, but denied having violated the statute or having infringed upon the rights of the authorized ferrymen. The ferry license authorized John T. Dill to carry passengers across the Ohio River, and gave him the exclusive right of doing this for pay. But it did not forbid others than the ferrymen to transport passengers to the middle of the stream.

Of course, Lincoln won the case and was acquitted.

V. The Lawyer Who Resembled A Steamboat [5]

In one lawsuit Lincoln was opposed by a lawyer who was a glib court room orator but a shallow thinker given to reckless and irresponsible statements.

"My friend on the other side," Lincoln said, "is all right, or would be all right if it were not for a physico-mental peculiarity which I am about to explain.

"His habit—of which you have witnessed a very painful specimen in his argument to you in this case—of reckless assertion without grounds need not be imputed to him as a moral fault or blemish. He can't help it. The oratory of the gentleman completely suspends all action of his mind.

"I never knew of but one thing which compared with my friend in this particular. That was a steamboat. Back in the days when I performed my part as a keelboatman, I made the acquaintance of a trifling little steamboat which used to bustle and puff and wheeze about in the Sangamon

---

[5] As told by Senator Daniel W. Voorhees. From *Lincoln Talks*, A Biography in Anecdote, Collected, Collated, and Edited by Emanuel Hertz, p. 44. Copyright, 1939, by the Viking Press, Inc. New York.

River. It had a five-foot boiler and a seven-foot whistle, and every time it whistled the boat stopped."

VI. THE LOST APPLE [6]

On a late occasion when the White House was open to the public, a farmer from one of the border counties in Virginia told the President that the Union soldiers, in passing his farm, had helped themselves not only to hay, but his horse, and he hoped the President would urge the proper officer to consider his claim immediately.

"Why, my dear sir," replied Lincoln, blandly, "I couldn't think of such a thing. If I consider individual cases, I should find work enough for twenty Presidents."

Bowie urged his needs persistently; Mr. Lincoln declined good-naturedly.

"But," said the persevering sufferer, "couldn't you just give me a line to Colonel ———— about it? Just one line?"

"Ha, ha, ha!" responded the amiable Old Abe, shaking himself fervently and crossing his legs the other way, "that reminds me of old Jack Chase, out in Illinois."

At this the crowd huddled forward to listen:

"You've seen Jack—I know him like a brother—used to be lumberman on the Illinois, and he was steady and sober, and the best raftsman on the river. It was quite a trick twenty-five years ago, to take the logs over the rapids, but he was skilful with a raft and always kept her straight to the channel. Finally a steamer was put on, and Jack—he's dead now, poor fellow!—was made captain of her. He always used to take the wheel, going through the rapids. One day, when the boat was plunging and wallowing along the boiling current and Jack's utmost vigilance was being exercised to keep her in the narrow channel, a boy pulled his coat-tail and hailed him with: 'Say, Mister Captain! I wish you would just stop your boat a minute—I've lost my apple overboard!'"

Uncle Abe

I. UNCLE ABE AS A PILOT [1]

The captain of one of the Mississippi River steamers one morning, while his boat was lying at her moorings at New Orleans, waiting for the tardy

[6] From *The Picket Line and Camp Fire Stories,* A Collection of War Anecdotes, Both Grave and Gay, Illustrative of the Trials and Triumphs of Soldier Life; with a Thousand-and-One Humorous Stories, told of and by Abraham Lincoln, together with a Full Collection of Northern and Southern War Songs, by a Member of the G.A.R., "Old Abe's Jokes, Fresh from Abraham's Bosom," pp. 77–78. New York: Hurst & Co., Publishers. [N.d.]

[1] From *Lincolniana;* or The Humors of Uncle Abe, Second Joe Miller, by Andrew Adderup, Springfield, Ill., pp. 68–69. Entered . . . 1864, by J. F. Feeks. New York.

pilot, who, it appears, was a rather uncertain sort of fellow, saw a tall, gaunt Sucker make his appearance before the captain's office, and sing out—

"Hello, cap'n! you don't want a pilot nor nothin' about this 'ere craft, do ye?"

"How do you know I don't?" responded the captain.

"Oh, you don't understand; I axed you s'posin' you did?"

"Then, supposing I do, what of it?"

"Well," said Uncle Abe, for it was he, "I reckon I know suthin' about that 'ere sort o' business, provided you wanted a feller of jest about my size."

The captain gave him a scrutinizing glance, and with an expression of countenance which seemed to say, "I should pity the steamer that you piloted," asked—

"Are you acquainted with the river, and do you know where the snags are?"

"Well, ye-as," responded Uncle Abe rather hesitantly, "I'm pretty well acquainted with the river, but the snags, I don't know exactly so much about them."

"Don't know about the snags?" exclaimed the captain, contemptuously, "don't know about the snags! You'd make a pretty pilot!"

At this Uncle Abe's countenance assumed anything but an angelic expression, and with a darkened brow and a fiercely flashing eye, he drew himself up to his full height, and indignantly roared back in a voice of thunder:

"What do I want to know where the snags are for, old sea-hoss? I know where they ain't, and there's where I do my sailing!"

It is sufficient to know that Uncle Abe was promptly engaged, and that the captain takes pleasure in saying that he proved himself one of the best pilots on the river.

(Wonder if Uncle Abe has forgotten how to sail in clear water?—A.A.)

II. UNCLE ABE GOES INTO PARTNERSHIP [2]

In the days when Uncle Abe plied the flatboat business on the Wabash and Sangamon, he made it a practice to troll for catfish and dispose of them to the planters in Mississippi when passing their plantations. This brought him quite a revenue, which was always expended for "forty-rod" whisky, or the fish were traded off direct for that fluid chain lightning. Once while passing the plantation of Mr. Percy he was bound to have some forty-rod, and went ashore with a fine lot of fish. A large party were assembled at the mansion of the aristocratic Percy when Julius Caesar informed him that Uncle Abe was below with some very fine fish. "Well," said Percy, "give him his forty-rod as usual—and let him go." "But, sah, he won't take it this time," said the slave. "He wants a hundred lashes on de bare back, well laid on, massa."

_____
[2] _Ibid._, p. 83.

Uncle Abe insisted to the surprise of every one on this strange price for his fish, and Mr. Percy, to humor him, complied, directing the overseer to cut him gently. When Uncle Abe had received the fiftieth lash, he cried, "Hold! I have got a partner in this business, to whom I have engaged to give half of whatever I should get for the fish—this overseer would not admit me only on that condition." Of course, the overseer had his share well paid and Abe got his forty-rod as usual, with something added.

Lincoln and the Rock Island Bridge Case

The year 1853 is important in railroad history in the Middle West, as it marks the beginning of the first of the railway bridges to span the Mississippi River. The conquest of the Far West was begun. This pioneer bridge when completed spanned the Father of Waters from Rock Island, Illinois, to Davenport, Iowa. At this point in the stream an island out in the channel—"Rock Island"—avoided the necessity of a straight span clear across.

As the Rock Island Company itself has explained: "The construction really involved three portions—a bridge across the narrow arm of the river between the Illinois shore and the Island; a line of tracks across Rock Island; and a long bridge between the island and the Iowa shore. The channel of the river passed very close to the west side of the island, and down the middle of this channel ran the boundary line between the two states."

The proposed bridge, on what is now a part of the main line of the Chicago, Rock Island and Pacific Railway, encountered bitter opposition. The very idea of the Mississippi being "obstructed" by a bridge of any sort aroused the antagonism of powerful river interests. Leading river towns —St. Louis in particular—saw that with such innovations they ran the risk of losing the commercial advantages, amounting almost to a monopoly, which they had hitherto enjoyed. The rivermen on their part foresaw in the coming of the railroads a formidable rival in the field of transportation. The building of bridges across "their" river was added fuel to the flame. They loudly insisted that such structures would interfere with the free transit of the stream.

This argument, so familiar to latter-day railroad people, was then new and brought many influential adherents into the camp of the opposition. Legal obstacles were put in the way of the Rock Island bridge, but the company was able to set them aside, and the bridge was built.

The opposition, however, did not end here; it only bided its time to make a test case of the whole matter. This soon came. In May, 1856, a steamboat, the *Effie Afton,* struck one of the piers of the bridge and was wrecked and totally destroyed by fire. The lawsuit which resulted prom-

---

From *Lincoln and the Railroads,* by John W. Starr, Jr., pp. 92–93, 97, 104–113, 115–116. Copyright, 1927, by Dodd, Mead and Company, Inc. New York.

ised to be one of the most important in the history of railroading up to that time. The owners of the steamboat instituted a damage suit against the company; while the latter maintained that the so-called accident was intentional. Incidentally, a portion of the bridge was burned.

This case with all its interesting legal angles derives further importance from the fact that our Sangamon County lawyer was retained for the railroad. It reveals Lincoln in the plentitude of his powers, holding his own against the best legal talent of that section. The time was but a few years before he became a national figure in politics.

* * * * *

The best legal talent available was engaged by both sides of the case. H. M. Mead, of Peoria, T. D. Lincoln, of Cincinnati, and Corydon Beckwith, of Chicago, represented the prosecution. Norman B. Judd, Abraham Lincoln, and Joseph Knox acted as counsel for the defense.

The trial opened on September 8 with the contending forces well primed. On account of its far-reaching influence Chicago was filled with people from far and near, interested in the proceedings.

* * * * *

On the 22nd, Abraham Lincoln commenced his argument before the jury.

* * * * *

Judge Blodgett, of Chicago, has left . . . detailed recollections of his impressions. "The two points relied upon by the opponents of the bridge," he says, "were: First, that the river was the great waterway for the commerce of the valley, and could not legally be obstructed by a bridge. Second, that this particular bridge was so located with reference to the channel of the river at that point as to make it a peril to all water craft navigating the river and an unnecessary obstruction to navigation.

"The first proposition had not at that time been directly passed upon by the Supreme Court of the United States, although the Wheeling Bridge case involved the question; but the court had evaded a decision upon it, by holding that the Wheeling Bridge was so low as to be an unnecessary obstruction to the use of the river by steamboats. The discussion of the first proposition on the part of the bridge company devolved mainly upon Abraham Lincoln.

"I listened with much interest to his argument on this point, and while I was not impressed by it as a specially eloquent effort (as the word eloquent is generally understood), I have always considered it as one of the ablest efforts I ever heard from Mr. Lincoln at the Bar. His illustrations were apt and forcible, his statements clear and logical, and his reasons in favor of the policy (and necessarily the right) to bridge the river, and thereby encourage the settlement and building up of the vast area of fertile country to the west of it, were broad and statesmanlike.

"The pith of his argument was in his statement that *one man had as good a right to cross a river as another had to sail up or down it;* that these were equal and mutual rights which must be exercised so as not to interfere with each other, like the right to cross a street or highway and the right to pass along it. From this undeniable right to cross the river he then proceeded to discuss the means for crossing. Must it always be by canoe or ferryboat? Must the products of all the boundless fertile country lying west of the river for all time be compelled to stop on its western bank, be unloaded from the cars and loaded upon a boat, and after the transit across the river, be reloaded into cars on the other side, to continue their journey east? In this connection he drew a vivid picture of the future of the great West lying beyond the river, and argued that the necessities of commerce demanded that the bridges across the river be a conceded right, which the steamboat interests ought not to be allowed to successfully resist, and thereby stay the progress of development and civilization in the region to the west.

"While I cannot recall a word or sentence of the argument, I well remember its effect on all who listened to it, and the decision of the court fully sustained the right to bridge, so long as it did not unnecessarily obstruct navigation."

Abraham Lincoln's argument lasted two days. At the end of the first day, as Joseph Knox, one of the associate counsel, sat down at the dinner table of Judd at whose home he was being entertained, he became greatly excited.

"Lincoln has lost the case for us," he said. "The admissions he made in regard to the currents in the Mississippi at Rock Island and Moline will convince the court that a bridge at that point will always be a serious and constant detriment to navigation on the river."

But Judd was not disturbed. He replied that Lincoln's admissions in regard to the currents were facts that could not be denied. They only proved that the bridge should have been built at a different angle to the stream, and that a bridge so built could not injure the river as a navigable stream.

The argument of Lincoln as preserved to us by [Robert R.] Hitt is worth noting in detail.[1] From a careful perusal of it, we observe that the points as recalled by Judge Blodgett were brought out in the first part of his plea, while the latter was devoted to more complicated matters: the river currents, their velocity, the position of the piers, engineering problems of river navigation, and the like, all being handled with mathematical precision.

Lincoln started in by saying that it was not his purpose to assail anybody, but that he expected to grow earnest as he proceeded.

"There is some conflict of testimony in the case, but one quarter of

---

[1] The stenographic report by Robert R. Hitt appeared in the *Chicago Daily News* for September 24, 1857.

such a number of witnesses seldom agree, and even if all were on one side, some discrepancy might be expected. We are to try to reconcile them and to believe that they are not intentionally erroneous as long as we can," he went on.

He said that he had no prejudice against the steamboats or steamboat-men, nor against St. Louis. Their feelings were only natural. "But," he continued, "there is a travel from east to west whose demands are not less than that of those of the river. It is growing larger and larger, building up new countries with a rapidity never before seen in the history of the world. This current of travel has its rights as well as that of north and south. If the river had not the advantage in priority and legislation, we could enter into free competition with it and we could surpass it."

It was at this point that he dilated upon the growing West, picturing it in glowing colors, as recalled by Blodgett.

"This particular railroad line," he went on, "has a great importance and the statement of its business during a little less than a year shows this importance. It is in evidence that from September 8th, 1856, to August 8th, 1857, 12,586 freight cars and 74,179 passengers passed over this bridge. Navigation was closed four days short of four months last year, and during this time while the river was of no use this road and bridge were valuable. There is, too, a considerable portion of time when floating or thin ice makes the river useless, while the bridge is as useful as ever. This shows that this bridge must be treated with respect in this court, and is not to be kicked about with contempt. . . . The proper mode for all parties in this affair is to 'live and let live,' and then we will find a cessation of this trouble about the bridge.

"What mood were the steamboat men in when this bridge was burned? Why, there was a shouting and ringing of bells and whistling on all the boats as it fell. It was a jubilee, a greater celebration than follows an exciting election."

He then referred rather sarcastically to the decrease in the number of accidents occurring.

"From April 19th, 1856, to May 6th—seventeen days—there were twenty accidents, and all the time since then there have been but twenty hits, including seven accidents, so that the dangers of this place are tapering off and as the boatmen get cool, the accidents get less. We may soon expect if this ratio is kept up that there will be no accidents at all."

Lincoln then discussed the alleged difference between a "float" and a "boat," and the angular position of the piers, but said that he would not take up the question, "What is a material obstruction?" as he was willing to trust Judge McLean's instructions on that technical point.

"What is reasonable skill and care?" was his next point. "This is a thing of which the jury are to judge. I differ from the other side when it says that they are bound to exercise no more than was taken before the building of the bridge. If we are allowed by the Legislature to build the bridge which will require them to do more than before when a pilot comes along, it is unreasonable for him to dash on heedless of this structure which has been legally put there. The *Afton* came there on the 5th, and lay at Rock Island until next morning. When a boat lies up the pilot has a holiday, and would not any of these jurors have then gone around the bridge and gotten acquainted with the place? Pilot Parker has shown here that he does not understand the draw. I heard him say that the fall from the head to the foot of the pier was four feet; he needs information. He could have gone there that day and seen there was no such fall. He should have discarded passion and the chances are that he would have had no disaster at all. He was bound to make himself acquainted with the case.

"McCammon says that the current and the swell coming from the long pier drove her against the long pier. In other words, drove her toward the very pier from which the current came. It is an absurdity, an impossibility. The only recollection I can find for this contradiction is in a current which White says strikes out from the long pier and then like a ram's horn turns back, and this might have acted somehow in this manner."

He then went into a lengthy discussion of the currents of the stream, their velocity, the average speed of the destroyed boat, the absence of cross currents.

"Next I shall show," he said, "that she struck first the short pier, then the long pier, then the short one again, and there she stopped."

The testimony of eighteen witnesses was then cited.

"My next proposition is that after she struck the short and long pier and before she got back to the short pier, the boat got right with her bow up."

At this point court adjourned until the following day.

On the fourteenth day of the trial, it was observed that Abraham Lincoln had a model of a boat in the court room. After he had resumed his argument it was seen just why he had that model, when he used it in explaining to the jury that the "splash door" on such a boat was just behind the wheel. This was necessary for their understanding of his contentions.

"The boat struck," he said, "on the lower shoulder of the short pier as she swung around in the splash door, then as she went on around she struck the point or end of the pier where she rested.

"Her engineers say," he went on, "that the starboard wheel was then rushing around rapidly. Then the boat must have struck the upper point of the pier so far back as not to disturb the wheel. It is forty feet from the stern of the *Afton* to the splash door, and thus it appears that she had but forty feet to go to clear the pier. How was it that the *Afton*, with all her power, flanked over from the channel to the short pier without moving one foot ahead? Suppose she was in the middle of the draw, her wheel would have been thirty-one feet from the short pier. The reason she went over thus is her starboard wheel was not working. I shall try to establish the fact that the wheel was not running and that after she struck she went ahead strong on this same wheel. Upon the last point the witnesses agree that the starboard wheel was running after she struck, and no witnesses say that it was running while she was out in the draw flanking over."

He then cited various witnesses proving that the starboard wheel was not working while the *Afton* was out in the stream, and that this was not unknown to the captain of the craft.

"The fact is undisputed," he stated, "that she did not move one inch ahead while she was moving this thirty-one feet sideways. There is evidence proving that the current there is only five miles an hour, and the only explanation is that her power was not all used—that only one wheel was working. The pilot says he ordered the engineers to back her up. The engineers differ from him and said they kept one going ahead. The bow was so swung that the current pressed it over; the pilot pressed the stern over with the rudder, though not so fast but that the bow gained on it and only one wheel being in motion the boat nearly stood still so far as motion up and down is concerned, and thus she was thrown upon the pier.

"The *Afton* came into the draw, after she had just passed the *Carson*, and as the *Carson* no doubt kept the true course, the *Afton* going around her got out of the proper way, got across the current into the eddy which is west of a straight line drawn from the long pier, was compelled to resort to these changes of wheels which she did not do with sufficient adroitness to save her.

"Was it not her own fault that she entered wrong, so far wrong that she never got right? Is the defense to blame for that?"

Then he indulged in a little irony. "For several days," he said, "we were entertained with depositions about boats 'smelling a bar.' Why did the *Afton* then, after she had come up smelling so close to the long pier, sheer off so strangely? When she got to the center of the very nose she was smelling, she seemed suddenly to have lost her sense of smell and to have flanked over to the short pier.

"The plaintiffs have to establish," he said in closing, "that the bridge is a material obstruction and that they have managed their boat with reasonable care and skill. As to the last point, high winds have nothing to do with it, for it was not a windy day. They must show due skill and care. Difficulties going down stream will not do, for they were going up stream. Difficulties with barges in tow have nothing to do with the accident, for they had no barge."

With this Lincoln rested his case, saying that he had much more to say and many things yet to suggest to the jury, but would close to save time.

The jury failed to agree and was discharged.

Carrying the case to a conclusion, we learn that it was not until 1862 that it was finally settled by the Supreme Court of the United States, permitting the bridge to remain and settling the question for all time.

* * * * *

In a lengthy argument filed within recent years by prominent attorneys, in a case in chancery, in Illinois, a significant reference is made to the important bearing which the Rock Island Bridge case exercised upon later legislation. The report in part:

The same bridge was the subject of the unsuccessful suit to abate, brought in the Iowa District in 1858, and in which the abatement order by the United States District Court of Iowa was reversed, and the bill dismissed by the United States Supreme Court. The case is valuable as marking the evolution of the Lincoln doctrine that a man has as good right to go across a river as another has to go up or down the river, that the two rights are mutual, that the existence of a bridge which does not prevent or unreasonably obstruct navigation is not inconsistent with the navigable character of the stream. Mr. Lincoln exerted a powerful influence upon the development of the transportation system of the continent. He is the author of the American doctrine of bridges.

Timber Cruiser

A good cruiser, the old saying ran, was born to the trade.

Swan Helstrom was a good one. In fact he was famous. He cruised timber through the wildest and roughest country of the North, from the Tomahawk River all the way up Keweenaw Peninsula in Lake Superior.

Picture him with his blond hair and his blue eyes, six-feet-three on his snowshoes or in his moccasins, traveling over rough country with a hundred pounds of supplies and equipment on his back. He is fifty miles from the nearest settlement and he'll be many miles farther before he swings around south again. Instinctively he finds his way through country no white man has ever seen before, and all the time his mind is busy: locating his range by a pocket compass, counting his paces, sweeping the forest with his keen blue eyes, sorting out pine from the rest of the timber, studying the soil to judge what lies out of sight (white pine in sandy soil, jack pine and Norway pine in heavier soil), his memory recording this country like a camera. At the end of the day, while his kettle boils on the fire, he jots down his notes: the terrain he has been over, what running water he has found, the various stands of timber in that section, and to the thousand board feet what the pine tracts will produce. A day's work. And there will be many days passing through swamp and along pine-shadowed rivers before he changes his

From *Upper Mississippi,* A Wilderness Saga, by Walter Havighurst, pp. 159–161. Copyright, 1937, by Walter Havighurst. *The Rivers of America,* editor, Constance Lindsay Skinner, assistant editor, Elizabeth L. Gilman. New York & Toronto: Farrar & Rinehart, Inc.

campfire for a supper table. Alert, resourceful, intuitive, he knows the forest like a Chippewa and he carries whole counties in his mind. Whole counties without a footprint in them, except his own.

This man with the slow smile and gentle singsong voice, like wind and like water, had the most skilled trade in all the North.

As logging grew into its epic proportions, every company sent cruisers into new country to bring back reports of potential lumber production. Behind the cruiser came the big camps, the tote roads, the spring river choked with a billion feet of pine, the whine and snarl of the mills. He was a forerunner of the whole vast enterprise.

Yet the cruiser was a man of the forest who lived off the country for whole seasons at a stretch. Between cruising assignments he turned back instinctively to the woods. A natural hunter, he might turn professional for a season, sledding great loads of deer, elk, bear, wolves, wildcats to the railroads to be shipped to the Chicago game markets. Einer Brandt, a veteran Norwegian cruiser in Pierce County along the Mississippi, once killed ninety-six deer and three elk between Thanksgiving and Christmas. One day in the following spring he shot a bear and three cubs and caught the fourth cub alive. He carried all five of them seven miles back to town, the live one inside his shirt. When he got there he said the live one gave him more trouble than all the others put together.

Timber cruising attracted hardy men who were not afraid of the loneliness of remote country. There were noted Irish and French-Canadian cruisers, and there were occasional halfbreeds who chose to follow this lonely and demanding life. But inevitably many of the cruisers were Norse woodsmen. In the mind of this race was a kinship with the wilderness. They were men of powerful frame, and they were woodsmen at heart. They were at home in a tamarack swamp or under the moan of pine boughs. For they were an elemental people, hardy and resourceful, meditative and self-contained. They marked the way up hidden rivers, into the gloom of ancient forests.

Pierre Pauquette, "Wisconsin Samson"

I [1]

Pierre Pauquette lived opposite Fort Winnebago on what was called the Agency Hill. He was a half-breed Winnebago Indian and French trader, who kept fifteen or twenty yoke of oxen to haul goods across the [Fox-Wisconsin] portage. He was born at St. Louis, Missouri, in 1876, and engaged in the Indian trade at an early day. He was a fine specimen of manhood—six feet, two inches in height, large, and very heavy. He was

---

[1] From *Old Forts and Real Folks*, by Susan Burdick Davis, pp. 250–252. Copyright, 1939, by Susan Burdick Davis. [Madison, Wisconsin] Published by Zoe Bayliss and Susan Davis.

handsome and good natured. His flesh was hard and is said to have been more like bone than like muscle. His thigh was as large around as an ordinary person's waist. He was extraordinarily strong. He could pick up a barrel of pork and throw it into a wagon as easily as a ten gallon keg. He once lifted off the ground a cask with eight hundred pounds of white lead in it. At one time, the story is told that, as he was hauling a boat across the portage with ox teams, one of the oxen gave out and would not pull. Pauquette took off the bow, pulled the ox to one side, and taking hold of the yoke, pulled beside the other ox. Another time Pauquette came upon some men on the river bank lifting and swinging heavy sledges—making sort of a game of it. Pauquette joined them and at once made for the heaviest hammer of all. The other men warned him not to try it, saying that that hammer or sledge was much too heavy for any of them. With a trial swing or two, Pauquette gave it a mighty heave, and into the river it flew, never to be seen again. Many other feats of his strength were related.

In spite of his strength, he was considered of a mild disposition. He could neither read nor write, but spoke Winnebago, English, and French. He had a fine sense of honor. All who knew him trusted him completely.

After traveling over much of the Northwest, Pauquette had settled at the portage for the purpose of trading with the Indians. They, too, trusted him and took his advice always. He was the only competent Winnebago interpreter in the country. In his trade with the Indians he always kept their accounts in his head. You would have thought that during the long winter he would have forgotten or become confused in regard to the many different items and accounts. When the Indians returned in the spring, however, he could tell at once just how much each one owed him. The Indians took his word and apparently were always satisfied with his accounts and bargains.

* * * * *

During one of the Indian uprisings, a company of Illinois rangers, it was said, were camped on the bank of the Wisconsin River. Pauquette happened to be walking past the camp and stopped to look at the soldiers. One of them, a large man, kicked a small dog that was following Pauquette, who at once said:

"Don't kick that dog; he is mine."

"I'll kick you, if you say too much," replied the soldier. "Who are you, anyway?"

"My name is Pauquette."

"Oh," said the man. "You are the very fellow I want to see. I have heard of you and came up here on purpose to lick you."

Thereupon the fellow pitched into Pauquette, who struck him but once, knocking him down. Then Pauquette picked the soldier up by the throat and shook him like an aspen leaf, asking him again and again if he called himself a man.

"I was a man where I came from, but I see I ain't here," was the reply.

II [2]

Andrew Jackson Turner contended that "the name of Pierre Pauquette was probably more frequently on the tongues of men than that of any other man in Wisconsin." When he was killed in a dispute with the Indian, "Iron Walker," they told throughout the Northwest of his last words, spoken as he bared his chest to the revolver barrel: "Shoot, and see a brave man die!" They recalled and told again the Pauquette stories. Satterlee Clark, once the sutler at Fort Winnebago, and the giant's intimate friend, had seen Pauquette swing over his head a pile-driver weighing more than two thousand pounds. Clark had cracked hickory nuts with a sledge hammer on the muscles of Pauquette's naked arms. . . .

Whisky Jack Yarns

Whisky Jack was a mythical character of the Wisconsin River in the years before the coming of the railroads, when pine logs were sawed into lumber at sawmills in towns on the upper reaches of the river and floated down the stream. The lumber was made up into rafts which were rowed with large sweep oars to St. Louis and other towns on the Mississippi River. Each raft consisted of a number of sections called "cribs." A certain number of cribs fastened together made a "rapids piece" and a number of these a raft.

Lumber raft navigation was a hard and dangerous employment. There were rapids to be run, river crossings to be made, and snags and sandbars to be encountered. Rafts had to be taken apart and put together again. The raft crew was often in the water for hours at a time. Each raft was in charge of a pilot and carried a cook and helper to prepare meals for the crew. At night the raft was made fast by ropes to the river bank. After supper the men amused themselves by singing river songs and ballads and telling stories. The Whisky Jack yarns had their origin in the adventures of particularly strong and daring pilots and raftsmen. Whisky Jack was their Paul Bunyan.

I. WHISKY JACK AND HIS CREW

Whisky Jack was famous for his great feats of strength. He was over seven feet tall and a Samson in power. In a brawl he was never bested by

[2] From *Early Wisconsin through the Comic Looking Glass,* edited by Jonathan W. Curvin, pp. 5–6. Madison, Wisconsin: The Wisconsin Idea Theatre and the Badger State Folklore Society. 1951.

From *Whisky Jack Yarns,* Short Tales of the Old Time Lumber Raftsmen of the Wisconsin River and Their Mythical Hero, Raft and River Bank Tales, [compiled by Charles E. Brown], pp. 1–2, 8. Madison, Wisconsin: Charles E. Brown, Wisconsin Folklore Society. 1940.

any man on the river or on its banks. He licked all of the other fighting raft pilots, all of the town bullies, and all of the wild Indians along both the Wisconsin and Mississippi Rivers. He and his crew were heavy drinkers and with an unbounded thirst for liquor, so that when word reached them that Whisky Jack and his crew were coming down stream, all of the taverns in the river towns laid in extra quantities of "forty-rod" and "tanglefoot" for their particular benefit.

If there was a wedding or other festivity afoot in any river hamlet, when this famous pilot and his men floated down river, Whisky Jack would tie up his "sticks" at the bank and never loose a rope or move a sweep oar until the celebration ended. This merrymaking often lasted several days, but the big pilot made up for lost time by rigging a sail on the raft and taking every possible shortcut over islands, sandbars, and other obstructions. With such maneuvers as these his raft would often reach Alton or St. Louis a week or several weeks ahead of schedule. In seasons of low water, if his raft ran aground on a sandbar, Whisky Jack thought nothing at all of picking up the raft, crib by crib, and carrying it into the deeper water beyond. When the raft progress was too slow to suit him he would sometimes jump into the water and himself tow it for a considerable distance.

II. The Bundle of Lath

On one occasion Whisky Jack's raft was tied to the bank at Richland City, a once thriving Wisconsin River town, but now off the map or largely in the river bed. The crew were mighty thirsty, but they had no money with which to buy drinks. This was a serious dilemma. Finally, one of the men took a bundle of lath from the raft and walked to the tavern. The tavernkeeper was willing to trade drinks for the lath. He told the raftsman to place the bundle outside the rear door of the tavern. When the man left by this door he picked up the lath and handed it to another member of the crew who was coming up. This man also traded the lath for drinks, leaving the bundle outside the door for another raftsman when he departed. This process was repeated again and again until every member of the raft crew had been served with drinks. When all had gone the tavernkeeper looked out of the rear door and was greatly disappointed to find but one bundle of lath instead of the several dozen bundles he expected to see there.

III. The Raft Cook

Cooking on the lumber rafts was done under some difficulties. The cookstove was mounted in a sand-box placed on one of the cribs near the middle of the raft. On windy days a rough screen shelter was erected to protect the cook and his cooking. The raft crew ate their meals from a rough board table, near by. The cooking utensils were a frying pan, coffee pot, and a few pots and kettles. The tableware consisted of tin cups, plates, knives, and forks.

Big John Marshall was the cook on one of Whisky Jack's rafts. He was a good enough lumberjack cook, but one day the crew complained about the meals. They were all pretty much the same, day after day. Whisky Jack thought that the meals could be better, so he talked with Big John and asked him whether he had ever had or seen a cook book. And the cook said, "I got one of them cookery books once but I never could do anything with it. It was just of no use to me." "Was it too fancy for you?" asked Jack. "That was it," said Big John, "every one of the recipes began the same way, 'Take a Clean Dish.' And that settled me."

Big John dished up a lot of hash. It was good, and one of the crew asked him if he had a regular recipe for making it. "No," said the cook, "it just accumulates."

IV. SIGNING HIS NAME

Whisky Jack was no scholar. He didn't care to read, and he could not write. When he signed the payroll or any other document at the sawmill or lumber yard offices, he signed with a big "X" instead of his name. He did this for a long time. But one day he signed with an "X X" instead of just an "X." The bookkeeper wondered at this and asked him why he signed with two "X's" instead of just one. And Whisky Jack explained to him that he and a milliner lady in one of the river towns had just got "spliced," and he thought that now, being a married man, he ought to change his name. . . .

The Hunting and Fishing Adventures of Bob Hooter

I. COON HUNT

. . . Bob Hooter, a great-grandson of Mike Hooter and legendary Delta character, . . . is naturally an expert in the difficult art of coon hunting. Nowadays just finding one somewhere in a slough or swamp is a satisfactory conclusion for most hunts, but Bob and the three coon dogs he always keeps are never content with anything less than a coon den.

One night he was walking along a road near his house with two companions, when two of the dogs raced past on the heels of a fleeing coon. Bob and his friends quickly grabbed some tree limbs that would serve as clubs and followed up the chase. They found the dogs barking at the foot of a large tree on the edge of a slough. A hole at the bottom of the old oak was the only entrance and exit to what they agreed was a large den.

Bob rapped on the trunk with his club several times, and that started a stampede of the trapped coons. They poured out in a steady stream, and Bob and his friends lined up at the entrance and proceeded to give each

From *The Yazoo River,* by Frank E. Smith, pp. 231–239. Copyright, 1954, by Frank E. Smith. *The Rivers of America,* edited by Carl Carmer. New York & Toronto: Rinehart & Company, Inc.

one a healthy lick as it emerged. The coons continued to come out for a solid hour, to make a total that was estimated variously from one to five hundred.

When the last one had come forth, the hunters built a fire to check on the results of their endeavors.

"We didn't kill a coon," Bob says, "but we did beat off four hundred pounds of fur."

II. THE RATTLESNAKE-BIT HOE HANDLE

No man has a healthier respect for rattlesnakes than Bob. One day he was making one of the very infrequent inspection tours of his farm when he encountered a rattlesnake pilot coiled at the edge of a turnrow. He ran back quickly and grabbed a hoe leaning against the side of tenant's house.

The regular hoe handle had been broken and in its place was a sassafras sapling. Bob took the makeshift hoe and swung at the snake. But the rattler had already begun to strike, and Bob missed him. The snake sunk its fangs into the handle, and, Bob concludes the story, "That handle swelled up so big that we split it up and made four fence posts."

III. BATTLING BOLL WEEVIL

Bob was telling the boys down at the barbershop why he had laid by his cotton crop so early in the summer.

"One night I heard a big noise in my back yard and got up to see what it was all about. A big boll weevil had a little one across the wood block and was giving it a beating with an ax handle because it couldn't strip more than one row of cotton at a time. I figgered then and there that I'd better hand it all over to them, or they might take it out on me."

IV. TURKEY SHOOT

There are few chances for turkey shoots in the Delta any more, but it hasn't been many years since a man could get a turkey dinner by spending a few minutes in the nearest patch of woods.

Bob and a friend were on a turkey hunt one morning when one of his near perfect calls pulled one strutting gobbler out into the open. Bob and his friend crawled to the edge of the bush that screened them from view. The cautious bird came as far as a log twenty yards away and stuck up its head.

Bob was using a rifle, and it was decided that he should take the shot, because the noise of his friend's shotgun might scare away any near-by birds. He carefully drew a bead on the gobbler's head and fired. The turkey ducked down immediately, and for a few seconds not a sound was heard. Then the head showed up again and Bob cracked down for the second time. Seconds passed, and then the head was up again—was up once more for another shot from the hunter.

The whole action was repeated nine times more, with each attempt bringing new curses from Bob over the failure of his usually perfect accuracy.

After the twelfth shot he decided to get a better look at the turkey with the charmed life. Moving slowly out to the log, he quickly peered over. Scattered over the ground on the other side were twelve gobblers, all shot in the neck!

V. THE GRATEFUL MINNOW

On a warm day Bob was fishing for perch in the middle of Round Lake. His luck had been so bad that he had to rely for his sole amusement on the quart of liquid refreshment that was part of every fishing trip. By the time half of it was gone he had become rather unsteady, and it was fortunate that half of the remaining pint was spilled into the minnow bucket.

Bob baited his hook with a fresh minnow several minutes later and dropped it listlessly over the side. The line started a wild dash out and around the boat, and a few seconds later he felt the tug of a speckled two-pounder, which he immediately pulled in. The fish had not swallowed the hook in the attempt to get the minnow, however. The pleasantly alcoholized minnow had bitten the big perch in the back of the neck and pulled him in with the assistance of the line.

In half an hour, with the assistance of several refreshing rests in the minnow bucket, the bait had dragged in the day's limit.

VI. FISH SCALES

Telling the story about the fish scales is the only way to quiet Bob. The scales came into prominence when one of Dan Taylor's annual offspring came into the world.

Dan took a notion all of a sudden to see how much his new son weighed. Bob Hooter was his nearest neighbor, so Dan went up the road to see if he had any scales. Bob was out fishing, and the only thing Mrs. Hooter could find around the house was the pair that Bob used when he weighed his fish catches. They put the baby on these scales, and it weighed thirty-seven pounds.

VII. THE POINTER

Bob had a great bird dog that was his pride and joy and the subject of endless bragging about his merits. There was some question, however, on the day the dog came to a point right on the main street of the county seat. There wasn't even a sparrow in sight, and Bob called to the dog, at first quietly, and then half mad, but still Tige made a perfect point.

Finally Bob had an idea. There was a stranger loafing in the shade across the street, and Bob approached and asked his name. The man answered, "My name is Bob White," and that explained everything.

VIII. THE BEST COON-AND-POSSUM DOG

Another one of Bob's prize dogs was a hound that he called the best coon-and-possum dog in Mississippi. All he had to do was to show the dog a board, and the dog would go off and find a possum or coon whose hide would fit the board. This saved Bob the trouble of hunting up a board to fit a hide, and he never had to worry about the quality of the possum or coon skin.

One day, though, the dog disappeared and when he had been missing for three days, Bob took to the woods himself to see if he could find any trace of the faithful animal. After hours of searching, he found the dog, so worn out and exhausted that Bob had to carry him home in his arms.

The incident puzzled Bob for a while, but he finally figured it out. His wife had left the ironing board out leaning against the back porch, and the dog saw it and went out in the woods and wore himself out trying to find a possum or coon with a hide big enough to fit the ironing board.

IX. A Fall

Speaking of coons and coon dogs, Bob tells about the one where the pack treed a coon after a long chase, but there was no way to get him out except for one of the boys in the hunting party to climb up and knock him down. In the midst of the climbing, a rotten limb gave away, and the boy fell to the ground, sustaining a broken neck.

His companions bore the boy home sadly, but the injured youth's father received the news philosophically.

"It coulda been worse," he observed. "George mighta fell on one of the dawgs."

X. Quail Dog

But on the subject of remarkable bird dogs, Bob says that one he heard of in Texas should take a few prizes. The specialty of this dog was to run a covey of quail down a prairie-dog hole, put his paw over the opening until the hunter was ready, then lift his paw just long enough for one bird at a time to fly out.

XI. The Eel and the Catfish

On a fishing trip one spring, Bob had been fishing all day in one spot before he decided to move on to a better location. The sum total of his catch up to then was a slender little eel, but even an eel tastes good when there is nothing else to eat at camp, so he tied it to a string and left it dangling in the water near the bank, planning to come back by and get it on the way in.

Coming back in the late afternoon, Bob reached down to pull in the eel, which he was going to have to use after all. The minute he took the line in his hand, his arm was nearly jerked out of its socket. Fighting hard to keep from going into the lake after the eel, he finally got a foothold and began a tug-of-war with whatever was on the other end of the line. After a twenty-minute fight, he pulled in a twenty-pound catfish. The eel was still on the line and wiggling happily!

It took a minute to figure out what had happened. The catfish had tried to swallow the eel, but the eel had other ideas about the matter. It had slipped out through the cat's gills after the big fish had taken it into its mouth, and then coiled the line around tightly enough to hook the fish with complete effectiveness.

III. STAR PERFORMANCES

When Noah Ludlow Sang "The Hunters of Kentucky"

The "benefits" of this season commenced sometime early in May, my own being about the fourth or fifth one. I do not remember the pieces acted on that occasion, but I do recollect that I did on that night something entirely out of my line of business, which created quite a sensation, and was the source of considerable annoyance to me for more than a year afterwards. It was this: A brother of mine, in the city of New York, had cut out of the New York *Mirror*, a periodical of that city, some lines that "tickled his fancy," called "The Hunters of Kentucky, or the Battle of New Orleans," written by Samuel Woodward, of New York, author of that well-known piece of poetry, entitled the "Old Oaken Bucket." Those lines above referred to my brother sent to me in a letter, which I received about a month prior to my benefit. The lines pleased me, and I thought would please the people of New Orleans; so I determined to sing them on the occasion of my benefit. The tune, to which they seemed adapted, was taken from the comic opera of "Love Laughs at Locksmiths," being Risk's song of *Miss Baily*. When the night came I found the pit, or parquette, of the theatre *crowded full* of "river men"—that is, keel-boat and flat-boat men. There were very few steamboat men. These men were easily known by their linsey-woolsey clothing and blanket coats. As soon as the comedy of the night was over, I dressed myself in a buckskin hunting shirt and leggins, which I had borrowed of a river man, and with moccasins on my feet, and an old slouched hat on my head, and a rifle on my shoulder, I presented myself before the audience. I was saluted with loud applause of hands and feet, and a prolonged whoop, or howl, such as Indians give when they are especially pleased. I sang the first verse, and these extraordinary manifestations of delight were louder and longer than before; but when I came to the following lines:—

From *Dramatic Life As I Found It:* A Record of Personal Experience; with an Account of the Rise and Progress of the Drama in the West and South, with Anecdotes and Biographical Sketches of the Principal Actors and Actresses Who Have at Times Appeared upon the Stage in the Mississippi Valley, pp. 237–238, 250–251. Entered . . . 1880, by N. M. Ludlow. St. Louis: G. I. Jones and Company.

But Jackson he was wide awake, and wasn't scared with trifles,
For well he knew what aim we take with our Kentucky rifles;
So he marched us down to "Cypress Swamp"; the ground was low and mucky;
There stood "John Bull," in martial pomp, *but here was old Kentucky.*

As I delivered the last five words, I took my old hat off my head, threw it upon the ground, and brought my rifle to the position of taking aim. At that instant came a shout and an Indian yell from the inmates of the pit and a tremendous applause from other portions of the house, the whole lasting for nearly a minute, and, as Edmund Kean told his wife, after his first great success in London, "the house rose to me!" The whole pit was standing up and shouting. I had to sing the song three times that night before they would let me off.

* * * * *

A few nights after [Mr. James H. Caldwell's] first performance in the Camp Street Theatre, an incident occurred that came near being an unpleasant one for me. The "Hunters of Kentucky" still pursued me like some evil genius. The manager requested me to sing that song, now become so popular that you could hear it sung or whistled almost any day as you passed along the principal thoroughfares of the city. The night on which I sang it, as just referred to, the theatre was crowded with people; and at the conclusion of the verse ending with the words, "There stood John Bull, in martial pomp, but here was old Kentucky," when I threw my hat off and raised my rifle, something passed swiftly by my head, within a few inches of it, and fell upon the stage a little way behind me. On the instant there was an evident commotion among the audience, a general running to and fro, with a rush for the upper tiers of the theatre, and a cry of "Turn him out" and "Pitch him over." I ceased singing, for I knew I could not be heard, so picking up the missile, and taking it to the front lights, found it was a piece of iron gas-pipe, about eighteen inches long and the thickness of a man's finger. I held it up before the audience without speaking, bowed, and retired from the stage. It was ten or fifteen minutes before order was restored among our auditors. Several of my friends and two of the police guards came to the stage-door to inquire if I knew who the offender was. I told them I had not the remotest idea who; and the conclusion generally, I believe, was that the disturber was most likely some Englishman, in whose bosom the "British lion" had been suddenly aroused by the words of the song.

It was not until about eighteen years after the event that the real offender became known to me, and it was in this wise: About the time mentioned, passing up the Mississippi River by steamboat, I was sitting late at night conversing with some of the officers of the boat, and listening to their jokes and witticisms, when a man, who had been sitting there silent for some time, said to me: "Mr. Ludlow, did you ever discover who it was that threw a piece of gas-pipe at you when you were singing the 'Hunters of Kentucky,' many years ago?" To which I replied, I never had. He lowered his eyes for a few seconds, then looking at me, in a jocular manner said: "Well, sir, it was me." I give his own words. "You?" I said, somewhat astonished. "Yes, sir, me!" "Well," I said, "why did you do it? How had I offended you?" "Offended!" he exclaimed; "so far was I from being offended that I believe I would have knocked any man down who would have dared hiss you." "But why did you throw at my head what, had it hit me, would most likely have hurt me very seriously?" Said he: "Mr. Ludlow, I have mentioned this matter for the purpose of apologizing to you for what was done under great excitement. I hope you will pardon me for an act that has hurt me more since than it was possible for you to have been, had the pipe hit you. These are the facts, sir: I am a Kentuckian; I was at the battle of New Orleans, under the command of Gen. Jackson; I went to the theatre for the purpose of hearing that song sung by you, of which I had heard many persons speak. I accidentally picked up a piece of gas-pipe in the lobby of the second tier, and was carelessly tossing it to and fro in my hands when you commenced the song, and when you spoke of Cypress Swamp and the old general, *I let her went*; and if it had been a gold repeater watch, it would have gone in the same way." This man was the principal engineer of the boat on which I was then travelling. We had a drink together that night, and were good friends ever after. He is dead now, poor fellow!

Lafitte at the Battle of New Orleans

At different times the English had sought to attack the pirates at Barataria, in hopes of taking their prizes, and even their armed vessels. Of these attempts of the British, suffice it to instance that of June 23rd, 1813, when two privateers being at anchor off Cat Island, a British sloop of war anchored at the entrance of the pass, and sent her boats to endeavor to take the privateers; but they were repulsed with considerable loss.

Such was the state of affairs, when on the 2d Sept., 1814, there appeared an armed brig on the coast opposite the pass. She fired a gun at a vessel about to enter, and forced her to run aground; she then tacked and shortly after came to an anchor at the entrance of the pass. It was not easy to understand the intentions of this vessel, who, having commenced with hostilities on her first appearance, now seemed to announce an amicable disposition. Mr. Lafitte then went off in a boat to examine her, venturing so far that he could not escape from the pinnace sent from the brig, and making towards the shore, bearing British colors and a flag of truce. In this pin-

From "Life of Lafitte, The Pirate of the Gulf," in *The Pirates Own Book,* or Authentic Narratives of the Life, Exploits, and Executions of the Most Celebrated Sea Robbers, with Historic Sketches of the Joassamee, Spanish, Ladrone, West India, Malay, and Algerine Pirates, pp. 71–80. Entered . . . 1837, by Samuel N. Dickinson. Portland [Me.]: Published by Francis Blake. 1855.

nace were two naval officers. One was Capt. Lockyer, commander of the brig. The first question they asked was, Where was Mr. Lafitte? He, not choosing to make himself known to them, replied that the person they inquired for was on shore. They then delivered to him a packet directed to Mr. Lafitte, Barataria, requesting him to take particular care of it, and to deliver it into Mr. Lafitte's hands. He prevailed on them to make for the shore, and as soon as they got near enough to be in his power, he made himself known, recommending to them at the same time to conceal the business on which they had come. Upwards of two hundred persons lined the shore, and it was a general cry amongst the crews of the privateers at Grand Terre, that those British officers should be made prisoners and sent to New Orleans as spies. It was with much difficulty that Lafitte dissuaded the multitude from this intent, and led the officers in safety to his dwelling. He thought very prudently that the papers contained in the packet might be of importance towards the safety of the country and that the officers if well watched could obtain no intelligence that might turn to the detriment of Louisiana. He now examined the contents of the packet, in which he found a proclamation addressed by Col. Edward Nichalls, in the service of his Britannic Majesty, and commander of the land forces on the coast of Florida, to the inhabitants of Louisiana. A letter from the same to Mr. Lafitte, the commander of Barataria; an official letter from the honorable W. H. Percy, captain of the sloop of war *Hermes,* directed to Lafitte. When he had perused these letters, Capt. Lockyer enlarged on the subject of them and proposed to him to enter into the service of his Britannic Majesty with the rank of post captain and to receive the command of a 44 gun frigate. Also all those under his command, or over whom he had sufficient influence. He was also offered thirty thousand dollars, payable at Pensacola, and urged him not to let slip this opportunity of acquiring fortune and consideration. On Lafitte's requiring a few days to reflect upon these proposals, Capt. Lockyer observed to him that no reflection could be necessary respecting proposals that obviously precluded hesitation, as he was a Frenchman and proscribed by the American government. But to all his splendid promises and daring insinuations, Lafitte replied that in a few days he would give a final answer; his object in this procrastination being to gain time to inform the officers of the state government of this nefarious project. Having occasion to go to some distance for a short time, the persons who had proposed to send the British officers prisoners to New Orleans went and seized them in his absence, and confined both them and the crew of the pinnace in a secure place, leaving a guard at the door. The British officers sent for Lafitte; but he, fearing an insurrection of the crews of the privateers, thought it advisable not to see them until he had first persuaded their captains and officers to desist from the measures on which they seemed bent. With this view he represented to the latter that, besides the infamy that would attach to them if they treated as prisoners people who had come with a flag of truce, they would lose the opportunity of discovering the projects of the British against Louisiana.

Early the next morning Lafitte caused them to be released from their confinement and saw them safe on board their pinnace, apologizing [for] the detention. He now wrote to Capt. Lockyer the following letter:

To Captain Lockyer.

Barataria, 4th Sept. 1814

Sir—The confusion which prevailed in our camp yesterday and this morning, and of which you have a complete knowledge, has prevented me from answering in a precise manner to the object of your mission; nor even at this moment can I give you all the satisfaction that you desire; however, if you could grant me a fortnight, I would be entirely at your disposal at the end of that time. This delay is indispensable to enable me to put my affairs in order. You may communicate with me by sending a boat to the eastern point of the pass, where I will be found. You have inspired me with more confidence than the admiral, your superior officer, could have done himself; with you alone, I wish to deal, and from you also I will claim in due time the reward of the services, which I may render to you.

Yours, &c.,

J. Lafitte

His object in writing that letter was, by appearing disposed to accede to their proposals, to give time to communicate the affair to the officers of the state government, and to receive from them instructions how to act, under circumstances so critical and important to the country. He accordingly wrote on the 4th September to Mr. Blanque, one of the representatives of the state, sending him all the papers delivered to him by the British officers with a letter addressed to his excellency, Gov. Claiborne of the state of Louisiana.

To Gov. Claiborne.

Barataria, Sept. 4th, 1814

Sir—In the firm persuasion that the choice made of you to fill the office of first magistrate of this state was dictated by the esteem of your fellow citizens, and was conferred on merit, I confidently address you on an affair on which may depend the safety of this country. I offer to you to restore to this state several citizens, who perhaps in your eyes have lost that sacred title. I offer you them, however, such as you could wish to find them, ready to exert their utmost efforts in defence of the country. This point of Louisiana, which I occupy, is of great importance in the present crisis. I tender my services to defend it; and the only reward I ask is that a stop be put to the proscription against me and my adherents, by an act of oblivion, for all that has been done hitherto. I am the stray sheep wishing to return to the fold. If you are thoroughly acquainted with the nature of my offences, I should appear to you much less guilty, and still worthy to discharge the duties of a good citizen. I have never sailed under any flag but that of the republic of Carthagena, and my vessels are perfectly regular in that respect. If I could have brought my lawful prizes into the ports of this state, I should not have employed the illicit means that have caused me to be proscribed. I decline saying more on the subject, until I have the honor of your excellency's answer, which I am persuaded can be dictated only by wisdom. Should your answer not be favorable to my ardent desires, I declare to you that I will instantly leave the country, to avoid the imputation of having cooperated towards an invasion on this point, which cannot fail to take place, and to rest secure in the acquittal of my conscience.

> I have the honor to be
> your excellency's, &c.
> J. Lafitte

The contents of these letters do honor to Lafitte's judgment, and evince his sincere attachment to the American cause. On the receipt of this packet from Lafitte, Mr. Blanque immediately laid its contents before the governor, who convened the committee of defence lately formed of which he was president; and Mr. Rancher, the bearer of Lafitte's packet, was sent back with a verbal answer to desire Lafitte to take no steps until it should be determined what was expedient to be done; the message also contained an assurance that, in the meantime, no steps should be taken against him for his past offences against the laws of the United States.

At the expiration of the time agreed on with Captain Lockyer, his ship appeared again on the coast with two others, and continued standing off and on before the pass for several days. But he pretended not to perceive the return of the sloop of war, who, tired of waiting to no purpose, put out to sea and disappeared.

Lafitte having received a guarantee from General Jackson for his safe passage from Barataria to New Orleans and back, he proceeded forthwith to the city where he had an interview with Gov. Claiborne and the General. After the usual formalities and courtesies had taken place between these gentlemen, Lafitte addressed the Governor of Louisiana nearly as follows.

"I have offered to defend for you that part of Louisiana I now hold. But not as an outlaw, would I be its defender. In that confidence, with which you have inspired me, I offer to restore to the state many citizens, now under my command. As I have remarked before, the point I occupy is of great importance in the present crisis. I tender not only my own services to defend it, but those of all I command. And the only reward I ask is that a stop be put to the proscription against me and my adherents, by an act of oblivion for all that has been done hitherto."

"My dear sir," said the Governor, who together with General Jackson, was impressed with admiration of his sentiments, "your praiseworthy wishes shall be laid before the council of the state, and I will confer with my august friend here present, upon this important affair and send you an answer to-morrow."

As Lafitte withdrew, the General said, "Farewell; when we meet again, I trust it will be in the ranks of the American army."

The result of the conference was the issuing of the following order.

The Governor of Louisiana, informed that many individuals, implicated in the offences heretofore committed against the United States at Barataria, express a willingness at the present crisis to enroll themselves and march against the enemy—

He does hereby invite them to join the standard of the United States and is authorised to say, should their conduct in the field meet the approbation of the Major General, that that officer will unite with the Governor in a request to the president of the United States to extend to each and every individual, so marching and acting, a free and full pardon.

These general orders were placed in the hands of Lafitte, who circulated them among his dispersed followers, most of whom readily embraced the conditions of pardon they held out. In a few days many brave men and skilful artillerists, whose services contributed greatly to the safety of the invaded state, flocked to the standard of the United States, and by their conduct received the highest approbation of General Jackson.

The morning of the eighth of January was ushered in with the discharge of rockets, the sound of cannon, and the cheers of the British soldiers advancing to the attack. The Americans, behind the breastwork, awaited in calm intrepidity their approach. The enemy advanced in close column of sixty men in front, shouldering their muskets and carrying fascines and ladders. A storm of rockets preceded them, and an incessant fire opened from the battery which commanded the advanced columns. The musketry and rifles from the Kentuckians and Tennesseeans joined the fire of the artillery, and in a few moments was heard along the line a ceaseless, rolling fire, whose tremendous noise resembled the continued reverberation of thunder. One of these guns, a twenty-four pounder, placed upon the breastwork in the third embrasure from the river, drew, from the fatal skill and activity with which it was managed, even in the heat of battle, the admiration of both Americans and British; and became one of the points most dreaded by the advancing foe.

Here was stationed Lafitte and his lieutenant Dominque and a large band of his men, who during the continuance of the battle fought with unparalleled bravery. The British already had been twice driven back in the utmost confusion, with the loss of their commander-in-chief, and two general officers.

Two other batteries were manned by the Baratarians, who served their pieces with the steadiness and precision of veteran gunners. In the first attack of the enemy, a column pushed forward between the levee and the river; and so precipitate was their charge that the outposts were forced to retire, closely pressed by the enemy. Before the batteries could meet the charge, clearing the ditch, they gained the redoubt through the embrasures, leaping over the parapet and overwhelming by their superior force the small party stationed there.

Lafitte, who was commanding in conjunction with his officers, at one of the guns, no sooner saw the bold movement of the enemy than, calling a few of his best men by his side, he sprung forward to the point of danger, and clearing the breastwork of the entrenchments, leaped, cutlass in hand, into the midst of the enemy, followed by a score of his men, who in many a hard fought battle upon his own deck had been well tried.

Astonished at the intrepidity which could lead men to leave their entrenchments and meet them hand to hand, and pressed by the suddenness of the charge, which was made with the recklessness, skill and rapidity of practised boarders bounding upon the deck of an enemy's vessel, they began to give way, while, one after another, two British officers fell before the cutlass of the pirate, as they were bravely encouraging their men. All the energies of the British were now concentrated to scale the breastwork, which one daring officer had already mounted, while Lafitte and his followers, seconding a gallant band of volunteer riflemen, formed a phalanx which they in vain essayed to penetrate.

The British, finding it impossible to take the city, and the havoc in their ranks being dreadful, made a precipitate retreat, leaving the field covered with their dead and wounded.

General Jackson, in his correspondence with the secretary of war, did not fail to notice the conduct of the "Corsairs of Barataria," who were, as we have already seen, employed in the artillery service. In the course of the campaign they proved, in an unequivocal manner, that they had been misjudged by the enemy, who, a short time previous to the invasion of Louisiana, had hoped to enlist them in his cause. Many of them were killed or wounded in the defence of the country. Their zeal, their courage, and their skill were remarked by the whole army, who could no longer consider such brave men as criminals. In a few days peace was declared between Great Britain and the United States.

The Capture of New Orleans

While [the] gigantic contest [between the Union and Confederate fleets] was going on in the river abreast of the forts [St. Philip and Jackson, in the early morning of April 24, 1862], the people of New Orleans were thronging the streets, listening to the unceasing roar of the great guns and discussing, with pale faces and anxious hearts, the outcome of the fight. "Farragut can never pass our forts. His wooden ships will be blown to pieces by their fire or dashed into atoms by the *Manassas*," the people said. But many listened in silence; they had husbands, sons, or brothers in that fearful fight, and who could tell that they would return alive? By and by the firing ceased. Only an occasional shot broke the stillness of the morning. Then came the suspense. Had the fleet been beaten back, or was it above the forts, and even now sullenly steaming up to the city? Everybody rushed for the house-tops to look to the southward, over the lowland through which the Mississippi winds. An hour's waiting, and they see curls of smoke rising above the trees, then slender dark lines moving along above the treetops. "Are they our ships?" every one cries; and no one answers until the dark

From *Blue Jackets of '61*, A History of the Navy in the War of Secession, by Willis J. Abbot, pp. 237–242. Copyright, 1886, by Dodd, Mead and Company. New York.

lines are seen to be crossed by others at right angles. They are masts with yard-arms, masts of sea-going vessels, the masts of the invader's fleet. A cry of grief, of fear, of rage, goes up from the house-tops. "To the levee!" cry the men, and soon the streets resound with the rush of many feet toward the river. "The river is crooked and its current swift. It will be hours before the Yankees can arrive; let us burn, destroy, that they may find no booty." Let one who was in the sorrowful city that terrible April day tell the story.

"I went to the riverside. There, until far into the night, I saw hundreds of drays carrying cotton out of the presses and yards to the wharves, where it was fired. The glare of those sinuous miles of flame set men and women weeping and wailing thirty miles away, on the farther shore of Lake Pontchartrain. But the next day was the day of terrors. During the night, fear, wrath, and sense of betrayal had run through the people as the fire had run through the cotton. You have seen, perhaps, a family fleeing, with lamentations and wringing of hands, out of a burning house; multiply it by thousands upon thousands; that was New Orleans, though the houses were not burning. The firemen were out; but they cast fire on the waters, putting the torch to the empty ships and cutting them loose to float down the river.

"Whoever could go was going. The great mass that had no place to go, or means to go with, was beside itself. 'Betrayed! betrayed!' it cried, and ran in throngs from street to street, seeking some vent, some victim for its wrath. I saw a crowd catch a poor fellow at the corner of Magazine and Common Streets, whose crime was that he looked like a stranger and might be a spy. He was the palest living man I ever saw. They swung him to a neighboring lamp-post; but the Foreign Legion was patrolling the town in strong squads, and one of its lieutenants, all green and gold, leaped with drawn sword, cut the rope, and saved the man. This was one occurrence; there were many like it. I stood in the rear door of our store, Canal Street, soon after reopening it. The junior of the firm was within. I called him to look toward the river. The masts of the cutter *Washington* were slowly tipping, declining, sinking—down she went. The gunboat moored next her began to smoke all over and then to blaze. My employers lifted up their heels, and left the city, left their goods and their affairs in the hands of one mere lad—no stranger would have thought I had reached fourteen—and one big German porter. I closed the doors, sent the porter to his place in the Foreign Legion, and ran to the levee to see the sights.

"What a gathering!—the riffraff of the wharves, the town, the gutters! Such women! such wrecks of women! and all the juvenile ragtag. The lower steamboat landing, well covered with sugar, rice, and molasses, was being rifled. The men smashed; the women scooped up the smashings. The river overflowing the top of the levee. A rainstorm began to threaten. 'Are the Yankee ships in sight?' I asked of an idler. He pointed out the tops of their naked masts as they showed up across the huge bend of the river. They were engaging the batteries at Camp Chalmette, the old field of Jackson's renown. Presently that was over. Ah, me! I see them now as they come slowly round Slaughterhouse Point, into full view, silent, so grim and terrible, black with men, heavy with deadly portent, the long banished stars and stripes flying against the frowning sky. Oh for the *Mississippi*, the *Mississippi!* Just then she came down upon them. But how? Drifting helplessly, a mass of flames.

"The crowds on the levees howled and screamed with rage. The swarming decks answered never a word; but one old tar on the *Hartford*, standing with lanyard in hand, beside a great pivot gun, so plain to view that you could see him smile, silently patted its big black breech and blandly grinned."

As the masts of the fleet came up the river, a young man stepped out upon the roof of the City Hall, and swiftly hoisted the flag of the State of Louisiana. When the ships came up, two officers were sent ashore to demand the surrender of the city; and shoulder to shoulder, the two old sailors marched through a howling, cursing mob to the City Hall. The mayor refused to surrender the city, saying that Farragut already had captured it. The officers went back to their ships, and the flag still floated. Two days later the officers, with a hundred sailors and marines, returned and demanded that the flag be hauled down. No one in the city would tear it down, and the Federals went up to the roof to lower it themselves. The street and surrounding housetops were crowded with a hostile people, all armed. No one could tell that the fall of the flag would not be followed by a volley from the undisciplined populace. The marines in front of the building stood grouped about two loaded howitzers that bore upon the darkly muttering crowd. Violence was in the air. As the two officers rose to go to the roof, the mayor, a young Creole, left the room and descended the stairs. Quietly he stepped out into the street, and without a word stood before one of the howitzers, his arms folded, eyeing the gunner, who stood with lanyard in hand, ready to fire at the word of the commander. The flag fell slowly from the staff. Not a sound arose from the crowd. All were watching the mayor, who stood coldly looking on death. The Federal officers came down carrying the flag. A few sharp commands, and the marines tramped away down the street, with the howitzers clanking behind them. The crowd cheered for Mayor Monroe, and dispersed, and New Orleans became again a city of the United States.

Donelson's Voyage

December 22, 1779.—Took our departure from the fort and fell down the river to the mouth of Reedy creek, where we were stopped by the fall of water and most excessive hard frost; and after much delay, and many difficulties, we arrived at the mouth of Cloud's Creek on Sunday evening, the

From *Journal of a Voyage,* intended by God's permission, the good boat *Adventure,* from Fort Patrick Henry, on Holston river, to the French Salt Springs on Cumberland river, kept by John Donelson. Reprinted in *Early Travels in the Tennessee Country,* 1540–1800, with Introductions, Annotations and Index, by Samuel Cole

20th February, 1780, where we lay by until Sunday, the 27th, when we took our departure with sundry other vessels bound for the same voyage, and on the same day struck the Poor-valley shoal, together with Mr. Boyd and Mr. Rounsifer, on which shoal we lay that afternoon and succeeding night in much distress.

Monday, February 28th, 1780.—In the morning, the water rising, we got off the shoal, after landing thirty persons to lighten our boat. In attempting to land on an island, received some damage, and lost sundry articles, and came to camp on the south shore, where we joined sundry other vessels also bound down.

Tuesday, 29th.—Proceeded down the river and encamped on the north shore, the afternoon and following day proving rainy.

Wednesday, March 1st.—Proceeded on, and encamped on the north shore, nothing happening that day remarkable.

March 2d.—Rain about half the day; passed the mouth of French Broad river, and about twelve o'clock Mr. Henry's boat, being driven on the point of an island by the force of the current, was sunk, the whole cargo much damaged, and the crew's lives much endangered, which occasioned the whole fleet to put on shore, and go to their assistance, but with much difficulty baled her out and raised her, in order to take in her cargo again. The same afternoon Reuben Harrison went out a hunting, and did not return that night, though many guns were fired to fetch him in.

Friday, 3rd.—Early in the morning fired a four-pounder for the lost man, sent out sundry persons to search the woods for him, firing many guns that day and the succeeding night, but all without success, to the great grief of his parents and fellow-travelers.

Saturday, 4th.—Proceeded on our voyage, leaving old Mr. H. Harrison, with some other vessels, to make further search for his lost son; about ten o'clock the same day found him a considerable distance down the river, where Mr. Ben Belew took him on board his boat. At three o'clock P.M., passed the mouth of Tennessee River, and camped on the shore, about ten miles below the mouth of Tennessee.

Sunday, 5th.—Cast off and got under way before sunrise; twelve o'clock, passed mouth of Clinch; at three o'clock P.M., came up with the Clinch river company, whom we joined, and camped, the evening proving rainy.

Monday, 6th.—Got under way before sunrise: the morning proving very foggy, many of the fleet were much bogged: about ten o'clock lay by for

Williams, pp. 233–242. Copyright, 1928, by the Watauga Press. Johnson City, Tennessee.

Because of its romantic phases and because of the notable contribution the company of voyagers made to the Cumberland Settlements, the voyage in 1779–80 of the flotilla under the leadership of Colonel John Donelson down the Holston and Tennessee and up the Cumberland Rivers is well known to Tennesseans. . . . The boat *Adventure* was fitted and supplied at the Boatyard (Kingsport) and wa but one of above thirty in the flotilla, which grew in number of vessels æs the voyage proceeded. No other migration group meant so much to the new country as this. Among the voyagers [was] Rachel Donelson (Mrs. Andrew Jackson).—S.C.W., *ibid.*, pp. 231–232.

them; when collected, proceeded down: camped on the north shore, where Captain Hutching's Negro man died, being much frosted in his feet and legs, of which he died.

Tuesday, 7th.—Got under way very early: the day proving very windy, a S.S.W., and the river being wide, occasioned a high sea insomuch that some of the smaller crafts were in danger, therefore came to at the uppermost Chickamauga town, which was then evacuated, where we lay by that afternoon and camped that night. The wife of Ephraim Peyton was here delivered of a child. Mr. Peyton has gone through by land with Captain Robertson.

Wednesday, 8th.—Cast off at ten o'clock, and proceeded down to an Indian village, which was inhabited, on the south side of the river: they invited us to "come ashore," called us brothers, and showed other signs of friendship, insomuch that Mr. John Caffrey and my son, then on board, took a canoe which I had in tow, and were crossing over to them, the rest of the fleet having landed on the opposite shore. After they had gone some distance, a half-breed, who called himself Archy Coody, with several other Indians, jumped into a canoe, met them, and advised them to return to the boat, which they did, together with Coody, and several canoes, which left the shore and followed directly after him. They appeared to be friendly. After distributing some presents among them, with which they seemed much pleased, we observed a number of Indians on the other side embarking in their canoes, armed and painted with red and black. Coody immediately made signs to his companions, ordering them to quit the boat, which they did, himself and another Indian remaining with us, and telling us to move off instantly. We had not gone far before we discovered a number of Indians armed and painted, proceeding down the river, as it were to intercept us. Coody, the half-breed, and his companion sailed with us for some time, and telling us that we had passed all the towns, and were out of danger, left us. But we had not gone far until we come in sight of another town, situated likewise on the south side of the river, nearly opposite a small island. Here they again invited us to come on shore, called us brothers, and observing the boats standing off for the opposite channel, told us that "their side of the river was better for boats to pass."

And here we must regret the unfortunate death of young Mr. Payne, on board Captain Blackemore's boat, who was mortally wounded by reason of the boat running too near the northern shore, opposite the town where some of the enemy lay concealed; and the more tragical misfortune of poor Stuart, his family and friends, to the number of twenty-eight persons. This man had embarked with us for the Western country, but his family being diseased with the small-pox, it was agreed upon between him and the company that he should keep at some distance in the rear, for fear of the infection spreading; and he was warned each night when the encampment should take place by the sound of a horn. After we had passed the town, the Indians having now collected to a considerable number, observing his helpless situation, singled off from the rest of the fleet, intercepted him, killed and took prisoners the whole crew, to the great grief of the whole company, uncertain how soon they might share the same fate: their cries were distinctly heard by those boats in the rear.[1] We still perceived them marching down the river in considerable bodies, keeping pace with us until the Cumberland Mountain withdrew them from our sight, when we were in hopes we had escaped them.

We are now arrived at the place called Whirl, or Suck, where the river is compressed within less than half its common width above, by the Cumberland Mountains, which juts in on both sides. In passing through the upper part of these narrows, at a place described by Coody, which he termed the "boiling pot," a trivial accident had nearly ruined the expedition. One of the company, John Cotton, who was moving down in a large canoe, had attached it to Robert Cartwright's boat, into which he and his family had gone for safety. The canoe was here overturned, and the little cargo lost. The company, pitying his distress, concluded to halt and assist him in recovering his property. They had landed on the northern shore, at a level spot, and were going up the place, when the Indians, to our astonishment, appeared immediately over us on the opposite cliffs, and commenced firing down upon us, which occasioned a precipitate retreat to the boats. We immediately moved off. The Indians, lining the bluffs along, continued their fire from the heights on our boats, below, without doing any other injury than wounding four slightly. Jennings's boat is missing.

We have now passed through the Whirl. The river widens with a placid and gentle current, and all the company appear to be in safety, except the family of Jonathan Jennings, whose boat ran on a large rock projecting out from the northern shore, and partly immersed in water immediately at the Whirl, where we were compelled to leave them, perhaps to be slaughtered by their merciless enemies. Continued to sail on that day, and floated throughout the following night.

Thursday, 9th.—Proceeded on our journey, nothing happening worthy of attention to-day; floated until about midnight, and encamped on the northern shore.

Friday, 10th.—This morning about four o'clock we were surprised by the cries of "Help poor Jennings," at some distance in the rear. He had discovered us by our fires, and came up in the most wretched condition. He states that as soon as the Indians had discovered his situation, they turned their whole attention to him, and kept up a most galling fire on his boat. He ordered his wife, a son nearly grown, a young man who accompanied them, and his two Negroes, to throw all his goods into the river, to lighten their boat for the purpose of getting her off; himself returning their fire as well as he could, being a good soldier and an excellent marksman. But before they had accomplished their object, his son, the young man, and the Negro

[1] It was a tradition among the Cumberland folk that the Chickamaugas suffered retribution in losses from small-pox from infection by the unfortunate emigrants. —S.C.W.

man jumped out of the boat and left them: he thinks the young man and the Negro were wounded. Before they left the boat, Mrs. Jennings, however, and the Negro woman succeeded in unloading the boat, but chiefly by the exertions of Mrs. Jennings, who got out of the boat, and shoved her off; but was near falling a victim to her own intrepidity, on account of the boat starting suddenly as soon as loosened from the rocks. Upon examination he appears to have made a wonderful escape, for his boat is pierced in numberless places with bullets. It is to be remarked that Mrs. Peyton, who was the night before delivered of an infant, which was unfortunately killed in the hurry and confusion consequent upon such a disaster, assisted them, being frequently exposed to wet and cold then and afterwards, and that her health appears to be good at this time, and I think and hope she will do well. Their clothes were very much cut with bullets, especially Mrs. Jennings's.

Saturday, 11th.—Got under way after having distributed the family of Mrs. Jennings in the other boats. Rowed on quietly that day, and encamped for the night on the northern shore.

Sunday, 12th.—Set out, and after a few hours' sailing we heard the crowing of cocks, and soon came within view of the town: here they fired on us again without doing any injury. After running until about ten o'clock, came in sight of the Muscle Shoals. Halted on the northern shore at the upper end of the shoals, in order to search for the signs Captain James Robertson was to make for us at that place. He set out from Holston early in the fall of 1779, and was to proceed by the way of Kentucky to the Big Salt Lick on Cumberland river, with several others in company, was to come across from the Big Salt Lick to the upper end of the shoals, there to make such signs that we might know he had been there, and that it was practicable for us to go across by land. But to our great mortifications we can find none, from which we conclude that it would not be prudent to make the attempt; and are determined, knowing ourselves to be in such imminent danger, to pursue our journey down the river. After trimming our boats in the best manner possible, we ran through the shoals before night. When we approached them they had a dreadful appearance to those who had never seen them before. The water being high made a terrible roaring, which could be heard at some distance among the drift-wood heaped frightfully upon the points of the islands, the current running in every possible direction. Here we did not know how soon we should be dashed to pieces, and all our troubles ended at once. Our boats frequently dragged on the bottom, and appeared constantly in danger of striking: they warped as much as in a rough sea. But, by the hand of Providence, we are now preserved from this danger also. I know not the length of this wonderful shoal: it had been represented to me to be twenty-five or thirty miles; if so, we must have descended very rapidly, as indeed we did, for we passed it in about three hours. Came to, and encamped on the northern shore, not far below the shoals, for the night.

Monday, 13th.—Got under way early in the morning, and made a good run that day.

Tuesday, 14th.—Set out early. On this day two boats, approaching too near the shore, were fired on by the Indians; five of the crew were wounded, but not dangerously. Came to camp at night near the mouth of a creek. After kindling fires and preparing for rest, the company were alarmed on account of the incessant barking our dogs kept up; taking it for granted the Indians were attempting to surprise us, we retreated precipitately to the boats, fell down the river about a mile, and encamped on the other shore. In the morning I prevailed on Mr. Caffrey and my son to cross below in a canoe, and return to the place, which they did, and found an African Negro we had left in the hurry, asleep by one of the fires. The voyagers then returned and collected their utensils which had been left.

Wednesday, 15th.—Got under way, and moved on peaceably on the five following days, when we arrived at the mouth of the Tennessee on Monday the 20th, and landed on the lower point, immediately on the bank of the Ohio. Our situation here is truly disagreeable. The river is very high and the current rapid, our boats not constructed for the purpose of stemming a rapid stream, our provision exhausted, the crews almost worn down with hunger and fatigue, and know not what distance we have to go, or what time it will take us to our place of destination. The scene is rendered still more melancholy, as several boats will not attempt to ascend the rapid current. Some intend to descend the Mississippi to Natchez; others are bound for the Illinois—among the rest my son-in-law and daughter. We now part, perhaps to meet no more, for I am determined to pursue my course, happen what will.

Tuesday, 21st.—Set out, and on this day labored very hard, and got but a little way: camped on the south bank of the Ohio. Passed the two following days as the former, suffering much from hunger and fatigue.

Friday, 24th.—About three o'clock came to the mouth of a river which I thought was the Cumberland. Some of the company declared it could not be, it was so much smaller than was expected. But I never heard of any river running in between the Cumberland and the Tennessee. It appeared to flow with a gentle current. We determined, however, to make the trial, pushed up some distance, and encamped for the night.

Saturday, 25th.—Today we are much encouraged; the river grows wider; the current is very gentle: we are now convinced it is the Cumberland. I have derived great assistance from a small square sail, which was fixed up on the day we left the mouth of the river; and to prevent any ill effects from sudden flaws of wind, a man was stationed at each of the lower corners of the sheet, with directions to give way whenever it was necesssary.

Sunday, 26th.—Got under way early; procured some buffalo meat: though poor, it was palatable.

Monday, 27th.—Set out again; killed a swan, which was very delicious.

Tuesday, 28th.—Set out very early this morning; killed some buffalo.

Wednesday, 29th.—Proceeded up the river; gathered some herbs on the bottoms of the Cumberland, which some of the company called "Shawnee salad." [2]

Thursday, 30th.—Proceeded on our voyage. This day we killed some more buffalo.

Friday, 31st.—Set out this day, and after running some distance, met with Col. Richard Henderson, who was running the line between Virginia and North Carolina. At this meeting we were much rejoiced. He gave us every information we wished, and, further informed us that he had purchased a quantity of corn in Kentucky, to be shipped at the Falls of Ohio, for the use of the Cumberland settlement. We are now without bread and are compelled to hunt the buffalo to preserve life. Worn out with fatigue, our progress at present is slow. Camped at night near the mouth of a little river, at which place, and below, there is a handsome bottom of rich land. Here we found a pair of hand millstones, set up for grinding, but appeared not to have been used for a great length of time. Proceeded on quietly until the 12th of April, at which time we came to the mouth of a little river running in on the north side, by Moses Renfroe and his company called "Red River," up which they intended to settle. Here they took leave of us. We proceeded up Cumberland, nothing happening material until the 23rd, when we reached the first settlement on the north side of the river, one mile and half below the Big Salt Lick, and called Eaton's Station, after a man of that name, who, with several other families, came through Kentucky and settled there.

Monday, April 24th.—This day we arrived at our journey's end at the Big Salt Lick, where we have the pleasure of finding Capt. Robertson and his company. It is a source of satisfaction to us to be enabled to restore to him and others their families and friends, who were intrusted to our care, and who, some time since, perhaps, despaired of ever meeting again. Though our prospects at present are dreary, we have found a few log-cabins which have been built on a cedar bluff above the Lick by Capt. Robertson and his company.

Bill M'Coy's Honor

As an illustration of [the keelboatmen's] rude code of honor is remembered the story of Bill M'Coy. He was a master-spirit, and had successfully disputed for championship upon almost every famous sandbar visible

---

[2] Putnam says that the locality was long known as "Pat's Injun Patch." Col. Donelson's old Negro woman cook, Patsy, gathered and cooked onion greens there for the party, well-nigh famished for vegetable food.—S.C.W.

From "Remembrances of the Mississippi," by T. B. Thorpe, *Harper's New Monthly Magazine*, Vol. XII (December, 1855), No. LXVII, p. 31. New York: Harper & Brothers, Publishers.

at low water. In a terrible row, where blood had been spilled and a dark crime committed, Bill was involved. Momentarily off his guard, he fell into the clutches of the law. The community was excited—a victim was demanded to appease the oft-insulted majesty of justice. Brought before one of the courts holding at Natchez, then just closing its session for the summer vacation, he was fully committed, and nothing but the procurement of enormous bail would keep him from sweltering through the long months of summer in durance vile. It was apparently useless for him to expect any one to go upon his bond; he appealed, however, to those present, dwelt upon the horrors, to him more especially, of a long imprisonment, and solemnly asseverated that he would present himself at the time appointed for trial. At the last moment, Colonel W——, a wealthy, and on the whole rather a cautious citizen, came to the rescue, and agreed to pay ten thousand dollars if M'Coy did not present himself to stand his trial. It was in vain that the Colonel's friends tried to persuade him not to take the responsibility; even "the Court's" suggestion to let the matter alone was unheeded. M'Coy was released. Shouldering his rifle, and threading his way through the Indian nation, in due time he reached his home in "Old Kaintuck."

Months rolled on, and the time of trial approached. As a matter of course, the probabilities of M'Coy's return were discussed. The public had doubts—the Colonel had not heard from him since his departure. The morning of the appointed day arrived, but the prisoner did not present himself. The attending crowd and the people of the town became excited —all except the Colonel despaired—evening was moving on apace—the court was on the point of adjourning, when a distant huzza was heard; it was borne on the wings of the wind, and echoed along, each moment growing louder and louder. Finally the exulting cry was caught up by the hangers-on about the seat of justice. Another moment and M'Coy—his beard long and matted, his hands torn to pieces, his eyes haggard, and sun-burnt to a degree that was painful to behold—rushed into the courtroom, and from sheer exhaustion fell prostrate upon the floor.

Old Colonel W—— embraced him as he would have done a long-lost brother, and eyes unused to tears filled to overflowing when M'Coy related his simple tale. Starting from Louisville as "a hand on a boat," he found in a few days that, owing to the low stage of water in the river and other unexpected delays, it was impossible for him to reach Natchez at the appointed time by such a mode of conveyance. No other ordinary conveyance, in those early days, presented itself. Not to be thwarted, he abandoned "the flat," and, with his own hands, shaped a canoe out of the trunk of a fallen tree. He had rowed and paddled, almost without cessation, *thirteen hundred miles*, and had thus redeemed his promise almost at the expense of his life. His trial in its progress became a mere form; his chivalrous conduct and the want of any positive testimony won for him a verdict of not guilty, even before it was announced by the jury or affirmed by the judge.

A Fortune in Pecans

Gerard Brandon [of Brandon Hall] was one of the most picturesque characters that ever settled in the Natchez country. . . . He was a successful planter, and for many years raised more indigo than any one else in that section. He was also a pioneer in pecan growing. . . .

A weary stranger begged for lodging one night and the next morning after a hearty breakfast asked for a reckoning.

"I charge you nothing, sir," said the generous host.

"I intended paying," remonstrated the stranger, "but if you will take no money, you'll at least accept these." He held in his hand the first pecans ever seen in the Natchez country.

As he rode away, he called out:

"Plant them. They'll make you a fortune!"

The pecans were planted and in due time brought forth abundantly. Today (1936) there are five hundred bearing pecan trees on the plantation. Last year, one crop alone brought $2300, and everywhere young trees are springing up.

"It Granulates!"

. . . Etienne de Boré . . . was a man of fifty-four, a Creole of the Illinois district, but of a distinguished Norman family; he had lived in France from the age of four to thirty-two, had served with the king's *mousquetaires*, had married a lady whose estate was in Louisiana near New Orleans, and returning with her to the province, had become an indigo planter. The year 1794 found him face to face with ruin. His father-in-law, Destréhan, had in former years been one of the last to abandon sugar culture. His wife and friends warned him against the resolution he was taking; but he persisted in his determination to abandon indigo, and risk all that was left to him on the chance of a success which, if achieved, would insure deliverance and fortune to himself and the community. He bought a quantity of canes from Mendez and Solis, planted on the land where the Seventh District (late Carrollton) now stands, and while his crop was growing erected a mill and prepared himself for the momentous season of "grinding."

His fellow-planters looked on with the liveliest—not always with the most hopeful—interest, and at length they gathered about him to see

From *In Old Natchez*, by Catharine Van Court, pp. 60–61. Copyright, 1937, by Catharine Van Court Myrick. Garden City, New York: Doubleday, Doran & Company, Inc.

From *The Creoles of Louisiana*, by George W. Cable, pp. 111–113. Copyright, 1884, by Charles Scribner's Sons. New York.

the issue of the experiment in which only he could be more deeply concerned than they. In the whole picturesque history of the Louisiana Creoles few scenes offer so striking a subject for the painter as that afforded in this episode: The dark sugar-house; the battery of huge cauldrons, with their yellow juice boiling like a sea, half-hidden in clouds of steam; the half-clad, shining Negroes swinging the gigantic utensils with which the seething flood is dipped from kettle to kettle; here, grouped at the end of the battery, the Creole planters with anxious faces drawing around their central figure as closely as they can; and in the midst the old *mousquetaire*, dipping, from time to time, the thickening juice, repeating again and again his simple tests, until, in the moment of final trial, there is a common look of suspense, and instantly after it the hands are dropped, heads are raised, the brow is wiped, and there is a long breath of relief— "it granulates!" [1]

Eliza Crosses the Ice

In consequence of all the various delays, it was about three quarters of an hour after Eliza had laid her child to sleep in the village tavern that the [slave trader's] party came riding into the same place. Eliza was standing by the window, looking out in another direction, when Sam's quick eye caught a glimpse of her. Haley and Andy were two yards behind. At this crisis, Sam contrived to have his hat blown off, and uttered a loud and characteristic ejaculation, which startled her at once; she drew suddenly back; the whole train swept by the window, round to the front door.

A thousand lives seemed to be concentrated in that one moment to Eliza. Her room opened by a side door to the river. She caught her child, and sprang down the steps towards it. The trader caught a full glimpse of her, just as she was disappearing down the bank; and throwing himself

---

[1] Etienne de Boré marketed $12,000 worth of superior sugar. The absence of interdictions that had stifled earlier trade enabled him to sell his product to advantage. The agriculture of the Delta was revolutionized; and seven years after, New Orleans was the market for 200,000 gallons of rum, 250,000 gallons of molasses, 5,000,000 pounds of sugar. The town contained some twelve distilleries—probably not a subject for unmixed congratulation—and a sugar refinery which produced about 200,000 pounds of loaf sugar; while on the other hand the production of indigo had declined to a total of 3,000 pounds and soon after ceased.—G.W.C.

From *Uncle Tom's Cabin;* or Life among the Lowly, by Harriet Beecher Stowe, pp. 73–76. Copyright, 1851, 1878, 1879, by Harriet Beecher Stowe. Boston: Houghton, Mifflin and Company. 1894.

For Eliza Harris's own story of her escape across the Ohio River, near Ripley, Ohio, as told to Levi Coffin, see *A Treasury of Southern Folklore* (1949) pp. 349–351.

For further testimony relating to the incident, see Harriet Beecher Stowe's *The Key to Uncle Tom's Cabin; Presenting the Original Facts and Documents upon which the Story is Founded* . . . (London, 1853), pp. 34–36.

from his horse, and calling loudly on Sam and Andy, he was after her like a hound after a deer. In that dizzy moment her feet to her scarce seemed to touch the ground, and a moment brought her to the water's edge. Right on behind they came; and, nerved with strength such as God gives only to the desperate, with one wild cry and flying leap, she vaulted sheer over the turbid current by the shore, on to the raft of ice beyond. It was a desperate leap—impossible to anything but madness and despair; and Haley, Sam, and Andy instinctively cried out, and lifted up their hands, as she did it.

The huge green fragment of ice on which she alighted pitched and creaked as her weight came on it, but she stayed there not a moment. With wild cries and desperate energy she leaped to another and still another cake;—stumbling—leaping—slipping—springing upwards again! Her shoes are gone—her stockings cut from her feet—while blood marked every step; but she saw nothing, felt nothing, till dimly, as in a dream, she saw the Ohio side, and a man helping her up the bank.

"Yer a brave gal, now, whoever ye ar!" said the man, with an oath.

Eliza recognized the voice and face of a man who owned a farm not far from her old home.

"O, Mr. Symmes!—save me—do save me—do hide me!" said Eliza.

"Why, what's this?" said the man. "Why, if 't an't Shelby's gal!"

"My child!—this boy!—he's sold him! There is his Mas'r," said she, pointing to the Kentucky shore. "O, Mr. Symmes, you've got a little boy!"

"So I have," said the man, as he roughly, but kindly, drew her up the steep bank. "Besides, you're a right brave gal. I like grit, wherever I see it."

* * * * *

Haley had stood a perfectly amazed spectator of the scene, till Eliza had disappeared up the bank, when he turned a blank, inquiring look on Sam and Andy.

"That ar was a tolable fair stroke of business," said Sam.

"The gal's got seven devils in her, I believe!" said Haley. "How like a wildcat she jumped!"

"Wal, now," said Sam, scratching his head. "I hope Mas'r 'll scuse us tryin' dat ar road. Don't think I feel spry enough fer dat ar, no way!" and Sam gave a hoarse chuckle.

"*You* laugh!" said the trader, with a growl.

"Lord bless you, Mas'r, I couldn't help it, now," said Sam, giving way to the long pent-up delight of his soul. "She looked so cur's, a-leapin' and springin'—ice a-crackin'—and only to hear her—plump! ker chunk! ker splash! Spring! Lord, how she goes it!" and Sam and Andy laughed till the tears rolled down their cheeks.

Ferry to Freedom

Most of the slaves didn't know when they was born, but I did. You see, I was born on a Christmas morning—it was in 1840. I was a full-grown man when I finally got my freedom.

Before I got it, though, I helped a lot of others get theirs. Lord only knows how many; might have been as much as two-three hundred. It was 'way more than a hundred I know.

But that all came after I was a young man—grown enough to know a pretty girl when I saw one, and to go chasing after her, too. I was born on a plantation that belonged to Mr. Jack Tabb in Mason County, just across the river in Kentucky.

Mr. Tabb was a pretty good man. He used to beat us, sure; but not nearly so much as others did, some of his own kin people, even. But he was kinda funny sometimes; he used to have a special slave who didn't have nothing to do but teach the rest of us—we had about ten on the plantation, and a lot on the other plantations near us—how to read and write and figure. Mr. Tabb liked us to know how to figure. But sometimes when he would send for us, and we would be a long time coming, he would ask us where we had been. If we told him we had been learning to read, he would near beat the daylights out of us—after getting somebody to teach us! I think he did some of that so that the other owners wouldn't say he was spoiling his slaves.

He was funny about us marrying, too. He would let us go a-courting on the other plantations near any time we liked, if we were good, and if we found somebody we wanted to marry, and she was on a plantation that belonged to one of his kinfolks or a friend, he would swap a slave so that the husband and wife could be together. Sometimes, when he couldn't do this, he would let a slave work all day on the plantation and live with his wife at night on her plantation. Some of the other owners was always talking about his spoiling us.

He wasn't a Democrat like the rest of 'em in the county; he belonged to the Know Nothing party, and he was a real leader in it. He used to always be making speeches, and sometimes his best friends wouldn't be speaking to him for days at a time.

Mr. Tabb was always specially good to me. He used to let me go all about—I guess he had to; couldn't get too much work out of me even when he kept me right under his eyes. I learned fast, too, and I think he kinda liked that. He used to call Sandy Davis, the slave who taught me, "the smartest nigger in Kentucky."

From *Lay My Burden Down*, A Folk History of Slavery, edited by B. A. Botkin, pp. 185–189. Copyright, 1945, by the University of Chicago. Chicago: University of Chicago Press. As told to Martin Richardson by Arnold Gragston, age 97, Eatonville, Florida.

It was 'cause he used to let me go around in the day and night so much that I came to be the one who carried the running-away slaves over the river. It was funny the way I started it, too.

I didn't have no idea of ever getting mixed up in any sort of business like that until one special night. I hadn't even thought of rowing across the river myself.

But one night I had gone on another plantation courting, and the old woman whose house I went to told me she had a real pretty girl there who wanted to go across the river, and would I take her? I was scared and backed out in a hurry. But then I saw the girl, and she was such a pretty little thing, brown-skinned and kinda rosy, and looking as scared as I was feeling, so it wasn't long before I was listening to the old woman tell me when to take her and where to leave her on the other side.

I didn't have nerve enough to do it that night, though, and I told them to wait for me until tomorrow night. All the next day I kept seeing Mr. Tabb laying a rawhide across my back, or shooting me, and kept seeing that scared little brown girl back at the house, looking at me with her big eyes and asking me if I wouldn't just row her across to Ripley. Me and Mr. Tabb lost, and soon as dusk settled that night, I was at the old lady's house.

I don't know how I ever rowed the boat across the river. The current was strong, and I was trembling. I couldn't see a thing there in the dark, but I felt that girl's eyes. We didn't dare to whisper, so I couldn't tell her how sure I was that Mr. Tabb or some of the others' owners would tear me up when they found out what I had done. I just knew they would find out.

I was worried, too, about where to put her out of the boat. I couldn't ride her across the river all night, and I didn't know a thing about the other side. I had heard a lot about it from other slaves, but I thought it was just about like Mason County, with slaves and masters, overseers and rawhides; and so I just knew that if I pulled the boat up and went to asking people where to take her I would get a beating or get killed.

I don't know whether it seemed like a long time or a short time, now— it's so long ago; I know it was a long time rowing there in the cold and worrying. But it was short, too, 'cause as soon as I did get on the other side the big-eyed, brownskin girl would be gone. Well, pretty soon I saw a tall light, and I remembered what the old lady had told me about looking for that light and rowing to it. I did; and when I got up to it, two men reached down and grabbed her. I started trembling all over again, and praying. Then, one of the men took my arm and I just felt down inside of me that the Lord had got ready for me. "You hungry, boy?" is what he asked me, and if he hadn't been holding me, I think I would have fell backward into the river.

That was my first trip; it took me a long time to get over my scared feeling, but I finally did, and I soon found myself going back across the river, with two and three people, and sometimes a whole boatload. I got so I used to make three and four trips a month.

What did my passengers look like? I can't tell you any more about it than you can, and you wasn't there. After that first girl—no, I never did see her again—I never saw my passengers. It would have to be the black nights of the moon when I would carry them, and I would meet 'em out in the open or in a house without a single light. The only way I knew who they were was to ask them: "What you say?" And they would answer, "Menare." I don't know what that word meant—it came from the Bible. I only know that that was the password I used, and all of them that I took over told it to me before I took them.

I guess you wonder what I did with them after I got them over the river. Well, there in Ripley was a man named Mr. Rankins; I think the rest of his name was John. He had a regular "station" there on his place for escaping slaves. You see, Ohio was a free state, and once they got over the river from Kentucky or Virginia, Mr. Rankins could strut them all around town, and nobody would bother 'em. The only reason we used to land 'em quietly at night was so that whoever brought 'em could go back for more, and because we had to be careful that none of the owners had followed us. Every once in a while they would follow a boat and catch their slaves back. Sometimes they would shoot at whoever was trying to save the poor devils.

Mr. Rankins had a regular station for the slaves. He had a big light-house in his yard, about thirty feet high, and he kept it burning all night. It always meant freedom for the slave if he could get to this light.

Sometimes Mr. Rankins would have twenty or thirty slaves that had run away on his place at a time. It must have cost him a whole lot to keep 'em and feed 'em, but I think some of his friends helped him.

Those who wanted to stay around that part of Ohio could stay, but didn't many of 'em do it, because there was too much danger that you would be walking along free one night, feel a hand over your mouth, and be back across the river and in slavery again in the morning. And nobody in the world ever got a chance to know as much misery as a slave that had escaped and been caught.

So a whole lot of 'em went on North to other parts of Ohio or to New York, Chicago, or Canada. Canada was popular then because all of the slaves thought it was the last gate before you got all the way *inside* of heaven. I don't think there was much chance for a slave to make a living in Canada, but didn't many of 'em come back. They seem like they rather starve up there in the cold than to be back in slavery.

The army soon started taking a lot of 'em, too. They could enlist in the Union army and get good wages, more food than they ever had, and have all the little gals waving at 'em when they passed. Them blue uniforms was a nice change, too.

No, I never got anything from a single one of the people I carried over the river to freedom. I didn't want anything; after I had made a few trips

I got to like it, and even though I could have been free any night myself, I figured I wasn't getting along so bad so I would stay on Mr. Tabb's place and help the others get free. I did it for four years.

I don't know to this day how he never knew what I was doing. I used to take some awful chances, and he knew I must have been up to something. I wouldn't do much work in the day, would never be in my house at night, and when he would happen to visit the plantation where I had said I was going I wouldn't be there. Sometimes I think he did know and wanted me to get the slaves away that way so he wouldn't have to cause hard feelings by freeing 'em.

I think Mr. Tabb used to talk a lot to Mr. John Fee. Mr. Fee was a man who lived in Kentucky, but Lord! how that man hated slavery! He used to always tell us (we never let our owners see us listening to him though) that God didn't intend for some men to be free and some men to be in slavery. He used to talk to the owners, too, when they would listen to him, but mostly they hated the sight of John Fee.

In the night, though, he was a different man. For every slave who came through his place going across the river he had a good word, something to eat and some kind of rags, too, if it was cold. He always knew just what to tell you to do if anything went wrong, and sometimes I think he kept slaves there on his place till they could be rowed across the river. Helped us a lot.

I almost ran the business in the ground after I had been carrying the slaves across for nearly four years. It was in 1863, and one night I carried across about twelve on the same night. Somebody must have seen us, because they set out after me as soon as I stepped out of the boat back on the Kentucky side; from that time on they were after me. Sometimes they would almost catch me. I had to run away from Mr. Tabb's plantation and live in the fields and in the woods. I didn't know what a bed was from one week to another. I would sleep in a cornfield tonight, up in the branches of a tree tomorrow night and buried in a hay pile the next night. The river, where I had carried so many across myself, was no good to me; it was watched too close.

Finally, I saw that I could never do any more good in Mason County, so I decided to take my freedom, too. I had a wife by this time, and one night we quietly slipped across and headed for Mr. Rankins' bell and light. It looked like we had to go almost to China to get across that river. I could hear the bell and see the light on Mr. Rankins' place, but the harder I rowed, the farther away it got, and I knew if I didn't make it I'd get killed. But finally I pulled up by the lighthouse and went on to my freedom—just a few months before all of the slaves got theirs. I didn't stay in Ripley, though; I wasn't taking no chances. I went on to Detroit and still live there with most of ten children and thirty-one grandchildren.

The bigger ones don't care so much about hearing it now, but the little ones never get tired of hearing how their grandpa brought emancipation to loads of slaves he could touch and feel but never could see.

Running the Vicksburg Blockade with the Confederate Mail

Before I left St. Louis on May 12 [1863] I gave all our mail to Miss Bowen to carry on the *Graham* to Memphis, from which place she and Miss Perdue took it to Colonel Selby's home. Miss Selby had returned home about ten days before I arrived in Paducah on the thirteenth. Bob came in next night with Miss Sudie Kendall. On the fifteenth we left for Dixie, stopping at Colonel Selby's for the Missouri mail. Before arriving at Grenada we learned through the Northern papers that Pemberton's whole army was penned up in Vicksburg by General Grant's troops and we were undecided what to do with the mail we had for them. There were two or three small steamboats running on the Yallabusha and Yazoo rivers to Haines' Bluff, so we went to Yazoo City on the *Dew Drop,* a stern-wheel boat. We learned that our troops were hemmed in at the rear by Grant's troops and by Porter and Foote's fleets of gunboats on the Mississippi River front. For once we felt that we were checkmated. The night of the twenty-fifth, while Bob and I lay in bed together in a hotel in Yazoo City, we discussed the situation and determined that the two thousand letters we had brought should go into Vicksburg before forty-eight hours or we would die in the attempt. Neither of us had a wink of sleep that night as we lay there planning to run the blockade of the Federal fleet.

After breakfast we went to a tin shop and had four large square boxes made and had the tinner bring his soldering outfit to our room. We packed all our mail in the boxes and soldered them up water-tight. We procured from a fisherman a good, double-ended skiff, pointed at each end like a canoe. We bought an extra pair of new oars and painted them and the boat a light lead color. We then procured two saucepans with long handles, two light dog-chains, some wire and staples, a hammer, and a pair of pliers to cut wire with. Last but by no means least, some ladies prepared a basket of lunch for us. We boarded a steamboat with our outfit that evening and soon arrived at Haines' Bluff, where a large raft of logs had been so arranged as to block the passage of boats either up or down the Yazoo.

On May 25 we wired our mail boxes and stapled them down in the bottom of the boat, two boxes at each end. Near each end, on opposite sides of the boat, we fastened a saucepan by means of a chain and staples. Then we arranged wire loops to stick the oars in so they would not float off or out of the locks. After we had everything in readiness we concluded to make a trial trip in the boat. We stripped off our clothing, fastened the oars inside the boat, and bore down on one side of the boat until it was filled with water to within three inches of the top. Each of us took

From *Absalom Grimes,* Confederate Mail Runner, edited from Captain Grimes' Own Story by M. M. Quaife, of the Burton Historical Collection, pp. 122–128. Copyright, 1926, by Yale University Press. New Haven.

a position at one end of the boat and with the saucepans (the handles of which passed through the loops of wire) we could paddle it anywhere we wanted to go, using one hand under water on the saucepan, and holding to the edge of the boat with the other hand. After paddling around awhile we used the saucepans to bail the water out of the boat, then we climbed in and rowed back to where we had left our clothing on the bank. We were delighted with the way our scheme worked.

At six o'clock we bad adieu to Captain Henry and the company of Confederates stationed at Haines' Bluff. "God bless you and see you safe through!" were the captain's parting words to us. It was dark when we reached the Mississippi River to make our start for Vicksburg. That morning I had procured a pair of field glasses and gone on top of the high bluff where I could get a good view of the location of many of the boats of the Federal fleet. Most of the transports were two or three miles above the gunboats and lay along the shore of the left bank. The gunboats lay in the middle of the stream, slightly nearer to the Vicksburg side. I planned our trip through the fleet accordingly. We kept our boat to the east bank until well past the transports; then we secured our oars inside the skiff and got out into the water with our clothes on.

After we had gone nearly across to the west side, using our saucepans under water as oars, we tipped and sank the boat to within three inches of the top edge and then went on west. The current carried us forward, and by the time we were within twenty yards of the west bank we were below the transports and all other noncombatant craft and immediately abreast of and opposite the gunboats. We found these pretty well spread out across the river, and had to pass within three or four hundred yards of the extreme western gunboat. We were afraid to get in too close to shore as we might attract the attention of the camp guards there. Three of the boats kept their lights moving all the time, and we did not dare use the saucepans too vigorously for fear our speed might attract attention to us. Our boat, sunk low in the water, presented little to arrest the eye of a lookout, but every little flash of light from those eight or ten gunboats made us expect an unfriendly bullet. Although it seemed a long time to us, I think it was really not more than an hour from the time we reached the danger line until we were beyond reach of the searchlights of the gunboats. We now employed the saucepans to bail out the skiff and soon were riding in it. Later we lighted our small, water-proof dark-lantern and headed across the river for the Vicksburg wharf. It was more than a mile across, and every few moments we waved our lantern to let the guards know that we intended to land in Vicksburg, and were not trying to run their blockade. Although it was midnight when we landed, at least fifty soldiers were waiting on the wharf to receive us.

The two guards said they would take good care of our boat and its precious contents until morning. We were then conducted to a rooming-house, where we were provided with night clothes while the folks in the house took our wet clothing and had it dry for us by six o'clock next morning. The news of our arrival in Vicksburg spread rapidly over the town, and when we stepped out of the house we found more than two hundred soldiers around the place. The crowd was composed mostly of Missouri and Kentucky soldiers whom we knew. We were simply crushed in their excited joy to see us once more and under such unfavorable circumstances and surroundings. They carried us about on their shoulders and cheered lustily. Many of them went with us to our boat and got the mail boxes. We had a tinner unsolder them carefully in order that we might use them to carry mail out of Vicksburg. I shall not attempt to describe the reception we had when we reached the Missouri and Kentucky sections of the camp. It would be impossible. However, all our vain ambitions, the glory of our perilous trip through the fleet, and the pleasure we had in the meeting were soon reversed when we were shown a list of the dear, heroic comrades who had been sacrificed at Port Gibson, Grand Gulf, Baker's Creek, and in the vicinity of Vicksburg since we had bade them such a happy farewell at the camp at Grand Gulf a little more than a month since. Oh, how dreadful the memory of that trip into Vicksburg, though now more than forty years ago! Over two hundred of those happy faces and eager hands that had been extended to receive loving messages from home were to be seen no more. How the joys of the mail-carrier in camp can so quickly be turned into grief and sorrow can scarcely be realized. I felt as if I never wanted to make another trip in the mail carrying business.

Bob and myself were so grieved that we had about decided to notify the troops that they need not expect us in with any more mail, but when we mentioned the subject to Generals Gates, Cockrell, and Breckinridge and the men in the ranks they cried out in dismay at such a proposition. The result was we assured them that we would continue to serve as long as life was in our possssion and that thereafter our ghosts would wait upon them in their dreams of home unless the Yanks detained us involuntarily. Shame on us to think of deserting them! But the sad faces and down-hearted expressions of those noble men, coupled with the absence of hundreds whom we were accustomed to meet and render happy with letters, made our existence miserable and we felt as if we must get out of that horrid place as soon as possible.

We had been so interested in getting into Vicksburg that we had laid no plans for getting out. However, we were not long planning a way north. We borrowed General Cockrell's field glasses and spent two or three hours on the bluff at the north end of the fortification. We decided that instead of floating south we would row north, whence we had come. We discovered that for a long way below where the transports lay and as far down as the gunboats there were skiffs, launches, and other small craft rowing and moving freely about between points where camps were established along the canal some distance back from the river. I knew that with two good sets of oars we could make fair time upstream.

The boys in Vicksburg soon made ready a large return mail for our care and distribution. It filled our four boxes as full as they could be packed and we had them soldered as before, water-tight. Instead of wiring the boxes inside the skiff, as we had brought them down, we turned the boat bottom up on the bank and wired the boxes in a row, end to end, to the bottom of the boat. The boxes were a foot wide, eighteen inches long, and eight inches deep. We put them underneath the boat so that in the event we passed any boat or persons on the bank they would find nothing inside the boat. Before starting we exchanged our clothing for Federal uniforms, which were plentiful in our camp. One of the saddest good-byes I ever expect to undergo in all my life took place in the trenches, in the camps, and on the wharf at Vicksburg the night previous to our departure.

After our parting with the men, whom we never expected to see again, we slept, or rather we retired, in a house on the levee. At two o'clock in the morning we pulled across the river to the west bank, and keeping in its shadow, as it was a fine starlight night, rowed upstream. By daylight we were directly across from the gunboats, without having received a single challenge from anyone. We were wearing Federal uniforms and our act was such a barefaced exhibition of lunacy and nerve that no one on the fleet suspected our character as we rowed up past the transports in full view and not more than a hundred yards from the boats of the fleet.

We rowed on up the western shore until we passed around a point three or four miles above the fleet. Here we landed and pulling our boat out of the water removed the mail boxes from the bottom, as they made it so much harder to row. Oh, what a relief to our overtaxed muscles, as well as our nerves and minds! We rested a short time and then launched our boat and made fine time rowing upstream. By one o'clock we were in the mouth of the Yazoo River, having been absent just six days. We received a hearty welcome from Captain Henry and our men at Haines' Bluff.

The Race of the *Natchez* and the *Robert E. Lee*

There has been a great deal written and printed about the race in which the pilots and the captains had the floor, but this article is to record the things that happened in the engine room, and show what the men down there did and how their devotion to their captain and to duties won at last.

John Wiest, the head steam engineer of the Louisville Water Company, one of the engine room force [of the *Lee*], has recorded his account of

From "Race of the *Robert E. Lee* with the *Natchez* Retold by a Member of the Crew, Daring Heroism by Louisville Man Made Possible Famous Victory. Boilers Began to Leak. John Wiest Climbed over Firebox and, Despite Heat, Repaired Damage," by Alfred Pirtle. Mounted newspaper clipping in Science and Technology Room, New York Public Library. No source or date given, but internal evidence indicates Louisville, 1916.

those memorable days of the race and has given full permission to extract whatever may seem useful in this record.

Mr. Wiest says: "Her engineers were William Perkins, first engineer; Thomas Berry, second engineer; John Wiest, assistant engineer; George Brown, assistant engineer; and Joseph McCrory and Thomas Hayden, strikers." It may be well to explain that a "striker" is one who is not yet accomplished enough to go up for examination for his license as an engineer, but is reliable and handles an engine sufficiently to "stand a watch," that is, to be an assistant to the engineer who is in charge of the boat's entire machinery for that part of the twenty-four hours for which the engineer is responsible. The striker that has had the most experience is sometimes known as the third engineer. In looking up the history of the engine room men, the writer has learned that William Perkins, Thomas Berry and John Wiest were from Louisville. This was interesting, so it was afterward ascertained that Captain Cannon, Pilot Ostrander, and Pilot Pell were also Kentuckians, which was likewise gratifying. Very likely, more Kentuckians in the crew could have been found.

The *Robert E. Lee* was a large boat in every respect. The dimensions do not give the feeling of strength and roominess that one felt on board. Being intended to carry cotton in large masses, the timbers were all massive, the spaces large, the hull deep, and the width great. Her hull was 297 feet long, 45 feet wide, and 9 feet deep. The guards, or that part projecting beyond the hull on each side, were twenty feet in front of the paddle wheel houses, so that (for want of exact figures) it may be said she was about 86 feet wide over all. They said that in the days of the race her chimney tops were 140 feet above the water. The fact that she was built primarily to carry cotton, which is very inflammable, and the fuel was wood [was] the [cause] of such high chimneys. Her between decks measured twenty-five feet, so that she sat high at all times. Her cabin was full length and was luxurious in every particular. The superstructure, that is the cabin and all above it, rested directly over the hull, leaving the guards without such covering as the boats on the Ohio River have, and this space was used for piling cotton, sometimes up to the height of the uppermost or "hurricane" deck. At intervals on each there were groups of heavy timbers, made part of the deck and called "knees," which prevented another boat from coming aboard. . . .

Now we will go aboard, in the engine room, where John Wiest says: "Her engines were 40 inches in diameter, 10 feet stroke; eight boilers, 42 inches in diameter, 32 feet long, four flues in each boiler; her paddle-wheels were 39 feet in diameter, paddles 18 feet long, with 3 feet dip." There is no such machinery afloat now—the nearest approach is that of the *City of Louisville*, whose dimensions are here given: Cylinders 30 inches in diameter and 10 feet stroke; seven boilers 26 feet long and 42 inches in diameter, with ten flues in each boiler. The boat is 301 feet long, 43 feet wide in the hull, and 7 feet deep. While strong, she is not required to carry such tremendous tonnage as the *Lee* was, and therefore is not so massive in her timbers. Her best speed for a long distance is not quite fourteen miles an hour, which is better than any speed made on the upper Ohio for a long run.

Mr. Wiest then says, "I remained on her [the *Lee*] for three years, then went with Commodore Parisot (a well-known steamboat owner on the lower Mississippi) up the Yazoo River, to take charge of the engines of one of his best boats out of Vicksburg.

"The steamboat *Natchez* came out in 1869, built at Cincinnati, expressly designed to be faster than the *Robert E. Lee.* The two boats were soon running in the same trade from New Orleans to Vicksburg, called 400 miles, the *R. E. Lee* leaving every Tuesday and the *Natchez* every Saturday, and great rivalry sprang up between the friends of the two boats as to which one was the faster. In the spring of 1870, the *Lee* left the Vicksburg trade and went into the New Orleans & Louisville trade, leaving New Orleans every other Thursday; the *Natchez* dropping out of the Vicksburg trade and going into the St. Louis trade, leaving New Orleans on a Saturday.

"The talk became so general about the two boats that Captain T. P. Leathers, of the *Natchez*, published that he would leave on the *Lee's* day and show that the *Natchez* was the faster boat of the two; so that threw the gauntlet down to Captain Cannon. On the arrival of the *Lee* at Vicksburg from New Orleans, on his trip to Louisville, I went aboard and asked Captain Cannon if he was going to make the race. He said, 'No.' Yet when he reached the Ohio river, and all along shore up and down the merchants got after him so hard he changed his mind, and on reaching Cairo, on his down trip, he telegraphed me to be ready to go on his boat to New Orleans, which satisfied me the race was coming off. We arrived at our destination Tuesday evening, and went to work to prepare for the race Thursday evening at 5 o'clock."

We must leave Mr. Wiest a moment to go back to the *Lee*. When nearing Louisville, going up the Ohio, Captain Cannon is said to have suggested to Chief Engineer Perkins to give the *Natchez* a race on the return trip, to which Perkins objected on the grounds that he had not had a chance to overhaul any of the machinery; that in fact the boat had been under steam almost all the time for seventeen weeks. And Engineer Perkins thought he had won the Captain over to his way of thinking, until the friends of the boat at Louisville overpersuaded Captain Cannon, and then Mr. Perkins yielded, entering into the plans with great enthusiasm, as if renewing his youth, making repairs that would be necessary in case the race came off.

We will now go back to New Orleans, June 28, 1870, where we left the *Lee* stripping for the race.

The friends of the two boats spread the news on Tuesday that the *Natchez* would leave for St. Louis at the same time as the *Lee,* and it is said a great deal of money was wagered on both boats, though it was said neither captain bet a cent.

The *Lee* removed all the glass in the pilot house, the two escape pipes and all other possible "wind catchers" on the hurricane deck; the glass doors in the front of the social hall, the windows at the extreme end of the ladies' cabin, the gangway doors at the sides of the wheelhouses, the splash boards behind the wheels; in a word, anything that would catch wind and hold her back. The decks aft (or back) of the wheels had every other plank taken up to allow the spray to fall through at once. The derricks, and rigging, the spare anchors, mooring chains, in fact everything that could be spared on the main deck or in the hold went ashore with all the other portable articles.

Announcement was made by the agent that the boat would take no freight nor any way passengers though they would carry passengers for Louisville or St. Louis; that the boat was not going to put out a line or make a landing. The taste of sport was so great that 125 passengers were booked under the conditions. Reports were coming to the *Lee* constantly about the *Natchez* following in the footsteps of the *Lee* in everything the *Lee* was doing.

On the down trip the *Lee* had taken on a quantity of pine knots and pine "slivers," or pieces of six feet or less, and in New Orleans loaded her main deck with coal enough to put her down to five and one-half feet forward and six feet aft.

Mr. Wiest says: "Thursday Captain Cannon called all the officers together for instructions for leaving; he wanted everybody ready at 5 o'clock, the pilot in his house, but not in sight; the engineers at the throttle valves, the mate to have only one stage out and that at a balance so that the weight of one man on the boat end of the stage would lift it clear of the wharf. There would be a single line out, fast to a ring bolt, with a man stationed there, ax in hand, to cut and run for the end of the stage, the moment he heard a single tap of the big bell, and come aboard on the run or get left. Everybody reported to the captain that he understood his particular duty. The United States steamboat inspector, Whitmore, came aboard just before we left, examined the safety valves on each boiler, particularly the one that could be locked, locked it and sealed it with a government lead seal. There was no ringing of the big bell to signal that the boat was about to leave, yet the wharf was lined for miles with the crowds eager to see the race begun. Precisely at 5 o'clock one tap was given, everybody leaped to his place, the line was cut, and we were away, and the 'Wild Bob Lee' was off.

"The reason of this was because Captain Leathers, of the *Natchez,* had made his boasts that she would not leave until after the *Lee,* for he was going to pass her within sight of New Orleans. As we passed St. Mary's Market, where the time had been taken from, a cannon was fired, and as the *Natchez* passed the same point a cannon was also fired, only one minute and some seconds after our signal, and that was the nearest she ever came to us."

It might as well be mentioned here that the excitement thus begun at

New Orleans was exhibited all along the great river, at every town, village, city and landing. We cannot now understand it, but this race was a great event in the times we speak of, as all the world likes sport more or less, and here was a contest for speed supremacy that never was surpassed in dramatic setting and munificent completeness.

The *Lee's* machinery was not exactly located as it would be now. The "doctor" is the name given to the engine used exclusively to pump water into the boilers, or, in case of fire, to supply the hose, or if a leak was sprung, to pump out the water. The steam, after doing its duty in the cylinder, is escaped into large steel cylinders called heaters, to give out its heat to the water pumped into the heater directly from the river. This hot water is taken from the heater by another pipe from the "doctor" and forced into the boiler as hot as possible. The heaters on the *Lee* were two, one attached to each engine, and not, as nowadays, attached to the "doctor." This explanation is inserted here because Mr. Wiest begins his narrative, after leaving New Orleans, thus: "Now for our difficulties:

"We had a five-inch hot water pipe to pull apart in the hold, but repaired it without stopping—this happened five minute from New Orleans. Late in the night we sprung a leak in one of our boilers, which began to look like we would have to go to the bank (that is, land), for it was putting out the fire under the boilers and we were hardly able to supply it with the 'doctor,' the leak was so bad."

Mr. Perkins, the head engineer, was rather too old for such jobs; Mr. Berry was too stout for the same, making thus Mr. Wiest as the man to find out just what and where the leak was.

The bravery and self-sacrifice when duty called that had raised John Wiest from a private to first lieutenant of Company G, Third Kentucky (Union) cavalry, now brought Wiest equal to the situation.

The water of the Mississippi river holds great quantities of mud in suspension which the steam engines found early could be collected near the bottom of the boilers. Then they planned to allow the water to settle in a cylinder below the boiler, which they called the mud drum; thus each boiler had a mud drum below it and connected with the boiler by a leg. A mud drum leg made of iron or steel may be compared to an old-fashioned beaver hat with a top brim as well as a lower brim, though the top brim turned up all around upward, while the bottom brim turned downward, in order that they would fit the cylindrical surface of the boiler or the mud drum. The mud drum that was leaking so heavily on the *Lee* was attached on its upper end to the bottom of the fourth boiler from the right hand side of the row of boilers, and in the midst of probably the very hottest point of the under surface of the boiler. To reach it the fire bed would have to be broken into in order to see just what the leak was and where.

John Wiest had but little preparation to make. He removed all his clothing, putting on a complete suit of old overalls, tied a handkerchief close to his head, and provided a heavy pair of gloves. His tools were a hammer, cold chisel, and a poker from the fire doors. The fire bed was of sheet iron lined with fire tiles and was very hot, so that the hose was laid and water used freely to dampen down the iron of the fire bed. Crawling under the boiler as far as he could get toward the mud drum he had selected, he attacked the metal, not knowing whether he would be scalded or perhaps suffocated by the flames of the fires that swept over his head, as he lay on his back, and cut away the rivets of the fire bed; this done, he pried apart the sheets of iron, and then on his hands and knees, wielding the poker, he broke a hole in the tiling not a foot from the bottom of the boiler, close to the drum, so that he could see that the many leaks were in the top flange of the mud drum he had decided was the seat of the leak. One good glance was all he got, at that moment, and the next thing he knew Captain Cannon, who had been watching him at work, together with two other steamboat captains, were dragging him out upon the starboard guard, where he soon recovered his speech and told what he had seen. The hole in the fire bed was enlarged, so it was decided to try to stop it and not land. It was for a long time known that objects floating in a boiler fell into the currents made by the springing of a leak, and sometimes these minute articles in time stopped the leak.

Now we go back to Mr. Wiest's account and see how simply, it seemed to him, that they managed the matter: "We took hemp packing that we had in our supplies, and cut it into fine bits, and would stop the doctor pumps and put a little hemp in the cold water suction valve, and start the pump and force the hemp into the boiler, and repeat it frequently, putting only a little hemp in at a time, until finally we got the leak stopped. All this time the *Natchez* was pulling up on us. Just before daylight I stepped out on the guards to see how close she was, and just at that time they opened her fire doors; I thought she was within about 400 yards of us. At that time we were getting into shape again, and then we began to pull away from her.

"Some time in the morning Captain Cannon came into the engine room and requested Mr. Perkins not to run the boat so fast, as they were rapidly pulling away from the *Natchez*. Mr. Perkins replied that the *Natchez* was not bothering him at all; that he was after beating the time of the *Princess* to Natchez, which was the fastest up to that time, but Captain Cannon said we were too far behind to take the horns,[1] but we

---

[1] "She takes the horns" is an old Mississippi River expression. The fastest boats on the river wore a pair of gilded deer antlers as a symbol of prowess. Sometimes these emblems were mounted on top of the big bell on the hurricane roof, sometimes on the front of the pilot house; always in plain view, at any rate, for all to observe. These decorative antlers were much coveted. They were a brag to all and sundry usually that the owning boat had "shortened the pegs" in a speed sprint between two major cities—that she had done it honestly, in the presence of qualified witnesses, with no "time out" deductions for any delays.

River etiquette dictated that no boat owned these horns, or had a right to wear them, save for the period of her championship. When a new contender successfully

took them anyway, for as we reached Natchez we slowed down both engines and just scraped the wharfboat when our agent jumped aboard with the horns, all trimmed with flowers and ribbons.

"When we arrived at Vicksburg, there was a tug out in the river, with two floats, between which we ran at slow speed and took them in tow, one on each side, until the coal had all been thrown on the *Lee,* and we turned the floats loose.

"We saw the *Natchez* at Vicksburg for the last time; though as the river is all very crooked we saw her smoke many a time across the bends. Above Vicksburg, some distance near Greenville, we met the steamer *Pargaud,* which had 125 cords of pine knots for us. She came alongside and lashed to us, and we steamed at a reduced speed until the wood was transferred to the *Lee.*"

The *Thompson Dean,* a large boat, had left New Orleans several days before the *Lee,* heaving in sight of Memphis about the time of the night when the *Lee* was due. The friends of the *Lee* had prepared a grand display of fireworks with which to welcome the *Lee,* but someone started the idea that the *Thompson Dean* was the *Lee,* and Memphis gave her the benefit of the fireworks. The *Lee* had the pleasure of enjoying them from down about President Island. At Memphis the plan of coaling was carried out as it had been at Vicksburg, giving the crowd the opportunity to shout themselves hoarse for the *Lee.*

The *Idlewild* was the Cairo & Evansville packet, with which Captain Cannon had arranged to come down the Mississippi a few miles to transfer to her the Louisville and Cincinnati passengers that the *Lee* might have. The captain of the *Idlewild* took a party on at Cairo, who wanted to go to St. Louis on the *Lee,* two pilots for the river from Cairo up, and a lot of excursionists, making pretty nearly three hundred people. They met the *Lee* just about Island No. 1, and rounded to, having an idea of measuring their speed with the *Lee's,* but that idea was banished in a few minutes, and the *Idlewild* performed the same act as the *Pargaud* had done, the *Idlewild* casting off as soon as the eighty passengers and baggage had been transferred, while the *Lee* resumed full speed, passing Cairo thus, and must have made a fine sight, for the entire town had turned out.

Early in the night of Sunday, the 3d of July, a fog descended upon the river so thick that ordinarily the boat would have laid up to wait for it to clear away, but those St. Louis pilots were game and never said anything about quitting, except to let it be known they wanted the help of

---

made a faster trip, the vanquished boat must give up her horns. This actual transfer was often an occasion for gay parties, banquets and general celebrations.

Where or when this custom arrived on the scene is not clear. During the early period of steamboating on the Mississippi, use was made of a broom for the same purpose, undoubtedly a fashion brought inland from the seaboard. These brooms were nailed to the side of the pilothouse and were symbolic of a "clean sweep." Their use had been abandoned by the time of the 1840's. Deer horns replaced them.
—Frederick Way, Jr., *"She Takes the Horns"* (Cincinnati, 1953), pp. 9–10.

all the best eyes on board. To work out this suggestion, the two pilots remained at the wheel; the Ohio river pilots placed themselves out forward of the pilot house on top of the Texas. Captain Cannon took his stand at the break of the deck, where he could hear any hail that might come from the three men he had stationed near the jackstaff to call to him if they saw the shore too near. In the engine room they were using a moderate head of steam, with a man at the throttle of each engine. If the cry came, "Hard a starboard," the pilot stopped a wheel until the boat headed away from the shore, and used the same tactics reversed if the shore was too close on his left, and then when he got a good glimpse of the shore he would work her hard until he was again warned. This is a good place to remark that John Wiest says that there was one engine at least "working ahead" the entire run. True, it was quite slow at Natchez, Vicksburg, and Memphis, but "Bad Bob" never took "back water" the whole way.

The voyage so far had been quite an ovation to the *Lee* as the banks had people on the lookout day and night to see the boats go by, for Captain Leathers had filled the papers with the idea that it would be a close struggle the whole way. Two years after the race, John Wiest met a friend who had been one of a party who came fifty miles to the Mississippi to see the race at a point some twenty miles above New Orleans, but "they had their jugs with them and sampled them too often, so that they went to sleep and never woke up until daylight, when the boats were up about Red River." There were also many excursions run out of New Orleans, "to see the boats go by." And these shore camps had some way to make a noise with guns and horns.

As soon as daylight came the welcome began above Cairo and lasted till the *Lee* landed at St. Louis. There were excursion boats as far as twenty miles from the city, crowded with cheering people. At Jefferson Barracks (then two miles below the city, though now part of St. Louis), they were honored with a salute. The Iron Mountain railroad runs along the river for miles and miles, affording fine views of the winner of the race to thousands taking that method of seeing the boat and a Fourth of July excursion. The long wharf at St. Louis was black with the crowd, which will seem strange to most of the readers of this, but you must try to enter into the feelings of the people of those days, to whom the steamboat such as the *Lee* was "a thing of beauty and a joy forever."

The *Lee* passed the New Orleans wharfboat at St. Louis, which was the point to mark the end of the race, Monday, July 4, 1870, at 11:25:14 A.M, three days, eighteen hours and fourteen minutes out, but in order to make a finish worthy of such a race, the engines were not stopped until "she reached the foot of Bloody Island." It would take a United States survey now to find the foot of Bloody Island in East St. Louis, but it was above the site of the Eads Bridge, say near Biddle Street.

Then she rounded to and steamed back and made fast to the wharfboat, where the crowd took possession and held the boat for hours, but at last the men not on watch had a chance to slip away and get some badly needed sleep. Mr. Wiest says he don't remember having been asleep at all, though he laid down frequently when off watch, yet the excitement and sense of responsibility may have prevented any sound sleep.

Did it pay the owners to make the race? Only in the way of advertisement, which went around the world. What the cost was no one save Captain Cannon and the head clerk knew, and they never told.

Billy King and the *J. M. White*

The [*J. M.*] *White* was built at Elizabeth [Pennsylvania], in the summer of 1844, in the Upper Yard, then owned by Samuel Walker. She was the third steamboat of the name, which was that of a wealthy man prominent in steamboat circles in St. Louis. The first was built at Webster, on the Monongahela River, the second at Elizabeth about 1833. The *White* of which we write, whose speed made the name famous, was built by J. M. Converse, of St. Louis, the money she cost being largely furnished by Robert Chouteau, of that city. Her power was 24-inch cylinders with 10-foot stroke. She was 210 feet straight keel, 240 feet on deck, 50 feet beam and 8 feet depth of hold. The buckets of her wheels were 12 feet long and 24 inches wide.

The *White* was drafted by William King, familiarly called "Billy," and it was in her draft that she got her great speed. So complete was King's calculation that when under way the boat turned two swells. One rose about midway of the boilers and the other under the wheels. King knew where those swells would come, and placed the wheels where they would catch the after ones. It was in the placing of the wheelbeams that a dispute arose between King and Converse that almost spoiled the boat. King was a man of but few words. When he had taken his men to cut down for the wheelbeams, Converse interfered, for he saw that the beams would be probably 20 feet farther aft than such beams were usually put, and he feared that the boat would be ruined. He objected to having the beams cut down where King had marked them, and King simply told the men to let the matter rest for the present, and walked away.

Converse went to Walker and told him where King wanted to place the beams and what he had said to King. "And what did King say?" asked

From the *Elizabeth* (Pennsylvania) *Herald,* Boat-Building Centennial Edition, June 7, 1900. Reprinted in *Elizabeth and Her Neighbors,* by Richard T. Wiley, pp. 340–342. Copyright, 1936, by Richard T. Wiley. Butler, Pennsylvania: The Ziegler Company.

Written about three years ago [1897] by John A. Lambert, of the *Somerset* (Pa.) *Standard,* a native of Elizabeth, for a Pittsburgh paper and . . . reprinted in this paper. . . . The gentleman referred to, who took the model to St. Louis, was his father, John Lambert, Sr., [who] stoutly maintains the correctness of the story.— Editor, *Elizabeth Herald.*

Walker. "He didn't say anything." "Well," said Walker, "if he has made up his mind to put them there, he'll do it or he won't finish the boat. You had better write Chouteau and ask his advice."

Converse wrote to Chouteau at once, explaining the matter fully, saying if the wheels were placed where King wanted to put them, the boat would be spoiled. The reply came in due time and it was brief enough: "Let King put beams where he pleases." That settled it, and Converse did not interfere further with King's plans. The keenness of King's judgment was eloquently told by his masterpiece, the *White*, when she made her famous run from New Orleans to St. Louis in 3 days, 23 hours, and 9 minutes.

That run of the *J. M. White* made Billy King famous, and the steamboat owners of St. Louis besought him with princely offers to draft a boat that would beat her time, but he refused to do so. He simply said: "If any man drafts a boat that shall beat her time, I will then draft one to beat that." After the *J. M. White* had been worn out, it dawned upon steamboatmen that there had never been a boat that equalled her speed, and they tried to secure her draft. This King refused to surrender, and no other man had a copy of it or could duplicate it.

It was not known that King had made a model of the *White*, but he had. After building the *White*, he went to St. Louis in the employ of a boat-building company. His wife remained at Elizabeth for some time. About four months after he had gone to St. Louis, King wrote to a friend of his in Elizabeth—one who had worked with him on the *White*—and this is briefly the substance of what he said in his letter:

"Bring my wife to St. Louis as soon as she can get ready. Go into the attic of my house and close under the comb of the roof you will find a model in a box. Bring that box with you, and don't open it or allow any one to see it. Lock it in a stateroom on the boat, and leave it there until you reach St. Louis. I will pay all expenses."

When the gentleman went to see Mrs. King with the letter, she knew nothing of the model. "If there is one in the attic," she said, "I don't know when he put it there." The box was found, however, where King said it was, and was taken to St. Louis, as requested.

King met his wife and the gentleman on their arrival, and his first inquiry after greeting them was concerning the model. Being told that it was locked up on the boat, he went for it and carried it to his home, where he at once opened the box in the presence of the gentleman who had taken it to St. Louis. It was probably never seen by any other person than King, his wife, and the gentleman referred to. It was a beautiful model, made of pine and black walnut. It was 10 feet, 2 inches long and otherwise in beautiful proportions. Without saying a word, King went to his tool chest, took therefrom a saw and cut the model into several pieces. Then with a hatchet he completed the destruction by cutting it into kindling wood. The gentleman present said: "Why, Billy, I could have done that at home just as well as you here, and saved you the expense of bringing it here." "That may all be," replied King, "but I never would have been satisfied that it had been done."

King said at the time that he had a draft of the *White* on paper, but, although it was sought for time and again by men who would have given a fortune for it, it has never been found, and the equal of the famous *J. M. White* has never been built.

How the *Far West* Brought the News of the Custer Massacre

By the time the *Far West* was ready to start down the [Yellowstone] river, fourteen of the wounded men were so far recovered as to be able to remain at the camp. They went ashore, as did General Terry and Major Brisbin, and at five o'clock on the afternoon of July 3rd [1876] the steamer, followed by the cheers and fervent good wishes of the assembled troops, backed away from the bank and started her paddles for Bismarck and Fort Lincoln, 700 miles away. Thirty-eight sorely wounded soldiers were still in her deck hospital, and in her cabin traveled Capt. E. W. Smith, aide-de-camp to General Terry, on his way to Bismarck with the dispatches for Division Headquarters at Chicago, and carrying, besides, a bag full of letters from other members of the expedition and a great number of messages to be put on the wire for distant friends.

The boat had scarcely left the bank before she was under a full head of steam. There was to be no tying up for darkness that night. Captain Marsh's orders were to reach Bismarck in the shortest possible time and, as always, he took them literally. Every man on board was steeled to do his utmost and nobly performed his part. The river was fortunately high, but even so, it was perilous work driving a steamboat at top speed down such a channel.

Through the hours of the short midsummer night and the glaring sunlight of the next day the *Far West* rushed on, Foulk and John Hardy crowding on the steam until a glance at the gauge turned them dizzy; Marsh and Campbell, in four-hour reliefs "on the roof," holding the wheel with iron grip as they strained their eyes over the narrow channel ahead and spun the boat in and out between islands and rocks.

From *The Conquest of the Missouri*, Being the Story of the Life and Exploits of Captain Grant Marsh, by Joseph Mills Hanson, pp. 303–314. Copyright, 1909 and 1937, by A. C. McClurg & Company; 1946, by Rinehart & Company, Inc. New York and Toronto.

It has been claimed at different times and by various authorities (see *History of Early Steamboat Navigation on the Missouri River*, by Col. H. M. Chittenden, U. S. A., for example) that Captain Marsh and the *Far West* did not bring the first news of the battle of the Little Big Horn to the outside world, the credit being given instead to "Muggins" Taylor. Such claims are without foundation in fact. The *Far West* brought the first news of a credible nature, though from Montana emanated at about the same time a few garbled rumors which received publication but no credit from persons in a position to judge their value.—J. M. H. *ibid.*, p. 309.

On the *Far West* few thoughts were given to the significance of the day, that Fourth of July. Thousands of miles away in the palaces of the Centennial Exposition at Philadelphia, vast throngs were bidding welcome to the one hundredth anniversary of the Nation's birth. From the peaceful hamlets nestled among New England's hills to the mining camps of the Sierra Nevada, the freemen of Columbia were giving themselves over to joyous celebration of the great event. Yet surely nowhere beneath the shadow of the Stars and Stripes were men engaged in more patriotic duty than those who trod the decks of the *Far West*. From bow to stern her timbers were quivering to the incessant clang and cough of the machinery as shirtless firemen, sweating and grimy, stood before the furnaces, cramming fuel into the hungry flames.

Now and then the hoarse bellow of the whistle sent its echoes reverberating along the bald cliff sides, startling the grazing herds of buffalo and elk to wild stampede from the fiery monster that came tearing, like a demon of destruction, into their solitudes. Now and then the keel scraped along a projecting bar and sheered off violently, throwing the men to the deck like tenpins. A hundred times it seemed as if she would be dashed to pieces, but each time the skill of the pilots saved her and she sped on with her message of disaster to a waiting nation, and her burden of suffering humanity groaning for relief. General Godfrey says of the run of the *Far West:* "I remember how thrilled we were to hear Colonel Smith, Assistant Adjutant-General of the expedition, when relating his experiences of the down river trip; how the boat would skim over a bar; how, in turning a bend, the treacherous current would push her bow over so as to run her nose into the bank, but more often would carom her hull against it. But Grant Marsh never hesitated to take reasonable chances to save distance or to make speed, and he made good."

The heroic Dr. Porter, working without interruption, lost one of his patients in the early morning hours of the 4th, Private William George, of H Troop, shot through the left side on Reno's Hill. At Powder River the boat stopped long enough to have his body interred and to confirm the news of battle to Major Moore's little garrison, still encamped there, who had hardly believed Reno's stampeded Arikaree scouts. Then, after taking on board the private property of the officers killed on the Little Big Horn, which had been left at the Powder with the wagons, she was off again. Near old Stanley's Stockade she passed the *Josephine*, Captain Mart Coulson, upward bound with supplies for Terry's column, but the *Far West* merely hailed as they hauled abreast without abating her speed. Then out of the Yellowstone she shot into the Missouri, whose channel seemed spacious indeed after the mountain stream she had been threading. At Fort Buford there was a momentary stop to put off a wounded Arikaree scout. The garrison went wild with excitement. Men crowded upon the boat, shouting and begging for news. Their questions were not half answered when they were cleared from the decks and the boat was out in the stream again. At Fort Stevenson, during the afternoon of the 5th, she halted once more, and again leaving a garrison convulsed with unsatisfied anxiety, she leaped out on the last lap, straight away for Bismarck. After leaving Stevenson, Captain Marsh, in accordance with General Terry's order, draped the derrick and jack-staff of the boat with black and hoisted her flag at half-mast, in honor of the dead and wounded.

Night and day all had been the same on the *Far West*. But when through the darkness the lights of Bismarck loomed ahead, men looked at their watches and saw that it was eleven o'clock as her bow touched the bank and she came to rest at her journey's end, just fifty-four hours out from the mouth of the Big Horn. She had covered 710 miles at the average rate of thirteen and one-seventh miles per hour and, though no one stopped to think of it then, she had made herself the speed champion of the Missouri River, with a record unequaled by any other craft that had ever floated on the turbulent stream or its tributaries, from St. Louis to Fort Benton. Her accomplishment had been performed in the line of duty alone, with no desire for the winning of laurels other than the gratitude of those she served.

The boat had barely touched the bank when her officers and men were off, running up the streets and rousing the sleeping town. It was like the night that Concord was startled from slumber by the hoof-beats of Paul Revere's horse, galloping down the elm-shadowed streets on his mission of warning. Men ran from their houses half-dressed and disheveled, in every direction lights flashed at the windows. The first men routed from their beds were C. A. Lounsberry, the editor of the Bismarck *Tribune*, and J. M. Carnahan, the telegraph operator. They, together with Captain Marsh, Dr. Porter, Captain Smith, and a number of others from the boat, hurried to the telegraph office and Carnahan took his seat at the key, from which he scarcely raised himself for twenty-two hours.

Editor Lounsberry, who was also the accredited correspondent of the New York *Herald*, prepared copy, handing it over to Carnahan as fast as the latter could send it.[1] None of them thought of tiring, for it was the most thrilling work they had ever done. The words they were sending would soon be flashing around the world. The first message was a brief bulletin to the New York *Herald*, reading as follows:

Bismarck, D.T., July 5, 1876.—General Custer attacked the Indians, June 25, and he, [and] every officer and man in five companies, were killed. Reno with seven companies fought in intrenched position three days. The Bismarck *Tribune's* special correspondent was with the expedition and was killed.

Then the little party in the telegraph office settled down to work in earnest, Lounsberry's hand flying over sheet after sheet as he wove the

---

[1] The details of the work done that night, as well as the facts relating to the question of whether the *Far West* brought the first authentic news of the battle, have been largely gathered from Col. C. A. Lounsberry who, in correspondence with the author, has kindly furnished him with full information.—J.M.H.

tremendous story poured into his ears by the participants. There was over a column of notes on the campaign up to the date of battle, written by Mark Kellogg and rescued by General Terry himself from the pouch beside the correspondent's body. There were two columns of comment and description sent down by Major Brisbin. Then came interviews with Captain Smith, Dr. Porter, Captain Marsh, Fred Girard, and the stories of General Terry, of Curley, of some of the wounded, and of the death of Charlie Reynolds. During a lull when Carnahan's key for a moment ceased clicking, Lounsberry flung over to him a copy of the New Testament, exclaiming: "Take this! Fire it in when you run out of copy. Hold the wires. Tell 'em it's coming and to hold the key!"

Now followed the full list of the killed and wounded, and now, in the early morning hours, the message written by Captain Smith for the widows at Fort Lincoln, which was being carried to them by the *Far West,* dropping down to the fort with the wounded. Through the day the story grew until, when it was finished, more than 15,000 words had been transmitted. It cost the New York *Herald* $3,000, but it was worth the money, for it was the biggest "beat" in newspaper history. The *Herald* at once adopted Kellogg as having been its special correspondent. That it did so was well for his widow and children for the great metropolitan daily sent $2,000 to them. But it was not strictly true. Colonel Lounsberry was the *Herald's* correspondent and up to the moment when Custer's column left for the field he had expected to accompany it. Then his wife fell ill and Kellogg, a reporter employed by him on the *Tribune,* went instead.

*　*　*　*　*

After her arrival at Bismarck, the *Far West* lay there only a few hours. Then Captain Marsh returned on board and she started for Fort Lincoln with the wounded and Captain Smith's message for the widows. In the twilight just before sunrise she arrived. . . .

*　*　*　*　*

There were twenty-eight widows in stricken Fort Lincoln that morning, and Captain Marsh never witnessed such a scene as followed the announcement of the awful tidings. Every one in the post was frantic, and men, women, and children came running to the boat, sobbing and moaning as they begged for news. Some of the poor, frightened families of the men in ranks received the blessed assurance that their dear ones were safe, but to many the only answer could be a sad confirmation of their fears, from which they turned away with breaking hearts. Two days after the arrival of the *Far West,* when the wounded had been made comfortable in the post hospital, Mrs. Custer sent Dr. Middleton in her carriage to the boat landing with the request that Captain Marsh come up and see her and the other bereaved women. But he could not bear the thought of witnessing their grief, and declined. He never saw one of them after that bright May morning when, happy and light-hearted, they had lunched with him in the cabin of the *Far West*, little anticipating the sorrow which was so soon to be theirs.

The Great Calliope Duel

The meeting between the *American* and the *Wonderland* at Bonnett's Mill on the Missouri in 1915 will live long in showboat history. Needham and Steiner's trim *American*, headed upriver, was edging in toward the landing about eleven in the morning, preparatory to tying up for the evening performance. Calliope Red [whose real name was Bobby Wills] sat at the steaming keyboard, announcing the showboat's arrival with her favorite, "Oh, Dem Golden Slippers."

Suddenly Cooley and Thom's big *Wonderland* rounded the bend just above, on her way down the river, evidently with identical intentions as to an evening performance. The calliope player on *Wonderland* hurled the first insult with "What You Goin' Do When the Rent Comes Round?" Those on board the *American* understood: Their rival was implying that they and their boat were discards, no longer able to make a living. They turned to Calliope Red.

"You ain't gonna stand for that, are you, Red, from that bunch of hams?"

Calliope Red, aged twenty-three, with face and hair burnt to the same rich bronze, was surcharged with passionate loyalty for the *American* and all things associated with her. His second love was ragtime music, whether it came from a jug, a saw, the tinny piano in the front of the auditorium, or the iron-lunged monster now before him. He was already rolling up his sleeves for the duel. "I'll make that fake musician jump in the river when I get through with him," he growled. Then he called down to George Emmich, the engineer: "Turn on full steam, Chief. We're gonna play calliope music till they're black in the face!"

His reply to the *Wonderland's* insult was "Mornin', Si," which means in calliope language that the persons addressed are clumsy clodhoppers, antiquated theatrical mistakes, fitted only to be tillers of the soil.

In turn the *Wonderland* fired back with the deliberately chosen indignity, "Goodbye, Little Girl, Goodbye," which freely translated meant, "Your usefulness being passed, it's time for you to leave."

Calliope Red grinned contemptuously and replied with "Sit Down, You're Rocking the Boat."

His antagonist, in desperation, played "I Don't Like Your Family." Red countered with "Silver Threads among the Gold," a pointed reference to the age of the *Wonderland*.

From *Showboats*, The History of an American Institution, by Philip Graham, pp. 141–142. Copyright, 1951, by Philip Graham. Austin: University of Texas Press.

The calliope man on the *Wonderland's* top deck lost his temper, and his whistles screamed out, "When I Get You Alone Tonight," certainly intended as a threat.

Calliope Red acted instantly to win the day with "Get Out and Get Under." Since getting under a boat meant death, and since, according to Red's conception, death for his enemy would mean eternity in an unpleasant place, by one master stroke he had said, "Go to hell!" Truly a difficult message to send via calliope!

The whistles on the *Wonderland* became silent, and her defender slunk from the upper deck. . . .

PART THREE
Pirates, Outlaws and Sharpers

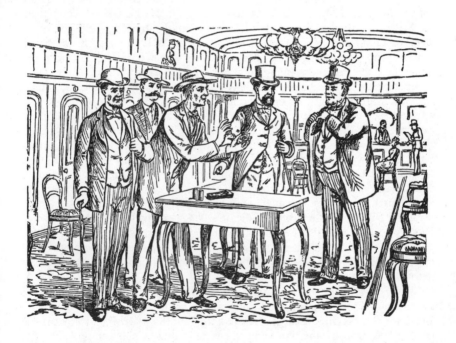

Introduction

"The frontier," wrote Judge Hall in 1828, "is often the retreat of loose individuals who, if not familiar with crime, have very blunt perceptions of virtue." All kinds and degrees of scoundrels and desperadoes—robbers and murderers, land and river pirates, dealers in stolen horses and slaves, gamblers and thimbleriggers, confidence and patent-medicine men—were attracted to the wide-open rivers and river country, with their easy hiding places and means of escape, their abundant flow of goods and money.

That there was not always a clear-cut line between the lawless and the law-abiding is evidenced by the boast of the Great Western Land Pirate, John A. Murrell,[1] that at least one half of the Grand Council of his Mystic Clan was made up of "men of high standing, and many of them in honorable and lucrative offices." It was doubtless one of these officials who exclaimed, when Murrell was about to make a death-bed confession, "Great God, John, don't give us all away!"

Second only to this land-pirate mastermind in strategy, if not in fiendish atrocity, were the outlaws of Cave-in-Rock, near the mouth of the Ohio, who preyed upon both river and overland travelers. The cave and its vicinity were for many years the stronghold of Samuel Mason (alias "Wilson"), whose "Liquor Vault and House of Entertainment" lured many an unwary flatboat captain and passenger into his hands. Mason later moved to Natchez, where he continued to rob boatmen and travelers passing through the Indian country, along the Natchez Trace. Here he was joined, and soon betrayed and beheaded for the reward, by Little (Wiley) Harpe, whose brother Micajah had already lost his head. James Ford, who maintained a first-class ferry and road and a dubious respectability as a front, stood out from the bloodthirsty monsters who slaughtered, burned and destroyed from "a deep-rooted malignity against human nature."

Comic relief from the lurid tales of the Ohio River outlaws is furnished by the picaresque tricks, close calls and masquerades of river gamblers and card sharks like George Devol and Jonathan Greene. Perhaps the most widespread of the gambling yarns tells how a sharper is found out and makes his getaway from his vengeful pursuers by disguising himself as a Negro deckhand or cook.

The greatest of the three-card monte men, Canada Bill, who started life as a Yorkshire gypsy, had a genius for snaring suckers by playing the part of the "greenest sort of a country jake." For this he was admirably fitted by nature. "Imagine," wrote his pal Devol, "a medium-

---

[1] For "John A. Murrell's Own Story" see *A Treasury of Southern Folklore* (1949), pp. 221–228.

sized, chicken-headed, tow-haired sort of a man with mild blue eyes, and a mouth nearly from ear to ear, who walked with a shuffling, half-apologetic sort of a gait, and who, when his countenance was in repose, resembled an idiot. . . . He had a squeaking, boyish voice, and awkward, gawky manners, and a way of asking fool questions and putting on a good-natured sort of a grin that led everybody to believe that he was the rankest kind of a sucker."

Ironically, Canada Bill was a kind of sucker. He had a soft heart, giving liberally to the Sisters of Charity, and on at least one occasion, returning $200 he had won from a man whose little boy came running down the cabin. Moreover, he was "a fool at short cards," which kept him poor. But, as he often said, "Suckers had no business with money."

B. A. B.

Harpe's Head

Many years ago, two men named Harpe appeared in Kentucky, spreading death and terror wherever they went. Little else was known of them but that they passed for brothers, and came from the borders of Virginia. They had three women with them, who were treated as their wives, and several children, with whom they traversed the mountains and thinly settled parts of Virginia into Kentucky, marking their course with blood. Their history is wonderful, as well from the number and variety as the incredible atrocity of their adventures; and as it has never yet appeared in print, I shall compress within this letter a few of its most prominent facts.

In the autumn of the year 1799, a young gentleman, named Langford, of a respectable family in Mecklenburgh County, Virginia, set out from this state for Kentucky, with the intention of passing through the Wilderness, as it was then called, by the route generally known as Boon's Trace. On reaching the vicinity of the Wilderness, a mountainous and uninhabited tract, which at that time separated the settled parts of Kentucky from those of Virginia, he stopped to breakfast at a public house near Big Rockcastle River. Travelers of this description—any other indeed than hardy woodsmen—were unwilling to pass singly through this lonely region; and

From *Letters from the West;* Containing Sketches of Scenery, Manners, and Customs; and Anecdotes Connected with the First Settlements of the Western Sections of the United States, by the Hon. Judge [James] Hall, pp. 265–281. London: Henry Colburn. 1828.

The principal scene of Harpe's atrocities and of his death was in that part of Kentucky which lies south of Green River, a vast wilderness then known by the general name of the Green River Country.—J.H.

they generally waited on its confines for others, and traveled through in parties. Mr. Langford, either not dreading danger, or not choosing to delay, determined to proceed alone. While breakfast was preparing, the Harpes and their women came up. Their appearance denoted poverty, with but little regard to cleanliness; two very indifferent horses, with some bags swung across them, and a rifle gun or two composed nearly their whole equipage. Squalid and miserable, they seemed objects of pity rather than of fear, and their ferocious glances were attributed more to hunger than to guilty passion. They were entire strangers in that neighbourhood, and, like Mr. Langford, were about to cross the Wilderness. When breakfast was served up, the landlord, as was customary at such places, in those times, invited all the persons who were assembled in the common, perhaps the only room of his little inn, to sit down; but the Harpes declined, alleging their want of money as the reason. Langford, who was of a lively, generous disposition, on hearing this invited them to partake of the meal at his expense; they accepted the invitation, and eat voraciously. When they had thus refreshed themselves, and were about to renew their journey, Mr. Langford called for the bill, and in the act of discharging it imprudently displayed a handful of silver. They then set out together.

A few days after, some men who were conducting a drove of cattle to Virginia, by the same road which had been traveled by Mr. Langford and the Harpes, had arrived within a few miles of Big Rock-castle River, when their cattle took fright, and, quitting the road, rushed down a hill into the woods. In collecting them, the drovers discovered the dead body of a man concealed behind a log, and covered with brush and leaves. It was now evident that the cattle had been alarmed by the smell of blood in the road, and as the body exhibited marks of violence, it was at once suspected that a murder had been perpetrated but recently. The corpse was taken to the same house where the Harpes had breakfasted, and recognized to be that of Mr. Langford, whose name was marked upon several parts of his dress. Suspicion fell upon the Harpes, who were pursued and apprehended near the Crab Orchard. They were taken to Stanford, the seat of justice for Lincoln County, where they were examined and committed by an inquiring court, sent to Danville for safe keeping, and probably for trial, as the system of district courts was then in operation in Kentucky. Previous to the time of trial, they made their escape, and proceeded to Henderson County, which at that time was just beginning to be settled.

Here they soon acquired a dreadful celebrity. Neither avarice, want, nor any of the usual inducements to the commission of crime, seemed to govern their conduct. A savage thirst for blood—a deep rooted malignity against human nature, could alone be discovered in their actions. They murdered every defenceless being who fell in their way without distinction of age, sex, or color. In the night they stole secretly to the cabin, slaughtered its inhabitants, and burned their dwelling—while the farmer who left his house by day returned to witness the dying agonies of his wife and children, and the conflagration of his possessions. Plunder was not their object: travelers they robbed and murdered, but from the inhabitants they took only what would have been freely given to them, and no more than was immediately necessary to supply the wants of nature; they destroyed without having suffered injury, and without the prospect of gain. A Negro boy, riding to a mill with a bag of corn, was seized by them, and his brains dashed out against a tree; but the horse which he rode and the grain were left unmolested. Females, children, and servants no longer dared to stir abroad; unarmed men feared to encounter a Harpe; and the solitary hunter, as he trod the forest, looked around him with a watchful eye, and when he saw a stranger, picked his flint and stood on the defensive.

It seems incredible that such atrocities could have been often repeated in a country famed for the hardihood and gallantry of its people; in Kentucky, the cradle of courage, and the nurse of warriors. But that part of Kentucky which was the scene of these barbarities was then almost a wilderness, and the vigilance of the Harpes for a time ensured impunity. The spoils of their dreadful warfare furnished them with the means of violence and of escape. Mounted on fine horses, they plunged into the forest, eluded pursuit by frequently changing their course, and appeared, unexpectedly, to perpetrate new enormities, at points distant from those where they were supposed to lurk. On these occasions, they often left their wives and children behind them; and it is a fact, honourable to the community, that vengeance for these bloody deeds was not wreaked on the helpless, but in some degree guilty, companions of the perpetrators. Justice, however, was not long delayed.

A frontier is often the retreat of loose individuals, who, if not familiar with crime, have very blunt perceptions of virtue. The genuine woodsman, the real pioneer, are independent, brave, and upright; but as the jackal pursues the lion to devour his leavings, the footsteps of the sturdy hunter are closely pursued by miscreants destitute of his noble qualities. These are the poorest and the idlest of the human race—averse to labour, and impatient of the restraints of law and the courtesies of civilized society. Without the ardor, the activity, the love of sport, and patience of fatigue, which distinguish the bold backwoodsman, these are doomed to the forest by sheer laziness, and hunt for a bare subsistence; they are the "cankers of a calm world and a long peace," the helpless nobodies, who, in a country where none starve and few beg, sleep until hunger pinches, then stroll into the woods for a meal, and return to their slumber. Frequently they are as harmless as the wart upon a man's nose, and as unsightly; but they are sometimes mere wax in the hands of the designing, and become the accessories of that guilt which they have not the courage or the industry to perpetrate. With such men the Harpes are supposed to have sometimes lurked. None are known to have participated in their deeds of blood nor suspected of sharing their counsels; but they sometimes crept to the miserable cabins of those who feared or were not inclined to betray them.

Two travelers came one night to the house of a man named Stegal, and, for want of better lodgings, claimed under his little roof that hospitality which in a new country is found at every habitation. Shortly after, the Harpes arrived. It was not, it seems, their first visit; for Mrs. Stegal had received instructions from them, which she dared not disobey, never to address them by their real names in the presence of third persons. On this occasion they contrived to inform her that they intended to personate Methodist preachers, and ordered her to arrange matters so that one of them should sleep with each of the strangers, whom they intended to murder. Stegal was absent, and the woman was obliged to obey. The strangers were completely deceived as to the character of the newly arrived guests; and when it was announced that the house contained but two beds, they cheerfully assented to the proposed arrangement: one crept into a bed on the lower floor with one ruffian, while the other retired to the loft with another. Both the strangers became their victims; but these bloody ruffians, who seemed neither to feel shame, nor dread punishment, determined to leave behind them no evidence of their crime, and consummated the foul tragedy by murdering their hostess and setting fire to the dwelling.

From this scene of arson, robbery, and murder, the perpetrators fled precipitately, favoured by a heavy fall of rain, which, as they believed, effaced their footsteps. They did not cease their flight until late the ensuing day, when they halted at a spot which they supposed to be far from any human habitation. Here they kindled a fire, and were drying their clothes, when an emigrant, who had pitched his tent hard by, strolled towards their camp. He was in search of his horses, which had strayed, and civilly asked if they had seen them. This unsuspecting woodsman they slew, and continued their retreat.

In the meanwhile, the outrages of these murderers had not escaped notice, nor where they tamely submitted to. The Governor of Kentucky had offered a reward for their heads, and parties of volunteers had pursued them; they had been so fortunate as to escape punishment by their cunning, but had not the prudence to desist, or to fly the country.

A man named Leiper, in revenge for the murder of Mrs. Stegal, raised a party, pursued, and discovered the assassins, on the day succeeding that atrocious deed. They came so suddenly upon the Harpes that they had only time to fly in different directions. Accident aided the pursuers. One of the Harpes was a large, and the other a small man; the first usually rode a strong, powerful horse, the other a fleet, but much smaller animal, and in the hurry of flight they had exchanged horses. The chase was long and hot: the smaller Harpe escaped unnoticed; but the other, who was kept in view, spurred on the noble animal which he rode, and which, already jaded, began to fail at the end of five or six miles. Still the miscreant pressed forward; for, although none of his pursuers were near but

Leiper, who had outridden his companions, he was not willing to risk a combat with a man as strong and perhaps bolder than himself, who was animated with a noble spirit of indignation against a shocking and unmanly outrage. Leiper was mounted upon a horse of celebrated powers, which he had borrowed from a neighbour for this occasion. At the beginning of the chase, he had pressed his charger to the height of his speed, carefully keeping on the track of Harpe, of whom he sometimes caught a glimpse as he ascended the hills, and again lost sight in the valleys and the brush. But as he gained on the foe, and became sure of his victim, he slackened his pace, cocked his rifle, and deliberately pursued, sometimes calling upon the outlaw to surrender. At length, in leaping a ravine, Harpe's horse sprained a limb, and Leiper overtook him. Both were armed with rifles. Leiper fired, and wounded Harpe through the body; the latter, turning in his seat, leveled his piece, which missed fire, and he dashed it to the ground, swearing it was the first time it had ever deceived him. He then drew a tomahawk, and waited the approach of Leiper, who, nothing daunted, unsheathed his long hunting knife and rushed upon his desperate foe, grappled with him, hurled him to the ground, and wrested his only remaining weapon from his grasp. The prostrate wretch—exhausted with the loss of blood, conquered, but unsubdued in spirit—now lay passive at the feet of his adversary. Expecting every moment the arrival of the rest of his pursuers, he inquired if Stegal was of the party, and being answered in the affirmative, he exclaimed, "Then I am a dead man."

"That would make no difference," replied Leiper, calmly; "you must die at any rate. I do not wish to kill you myself, but if nobody else will do it, I must." Leiper was a humane man, easy, slow-spoken, and not quickly excited, but a thorough soldier when roused. Without insulting the expiring criminal, he questioned him as to the motives of his late atrocities. The murderer attempted not to palliate or deny them, and confessed that he had been actuated by no inducement but a settled hatred of his species, whom he had sworn to destroy without distinction, in retaliation for some fancied injury. He expressed no regret for any of his bloody deeds, except that which he confessed he had perpetrated upon one of his own children. "It cried," said he, "and I killed it: I had always told the women I would have no crying about me." He acknowledged that he had amassed large sums of money, and described the places of concealment; but as none was ever discovered, it is presumed he did not declare the truth. Leiper had fired several times at Harpe during the chase, and wounded him; and when the latter was asked why, when he found Leiper pursuing him alone, he did not dismount and take to a tree, from behind which he could inevitably have shot him as he approached, he replied that he had supposed there was not a horse in the country equal to the one which he rode, and that he was confident of making his escape. He thought also that the pursuit would be less eager, so long as he abstained from shedding the blood of any of his pursuers. On the arrival of the rest of the party, the wretch was dispatched, and he died as he had lived, in remorseless guilt. It is said, however, that he was about to make some disclosure, and had commenced in a tone of more sincerity than he had before evinced, when Stegal advanced and severed his head from his body. This bloody trophy they carried to the nearest magistrate, a Mr. Newman, before whom it was proved to be the head of Micajah Harpe; they then placed it in the fork of a tree, where it long remained a revolting object of horror. The spot which is near the Highland Lick, in Union (then Henderson) County, is still called Harpe's Head, and a public road which passes it, is called the Harpe's Head Road.

The other Harpe made his way to the neighbourhood of Natchez, where he joined a gang of robbers headed by a man named Meason, whose villainies were so notorious that a reward was offered for his head. At that period, vast regions along the shores of the Ohio and Mississippi were still unsettled, through which boats navigating those rivers must necessarily pass; and the traders who, after selling their cargoes at New Orleans, attempted to return by land, had to cross immense wildernesses, totally destitute of inhaibtants. Meason, who was a man rather above the ordinary stamp, infested these deserts, seldom committing murder, but robbing all who fell in his way. Sometimes he plundered the descending boats; but more frequently he allowed these to pass, preferring to rob their owners of their money as they returned, pleasantly observing that "those people were taking produce to market for him." Harpe took an opportunity, when the rest of his companions were absent, to slay Meason, and putting his head in a bag, carried it to Natchez, and claimed the reward. The claim was admitted; the head of Meason was recognized; but so also was the face of Harpe, who was arrested, condemned, and executed.

In collecting oral testimony of events long past, a considerable variety will often be found in the statements of the persons conversant with the circumstances. In this case, I have found none, except as to the fact of the two Harpes having exchanged horses. A day or two before the fatal catastrophe which ended their career in Kentucky, they had murdered a gentleman named Love, and had taken his horse, a remarkably fine animal, which big Harpe undoubtedly rode when he was overtaken. It is said that little Harpe escaped on foot, and not on his brother's horse. Many of these facts were disclosed by the latter, while under sentence of death.

After Harpe's death the women came in and claimed protection. Two of them were the wives of the larger Harpe, the other one of his brother. The latter was a decent female, of delicate, prepossessing appearance, who stated that she had married her husband without any knowledge of his real character, shortly before they set out for the west; that she was so much shocked at the first murder which they committed that she attempted to escape from them, but was prevented, and that she had since made similar attempts. She immediately wrote to her father in Virginia, who came for her, and took her home. The other women were in no way remarkable. They remained in Muhlenburgh County.

The Big Kentuckian's Pants

Mr. [John L.] Swaney carried the mail on horseback from Nashville to Natchez in early times, and frequently saw and talked with the noted robber [Samuel] Mason, the leader of a band who laid in ambush in the Choctaw Nation, and robbed traders and boatmen as they returned from New Orleans and Natchez. He began carrying the mail about 1796 or '97, and continued in this employment for nearly eight years. . . .

* * * * *

[Samuel] Mason lived several years near Cross Plains, in Robertson County. He went from there to Natchez, where he organized his band, which consisted of himself and his two sons, Tom and John, and seven or eight other men. The leader of this band was then about fifty years old, weighed about two hundred pounds, and was a fine-looking man; rather modest and unassuming, and had nothing of the raw-head-and-bloody-bones appearance which his character would indicate. He frequently sought interviews with the mail-carriers, and was always anxious to know what was said of him by the public. Mason told Mr. Swaney that he need not be afraid of him, as he had nothing but the mail, while he (Mason) wanted nothing but money. Mason told Swaney repeatedly that he did not desire to kill any man; that money was all he was after, and that if he could get that without taking life, he would certainly shed no blood. Mason's band was a great terror to the boatmen and travelers who came through the Indian nation. Before leaving Natchez those who were coming through supplied themselves with provisions to last them until they should reach the agencies or all the way through, and capturing these supplies gave Mason and his men ample means to support themselves. This band knew every foot of the road, and every place where parties would be likely to camp, particularly the springs, etc., which enabled them "to ply their vocation" the more successfully.

Among Mason's first robberies was a party of Kentucky boatmen returning from Natchez. They had camped at what was called Gum Springs, in the Choctaw Nation. They ate supper, and as a matter of precaution, were putting out pickets before retiring for the night. In going to their positions, one of the pickets stepped on one of Mason's men, who were hid in the cane and grass, awaiting an opportunity to pounce upon the boatmen. The robber, thus carelessly trod upon, jumped up and gave a yell and fired off his gun, calling upon his comrades to shoot and kill every boatman. This was so unexpected to the Kentuckians that they became panic stricken and ran off in the wildest confusion, leaving everything, some even their wearing apparel. Mason and his men went to the camp

From *Old Times in Tennessee,* with Historical, Personal, and Political Scraps and Sketches, by Jo[sephus] C. Guild, pp. 93–96. Nashville: Tavel, Eastman, & Howell. 1878.

and carried away everything. The next morning, just at daylight, Mr. Swaney came along, and seeing the campfires burning, rode out but could find no one. He was going toward Natchez, and having met no party that morning, he instinctively knew that something was wrong, and he began to blow his bugle. The boatmen recognized the familiar sound, and commenced coming to Mr. Swaney, one and two at a time, who asserted that they were the worst scared, worst looking set of men he ever saw, some of them having but little clothing on, and one big fellow had only a shirt. They immediately held a sort of council of war, and it was unanimously agreed to follow the robbers and capture their property. It was an easy matter to follow their trail through the cane and grass. Their plan was, as they had no arms, to provide themselves with sticks and knives, and when they should overtake Mason and his men, attack them by a vigorous charge, knocking down right and left with their shillelahs, and if those in front fell at the fire of the robbers, those in the rear were to rush upon, overpower, and capture the robbers and recover their property. They started in pursuit of the robbers, under the lead of the big Kentuckian.

They had gone about a mile, when they began to find articles of clothing which had been thrown away by the robbers. The big Kentuckian found his pants, in the waistband of which he had sewed four doubloons, and to his great joy the robbers had not found them. After this it was noticed that the big Kentuckian's valor began to fail him, and soon he was found in the rear. The pursuit was kept up about two miles further, when they were suddenly halted by Mason and his men, who were hid behind trees, with their guns presented, and who ordered them to go back or they would kill the last one of them. This caused a greater stampede than that of the night before, and the big Kentuckian distanced the whole party in the race back to camp. They abused the big Kentuckian at a round rate for his want of courage, but he only laughed at them, saying he had everything to run for. But to his credit be it said, he spent his last dollar in procuring supplies for his companions.

Adventure at Cave-in-Rock

The earliest connection of Cave-in-Rock with the name of any outlaw who became famous was in 1797, when Samuel Mason, of Revolutionary fame and hideous fate, seems to have occupied it as a main trap for his carefully worked out scheme of river piracy on a large scale. He

From *The Outlaws of Cave-in-Rock,* Historical Accounts of the Famous Highwaymen and River Pirates Who Operated in Pioneer Days upon the Ohio and Mississippi Rivers and over the Old Natchez Trace, by Otto A. Rothert, pp. 46–47, 285–293. Copyright, 1923, by Otto A. Rothert. Cleveland, Ohio. 1924. Reprinted by permission of The Arthur H. Clark Co.

erected a great rude sign on the river bank near the mouth of the Cave, proclaiming to every passer-by that his "Liquor Vault and House for Entertainment" was open to the public. Many captains and their crews and many flatboat passengers were lured to it. After Mason and his family left for the South, most of the succeeding bands, during their necessarily short stay, operated a gambling and drinking place on the same principle.

It was a common practice among outlaws frequently to change not only their headquarters but their names. While at Cave-in-Rock Mason was also known as "Wilson." Thomas Ashe, who wrote about it [in *Travels in America Performed in 1806*, London, 1808], probably did not know that the Wilson he described was Samuel Mason. Among the various men who appeared after the departure of Samuel Mason, alias "Wilson," was one Jim Wilson. Whether Jim Wilson was his real name is not known. However, between Samuel Mason as "Wilson" and a later man known as "Jim Wilson" there has been more or less confusion for almost a century, especially in tradition. In 1897 William Courtney Watts wrote a historical romance, *Chronicles of a Kentucky Settlement*, in which he presents James Ford, of Ford's Ferry notoriety, as "James Wilson." James Ford was in no way connected with Mason or with Wilson, but his presentation under the fictitious name of "James Wilson" had added to the already existing confusion.

*   *   *   *   *

Among the men who figure in the romance, and whom Watts personally knew was Dr. Charles H. Webb, of Livingston County, of which Smithland is the seat. Dr. Webb married Cassandra Ford, the daughter of James Ford. He related the story of his life to Watts and thus contributed a chapter to history that stands alone. There exists in more or less abundance data relative to some of the methods employed by the bands of robbers at Cave-in-Rock to entice boats to land at the Cave and get possession of victims. All these, however, are . . . stories based on statements made, not by men who spoke from actual observation, but by persons who had heard others relate another man's experience. In Dr. Webb we actually touch hands with a well-known and highly respected citizen who was lured to the Cave by some of the tricks suggested—tricks regarding which few lived to tell the tale, and of which nobody else left any direct authoritative account.

Dr. Charles H. Webb and his brother John, both young men, left South Carolina in 1822 for Philadelphia and shortly thereafter set out for the West in search of fortune, with St. Louis as their destination. At Cave-in-Rock, on their way down the Ohio, they met their great adventure and were separated as the narrative records. Dr. Webb, having lost all, settled at Salem. There he subsequently met and knew Watts. The two became fast friends when Watts, much the younger of the two, had grown up. It was from Dr. Webb, in the flower of his middle age, that Watts had this story:

My brother and I descended the Ohio River from Pittsburgh to Louisville in a flatboat, and after remaining a few days in Louisville we again
started on another flatboat, intending to go on it as far as the mouth of
the Ohio River, or near there. . . . The boat, a "broadhorn," was in
charge of one Jonathan Lumley, who owned a large proportion of the
cargo which consisted of corn, provisions, and whisky. With Mr. Lumley
were three other stout young men as hands, making, with my brother and
myself, who had agreed to work our way for food and passage, six persons
on board.

Day after day, as we floated along, the better I got acquainted with my
companions . . . the more I found that, under a rough exterior, they were
warm-hearted, generous, and confiding fellows, equally ready for a jig
or a knockdown, for a shooting match or a drinking bout, for a song or a
sermon.

I was playing on my flute as our boat was nearing Cave-in-Rock, and
when within full view of the high rocky bluffs, at the base of which is the
entrance to the cave, we observed a woman on the top of the bluff hailing
us by waving a white cloth, whereupon our captain, as we called Mr. Lumley, ordered us to pull in close to shore, within easy speaking distance, so
as to learn what was wanted.

Presently a man came from the entrance of the Cave, and called out:
"Hey, Cap! have you enny bacon or whisky on board?"

"I-yie!" shouted back our captain.

"Won't yer land? We're short on rations here, an' want ter buy right
smart!" said the man.

"Goin' to the lower Mississippi!" answered our captain, "and don't
want to break bulk so high up."

"But, Cap, we'ud be mi'ty obleeged ef you'd lan'. An' we've got a
woman here an' a boy who want passage down ter the mouth er Cumber-
lan'. They've bin waitin' a long time, an'll pay passage."

"All right, then," replied the captain, "I'll land; but let them come
aboard at once."

And land we did some two hundred yards below the Cave, when the
captain and three others—my brother being one of them—went ashore
and walked up to the entrance. After waiting for more than an hour, and
none of our men returning, I asked my remaining companion to go up
to the Cave and see what was detaining them. Another hour passed away;
the sun had gone down, and night, with clouds, was rapidly coming on.

I began to feel uneasy, and to add to my uneasiness, a large dog which
we had on board began howling most dismally. Presently, by the dim twilight, I saw three men approaching the boat from the Cave. At first I
thought them a part of our crew, but I was soon undeceived, for they came
on board, and with pistols drawn, demanded my surrender. Resistance was
useless; my arms were soon bound behind my back, and I was told that
if I made any row my brains would be blown out. I asked about my
friends but was only told that they were "all right," that the captain had

"sold the boat and cargo" and that what little information they had given was "enough" for me "to know."

I was then blindfolded, and when my money had been taken from me, I was assisted—I should say lifted—into a skiff, into which two of the three men, so I thought, entered. I begged to know what had become of my brother, and told them that he and I were passengers on the boat and no part of the crew proper. I did this, hoping that if they knew we were passengers and had no direct interest in the boat and cargo they would think us less likely to return to the Cave and molest them. But the only answer I got was that the "fewer questions" I asked, the better it would be for me, "by a d—— sight."

The skiff was then rowed away—in what direction I could not tell, but in some five minutes there was a pause in the rowing, and soon a slight jar as of two skiffs coming together, followed by a conversation in low tones, the purport of which I could not catch. Very soon, however, one of the men approached me and whispered in my ear. There seemed to be a remnant of mercy in the intonation of his words, rather than in the words themselves. He said: "We're goin' ter vi'late orders a little, an' turn yer loose here in the middle er the river. An' the furder yer float away frum here 'fore yer make enny noise, the better for yer by a d—— sight. Yer'd better lay low an' keep dark till mornin' comes." The speaker then slackened the cords that bound my arms, after which he again whispered: "Yer ken work 'em loose when we're gone, say in 'bout an hour, but not sooner, er yer may get inter trouble. An' don't yer never come back here to ax enny questions, or yer'll fare worse, an' do nobody enny good."

The man then left me seated in the stern of the skiff, and I could tell from the motion and the rattling of a chain that a second boat was being pulled alongside it, into which the man stepped, leaving me alone. I strained my ears to catch the slightest sound, but I could neither hear the click of oars nor the dip of a paddle; the latter, however, might have been used so noiselessly as to be unheard. I was therefore in doubt. I thought possibly the other boat might be floating close to me and that I was being watched. This brought to my mind the man's caution not to try to free my arms for an hour. I therefore remained quiet for about that length of time. No sound reached me except the moaning of the night winds among the forest trees that lined each shore, the occasional barking of wolves, and the weird cry of night-fowls—particularly the blood-curdling hooting of great owls. . . .

After a long and painful effort I succeeded in releasing my arms and freeing my eyes from the bandage. Looking around, I found the heavens overcast; the night was so intensely dark that I could see only a dim outline of the shore. I discovered there were neither oars nor paddle in the skiff, but I was floating some two or three miles an hour, and it might be many hours before I would pass any habitation. I therefore made up my mind to lie down in the skiff, try to get some sleep and await the coming of morn. But the distant growling thunder was creeping nearer and nearer; flash after flash lit up the heavens, followed by almost deafening discharges that rolled, crashed and reverberated along the river and among the forests, which moaned and groaned under the pressure of the rising wind. The waves in the river were momentarily increasing, and were dashing my little skiff about in a way that was alarming. . . .

I knew if the downpour continued for many minutes my skiff would fill and sink. There was but one way to bail it out—to use one of my thick leather shoes as a scoop. I worked manfully while the rain lasted, which, fortunately, was not for more than an hour.

The long night finally passed, but the heavens were still overcast. I peered along both banks—looked, hoping to see smoke curling above some cabin chimney—but there was no sign of human habitation. Occasionlly I raised my voice to its highest pitch—gave a loud halloo—but no answering voice was returned. However, about an hour later, I saw an island ahead of me; it was evidently inhabited, for notwithstanding the leaden aspect of the skies, I could see smoke ascending from among the trees. I used my hands as paddles as vigorously as I could so as to drift against the head of the island, and in this I succeeded. Having secured my boat, I soon found the cabin, and was kindly received by a Mr. Prior and his wife, who gave me a good breakfast. I told them of my misfortune, and they expressed much sympathy for me. Mr. Prior, who seemed to be an honest and intelligent man, told me that he was one of the earliest settlers in those parts. He said he had often heard of the depredations of the Wilson gang about the Cave and that I was lucky to have escaped with my life. He advised me to stop at Smithland, at the mouth of the Cumberland River, where I might obtain assistance and directions as to what was best for me to do. Mr. Prior then made me a paddle out of a clapboard, and bidding him and his kind wife goodby, I returned to my skiff, pushed off, and that evening arrived in Smithland.

At Smithland young Webb was directed to Salem, "which then contained a population, white and black, of about two hundred and fifty." There, in turn, he was advised by Judge Dixon Given to consult Colonel Arthur Love relative to the best method of gaining information regarding his brother who had been captured at the Cave. Colonel Love, a highly esteemed citizen, lived a few miles from the home of James Ford, who was suspected by many of being a leader of the Cave-in-Rock band. No crime, however, had ever been traced to Ford, "with sufficient clearness to cause his arrest and trial." On his way to Colonel Love's farm Webb fell from his horse and sprained his ankle, and it so happened that Cassandra Ford, daughter of James Ford, found the helpless young man lying in the road. She took him to her home, and he soon discovered he was in the house of the very man he dreaded most. But his fears rapidly vanished, for his rescuer had become very much attached to him and he to her. He was shown the flute of which he had been robbed near the Cave. The mother and daughter revealed to him the fact that they, like many of their neighbors, felt somewhat suspicious that James Ford was, in some way, connected with the notorious crowd at the Cave. Ford, who was away from home much of the time, did not return until about a week after the crippled man was admitted. Then Webb saw the "masterful, self-willed, dreaded, and almost outlawed man." He gave a description of him as he appeared at that time:

"He was about six feet in height, and of powerful build, a perfect Hercules in point of strength; but he has now grown too corpulent to undergo much fatigue. His head is large and well shaped; his sandy brown hair, now thin, is turning gray; for he must be fully fifty years old; his eyes, of a steel-gray color, are brilliant and his glance quick and penetrating; his nose rather short and thick; his upper lip remarkably long, his mouth large, and his lips full and sensuous. He has a broad, firm double chin, and his voice is deep and sonorous. His complexion is very florid, and he converses fluently. On the whole, when in repose, he gives one the idea of a good-natured rather than a surly bulldog; but, if aroused, I should say he would be a lion tamer."

When Webb's foot was sufficiently healed to permit his leaving the Ford home, he took his flute and crutches and returned to Salem. Shortly thereafter he made the first of his many calls on Miss Ford. In the meantime, learning that his brother had been allowed to depart from the Cave unhurt, he wrote letters to various places and finally located him. Later he "went to Fort Massac on a flatboat and from there walked to St. Louis," where he found his brother established in business. The two spent several months together in the city, and, according to the story as related in *Chronicles*, it was during his absence from Kentucky that Ford, the "almost outlawed man," passed beyond the reach of law.

The Tragedy of Potts' Hill

It was at Ford's Ferry that many emigrants going to the Illinois country crossed the Ohio. In Ford's day the ferry at Shawneetown and another at Golconda also were thriving, and the three were, in a sense, rivals.

A river crossing with the reputation of having the best roads leading to and from it was usually given the preference. Ford, realizing this, placed sign-boards at a number of road crossings, and cards in some of the taverns, advertising the highway to his ferry. What was known as the Ford's Ferry Road extended, in Kentucky, some eight miles south of the ferry and, in Illinois, about twelve miles north of it. That part of it in Kentucky running north from Pickering Hill to the ferry, a distance of four miles, was well maintained by the county through Ford's influence. The road leading from his ferry into Illinois was an equally important one, but its condition depended solely upon his interest and efforts in the matter. He attempted to persuade the local authorities in Illinois to change the old

Ibid., pp. 293–298.

Low Water Road running through the bottoms to Potts' Hill, a distance of twelve miles, to one over higher ground. Failing in this effort, he, at his own expense, opened up a new road ever since known as Ford's Ferry High Water Road.

Thus, with about twenty miles of comparatively good road through a densely wooded country and with a first class ferry, and by proper advertising, he succeeded, as one man expressed it, "in having things come his way." Many people, it is true, were molested at the ferry and along the highways leading to and from it; but such misfortunes were then likely to befall any traveler at any place. If a robbery occurred along the Ford's Ferry Road, the news of the hold-up invariably ended with the report that "Jim Ford found the robbers and ran them out of the country." And so, for many years, the Ford's Ferry Road and Ford's Ferry maintained the reputation of being "safe again." In the meantime, strangers continued to travel over it, and many fell into the well-set trap.

At the foot of Pickering Hill, near Crooked Creek, newcomers frequently met, as though by chance, some "strangers" who explained that they were on their way to Illinois. The unwary emigrants continued their travel accompanied by persons who seemed honest men. The "strangers" soon gained their confidence, and if, by the time Ford's Ferry was reached, the desirability and possibility of a hold-up had not been ascertained, the united party crossed over into Illinois. At Potts' Hill, or before reaching that wayside tavern on the south hillside, the newcomer was either robbed or permitted to continue his journey unmolested. It is said that many a traveler who was found weak and destitute by the "strangers" was given money and help by them. On the other hand, the traveler who exhibited evidence of wealth and prosperity almost invariably met his fate along the road, at the ferry or at Potts' Hill.

Billy Potts was the strategist on whom the highwaymen relied as their last and best man to dispose of any encouraging cases that had not been settled before they reached his house. Potts, by one means or another, succeeded in persuading the selected travelers to remain all night at his inn. His log house was large and comfortable, and stood near a good spring which, then as now, offered an abundant supply of water for man and beast. Tradition says many a man took his last drink at Potts' Spring and spent his last hour on earth in Potts' House. Human bones are still turned up by plowmen in the Potts' Old Field, and since there is nothing to indicate that they are the remains of Indians, the conclusion is they represent some of the victims of the mysterious Ford's Ferry band. The log house occupied by Billy Potts is still standing. Many years ago it was converted into a barn. On its floor and walls there can still be seen a number of large dark spots. Tradition has it that they are stains made by human blood. Some of the old citizens living in the neighborhood insist that they are as distinct today as they were more than half a century ago, notwithstanding the ravages of time.

There are many traditions of mysterious murders attributed to the Ford's

Ferry highwaymen. Every one is a fearsome tale, and has evidently undergone many changes since it was first told. Some seem to have more versions
than they are years old. None, so far as is now known, can be verified by
documentary or other positive evidence. All these tales are apparently based
on facts, but it is also evident that each is much colored by fiction. A version of the tradition relating to Billy Potts and his son is here retold:

A traveler was riding north on the Ford's Ferry Road one day, and after
crossing the ferry was overtaken by the son of Billy Potts. Young Potts
expressed a delight at having found a man with whom he could ride, and
thus not only pass the time away more pleasantly but also travel with greater
safety. After going a few miles young Potts gained sufficient information
to convince him that the man was well worth robbing. When they reached
a point along the road where a hold-up could be made with the least danger
of exposure, Potts pulled out his pistol, forced the man to throw up his
hands and then proceeded to rob him. While Potts was in the act of taking
his victim's money, two farmers living in the neighborhood happened upon
the scene. Not being in sympathy with the gang of highwaymen and having
recognized young Potts, they informed others what they had witnessed and
reported the robbery to the authorities. Ford, so runs the story, realizing
that one of his men had been detected and that much evidence could be
produced to convict the guilty one, advised him to leave for parts unknown,
and thus not only save himself but also shield his confederates from further
suspicion. The young man left, and a few days later, rumors emanating
from the gang to the effect that young Potts had been driven out of the
country by Jim Ford circulated freely. The disappearance of Potts substantiated the report, and Ford received the credit for ridding the community
of an undesirable citizen.

Young Potts wandered around for several years, in the meantime growing a beard and gaining in weight. He evidently changed in appearance to
such an extent that he felt confident no one—not even his mother—would
recognize him, and that he could return home without the least fear of detection. He reached Pickering Hill on his homeward journey and there met
a number of "strangers" who informed him that they were resting preparatory to resuming their travel to the Illinois country. Potts recognized in
these men his old companions in crime, but none suspected who he was.
He rode with them to Ford's Ferry, in the meantime keeping the men in
ignorance as to his identity. When they reached the Ohio he saw that active
preparations were being made to rob him and, if necessary, to murder him.
He then revealed his identity. But it was only after producing considerable
proof that he convinced the men that he was their long gone accomplice.
A great rejoicing followed.

Early in the evening young Potts started alone over Ford's High Water
Road to his father's house, where he arrived shortly after dark. He found
his father and mother at home, and, as he had anticipated, was not recognized by them. He decided to attempt to conceal his identity until late in
the night, for he concluded that if before making himself known he could

impress his father with the fact that his wandering boy had accumulated money, the surprise which he was soon to give him would be even greater. With this double surprise in view, young Potts displayed a large roll of money and whispered to his unsuspecting host that he knew he was in a safe place for the night. The two men had chatted in the candle lighted room for an hour or more, when the guest asked for a drink of water. Out into the dark they walked and down to the Potts Spring, a distance of some three hundred feet. The young man, getting down on his knees, leaned over the rock-lined spring. While in the act of drinking he was stabbed in the back, under the left shoulder blade, and instantly killed.

The murderer took the money from his victim's pocket, but failed to find anything to indicate who he was, from where he came, or to what place he intended to go. Old Potts dug a shallow grave and in it buried all evidence of the crime. He returned to the house, and after reporting to his wife that he had "made a good haul," retired for the night.

The next morning some of the Ford's Ferry gang rode to Potts' Hill to celebrate the return of their friend. Before they had an opportunity to explain the object of their coming, Potts recited the details of how he had disposed of an "easy" man the night preceding. One of them then began the story of how they had met the young fellow and how, when they were at the point of carrying out their intention of robbing and killing him, he made himself known and proved beyond doubt that he was young Potts, their former associate. But before the account was finished old Potts and his wife accused the crowd of concocting this story and cursed the men for plotting against them. But, persisting and giving every detail of what happened during the time the victim was in their presence, the men created doubt in the minds of Potts and his wife, though Potts asserted that in his opinion the man he had killed was not his son, but perhaps a friend in whom his son had confided to such an extent that he was able to convince them that he was young Potts himself.

At this point in the discussion Mrs. Potts recalled that her son had a small birthmark under one of his shoulder blades, but which shoulder blade she could not remember. Upon learning this, the men, hoping to find such evidence as would convince the parents of the identity of their son, repaired to the grave. It was shallow and the soil loose. In a little while the body was uncovered. Without waiting for it to be taken from the grave, Potts bent forward and began to rip the clothing from the corpse. The back showed no mark on the right side. The bloody wound made by the dagger that had pierced the heart was then examined. It revealed the presence of the remembered birthmark.

Foiled by the Murrell Clan

[In the old times] Randolph . . . was the most flourishing business river town in West Tennessee, on the Mississippi. It was the "receiving and forwarding" town for Tipton, Haywood, Fayette, Madison, and Hardeman. Eligibly situated immediately below the mouth of the Big Hatchie, which was navigable for small steamboats as high up as Bolivar, it received a considerable trade from the counties east of Madison and Hardeman.

* * * * *

Randolph came in for her share of the Murrell excitement, prevalent in those days. The "Murrell Clan" were not myths; they were veritable men of extraordinary boldness and daring. They counted their numbers by hundreds, and ranged from the Walnut Hills, at the mouth of the Yazoo, to the mouth of the Big Hatchie. They held their "Grand Council" in the deep, dark woods of the Mississippi Bottom, in Arkansas, twelve or more miles below Randolph and some six miles from the river, near Shawnee Village. The writer yet retains a lively recollection of the many scenes and incidents of that thrilling and eventful period. Robbery, theft, and murder occupied and filled the minds and engaged the attention of the people from Vicksburg to New Madrid. It was the theme in the quiet family circle, as well as public talk, and the subject of municipal ordinances and regulations. Every town along the river had its vigilant committee and patrol, for the protection of life and property. Randolph had its vigilant committee and organized patrol, and every stranger that entered the town and neighborhood was "spotted" until his business and person became satisfactorily known to the guardians of the town.

The Clansmen's most usual place of crossing the Mississippi was a short distance below the "Benton place." In tracking their way to and from the "Grand Council Tree," a notable sycamore standing in the thickest of the deep forest, towering above all other trees—discernible for miles around—a beacon to guide the footsteps of the Clan in gathering, they seldom traveled over the same trail more than once, that they might elude the vigil of all who were not of their clan. The size of the "Council Tree" at its base equaled the notable Indiana sycamore at the mouth of the Big Pigeon, which is said to measure, at its base, seventy-five feet around and is capable of stabling in its capacious hollow twenty-four horses at a time. It was at this tree, and in its great hollow, that John A. Murrell and his Clansmen met in grand council and formed their dark plots and concocted their hellish plans. Most of their depredations were committed along the river and in

From *Old Times in West Tennessee,* Reminiscences—Semi-Historic—of Pioneer Life and the Early Emigrant Settlers in the Big Hatchie Country, by a Descendant of One of the First Settlers [Joseph S. Williams], pp. 194, 200, 203–205. Entered . . . 1873, by Joseph S. Williams. Memphis: W. G. Cheeney, Printer and Publisher.

the nighttime. Seldom a night passed at Randolph without the capture of suspicious persons. . . .

It was during those bloody days that an occurrence happened some twelve miles below Randolph that shocked the whole country. A most atrocious and diabolical wholesale murder and robbery had been committed on the Arkansas side. The crew of a flatboat had been murdered in cold blood, disemboweled, and thrown in the river, and the boat-stores appropriated among the perpetrators of the foul deed. The Murrell Clan were charged with the inhuman and devilish act. Public meetings were called in different parts of the country to devise means to rid the country and clear the woods of the Clan, and to bring to immediate punishment the murderers of the flatboat men. In Covington a company was formed to that end, under the command of Maj. Hockley and Grandville D. Searcey, and one, also, formed in Randolph, under the command of Colonel Orvil Shelby. They met at Randolph and organized into one company, under command of Colonel Shelby. A flatboat, suited to the purpose, was procured, and the expedition, consisting of some eighty or an hundred men, well armed, with several days' rations, floated out from Randolph, and down to the landing where the wholesale murder had been committed. Their place of destination was Shawnee Village, some six or more miles from the Mississippi, where the Sheriff of the county resided. They were first to require of the Sheriff to put the offenders under arrest and turn them over to be dealt with according to law. To Shawnee Village the expedition moved in single file, along a tortuous trail through the thick cane and jungle, until within a few miles of the village, when the whole line was startled by a shrill whistle at the head of the column, answered by the sharp click! click! click! of the cocking of the rifles in the hands of the Clansmen, in ambush, to the right flank of the moving file, and within less han a dozen yards.

The chief of the Clan stepped out at the head of the expedition, and in a stentorian voice commanded the expedition to halt, saying:

"We have man for man; move forward another step and a rifle bullet will be sent through every man under your command."

A parley was had, when more than man for man of the Clansmen rose from their hiding places in the thick cane, with their guns at a present. The expedition had fallen into a trap; the Clansmen had not been idle in finding out the movements against them across the river. Doubtless many of them had been in attendance at the meetings held for the purpose of their destruction. The movement had been a rash one, and nothing was left to be done but to adopt the axiom that "prudence is the better part of valor." The leaders of the expedition were permitted to communicate with the Sheriff, who promised to do what he could in having the offenders brought to justice; but alas for Arkansas and justice! the Sheriff himself was thought to be in sympathy with the Clan, and the law was in the hands of the Clansmen. The expedition retraced their steps. Had it not been so formidable and well known by the Clansmen, every member of it would have found his grave in the Arkansas swamp.

Lafitte, the Pirate

Jean Lafitte, the pirate, was a blacksmith from Bordeaux, France, who kept his forge at the corner of Bourbon and St. Philip streets [New Orleans], in a building which remains to this day. He had an older brother, Pierre, who was a seafaring character, and had served in the French navy.

Shortly after the cession of Louisiana to the United States, a series of events occurred which made the Gulf of Mexico the arena of a most extensive and profitable privateering. First came the war between France and Spain, which afforded the inhabitants of the French islands a good pretence to depredate upon the rich commerce of the Spanish possessions, the most valuable and productive in the New World. The Gulf of Mexico and the Caribbean swarmed with privateers. Shortly after this the United States of Columbia declared its independence of Spain, and invited to its port of Carthagena all the privateers and buccaneers of the gulf. Commissions were promptly given or sold to them to sail under the Columbian flag and prey upon the commerce of poor old Spain. The privateers selected as their headquarters the little bay or cove of Grand Terre. It was called Barataria, and several huts and storehouses were built there, and cannon planted on the beach. Here rallied the privateers of the Gulf with their fast-sailing schooners armed to the teeth and manned by fierce-looking men, armed with cutlasses—desperadoes of all nations.

Besides its inaccessibility to vessels of war, the Bay of Barataria recommended itself by another important consideration. It was near to New Orleans, where the spoils of the privateers, or as they can well be styled, pirates, could be disposed of. A regular organization was established, officers chosen and agents appointed in New Orleans to enlist men and negotiate the sale of goods.

Among these agents was the blacksmith Jean Lafitte, who by his address, enterprise and success soon obtained such ascendancy over the lawless congregation at Barataria that they elected him their captain or commander.

There is a tradition that this choice gave great dissatisfaction to some of the more warlike of the pirates, and particularly to one Gambio, a savage, grim Italian who did not scruple to prefer the title and character of pirate to the puling hypocritical one of privateer; and Lafitte found it necessary when one of Gambio's followers resisted him to shoot him through the heart before the whole band. His vigor and determination gave him supreme command of the pirates and he certainly conducted his administration with energy and ability. A large fleet of small vessels rode in the harbor, besides others that were cruising in the Gulf. Their storehouses were filled with valuable goods. Hither resorted merchants and traders from all parts of the country to purchase goods which, being cheaper obtained, could be retailed

From *Historical Sketch Book and Guide to New Orleans and Environs*, edited and compiled by several leading writers of the New Orleans Press, pp. 188–190. Entered . . . 1885, by Will H. Coleman. New York.

at a large profit. A number of small vessels were employed in transporting these goods to New Orleans, into which city they were carried by night and disposed of by the agents of the pirates there.

Several attempts were made to break up the band and the U.S. Grand Jury more than once indicted Lafitte, but the government could never arrest him. At the very time when a Federal force was being equipped to descend upon the settlement of Barataria, the pirates were able to do the United States a great service, which saved New Orleans from capture by the British, and won for Lafitte the title of the "pirate patriot." When the British were arranging their expedition against the city, they prepared to advance on it by way of Barataria, and sent a man-of-war to the island, to make terms with Lafitte and secure the cooperation of the pirates in capturing New Orleans, offering as a bribe a large sum of money and to Lafitte personally a commission as captain in the British navy.

Lafitte affected acquiescence in these proposals, but at the same time warned Governor Claiborne of the approach of the British, and thus enabled the United States to take steps for the defence of the city and to send General Jackson there.

At the battle of New Orleans, General Jackson being short of gunners, appointed several of Lafitte's men to the artillery, where they did good service.

Notwithstanding Lafitte's services, an expedition was fitted up against the pirates and the settlement captured. The Baratarians were ironed and committed to the calaboose at New Orleans, and their spoils, consisting of an immense amount of valuable goods, money, etc., seized and conveyed to the city.

After the expedition against Barataria, the pirates were scattered in every direction. Some of them fled the country, and may have fallen into loose ways and sought to trade upon the name of Lafitte, thereby giving circulation to the fictitious stories, and multiplying the name and form of the pirate. Others remained in New Orleans and took to honest and regular pursuits, and several prospered and became rich and important personages. Two of them, who were famous fighting men, You and Bluche, managed to secure the admiration and respect of General Jackson to such a degree that he gave the latter, Bluche, a high certificate and recommendation, which procured him an appointment to the command of the fleet of one of the South American republics, and the other, Old Dominique, was the first person the General inquired for on his last visit to the city. He lived to an advanced age, in great poverty, but with undiminished pride in his achievements as a warrior, and at his death was buried in the St. Louis Cemetery, where a pompous tomb was erected over him, and a quotation from Voltaire's "Henriade" testifies to his greatness as a hero and warrior, "The victor in a hundred fights on sea and land."

Lafitte himself returned to his old pursuits, and being unable to remain at Grand Terre, removed to Galveston (then known as Campeachy) island in 1817. Here he built a small town, having his quarters in a commodious house, painted red, where he was visited in 1819 by Col. W. D. C. Hall, in the endeavor to secure his cooperation with Gen. Long in his expedition to Mexico, but without success.

Lafitte's person is thus described: He was a well-formed, handsome man, about six feet two inches in height, strongly built, with large hazel eyes and black hair, and generally wore a moustache. He dressed in a green uniform and otter-skin cap. He was a man of polite and easy manners, of retired habits, generous disposition, and of such a winning address that his influence over his followers was almost absolute. He located his town on the ruins of Aury's village, built a house which he painted red, and threw up around it a fort.

While Lafitte was located on the island he had five or six armed vessels, and a large number of followers. In 1819 the island was visited by a severe storm, and several of the vessels were driven ashore on the mainland. Shortly after the occupation, one of Lafitte's men stole a squaw from the Caranchua tribe of Indians, who often resorted to the west end of the island, and kept possession of her. This so enraged the Indians that they attacked a hunting party of the buccaneers and killed two of them. In return the Indians were attacked by Lafitte with two hundred men and two cannon, and a skirmish ensued, lasting two days, when the Indians were forced to flee to the mainland, after having thirty warriors slain.

While at Grand Terre, Lafitte had dealt largely in Negroes taken from Spanish slavers, and continued the business during his stay here, and it was not a great many years since there were living witnesses that the price of an able-bodied Negro was at that period only $40. In 1819 a desperado named Brown plundered an American vessel and was pursued to Galveston by the United States revenue cutter *Lynx*, Captain Madison. Brown arrived before the cutter, and Lafitte, getting wind of the affair, had him hung on a little island near the present harbor improvement works, then known as "Little Campeachy," and separated from the larger island by a channel seven or eight feet in depth. He also hung another of his men named Francois for engaging in a plot to rob and murder a Mr. Kuykendall, who, it is quite probable, visited the island for the purpose of purchasing a few of Capt. Lafitte's likely Africans.

The United States becoming tired of Lafitte's establishment, owing to the numerous complaints of depredations on American vessels, determined to break it up, and dispatched a naval force under Lieut. Kearney, with orders to see that Capt. Lafitte left. The pirate chief received the officer courteously, entertained him sumptuously at the Red House, and issued instructions to his followers to prepare to depart. The buccaneers having everything in readiness, Lafitte ordered the town to be set on fire, and embarking on the *Pride*, his favorite vessel, sailed from the island on the twelfth of May, 1820, never to return. After cruising in the Caribbean Sea for several years he located on the island of Mugeres, off the coast of Yucatan, where, according to the traveler Stevens, he died in 1826, leaving a widow and a hecatomb of turtle shells to honor his memory.

Jim Girty's Skirmish with the Natchez Gamblers

The hero of the following narrative is now dead and gone. I knew him well, and when I mention his name, many other boatmen will recollect him. It was James Girty, familiarly known as Dad Girty, and a nephew of the Girtys of Indian notoriety. He was a man of common stature, but of uncommon strength and courage, and was, in the old barging times, generally engaged as captain of a keelboat or a barge, and was never known to hire a hand without he *could* and *would* fight. The last boating he ever did was steering a keelboat for me from the mouth of the Cumberland River to Nashville, during which voyage he was taken sick and never recovered. I had often heard of a skirmish in which he and his crew had been engaged with some gamblers at Natchez-under-the-Hill; and whilst sitting by his bunk one night, I asked him some questions concerning it, when he related the following narrative:

In the year 1814 I was captain of the barge *Black Snake* (a nickname he gave the barge, whose right name I do not recollect) belonging to the Pointses, at Maysville, Kentucky. I started for New Orleans in the latter part of November, with the barge about two-thirds loaded. When I came to the mouth of the Cumberland, I found arms in possession of the United States officers, destined for the defense at New Orleans. They were waiting for a keelboat which they had been expecting for many days, and for fear of being disappointed, were anxious that I should take them on board the *Black Snake,* and proceed on with all possible dispatch in my power, which I contracted to do. I arrived in New Orleans on the 3rd of January, 1815, with all the arms in my charge and eager to be in the fight. I immediately reported myself to General Jackson. Martial law was in force, and from my own solicitation, I got an appointment as captain of a company, for the purpose of pressing barge and keelboat men into the service, at which I went to work without delay. You know how the battle was ended. After the glorious 8th of January, and everything in the shape of a redcoat had disappeared, I discharged the remaining part of my cargo and crew. I had no further use for my crew until I could get a freight for up the river, which I did not get until the latter end of May, when I hired a crew, and started for Pittsburgh. Some time in June, I landed at Natchez. It was the custom of that day to give the hands a holiday at Natchez, and a holiday at the mouth of the Ohio, and one at Louisville or Shippingsport. It was four o'clock, P.M., that we threw up our poles and fastened our bow-lines at Natchez. My men were eager for a dance, and some would not wait for supper, but scampered away for the dance houses under the hill. I got my supper and went up also—looked at them until 11 or 12 o'clock at night,

From *The Earthquake of 1811 at New Madrid and along the Mississippi Valley,* together with Other Tales, by Capt. Chas. Ross, pp. 9–13. Entered . . . 1847, by George Conclin. Cincinnati.

and when I found all my entreaties unavailing to get them on board, I left them, some dancing and some betting on the roulettes with the gamblers, and went on board. By the time daylight came, all hands were on board, but some had their heads badly bruised. It appeared that the gamblers had won all their money, and a fight ensued—the gamblers came off victorious. After breakfast, I found, from the threats of my hands, and their general behavior, it was advisable to get the *Black Snake* under weigh, and undertook it, but not a man would raise a pole until they had their accustomed frolic; and I gave that up, determined to leave at 4 o'clock, when the day would be up. Four o'clock came, but not a man would stir a peg until they were revenged; and they had made it up amongst themselves that they would help me no farther without I went up with them and helped them to whip the gamblers. I found no other alternative, and, after supper, I repaired with my whole crew to the dance houses, armed with knives, axes, and setting poles. The gamblers expected us, and were armed with pistols, knives, and guns. The fight immediately commenced. They at first gave us a hard fight, but their ammunition was soon spent, and they gave ground, leaving three dead on the spot. One of our men was mortally wounded, but he walked to the barge and was dead in half an hour. We cut cable and crossed the river, worked the *Black Snake* three miles up the river, and came to for the night. About daylight the next morning, while burying the dead man, the sheriff and a posse of near a hundred men came up and took us all. They left a man of the posse in charge of the barge, and took us down to the ferry boat and across to Natchez—took us before a judge and tried us, and found no evidence against any but myself and Bill Lloyd. The rest of the crew were set free; but myself and Bill were sent out to Washington jail. My barge was sent on, and I was destined to stay in the jail until court, which was to sit the first Monday in October. After I had been in jail about two weeks, one of the associate judges of the court where I was to be tried came out to Washington to see me. I found in him an old Pennsylvania acquaintance, on whom I had some claims. He gave me poor encouragement and told me he feared the court would not let me out on bail. I told him I had $2700, which I could leave with my security. Still he discouraged me. He said the evidence was point blank against me and Lloyd, but promised to call again, and ordered the jailer to see that I did not want for anything. In about a week he came again and told me he had succeeded in making it a bailable case of three thousand dollars, and had also obtained a man to go my security. The door was opened, and I gave the judge $2700, and the necessary security. The judge advised me to leave immediately and never show myself again in Natchez. He would willingly pay the $300 if I would keep away. I told him I would be in Washington at the sitting of the court if I lived—on this I was determined. That afternoon I wrote a letter to Natchez to a friend of mine,[1] requesting her to get clear

---

[1] This was a woman that kept a dance house, now living and wealthy and, of course. respectable.—C.R.

of the evidence against me, and got an answer the next morning, assuring me I need not fear anything—to come back—there would be no evidence against me when court sat. The same day I left for Pittsburgh on foot, and arrived there in the latter part of July. I immediately went to work, raised all the money I could, amounting to $1500, and started for Natchez in the last days of August, in a large covered skiff. It had two pairs of oars, and I took on board three Yankees, to work their passage as far as Cincinnati; and our oars never rested until we got there. Here I hired a man to help me all the way, but he got tired and run off at Louisville. I crossed the falls by myself, and landed at Shippingsport, in quest of another hand, when the first man that met my eye was Bill Lloyd. You may wonder at my astonishment when I saw him. My first words were, "Why, Bill, how did you get here?"

"Why, I walked most of the way."

"Well, how did you get out of jail?"

"Oh," said he, "it got so d——d sickly amongst the thieving scoundrels in there that the jailor was obliged to open the door for me, that I might take care of the sick; and I opened for the rest, and all went out that could walk out, and then I walked off, and walked to the mouth of the Tennessee, and there I got a chance to push up on that keel-boat there" (pointing to it).

"Well, Bill," said I, "you need not fear anything while you are with me; I am going back to stand my trial, and I want to hire a hand to help me now; I fear I won't get there in time."

I struck a bargain with Bill, for a dollar a day, agreeing to let him off at the Walnut Hills, if he wished, and he came on with his horn and blanket, and we were off in a jiffy. Bill was a bad man, and I knew it; yet he was a stout man, and a good oarsman. He was not long with me until he found out that my chest was heavy, and I watched him close. When we came near the mouth of the Ohio, he became dissatisfied with his going any further towards Natchez, and insisted on our going up the Mississippi a-trapping, and told a great many things that could be done on the Missouri river. I paid very little attention to his entreaties, but kept on down the river, and told him, if he wanted to stop, to stop—I was going to Natchez. He said no more until we were in the bend above Beef Island, when he broke out afresh and accused me of suspicioning him of a wish to rob me. I told him I was not afraid of him in any shape, while I had my senses. A fight ensued, which was to end in death, and the victor's spoils were to be the skiff and my money. The fight soon ended in my getting him overboard. I put the blade of an oar against him, shoving him off from the skiff, and threw it to him, and told him to save his life, if he wished. He clinched the oar and threw it back to me, and told me to go to h——l, and swam about fifty yards, and landed safe on the head of Beef Island.

I will drop Bill now, and go on to Natchez, where I landed at one o'clock in the morning of the first Monday in October. I left my skiff, and with my chest on my shoulders, walked up to the dance-house. My friend had not went to bed yet—there were several up—I deposited my chest with her, and looking around the room, I spied the most important witness against me. I turned to her and reminded her of her promise. She told me she had been trying to get clear of him all summer; that he was the only evidence left in the country against me, and she would get clear of him. I told her the time was short; and called him to us and told him I would give him $500 to leave the place and not appear. He swore he would appear against me—that he had braved through the worst of the yellow fever for that purpose—that there was no use to talk to him, he was determined. My friend told me not to fear—all would be right. It was now drawing towards day, and I was about bidding her and the witness goodbye, when she proposed a gin sling, before I started; she mixed one and gave it to witness, one for me, and one for herself. We drank, and I started. I got out to Washington about nine o'clock, A.M., and being tired, I laid down on the door steps of the courthouse and fell fast asleep; and I did not wake until the noise of the Sheriff calling court awakened me. Everybody seemed astonished at my presence. However, my case was the first one called, and I answered to my name. The judge asked me if I was ready for trial. My counsel did not happen to be in court, and I answered that as I was as ready now as I ever would be—that I had no evidence when I was sent to jail, and I had none now. The attorney for the commonwealth wished to call the names of the witnesses to see if he was ready for trial. This wish was granted, and he called eleven names, and not one [was] present, but some one to answer as their names were called, telling the court what had become of them; some had left the country, and some had died with the yellow fever, until the name of the one I had left at Natchez was called, and the answer was—he died this morning at half past eight. My mind was immediately made up that she had killed or poisoned him. No evidence appearing against me, of course I was at liberty, and went the same evening into Natchez. I questioned her as to the cause of the sudden death of the evidence; she gave me no farther satisfaction than that it was natural, nor could I get any other satisfaction from her. Next day I called on my security, settled my business with him, went to my friend's house, opened my chest, and counted $500 for her. She perceived what I was doing, and told me if I wanted to make her mad, I could have a chance, and if I dared to offer her money, she would blow out my brains. I made several excuses to make her take the money—told her I honestly owed it to her, for her kind treatment of me, and not for anything dishonorable she might imagine; but she told me if I wanted her friendship continued, I must not offer her money. I bade this queer and extraordinary woman adieu, and before dark, my skiff, self, and chest were on the way for New Orleans.

Such was the narrative of this man, who at this day would be trusted nowhere in this Union; but, in his day, thousands were committed to his care. He was never known to violate a trust, and in all his pecuniary dealings he was considered correct.

The Exterminating War on the Gamblers of Vicksburg

We cannot pass over the fate of the gamblers on the river, in 1835–7, without giving them a passing notice.

At this period the river towns were beset, infested, with hordes of the most infamous and abhorrent scoundrels ever known in a civilized country. The Yazoo and Natchez country was overrun with these miscreants. As this region became more populous and towns sprang up, the rogues thronged the towns, and from being river pirates and land robbers, they became genteel gamblers and counterfeiters, infesting steamboats and hotels, and even establishing themselves in houses of their own, where they openly exposed their gambling tables, heaped with gold, to the eyes of the passers-by.

The morals of this out-of-the-way part of the States were not of the straightest kind, and as there was but little excitement,—few theatres, circuses, or horse-racing, &c.,—men were readily tempted to *play*. Even magistrates passed whole evenings at the roulette or faro table, and gamblers contributed to the income of the town by paying large license money into its treasury.

Matters went on this way till there was scarcely a town on the Mississippi that had not, for every five of its male citizens, at least one genteel gamester. We know that in 1836 there were living in Natchez not less than one hundred genteel blacklegs—men who dressed richly, lived in style in their gaming houses, betted largely at the races, where they appeared in their barouches with their mistresses, and who affected the fine gentleman in everything. The chief place of abode of these gentry was at "Natchez-under-the-Hill," a place of infernal fame all the world over. It consisted then (for it was since destroyed by a tornado) of a single street, skirting the base of a bluff on which the upper town, like Quebec, stands, and was lined with gaming-houses, brilliantly lighted by night, the upper stories being inhabited by gamblers. These gentry got to regard this street as their own proper territory, and it was dangerous to pass through it at night, and in the day time with ladies; yet it was the only thoroughfare between the town and the steamboat landing. Many a murder had been committed there, of the secret of which the dark tide of the Mississippi is the depository.

Vicksburg also had its horde of gamblers; but there they were bolder than in Natchez, and instead of keeping in one quarter of the town, planted themselves all over the city; nevertheless there was one short street which was exclusively occupied by them.

Emboldened by the license given them, and by the freedom and familiarity with which the planters played at their tables and drank and talked with

---

From *Dan. Marble; A Biographical Sketch of that Famous and Diverting Humorist, with Reminiscences, Comicalities, Anecdotes, Etc., Etc.,* by Falconbridge, pp. 118–123. Entered . . . 1851, by Dewitt & Davenport. New York.

Cf. the account by Captain F. Marryat, *A Diary in America* (Philadelphia, 1839), Vol. II, pp. 196–201.

them, they began to be presuming; and to even intrude at hotel tables, an offence the Southerner could not overlook; for a gentleman may game with a gambler by the hour, and yet despise him and refuse to recognize him afterwards.

At Natchez, confident in their numbers, they had become very insolent, and several gentlemen who had won money of them, had been harshly dealt with by them. Their increase had for some time begun to alarm the better class of citizens, and many a wish was expressed that they could be got rid of.

At length, at Vicksburg, a young planter who was known to enter one of their gaming houses with a large sum of money never re-appeared. Rumor had it that he had been murdered and robbed; and this report was confirmed by the sudden absence of two or three noted gamblers who had lodged in the house. The citizens of Vicksburg had long felt the necessity, if they would dwell in peace and have their town prosper, of getting rid of these desperadoes, who numbered nearly two hundred, a large proportion of the male population. Many of them also had their mistresses, who were an abandoned set, and quite as impudent as their male companions.

But a few days had elapsed after the disappearance of the young planter, when a gentleman, passing through their street with a lady on his arm, was most grossly insulted, as well as the lady. This conduct exasperated the citizens, and taken together with countless other outrages, made them resolve to take some resolute steps to rid the town of these nuisances; for, aside from their dangerous presence among them, they kept business men from establishing themselves in a community, a large portion of which was composed of gamblers.

The next day was the Fourth of July; and a public dinner was given at the Court-house. After the guests were seated, it was found that a notorious gambler had coolly seated himself at the table. He was at once ordered to leave the hall. He refused to do so, when three or four gentlemen disarmed him as he was drawing a pistol and put him out.

In a little while he returned, with one or two others, and reentered the hall. An uproar ensued, in which they were ejected and the hall doors closed. In all this you will say that the citizens acted with great forbearance. After the dinner was over, a gentleman proposed that a public meeting should be called by ring of bell at the Court-house, for the purpose of taking into consideration the expediency of the immediate expulsion of the gamblers from Vicksburg.

The meeting was largely attended, scarcely a citizen being absent. The meeting was addressed in an eloquent manner by several gentlemen, who recounted the outrages which had been long quietly borne from the gamblers. The result was that the resolutions were passed unanimously that public proclamation by crier and printed placards should be made, giving "all such persons who could not show some honest mode of livelihood, or give a satisfactory account of their mode of subsistence, *twenty-four hours* to leave the town"; and adding that "all such persons found within the town limits after the expiration of this time, shall receive thirty-nine lashes at the public whipping post!"

This *pronunciamento*, you see, included all the gambling fraternity. The resolutions being printed upon placards and posted up throughout the place, the citizens waited quietly to see the effect. Before half the time had expired, there was a very perceptible movement among the gentry against whom the placard was aimed. The steamers that passed took on board a large number of gamblers, and many left for the interior, some on foot and others by such conveyances as offered.

As the twenty-four hours drew to a close, the citizens were gratified to see that nearly all the blacklegs had taken warning and departed, or were busily getting their goods together to leave. The gamblers had fairly taken fright by the resolute stand and determined bearing of the Vicksburgians, and saw that they were not to be tampered with. At the expiration of the time, the Court-house bell called the citizens together again, and a report of the committee of vigilance showed that all the gamblers, with their women, had taken leave, save five or six of the most desperate, who had barricaded themselves in their dwellings, and defied all Vicksburg to eject them!

Upon hearing this, the meeting of citizens delegated a committee to wait upon these gentlemen and order them to leave at once, or suffer the consequences. The Vicksburg volunteer company was also ordered out to help to keep the peace. The committee was accompanied on its mission by a large number of the citizens, to witness the result. The gamblers defied them, and swore they would fire on the first man who attempted to enter the house. A party of citizens made a rush to the door when several shots were fired from within, and Dr. Bodley, one of the most popular young men in Vicksburg, fell dead, being shot through the lungs.

At seeing him fall, the citizens, as may easily be imagined, became exasperated. The barricaded house was in a moment carried by storm, and the five gamblers made prisoners, after desperately defending themselves. One of them was dangerously wounded in the conflict, and doubtless would have died before night if he had *not* been *hanged*!

Upon getting these desperadoes into their hands, the citizens, with one voice, cried—"To the Court-house! There let us judge them!"

The volunteer company now formed a hollow square; the prisoners were placed in the centre, the wounded man in a cart, which someone had provided. Somebody else provided ropes, and somehow or other they were noosed about the gamblers' necks, nobody could tell by whom. All seemed done by one impulse, as if one spirit only governed the multitude. To the sound of a dirge they were marched to the green in front of the Court-house, the citizens falling in behind the soldiers in orderly procession. Arriving at the Court-house, they marched silently on and enclosed the gallows that stood near. No voice had said, "To the gallows!" Not a tongue had breathed *hanging*! Yet each man instinctively felt what was going to take place—each read it in his neighbor's looks!

The gallows was surrounded in profound silence. Three men stepped out

and lifted the wounded man from the cart and placed him on the lower step
of the gallows. Others led the four desperadoes to the beam and fastened
the end of the cords to the cross bar. The fifth was secured in his place
beside them.

Up to this time nothing had been said by anyone of what was to be done.
Nobody had given an order of any kind. Men acted as if moved by one
emotion—as if the whole proceedings had been long before decided upon.
The gamblers too had preserved a dogged silence.

The leader of the five, a desperate villain, black with crimes, now spoke,
his face as pale as death; for he saw in the stern eyes around him that this
was likely to be no farce, as he and his companions had up to this moment
evidently supposed it to be.

"Good God!" he cried, "you are not going to hang us, gentlemen!"

There was no reply. One or two men advanced towards the pulley that
sustained the drop. The gambler implored, shrieked, cursed, and————;
the next moment, with his four comrades, he was dangling in mid-air!

After hanging about half an hour, the five bodies were cut down and
buried in graves, still visible at the gallows' foot. The concourse of citizens
then re-entered the Court-house, and passed resolutions which called upon
the citizens of Natchez and other towns on the river to deny shelter to the
gamblers which had been banished. They then quietly dispersed to their
homes. A committee left in the next boat for Natchez, and reported there
what had been done at Vicksburg. The citizens of Natchez at once called a
public meeting, unanimously adopted the resolutions of the Vicksburg meeting, and gave their gambling friends twenty-four hours to depart.

The news of the fate of the five gamblers produced among their *confrères*
at Natchez the greatest consternation. They did not wait for steamers to
take them off, but hired flat-boats, and crowded them by scores, male and
female. One of these boats was picked up a hundred miles below Natchez,
drifting with the current, with thirty persons, male and female, on board,
nearly perishing with exposure and hunger, and fearing to land anywhere.
The Captain humanely took them to New Orleans, where doubtless the
most of the others ultimately found their way. Some of the more desperate
flew armed to the woods; but horse patrols were organized, and they were
hunted like wild beasts till they were taken, or made their escape to the
river. Those who were taken were not hanged, but whipped and sent off
down the river.

By this severe but needful administration of even-handed justice, the
towns on the river became purified from a moral pestilence which the law
could not cure. It was not the act of a lawless *mob,* but the deliberate procedure of the citizens of a whole town, for every inhabitant of Vicksburg,
to a man, took part in this work of purification. Since this, Vicksburg has
risen to be an important commercial town. Gamblers, though almost forgetting their past treatment, are still shy of it; and gambling since this affair
is not quite so *genteel* as formerly.

Thimblerigging in Court

In the early days of the West, when justice was dispensed after a free-and-easy fashion in log-cabin courthouses, a case was on trial in which the plaintiff sought to avoid payment of a gambling debt on the ground that the money had been won by "thimblerigging." His counsel, who was an expert in the game, was giving an illustration of its operation to his Honor and the jury. "Then, may it please the court, the defendant, placing the cups on his knee, *thus,* began shifting them *so,* offering to bet that my client could not tell under which cup was the 'little joker'—meaning, thereby, may it please the court, this ball—with the intention of defrauding my client of the sum thus wagered. For instance, when I raise the cup *so,* your Honor supposes that you see the ball."

"*Suppose* I see!" interrupted the judge, who had closely watched the performance, and was sure that he had detected the ball as one of the cups was accidentally raised. "Why, any fool can see where it is, and bet on it and be sure to win. There ain't no defraudin' *thar.*"

"Perhaps your Honor would like to go a *V* on it," insinuated the counsel.

"Go a *V*! Yes, and double it too, and here's the rhino. It's under the middle cup."

"I'll go a *V* on that," said the foreman of the jury.

"And I, and I," joined in the jury, one after another, until each one had invested his pile.

"Up!" said his Honor.

"Up" it was, but the "little joker" had mysteriously disappeared. Judge and jury were enlightened, and found no difficulty in bringing in a verdict in favor of the plaintiff on the ground that "it was the biggest kind o' defraudin'." His Honor adjourned the court, and "stood for drinks all round" in consideration of being "let off" from his wager.

Thimblerig's Account of the Spanish Burial Trick

. . . Natchez under the Hill—where, oh! where shall I find words suitable to describe the peculiarities of that unholy spot? 'Tis, in fact, the

From *The Lance, Cross and Canoe;* The Flatboat, Rifle and Plough in the Valley of the Mississippi, The Backwoods Hunter and Settler, The Flatboatman, The Saddle-Bags Parson, The Stump Orator and Lawyer, as the Pioneers of Its Civilization, Its Great Leaders, Wit and Humor, Remarkable Extent and Wealth of Resource, Its Past Achievements and Glorious Future, by W. H. Milburn, pp. 577–578. Entered . . . 1892, by William Henry Milburn. New York and St. Louis: N. D. Thompson Publishing Company.

From *Life of David Crockett,* The Original Humorist and Irrepressible Backwoodsman, Comprising His Early History, His Bear Hunting and Other Adventures, His Services in the Creek War, His Electioneering Speeches and Career in Congress, with

jumping off place. Satan looks on it with glee, and chuckles as he beholds the orgies of his votaries. The buildings are for the most part brothels, taverns, or gambling houses, and frequently the whole three may be found under the same roof. Obscene songs are sung at the top of the voice in all quarters. I have repeatedly seen the strumpets tear a man's clothes from his back and leave his body beautified with all the colors of the rainbow.

One of the most popular tricks is called the "Spanish burial." When a greenhorn makes his appearance among them, one who is in the plot announces the death of a resident, and that all strangers must subscribe to the custom of the place upon such an occasion. They forthwith arrange a procession; each person, as he passes the departed, kneels down and pretends to kiss the treacherous corpse. When the unsophisticated attempts this ceremony, the dead man clinches him, and the mourners beat the fellow so entrapped until he consents to treat all hands; but should he be penniless, his life will be endangered by the severity of the castigation. And such is Natchez under the Hill.

River Sharpers' Tricks

The games which were mostly played in those days on river steamers were poker, brag, whist, Boston, and old sledge; and if banking games were set up in the social hall, they were usually *vingt-et-un*, chuck, and sometimes faro. According to the rules of these steamers, all gambling was prohibited after ten o'clock in the evening; but in many instances these rules were a dead letter, and the morning sun frequently found one or more parties at the card-table engaged at their favorite games. In these jolly times the steamboat officers mingled with the passengers in the cabin as equals, and it was no uncommon thing to see uncouth pilots, mates, and greasy engineers engaged at the card-tables with well-dressed travelers. Passengers were privileged to amuse themselves just as they pleased, so long as they did not infringe upon the rights of others, or interfere in any respect with the duties of the officers or crew. This latitude sometimes led to some rather strong contrasts; for instance, there might frequently be seen in the ladies' cabin a group of the godly praying and singing psalms, while in the dining-saloon, from which the tables had been removed, another party were dancing merrily to the music of a fiddle, while farther along, in the social hall, might be heard the loud laughter of jolly carousers

His Triumphal Tour through the Northern States and Services in the Texan War, to Which Is Added an Account of His Glorious Death at the Alamo while Fighting in Defence of Texan Independence, pp. 308–309. Entered . . . 1860, by John E. Potter and Company. Philadelphia.

From *Wanderings of a Vagabond*, An Autobiography, edited by John Morris [John O'Connor], pp. 422–425. Entered . . . 1873, by John Morris. New York: Published by the Author.

around the drinking bar, and occasionally chiming in with the sound of the revelry, the rattling of money and checks, and the sound of voices at the card-tables.

Previous to the appearance of the card sharper and his newly invented schemes for cheating, on the river the card-tables of a steamer were free to all persons of gentlemanly habits and manners. The gambler was not excluded from a seat there on account of his superior skill at play; or, at least, it was an exceedingly rare thing for one person to object to another on these grounds. Pride would not permit the humiliating confession. Neither would men holding real or equivocal positions in society, and who, by the arbitrary laws of that society, felt themselves compelled to shun a professional gambler on the street, think their reputation compromised by meeting him as an equal on board a steamer at the card-tables.

The votaries of chance were not yet aroused to the fact that they could be insidiously robbed at the card-table when everything seemed perfectly fair and aboveboard; but when the enlightening took place, the gambler was immediately classed with the sharper, because the verdant were unable to understand where the gambler left off and the thief began. Thimble-riggers, dice-coggers, trigger-wheel players, strop-players and card sharpers of every description were classed as gamblers.

*   *   *   *   *

It is said that bottom-dealing was first brought to perfection by a man named Wilson. This desirable consummation was reached in 1834, and about this time first made its appearance on the western rivers, where it was rendered, in the course of a few years, entirely useless, through the blunders of bungling operators, and the verdant learned to protect themselves against the fraud.

Means swifter and more sure were gradually brought into requisition for robbing the votaries of chance of their money. It is a strong advantage undoubtedly to know the strength of your adversary's hand at poker; but the work was too tedious for your fast sharper. Luck would sometimes protect a "sucker" against "iteming," stamped cards, and bottom-dealing. In the good old times, before draw poker became fashionable, straight poker was the favorite brag game. At this game the cards were dealt by the winner of the pool, who could, of course, keep on dealing as often as he could win. This rule enabled the bottom-dealer to help himself to good cards as often as he dealt; but he might win twenty pools in succession without securing scarcely any money, should his adversaries hold poor hands, and in the meantime one of them might get, by good luck, better cards than those he held, and thus win from him a large stake. True, if he had a partner who was posted in the game he could give the "sucker" a big hand from the bottom, while his partner raised from his lap a bigger one to beat it, but it was rather dangerous to attempt such a thing too often, and the least bungling was sure to lead to detection.

Young men perfected themselves in the science of false cutting and shuffling, "running-up" hands, "palming out" cards, and "ringing them in," ringing in cold packs, double discarding, etc. . . . These ambitious tyros were taken under the fostering care of some patriarch of the sharper tribe, who assisted them in getting up their games and furnished them with money when that article was needed, which, with this kind of sharpers, was generally the case, when a trip on the river was in prospect.

The popular game of draw poker, which has entirely superseded straight poker and brag, was the invention of river sharpers, and was first put into practice on the Mississippi steamboats. This game offers to the manipulator a hundred-fold better facilities for fleecing the unwary than either of the old games. The skilful operator can give his victim, with perfect ease, as many big hands as he chooses, and at the same time arm himself or his partner with better ones to beat them. But a shrewd swindler seldom gives a sucker more than an ace-full. He first tempts his appetite with two large pairs; then threes of various kinds; after these are expended, he hoists him up a flush or a full hand of a small denomination, and gradually increases them in size till he beats an ace-full for him; beyond this he is not likely to go. Whenever they find customers who will not stand running-up hands, false shuffling and cutting, double discarding is practised upon them; an advantage peculiar to draw poker, and not applicable to any other game. Scores of those who have grown gray in the service of the fickle goddess, and who were the most wary among her votaries, have come to grief through the following artful piece of chicanery:

The partners being seated next to each other, one attends to the betting department, while the latter manipulates the cards. He goes out with three aces, we will say for example, which he conceals in the joint of his knee until it comes his turn to deal. The cards having been dealt, he is ready to help the discarded hands, and he now conveys from their hiding place the stolen cards, in the palm of his hand, and places them upon the top of the pack while in the act of lifting it from the table. These cards are now drawn by his partner, who is informed by a secret "item" of their denomination, and discards his hand accordingly for their reception. As he has the first "say" or "age," and the other players may perhaps not chip in for the pool, it is not necessary to bring out the hidden cards; that is, if any of the players chip in, then he tries, by making a large brag, to run them out; but should any of them prove obstinate and stand the raise, then the three aces are brought into action. The persons who can perform this trick well are by no means numerous.

The rough handling frequently received by sharpers at the hands of their victims, during their various pilgrimages up and down the river, finally caused them to be a little more wary, and it was only when the steamer was about to make a woodpile or some port that they would venture to put the finishing stroke to their nefarious work by dealing a big hand to their victim and then beating it for him.

When they had accomplished this, they would leave the boat as quickly as convenient, and get upon the next steamer which stopped at their place of sojourn, whether going up or down mattered very little to them; and having leeched what "suckers" they found on her, abandon her, in turn, for another which offered them subjects for plunder.

Gambling on the Upper Mississippi

Volumes have been written, first and last, on the subject of gambling on the Mississippi. In them a small fraction of truth is diluted with a deal of fiction. The scene is invariably laid upon a steamboat on the lower Mississippi. The infatuated planter, who always does duty as the plucked goose, invariably stakes his faithful body servant or a beautiful quadroon girl against the gambler's pile of gold and as invariably loses his stake. Possibly that may occasionally have happened on the lower river in ante-bellum days. I never traveled the lower river, and cannot therefore speak from actual observation.

On the upper river, in early times, there were no nabobs traveling with body servants and pretty quadroons. Most of the travelers had broad belts around their waists, filled with good honest twenty-dollar gold pieces. It was these belts which the professional gamblers sought to lighten. Occasionally they did strike a fool who thought he knew more about cards than the man who made the game and who would, after a generous baiting with mixed drinks, "set in" and try his fortune. There was, of course, but one result—the belt was lightened, more or less, according to the temper and judgment of the victim.

So far as I know, gambling was permitted on all boats. On some, there was a cautionary sign displayed, stating that gentlemen who played cards for money did so at their own risk. The professionals who traveled the river for the purpose of "skinning suckers" were usually the "gentlemen" who displayed the greatest concern in regard to the meaning of this caution, and who freely expressed themselves in the hearing of all to the effect that they seldom played cards at all, still less for money; but if they did feel inclined to have a little social game it was not the business of the boat to question their right to do so, and if they lost their money they certainly would not call on the boat to restore it.

After the expression of such manly sentiments, it was surprising if they did not soon find others who shared with them this independence. In order to convey a merited reproof to "the boat" for its unwarranted interference with the pleasure or habits of its patrons, they bought a pack of cards at the bar and "set in" to a "friendly game." In the posting of this inconspicuous little placard, "the boat" no doubt absolved itself from all responsibility in what might and surely did follow in the "friendly games"

From *Old Times on the Upper Mississippi*, The Recollections of a Steamboat Pilot from 1854 to 1863, by George Byron Merrick, pp. 138–141. Copyright, 1909, by George Byron Merrick. Cleveland, Ohio. Reprinted by permission of The Arthur H. Clark Co.

sooner or later started in the forward cabin. Whether the placard likewise absolved the officers of the boat from all responsibility in the matter is a question for the logicians. I cannot recollect that I had a conscience in those days; and if a "sucker" chose to invest his money in draw poker rather than in corner lots, it was none of my business. In that respect, indeed, there was little choice between "Bill" Mallen on the boat with his marked cards and Ingenuous Doemly at Nininger, with his city lots on paper selling at a thousand dollars each, which today, after half a century, are possibly worth twenty-five dollars an acre as farming land.

Ordinarily, the play was not high on the upper river. The passengers were not great planters, with sacks of money, and Negroes on the side to fall back upon in case of a bluff. The operators, also, were not so greedy as their real or fictitious fellows of the lower river. If they could pick up two or three hundred dollars a week by honest endeavor, they were satisfied and gave thanks accordingly.

Probably by some understanding among themselves, the fraternity divided themselves among the different boats running regularly in the passenger trade, and only upon agreement did they change their boats; nor did they intrude upon the particular hunting ground of others.

The *Fanny Harris* was favored with the presence, more or less intermittently, of "Bill" Mallen, "Bill" and "Sam" Dove, and "Boney" Trader. "Boney" was short for Napoleon Bonaparte. These worthies usually traveled in pairs, the two Dove brothers faithfully and fraternally standing by each other, while Mallen and "Boney" campaigned in partnership.

These men were consummate actors. They never came aboard the boat together, and they never recognized each other until introduced—generally through the good offices of their intended victims. In the preliminary stages of the game, they cheerfully lost large sums of money to each other; and after the hunt was up, one usually went ashore at Prescott, Hastings, or Stillwater, while the other continued on to St. Paul. At different times they represented all sorts and conditions of men—settlers, prospectors, Indian agents, merchants, lumbermen, and even lumberjacks; and they always dressed their part, and talked it, too. To do this required some education, keen powers of observation, and an all-around knowledge of men and things. They were gentlemanly at all times—courteous to men and chivalrous to women. While pretending to drink large quantities of very strong liquors, they did in fact make away with many pint measures of quite innocent river water, tinted with the mildest liquid distillation of burned peaches. A clear head and steady nerves were prerequisites to success; and when engaged in business, these men knew that neither one nor the other came by way of "Patsey" Donnelly's "Choice Wines and Liquors." They kept their private bottles of colored water on tap in the bar, and with the uninitiated passed for heavy drinkers.

The play was generally for light stakes, but it sometimes ran high. Five dollars ante, and no limit, afforded ample scope for big play, provided the players had the money and the nerve. The tables were always surrounded by a crowd of lookers-on, most of whom knew enough of the game to follow it understandingly. It is possible that some of the bystanders may have had a good understanding with the professionals, and have materially assisted them by signs and signals.

The chief reliance of the gamblers, however, lay in the marked cards with which they played. No pack of cards left the bar until it had passed through the hands of the gambler who patronized the particular boat that he "worked." The marking was called "stripping." This was done by placing the high cards—ace, king, queen, jack, and ten-spot—between two thin sheets of metal, the edges of which were very slightly concaved. Both edges of the cards were trimmed to these edges with a razor; the cards so "stripped" were thus a shade narrower in the middle than those not operated upon; they were left full width at each end. The acutely sensitive fingers of the gamblers could distinguish between the marked and the unmarked cards, while the other players could detect nothing out of the way with them. "Bill" Mallen would take a gross of cards from the bar to his stateroom and spend hours in thus trimming them, after which they were returned to the original wrappers, which were carefully folded and sealed and replaced in the bar for sale. A "new pack" was often called for by the victim when "luck" ran against him and Mallen himself would ostentatiously demand a fresh pack if he lost a hand or two, as he always did at the beginning of the play.

I never saw any shooting over a game, but once saw pistols drawn. That was when the two Doves were holding up a "tenderfoot." There was a big pile of gold on the table—several hundred dollars in ten- and twenty-dollar gold pieces. The losers raised a row and would have smashed the two operators but for the soothing influence of a cocked Derringer in the hands of one of them. The table was upset and the money rolled in all directions. The outsiders decided where the money justly belonged, in their opinion, by promptly pocketing all they could reach while the principals were fighting. I found a twenty myself the next morning.

A Game of Brag with a Sequel

The *Wheeling Gazette* has revamped an old yarn which was published years ago. As it is a capital story, however, we will give it a place, merely remarking that the "clerk" mentioned was no less a personage than "Old Poins."

A clerk left New Orleans for Pittsburgh with $100,000 belonging to one of the banks. A gang of sharpers found it out, and determined to "pluck"

From *The Spirit of the Times*, A Chronicle of the Turf, Agriculture, Field Sports, Literature and the Stage, edited by William T. Porter, Vol. XII (October 22, 1842), No. 34, p. 398. New York.

him; for which purpose they took passage on the same boat. Before they had proceeded far cards were introduced, and the clerk joined them in a game of "brag." For the purpose of drawing him on, he was allowed to win a considerable sum, and then came the time for the big rush. Accordingly the "hands" were dealt out and "two bullets and a bragger" given to the boss gambler and the clerk, the former having the "age." They both bet largely until at length the gambler, believing he had all his competitor's money on the table, "saw" his last bet and went him five thousand dollars better. He was correct in his suppositions—the clerk said his pile was up and asked for a "sight." The gambler refused to grant it, and after some expostulation, sang out emphatically:

"I go you five thousand better and give you five minutes to raise the money."

The clerk spent three of the minutes in endeavoring to persuade the gambler to "show"; but finding all his efforts in vain, slowly arose from the table, unlocked his trunk, and returned with the package of money entrusted to his care.

"You will not give me a sight for my money?" said the clerk.

"No, sir," replied the gambler, "I went five thousand dollars better and gave you five minutes to raise the money—but one minute of the time remains."

"Then, sir," exclaimed the clerk, throwing his package upon the table, "I see your five thousand and go you ninety-five thousand dollars better and give you *five minutes to raise the money in!*"

The pile was too big. The gamblers left the table precipitately. At the first stopping place they left the boat and returned to New Orleans perfectly used up.

The One-Eyed Gambler

One of the old-time river gamblers was an individual, blind in one eye, known as "One-Eyed Murphy." Murphy was an extremely artful manipulator of cards and made a business of cheating. One day, shortly after the *Natchez* had backed out from New Orleans and got under way, Marion Knowles, a picturesque gentleman of the period and one who had the reputation of being polite even in the most trying circumstances, and no matter how well he had dined, came in and stood for a time as a spectator beside a table at which Murphy was playing poker with some guileless planters. Mr. Knowles was not himself guileless, and very shortly he perceived that the one-eyed gambler was dealing himself cards from the bottom of the

From *American Adventures,* A Second Trip "Abroad at Home," by Julian Street, pp. 516–517. Copyright, 1917, by the Century Company; 1916, 1917, by P. F. Collier & Son, Inc. New York: The Century Company.

pack. Thereupon he drew his revolver from his pocket, and rapping with it on the table, addressed the assembly:

"Gentlemen," he said, speaking in a courtly fashion, "I regret to say that there is something wrong here. I will not call any names, neither will I make any personal allusions. *But if it doesn't stop, damn me if I don't shoot his other eye out!*"

Colonel Starr

[There was] an old gambler [named "Colonel" Charles Starr] who at one time was a prominent figure all along the Mississippi Valley and whose face was as familiar to patrons of the river steamers as were the sandbars which blocked the channel. . . . His long yarns were proverbial. According to his own story, he owned half the plantations skirting the river. Occasionally some one would "pick him up" by telling him that he (the skeptic) was the owner of those broad acres. No such trifling circumstance as this abashed the "Colonel" in the least. Like Banquo's ghost, he peremptorily and perennially refused to "down." Stories about him were . . . plentiful. . . . It is said that once at an Arkansas watering place he was approached by an itinerant blackleg who asked for half a dollar with which to get something to eat. The "Colonel" surveyed him leisurely, from head to foot, before either granting or refusing his request. Finally he said: "How long did you say it was, young man, since you had anything to eat?"

"Two days, Colonel."

"Well," drawled Starr, "I reckon I don't want to give you half a dollar, but if you go without eating two days longer, I'll give you a hundred dollars for your appetite."

Starr was a gourmand, though a dyspeptic, and withal rather selfish. He went into a restaurant in New Orleans one day and ordered a sumptuous repast. A hungry, penniless gambler entered while he was eating, and approaching him, said: "Colonel, I'm hungry and I'm dead broke. Can't you 'stake' me with some of that?"

"Oh, no," answered Starr, "you see, I'm a capper for the house, and my play doesn't go."

He accumulated a fair competence, but gambling and dissipation re-

---

From *Fools of Fortune*, or Gambling and Gamblers, Comprehending a History of the Vice in Ancient and Modern Times, and in Both Hemispheres; an Exposition of Its Alarming Prevalence and Destructive Effects; with an Unreserved and Exhaustive Disclosure of Such Frauds, Tricks, and Devices as are Practised by "Professional" Gamblers, "Confidence Men," and "Bunko Steerers," by John Philip Quinn, who modestly, yet with sincerity, tenders to the world what he hopes may extenuate his twenty-five years of gaming and systematic deception of his fellowmen, p. 213. Copyright, 1890, by John P. Quinn. Chicago.

duced him to poverty, and he died a pauper. The evening of the day preceding his death, he entered a fashionable restaurant and ordered a dinner costing some seven or eight dollars. The proprietor called him on one side, and told him frankly that he did not feel disposed to "carry" him any longer, that he must pay cash for his order or it would not be filled. Starr said nothing, but went out and borrowed five dollars from a friend; returning, he threw it on a table and ordered the best meal obtainable for that sum. When it was set before him, he deliberately turned every dish upside down upon the cloth, and walked out of the place. The following morning he died.

Martin and Walton's Game

. . . While traveling in partnership with a man named Sam Martin . . . , we were going down the Mississippi in a steamboat. Martin had placed a number of packs of marked cards with the barkeeper, with instructions to "ring them in," that is to sell them to customers asking for playing cards. We wandered about the boat, separately, looking for victims. At length I formed the acquaintance of a tall, handsome man, who suggested a game of euchre for the cigars. We had not played long when the stranger proposed poker for a small ante. I said that I was not accustomed to playing for money, but that if he would promise not to expose me if I lost I would chance a few dollars. Martin was in the cabin waiting for me to give him a signal to approach. On receiving it he drew near the table and I accosted him with: "Well, stranger, will you join us in a game for a small ante?" He answered that he would if my friend had no objections, although it was near his bed time. We played a few games and quit losers. We knew that our "mark" was going to Memphis, and that we would have an abundance of time in which to win our money back.

The next morning we resumed play. I lost fifty dollars (which of course was won by Martin), and said that I would have to withdraw from the game, unless they would consent to place stakes against a draft. (In those days I always traveled with a liberal supply of worthless checks.) I left the table and Martin and the stranger (who gave his name as Walton) played single handed, which was precisely what the former wanted. They were using the marked cards which my partner had placed with the barkeeper. It was not long before Martin had won all the stranger's money—some $800—besides a valuable gold watch and chain. At the conclusion of the game, the winner invited his dupe to take a drink at the bar, which invitation was accepted.

As they were drinking, Walton looked at Martin and said: "You are a very lucky man. I believe that you might fall overboard without getting

Ibid., pp. 241–242.

wet, and I certainly should expect to see your body floating up stream. You have all my money, and I don't mind telling you, now, that I was cheating all the time. I was 'holding out' and playing the 'double discard' from the beginning, and I don't see how you managed to come out ahead."

"Well," said Martin, "since you have been so frank, I will be equally so. I am an expert marked card player, and each pack that we played was one of mine. I knew that you were cheating, but didn't care. My 'percentage' was too strong for you. Here is your watch and chain and fifty dollars for a 'stake.' But I can tell you right here that you won't ever have any show against an artist who can read your hand at sight and remember it."

And there is no doubt that Sam was right. Yet if an accomplished card sharp like Walton can thus be taken in, even while practising his professional tricks, what possible chance remains to a greenhorn?

They Woke Up the Wrong Passenger

I had been in Natchez from the time of Mose Way's horse-race until poor Clifton received his second Spanish burying. I left on board of the *Tippecanoe*, a snug little boat, running in the cotton trade between Natchez and Princeton, and commanded by Captain Simon Miller, of Louisville. As gamblers are accustomed to do, soon after going on board, I endeavored to ascertain what the prospects were for game. The usual way of doing this is by going around and forming acquaintances among the players in a friendly game of whist, eucher, boston, seven-up, or old sledge. This is done to draw in the unsuspecting, to see who play, and what amount of money they carry upon their persons. Then, if they cannot get the money by gambling, there are but few who will not try to secure it in another way. . . .

I soon found that my prospects were dull enough, for I could not start a game, even for amusement. So I took my berth, thinking I would sleep upon it. A curious set of passengers, thought I, afraid to play with a beardless boy. But as I lay in my berth thinking over the matter, the boat stopped her engines—passengers had hailed her. The yawl was sent out, and two elderly men, planters in appearance, came on board. They were evidently under the influence of liquor. They had scarcely reached the boat before they sung out, "Barkeeper, have you any cards on board?" Being answered in the affirmative, they asked if there were any gentlemen that would play. The barkeeper could not inform them, but remarked they could satisfy themselves by inquiry. Upon this, they advanced to

From *Gambling Unmasked!* or the Personal Experience of J. H. Green[e], the Reformed Gambler, Designed as a Warning to the Young Men of This Country, written by Himself, pp. 189–193. Entered . . . 1844, by Jonathan H. Green. Philadelphia: G. B. Zieber & Co. 1847.

where several persons were seated, whom I had annoyed very much by urging them to play. They all refused again. "But you must play," said one of the old men; "we will have a game." Some one of them pointed to my berth, and said there was a gentleman there who would probably be happy to accommodate them. He was right, and if they had not called upon me, I would soon have called upon them, to accommodate them with a game of poker. The old man turned round and felt his way along to the berth where I lay, as he supposed, asleep. But "all men do not sleep when their eyes are shut." He gave me a hearty shake, crying out, "Halloo! get up, get up." I affected the sleeping man, muttered out my surprise, asked him if the boat was sinking, and so forth. He was perfectly deceived, and continued to bawl out, "Get up, get up, and play poker."

"Well, if I must, I must," said I. "Go and get the table and cards ready, and I will be with you as soon as possible." I soon heard him giving orders to the steward to bring a table and cards. While things were making ready, I was very busy in finding and arranging my wearing apparel, and saw, from the run of their conversation, that they were expecting a rich treat, and had agreed to play against me in partnership. . . . Their agreement I overheard. Said one of them, "You, sir, set your foot on mine, and for one pair, kick me once; for two pairs, twice; for three, three times; for four, four times, and for a 'full,' once very hard." I knew that, with this arrangement, unless I should counterplay, they would soon fleece me. Soon after the game began, I found them feeling for feet, and being of an accommodating disposition, I gave them a foot apiece. Kick after kick did I get, and answer; and soon found myself winner by six hundred dollars, and my opponents in a very disagreeable mood for amusement players, as they assured me they were. We had about forty dollars in silver to play with, and as fast as I won it, they would give me bank-notes in exchange. When I had won the six hundred dollars, and all the silver, they wished to play upon credit. This I refused; and as they were getting very quarrelsome, I determined to close. They objected to this, and insisted that if I did quit, I should leave the silver. I did so, and they soon were playing high against each other. It is a natural consequence that, when two gamblers in partnership have been unsuccessful, they will turn upon one another. I lay in my berth, well pleased with my night's work. Unpleasant and harsh words passed between the old men.

"You did not play the game according to bargain, Mr. ———."

"I not play! Do you mean me, Mr.?"

"I mean you, ———."

"Don't say that, Mr. ———. No, sir, it will not do to accuse me, when you did not kick me right one time during the whole night."

"Hold! hold! Did you kick me according to the arrangement? Mr. ———, we are neighbors, and I thought friends, till this evening's play; but I must confess I am somewhat—"

"Ashamed of yourself, I suppose," said ———, taking the words out of his mouth.

"No, sir; one proposition, and leave the balance until tomorrow."

"Propose," said ———.

"That we settle our play tonight, and leave the matter of the incorrect kicking to be settled another time."

"Very willing; how do you say we stand?"

"I owe you one hundred and seventy-five dollars," said ———.

"You are a correct man, sir."

"That I am, and this settlement will prove it; but let me ask you how you like our night's play?" said ———.

"Don't like it at all," said ———.

"And the boy that played, what do you think of him?"

"I think just this, ———; I think we *waked up the wrong passenger!*"

"I think so, too; we are perfectly agreed, ———. And now, neighbor ———, you know I have a great respect for you, and hope you may not lose; but I must cast up my account against you, and see how much you are indebted to me."

"Account against me!" exclaimed ———; "I will submit to no such thing, I assure you."

"Just look over that list, and—keep cool, friend—keep cool, sir—it says you owe me two hundred and twenty-five dollars; bringing you in my debt fifty dollars. Is not that right?"

"Too late to rectify mistakes, sir."

"But you are bound to rectify this one. What do you think of that?"

"I think as I did of the boy—that I *waked up the wrong passenger,*" said he, at the same time sliding his claim from the table, badly beaten.

These two old men had come on board on purpose to fleece some inexperienced card-player, while they pretended that *amusement* was all they wanted in playing. I was, probably, the only individual on board whom they could not have beaten. Beware of the men who say they play merely for amusement. . . . Beware, too, of those who advocate such playing; for, while here and there one may do it from ignorance, it is generally done by dishonest, unprincipled men, as a cloak for their own knavery and crime. The only safe course is total abstinence. Touch not, handle not, the implements of the gambler. . . .

Grampin and the Sea Captain Who Won at Roulette

. . . On their way [to take their lodgings on the boat in New Orleans, W. and the young planter] passed "No. 9," a place in which W. professed to be greatly interested. He said he expected to receive several hundred dollars from the managers in passage money, as all the licensed gamblers would travel north in the summer season.

Ibid., pp. 157–162.

Although it was late, W. proposed to go in. Upon entering, he stepped
forward to an old gambler by the name of Grampin, who was seated behind a faro table counting his doubloons, and addressed him thus:

"Monsieur Grampin, what is the news this evening?"

"Bad news, Monsieur W.," replied Grampin, "bad news; we have lost
a great deal of money, sir; ten thousand dollars will not make us even
upon this night's play."

"Who beats the game so bad to-night, Monsieur?" asked W., turning
his eye where several were then sitting, betting small sums upon the roulette
and twenty-one table. The "Sweat-cloth" was also covered with bets. . . .

"Oh, sir, you look to the wrong part of the house for the winner; look
to the other corner—then you will see the lucky man," said the Frenchman, grinding his teeth and disfiguring his face with a fiendish grin. "Five
hundred thousand dollars, after paying our license, have we made, without
ever before sustaining such a loss; and no man ever left this table before
so much the winner."

Then he broke out in oaths, imprecations, and curses against the
Almighty for sending him such "bad luck." It was enough to make humanity shudder to hear the blasphemies which came from his polluted
lips.

W., turning his eye to the corner mentioned, and seeing a corpse, exclaimed—"What, a corpse here, Monsieur?"

"Yes, a corpse!" said the Frenchman. "I tell you, Captain, God Almighty never permits living men to win so large a sum from 'No. 9.'"

In the corner of the room, upon a couple of barrels, were laid two
planks, and upon these were the lifeless remains of a sea captain! He died
while at play!

The circumstances of his death were as follows: He was a man fond
of amusement and sport; but was not considered either a drunkard or
a gambler; he had never been seen intoxicated when in port. But he used
to pay frequent visits to "No. 9," when he would sit for hours and bet
upon the roulette. Twenty-five cents, however, was his highest bet. If he
lost, he went no higher; if he gained, it was the same. . . . On the evening
of his untimely death, he came in as usual, and took his seat at the table.
The roulette table has two colors—one of red and one of black. Betting
on either color separately affords the same chance of winning, as the
colors are divided equally and figures correspond. If the ball which is
rolled is permitted to fall where it chances, the game is equal; and as the
banker also throws the ball, he has to pay an amount equal to the sum
you bet. If you bet upon the color, and place, for instance, one dollar on
the red, the banker starts the wheel and ball with great rapidity, and as
the wheel ceases to revolve, the ball rolls into its color and the bet is decided; and if your bet be upon the same color where the ball stops, he
pays you an amount equal to the sum you have laid down. The roulette
tables at that time were constructed on a fairer principle than they are at
the present day, and it sometimes happened that the banks were broken

by the bettors. The wheel is marked with numbers from one to thirty-six, and has three bars placed in the bed, dividing the figures into equal parts; every twelve figures has a bar, one of which is marked with an Eagle, another with a single *0*, and the third with a double *00*. If, when you bet on the colors, the ball falls into either of these bars, the banker is entitled to all you bet.

The sea captain, having placed his bet upon the red, sat with his head leaning upon his hands, as if to wait the result of the game. The ball fell into the column, and he was the winner. The wheel started again, but the Captain did not move, and, contrary to his usual practice, the amount of his bet was doubled. He won the second, third, fourth, and fifth, the sum doubling each time. Thus it went on to the eighth time, when the gamblers began to be excited, and, uttering loud curses, exclaimed, "He wins again!"

At this, many who were in the room gathered around the table. The result of the ninth and tenth being the same, one cried out, "He is a fool! Why don't he make sure of what he has won?"

The eleventh, twelfth, and thirteenth brought the same result, and many exclaimed, "He is mad!"

But the game went on, and the Captain continued heedless. The fourteenth was in his favor. At the fifteenth, thousands were at stake, from the small beginning of twenty-five cents, and all eyes seemed fixed in amazement. Still he won. The sixteenth was the same. The bankers vociferated curses upon the wheel-player. Others urged the Captain to withdraw at least a part of his winnings. Sixteen thousand dollars was at stake for the seventeenth. The ball flew like lightning, but there was no change. The money was piled up before the Captain in heavy bank notes, but he moved not a finger, nor uttered a word.

At this juncture, a husky voice, in seaman's phrase, was heard.

"Haul in, old Captain! You don't bet all that pile against this set of land pirates! Haul in!" and a hand was stretched forth from one at the table, grasping the money and depositing it in a hat. It was the first mate of the captain's vessel. Having thus secured the money, he seized the captain by the shoulder, saying, "Come, you have a full cargo; it's time to hoist sail"—when, horrible to relate, the corpse of the Captain fell against him. He had been sitting with his head upon his hand through all this exciting scene, having died in the act of betting his first quarter. The mate called for water, and dashed it into his face; then for spirits; but all efforts to resuscitate him were in vain. Life was extinct.

The gamblers then demanded that the money should be refunded; but the mate had rolled it up in a handkerchief, put it into the hand of a cabin boy, and charged him to run with it for his life to the ship, and deliver it to the clerk and summon the crew to the gambling house. The tumult and confusion were so great that the boy slipped away unnoticed.

When the corpse was laid on the plank, the gamblers again demanded the money of the mate, stating that, as the Captain had undoubtedly died while betting the first quarter, justice required that it should be returned to the bankers. The mate, in a tone of defiance, replied that the orphan children of the Captain needed the money, and should have it. Force was then threatened if he refused to deliver it up. Seeing that their threats were unheeded, they rushed upon him with violence, seized his hat, and bore it off, supposing they had thus secured the money; but to their surprise the hat was empty. A large number who were present took the part of the mate, and great excitement prevailed throughout the house. An assault was made upon the mate. Some cried one thing, and some another. "Down with him!" "Get the money." "Let him alone." "You have no right to rob him"—mingled with oaths and imprecations and curses. At this moment twenty or thirty of the ship's crew rushed in, and one word from the mate brought them to his rescue, and the gamblers were soon made to stand at a distance.

Something was said respecting the money, which led the sailors to suppose that the mate had been robbed, and they were about rushing upon Monsieur Grampin, as the proper person to indemnify him for any loss he might have sustained, but were diverted by the entrance of some twenty of the city watch, armed with short swords. The sailors knew the character of the posse, made up of what were called among them "wharf-rat-Frenchmen," and were no more daunted by their array of force than they would have been by the display of tin swords in the hands of so many trained monkeys. A fracas was, however, prevented between the sailors and the watch by the assurance of the mate that the money was safe and a request from him that they would return quietly to the vessel. He proposed to take the corpse on board, but was informed by the Captain of the Watch that a coroner's inquest must be held over it before it could be removed. He then seated himself by the corpse of his Captain, to watch over it during the rest of the night; and the gamblers returned to the common work of darkness, playing cards and drinking liquor the meanwhile, now and then uttering curses upon the dead body of the Captain.

Before W. and the young planter left the room, they stepped to the spot where the corpse was laid, to take another view of it. "This is a dreadful scene, indeed!" said W.

"Yes," replied the young man, "a corpse in one part of the room, and faro, roulette, game twenty-one, and chuckerluck in another."

Here Grampin, interfering, said, "I have paid my license, and if it were necessary I would play the game upon the corpse."

The young man, shocked at this horrid depravity, immediately left the room, followed by W.

"He is the most hardened wretch I ever knew!" exclaimed the former, to which the latter coolly replied, "Oh, he is only a little excited. Had the Captain not died, and won the same amount, and played daily, it would all have passed off as a common thing. In twelve hours he will be as good a man as need be."

The reader may be shocked at such an instance of the absence of all moral sensibility. But such was the state of things among the gambling fraternity in the years 1830–1–2–3–4–5.

An inquest was held upon the corpse in the morning and the verdict returned was, death by a fit of apoplexy; after which the mate was permitted to remove it. We never learned any further particulars of this horrid incident.

A Gambler's Punishment

On one trip [on the Mississippi River], on board the *Eclipse* (which was afterwards torn to pieces by a tornado at New Orleans), a man by the name of Smith Mace won $1,000 of a young man, at three-card monte. This being a "sure thing game," and contrary to all the traditions of the sporting fraternity, the winner was looked upon as a thief, and so an indignation meeting was improvised, a committee appointed to institute proceedings, a jury was impaneled, the culprit duly and formally tried, found guilty of violation of all the rules, customs, and proprieties of sporting, and was sentenced either to refund the money at once or to be tied for an hour to the horizontal piston rod, where there would be just room for him to walk back and forth with each movement of the rod. Mace refused to give up the money, and a rope was fastened to the piston rod and tied around his neck in such a manner as to allow him to turn, and he commenced his walk of almost ten feet and back. He only made one remark during the whole hour. After he had walked a while, one of the committee asked him if he would give up the money. He answered, "Go away, I have no time to talk," and he did not have much. It was absolutely necessary for him to keep his eye on the rod and turn exactly with its backward movement or it would have torn his head from his shoulder. He walked his hour, was released, and sent to Coventry for the rest of the trip.

Adventures of George Devol

I. A Leap for Life

Another time I was coming up on the steamer *Fairchild* with Captain Fawcett, of Louisville. When we landed at Napoleon, there were about

From *Life and Adventures of Henry Edward Hugunin, or Thirty Years a Gambler,* Incidents, Places Visited, Persons Met, with Some Account of Different Games, the Evils of Gambling, and How Never to Lose, written by Himself, p. 35. Oswego, New York: B. J. Oliphant, Book-binders and Stationers. 1879.

From *Forty Years a Gambler on the Mississippi,* A Cabin Boy in 1839; Could Steal Cards and Cheat the Boys at Eleven; Stack a Deck at Fourteen; Bested Soldiers

twenty-five of the "Arkansas Killers" came on board, and I just opened out and cleaned the party of money, watches, and all their valuables. Things went along smoothly for a while, until they commenced to drink pretty freely. Finally one of them said: "Jake, Sam, Ike, get Bill and let us kill that d——d gambler who got our money." "All right," said the party, and they broke for their rooms to get their guns. I stepped out of the side door, and got under the pilot-house, as it was my favorite hiding place. I could hear every word down stairs, and could whisper to the pilot. Well, they hunted the boat from stem to stern—even took lights and went down into the hold—and finally gave up the chase, as one man said I had jumped overboard. I slipped the pilot $100 in gold, as I had both pockets filled with gold and watches, and told him at the first point that stood out a good ways to run her as close as he could and I would jump. He whispered, "Get ready," and I slipped out and walked back, and stood on the top of the wheelhouse until she came, as I thought, near enough to make the jump, and away I went; but it was farther than I expected, so I went down about thirty feet into the river, and struck into the soft mud clear up to my waist. Some parties who were standing on the stern of the boat saw me, and gave the alarm, when the "killers" all rushed back and commenced firing at me, and the bullets went splattering all around me. The pilot threw her into the bend as quick as he could, and then let on she took a sheer on him, and nearly went to the other side. The shooting brought the Negroes from the fields to the bank of the river. I hallooed to them to get a long pole and pull me out, for I was stuck in the mud. They did so, and I got up on the bank and waited for another boat.

II. THE QUADROON GIRL

I got on the *Belle Key* one afternoon at Vicksburg; and as I claimed to be a planter from White River, I soon became acquainted with some planters that lived on the coast. There was a game of poker started, and I was invited to sit in. We played until supper was ready. I had played on the square, and had won a few hundred dollars. After supper they got up a dance, and that spoiled the game. I was sitting in the hall, when one of the planters came to me and said, "Don't you dance?" "No, I don't care to dance where I am not acquainted." "You are like me in that respect; I had rather play poker; but as those gentlemen who were playing in the game today have all got their families on board, they will not play, so what do you say to us having a game?"

I said I did not care to play a while, but I would rather be a little more private, and that we might go up into the Texas and play. We

on the Rio Grande during the Mexican War; Won Hundreds of Thousands from Paymasters, Cotton Buyers, Defaulters and Thieves; Fought More Rough-and-Tumble Fights than Any Man in America and Was the Most Daring Gambler in the World, by George H. Devol, pp. 29–30, 75–76, 172. Entered . . . 1887, by George H. Devol. New York. 1892.

got the checks at the bar (and the barkeeper did not forget a deck of my cards). We went up and had just got seated when up came my partner and said, "Gentlemen, are you going to sport a little?" "We are; will you join us?" said the planter. "What are you going to play?" "Poker, of course." He sat in, and then it was a very nice, gentlemanly game. We played on the square for a while (that is, if the cards had been square). Finally I could put it off no longer, so I ran up two hands, giving the planter three eights, and then downed him for over $400. We played a little while longer, and then I ran up two more hands, and guarded them so that nothing could fall in that time. I gave my partner the best hand, and he took in about $600. The planter was then over $1,000 loser, so he excused himself for a few minutes, and I knew that he had gone after more money. He soon returned with $1,500, and that lasted him about one hour. He got up and said, "Boys, I must have some more money." My partner and I went down with him, as I did not think he could get any more. We were at the bar taking a drink when he turned to me and said, "I would like to play some more, but I can't get any more money, unless you will loan me some on my Negro, as I have one on board that I paid $1,500 for, and she is one of the most likely girls you ever saw." I winked at my partner to loan him some money on his wench. He went back and brought out one of the prettiest quadroon girls, about seventeen years old, that I ever saw. My partner loaned him $1,000, and got the clerk to draw up a bill of sale; then we resumed the game; but that did not last him but about half an hour, for I beat him out of nearly the whole amount on one hand, and that broke up the game. He had but seventy-five dollars left. We went down and took a drink, and then went to bed.

The next day he got the money and redeemed his girl; then he said to me, "I have got about $700, so let us go up and play single-handed." We went up, and I soon got that money. He said, "In all my poker-playing, I never played so unlucky in my life." He went to my partner and borrowed $1,000 more on the girl, and I took that in. He then went to Captain Keys, tried to borrow the money to redeem his girl again, but the Captain would not loan it to him. He found a man that loaned him the money, and he redeemed her again. He was considerable loser, but he got some more wine in him, then he wanted more poker; but I told my partner not to have anything more to do with his Negro, for it was making too much talk on the boat already. When he got to his landing, he and his Negro left the boat, and I tell you she was a dandy.

III. BAD COMPANY

On one occasion while traveling from New Orleans to Baton Rouge, I espied a gentleman who was a Judge at the latter place. He was a man of aristocratic bearing and somewhat haughty in his manners. I started up my wheel after supper, and soon had a fine game. It was not long before I noticed a slick young man that I knew was from Cincinnati, walking arm in arm with the Judge, and apparently on terms of the utmost intimacy with him. This slick young Cincinnatian had introduced himself as a son of the late Nicholas Longworth, who was well known up and down the river. He claimed that he was traveling for his health.

I had made up my mind that he was playing a dead card, as I did not think the Judge was of much force, though he always appeared to have plenty of money. They soon were playing euchre, and began talking about poker, and presently the Judge came to me and said, "Devol, will you loan me $500? I will pay you when Baton Rouge is reached. I am a sure winner," he continued, and looking at his hand, I saw the old familiar four queens and an ace, with which I had downed so many suckers. I must say that I wanted to see him get it in the neck, and I was not disappointed. I took chances, and loaned him $500, and when I saw Longworth's would-be son putting it in his pocket that was the last time I ever beheld that money. The Judge never recognized me again. This is what an honest man gets when in bad company.

The Race Riot on the *Dubuque*

In July, 1869, the packet *Dubuque,* of the old Northern Line, one of the best boats that ever ran on the Mississippi, took on board at St. Louis four raft crews numbering about one hundred and twenty. They had deck passage with certain harvest hands, number unknown, that were bound for the wheat harvest along the upper river. Harvest hands were also more or less of the jungle. Of cabin passengers, traveling upstairs, the lists were full, for this was a popular boat.

She reached Davenport on the evening of July 23 and tied up for the night. There seems to have been low water and the captain was unwilling to run the Rapids at night.

Many passengers went ashore; among them the raftsmen and harvest hands, who tanked up on the usual beverages.

At daybreak the *Dubuque* pulled out. Half an hour later a big raftsman, in the belligerent lees of intoxication and followed by a crowd of his compeers in the same state, climbed the companionway to the upper deck and demanded breakfast in the saloon.

The steward was a colored man; the waiters and deck-hands were of the same unfortunate race.

The steward explained that only passengers having first-class tickets were served on the upper deck and that breakfast for the others would be served on the deck below.

The raftsmen jeered at this information and tried to push their way

From *A-Rafting on the Mississip'* by Charles Edward Russell, pp. 200–204. Copyright, 1928, by Charles Edward Russell. New York and London: The Century Company.

into the saloon. The steward opposed them. In the scuffle he got the big drunken raftsman close to the companionway and sent him reeling downstairs.

His companions swore vengeance. Raftsmen were not to be insulted by Negroes.

They trooped to the captain and told him that unless the impudent Negro steward was punished they would set fire to the boat.

River men had one handy and common way of settling disputes. The captain, who realized the danger he was in, tried to quiet the rioters by reminding them of their favorite tribunal. Let the raftsman and the steward meet on the forecastle and fight it out with their fists.

The raftsman refused to fight a black man. Part of the deck-load was baled hay. The rioters now approached it with lighted matches to set it afire. All were armed; every raftsman went armed in those days. While part of the mob threatened the captain, the rest sought out the deck-hands to kill them, for by this time had come the strange and terrible frenzy that we have since seen in many a race riot, and madness reigned.

The terrified deck-hands had scattered into hiding-places. Raftsmen relentlessly trailed them. An incessant fusillade of pistol shots produced wild panic on the upper decks. The boat was now fighting the swift current of the Rapids. Even the coolest of the passengers could see nothing but death ahead of them; either the boat would be fired or she would be wrecked on a reef.

A colored man had hidden in the forward hold. The raftsmen hunted him out. He eluded them and ran aft, followed by a cursing crowd. At the end of the afterguard he suddenly turned, whipped out a knife, stabbed to the heart one of his pursuers, and leaped into the water. Two men that had been fishing in a skiff started to row to him. The raftsmen fired at his head as he swam along. I cannot tell now whether they hit him, but, just before the skiff could reach him, he sank from sight and the mob cheered.

The barber hid in a closet. A rioter dragged him forth and stabbed him with a bowie-knife. He ran aft and begged a woman passenger to save his life. She hid him in her stateroom and bound up his wound. The rioters trailed him by his blood to her door and demanded their prey. She stood like a statue and poured upon them a torrent of such scorn that they sneaked away.

A deck-hand hid on the after-guard. Strange as it may seem, the boat continued all this time to make her regular landings. At the town of Hampton, Illinois, this fugitive attempted to escape. He was discovered and beaten into the water, where he was pelted with missiles until he sank and drowned.

The captain had managed at Hampton to get a passenger ashore with telegrams for help to be sent to the sheriff at Rock Island and other authorities. When the *Dubuque* was again upon her way, three more deck-hands were stabbed or shot and the bodies thrown into the river. Now the rioters sought the captain and demanded that the boat be run ashore, every black man on board be disembarked, and the voyage resumed with themselves as deck-hands. But they made a condition that the captain and officers should make no resistance, the boat should be run as they directed, no arrests must be made, and no information given. If the captain refused, the boat would be fired.

He consented to these terms and ran the boat to shore, where all the black men were landed. After this the rioters were quiet and the boat proceeded.

At Camanche, a few miles above Le Claire, the truculent ruffian that had started the trouble slipped ashore and disappeared.

Clinton was the next stop. The rioters by this time became impatient and demanded that the boat should speed up for St. Paul without stopping. There was a railroad bridge at Clinton and its draw was closed. The captain of the *Dubuque,* to gain time, told the rioters that the draw could not be opened. While they were arguing about this, a special train passed over the bridge, and the next the rioters knew a company of regular soldiers from the Rock Island arsenal marched down the levee. In answer to the captain's appeal they had been sent by train up the Illinois shore. At the sight of the uniforms and rifles the rioters broke and ran for a vacant warehouse. Soldiers and the gathering citizens surrounded it. The commandant summoned the men to surrender. They made some show of resistance but finally gave in and were marched in irons back to the *Dubuque.* With all her passengers she started back to Rock Island. The passengers were desired as witnesses.

The trial was short. Eleven of the rioters were convicted on the spot and taken to the penitentiary. Some days in the county jail was the sentence for the rest.

But the man that launched that day of horror, the ringleader that slunk ashore at Camanche, was never caught. All the country was scoured for him, vigilantes rode in every direction, the telegraph was used, and all to no result. Once the scouts got a trace of him. Far in the interior he had stopped at a lonely farmhouse and asked for a drink of milk. Then he disappeared. On the river he had been well-known for years as "Pock-Marked Lynch." In behalf of my river and its renown, I set down with emphasis that he was not really a riverman. He was a parasite. His business was to carry a faro layout up and down and relieve raft crews of their wages. He had a partner named Frazier, who managed to escape at Clinton. Years afterward interest was revived in this story by a report that Frazier had returned to the river and had been seen and recognized. If so, his visit was brief. As to Lynch, his description was widely published, but so far as any record shows he was lost to the sight of men.

Lew Brown: Mean Mate for Rough Rousters

The rouster was always telling tales about the mates. To him the mate then over him was the toughest on the river. Sooner or later he got around to the stories about Lew Brown, certainly the most sinister of his brutal kind. No one knew where "One-arm Lew" came from; some said Vicksburg, some St. Louis. He had, they said, been a thug hired as a strikebreaker in the latter city; or a waterfront rat in Vicksburg. No one knew how he had lost his left arm—lost it in a pistol shooting in a barroom; Negro shot it off; an overseer winged him at a private wharf near Vicksburg. A river captain who believed the last story said Lew struck a field hand who was helping the rousters at a plantation landing. The overseer, angered at Lew's whacking his Negro, grabbed the mate's arm to prevent a second blow. Lew smashed out with his fist. The overseer came up shooting, severing the bones of Lew's arm. Lew killed the overseer by shooting him in the stomach. "Self-defense," said the judge.

But people didn't ask a man like "One-arm Lew" about his past. He stood six feet tall and could throw his two hundred pounds behind his right fist for an impact that had the finality of an oak maul. But after losing his left arm he didn't use his famous right. A hickory blackjack loaded with lead and a forty-four in a belly holster became the tools of his trade, and he was nervous with both—especially after the long hours and strain of a mate's life caused him to start "doping," and, before that, when he was well-liquored. Then his black eyes, crooked nose, and bitter mouth made him a holy terror to the rousters and a man for whites to avoid.

Old rivermen said Lew wasn't a killer before he lost his arm. But afterward he developed a grudge against the whole world. He said his *left* elbow hurt him all the time. If he could find his amputated arm and straighten out that elbow, he thought the pain would stop. Not only did he suffer from this throbbing arm stump, but he suffered also from the strain of being more terrible than other mates with two fists. No rouster would fear a one-armed mate in a fight, but he would fear a killer. When the clerk stopped the loading to check, Lew liked to call a rouster whom he suspected of threatening talk. "Come here, nigger, and roll me a cigarette!" With his hand on the butt of his pistol Lew stared at the rouster, trying to make the Negro quail or his fingers shake. "Stop," said Lew, "don't you lick it! Hold it up here!"

Coming back to the boat from an uptown drunk, Lew, on reaching the waterfront, would fire over bunches of Negroes to clear his way. The

From *Memphis Down in Dixie,* by Shields McIlwaine, pp. 213–219. Copyright, 1948, by Shields McIlwaine. New York: E. P. Dutton and Company, Inc.

Mr. William McCaskill, formerly my college student in Southwestern at Memphis, did all the interviewing of old river captains and roustabouts for "Mean Mates and Rough Rousters". . . .—S.M., *ibid.,* p. 387.

rousters said he fired right into them. Rivermen relay the story about Lew's "killing" six Negroes while trying to get a rescue crew during a flood time. Not only money, but human life was at stake. When the clerk failed to sign up the quota of rousters—they knew the emergency and were hanging back for big money—he turned over the tickets to Lew, the first mate. Lew strode up the cobblestones toward the cotton bales on which the rousters had been lolling, contemptuous of the clerk. All muttering ceased. A moment of fixity and silence—then the blacks disappeared among the bales. Lew pulled up within shouting distance and turned on the barrage of abuse that other mates tried in vain to copy. "You lazy black bastards!" he snarled. "You white-livered mud rats, get down on your bellies and beg, 'cause I'm on a nigger-killin' drunk. Dog! You sons-o'-bitches, dog!" Then a few panicky Negroes bolted for the top of the Bluff. This was what Lew had been waiting for. He fired over the head of the flying blacks. Then he waved the tickets. "Do I get six live rousters or six dead ones?" He got his pick of the whole crowd.

Very likely Lew never slaughtered a half-dozen Negroes on the Memphis waterfront in the 1880's, or 1890's; he didn't need to do that to get a crew; besides, the law, local and Federal, had tightened its control over the river world since Reconstruction. Lew killed rousters down river and at small landings—the Negroes say over twenty. Nobody knows how many, because people were afraid of telling, or at least, of being specific. When, according to the river Negroes, nearly every mate was the toughest and had killed rousters and rolled them in the river for the gars, Lew's killings must have in reality been numerous, for his evil reputation led all the rest. That the Lee Line and the Anchor Line employed Lew Brown shows what the staple in mates was. The scoundrel got results.

Certainly rousters found thrill and pride in working for him. The tough old-time Negro loved to brag about how hard, how hellraising, how generous his bossman was. A Negro who had survived a season with "One-arm Lew" was a man-in-full, an A No. 1 rouster. One day, a stringy brown man asked a stevedore about a job, saying he had worked for Mista Lew. The stevedore snatched off the newcomer's cap and rubbed his hand over the Negro's smooth head. "Git off'n dis boat, you lyin' coon!" he cried. "You ain't nevah worked fuh Mista Lew. Yo' head's smooth ez a billiard ball." Mista Lew's rousters, of course, were all supposed to have knotty heads scarred by the loaded stick.

No thin-legged rouster could stand the killing pace set by Lew Brown. During the fall cotton-carrying, "Old One-arm" was tireless and demonic. With oaths, threats, and directions he blasted the sluggish men into high gear. Most mates let their gangs use "lead niggers," strapping fellows that set the pace and led the rouster line up the stage. Lew would have no lost motion; he used a human conveyor belt that moved without stop for many hours. "I don't want no leadman!" he would yell. "Gimme a closed circle!" He scorned picayune loads and soft "chain-barrel" mates who allowed two rousters to carry one barrel with a device made of two poles with connecting chain. "A good load," Lew said, "is what two men can pick up and one can carry."

If a new rouster's legs began to shake or his load to sway crazily, Lew fired him. "Old One-arm" tolerated neither weakness nor error. Once at a slippery landing a rouster rolling a cotton bale down the stageplank lost control of it. "Hold onto that cotton!" Lew cried. "Hold it, you sorry bastard!" The Negro held and was carried with the bale into the river. Some one started to throw the rouster a rope. "Let the no-good bastard go!" Lew yelled. "Get that cotton!"

Though he cared no more about a rouster's life than a mud turtle's, he dealt out his terrors and rewards with even hand. No pets for Lew. Nor did he frighten them off the boat just before the end of the run to cheat them out of their wages. No steamboat owner or officer ever made him party to such deviltry. "Here's a hundred-dollar ticket, nigger," the mate of a crooked boat would shout, "and I'll bet you another hundred you won't last the trip." Such dealing was not only low, but short-sighted. It made trouble. The next time the guilty captain tried to sign a crew the rousters would "holler the mate off," that is, they would stand on the cobblestones and yell at the bidder: "Won't go wid dat mate! Won't go wid dat mate!" until the captain sent the officer to another boat or fired him. Lew expected work, expected to pay for it. When he thought the crew had done its duty, he sent them to the bar for a round of liquor—on the house! Sometimes, after a grueling stint, he would toss a sack of tobacco to a spirited, hard-driving rouster and say with a sneering grin: "Here, you black rascal, smoke some o' that stink off'n you!" "Dat man!" would mutter the pleased rouster. "Dat duh meanest man ever cussed a po' rousta, but he ain't no damn peckerwood! Naw, suh."

To old rivermen this confused idolatry of Lew by rousters was no mystery. A killing mate was the rousters' Jesse James, Billy the Kid, and John Dillinger, rolled into one terrible man. "Meanest mate on duh rivah . . . kill a rousta ev'ry trip . . . kill you fuh lookin' at 'im." Out of Negroes' loose mouths rolled the awesome names of the meanest mates on the river—"Finn" Starr, Johnny Britton, Mike Carkin, Hughey McGory. . . . Remember old Hughey, "Bull-whip Shorty," down river away from the big towns, used to drive his rousters with a long snake whip, cut a patch out of a rouster's shirt, wham! Sound like a gun. Around such men rousters could smell death, and like all brutish ignorant men they enjoyed the brimstone air of danger in their big nostrils. Mates knew this. One of them had killed a rouster below Memphis and buried him in a box on the bank to avoid any questions from the Federal authorities. The river and the rains cut into the bank and exposed the end of the coffin. Afterward, when the mate's boat was passing the box, he would point to it and say, "Niggers, you see that coffin end over there? Don't you forget it. That's what happens to uppety niggers." Lawd, lawd, meanest mate on duh river!

This hero worship among rousters was a crazy thing. The black man hated the mate, swore he would put a knife into him some dark night, bash his head in with a cotton hook. But, my, what a killin' mate! Worse than a bad, blue-gummed Geechee. Even "Goggle-eye" Austin, an Anchor Line mate that never killed a Negro, was made out by the rousters to be a bad, bad man:

> Where dat ole rousta now?
> Out on some big boat tryin' to fly
> Out'n duh way uv ole Goggle-eye.

Negroes were always killing each other. To be a "bad nigger" was to cut a big figure. No wonder the rousters invented Stackolee, the bad black man, who was like a tough mate, "doin' nothin' but killin' up good men." [1]

Foreigners and refined people were horrified, also puzzled, when they saw and heard Lew Brown and his kind of action. Captains told a joke— about an Englishman, of course—who went to bed on a steamboat after being filled with ghastly stories about those human scourges, the mates. Later he started out of his sleep. He heard a terrible barrage of words outside: "Cut that niggerhead! Cut it! Cut it again! Lay it there! Now hold it!" The Briton slept no more after that. Next morning he was re- lieved to see the Memphis wharf uncluttered by rousters' heads and head- less bodies. He felt entirely relieved—and perhaps foolish—when the cap- tain explained that a "niggerhead" was a long pole with a block on the end used in guiding a line of rolling barrels down the stage. People new to the river did not know that sluggish, dull-witted rousters paid no atten- tion to ordinary commands delivered in an ordinary voice. You might as well tickle a mule's iron hide with a feather. Nor was it alone the mate's foul roaring that got results. Didn't rousters sing scornfully:

> Rousters a-walkin' an' a-walkin',
> Old Mate's a-doin' nothin' but talkin'.

Only what the Lew Browns could and might do with their fists, black- jacks, and pistols, if the rouster didn't hump it, had any meaning.

In the end neither mate nor rouster won the "battle." Elemental crea-

---

[1] [Stacker Lee], a dashing Confederate cavalryman, son of a great old river captain, a steamboat officer, and a powerful lovin' man—no wonder more colored kids were named Stack Lee than there were sinners in hell. One of them, a short, black fellow, a cabin boy on the Anchor Line, by one of those queer turns of folk- lore gave to the name of Jim Lee's son a mistaken immortality. For Stack Lee, the Negro, was a killer and the rousters sang:

> Stack-o-Lee's in de Bend,
> He ain't doin' nothin' but killin' up good men.

And so it came about that the glamour about the white man's name among the Negroes passed to a black with a bad eye who was celebrated in the ballad, "Stack-o- Lee," or in the loose-mouthed, slow-drag version, "Stagolee." The final irony is that some old rivermen always thought the song was about that rounder, Captain Stacker Lee.—S.M., *ibid.*, p. 200.

For the song and story of "Stackalee," see *A Treasury of American Folklore* (1944), pp. 122–130.

tures thrown up in a time of flux and geared together to grind out wealth for steamboat owners—both were used up and thrown away. "One-arm Lew" killed himself in a low hotel. To both, as greenhorns, the river had meant glamor and freedom. More than likely the tough mate had been a poor illiterate boy who had run away to find adventure aboard steamboats. During long years he worked up the ladder: scrubber, deck hand, fourth mate, third mate, second mate, and, finally, first mate. Not many of his crude sort had hopes of a master's, that is, a captain's license. (A captain's son working his way up was another matter.) The tough mate belonged and didn't belong at the captain's table for, iron-ically enough, he assumed for the captain and the owners the odium of driving Negroes. He was the plantation overseer afloat. On riverside cotton lands the field slave had stopped hoeing to yell when he heard a steam-boat blow. To ride up and down the Mississippi on a boat would make every day like Saturday. But later as a freedman he found that roustering was no joy ride. In 1883, on the Memphis wharf, Joseph Pennell found such a Negro named Billy, and the great artist put down the rouster's talk and sketched him. "I's jist nobody," Billy said; "I's de most lone man dere is . . . Fo' duh war I was a slabe, now I's free . . . now I's a slabe to dis hyar steamboat."

Maybe, despite their "battle," both mate and rouster at times had an inkling of their common bond as slaves to the river. Maybe that explains what happened one night in Vicksburg after "Old One-arm" had beaten up a saloonkeeper and, on his way back to the boat, was being taken apart by the victim's sons. One of Lew's rousters, "Buttin'-Head Joe" charged. Soon that cast-iron battering-ram had discouraged the attackers and saved the man hated by more rousters than any other on the river.

Mean mates and rough rousters—both losers, both gone with the steam-boats. . . .

Law Comes to the River

In those palmy days, steamboat officers did what seemed good in their own sight, with none to molest or make them afraid. They neither dreaded courts of justice nor were they one whit restrained by fear of public opinion, from committing the most brutal outrages on inoffensive persons placed in their charge. The mate or engineer who could wield a billet of wood or a bar of iron the most scientifically on the heads of deck-hands, firemen, and deck-passengers, was considered "a regular screamer," and received the highest wages. When laborers were plenty on the levee at New Orleans, it was common for steamers to hire twenty-five

From *Wanderings of a Vagabond*, An Autobiography, edited by John Morris [John O'Connor], pp. 419–422. Entered . . . 1873, by John Morris. New York: Published by the Author.

or thirty more than the complement required for her crew, in order to facilitate the taking in of sufficient pine wood to run the seven or eight hundred miles up the river, and to discharge whatever way-cargo she might have between New Orleans and Vicksburg. These men would be discharged at the different landings on the river as fast as their services were no longer required, having shipped with the idea that they would be wanted for the round trip. They did not, of course, expect that, after a few days' hard labor, they would be discharged in a place where it was impossible for them to get anything to do, and where it would cost them more money than they had earned to take them back to New Orleans. These hands were sometimes—as a punishment for incurring the displeasure of some of the petty officers—set ashore in impenetrable cane-brakes, or on lonely islands, and any murmurings or remonstrances on their part were instantly silenced by a blow on the head with a billet of wood, and not unfrequently the knife and the bullet were brought into requisition. Nor were passengers exempt from these brutalities. To those of wealth and influence the most slavish attention was shown, while modest and unassuming strangers were neglected and treated with rudeness and contempt if they dared demand their rights. The smallest infringement of the rules of the boat has planted many a one in a solitary state on the edge of a cane-brake with his luggage beside him. Deck passengers were stowed like hogs on the lower deck of the steamer, where they were made to feel all the degradation of poverty in the brutal and disgraceful treatment they received from the petty officers belonging to the boat.

Maltreated crews of vessels and steamers, and also their passengers, had from time to time brought their wrongs before the tribunals of their country and clamored for redress. But it was impossible to obtain anything like justice, where capital was the defendant; and in no cities were these tribunals more blunted or deaf to the cries of justice than in St. Louis, Louisville, and New Orleans. In these cities the majority of the river steamers were owned by the wealthy merchants, and the officers of these steamers were their servants, whom they protected at all hazards. However flagrant their crimes, money and talent were ready to stand forth in their defense and save them from the lash of justice, and that justice was dispensed by a cultured class who were but too ready to pander to the power of the almighty dollar. What could ignorant crews or obscure passengers expect, whose only recommendation to justice was that they had been wronged, while opposed to them was money and talent in abundance—where obsequious Judges and prosecuting attorneys were eager to bow the knee before the shrine of wealth and influence. But let the accused be some ignorant boat-hand or some obscure passenger on trial for killing or maiming some brutal officer, who had perhaps tantalized him into committing the deed by his taunts and jeers, justice did not sleep then; but listened to the accusation, and condemned the guilty wretch as implacably as the presiding dignitary over the "Court of

Death," delineated by the masterly pencil of Rembrandt Peale, meted out his award to every culprit brought before him.

It is quite natural to suppose that men respecting no law save that of brute force would at times fall victims to their own dastardly deeds of violence. Such was in many instances the case among the steamboat officers. Numbers were openly killed or secretly assassinated by those whom they had maltreated. In the large cities these murderers were punished by law, when arrested; but if, after the commission of their deeds of blood, the perpetrators could gain the banks either of the Mississippi or Ohio River, at any point between the ports of St. Louis, Louisville, and New Orleans, they were safe from all punishment by the law. The people who lived in the scattered settlements along the banks of these rivers had conceived a deep and abiding hatred towards the generality of steamboat officials, on account of their brutal and overbearing conduct. The first season that I struck the Mississippi River, twenty-two steamboat officers fell by the bullet and the knife, in consequence of having violated the persons of their murderers. During the same summer and following winter eleven boats were snagged between St. Louis and New Orleans, and six were blown up by the bursting of their boilers, and over five hundred souls were hurried into the presence of their Maker. High old times were these on the Mississippi River.

The long suppressed murmuring of public opinion against the shameful atrocities perpetrated by rivermen on the western waters became now too formidable to be longer disregarded. Congress passed laws regulating the navigation of all inland steamers; the duties of steamboat officials were clearly defined; committees were appointed to examine into the capabilities of pilots and engineers, and also to ascertain the seaworthiness of vessels carrying freight and passengers; inspectors were appointed to look to boilers and machinery. About the same time the people of Louisana demanded of their legislators that severe laws defining the relations between steamboat officers and their crews should be passed, and the public voice compelled the courts to enforce these laws. The former brutal treatment of steamboat hands was no longer tolerated; such amusements became too costly to be indulged in by their officers. The wages of crews had to be settled before any other claims; and until that was done the boat could be held by the Sheriff. Public opinion frowned down steamboat racing, and fewer boilers were burst in consequence. The "knockdown and drag-out" officers of the "screamer" tribe were obliged to stand back and give place to such as could direct their men in the performance of their duty without resorting to oaths and violence. Steamboat officers were no longer permitted to gamble with passengers, or to enter the cabin with loud oaths, or seat themselves at the dinner-table in filthy garments or their shirt-sleeves. The mess-rooms and sleeping-rooms of the employees were separated from those of the passengers; and only the captain and his clerk and first officer, with the servants required there, were allowed entrance into the cabin. Humanity and courtesy has made mighty strides in this section of the country over cruelty and oppression. The recklessness and brutality which once characterized steamboat officials has totally disappeared from our western waters; and today the traveler can nowhere meet with kinder or more polite treatment than on board a river steamer, or with more civil and gentlemanly men than their officials.

Town-site Frauds

The town-site industry was on the same plane of deception and robbery as the banking frauds, but it found its victims "back East," instead of close at hand. Being Easterners, who had been educated to suppose that integrity and honesty were the basis of all business confidence, and themselves practised these old-fashioned virtues, they all too readily accepted the assurances of the land-sharks, and invested their money without seeing the property which was so glowingly described in the prospectuses sent out by the Western promoters. The result was that they were "taken in and done for" by the hundreds of town-site sharks who were operating all along the river, between Dunleith and St. Paul. I shall refer to but one of which I had personal knowledge and to another described to me by Captain Russell Blakeley.

The city of Nininger, as delineated on the large and beautifully-engraved and printed maps issued by Ingenuous Doemly, was a well-built metropolis capable of containing ten thousand people. As delineated, it had a magnificent court house, this city being the county seat of Dakota County, Minnesota. Four or five church spires sprang a hundred feet each into the atmosphere. It had stores and warehouses, crowded with merchandise, and scores of drays and draymen were working with feverish energy to keep the levee clear of the freight being landed from half a dozen well-known steamboats belonging to the Minnesota Packet Company or the St. Louis & St. Paul Packet Company. An imposing brick structure with cut stone trimmings, four stories high, housed the plant of the Nininger *Daily Bugle.*

This last-mentioned feature of the prospectus was the only one that had the remotest semblance of foundation in fact. There certainly was a *Daily Bugle,* issued once a week, or once in two or three weeks, depending upon the energy of the printer and his "devil," who jointly set the type, and the assiduity of the editors who furnished them with copy. This paper was printed upon the first power press that ever threw off a printed sheet in the Territory of Minnesota. It was a good press, and the paper printed upon it was a monument to the shrewdness and ingenuity of the honorable proprietor of the Nininger town-site. The sheet was filled with a wealth of

From *Old Times on the Upper Mississippi,* The Recollections of a Steamboat Pilot from 1854 to 1863, by George Byron Merrick, pp. 180–182. Copyright, 1909, by George Byron Merrick. Cleveland, Ohio. Reprinted by permission of The Arthur H. Clark Co.

local advertising—drygoods, groceries, hardware, millinery, shoe stores, blacksmith shops—every class of business found in a large and prosperous city, was represented in those columns. But every name and every business was fictitious, coined in the fertile brain of this chief of all promoters. It was enough to deceive the very elect—and it did. When the Eastern man read that there were six or eight lots, lying just west of Smith & Jones's drygoods store, on West Prairie Street, that could be had at a thousand dollars per lot if taken quickly, and that they were well worth twice that money on account of the advantageous situation, they were snapped up as a toad snaps flies on a summer day.

The paper was filled with local reading matter, describing the rush at the opening of the latest emporium; that Brown had gone East to purchase his spring stock; that Mrs. Newbody entertained at her beautiful new residence on Park Avenue, [with] the names of fifty of her guests. The whole thing was the plan of a Napoleonic mind, being carried out to the minutest detail with painstaking care by a staff of able workers, with the result that the whole prairie for two miles back from the river was sold out at the rate of ten thousand dollars an acre or upwards, and that before the proprietor had himself perfected his legal rights to the land which he was thus retailing.

Henry Lindergreen, the printer who did the mechanical work on the Nininger paper, was a chum of mine, we having set type in the same "alley" elsewhere, and that winter I went up to Nininger to help him out. The four-story brick block of the wood-cuts shrunk into a little frame building, the sides of which were made of inch boards set up on end and battened on the outside. Inside, it was further reinforced with tarred paper; and while I was there a pail of water ten feet from a red-hot stove, froze solid in a night, and the three printers had all they could do to feed the fire fast enough to keep themselves from freezing also, with the mercury down to forty degrees below zero. The editor, who, in the absence of the promoter himself in the East disposing of lots, was hired to improvise facts for the columns of this veracious sheet, lived in St. Paul, and sent his copy down to Hastings, as there was no postoffice at Nininger. If the editor or the proprietor had been found in Nininger in the following spring when the dupes began to appear, one or two of the jack oaks with which the city lots were plentifully clothed would have borne a larger fruit than acorns. Even the printer who set the type was forced to flee for his life.

One of the boldest-faced swindles I ever heard of was the so-called Rolling Stone colony. In the spring of 1852, some three or four hundred people, chiefly from New York City, came to seek their purchased lands in Rolling Stone. They brought with them beautiful maps and bird's-eye views of the place, showing a large greenhouse, lecture hall, and library. Each colonist was to have a house lot in town and a farm in the neighboring country. The colony had been formed by one William Haddock, and none of the members had the faintest shadow of experience in farming.

Boarding steamers at Galena, they expected to be put off at the Rolling Stone levee, for the views represented large houses, a hotel, a big warehouse, and a fine dock. But the steamboat officers had never heard of such a place. Careful questioning, however, seemed to locate the site three miles above Wabasha Prairie, on land then belonging to the Sioux Indians. As they insisted on landing, they were put off at the log cabin of one John Johnson, the only white man within ten miles. They made sod houses for themselves, or dug shelter burrows in the river banks; sickness came; many died during the summer and autumn; and when winter set in the place was abandoned. The people suffered severely, and the story of Rolling Stone makes a sad chapter in the early history of Minnesota.

Ghosts in Gallatin Street

There was a time when the very name would make a man shudder, but that has been a long time ago. It lies far down in the French Quarter, a street so hidden that one might pass it a dozen times and never notice it. It is the first thoroughfare parallel with the river, between the docks and Decatur Street. It stretches its length for two scant squares, from Ursuline to Barrack streets, from the French Market to the Mint.

Nowadays it is deserted, forgotten, given over to warehouses and storage rooms of produce merchants. It is permeated with the smells from the fish market, and with the odors of decaying garbage. Its narrow width is littered with trash and dirt—old shoes, broken barrels, rotting fruit. And yet, before the dark doors of one or two old houses, battered signs sway, signs proclaiming that "rooms" are for rent.

Even in daylight there is a sinister atmosphere in Gallatin Street, and at night—but we will speak of that later. Now let us try to turn back the hand of time, to the street as it used to be.

It was some time in the early eighties that Henry Parmalee disappeared. Vanished. It was a strange case, and men remembered it and talked of it long afterward. There were many theories, many surmises, but only one woman knew the truth, and fear kept her silent.

Briefly, it was like this: Parmalee was the son of a wealthy planter who lived "up the river." He was twenty-two years old and a handsome chap, well over six feet, and broad proportionately. He was blonde and sinewy, and he was very strong. Women liked him, and he liked them. He was engaged to marry the daughter of a prominent Creole attorney.

A week before the wedding a bachelor supper was given for the boy. The guests met in a small but fashionable restaurant in the French Quarter. There was champagne. Two of the guests dropped out of the party

From *Fabulous New Orleans*, by Lyle Saxon, pp. 291–300. Copyright, 1928, by The Century Company. New York and London.

and three young men walked over to the market "for coffee" some time after midnight. A policeman on duty in Decatur Street obligingly climbed a lamp-post and lighted a paper quill over the gas flame, in order that the men might light their cigars. Young Parmalee, the policeman said afterward, was gay but a little unsteady on his feet. When the officer saw them for the last time, they were entering a dance hall in Gallatin Street, arm in arm. The hall, a resort for sailors, was half-way along the lane of narrow, dark, tall houses.

And Parmalee was never seen again.

There was an investigation, of course, but it took place many days later. There was a hue and cry. But nothing happened. His friends told the same story; they had lost sight of him for a moment in the hall in the jostling crowd. When they failed to find him, they thought he had gone back into the street again. They called, they wandered about, but he was not found. So they thought that he had gone back to his hotel. The next day, when inquiries failed to find him there, they supposed that he had gone back to the plantation. It was not until several days later that the police were notified.

Gallatin Street was searched from end to end. Sailors' rooming-houses were visited, doors were opened, closets searched. But there was no trace of Parmalee. A year later a signet ring, identified as his property, was found in a Royal Street pawnshop. And the story was revived. But the man was never seen again.

So much for the old records, so much for old gossip. Now, let us see what occurred that evening, so many years ago.

Three young men, wearing immaculate evening clothes and swaying slightly as they walked, crossed the cobbled roadway beyond the French Market. Before them stretched the dark cañon of a narrow street, its dark buildings cutting the sky with a fantastic pattern. So narrow was the street, so high the buildings with their overhanging balconies, that it seemed that they leaned together in mid-air, like old hags, whispering together in the darkness.

It was a foggy night, clammy, damp, and it was cold, as weather is counted in New Orleans. Gas lamps flared dimly in the fog, and the street between was dark, save for those streaks of light which came out through the glass doors of the sailors' dance hall. From within there came the sound of ribald music, and the stamping feet. Only one or two of the houses were lighted, and the others seemed deserted—but the dark figures that lurked in the shadows knew better; they knew that there were dark alleys which led in to darker courtyards, where curving stairs led upward. Above were the rooms where the "ladies" lived, those harpies who preyed upon sailors, cheap women, companions for a night.

And an ugly crowd it was, too. Tough girls and older women, women of foreign tongue, Slav, Dutch, Danish; girls who could cry *skoal!* to the Scandinavian saliors as they held up their glasses of beer and cheap

whisky—girls and women from God knows where—the floatsam and jet-
sam, the riffraff of the world, drifted from near and far, to the shabby
rooms stuck above the bar-rooms of Gallatin Street.

One dance hall was kept by a man we shall call "Tony," although that
was not his name; for even across the bridge of the years he is still remembered in that street of shadows. And for Tony worked many girls.
There was Thelma and there was Hulda, Norwegians; there was Chris-
tine from Sweden—and there was Anna, who said she was English, and
looked it. And there were others. But it is of English Anna that we wish
to speak.

Anna was a "softy," according to the jargon of the other girls. She
was always falling in love with some sailor, and getting beaten in consequence. One of her front teeth was missing. Tony had struck her in the
mouth with his fist once, because she had tried to hold back part of her
earnings, in order to give it to "Big Hans" of the *Eberhard,* a vessel which
lay at anchor in the harbor. But drunken sailors can overlook a missing
tooth, and Anna was none the less popular because of it.

And it was Anna who saw young Parmalee that night when bad luck
brought him to Tony's dance hall. Anna had just come downstairs, after
a quarrel with Hans, and she was leaning against the bar, telling the
bartender that she was "feelin' bad." She turned to find a handsome
young gentleman at her elbow, a big fellow in immaculate evening clothes,
and with an overcoat over his arm. He was obviously drunk. The woman
smiled at him, and he bought her a drink—whisky at ten cents a glass.
Anna asked him to dance with her, but he refused, and was turning away
when she caught him by the arm.

If he wouldn't dance, she suggested, perhaps he would like to have
another drink. She knew of a quiet place where they could sit and talk,
and she wished to ask him something.

Now liquor plays strange pranks. In his sober moments Parmalee
would have paid no attention to Anna, but drunk and jovial, he followed
her through a swinging door which led into a hall at one side of the bar.
Even the bartender did not notice their departure.

Anna would have taken him to her room, but Big Hans was lying
across the bed. So she took him into Thelma's room instead, up another
flight of stairs; and it was there that a Negro waiter brought them drinks.
The girl was sitting upon his knee, her arm around his neck, and she
kept up a steady stream of chatter in her Cockney English. Drunken men
are easily amused. At intervals she explored his pockets with her free arm,
and succeeded in getting his wallet, and even some loose silver. As she
sat there, she listened to a conversation which came through the thin partition of boards which separated Thelma's room from Tony's "office"
at the back of the house. Tony sat talking business with the master of the
Eberhard, and Anna gathered that Tony was promising to get four sailors
before daylight. She knew what that meant. Four poor fellows, sodden

with drink, or drugged, were to be carried aboard the vessel before day-light. Shanghaied.

"Poor devils," thought Anna, thinking of her Hans who lay across the bed upstairs, and wondering if he would be called into service in securing the men.

And Anna sighed a little, forgetting the business in hand, as she mechanically stroked the hair of the blonde young man who was almost helpless now from liquor consumed. She heard Tony's door open and steps go down the hall. From below she could hear the beat of the music and the shouts of the sailors. Then other footfalls resounded on the stairs, and the door behind her was burst open.

A hand gripped her shoulder. Hans was standing there, towering above her, his great red face redder than usual. He snarled at her, brutal through jealousy.

"Honest, I wasn't doin' nothin'—honest, Hans!" cried Anna, springing up.

Young Parmelee tottered to his feet. But a blow from the fist of the sailor caught him squarely on the chin, and he fell backward across a broken chair, rolled over, and lay still upon the floor.

Hans stood over Anna, his fists clenched. "Give it to me!" he said, indicating the wallet that the girl held in her hand.

What happened in that room remained impressed upon Anna's mind long afterward—for Hans did a strange thing. Slowly, methodically, he began stripping the clothing from the boy's body. First the overcoat, then the coat, the trousers, the underclothing, until Parmalee lay naked upon the floor, his body white against the grimy carpet.

Within a few moments the boy was dressed in a pair of tattered trousers and a seaman's jacket. A cap was pulled down over his eyes, a cap which turned red with the blood which was running from a wound in his forehead.

Catching the body up, the sailor threw it across his shoulders, as he might have shouldered a sack of meal. With a curt word to Anna, he was gone. Cautiously, Hans carried Parmalee down a rear stairway, through an alley, across the dock, and aboard the *Eberhard*. For Parmalee was a strong and husky man—and the captain would pay ten dollars for an able-bodied sailor.

Hans and Anna parted that night, after a drunken debauch, and she never saw him again. For the *Eberhard* and all on board went down in some fiord of Norway, months later. And by the time that the news had filtered back to Tony's dance hall in Gallatin Street, Anna did not care; she had forgotten Hans for a dark-eyed Spaniard, who wore gold earrings in his ears, and who kissed and beat her, just as Hans had done.

And she never told Tony what had happened in Thelma's room that night. She was afraid of his fists. So Anna was unsuspected. Tony was righteously indignant when the police searched his house for the body of young Parmalee. And fear held Anna silent.

But the thing worried her; she found that she would dream of the young fellow as he lay naked upon the floor with the blood running down from the wound in his forehead. Anna had been guilty of things worse than her share in this—but this was the thing which worried her most. And she kept the signet ring which she had slipped from his finger and which Hans had overlooked, hidden away in a hole in the chimney. It was a year later that she pawned it, after Tony had turned her out, and with the money realized she bought food. And she gave a fictitious name to the pawnbroker. Anna never knew that the discovery of the ring in the pawnshop had caused the city to revive the old story again—for Anna lay dying not many days later, dying of a loathsome disease which destroyed her usefulness to Tony's dance hall, and which made it bad business to keep her in his employ.

When Anna was dying she told her story to an old woman who had befriended her. And the woman told her husband. The story must have been true, the old woman thought, because Anna told it so vividly that the old woman remembered every word of it, and often repeated it to her husband.

And it was the old man who told it to me, just as I have told it to you here.

But when I searched police records for the Parmalee case, I could find nothing of it. But there were other tragedies. There was the murder of one Lee, a drum major in the Federal army, who met his death in Gallatin Street during the Reconstruction period in New Orleans. There was the killing of a policeman in that shadowy street in 1887, and there was the murder of John Hurley by Frankie Lyons, years afterward. Old files of newspapers tell more of the horrors. For life was held cheaply under the flickering lamps of Gallatin Street.

"Yes, strange things have happened down there," an old policeman said, his dark eyes flashing at the recollection. "And what they tell you of the house of shanghaied sailors is true enough. I heard about the place time and again when I was a young man. And I know the name of the man who ran it, the one you call Tony. But even now it cannot be told, except in a whisper, because with the money he made in Gallatin Street, keeping that house of his, he went into politics, made more money, and became a popular politician.

"But he's dead now, and gone to a place where perhaps he'll meet some of those poor devils he sent to the bottom of the sea in rotten ships. Yes, he's gone, and so is the street. There's nothing left there now, only empty old houses."

* * * * *

No, there is nothing. Gone is young Parmalee, gone are his swaying companions. Anna is no longer here. Big Hans lies in the sea, half a world away.

There are only ghosts in Gallatin Street.

PART FOUR
Old Devil River

Introduction

"When God made the world," said the Mississippi orator, S. S. Prentiss, "He had a large amount of surplus water which He turned loose and told to go where it pleased; it has been going where it pleased ever since and that is the Mississippi River." In the mythology of the river country the Mississippi is half god—William Alexander Percy's "shifting, unappeasable god . . . feared and loved"—and half devil—Louisiana Negroes' "old Devil river, pushin' and shovin' at the levees."

Traditional nicknames for the Mississippi, from the Indian's Great Waters and Old-Big-Strong to the Negro's Old Man River and Ole Miss', stress its supremacy among rivers, its might and majesty, venerable wisdom and omnipotence. Its crookedness and mischievousness have endowed it with the personality of a trickster-hero, impishly moving farms and plantations from one state to another ("now taking from Arkansas to give to Mississippi and now robbing Mississippi to pay Arkansas"), now making a bank where its bed had been and now trying to get back into its old bed. But its "ownwayishness" and Indian-giving have also inspired fear and distrust of the river as a threat to human life and property. Thus Delta Negroes think of the Mississippi as a baleful witch "lying mighty peaceful and tender-like now, but . . . high-handed when she took a notion. Another thing, when time come to share up, Ole Miss' always took her part—the fattest calf, a strip of the blackest land, a child, or even a man. Yes, this land belong to Ole Miss' and Ole Miss' was bound to get her share." [1]

Not inappropriately in the minds of youngsters brought up by the river, "one of the earliest conceptions of the Missouri River from its appearance on the maps was the picture of some vast serpent, which, in a terrible convulsion of nature, had been hurled to the earth to bind together this continent." [2]

Nor is it surprising that the *gris-gris* river should give rise to superstitions, from the old rivermen's saying that "the Mississippi never lets go of a man who has his clothes on" to the belief of Louisiana Negroes that it is bad luck to throw an animal or fowl into it. On the credit side of the ledger, the yellow water of the Mississippi changes your luck from bad to good (when you wash your face in it) and brings fecundity to women.

In the unceasing battle of men against the rivers, radio broadcasters have taken their place among heroic flood fighters and relief workers,

---

[1] Ruth Bass, "Ole Miss'," *Folk-Say,* edited by B. A. Botkin (Norman, Oklahoma, 1931), p. 49.

[2] Col. DeWitt Clinton Allen, "Old Ballad Days in Western Missouri," *Glimpses of the Past,* Missouri Historical Society, Vol. II, November, 1935, No. 12, p. 146.

alongside civilian armies of levee workers and watchers, the Corps of Engineers of the United States Army, the Weather Bureau, and the American Red Cross. During the disastrous 1937 flood, high-water warnings broadcast from a loudspeaker in an airplane were said by Negroes to be the voice of God announcing the second Flood. More disconcerting in its effect was the voice of a Cincinnati broadcaster during a later rise in the Ohio. An old-time pilot was coming down river very fast with his tow, trying hard to run the last of the five Cincinnati bridges without hitting a pier. The captain had just tuned in a local station, from which a voice was heard saying: "Here's a thrilling picture. From our studio window we can see a towboat pushing a string of empty barges down the river. The tow is in the grip of that swirling yellow current. The skipper is fighting to make the Southern Railway Bridge. Folks, from here it looks to be a very grave question whether he will be able to make that bridge. It's a serious situation out there on the river. We may be witnessing one of the first casualties of the growing flood." This play-by-play description made the pilot so nervous that it took all his skill and all the captain's scoffing to avoid a catastrophe. "He and I," says the captain, "got some laughs out of it later, but that was his last trip on the river. He decided that he was getting too old for the work and that piloting these modern Diesel-driven towboats was for a younger man anyway." [3]

B. A. B.

"Quare and Mad-Like"

Pearl River [Mississippi], is said to be full of quicksand and dangerous to wade in. It is also full of undertows, and a number of people have been drowned when attempting to swim it at its full. The Negroes believe that the river has an evil spirit which becomes angry when anyones dares to swim across, "and it jerks him under and he is drown dead befo' he know what he's about. Dat ribber gets t' be a man when he's up and he acts quare and mad-like. Folks bettah stay on de land and den dey know whar dey is at. De Lawd made 'em outer dirt, and all dey is and all dey get is from de land. Folks and land goes t'gether. But dere ain't dependence t' be put in no big river o' water. De river he fool yuh, sho."

[3] As told by Captain Tommy Stevenson, Irving Crump, *Our Army Engineers* (New York, 1954), pp. 201–203.

By Elizabeth Bradley. Manuscripts of the Federal Writers' Project of the Works Progress Administration for the State of Mississippi. 1939.

The Crookedness You Can't See

"It's a very crooked river and swift," he says [of the Missouri]. "I suppose its crookedness makes it hard to remember and dangerous. And I hear that it shifts its bed, traveling sideways sometimes."

"Pshaw!" I says, "that ain't half of its crookedness. Anybody could see *that* crookedness just by looking."

"What other crookedness is there?" he says. "And doesn't the pilot go by looking?"

I seen he didn't know nothing.

"Well," I says, "seeing you don't know nothing, I'll tell you all about the river. Some rivers knows some tricks and other rivers knows others, but the Missouri knows the whole business and does it. This part of the river used to be about a mile over there where there's farms; and there used to be farms right here where we're running—that's how she shifts sideways sometimes. And sometime she might go back again if she don't like it here. That's easy enough for it to do, because the banks is awful crumbly where there ain't rock ridges. It eats under them, and when the bank is all hollow underneath and can't support its weight no more, it breaks away and falls in with a noise about like an elephant. She's always doing it one place and another—takes it way somewheres else if it needs it; and if it don't, she takes it down and drops it into the Gulf of Mexico and chokes up the Mississippi. That's why she's called the Big Muddy. But how she works it—that is a different thing. I'll tell you how she works it. Then you'll see what the pilot's got to get by heart and then forget.

"The bed of this river and the channel of it is two different things. The channel is just the deepest and swiftest part. You hear people say that still water runs deep but that ain't so—never was so. Deep water is the swiftest, because the top water slides along on the water below and it can naturally run slicker than shallow water that is rubbing along on bottom. This river is shallow where it looks deep and you couldn't hardly float a tub on it; and the pilot has to know where it's deep enough to go up, and not too swift; and he's got to know where it's good and swift when he's breaking the Fourth of July record like we're going down river right now.

"To look at it some people would think it was just a plain river running along in its bed at the same speed—but it ain't. The river runs crooked through the valley; and just the same way the channel runs crooked through the river. The river changes whenever it feels like it in the valley; and just the same the channel changes whenever it feels like it in the river. The crookedness you can see ain't half the crookedness

From *Partners of Providence,* by Charles D. Stewart, pp. 129–134. Copyright, 1907, by The Century Company. New York.

there is. Some rivers has the channel right down the middle, and that is the deepest and swiftest part. But this river ain't that way. Some places the channel runs down the middle; and some places it flows right up along one shore and then crosses over and flows along the other shore a while. That's how it comes to be moving sideways; and the way it works it you can see easy when I tell you. This channel ain't satisfied with nothing. Sometimes it ain't satisfied with the Missouri. So it keeps eating away one bank and caving it in and hurrying it away like you think it was going to break out sideways and start a river of its own. It *would* too; but the Missouri is too wise for it; it won't have no such a thing. When the channel gets right over to shore and the main waters is coming deep and swift and working away, the shallower water on the side is going along slower and thinking to itself and dropping down the mud it has been bringing hundreds of miles maybe. It says to itself, 'This thing has got to be settled right here'; so it settles down the mud to the bottom. That way it keeps building up one side; and when it is doing that it kind of slides sideways on it and builds up more; it keeps the river about the same width, no matter how fast it is eating on the other side. I guess this channel would a' left the river long ago, only the river follows it up and is too blame smart for it. The Missouri is a wise old river and it knows the tricks—but it's got a shifty channel to manage. Well, when that channel has gone sideways a while, maybe a new channel gets started in a mushier place on bottom; and when that is getting to be pretty much of a success, the main waters goes there to help a good thing along—same as people. Then the old channel ain't doing much and it has got to go to work and crawl back and build up where it tore down—that's the way it is; nothing certain about it. But mostly when she has struck a stone bluff the waters hurries along and is mad about it and stays right there, working hard and swift. That's why we are crossing back and forth to the bare bluffs so much. And when we go over the river that way it's a crossing. Pshaw! this is the greatest river in the world and the wisest river there is. Some rivers, if they didn't hit the trail oftener than this does, wouldn't know the way anywhere. They'd get so mixed up they'd start emptying into themselves, I guess. But you wouldn't know it to look at it; you'd think it was just a plain river running along between its banks."

The Dangerous Missouri

. . . A trip from St. Louis to St. Joseph took about as long as a voyage from New Orleans to St. Louis; Big Muddy's snags and shifting sandbars

By Dan Saults. From *Steamboating*, Sixty-Five Years on Missouri's Rivers, The Historical Story of Developing the Waterway Traffic on the Rivers of the Middlewest, by Captain William L. Heckman, "Steamboat Bill," p. 21. Copyright, 1950, by Burton Publishing Company. Kansas City.

made night travel a perilous feat. The dangerous stream claimed many a sidewheeler and sternwheeler, but "whisky sunk a third of them and carelessness another third."

At least, that was the verdict of Captain Bill Heckman, who lives at Hermann. Still vigorous and still holding a Missouri river pilot's license at 80, after sixty-four years on the river, he likes to say: "We used to separate the men from the boys at the mouth of the Missouri. The boys went up the Mississippi and the men up the Big Muddy."

The Big Gamble

It is a perpetual dissatisfaction with its bed that is the greatest peculiarity of the Missouri. It is harder to suit in the matter of beds than a traveling man. Time after time it has gotten out of its bed in the middle of the night, with no apparent provocation, and has hunted up a new bed, all littered with forests, cornfields, brick houses, railroad ties and telegraph poles. It has flopped into this prickly mess with a gurgle of content and has flowed along placidly, for years, gradually assimilating the foreign substances and wearing down the bumps in its alluvial mattress. Then it has suddenly taken a fancy to its old bed, which by this time has been filled with suburban architecture, and back it has gone with a whoop and a rush, as happy as if it had really found something worth while.

Quite naturally this makes life along the Missouri a bit uncertain. Ask the citizen of a Missouri River town on which side of the river he lives, and he will look worried and will say, "On the east side when I came away." Then he will go home to look the matter up and, like as not, will find the river on the other side of his humble home and a government steamboat pulling snags out of his erstwhile cabbage patch.

It makes farming as fascinating as gambling too. You never know whether you are going to harvest corn or catfish. The farmer may go blithely forth of a morning with a twine binder to cut his wheat, only to come back at noon for a trot-line—his wheat having gone down the river the night before.

These facts lead us naturally to the subject of the Missouri's appetite. It is the hungriest river ever created. It is eating all the time—eating yellow clay banks and cornfields, eighty acres at a mouthful; winding up its banquet with a truck garden and picking its teeth with the timbers of a big red barn. Its yearly menu is ten thousand acres of good rich farming land, several miles of railroad, a few hundred houses, a forest or two, and uncounted miles of sand bars.

This sort of thing makes the Missouri valley farmer philosophical in the extreme. The river may take away half his farm this year, but he feels sure

From "The Missouri River, Its Habits and Eccentricities Described by a Personal Friend," by George Fitch, *The American Magazine*, Vol. LXIII (April, 1907), No. 6, pp. 637–638. Copyright, 1906, 1907, by the Phillips Publishing Company. New York.

that next year it will give him the whole farm of the fellow above him. But he must not be too certain. At this point the law steps in and does a more remarkable thing than the river itself may hope to accomplish. It decrees that so long as there is a single yard of an owner's land left—nay, even so long as there is a strip wide enough to balance a calf upon, he is entitled to all the land that the river may deposit in front of it. But when that last yard is eaten up, even though the river may repent and replace the farm in as good order as when it took it, the land belongs to the owner of the land behind it. There is no way of getting around this decision. All the despoiled owner can do is to buy the farm back of the farm back of his erstwhile farm and wait patiently for the river to eat up his land. Then, if it recedes, he may not only get his old farm back but the one between his old one and his new one and possibly a few more for good measure. Roulette is child's play compared with it.

This thing happened in Kansas City not many years ago. A party of men owned a strip of land along the Missouri River bank. It was not handsome land, but it was valuable for factory purposes. They were offered portly prices for it, but held on.

One day they noticed that the strip was getting emaciated. They held a hurried diagnosis with a surveyor's tape and found that half it had wasted away. The next year half of the remainder had gone.

The men wanted to sell then, but the market seemed remarkably sluggish. The next year the river ate so vigorously that only a tiny strip about as wide as a piece of baby ribbon was left. The men were much depressed.

Suddenly the land began to increase. The Missouri had chosen the late manufacturing site to deposit a fine 160-acre farm upon which it had foreclosed up the river. Inside of six months that strip of land contained 200 acres. The men were jubilant, but still they could not sell. They wanted another 100 acres, they said. They strolled along the bank each day and urged the river, in proprietary tones, to build faster.

Then the river changed its mind once more and not only wiped out the extra 100 acres, but the original 100 acres, every foot of it. The next year it built up 500 acres in the same spot, but they all belonged to the man who owned the ground behind the original plot. They have stayed there ever since—that is, up to last reports. For high financing and property juggling, the Missouri makes a crooked lawyer look like a child. I hate to think what it would do for a man if it had a personal friendship for him.

Mud on the Missouri

Because the [Missouri] River is always busy dissolving farms and shifting sand bars it is the muddiest stream in the world. It is so thick that it cracks, sometimes, in working its way around the bends. At certain seasons

Ibid., p. 639.

of the year there is scarcely enough water to keep the mud moist and it has to be drunk with a fork. Throw a man into the Missouri and he will not often drown. It is more likely that he will break his leg. In every glass of good, ripe Missouri water there is at least a peck of sediment. Old residents claim to have made grindstones in the early days by running Missouri River water through a big pipe and cutting it into flat disks with handsaws as it came out.

Abolitionist River

. . . The channel of the Mississippi is the dividing line of the States between which it flows, and the action of the river often changes the location of real estate. There is sometimes a material difference in the laws of States that lie opposite each other. . . .

* * * * *

Once, while passing up the Mississippi, above Cairo, a fellow-passenger called my attention to a fine plantation situated on a peninsula in Missouri. The river, in its last flood, had broken across the neck of the peninsula. It was certain the next freshet would establish the channel in that locality, thus throwing the plantation into Illinois. Unless the Negroes should be removed before this event, they would become free.

"You see, sir," said my informant, "that this great river is an Abolitionist."

Low Water

Various stories were in circulation concerning the difficulties of navigation on the Upper Mississippi in a low stage of water. One pilot declared the wheels of his boat actually raised a cloud of dust in many places. Another said his boat could run easily in the moisture on the outside of a pitcher of ice-water, but could not move to advantage in the river between Lake Pepin and St. Paul. A person interested in the railway proposed to secure a charter for laying track in the bed of the Mississippi, but feared the company would be unable ot supply the locomotives with water on many portions of the route. Many other jests were indulged in, all of which were heartily appreciated by the people of St. Paul.

From *Camp-fire and Cotton-field; Southern Adventure in Time of War, Life with the Union Armies and Residence on a Louisiana Plantation,* by Thomas W. Knox, p. 458. Entered . . . 1865, by Blelock & Company. New York.

Ibid., pp. 290–291.

Cut-Offs, Rafts, Sawyers, Snags, and Planters

I[1]

The country through which [the Mississippi] flows is almost entirely alluvial. Not a stone is to be seen, save about its headwaters, but a dark rich earth that "looks eager for the hand of cultivation"; for vegetation lies piled upon its surface with a luxuriant wastefulness that beggars all description, and finds no comparison for its extent, except in the mighty river from which it receives its support. This alluvial soil forms frail banks to confine the swift current of the Mississippi; and, as might be imagined, they are continually altering their shape and location. The channel is capricious and wayward in its course. The needle of the compass turns round and round upon its axis, as it marks the bearings of your craft, and in a few hours will frequently point due north, west, east, and south, delineating those tremendous bends in the stream which nature seems to have formed to check the headlong current, and keep it from rushing too madly to the ocean.

But the stream does not always tamely circumscribe these bends; gathering strength from resistance, it will form new and more direct channels; and thus it is that large tracts of country once on the river become inland, or are entirely swept away by the current; and so frequently does this happen that "cut-offs" are almost as familiar to the eye on the Mississippi as its muddy waters. When the Mississippi, in making its "cut-offs," is ploughing its way through the virgin soil, there float upon the top of this destroying tide thousands of trees that covered the land and lined its caving banks. These gigantic wrecks of the primitive forests are tossed about by the invisible power of the current as if they were straws, and find no rest until with associated thousands they are thrown upon some projecting point of land, where they lie rotting for miles, their dark forms frequently shooting into the air like writhing serpents, presenting one of the most desolate pictures the mind can conceive.

These masses of timber are called "rafts." Other trees become attached to the bottom of the river, and yet by some elasticity of the roots they are loose enough to be affected by the strange and powerful current, which will bear them down under the surface; and the tree, by its own strength, will come gracefully up again, to be again engulfed; and thus they wave upward and downward with a gracefulness of motion which would not disgrace a beau of the old school. Boats frequently pass over these "sawyers," as they go down stream, presssing them under by their weight; but let some unfortunate child of the genius of Robert Fulton, as it passes up stream, be saluted by the visage of one of these polite gentry, as it rises ten or more feet in

---

[1] From "The Mississippi," in *The Mysteries of the Backwoods;* or Sketches of the Southwest: Including Character, Scenery, and Rural Sports, by T. B. Thorpe, pp. 172–174. Entered . . . 1845, by Carey & Hart. Philadelphia. 1846.

the air, and nothing short of irreparable damage or swift destruction ensues, while the cause of all this disaster, after the concussion, will rise above the ruin as if nothing had happened, shake the dripping water from its forked limbs, and sink again, as if rejoicing in its strength.

Other trees will fasten themselves firmly in the bottom of the river; and their long trunks, short of their limbs, present the most formidable objects to navigation. A rock itself, sharpened and set by art, could be no more dangerous than these dread "snags." Let the bows of the strongest vessel come in contact with them, and the concussion will drive through its timbers as if they were paper; and the noble craft will sometimes tremble for a moment like a thing of life, when suddenly struck to its vitals, and then sink into its grave.

II[2]

. . . As in most instances, a large body of earth is attached to the roots of the trees, it sinks those parts to the bottom of the river, whilst the upper parts, more buoyant, rise to the surface in an inclined posture, generally with the heads of the trees pointing down the river. Some of these trees are fixed and immovable, and are therefore termed *planters*. Others, although they do not remove from where they are placed, are constantly in motion; the whole tree is sometimes entirely submerged by the pressure of the stream, and carried to a greater depth by its momentum than the stream can maintain. On rising, its momentum in the other direction causes many of its huge limbs to be lifted above the surface of the river. The period of this oscillatory motion is sometimes of several minutes duration. These are the *sawyers*, which are much more dangerous than the *planters*, as no care or caution can sufficiently guard against them. The steersman this instant sees all the surface of the river smooth and tranquil, and the next he is struck with horror at seeing just before him the sawyer raising his terrific arms, and so near that neither strength nor skill can save him from destruction. . . .

The Treasure of the *Drennan Whyte*

Buried deep in the treacherous sands of the [Mississippi] river were many secrets, some of which a shifting, cutting current occasionally brought to light. A passenger from Tennessee, with whom John Williamson became

---

[2] From *Travels in the Interior of America, in the Years 1809, 1810, and 1811*, Including a Description of Upper Louisiana, together with the States of Ohio, Kentucky, Indiana, and Tennessee, with the Illinois and Western Territories, and Containing Remarks and Observations Useful to Persons Emigrating to Those Countries, by John Bradbury, pp. 202–203. Second Edition. London: Published by Sherwood, Neely, and Jones. 1819.

From *South of the Middle Border*, by Hugh P. Williamson, pp. 209–213. Copyright, 1946, by Dorrance & Company, Inc. Philadelphia.

acquainted, told him the story of the treasure ship, the *Drennan Whyte*. This boat was built on the upper Ohio, and in September of 1850 was bound upstream from New Orleans, carrying a mixed cargo, the most important of which was one hundred thousand dollars in English gold. A few miles above Natchez, Mississippi, she blew up and sank in forty-odd feet of water, within one hundred feet of the eastern bank. When word of the disaster reached her owners, they sent out a big boat, the *Evermonde*, to grapple for her. Somewhere near the watery grave of the *Drennan Whyte*, the *Evermonde* got afire and went to the bottom, carrying sixteen of her crew with her. After this setback, it was nearly a year before another attempt could be made.

In August of 1851 the *Ellen Adams*, fully equipped for salvage work, came on the scene. Meanwhile the river current had shifted to the west, and constant building and filling had been in progress. Two high waters had come and gone, but even so it was not thought that it would be difficult to locate the sunken *Drennan Whyte*. Drags were lowered and the river bed was combed in an ever-widening area which finally extended for twenty miles up and down the river. This continued until October, when the *Ellen Adams* herself struck a bar and partially sank. After some abortive attempts the following spring the whole costly business was given up and marked down to profit and loss, although the loss was indeed a heavy one. So it was that this boat passed into river legend. In the years that followed, fishermen and hunters sometimes reported that they had found her, and numerous expeditions were put out to recover her, all of which came to nothing. Gradually put down as lost for good and all, she was almost forgotten.

Ancil Fortune was the son of Caleb Fortune, who had been captain of the *Ellen Adams* when she went seeking the *Drennan Whyte*. He worked on the Ohio for a while, as a boy, gave it up, and bought a farm on the river near the town of Jeffris, Mississippi. He had a large family and little money. Luck seemed to go against him, and he was hard pressed to make ends meet. In the spring of '70 he went onto a piece of made land which lay within fifty feet of the river bank, with the intent to dig a shallow well for stock water. When he had got about eight feet down, his spade struck metal, which when uncovered proved to be the top of a steamboat smokestack. With growing interest he followed it down. This might be, and probably was, he thought, the fragment of a boat burned or blown up, but there was the chance that a steamboat lay buried below it—and that vessel might possibly be the *Drennan Whyte*, although this spot was far below the place of her sinking. To a poor man the thought that one hundred thousand dollars in gold might be only a few feet below him was exciting, but he did not lose his judgment or control. First of all his secret must be strictly kept. Unusual or prolonged digging on this spot would be sure to attract curious strangers. His title to this land was none too good, and if it was rumored that the old lost treasure ship lay here, there would be a dozen suits filed against him at once. He thought about this fact long and seriously, and as a result filled up the hole, sowed willow seeds about the place for four or five hundred feet in every direction, and did not again come near the spot for five years.

By that time the ground was a forest of young willow trees eight or ten feet high, and very dense. Then with ax and spade he went and made a clearing and started to dig. Fifteen feet down from the top of the once more uncovered smokestack he came upon the upper deck of a steamboat, and then his real labor had begun. Patiently and all alone, in what time he could spare from his farming, he dug, one weak man attempting the task of a giant. Three years went away with Fortune constantly tormented with the thought that though this was a lost boat which he had found yet it might not be the *Drennan Whyte*. Then one day as he worked down the side of the boat he came upon a heavy brass plate which bore, in corroded but not-to-be-mistaken letters, the words *Drennan Whyte*.

Sure of himself now, he settled down to his labor with renewed zeal, and after making a number of tunnels which ended nowhere, found himself in a cabin of the vessel. It was solidly packed with mud and sand. Bit by bit he cleared it out, and after three months concluded that it was not the one occupied by the captain, which was where the gold and all other valuables would be. He calculated his position and started digging again, and three years went by. Twice the entire excavation filled with water, which had to be bailed out a bucketful at a time. Many times parts of it caved in, but doggedly Fortune kept on. In the late winter of '81, he knew that at last he was near his long sought quarry, and on a day in May of that year he uncovered an iron chest, broke it open with a blow of his spade, and plunged his arms up to the elbows in pieces of gold. The treasure of the long lost *Drennan Whyte* was literally in his hands. He would go for sacks and return at once to begin removing the money. As he neared his home, he stumbled over a root, fell, and broke his right leg.

That night, as Ancil Fortune lay in his bed, rain began to fall, and continued to do so for a week. It fell far up the river, and on the watershed of many tributary streams which rushed down to meet and swell the June rise from the mountains. Suddenly the current changed and began to cut the willow point where the sunken ship lay. The helpless man could hear great chunks of earth fall into the water. A month later, when he was able to hobble, he crept to the door and looked out. Not a willow tree was to be seen on the point, and the shining river, gleaming in the morning sun, ran swiftly over the spot where only a short time before the *Drennan Whyte* lay buried. Forgetting his injury, forgetful of all except his lost treasure, Fortune plunged down to the river bank and straight into the roaring waters, never to be seen again. The river was like that, said the Tennessee man, shaking his head sagely. It gave things up, but it usually, in its own good time, took them back again. It was an Indian giver, that old river.

The Phantom Steamer of Raccourci

In the Indian tradition, Meschebe, or Mississippi—why on earth can't it be spelled Misisipi?—arose from his bed once in seven years and attacked the low country. Then the red men fled to their mounds or artificial hills, and as nobody tried to oppose him, he was kind to the land, leaving it more fertile after he had passed on. Only since the white man came in with his bridges, his levees, his walls, and the like undertakings, has he descended to quarreling and to drowning the cabin-dwellers. He no longer waits till the seventh year to pay his visits, either, and is never more delighted than when he can slip through some pretentious piece of engineering and, in a night, create a new passage for himself. His banks are skeined with old and forgotten channels.

About twenty leagues above Baton Rouge, Louisiana, he made the Raccourci cut-off, that shortened the river nearly thirty miles. For the Mississippi is a tortuous stream. Boats may have to go thirty-five miles around to get a half a mile ahead. Sometimes a planter who cannot go to the river brings the river to him, by digging a ditch across one of these necks, and in high water the map is changed over night. His farm and gardens now have a frontage on this majestic stream—if they are not washed away—and his neighbor, who formerly sent his produce to New Orleans by steamer, now sends it on a cart to the railroad, for his very wharf has been left high, dry, and distant. A ditch-cutter did not live long if the other planters caught him at his work. Not all the cut-offs are made by the ditchers; in fact, few people meddle with the course of the river in these railroad days. It is left to straighten itself. The crumbly soil is washed down to the Gulf of Mexico, or piled on the bottom to make the delta—400,000,000 tons a year—is rapidly torn to pieces in a freshet, and boats are seen gliding across what a few days before were orchards or canebrakes.

The nineteenth century had lost but twenty-five years when the change occurred at Raccourci. It happened suddenly, as usual, and had not been made known to the pilots of one of the steamers of that day which was splashing and wheezing down from Vicksburg. It was night when they entered the old channel, and a gray, drizzly night at that. Presently they felt the grind of a new bar under their vessel. They cleared it, and in another minute had rammed a reef that was entirely out of place. Failing to dislodge it, they backed into a lot of snags and began to punch holes in the bottom. Nearly ready to cry at the many and uncalled for perplexities that had come into the steering business since their last trip, the pilots resorted to profanity as a relief to their own and the passengers' feelings and to the delight of that gentleman who is never far away when people go wrong. Finally one of the men at the helm roared, in a rage, that he was blessed if

From *American Myths and Legends,* by Charles M. Skinner, Vol. II, pp. 36–39. Copyright, 1903, by J. B. Lippincott Company. Philadelphia and London.

he didn't hope the blinkety-blanked old ark would stay right there, in the vanishing river, and never get out. He was only a fresh-water sailor and had never heard of the Flying Dutchman. His wish was granted. The bend was filled up so long ago that none but the oldest men recollect when it was navigable for rowboats; yet every now and again tug captains and scow hands report a strange light in that dark and winding channel—a light as of fox-fire or phosphorus; and when the weather is not too thick, and the witnesses not too sober, they add to this tale a garnish of pale form, a phantom steamer, in short, with bell ringing funereally, engines faintly puffing, and voices using nearly forgotten "cuss words" in plaintive tones as the form bumps and staggers this way and that, ever seeking a channel that moved away for miles in a night.

The Story of Juno Island

The *Juno* was a side-wheeler that plied the Wabash in the sixties. John R. Hugo built and captained her, and his brother, Jenk Hugo, piloted her. They picked up cargoes of grain and cattle and occasionally carried a passenger or two. The *Juno* was not a floating palace, by any means. She had only one engine and a wooden cogwheel and you could hear her coming and recognize her without a whistle. Folks along the Wabash made up a song about her once that goes like this:

> She was warped in the hull and broad o' beam
> An' her engine whistled with the waste o' steam—
> An' a two-mile jog agin Wabash stream
> Was her average runnin' gait.

But the *Juno* served her purpose, and the Hugo brothers were proud of her.

On the night of February 18, 1865, the *Juno* was headed for New Orleans with a load of pork and flour. She had no passengers; but, in addition to Captain John and Pilot Jenk, the two engineers, and a co-pilot named Beal, Mrs. Jenk Hugo, Mrs. Beal and the Beal baby were aboard. The river was high and so were the spirits of the Hugo brothers, for they had a good cargo and every riverman liked the prospect of a trip to New Orleans. But when they approached Neal's Bend, a mile or so above New Harmony, their rejoicing came to an abrupt end. They were engaged in a heated and unprecedented quarrel.

It was all because of the middle shoal at Neal's Bend, which left two channels in the river. The west channel, on the Illinois side, was clear and wide. The east channel, on the Indiana side, was filled with snags. But the east channel was considerably shorter. Captain John, thinking of his cargo,

From *The Wabash*, by William E. Wilson, pp. 272–275. *The Rivers of America*, edited by Stephen Vincent Benét and Carl Carmer. Copyright, 1940, by William E. Wilson. New York and Toronto: Farrar & Rinehart, Inc.

was all for playing safe and taking the west channel. But Pilot Jenk, confident of his skill, held out for the east channel. For a half hour they argued,
while the *Juno,* paddling downstream, drew rapidly near the shoal. Captain
John had wisdom and the authority of ownership on his side. But Pilot
Jenk had determination—and something else that was even stronger. He
had the rank of pilot, and, on any boat under way, the pilot is king.

For that reason, when she arrived at the middle shoal at Neal's Bend,
the *Juno* swung eastward into the snag-infested Indiana channel.

There was nothing spectacular in the *Juno's* sinking. She simply struck
a snag, heaved up on one end, sighed heavily as the water rushed through
the gash in her belly, and then settled gently into a cradle of more snags,
which held her cabins up out of the water. Captain John swore and Pilot
Jenk tried to exonerate himself, but that was all the confusion the wreck
created aboard. The women, knowing the river as well as their husbands,
had no fear for their safety; and the engineers soon saw that the engine
could be salvaged. So eventually Captain John quieted down and began to
blow the distress whistle, and a farmer appeared in the dawn and rowed
all hands ashore.

The engine and the cargo were salvaged, but there was no saving the
Juno herself. The Hugos had to leave her to the river and to fate.

Fate appeared on the scene very shortly in the persons of half the towns-
people of New Harmony. They came in rafts and skiffs and swarmed about
the *Juno* like flies around sugar. They played their role well, stripping off
all the structure that could be pried loose and carrying it back with them
to the town. There, for years afterward, their houses and sheds and outside
stairways were patched with parts of the steamer's storm deck, and a half
dozen privies were graced with ornamental deck railing.

Fate having finished, the river took up its task; and it was the river that
won the *Juno* her place in Wabash history. First, the middle shoal began
to make down upon the steamboat, covering her decks and eventually her
cabins with silt and sand. This process lasted for a quarter of a century.
The river bottom slowly rose and engulfed the steamboat, like a growing
anthill. Driftwood piled up. Little islands sidled over and attached themselves. Trees began to sprout until a thick growth of them—willow and
cottonwood—covered the whole surface. At last, a large island had been
formed where the *Juno* sank.

"Juno Island" the people of New Harmony called it; and, for the next
thirty years, the shelving bar that ran out from it was a favorite bathing
point for young people born long after the wreck of the old steamboat.

But the river was not through. In the 1920's, it sent a cutoff through
another island upstream and began to eat away the sand and silt it had
piled over the *Juno* years before. The willows and the cottonwoods lost
their hold in the shifting soil, tumbled into the water, one by one, and
floated off downstream. The little islands that had scurried over to join
their fate with *Juno* broke away and dissolved or set up housekeeping elsewhere. Eddies dug into the earth that was left. Sand swirled upward and

was spewed out into the current. Finally, rising like a ghost from the river bed, the *Juno* reappeared.

For several years she stood in the middle of the river, gaunt, stripped, bleached, and sand-streaked. Then the river once more took pity on her and, in one surging flood, swept the old carcass and its whole foundation away.

Today, there is only a smooth, clear expanse of water where Juno Island used to be; but somehow it seems to tell, with mute eloquence, the whole story of the steamboats on the Wabash. They came. They conquered. They prospered. They grew extravagant and reckless. They vanished. And now there is only the silent water, flowing placid and undisturbed.

The Fate of Kaskaskia

When the French missionaries and traders found their way to the rich American Bottom, some of them located on a choice site on the neck of land between the Kaskaskia River and the Mississippi River. There they built a town that for more than a century was the chief settlement for hundreds of miles. From about the year 1700 until well into the nineteenth century it was famous locally, commercially, and politically. Its name was heard in Richmond, when the Illinois country was a county of Virginia, and its problems sometimes were considered by government officials at Washington. Early travelers were eager to visit it and were proud to write of it. Pioneer surveyors gave it prominent place on their maps of the Illinois country. But for many years most travelers to the region where Kaskaskia long ruled alone have been unconscious of their nearness to the site of the old town, and those who would find it named on a map must go to an old atlas, or to the records of the historian.

The early years of Kaskaskia were like those of other pioneer settlements. The surrounding Indians were on friendly terms with the peaceable French cottagers, though there were times of anxiety and danger when the savages were threatening. Adventurers toiled past the town on their way to the Missouri or to the upper Mississippi, or floated down toward the mouth of the Ohio and New Orleans. Scores of those whose names are written large in the history of the Mississippi Valley paused there, or lived there for a season.

But usually life was very tranquil there, even when the French gave way to the English and the English to the Americans. For Kaskaskia, like so many settlements of the Mississippi Valley, was a town of three flags.

* * * * *

From *The Romance of Forgotten Towns*, by John T. Faris, pp. 81–82, 88–89. Copyright, 1924, by Harper & Brothers. New York and London.

When Illinois became a territory, the pioneer legislature met at Kaskaskia on November 25, 1812. Both houses met in a large building of uncut limestone, which had a steep roof and a gable of unpainted boards. There were also dormer windows. The building, after the flood that caused the abandonment of Fort Chartres, had been used by the French as headquarters for the military commandant. This building remained the Capitol until the removal to Vandalia in 1818, when all the records were transferred in a single small wagon!

Forsaken by the legislature, Kaskaskia was not forsaken by the rivers between which its founders had located it. Gradually these encroached upon the site. Finally floods threatened to make Kaskaskia an island, the Mississippi reaching across the neck above the town to the Kaskaskia (or Okaw, as the river came to be called, because of the French way of saying that they were going *au Kau*, to Kaskaskia).

In vain the government strove to protect the Kaskaskia, but, following the heavy winter snows of 1880–81, the ice and floods swept down the river and carried away the protecting works. Then the Mississippi cut across the four-hundred-yard neck that separated the rivers. At first the water fell into the Kaskaskia with a six-foot fall, but soon the alluvial soil was swept away and a far wider channel for the river was made. The people stood by and watched the awful force of the flood waters as they tore across to the Kaskaskia, which was but six hundred feet wide at the point of the junction. The flood was flung against the farther bank of the Kaskaskia, where great trees were uprooted and carried downstream. Sometimes a half acre of ground would fall into the river at one time.

The relentless river then began to wear away the island on which Kaskaskia stood. One by one the houses slipped into the stream, and year after year there were less people in the town. Some lingered until 1898, but by that time there was little left. In 1906 a single chimney was standing on the bank of the stream—all that was left of old Kaskaskia!

Breaking Up of the Ice

While proceeding up the Mississippi above its junction with the Ohio, I found to my great mortification that its navigation was obstructed by ice. The chief conductor of my bark, who was a French Canadian, was therefore desired to take us to a place suitable for winter quarters, which he accordingly did, bringing us into a great bend of the river called Tawapatee

From *Audubon and His Journals,* by Maria R. Audubon, with Zoological and Other Notes by Elliott Coues, Vol. II, pp. 222, 224–225. Copyright, 1897, by Charles Scribner's Sons. New York.

This was on the journey made by Audubon and his partner, Ferdinand Rozier, from Louisville to St. Geneviève, then in Upper Louisiana. They left Louisville in the autumn of 1810, and Audubon returned in the spring of 1811.—E.C.

Bottom. The waters were unusually low, the thermometer indicated excessive cold, the earth all around was covered with snow, dark clouds were spread over the heavens, and as all appearances were unfavorable to the hope of a speedy prosecution of our voyage, we quickly set to work. Our bark, which was a large keel-boat, was moored close to the shore, the cargo was conveyed to the woods, large trees were felled over the water, and were so disposed as to keep off the pressure of the floating masses of ice. In less than two days, our stores, baggage, and ammunition were deposited in a great heap under one of the magnificent trees of which the forest was here composed, our sails were spread over all, and a complete camp was formed in the wilderness. Everything around us seemed dreary and dismal, and had we not been endowed with the faculty of deriving pleasure from the examination of nature, we should have made up our minds to pass the time in a state similar to that of Bears during their time of hibernation. We soon found employment, however, for the woods were full of game. . . .

* * * * *

Six weeks were spent in Tawapatee Bottom. The waters had kept continually sinking, and our boat lay on her side high and dry. On both sides of the stream, the ice had broken into heaps, forming huge walls. Our pilot visited the river daily, to see what prospect there might be of a change. One night, while, excepting himself, all were sound asleep, he suddenly roused us with loud cries of "The ice is breaking up! Get up, get up! Down to the boat, lads! Bring out your axes! Hurry on, or we may lose her! Here, let us have a torch!"

Starting up as if we had been attacked by a band of savages, we ran pell-mell to the bank. The ice was indeed breaking up; it split with reports like those of heavy artillery, and as the water had suddenly risen from an overflow of the Ohio, the two streams seemed to rush against each other with violence; in consequence of which the congealed mass was broken into large fragments, some of which rose nearly erect here and there, and again fell with thundering crash, as the wounded whale, when in the agonies of death, springs up with furious force and again plunges into the foaming waters. To our surprise the weather, which in the evening had been calm and frosty, had become wet and blowy. The water gushed from the fissures formed in the ice, and the prospect was extremely dismal. When day dawned, a spectacle strange and fearful presented itself: the whole mass of water was violently agitated, its covering was broken into small fragments, and although not a foot of space was without ice, not a step could the most daring have ventured to make upon it. Our boat was in imminent danger, for the trees which had been placed to guard it from the ice were cut or broken into pieces, and were thrust against her. It was impossible to move her; but our pilot ordered every man to bring down great bunches of cane, which were lashed along her sides; and before these were destroyed by the ice, she was afloat and riding above it. While we were gazing on the scene a tremendous crash was heard, which seemed to have taken place about a

mile below, when suddenly the great dam of ice gave way. The current of
the Mississippi had forced its way against that of the Ohio, and in less
than four hours we witnessed the complete breaking up of the ice.

During that winter, the ice was so thick on the Mississippi that, opposite
St. Louis, horses and heavy wagons crossed the river. Many boats had been
detained in the same manner as our own, so that provisions and other necessary articles had become very scarce, and sold at a high price. This was
the winter of 1810–11.

Walking the Levee

. . . A battlement of levees extends for a thousand miles on each side of
the river from Memphis to New Orleans, without break in the battlement
except where the hills crowd down to the bank for a glimpse of the old
yellow snake or where tributaries like the Arkansas, the White, the Yazoo,
and the Red join it with their own mighty contents. It towers forty feet
above the country it protects and its sloping thickness is a hundred feet
wide at the base.

All of us who grew up in the Delta have had experience aplenty in guard
duty, or "walking the levee," as we call it. The earliest reason given for
this custom was the fear that folks from the other side of the river would
sneak over in a dugout and dynamite our levees in order to relieve the
pressure on theirs. I doubt if any one on either side ever attempted such a
crime, but the tradition having been established, armed citizens must guard
the levee all night, listen for marauders in the willows, and shoot to kill.
A soberer reason for the custom was to discover weak spots in the levee,
particularly "boils."

A boil is a small geyser at the base or on the berm of the levee, on the
land side, of course. It is caused by the river's pressure fingering out some
soft stratum in the soil of the levee or by a crawfish hole. If the geyser
runs clear, it is being filtered and is comparatively harmless; but if it runs
muddy, it is in direct contact with the river and you'd better shoot your
pistol, yowl to the next guard, and do something quick. What you do, if
you have the gumption of a catfish, is build with sacks of earth a little
"run-around"—that is, a small levee around the geyser to the height of its
jet. That stabilizes the pressure, and the boil is safe, but should be flagged
and watched. The levee generally breaks from boils enlarging themselves
and not from the river running over the top.

So during every high-water scare Delta citizens walk the levee all night
with pistol and lantern, nowadays with flash-light. If you won't volunteer
for that duty, you should return to the hills from which obviously you
came. If a guard gets lonesome he may gig a frog, whose croaking makes

From *Lanterns on the Levee*, Recollections of a Planter's Son, by William Alexander Percy, pp. 245–247. Copyright, 1941, by Alfred A. Knopf, Inc. New York.

everything lonesomer, or take a little drink. During these times the river is a savage clawing thing, right at the top of the levee and sounding at night like the swish of a sword or the snarl of a beast. It puts ice in your heart when you're trudging the darkness on the slippery berm and hoping not to step on a snake. Each guard walks alone, and the tiny halo of his lantern makes our fearful hearts stouter.

Crevasse

The Creole planter in lower Louisiana piled up his first flimsy barricade with slaves and shovels, until parishes united in levee construction as a public work, when regiments of shaggy Irish began to trundle their barrows full of dirt. They used plank runways, dumping along the growing ridge, and being paid by the piece, at so much per cubic yard, they'd sneak in an empty barrel or box and cover it over—to measure in their yardage. Crawfish bored holes in the embankments which broke and furnished another job, so to this day a crawfish is known as "The Irishman's Friend."

As modern methods developed, a slip scraper and single mule, usually driven by a plantation Negro, supplanted the Irishman's barrow; then a double scraper and two mules that built more solid levees because the trampling of mules would pack the soft earth. For colossal projects in the past few years, machines of unthinkable power are employed, tractors, "revolving turrets" and "drag lines" whose ponderous "shovels" carry more material at one load in one minute than an Irishman's barrow might handle in a week.

All levees, however, could not at once be raised to "commission grade and standard" by which is meant the specifications of U.S. Engineers when Uncle Sam stepped into the picture. No standard embankment ever broke, weaker lower defenses always being first to give way.

"Come here, Gordon." Colonel Rye beckoned his manager into the office and whispered, "Don't start a panic, but send out half a dozen reliable tenants and round up all our stock. Then drive them to the hills."

"Yes, sir," the manager answered. "I'm afraid the levee's going out."

"Looks that way. Water's brimming over its top, with two more feet coming down from Cairo."

"How about the women and children?" Gordon asked. "Hadn't I better make them get ready, and if a break happens, rush everybody to the Indian mound?"

"No use, yet," the veteran planter shook his head. "You know how bullheaded our Negroes are about deserting their cabins. Won't believe an overflow's coming until it gets up to their necks."

From *The Story of King Cotton*, by Harris Dickson, pp. 119–125. Copyright, 1937, by Funk & Wagnalls Co. New York and London.

Delta people usually refused to believe that a crevasse might occur, and persisted in fighting to the last, thus often holding their leeves.

"Don't get excited, boy." Colonel Woodville patted Gordon on the shoulder and smiled through a silver-white mustache. "We've floundered through so much water that I've got webfooted. Save our stock and I'll try to hold the levee."

Men of sense realized that such embankments couldn't stand against a flood that would overtop them by three feet, so every planter fought to maintain his own defense, until the break and the destruction occurred at some other point.

When Colonel Woodville reached the river front and glanced at the levee, he felt a moment's restoration of confidence. From the land side these gigantic fortifications seemed impregnable, a towering titanic rampart that guarded the frontier of the world. He couldn't see the river, but knew that beyond the levees' crown, water was piling up, water, water, water, higher than any dyke could stand against.

Hundreds of men, white and black, were frantically filling sacks with dirt, while other hundreds marched up the slope in single file bearing sacks upon their shoulders to where they'd be laid in place. Along the ridge, north and south as far as he could see, still other thousands toiled; and unseen thousands stretched beyond his range of vision.

The planter leaped from his car and ran zigzag up the slope, noting that two additional tiers of sacks had been laid since he went home an hour ago. This he hoped might give them breathing time, but the river was mounting faster than bags could be laid.

The yellow monster attacked with incredible force, and human midgets were trying to beat him back. Hopeless. Hopeless.

The crown of Ruthven levee was less than six feet wide because the engineers had not yet got around and strengthened it. Along its outer edge, next to the devouring river, a temporary barricade of planks extended for miles to protect the loose dirt against wave wash. Half a gale blew, and ravenous waters licked at the soft earth that melted and fell away. White men and Negroes stood waist deep in the water, nailing on planks. With haggard eyes they gazed at Colonel Woodville, telling their story of defeat.

"Here, boy," the boss reached down and gave a hand to one of his Negroes, pulling him from the water, "go home and rest. You've worn out. Give me that hammer."

Colonel Rye had just started to take the tenant's place and drive nails, when a sudden cry burst out, "Help! Quick! Help!"

"Look dere!" a black man screamed, and turned gray with terror as he pointed at the crest. "Look! Look!"

The saturated levee was settling down like mush, slipping, sliding, caving into the river. A huge crack appeared; tons of dirt sloughed off to melt and wash away. "Run, men, run," Colonel Rye shouted.

Tenants scurried like rabbits, splashed through seepage water at the base of the levee and were gone. Colonel Woodville stood another moment and saw the last thin remnant as it broke. A sudden collapse, the earthen ridge sank gently, quietly. A gap showed at the top, a gap that filled with frothy bubbling water, as though myriads of triumphant demons were rushing through a breach in the conquered fortress. The planter stood fascinated by its sheer magnificence and watched a victorious mass that thundered through with a roar. Then he too ran down the slope.

On the lower level panicky autos were starting. They must beat the water to the highway; in two minutes more their plantation road would go out. Negroes scrambled on mules and raced off; others trusted to their legs.

When Colonel Woodville in his car reached the graveled road, water was already skimming over it. A flying Negro on a mule waved his hand and shouted, "Don't go dat way, Cunnel. Dis road's cut off at de bayou."

Soon the crevasse had widened until twice the downpour of Niagara swept across Ruthven. Logs went swirling past, and struggling animals. Waters rioted among the forest, carrying Negro cabins to smash against trees.

After gushing out from the jaws of the crevasse, the first mad torrent spread out and diffused itself across the flatlands, where thousands of isolated families lived, white farmers and black farmers, women, children, cows, mules, all helpless in the path of destruction which would end only at the bluffs of Vicksburg. Farmers in the back country had a little time to prepare, possibly a few hours. Small boats came, skiffs, dugouts, batteaux, rafts, every imaginable thing that would float, and bore them to safety. Day and night the rescuers searched every thicket, every cabin, telephone poles, trees, so that not one single person was overlooked.

Nearer the front, by wading, swimming, or using boats, farmers and most of their livestock were concentrated upon unbroken levees. There was nowhere else to go, for with a turbulent Mississippi on one side and crevasse rapids on the other, levees offered the only solid land.

For days this submerged area was a nightmare of hysteria, the saving of human life, picking up of cattle; then it settled down into a watery solitude from which all living creatures had departed. Only the vultures remained, circling around in empty skies and feeding on carcasses.

Steamboats nosed up to the levees bringing barges on which refugees were loaded thick as they could stand, and carried to the Gibraltar hills at Vicksburg.

The population of that town doubled overnight by the addition of twenty-five thousand wet, hungry, and impoverished cotton farmers.

The same catastrophe happened all over Southern Louisiana, where the magnitude of disaster appalled our nation. The Red Cross came, the U.S. Army, senators, representatives, and cabinet ministers to see for themselves, to witness damages far greater than would be the cost of prevention for all time.

Refugee

We are gathered together on the levee-top—white and black men, rich and poor—or, rather, yesterday we were rich and poor; tonight we are equal in misery, for the Mississippi has taken everything from us.

The old Devil river! Rightly enough do the Negroes call it so. "The old Devil river, pushin' and shovin' at the levees," they say. These walls of earth, man made, erected at tremendous cost and endless labor, are built higher and higher every year in order that our homes, lying behind the levees, may be safe from the ever-rising stream. And now—all useless, all washed away.

The broken levee-top is like a long narrow island. Twenty feet wide, perhaps, and water washing on both sides—black water that extends out in all directions, mile after mile, dotted now with wreckage of our homes and covering the land endlessly.

We are tired out, hungry, wet, miserable. There are perhaps fifty of us, near the end of the levee. Ahead of us lies the crevasse . . . the water rushing through, inundating the fields and cotton land deeper under the yellow flood. Yes, yellow by day, but at this hour only a vast black torrent, with never a light anywhere. There is no moon. There are no stars tonight. A soft rain has fallen, making us, shelterless, even more miserable.

We sit upon the ground, in groups, afraid to sleep, too miserable to cry, waiting, with forlorn hope, for a rescue boat.

We have been here for more than twenty-four hours, ever since the alarm came which sent us running out into the night. . . . Can it be only twenty-four hours ago? It seemes eternity.

We have no water except the yellow, foul stuff that is all about us. We drink sparingly of it, grimacing, wiping our lips. There is no food.

There is no wood. We have no fire. This afternoon some one broke up a packing-case, kindled a fire, and made coffee. There was only enough for a few. The aroma made the rest of us sick with its fragrance.

Only two white men. We sit with bowed heads, leaning forward, looking out into the darkness. Near-by a group of Negro men lies sleeping. A young Negro woman, separated from her family, lies moaning. She is going to give birth to a baby before morning, or so the old Negro women say who have gathered around her. She is having a hard time. They have tried every charm and spell they know, but nothing works.

What can you expect with the old Devil river pounding all around you, and with no help in sight?

The black woman cries. Sometimes she screams aloud. An old Negro man lies near her, his head pillowed in the lap of a woman almost equally old. The old man doesn't say anything. This afternoon we tried to talk to him,

From *Father Mississippi,* by Lyle Saxon, pp. 301–303, 309–313. Copyright, 1927, by The Century Company. New York and London.

but nothing was gained by it. His mind ran back to the old days, to other floods and disasters. This one, he says, is no worse than others. The old woman, his wife, grunts and groans and holds his head:

"De ole man's mighty bad," she says. " 'E won't las' long."

The girl's moans, muffled by the rushing of the water around us, worry the old man. He mutters to himself.

* * * * *

Behind us the Negro girl is screaming again. The old Negro women are trying to fortify her with one of their remedies—an open pocket-knife placed under her body, "to cut de pain"; but this seems to give no relief, although it is one of the Negroes' favorite superstitions. Over and over the woman cries out: "Oh, Jesus! Please, Jesus!"·

And the old Negro women nod, mumbling: "Gawd, help! Hab mussy!"

The big Negro man at my elbow leans forward, trying to see into the darkness. "Seems to me, I heahs screams in de wind," he says.

We shiver, relapse into silence.

After a time a woman's quavering voice is heard:

> In de time o' dyin'
> Ah wan't yuh all tuh draw nigh;
> Dey's one mo' favor dat I wan' to ask,
> Come close muh dyin' eye.

And then every Negro joining in the chorus, their voices rising sweet and clear above the rushing waters:

> Well! Well! He's a dyin'-bed maker!
> Well! A dyin'-bed maker!
> Well! Well! He's a dyin'-bed maker!
> Ah know he's goin' to make-up muh dyin'-bed!

The Negroes are excited; they move about in the darkness. They cry and moan aloud. The big Negro man leans toward me and says: "De ole man's done die."

The young black girl's screams of pain now blend with the moans for the dead man and the rushing sound of the water:

"Oh, Jesus!"

"Hab mussy!"

"Please, Jesus!"

"Gawd, help!"

There are two groups discernible in the darkness now. One group of the Negroes is around the old man, who still lies with his head in the lap of the old woman, and the other group is about the young woman.

The two white men, powerless to help, lean forward, burying heads on folded arms. The sky in the east is beginning to show gray.

The black man beside me speaks again: "Ah'm worried 'bout Mattie— Ah shore wish daylight wuz heah!"

"The sun will be up before long," says the civil engineer.

Another hour drags by. As the light increases we can see an old woman crouching at the levee's edge, holding something in her arms. She dabs a rag in the muddy water. And then, in the silence, comes a thin cry, like a cat mewing.

One man is dead, but there is another life on the levee-top. We all crowd around to see the baby, lying naked in the old woman's lap. The mother, covered with sacking, lies with closed eyes.

"Hit's a fine big boy!" the old woman announces.

Immediately there is a chorus of comment:

"Great day!"

"What yo' goin' tuh name 'im, sister?"

The black mother opens her eyes in the dawn and smiles a twisted smile. "Ah specks Ah'm goin' tuh name 'im Refugee," she says.

There is instant agreement.

"Dat's right!"

"Sho' nuff!"

The old woman, leaning with bowed head over the body of the old man, continues to moan to herself. Above the horizon comes the broad face of the sun, round and red.

We all look about. On all sides desolation. Only a strip of levee-top, an island, on which we are gathered, and beyond, to the left, the mighty river, roaring toward the Gulf, its surface dotted with drifting logs and uprooted trees. To our right are the inundated fields, with the tops of trees visible, and in the distance the tall tower of a sugar-house, standing clear of the flood. Wreckage is floating about—a chicken-coop, a barrel, a broken chair from some water-swept cabin.

"Thank Gawd! De boat done come!"

Slowly it draws nearer down the river. A small steamboat, the *Daisy B* —usually in some placid bayou—now playing its part as a rescue boat. Already the decks are crowded with other refugees, but there will be room for us. It is not dangerous for the boat to come near us now, for the water has stopped roaring through the crevasse ahead of us; the water in the fields is at the same level as the water in the river outside the levee.

A white man is in the bow. He greets us, hails the Negroes with a cry: "Well, we'll take you folks to land somewhere."

Negro men carry the body of the old man aboard. Those already on deck roll their eyes in superstitious awe. Bad luck for a boat to take a corpse aboard. But the bowed figure of the old woman quiets their comment. The young Negro mother with her new baby is greeted with a shout: "Lawzee! De flood done brought dat gal a baby! Um-Umph!"

The Negro man who sat at my elbow all night goes from group to group, asking for news of his wife: "Is yo' seen anything of a light brown gal dey calls Mattie?" he asks.

The white man in charge of the refugees asks where she was, and, on hearing his reply, becomes grave. He shakes his head: "No, I haven't seen her."

Then, turning to the civil engineer, he says: "How can I tell that black boy that fifteen Negro women were drowned up there at the schoolhouse? Yes, sir. The building collapsed some time yesterday. We were there this morning. There's not one of them alive."

From group to group the big Negro goes, asking his question: "Yo' ain't seen Mattie nowhere, have you? A light brown gal. . . . She wuz headed fo' de schoolhouse when I las' seed her. I just got tuh find Mattie. She's done got los' somewhere."

Floods and a County Seat

The most famous town to be wiped out of existence by floods in Arkansas was Napoleon—made famous by Mark Twain in *Life on the Mississippi*.

Napoleon was the county seat of Desha County (pronounced De-shay) and it was a town of some distinction with a good-sized Marine Hospital, churches, banks, a theater, courthouse and stores. It stood at the confluence of the Arkansas with the Mississippi and it was an important river point when Mark Twain was a steamboat pilot.

In *Life on the Mississippi* Mark Twain told of a fantastic errand he planned to perform at Napoleon. He described the utter amazement of the captain when his ex-pilot asked to be put ashore at Napoleon and how the captain finally recovered sufficiently to inform Mark Twain that the town didn't exist any more. He said: "The Arkansas River burst through it, tore it all to rags and emptied it into the Mississippi. . . . Just a fifteen minute job, or such a matter. Didn't leave hide nor hair, shred nor shingle of it, except the fag-end of a shanty and one brick chimney."

Actually the demolition of Napoleon took rather more than fifteen minutes. The destruction was accomplished, not by one catastrophic flood, but by a gradual caving of the land.

In the fall of 1865 the federal government deemed the location of Napoleon unhappy and moved the Marine Hospital, whereupon Desha County leased the big brick building for a county hall. Some of the hospital rooms were occupied by the city government for municipal purposes.

Occupancy of the building became dangerous by 1869 and two years later the county and city records were moved to a new building and the old hospital was abandoned to the river, which by that time had eaten under one end of the structure.

From *The Arkansas*, by Clyde Brion Davis, pp. 293–295. Copyright, 1940, by Clyde Brion Davis. *The Rivers of America*, edited by Stephen Vincent Benét and Carl Carmer. New York and Toronto: Farrar & Rinehart, Inc.

That same year the old jail was declared dangerously near the river and it was replaced by another.

During these six years both the Arkansas and the Mississippi had been crumbling away the banks, foot by foot. Every few weeks the residents would arise to note that a neighbor's house or store had disappeared in the night.

This all was discouraging to the chamber of commerce and county commissioners, who finally decided there was no way to cope with the two rivers and it would be the better part of valor to move the county seat elsewhere.

A public-spirited citizen named L. W. Watson offered to donate to the county five acres of land on the railroad to the south on condition that the new county seat be named Watson. The offer was accepted and Watson became county seat of Desha County, Arkansas, while the once proud city of Napoleon was abandoned.

However, in 1878, Jay Gould got tired of having the Arkansas River running over his railroad more often than his trains and moved his tracks westward to higher ground. That left the damp but thriving town of Watson several miles off the railroad and practically isolated back in the swamplands. The following year the Desha electorate voted to move its county seat once more and this time to Arkansas City.

Budge Cobb and the Army Engineers

. . . Flood waters often do surprising things and can perform this way or that, depending on factors that even Army Engineers can overlook or under- or overvalue. I believe that by 1937 they had begun to question their early calculations and to suspect that when they turned the Mississippi into the floodway the water might build up much deeper than they had first said it would. At any rate all the engineers from the Memphis office and elsewhere seemed to hold themselves responsible for the life of every inhabitant of the floodway, and they did a splendid job of getting people out under circumstances that could hardly have been more difficult.

But they did not take us into their confidence as to when and how they proposed to turn the great Mississippi into the floodway or whether they proposed to do so at all. They may have been reticent because they themselves were uncertain, or because old antagonisms still held over. The law had empowered them to cut down the so-called upper end or "fuse-plug" section of the riverfront levee three or four feet. They had not done so, and that was greatly to their credit because that clause of the law was obviously uncalled for.

* * * * *

From *From Missouri,* by Thad Snow, pp. 210–212. Copyright, 1954, by Thad Snow. Boston: Houghton Mifflin Company.

Budge Cobb . . . is an old-timer, a hunter and trapper, and he is perfectly happy only in time of flood. He is indigenous to the swamps and looks it. When Thomas Hart Benton, the artist, was down here sketching overflow scenes and faces, everybody told him to get Budge Cobb. But Budge was somewhere out in the water and we could not locate him.

Budge feels a deep proprietary interest in every flood and he has been drowned in every flood we have had, including this [1937] one. We believe it for a day or two until he shows up. This time we were sure of it until he came in and told us about his encounter with the United States Army.

It seems that Budge couldn't wait for the river to break into the floodway but had launched his boat on the riverside as soon as the water promised a satisfactory rise. He knew that the rabbits would leave the outside fields ahead of the water and go to the levee for a dry seat. Talk about the happy hunting grounds! He was patrolling the levee like the Army had reported, and he was not toting any rabbits with him to proclaim him a hunter. He'd come along later by boat to gather up the kill.

When he saw a uniformed landing party ahead, naturally he strolled toward it. It was the first dynamiting expedition. Budge looked the Army over and said absolutely nothing. The Army looked through Budge's startling whiskers and grizzly brows and saw the murder in his eye. It was only rabbit murder, but the Army didn't know that. Nobody said anything; but after a bit the Army silently withdrew, re-embarked, and headed upstream to make a trial landing two miles farther up.

But when they again saw Budge from afar, coming around a bend in the levee, and heard his old shotgun roar, the Army called it a day and crossed the river to Cairo for re-enforcements, not to return till next morning. Budge, having loaded his boat with rabbits the previous day, was elsewhere pursuing the myriad delights borne to him on the flood. Some say that hundreds owe their lives to Budge's heroic and successful, albeit unconscious and bloodless, repulse of the Army and the consequent delay in the opening of the fuse-plug.

Lightkeeper

From the bustling cities of St. Paul and Minneapolis, where the blinker lights flash in brilliant rhythm, to the green jetties far below New Orleans where a drowsy pelican sits on the post beside each polished lamp, the river lights mount their guard to protect the passing vessels from disaster. Their very names are touched with the strange and the bizarre—Hanging Dog Light, Dark Slough Light, Devil's Island Float Light; they are rich

From *Big River to Cross*, Mississippi Life Today, by Ben Lucien Burman, pp. 122–128, 136–137. Copyright, 1938, 1939, 1940, by Ben Lucien Burman. New York: The John Day Company.

calendars of local history and legend. The lighthouse service everywhere on the Mississippi is a thing of fascination; but the section of the river where the life of the lightkeeper goes on in the leisurely fashion of the olden days, unaffected by the turmoil of an ever-changing world, is the lower river between Memphis and New Orleans. Here cities and towns are infrequent and factories almost non-existent; there are only sunless woods and tangled swamps where long cranes fly like wandering ghosts and alligators crawl silently. Here there are no blinker lights powered by electricity; here there are only coal-oil lamps burning like the lights of those times in the past when the boats of today were unborn.

A river light possesses an importance that no mere land dweller can even faintly measure. It may mean life or death to a crew; it may mean the saving or destruction of a million-dollar cargo. I have been a cub pilot at night when a sudden fog descended, and I have stood beside the steersman, peering blindly ahead, while the vessel beneath us floundered helpless in the gray maze. And I know that feeling of exaltation when a spectral blur appeared faintly over the bow, that meant we had found the light we were seeking.

The lightkeeper knows his importance as well as the pilot. He knows that he has only one task: whatever the risk, he must make his way to the pole where a great brass lamp rests on a wooden bracket, and keep the light burning.

The perils of the lightkeeper's life are many. Though the wind is blowing a hurricane, lashing the river into mountainous waves that overwhelm his frail skiff and each instant threaten to capsize it; though a flood is raging, with wrecked houses, timbers, and broken bridges sweeping swiftly down upon him, he does not hesitate. Though the mist is so thick he cannot see the oars in his hands, he must grope his way across the river in constant terror of being crushed by the barges of some lost towboat.

But his greatest enemy is the caving bank, a perpendicular wall sometimes seventy or eighty feet high, on top of which his light is resting. As he moors his rowboat below, he must watch with all the vigilance of an Alpine climber expecting an avalanche, lest the great cliff suddenly topple and bury him alive. Many a keeper has died in this fashion, with only the crew of the lighthouse tender and the superintendent in far off St. Louis to know of his heroism.

The courage and devotion of the lightkeepers is shared by their children. When the father grows too old and the mother is feeble as well, the son or the daughter assumes the responsibility. . . .

* * * * *

Besides caving banks and floods, the keeper has other, lesser enemies. There are the willow bugs, great blundering creatures, who live just long enough to drop into a light, and cause the glass to become smoky and dull. There are human enemies as well. There is the coon hunter, who, when out in the swamp, finds there is no more oil in the miner's lamp he is wearing on his cap, and replenishes his supply at the Government light, as a traveler fills his fountain pen in the writing room of a hotel. Worst of all there is the moonshiner, who discovers that he has brought insufficient fuel for his bubbling mash, and considering his need greater than that of the passing steamboats, empties the reservoir of the lamp into his oil can and carries it away to his still.

"They sure got mighty fine coal oil in them Government lights," the overalled swamp dweller will confide as he sets out some jugs of his product for an expected customer. "Government always gets the best there is."

These latter practices are growing rare, however, for the Secret Service agents have been vigorous, and the too-casual woodsmen are in the penitentiary, pondering over the error of their ways.

* * * * *

With all its responsibilities and perils, the task of lightkeeper is one of the prizes of the river. For not only does it invest the holder of the post with the dignity of the Government—and there is no more ardent patriot than the riverman—but it provides him as well with a regular income of ten dollars a month for each light that he tends. And on the river where life is simple and money is rare, ten dollars is many times that sum in a great metropolis. In consequence, lights remain in the same family for generations; the waiting list is long and the jealousies intense. More than once, a lightkeeper has started on his daily round to find that his flatboat has been smashed with an ax during the night; or he has rowed a little way across the river only to find the water pouring through a half dozen leaks in the bottom of his boat where the seams have been carefully parted, and he has been compelled to swim for his life. More than one keeper has been found killed in some mysterious fashion; and all the Valley knows that an envious neighbor seeking his lights has been the murderer.

As the years pass, often a good keeper may acquire other lights, sometimes ten, even fifteen, and here he rises to the status of a merchant prince, a veritable captain of industry. And if, by some accident of fate, this fortunate individual should be a woman, she becomes a queen, to be assiduously wooed by all her male neighbors of the river, anxious to acquire a wealthy wife. They are excellent lightkeepers, the women, at times superior to the men, worried if a speck or smear mars the lamp's spotless surface.

The life of the lightkeeper is a happy one, filled with infinite variety. When his duties are not pressing, he can go out to fish in his pirogue, a dugout made of a single log, unchanged since the days of the Indians. He can chew tobacco and talk all day with the crews of the towboats who have come into shore to remake their tows, or philosophize with the Government men. . . .

The ordinary lightkeeper is a white fisherman. But there are a few who depart from the pattern. There are a score of Negroes, all excellent keepers, and even a Filipino. Some of the keepers live in shantyboats anchored near their lights, some in shantyboats beached on the shore. A few live in Choctaws, houses built on great hollow logs so that when the high water comes, the curious structures float off with no damage to the interior, and as the yellow flood slowly recedes, the occupants can set them down again wherever they will. One lightkeeper operates a little sawmill; one has a shantyboat store where he sells candy and pop to passing river travelers; another, whose lights are all on one side of the water, is the possessor of an old and faithful horse, and every day rides out with his lamps and supplies dangling from the animal's sides.

* * * * *

... A cutoff in the river may eliminate the light of a faithful tender and threaten him with the loss of the monthly ten dollars which is his very existence; the captain of the lighthouse boat tries to find some other light near by and avoid a tragedy. For the lighthouse service is loyal to its loyal servants.

Some years ago up one of the small tributaries a group of pilots came to the captain of the lighthouse tender in the region and asked that a light be moved from one side of the river to the other. The bank and the channel had changed, they declared, and the light must be placed on the other shore, if their labors were not to be increased tenfold and their vessels even wrecked.

The captain of the lighthouse boat, an old man grown gray at his post, became troubled. "I'll move her for you next week," he declared. "But I'm sure mighty sorry it's got to go. That light's kept by Aunt Mollie Snow, that's been having it for forty years, ever since her husband drowned going out to fix his lamp. The light money's all she's got to support herself and her two grandchildren. I don't think she'll ever be able to cross the river. She's too twisted up with rheumatism. I reckon she'll just have to lose it, that's all."

The pilots went away, looking worried. They returned the next morning. "Captain, we don't want that light changed at Greenpoint," said the spokesman. "We'll get along fine with the light where she is. Pilots can just be kind of extra careful going round her."

The captain of the lighthouse boat smiled and nodded.

And the light remained until Aunt Mollie was dead.

McGill's Miracle

During the . . . devastating Mississippi flood in 1927, the lamplighters once again covered themselves with glory. In that year the lower Missis-

From *Keepers of the Lights*, by Hans Christian Adamson, pp. 305–306. Copyright, 1955, by Greenberg: Publisher. New York.

sippi flooded about 700,000 people out of their homes. Rescue operations were greatly aided by the successful efforts of lightkeepers to maintain their post lights. With the river out of its banks, coursing through woods and over fields, few indications of the main channel remained. Of these, the post lights were the most important.

An incident . . . was told after the 1927 flood crest had passed, by William McGill, a lamp tender who included Windy Point Light on Grand Lake, Louisiana, among those on his rounds. But for the curiosity of the superintendent of lighthouses in New Orleans the story might never have been told. On June 1, 1927, he received a report from McGill which stated: "I am yet on the job, but the water has run me out of my house. I have the oil on some logs. I will stay out there. All is well."

Having heard that nearly all McGill's lights were showing and wondering how the miracle was wrought, the boss asked McGill for a full report. It arrived and it read: "Your letter of June 10 at hand asking for details of how I lived and cared for oil and things. On May 21 I had to leave my home. The water came in the floor at 11 A.M. I went out on the lake and gathered in some cottonwood logs and made a raft and I had a little outhouse 8 by 10. I jacked it up and ran these logs under it and so it floated, and I had a home to carry me through the water. But in the meantime, while doing this a boat passed and the waves set all of my oil afloat.

"I gathered it up again and put it on the roof. Then a Red Cross boat came down full speed, one of those United States rum chasers, and knocked the oil house off the blocks.

"Again, I saved the oil and wicks, but the chimneys went down to the bottom with the house. I don't know if they are broken or not. There are about 5 feet of water over them, but the house is not gone to pieces. Everything will be in the house when the water goes down. I have 4 feet of water over the floor in my house.

"On May 25 Captain Harvey took my wife out to Morgan City, but she is in the camp now with me. We are all well and safe if no storm comes. We are a long way from any land. We have a small boat of our own to go about. That is about all the details. When the water goes down I want to take a lay off and go on a trip to New Orleans while the mud is drying up."

How to Work With the River

When you come to consider it, there should be more collisions than there are on the river. Especially on some of the smaller tributaries, the bends are so sharp that there is no way to see around them; and the hills go up on both sides, hiding any trace of smoke that may warn a pilot of

From *Towboat River,* by Edwin and Louise Rosskam, pp. 204–208, 212–214. Copyright, 1948, by Edwin and Louise Rosskam. New York: Duell, Sloan and Pearce.

another tow. You might hear the other fellow's whistle, and then again you might not. It depends on the wind and the noises on your own boat. And so there you are, going downstream sticking that enormous snout of your tow out ahead of you across a point you can't see around. You'll be going slow, backing, probably. But you can't stop and you know it. It's just about impossible to stop a big tow going downstream, except by getting lines ashore and checking against some large trees. That takes a long time, and the big trees aren't always handy. And if you do find some of them, in high water when the current is strong, a heavy tow may snap a couple of hefty trees as if they were matchsticks. The boat will be backing full head. There might be a sharp report first, like that of a gun going off. That'll be one of the two-inch hawsers breaking as a thread breaks. A rope end will whip around, and you'll be lucky if none of your men is in the way of it; because it will shatter his leg or cut it off, sure. And then there'll be a cracking in the woods and a rustle in the leaves. And the men who have been making the shore tie will run, looking behind them and up, with afraid faces. Then the trees will come over, both of them at once, slowly at first, and then fast, and you'll be fortunate if they don't fall across your tow or on your boat. And you'll still be going down the river, with your boat backing full head, dragging a couple of big trees alongside in the water. If you meet another tow at that point it won't be funny, not funny at all. The chances are he'll be hugging the shore, plowing away right under the branches of the trees, more than likely on the inside of the bend. The same current that is sweeping you down the river is pushing him back; and he'll be trying to avoid the main stream of it, which usually goes down the center and the outside of the bend. He'll be looking for the still places, the slack water, as they call it on the river. Knowing this, you'll be coming around as far out as the channel allows. Even so, when you meet him, you may find yourself in a spot. The first thing you'll see is the head of his tow peeking around the point. Your tow, swinging slowly, will be at least a half a mile from him; but your throat will tighten as you ring the engine room to "Full stroke 'er!"

The emergencies on the river are awful in their slowness. You see them a long time ahead and you do what you can; and, if that's not good enough, you'll wish you hadn't ever come on the river, and you wait for the crash—ten or fifteen minutes with no way out, no way to stop it from happening. At a moment like that you realize how feeble you are, you and your little boat, with that huge load in front of it; how completely you are in the grip of the blind forces of the river—forces like wind and current that are impersonal and inevitable. You'll be swinging down on that other tow, and you'll try to borrow room where you know there shouldn't be any room, and, long before you're anywhere near the other fellow's barges, you'll know if you're going to hit or not.

"We were going down the river with a bunch of empties," one captain told us. "And this other boat was comin' up with loads. The signals were blown. It was understood how we were to pass, port to port, left side to

left side. We were figurin' on passin' a good distance apart. Everything
was gonna be just fine. But just before we met that other boat, a sudden
wind squall came up from our starboard. That wind caught our empties
and boat and blew us over in the path that the other boat was travelin'.
And that same wind caught his boat and swung him around so that his
head was pointed toward us. Just circumstance. Wouldn't happen again in
a thousand trips. The other man did the only thing he could do. He kept
goin' full speed and tryin' to steer his boat back against the wind to keep
her from turnin' around. And the only thing we could do was to keep goin'
full speed and try to steer into the wind. We had to hit. We knew that
pretty quick. But we could hope we would hit sideways glance. . . . Of
course, the pilot law says that in a case like that the both of you are
supposed to stop and back your engines and sound the danger signal. We
couldn'ta stopped, and if we'da backed the engines, why, it woulda been
too damned late for danger signals. . . . Along with the wind there was a
lot of rain. We couldn't see very well. If we'da backed, our empty barges
woulda swung crossways in the river and we would of dropped head-on
into his tow with our empty barges. And so we kept going. Oh, yes, we
hit. The head of his tow hit the side of our tow and rubbed along it. That
didn't cause any damage. But when he got back to the stern of our tow,
the wind blew us into the head of his tow—and his load of gas barges
went into the engine room of the boat I was on. Come right into the
engine room. That was something. That was really quite a time. Nobody
hurt. But the boat almost sunk, and it scared us all to death. No fire, no
explosion. We were lucky at that. . . ."

A man can't work against the river. He's got to work with it. It's a
matter of estimating the forces, current, wind, and drift, and of drawing
an average from the sum of them. You know what your engine can do;
you've studied your river report; you know where you want to go and
where the limits of the channel at that stage of water will let you go.
It's a lot of arithmetic to do in your head, but that isn't where you do
all of it. The final deciding thing, the know-how, the feel, is farther down
in your gut some place. You steer by it as an airplane pilot flies by the
seat of his pants. After you've done all the thinking and the calculating,
you reach into yourself and something tells you where to line up your lead
barge—not on the mark, not right on the government light or the day-
board in the turn, but just a little, just the right amount, to one side of
it. It worries you all the time. It's one potential emergency after another.
There's no rote and no rule. There are as many ways to run the river as
there are pilots. . . .

* * * * *

. . . You cannot steer a tow as you steer a light boat. The art is always
to make the river do part of the work. Many a bend is far too tight to steer.
You have to "flank" your tow or "drive" it, to get around. In each case
you back your engines; when you flank, you back your stern up to the

point; when you drive, you back your stern away from the point. In each of these two maneuvers your tow heads away from where you are going. Sometimes it seems to hang there crazily, stretching halfway across the river. In fact, you are making the river skid you around the bend, just as a racing car skids around a hairpin curve. Seen from the shore, a flanking tow looks like something drifting and disabled. Actually, flanking and driving are safety measures as well as maneuvers. They slow you up, but the diminished risk makes it worth while.

One pilot put it this way: "When I was a young feller, I used to think I had to steer every bend that I possibly could, because it was quickest. Well, it didn't take me long after I slid through several bends, and had my hair stand on end thinkin' of the big rocks I was rubbin' alongside of and wonderin' if I was gonna take the bottom out of the boat or the barges. . . . Several happenin's like that, and I changed my mind about steerin' some of these bends. I decided it would be better to flank 'em than to steer 'em and steer myself right out of a job. I learned that, yessir. It's no use takin' chances with a big tow like this. You take your time and you get in shape right, and then you let the current carry you around the bend."

Getting in shape is something a pilot does practically all the time. His tow is such a slow-moving, long, and clumsy mass that the pilot must forever be preparing for the next maneuver while he is executing the present one. That is what is called getting in shape. He has to get in shape for a bend, for a crossing, for a bridge, for a landing, or for a lock. If he's going to steer, he lines up the head of his tow. If he's going to flank, he lines up his stern, by some mark such as a tree or a hill or a house or a government light. This has to be most carefully done. While you're getting in shape for something you are going to do a mile or two farther on, while you are calculating the set of the current, the wind and the stage of the water as it is going to be in fifteen minutes, you are making the moves which will decide whether, later down there, you are going to go through smoothly or pile up. It is all very slow and very deliberate and unbelievably skilled. There is no excitement to it, no hurry, and it is beautiful to watch. Getting in shape involves all the river knowledge a man can have, his memory, his familiarity with the river, and his fine workmanship with the huge tool that he controls with his fingertips on a lever.

A few miles below Gallipolis, Ohio, there is a large permanent dam and a lock. We were coming down with a big tow, and we had tied off half our tow to some trees and were going downstream with the other half, our first lockage. We headed way out into the river, so that it looked as though we were getting ready to go crashing over the dam. The pilot grinned when we asked him about it. "You see," he said, "we got three sets of current here. Near the shore you've got a current which wants to set you into the shore. In other words, if you come down here too close to those sheet-steel pilings and you take the headway out of your boat, that current will set you in on that piling. Now if you got out too far, then you've got a strong current that goes through the dam. But right in between there's one narrow streak, that if you can get right in that narrow streak and stay there, you go right down to the end of the guide wall in perfect shape." He was quite unruffled, watching his tow and the dam and the river. Very gradually, as he had said it would, the tow started swinging inward toward the lock. "It'll be different at different stages," he said. "That's what makes it difficult for the man that doesn't know. Of course, if a man knows and has done this thing a whole lot, he knows just where that streak of neutral current is and he gets into it. See how she's swingin'? We had her in perfect shape all the time."

PART FIVE

River Boats and Rivermen

Introduction

"With the improvements the Corps of Engineers has made on the river and the way they maintain the channel," Captain Tommy Stevenson told Irving Crump, "I think navigating Ol' Man River is much easier today than it was back in the supposedly 'good ol' days.' " I had just seen some of the Engineers' improvements, and was eager to hear about the good old days in relation to the present from the captain of one of the last of the sternwheelers. So I visited Captain Dave Cook on board the Corps of Engineers' U. S. Steamer *Mississippi* at Ensley Mooring Site, outside Memphis.

"When I learned the river," Captain Dave told me, "there were no screw-wheel boats. Up to the 1930's the river was just like it was in Mark Twain's time. Jobs were scarce. There was a closed shop. You had to get a letter and be recommended before you could take the examinations for the pilot's license. They'd make you clean spittoons and all that to try to discourage you. I have had my pilot's license since 1932.

"It was a gradual change, though it seemed as if it happened over night. The sternwheelers dropped out, one by one. The Second World War just speeded up things, whereas without the war the change would have taken ten years. We had a business boom. They needed more boats and pilots. The Coast Guard formed schools to try to make pilots.

"It was not the passing of steam but the passing of the sternwheelers that made the difference. They called those boats 'she' because you had to fight them all the time, but they certainly got into your system. They have a soul and a personality that is not built into the modern boats, which are like trucks. The sidewheeler couldn't push, so it had to pass out of the picture. It took skill and judgment to be a pilot. You had to be a mile or two ahead of yourself to figure what you were going to do. You would stand at the wheel twenty minutes before it happened, but you couldn't do anything about it, except kick the wheel and back, etc. Yes, it's a lost art. You couldn't find three men today who know how to pilot in the old sense. When you get into one of those positions where you're out of shape, it ages you— it turns your hair gray.

"There were just a few boats on the river in the 1930's. The Standard Oil Line had five sternwheelers and the Federal Barge Line had a few. Once in a while one would come from Pittsburgh. Now without batting an eye you pass twenty-four boats in twenty-four hours.

"I'm glad I had the experience, but I wouldn't want to go back to the good old days. I wouldn't want to go back to the *Sprague,* though I didn't work for it; I worked for the *Charles F. Richardson.* People talk about the good old days because they remember the high spots. You were a lot younger then and you could take it. You don't remember the long hours or the drudgery. I belong to the transition period.

"Yes, the Corps of Engineers have an organization that can cope with anything that happens—it never fails. It takes an emergency now and then to wake you up. It gives you a feeling of pride. Like the time they were plugging the Tennessee Chute at Memphis and the high water came along and the fill wouldn't hold. People were on the bluff betting we couldn't do it. It was the same thing in the Omaha flood and in the tornado at Vicksburg. The engineers took over. Not a word was said."

Speaking of the old days, Captain Dave said that there are no boats like the *Mississippi* left. There have been five *Mississippi* boats, and this is a composite of them, dating from 1927. "Looks like a ghost," he said of the sheet-draped furniture as we passed through the cabin, where the hearings of the Mississippi River Commission are held. On the bow he pointed out the line of the old pointed prow marked by rivets in the floor. When the Engineers had decided to use the *Mississippi* as a towboat, the bow had been squared off.

Back in the pilothouse, he said proudly that this is the only boat left with the pilothouse set back behind the texas deck instead of right up forward, as on other boats, which look snub-nosed like a tug. He showed me the old pilot wheel kept for ornament—the modern tiller does the work. The signals, too, are now automatic. Passing the ship's bell, he struck it with a coin, to hear the fine ring. "Yes, it must have twenty silver dollars melted into it—that was the old custom." The boilers have held since 1927. "You don't have to watch them as you did in the old days when if you waited five minutes it might be too late."

When I asked about the other old boats, he told me that the *Gordon C. Greene* is a restaurant and tourist attraction at Owensboro. The *Sprague* is down at Vicksburg, where it is used as a yacht club, and for plays given by the little theater. "She is painted up on the shore side. But on the river side you can see the paint is off. She's rusty and has holes in her side. I wish she had burned up instead."

As we were walking back to the car, my guide said: "It would sure break Dave up to lose that boat, like losing one of his family."

B. A. B.

The Canoe and the Pirogue

The *canoe* was the simplest and most generally used of all the [pre-steamboat] rivercraft. It was the wooden canoe, or dugout, and not the

From *History of Early Steamboat Navigation on the Missouri River*, Life and Adventures of Joseph La Barge, Pioneer Navigator and Indian Trader for Fifty Years Identified with the Commerce of the Missouri Valley, by Hiram Martin Chittenden, Vol. I, pp. 91–94. Copyright, 1903, by Francis Harper. New York. Francis P. Harper.

bark canoe which was so much used where the proper material could be found. The Missouri River canoe was generally made from the logs of the cottonwood, though frequently from the walnut, and occasionally from cedar. The cottonwood in the river bottoms attained immense size, ample for the largest canoes, for these boats rarely exceeded thirty feet in length and three and one-half in width. The ordinary length was between fifteen and twenty feet. A suitable tree having been found, it was felled and a proper height of the trunk was cut out. The exterior was straightened with the broad-ax, and reduced to a round log shorn of all roughness and irregularity. The top was then hewn off, so as to leave about two-thirds of the log. The ends were given a regular canoe model, and were sometimes turned up on bow and stern with extra pieces for purpose of ornament. The log was then carefully scooped out from the flat surface so as to leave a thin shell about two inches thick at the bottom and one at the rim. To support the sides and give strength to the craft the timber was left in place at points from four to six feet apart, making solid partitions or bulkheads. A good-sized canoe was easily built by four men in as many days. They had tools especially adapted to the work, the most important being the *tille ronde,* or the round adz.

These log canoes made excellent craft, strong, light, and easily managed. A full crew generally consisted of three men, two to propel and one to steer. The paddle (French *aviron*) was always used. A mast was occasionally placed in the center and rigged with a square sail, but this could be used only with an aft wind, for fear of capsizing the canoe.

Sometimes these boats were made with a square stern, and were then called *pirogues;* but this name was more frequently used where two such boats were rigidly united in parallel position a few feet apart and completely floored over. On the floor was placed the cargo, which was protected from the weather by the use of skins. Oars were provided in the bow for rowing and a single oar in the stern between the boats for steering. Sails could be used with a quartering wind on these boats without danger of upsetting. Dubé's ferry, on the Mississippi, one of the earliest ferries of St. Louis, used a boat of this kind.

The principal use of the canoe was for the local business of the larger river posts. Often, however, they were used in making trips to St. Louis, even from the remotest navigable points of the mainstream or its tributaries. Many such a journey has been made with a single voyageur running the gauntlet of hostile tribes all the way from the mountains to the Mississippi. A common use of the canoe was for sending express messages down the river, and there are several records of their having been used to transport freight. An example of this last use was the shipment of bear's oil, which was extensively used in St. Louis as a substitute for lard in the early days when swine were scarce and black bears plentiful. The oil was extremely penetrating and could rapidly filter through skin receptacles. Barrels or casks not being available, the center apartment of the canoe was filled with the oil and tightly covered with a skin fastened to the sides of the boat. Honey was also transported in this way. In those days bee trees were exceedingly plentiful in the Missouri bottoms, and large quantities of honey were taken from them.

The Mackinaw Boat

The *mackinaw* boat, as the name implies, was an imported design, having already been used on the Eastern lakes and rivers. It was made entirely of timber, and before nails were carried up the river all the parts were fastened with wooden pins. The bottom was flat, and was made of boards about one and a half inches thick. On these rested cross-timbers, to which, and to the bottom, were fastened the inclined knees that supported the sides. The boats were sometimes made as large as fifty feet long and twelve feet beam. The plan was that of an acute ellipse, and the gunwale rose about two feet from the center of the boat toward both bow and stern. The keel showed a rake of about thirty inches from the bow or stern to the bottom. The hold had a depth of about five feet at the two ends of the boat, and about three and one half at the center.

The central portion of the boat was partitioned off from the bow and stern by two water-tight bulkheads or partitions. Between these the cargo was loaded, and piled up to a height of three or four feet above the gunwale and given a rounded form. Over the cargo lodge skins were drawn tight and fastened with cleats to the sides and gunwales of the boat, so as to make practically a water-tight compartment. In the bow were seats for the oarsmen, and in the stern an elevated perch for the steersman, from which he could see over the cargo in front, and give directions to the crew in the bow or study the river ahead.

The crew of the boat ordinarily consisted of five men, four at the oars and one at the rudder. The latter had charge of the boat and was called the *patron*. Only experienced, courageous, and reliable men were chosen for this responsible work.

These boats were only used in downstream navigation, and the labor of handling them was not arduous. The men found ample time for song and gossip, and every hour or so, after a vigorous pull, would take advantage of a good stretch of river to rest their oars (*laisser aller*) and take a smoke (*fumer la pipe*). Then they would let fall their oars (*tomber les rames*) and bend to their work for another hour. They ran from fifteen to eighteen hours a day and made from 75 to 150 miles. The boats carried about fifteen tons of freight, and the cost per day was about two dollars. Transportation by mackinaw boat was therefore inexpensive.

These boats were cheaply made and were intended only for a single trip down to St. Louis, where they were sold for four or five dollars apiece. After the advent of the steamboat the mackinaws were frequently carried

Ibid., pp. 94–96.

back to the upper rivers on the annual boat, for even steam did not absorb the peculiar field of usefulness of these craft. They were quite safe and were preferred to the keelboat for downstream navigation.

The lumber for the mackinaws was manufactured where the boats were built, or rather the latter were built where suitable timber could be found. There being no sawmills, the boards had to be sawed by hand, and for this purpose the logs were rolled upon a scaffold high enough for a man to work underneath. They were first hewed square, and were then sawed by two men, one standing above and the other below. At all important posts there was a *chantier* (French for boatyard) located where timber was to be had. Here all woodwork was done. The Fort Pierre chantier, always called the navy yard, was some fifteen miles above the post, and was a very active place. The Fort Union chantier was three miles below at the mouth of Chantier (now Shonkin) Creek. At all these workyards skilled artisans were employed.

The Bullboat

The *bullboat* of the fur traders, in distinction from the tubs which were used by some of the Missouri River tribes, was an outgrowth of the conditions of navigation on such streams as the Platte, Niobara, and Cheyenne. The excessive shallowness of these streams precluded the use of any craft drawing more than nine or ten inches. The bullboat was probably the lightest draft vessel ever constructed for its size, and was admirably fitted for its peculiar use. It was commonly about thirty feet long by twelve wide and twenty inches deep.

The frame of the bullboat was constructed by laying stout willow poles, three or four inches in diameter, lengthwise of the boat, and across these similar poles, the two layers being firmly lashed together with rawhide. The side frames were made of willow twigs about an inch and a half in diameter at the larger end and six to seven feet long. The smaller ends were lashed to the cross-poles, and about two feet of the larger ends were then bent up to a vertical position. Along the tops of the vertical portions and on the inside was lashed a stout pole like those forming the bottom of the framework. To this gunwale were lashed cross-poles, at intervals of four or five feet, to keep the sides from spreading. No nails or pins were used for fastenings, but rawhide lashings only. The frames so constructed were exceedingly strong, and its flexible quality, by which it withstood the continuous wrenching to which it was subjected, was an important element of strength.

The framework, being completed, was then covered with a continuous sheet of rawhide formed by sewing together square pieces as large as

Ibid., pp. 96–102.

could be cut from a single buffalo hide. Only the skins of buffalo bulls
were used for this purpose (hence the name of the boat), for they were
the strongest and best able to resist abrasion from rubbing on the bottom
of the river. The pieces were sewed together with buffalo sinew. Before
this work was done the hides were carefully dressed by the Indians so
as to be free of hair and perfectly flexible. When the covering was all
sewed together, it was thoroughly soaked and then placed over the framework, and the sides and ends made fast to the gunwale and the boat.
The hides would then dry and shrink until they were drawn as tight as
a drumhead.

The final operation in the work was to pitch the seams. The material
used was a mixture of buffalo tallow and ashes, and it was carefully
rubbed into all seams or cracks until the whole covering was watertight.

The boat so built was very light, and could be easily turned over by
two men. When in the water and ready for its cargo, a layer of loose
poles was laid lengthwise on the bottom so as to keep the cargo five or
six inches from the bottom and protect it from any water that might leak
in. The cargo nearly always consisted of furs, securely packed in bales
about thirty inches long, fifteen inches wide, and eighteen inches deep.
They were placed one bale deep over the bottom of the boat, leaving space
in bow and stern for the pole men. The bales were always laid flatwise,
so that if the water should reach them it would injure only the bottom
skins and not all, as it would if they were set edgewise. The cargo
rarely exceeded six thousand pounds.

The boat was handled by means of poles, and the crew generally consisted of two men. The draft of the boat, when placed in the water in the
morning, was about four inches, but the boat hide becoming soaked during
the day, and possibly some water leaking in, it would probably be as
much as six or eight inches by night. Every evening when camp was made
the boat was unloaded, brought up on the bank, and placed in an inclined
position, bottom side up, to dry. In this position it served as a shelter
for both cargo and crew. In the morning the seams were repitched, and
any incipient rents or abrasions were carefully patched. The boat was then
launched and reloaded and the voyage resumed.

Low water, even on the Platte, was generally preferred to high water
for bullboat navigation, because in high water the current was too strong.
Every little while the boat would glide into deep pockets, where the poles
could not touch bottom, and it was then necessary to drift with the
current until a shallower stretch would give the men control again. Sometimes in those wide and shallow expanses, which give the Platte such a
pretentious appearance in high water, the wind would play vexatious
pranks with the bullboat navigators. A strong prairie gale blowing steadily from one direction during the day would drift most of the water to
the leeward side of the stream. The boat would naturally follow the same
shore, and the night camp would be made there. If, as often happened,
the wind changed before re-embarkation, the river would very likely be

wafted to the other side of its broad bed, and the crew would find themselves with half a mile of sandbar between them and the water.

Bullboat navigation, as here described, was most frequently resorted to in bringing the trade of the Pawnees on the Loup Fork of the Platte to the Missouri, but it was likewise extensively used on the Cheyenne and Niobara and other tributaries. There were some very extensive bullboat voyages. A good many were made from Laramie River to the mouth of the Platte, but generally it was impossible to find enough water to make a continuous voyage. In 1825 General Ashley loaded one hundred and twenty-five packs of beaver into bullboats at the head of navigation on the Bighorn River, with the intention of conveying them in that way to St. Louis. But at the mouth of the Yellowstone he met General Atkinson, who offered him the use of his keelboats for the rest of the journey. In 1833 the Rocky Mountain Fur Company, Captain Bonneville and Nathaniel J. Wyeth, embarked all their furs, the product of a year's hunt, in bullboats on the Bighorn River, and together went downstream to the mouth of the Yellowstone. Sometimes these boats were actually given names, and we have a record of the bullboat *Antoine,* in which a free trapper, Johnson Gardner, shipped his furs from the "crossings of the Yellowstone" to Fort Union in 1832.

The boats just described were quite different from the hemispherical tubs used so extensively by the Mandans and other tribes of the upper Missouri. These little boats had a circular rim or gunwale, and the willow supports passed from one side entirely under the boat to the other. The frame was generally small enough to be covered with a single hide, and was designed to carry ordinarily but one person. A fleet of these boats, numbering a hundred or so, was one of the most singular sights ever witnessed on the river. The squaws often used them, on occasions of buffalo hunts above the village, to transport the meat downstream. In fact the women rather than the men were the navigators of this picturesque little craft.

The Keelboat

We come now to the *keelboat,* the representative river craft of ante-steamboat days. It was in this boat that the merchandise for the trade was transported to the far upper river, and it was used on all important military or exploring expeditions. It was a good-sized boat, sixty to seventy feet long, and built on a regular model, with a keel running from bow to stern. It had fifteen to eighteen feet breadth of beam and three or four feet depth of hold. Its ordinary draft was from twenty to thirty inches. It was built in accordance with the practice of approved shipcraft,

Ibid., pp. 102–109.

and was a good, stanch vessel. Keelboats were generally built in Pittsbugh at a cost of two to three thousand dollars.

For carrying freight the keelboat was fitted with what was called a cargo box, which occupied the entire body of the boat excepting about twelve feet at each end. It rose some four or five feet above the deck. Along each side of the cargo box was a narrow walk about fifteen inches wide, called the *passe avant*, the purpose of which will be explained further on. On special occasions when these boats were used for passenger traffic, as on expeditions of discovery or exploration, they were fitted up with cabins and made very comfortable passenger boats.

For purposes of propulsion the boat was equipped with nearly all the power appliances known to navigation except steam. The cordelle was the main reliance. This consisted of a line nearly a thousand feet long, fastened to the top of a mast which rose from the center of the boat to a height of about thirty feet. The boat was pulled along with this line by men on shore. In order to hold the boat from swinging around the mast, the line was connected with the bow by means of a "bridle," a short auxiliary line fastened to a loop in the bow and to a ring through which the cordelle passed. The bridle prevented the boat from swinging under the force of the wind or current when the speed was not great enough to accomplish this purpose by means of the rudder. The object in having so long a line was to lessen the tendency to draw the boat toward the shore; and the object in having it fastened to the top of the mast was to keep it from dragging, and to enable it to clear the brush along the bank.

It took from twenty to forty men to cordelle the keelboat along average stretches of the river, and the work was always one of great difficulty. There was no established towpath, and the changing conditions of the river prevented the development of such a path except along a few stable stretches. It was frequently necessary to send men ahead to clear the most troublesome obstructions away. In some places, where it was impossible to walk and work at the same time, a few men would carry the end of the line beyond the obstruction and make it fast, while the rest would get on board and pull the boat up by drawing in the line. This operation was called warping.

When the boat was being cordelled there stood at the bow, near where the bridle was attached, an individual called in French a *bosseman* (boatswain's mate), whose duty it was to watch for snags and other obstructions and to help steer the boat by holding it off the bank with a pole. There was selected for this place a man of great physical strength, prompt decision, and thorough knowledge of the river. The patron, or master of the boat, stood at the rudder, which was manipulated by means of a long lever from the rear end of the cargo box. This position gave him an elevated point of view, from which he could overlook everything.

There were many places where the keelboat could not be cordelled at all, as along sandbars where the water was too shallow for the boat to get near the shore, or the alluvium too soft for the men to walk in. At such times it was necessary to resort to the pole, as it was called. This was a turned piece of ash wood regularly manufactured at St. Louis. On one end was a ball or knob to rest in the hollow of the shoulder, for the voyageur to push against; and on the other was a wooden shoe or socket. In propelling the boat with these poles eight or ten voyageurs ranged themselves along each side, near the bow, facing aft, pole in hand, one in front of the other, as close together as they could walk. The whole operation was under the direction of the patron. At his command, *"À bas les perches"* (down with the poles), the voyageurs would thrust the lower ends into the river close to the boat and place the ball ends against their shoulders, so that the poles should be well inclined downstream. They would all push together, forcing the boat ahead, as they walked along the *passe avant* toward the stern, until the foremost man had gone as far as he could. The patron then gave the command, *"Levez les perches"* (raise the poles), upon which they would be withdrawn from the mud, and the men would walk quickly to the bow and repeat the operation. All steering was done while the poles were up, for the boat could not change direction while the men were pushing. It was always essential to give the boat sufficient momentum at each push to keep her going while the men were changing position. The *passe avant* had cleats nailed to it to keep the feet from slipping, and the men, when pushing hard, sometimes leaned over far enough to catch hold of the cleats with their hands, thus fairly crawling on all fours.

In some places, where the water was too deep for the poles and where cordelling was impracticable, oars were resorted to. There were five or six of these on each side of the bow. They often furnished assistance also when the boat was being cordelled.

A great reliance in propelling the keelboat, strange as it may seem considering the nature of Missouri River navigation, was the wind. A mast was rigged, with a square sail spreading about one hundred square feet of canvas, which often gave sufficient power to propel the boat against the swift current of the river. Unless the direction of the wind were altogether wrong, the sinuous course of the stream would every now and then give an aft or quartering breeze. In some places the wind seemed to follow the bends, blowing up or down the river clear around. Thus Brackenridge relates that when Manuel Lisa's boat, in June, 1811, was going around the Great Bend below Fort Pierre, where in the course of thirty miles the river flows toward every point in the compass, an aft wind was experienced all the way, and the entire circuit was made under sail. Some idea of sailing speed up the Missouri under favorable conditions may be gleaned from the fact that, on the day of passing the Great Bend, Lisa's boat made seventy-five miles, a portion of the distance being made at night by the light of the moon. And on another occasion on the same trip Brackenridge records that "we had an extraordinary run of forty-five leagues from sun to sun."

Thus by means of the cordelle and pole, the oar and the sail, the sturdy keelboat worked and worried its way up the turbulent Missouri in the early days. It was a slow and laborious process at best. A good idea of its maximum accomplishment under rather unfavorable conditions is furnished by Manuel Lisa's voyage, already referred to. It was made with an exceptionally fine boat, a picked crew, and the most untiring and energetic commander that ever ascended the Missouri. There was especial necessity for rapid progress, for it was of the greatest importance to overtake the Astorian expedition, which was a long distance ahead, before it should reach the dangerous Sioux country. The difficulties from wind and storm were greater than the average, and the rate of progress was not increased by any fortuitous aids. Lisa left St. Charles, 28 miles above the mouth of the Missouri, April 2, 1811. He overtook Hunt at 1132 miles, on the morning of June 11. He therefore made about 1100 miles in sixty-one days, or about 18 miles per day. This, however, was better than the average. A keelboat trip to the upper river was practically an entire summer's operation.

Above the mouth of the James or Dakota River, keelboating was easier than below because the natural obstacles of all sorts were less; but everywhere it was a very laborious process. Captain La Barge often remarked that it would be wholly impossible in this day to get men to undergo such exertions as were required of the keelboat crews. They worked early and late, in water and out, and often to the very limit of endurance. Their food was of the plainest description, consisting mainly of pork, lyed corn, and navy beans. From this allowance, slender as it was, meat was cut off as soon as the game country was reached. The cooking was done at the night camp for the following day. On top of the cargo box there was sometimes placed a cooking stove, in a shallow box filled with ashes or gravel to protect the roof from fire. The men's baggage was stored in the front of the cargo box, where there was also a place for any one to lie down who might fall sick. It was, however, a very poor place to be sick in. There were no medicines, no physicians, no nurses or attendants, and nothing but the coarsest food. The prospect itself was enough to frighten every one into keeping well.

The hired laborers who did the work on these river expeditions were called voyageurs, and were generally of French descent. They were an interesting class of people and presented a phase of pioneer life on the Missouri which has become wholly extinct. They were a very hard-working class, obedient, cheerful, light-hearted, and contented. It was a marvel to see them, after a hard day's work, dance and sing around the evening campfire as if just awakened from a refreshing sleep. The St. Louis Creoles were regarded as more desirable boatmen than the French Canadians. The American hunter was not so useful in river work as the French voyageur, but was far more valuable for land work and in situations involving danger or requiring the display of physical courage.

The Voyageur Who Refused to Chop Wood

. . . The Canadian voyageurs or engagés . . . were unlike any other class of men. Like the poet, they seemed born to their vocation. Sturdy, enduring, ingenious, and light-hearted, they possessed a spirit capable of adapting itself to any emergency. No difficulties baffled, no hardships discouraged them; while their affectionate nature led them to form attachments of the warmest character to their "bourgeois," or master, as well as to the native inhabitants among whom their engagements carried them.

* * * * *

It was a common saying, "Keep an engagé to his corn and tallow, he will serve you well—give him pork and bread, and he soon gets beyond your management." They regard the terms of their engagement as binding to the letter. . . .

* * * * *

On arriving at Mackinac, which was the entrepôt of the Fur Trade, a small proportion of the voyageur's wages was advanced him, to furnish his winter's outfit, his pipes and tobacco, his needles and thread, some pieces of bright-colored ribbons, and red and yellow gartering (quality binding), with which to purchase their little necessaries from the Indians. To these, if his destination were Lake Superior, or a post far to the north, where such articles could not be readily obtained, were added one or two smoked deerskins for moccasins.

Thus equipped, he entered upon his three years' service, to toil by day, and laugh, joke, sing, and tell stories when the evening hour brought rest and liberty.

There was not wanting here and there an instance of obstinate adherence to the exact letter of the agreement in regard to the nature of employment, although, as a general thing, the engagé held himself ready to fulfill the behest of his bourgeois as faithfully as ever did vassal those of his chief.

A story is told of M. St. Jean, a trader on the Upper Mississippi, who upon a certain occasion ordered one of his Frenchmen to accompany a party to the forest to chop wood. The man refused. "He was not hired," he said, "to chop wood."

"Ah! for what then were your hired?"

"To steer a boat."

"Very well; steer a boat, then, since you prefer it."

It was mid-winter. The recusant was marched to the riverside and placed in the stern of the boat, which lay fastened in the ice.

From *Wau-Bun, the "Early Day" in the Northwest*, by Mrs. John H. Kinzie, pp. 196–199. Entered . . . 1856, by Derby & Jackson. Chicago: D. B. Cooke & Co., Publishers.

After serving a couple of hours at his legitimate employment, with the thermometer below zero, he was quite content to take his place with the chopping-party, and never again thought it good policy to choose work for himself.

Flatboating in 1866

When I was eleven past, I raised a patch of potatoes—had three hundred bushels. They were a dollar a bushel. When they were sold I found out that they were Pap's potatoes. He gave me a note for them. My playmates laughed at me at school, said that was the way their dads did them and I'd never get a dang cent. I brooded over that thing and thought that my father being a class leader in church and would do me that way, religion didn't do him any good and wouldn't do me any good. So I used the note for thumb-paper in the school books and quit speaking in the church meetings. He just kept the money and I never saw it. We sold the potatoes to John Beard.

John Beard was a flatboat man. The thought then came to me that I'd just like to run away and go down on a flatboat. I kept talking about that till next fall. Dad thought he'd save my soul—soften matters, anyway—and consented to let me go with Wilf Watkins, a neighbor, who ran a flatboat.

I was firing a lime kiln one night. It was April, 1865, the day after Lee's surrender. People at New Amsterdam, our nearest town on the Ohio River, were celebrating the close of the war by firing anvils. Watkins and my father were at the celebration. They were told by friends that they'd better not go home the usual way because there were Southern sympathizers along the road waiting to kill them. So they came up the river road and came up through the woods to where we were burning lime. It was way after midnight, and I had roasted potatoes, had a lot o' coffee, and an oven full of cornpone, and a neighbor's chicken had got into the pot. And those men were hungry. While enjoying the feast Watkins wanted to know who had cooked that. Paw told him that I was the cook. Right away Watkins said that he wanted me to be the cook on his flatboat. That's how I became a cook on a flatboat at $12 a month when I was twelve.

The people made their flatboats out of their own timber. They cut down a poplar tree a hundred feet to the first limb, six feet in diameter, and ripped that into two gunwales. Gunwales was what they built the boat on, same as sled-runners to build a sled on. The bottom of the boat was two by twelve poplar boards, twenty feet long. Notches were cut out of the

As told by Cliff Frank to B. A. Botkin, Norman, Oklahoma. October 1, 1929.
For other chapters in Cliff Frank's Indiana boyhood, see *Folk-Say*, 1929, 1930, and 1931, edited by B. A. Botkin (Norman, Oklahoma).

side of the gunwales three inches down so that the boards set down on them. That made a flat bottom underneath. The gunwales were eight to twelve inches thick. Those boards were put on the bottom and a spike driven in each one; then with a two-inch augur we bored holes and put two-inch wooden pins in each end of the board. The pins fit so that they were hard to drive in. Soon as they got wet nothing could pull them out. Then we calked the bottom with oakum.

When the bottom was on, we put skids down and out far enough into the river where the boat would float. We put soft soap on the skids and let her loose. The boat went out into deep water but not deep enough there to turn it over, the bottom side being up. We took that boat down the river three miles to a deep place close to shore where there were big rocks and little rocks—no end of them—just a mass of rocks. We nailed a board on the outside, carried those big rocks from the shore all along the outside, kept carrying them until the outside went down, and in going down it gave enough momentum to turn it over. They had to bore holes in the bottom on account of the suction to let the air out before it would turn over. Those holes let the water out of that big hull. The poplar lumber being so much lighter, the water kept running out of the bottom and the boat kept coming up. Then we drove pins in the holes in the bottom and bailed out what little water was left, and then towed the boat back up to New Amsterdam, where we put the top on.

In making that boat we first had to have girders for those bottom planks to be spiked on to. We put a big piece of timber like the gunwale on each end of the gunwales and then put girders across from one gunwale to the other, dovetailed in and spiked down. Then we put on the streamers lengthwise. The next thing we did was to put stanchions all around. That made it eight feet from the floor to the roof. Then the siding was spiked to the stanchions. Then two rows of stanchions ran the full length of the boat in the middle, far enough apart for two barrels to be rolled lengthwise between and two feet higher than the outside stanchions, and then joists were placed on those. Then linn lumber was nailed on top of those stanchions, green, and it curved, it was so limber. They usually put three layers on so that it wouldn't leak, and about a two-by-six was spiked on along the outside edge, straight up from the gunwales, to hold the roof down on the outside. Linn is porous and in a little while it almost becomes a solid roof.

Then they put on the sweeps. There were six sweeps, two on a side and one on each end. Those are the oars to pull on—the end ones are to guide with. In the center, twenty feet from the stern, was a platform on top of the roof for the pilot to stand on. He held the oar that guided the boat. The cabin was in the stern, big enough to have two bunks, one on each side—big enough for four fellows to sleep in—stove, and a board for a table. When the boys were in the beds and the pilot wanted them out to help pull, he hit his oar three licks, and the pin that held the oar being right over the beds, that woke them all up. The crew was eleven, two men to the side sweeps making eight men, the pilot nine, and one to the bow ten, and the cook eleven. We hardly ever used the bow sweep. The captain used it only in a storm or in landing or leaving shore.

The boat was finished, and the farmers brought in their potatoes, two thousand barrels. We were ready to be off. News came that a seven-foot rise was on the way, that it would reach our town in three days. Looked like an army loading that boat. We were ready, though, when the rise came. The rising waters released the coal and ore boats, but we were ahead of them. Great side- and stern-wheel steamboats passed us, some going up and some going down the river.

My mother didn't want me to go with the river rats, as she called them, because they were such cussers. She gave me a little Testament to take along and an old hymn book and a blue-backed speller. I have them yet. I studied the words when I went down the river, learned to spell big words, to read the Testament, and sing the Methodist hymns. I had an old army musket my Uncle George gave me. I had an accordion and a watch. I raised enough turnips on the side of my acre potato patch to buy the watch and the accordion. I played for parties. Folks could dance to the accordion music but they couldn't dance to the fiddle. It was agin their dis-*ci*-pline and the ordinances of the church. I sold my turnips and got the accordion in the fall before that. I played all the old familiar tunes: "My Old Kentucky Home," "Old Dan Tucker," "Comin' through the Rye," and Sunday school songs. I bought my girl a knife out of the turnip money. I figured that out of my crop of potatoes I was going to get all these things, but the turnips saved me and I got her the pretty knife. And she said that a present of a knife always cuts love, and it just happened that way. We never hooked up.

Mother and Mrs. Watkins came down in the morning and showed me all day about cooking. They showed me how much soda and stuff to put in the flour and how much lard to put to make good light bread. I had made biscuit. I had learned at home, at the lime kiln. They forgot to tell me how to cook beans and dried apples. We had old black iron pots to cook in so they wouldn't break. One day I filled one full of beans and commenced boiling it. They kept swelling up and boiling over. I filled every crock and pan they had with beans and put the surplus in the tin washtub. You know, a pot full of beans would make a washtub full. We had the same experience with rice. The rice rared up, too, and kicked the lid off. And I had exactly the same experience later with dried apples. They laughed at me. They ate the beans till they got tired of them and then they threw them to the fish. But apples were different. They'd keep in the winter time, and the boys would come in, when not working, and eat bread and apples. Then I made an apple pie out of them and soon used up the apples. And one day I did make apple dumplings.

We had all kinds of stock food: bacon, ham, quarter of a beef, kraut —two two-gallon jars of kraut and they were empty by the time the apples boiled over. Then we had apples—green apples and dried apples—onions, and two thousand barrels of poatoes. We had fried potatoes and boiled potatoes and potato soup, then potatoes. Eleven people would eat potatoes every day. You had to keep them cooked because some one was up all night. You had to keep hot coffee. I'd cook enough and leave it on the stove. They'd pull on the oars and everything would be going all right, and they'd come down to eat and go to bed.

It wasn't routine, it was nothing regular. They'd get me out of bed in the night to make coffee or cook something. They didn't have no beginning or no ending. They had breakfast from daylight to midnight and dinner from midnight to daylight. We had no supper. Breakfast was pancakes and coffee and syrup made out of brown sugar. When we got further down the river we got New Orleans molasses. For dinner we'd boil a pot of meat and potatoes. We ran out of sweet stuff, out of sugar, down at Golconda, Illinois. The captain sent me out to Golconda with twenty-five cents to get brown sugar for eleven people. He was just that stingy. It didn't last at all. We did without for quite a while. He'd look at the boys while they'd put sugar in their coffee, with hell in his eye. One time he left me on that boat alone while he went over to Shreveport—didn't leave a cent. The rest of the men had got on boats and gone home—we were there with our potatoes, waiting to sell them, and there was no use for them. I ran out of bread and flour, ran out of meat, and I lived on potatoes for three or four days, and I'd have suffered then if it hadn't been for Hugh Trotter, who came over one day and asked me to eat at their boat, that lay alongside.

The second morning out we passed Uncle Martin's place about a hundred miles down the river. Uncle Martin ran a flatboat, and I had wanted to go with him, but he was a Democrat and my parents thought that I should be with a Republican. Besides, Captain Watkins' farm joined ours, and his flatboats were built, from gunwales to sweeps, from timber from our farm. Uncle Martin went through the war as a pilot on gunboats while Watkins got rich as a sutler in the army. A sutler is a man who by pull or for cash on the barrelhead secures the monopoly of selling the soldiers what the boys have to have. Nearly all profit—in many cases altogether so because they didn't pay the wholesale houses. I went to shore to see Uncle Martin in our skiff. His boat was nearly loaded, and he said he would pull out in two days and beat us to Memphis. The boys laughed at that when I told them, but when we were towed into Memphis by a tug we found Uncle Martin ready to go home. How did he gain four days on us?

The first thing that was big in my boy's mind was the sunken gunboats at Cairo. Uncle Martin knew where every boat had been sunk during the war. Some of the men on the boats had been soldiers. The wind was a little heavy to run the boat, so we landed right below the sunken monitors, and we all went up to look at them. The sterns and smokestacks stuck up out of the water. There were curios for sale on one little houseboat. The fellow on the houseboat took pictures and sold curios, and boys were out in skiffs selling relics—old army guns and shells and minnie balls and sabers and (I remember distinctly) pieces of the big chain that the Confederates put across the river at Island Number Ten to keep the Union boats from going down the river. The iron in the links must have been two inches in diameter and four to six inches long. The fellow on the boat had those links to sell for fifty cents apiece. And the kind that was cut was cheaper. Either one of them now offered would bring ten to fifteen dollars. They have them in museums now. I saw one of them at the World's Fair in Chicago. This chain was across the Mississippi at Island Number Ten, and during a storm a German boy floated down with his hack saw, raised the chain, and sawed it in two. And the next day the boats went through there.

My Uncle Martin, who was pilot on the *Storm* (that was a dispatch boat that ran from Louisville down the river and after that it went on down as far as New Orleans), he told me about passing a hail of cannon balls as he passed Island Number Ten. One cannon ball took off the captain's head right in front of the pilot house as he was giving orders. The pilot was in an iron-clad pilot house made up of railroad rails. It may have been below the Island. I don't want anyone to say that no captain's head was cut off near Island Number Ten. I lived with my Uncle Martin until I was grown (after the flatboat trip) and he told me these things. We saw the big cannon sticking out of the banks of Island Number Ten, a row of cannon trained on the river to get the boats that came to break the chain.

The next thing that sticks to me was a storm that came up down the river farther. The storm was coming from the Illinois side, and we pulled against the wind. In landing a flatboat you have to pull against the wind; if you land with the wind you run onto snags and rocks. Or it would run you off on a sand bar and you'd never get off. We had a time landing the boat and finally got to the shore through the blinding rain, and landed just a little above a town called Cave-in-Rock. We had to stay over that night and the next day because it wasn't safe to start out again. During the day we went up a short distance to the cave in the rock. It was known as John Murrell's cave. Murrell was a robber from Mississippi and would send a man up the river to get a job coming down on a flatboat, and the fellow would report to Murrell that the flatboat would be along about such time. Then the Murrell gang would go out and kill the crew and take the boat to Memphis or New Orleans and sell the produce. That was before the war. The government finally tracked him down and killed him. The old folks there at Cave-in-Rock told us about how he killed the men and tied the rocks on them to sink them. Some said they cut them open so they wouldn't swell up and float. They removed the entrails and put the rocks inside.

A boat had sunk there loaded with onions. They said it was a couple of years before that, and the owner of the boat had put the onions all over the floor of the cave to save them. Of course I don't know the size of the cave, but, as I remember now, it must have been a half acre or more—the different rooms of it. There were piles of old harness, trace chains, and saddles in the cave. Murrell put them in there. The fog from the river had destroyed the harness and moulded it, and the onions had dried out. Nothing was left there but the shells of the onions, and I waded through them ankle-deep, light as leaves. The cave is there yet if they haven't taken it away. I know it's high enough I could toss rocks up one place—oh, I should think, fifteen or twenty feet.

The next thing of any importance was the passing of the chalk banks. The chalk banks are so-called because there's a chalk formation there. The river washed it out in time. There are great holes in the bed of the river there between the rocks. And it's a sort of an incline down, and it's called the Chalk Falls. There are three or four of these washouts scattered zigzag with the water boiling up, and it's only dangerous when the water's low. It took everybody on the boat to pass that because the pilot had to know the exact thing to do and when to strike. It made such a noise that he couldn't give us orders, but he told us before reaching that place to keep our eyes on him and he'd motion with his hand which way to pull. That is, one side would pull and the other would back, and all at once the thing would be reversed and the fellows that were pulling back would be pulling forward and the other would be pulling back. This was the most exciting thing in my life. If the pilot didn't know when to reverse and turn, they'd go on to the rock—it was just solid rock.

One night we saw great lights along the shore. And the pilot said, "That's Memphis." He said we couldn't land there in the night. So he piloted the boat into Wolf Island, which is four or five miles above Memphis. Then the captain and someone went down and just as we got down there, where there were flatboats for half a mile or more, another tug pulled out an empty flatboat, and they put a timber across to keep the current from pressing the boats together; then our boat was shot into that opening.

That's all there was to it except selling. The commission men are always waiting for new boats to come in, bring their cards up and introduce themselves. The commission men have one price, but one would arrange to have the captain come and eat with him. He'd get solid with the captain and the one who got solid would do his business. He gave him something to drink and took him out to see the girls and to the theater.

The first Sunday we were there they had a Negro baptizing the upper end of the long line of flatboats because the boats made a sort of eddy above so they could wade out a piece and duck them. I walked from about the middle of the line of flatboats—walked all the way over the tops—and went up there and watched and heard the Negroes shout "hallelujah" and sing their songs. Oh, it's just a picture in my mind—milling around, a preacher soaking the men, women, boys, and girls—it must have been a half acre of them that were getting the second degree in the Baptist church.

We sold the two thousand barrels and then sold the boat for $100. We went home on the sidewheeler *Idlewild*. The rise in the river had filled the stream full of logs, and the captain didn't like to run much at night. They didn't have searchlights then. But he'd run it slowly and every little while a big log would bump, and we could feel it all over the boat. One day a green deck-hand—Negro—was getting a bucket of water for the straw boss, and he took the bucket—it had a long rope on it—went to the side of the boat, threw the bucket in, and it jerked him out into the river. I was on the back end of the top of the boat. The boat stopped suddenly and went to backing. I thought there was something going wrong with the boat. I saw the swinging yawl drop to the water, some men jumped into it, pulled down to where they thought the Negro was, but he evidently had gone through the wheel and couldn't hold himself up until they got to him. They never got him. I saw him up and struggling, saw the boat going to him, but he could only use one hand. He couldn't hold himself up that way. He must have had one of his arms broken. He went down; they never got him.

That's all except the joy of riding day and night on a river palace. I remember when I got home I thought maybe the folks would hardly remember me. We left in February and we got back about the first of April. That was a long time. To my astonishment the folks remembered me.

Shanty-Boat Migrants

By far the most interesting and peculiar features of a winter's row down the Ohio are the life studies offered by the occupants of the numerous shanty-boats daily encountered. They are sometimes called, and justly too, family-boats, and serve as the winter homes of a singular class of people, carrying their passengers and cargoes from the icy region of the Ohio to New Orleans. Their annual descent of the river resembles the migration of birds, and we invariably find those of a feather flocking together. It would be hard to trace these creatures to their lair; but the Allegheny and Monongahela region, with the towns of the upper Ohio, may be said to furnish most of them. Let them come from where they may (and we feel sure none will quarrel for the honor of calling them citizens), the fall of the leaf seems to be the signal for looking up winter-quarters, and the river with its swift current the inviting path to warmer suns and an easy life.

The shanty-boatman looks to the river not only for his life but also

From *Four Months in a Sneak-Box*, A Boat Voyage of 2600 Miles down the Ohio and Mississippi Rivers, and along the Gulf of Mexico, by Nathaniel H. Bishop, pp. 58–66. Copyright, 1879, by Nathaniel H. Bishop. Boston: Lee and Shepard, Publishers.

for the means of making that life pleasant; so he fishes in the stream for
floating lumber in the form of boards, planks, and scantling for framing
to build his home. It is soon ready. A scow, or flatboat, about twenty feet
long by ten or twelve wide, is roughly constructed. It is made of two-
inch planks spiked together. These scows are calked with oakum and rags,
and the seams are made water-tight with pitch or tar. A small, low house
is built upon the boat, and covers about two-thirds of it, leaving a cock-
pit at each end, in which the crews work the sweeps, or oars, which govern
the motions of the shanty-boat. If the proprietor of the boat has a family,
he puts its members on board—not forgetting the pet dogs and cats—
with a small stock of salt pork, bacon, flour, potatoes, molasses, salt, and
coffee. An old cooking-stove is set up in the shanty, and its sheet-iron
pipe, projecting through the roof, makes a chimney a superfluity. Rough
bunks, or berths, are constructed for sleeping quarters; but if the family
are the happy possessors of any furniture, it is put on board, and adds
greatly to their respectability. A number of steel traps, with the usual
double-barreled gun, or rifle, and a good supply of ammunition constitute the most important supplies of the shanty-boat, and are never forgotten. Of these family-boats alone I passed over two hundred on the
Ohio.

This rude, unpainted structure, with its door at each end of the shanty,
and a few windows relieving the barrenness of its sides, makes a very
comfortable home for its rough occupants.

If the shanty-man be a widower or a bachelor, or even if he be a married man laboring under the belief that his wife and he are not true
affinities, and that there is more war in the house than is good for the
peace of the household, he looks about for a housekeeper. She must be
some congenial spirit, who will fry his bacon and wash his shirts without
murmuring. Having found one whom he fondly thinks will "fill the bill,"
he next proceeds to picture to her vivid imagination the delights of "drifting." "Nothing to do," he says, "but to float with the current, and eat
fresh pork, and take a hand at euchre." The woods, he tells her, are full of
hogs. They shall fall an easy prey to his unfailing gun, and after them,
when further south, the golden orange shall delight her thirsty soul, while
all the sugar-cane she can chew shall be gathered for her. Add to these
the luxury of plenty of snuff with which to rub her dainty gums, with the
promise of tobacco enough to keep her pipe always full, and it will be
hard to find among this class a fair one with sufficient strength of mind
to resist such an offer; so she promises to keep house for him as long as
the shanty-boat holds together.

Her embarkation is characteristic. Whatever her attire, the bonnet is
there, gay with flowers; a pack of cards is tightly grasped in her hand;
while a worn old trunk, tied with a cord and fondly called a "Saratoga,"
is hoisted on board; and so, for better or for worse, she goes forth to meet
her fate, or as she expresses it, "to find luck."

More than one quarrel usually occurs during the descent of the Mississippi, and by the time New Orleans is reached the shanty-boatman sets his quondam housekeeper adrift, where, in the swift current of life, she is caught by kindred spirits, and being introduced to city society as the Northern Lily, or Pittsburgh Rose, is soon lost to sight, and never returns to the far distant up-river country.

Another shanty-boat is built by a party of young men suffering from impecuniosity. They are "out of a job," and to them the charms of an independent life on the river are irresistible. Having pooled their few dollars to build their floating home, they descend to New Orleans as Negro minstrels, trappers, or thieves, as necessity may demand.

Cobblers set afloat their establishments, calling attention to the fact by the creaking sign of a boot; and here on the rushing river a man can have his heel tapped as easily as on shore.

Tin-smiths, agents and repairers of sewing-machines, grocers, saloon-keepers, barbers, and every trade indeed is here represented on these floating dens. I saw one circus-boat with a ring twenty-five feet in diameter upon it, in which a troupe of horsemen, acrobats, and flying trapeze artists performed while their boat was tied to a landing.

The occupants of the shanty-boats float upon the stream with the current, rarely doing any rowing with their heavy sweeps. They keep steadily on their course till a milder climate is reached, when they work their clumsy craft into some little creek or river, and securely fasten it to the bank. The men set their well-baited steel traps along the wooded watercourse for mink, coons, and foxes. They give their whole attention to these traps, and in the course of a winter secure many skins. While in the Mississippi country, however, they find other game, and feast upon the hogs of the woods people. To prevent detection, the skin, with the swine-herd's peculiar mark upon it, is stripped off and buried.

When engaged in the precarious occupation of hog-stealing, the shanty-man is careful to keep a goodly number of the skins of wild animals stretched upon the outside walls of his cabin, so that visitors to his boat may be led to imagine that he is an industrious and legitimate trapper, of high-toned feelings, and one "who wouldn't stick a man's hog for no money." If there be a religious meeting in the vicinity of the shanty-boat, the whole family attend it with alacrity, and prove that their *belief* in honest doctrines is a very different thing from their daily *practice* of the same. They join with vigor in the shoutings, and their "amens" drown all others, while their excitable natures, worked upon by the wild eloquence of the backwoods preacher, seem to give evidence of a firm desire to lead Christian lives, and the spectator is often deceived by their apparent earnestness and sincerity. Such ideas are, however, quickly dispelled by a visit to a shanty-boat and glimpse of these people "at home."

The great fleet of shanty-boats does not begin to reach New Orleans until the approach of spring. Once there, they find a market for the skins of the animals trapped during the winter, and these being sold for cash, the trapper disposes of his boat for a nominal sum to someone in need of cheap firewood, and purchasing lower-deck tickets for Cairo or Pittsburgh, at from four to six dollars per head, places his family upon an up-river steamer, and returns with the spring birds to the Ohio River, to rent a small piece of ground for the season, where he can "make a crop of corn," and raise some cabbage and potatoes, upon which to subsist until it be time to repeat his southern migration.

In this descent of the river, many persons, who have clubbed together to meet the expenses of a shanty-boat life for the first time, and who are of a sentimental turn of mind, look upon the voyage as a romantic era in their lives. Visions of basking in the sunlight, feasting, and sleeping, dance before their benighted eyes; for they are all of the low, ignorant class I have described. Professors, teachers, musicians, all drift at times down the river; and one is often startled at finding in the apparently rough crew men who seem worthy of a better fate. To these the river experiences are generally new, and the ribald jokes and low river slang, with the ever-accompanying cheap corn whisky and the nightly riots over cut-throat euchre must be at first a revelation. Hundreds of these low fellows will swear to you that the world owes them a living, and that they mean to have it; that they are gentlemen, and therefore cannot work. They pay a good price for their indolence, as the neglect of their craft and their loose ideas of navigation seldom fail to bring them to grief before they even reach the Mississippi at Cairo. Their heavy, flat-bottomed boat gets impaled upon a snag or the sharp top of a sawyer; and as the luckless craft spins round with the current, a hole is punched through the bottom, the water rushes in and takes possession, driving the inexperienced crew to the little boat usually carried in tow for any emergency.

Into this boat the shanty-men hastily store their guns, whisky, and such property as they can save from the wreck, and making for the shore, hold a council of war.

There, in the swift current, lies the center of their hopes, quickly settling in the deep water, soon to be seen no more. The fact now seems to dawn upon them for the first time that a little seamanship is needed even in descending a river, that with a little care their Noah's Ark might have been kept afloat, and the treacherous "bob sawyer" avoided. . . .

Destitute of means, these children of circumstance resolve never to say die. Their ship has gone down, but their pride is left, and they will not go home till they have "done" the river; and so, repairing to the first landing, they ship in pairs upon freighters descending the stream. Some months later they return to their homes with seedy habiliments but an enlarged experience, sadder but wiser men.

And so the great flood of river life goes on, and out of this annual custom of shanty-boat migration a peculiar phase of American character is developed, a curious set of educated and illiterate nomads, as restless and unprofitable a class of inhabitants as can be found in all the great West.

Steamboatmen *versus* Flatboatmen

. . . On the great rise, down came a swarm of prodigious timber-rafts from the headwaters of the Mississippi, coal-barges from Pittsburgh, little trading-scows from everywhere, and broadhorns from "Posey County," Indiana, freighted with "fruit and furniture"—the usual term for describing it, though in plain English the freight thus aggrandized was hoop-poles and pumpkins. Pilots bore a mortal hatred to these craft, and it was returned with usury. The law required all such helpless traders to keep a light burning, but it was a law that was often broken. All of a sudden, on a murky night, a light would hop up, right under our bows, almost, and an agonized voice, with the backwoods "whang" to it, would wail out:

"Whar'n the ———— you goin' to! Cain't you see nothin', you dash-dashed aig-suckin', sheep-stealin', one-eyed son of a stuffed monkey!"

Then for an instant, as we whistled by, the red glare from our furnaces would reveal the scow and the form of the gesticulating orator, as if under a lightning flash, and in that instant our firemen and deck-hands would send and receive a tempest of missiles and profanity, one of our wheels would walk off with the crashing fragments of a steering-oar, and down the dead blackness would shut again. And that flatboatman would be sure to go to New Orleans and sue our boat, swearing stoutly that he had a light burning all the time, when in truth his gang had the lantern down below to sing and lie and drink and gamble by, and no watch on deck. Once, at night, in one of those forest-bordered crevices (behind an island) which steamboatmen intensely describe with the phrase "as dark as the inside of a cow," we should have eaten up a Posey County family, fruit, furniture, and all, but that they happened to be fiddling down below and we just caught the sound of the music in time to sheer off, doing no serious damage, unfortunately, but coming so near it that we had good hopes for a moment. These people brought up their lantern, then, of course; and as we backed and filled to get away, the precious family stood in the light of it—both sexes and various ages—and cursed us till everything turned blue. Once a coalboatman sent a bullet through our pilot-house when we borrowed a steering-oar of him in a very narrow place.

From *Life on the Mississippi*, by Samuel L. Clemens, pp. 91–92. Copyright, 1874 and 1875, by H. O. Houghton & Company; 1883, 1899, 1903, by Samuel L. Clemens; 1911, by Clara Gabrilowitsch. New York and London: Harper & Brothers, Publishers.

Rip-roaring Raftsmen

Raftsmen were known up and down the river as the most riproaring of all sons of perdition. When a raft tied up and the crew came to town they began with a dozen rounds of forty-rod whisky and ended with a free-for-all battle in which the barkeeper might be driven out of his saloon and the whole place left a shambles. "A raftsman would just as soon stab you as look at you," said Deacon Condit who kept the hotel at Le Claire and had been three times to St. Louis. Most people in the river towns were of the opinion that rafting was but a diversion for the crews; their true calling was battle, murder, and sudden death. It was a fact that when a raft tied up at Guttenberg Bend the widow Fowler hid her silver spoons.

Between violent trips ashore the men danced in their bare feet on the logs and wrestled with each other when there was no heavy work to use their energy. For quiet diversions there were hunting and fishing, which could be carried on as they moved down the river. One fine day below the hills of Hannibal, Olsen Skam caught a channel catfish that weighed a hundred and eighty pounds. Jack Grunow made himself a small howitzer and mounted it at the forward end of a raft. He shot into flocks of geese, where they had settled on the sloughs, killing dozens at a shot. He could wade in and gather a good mess of them and still climb aboard the tail end of the raft as it came along.

Making a Raft

To make a raft, this was the receipe. The logs were placed side by side and lengthwise of the stream. At each end of each log great holes were bored. A limb of birch was laid across, a binding withe of split burr-oak was bent over it as a staple, and pegs were driven into the holes to hold the staple fast; contrary to precept: square pegs into round holes. It was wasteful, extravagantly wasteful; there is no doubt of that. The holes spoiled the ends of the logs, and the birch and burr-oak were increasingly difficult to come by. But what cared we? The resources of the continent, bestowed upon us because of our great deserving—would they not last forever? On with the dance and the hole-boring!

From *Upper Mississippi*, A Wilderness Saga, by Walter Havighurst, pp. 193–194. Copyright, 1937, by Walter Havighurst. *The Rivers of America*, editor, Constance Lindsay Skinner; assistant editor, Elizabeth L. Gilman. New York & Toronto: Farrar & Rinehart, Inc.

From *A-Rafting on the Mississip'*, by Charles Edward Russell, pp. 78–79. Copyright, 1928, by Charles Edward Russell. New York and London: The Century Company.

Each section of logs thus bolted together extended the length of the raft and was called a string. In making up the strings, which were units of the raft, care was had to put side by side logs of different lengths, where that was possible, that there should be few even breaks at the joints. This was necessary to keep the whole thing from tearing apart as it went around the bends. But at best the texture was uncertain, and when a forward corner of a raft hit the bank the birch lashings would crumple up anl the logs start forth like sheep loosed from a pen.

At each end of each string was a great sweep-oar made of a plank bolted to the butt of a young tree. A raft with ten oars at each end was a ten string raft. I have seen rafts of fifteen strings, when they covered more than three acres and looked like a vast plowed field gone afloat.

When the raft had been constructed after this fashion, the boom that had held the logs in Beef Slough or elsewhere was opened and the raft slid out upon the river.

Raftsmen's Biscuits

The unwritten rule of the river was that each man in a rafting crew should take his turn at cooking aboard. Nobody cared much about cooking, it was considered a sort of effeminate job. So the men took turns "getting" the meals in the shanty and the custom was for a man to go on cooking till he "wore out," or until the others got so tired of his biscuits and stews they couldn't stand them any longer. [Then the first man who complained had to take his turn in the galley.]

On one raft that Charley Chase piloted to Cincinnati there were some signally bad cooks among the men. When they started from Warren [Pennsylvania], Otto Barnes was keeping the fires going in the galley, cooking the salt pork and potatoes and green tea which the men consumed in enormous quantities. The men stood Otto's cooking till the raft was below Pittsburgh; then Jem Wilson was pressed into service cooking, "to save our lives," as the crew declared.

After a couple of days Jem was sick and tired of his job. He made up his mind to sicken the men of his cooking and get back on his old job at the oars. So he mixed a batch of biscuits, a favorite with raftsmen, and dumped in enough salt to salt a keg of pork. When the men sat down to their dinner Rant Findlay bit into one of the biscuits and exclaimed, "Great guns, these here dam biscuits is saltier than hell!" It then flashed upon Findlay that in case of a change he would be slated as the next cook, and he hastily added—"but they're certainly fine."

From *Old Time Tales of Warren County*, A Collection of the Picturesque and Romantic Lore of Early Days in Warren County, Pennsylvania, by Arch Bristow, pp. 127–128. Meadville, Pa.: Press of Tribune Publishing Co. 1932.

. . . Through a conversation with that grand old gentleman Charles M. Chase, of Russell.—A.B.

Oil on the Waters

Titusville had no railroad. The roads around it were narrow, almost impassable. The problem was to get the oil to Pittsburgh. Oil Creek, under certain circumstances, provided the only outlet. The crooked, twisting creek, however, was extremely shallow in many places, so shallow that the waters would not float a loaded boat. To overcome this, to make the creek bed passable, the big millpond would be filled to overflowing. When the water was released it raised the creek level from two to three feet, and for a few hours heavily laden boats would pass down the fifteen mile channel to Oil City where the barrels of oil could be transferred to bigger boats and thence floated down the Allegheny River to Pittsburgh.

The opening of the dam gates required a nice sense of timing. The hundreds of loaded boats had to be properly aligned below the dam. They had to be manned with pilots who knew the entire channel, men who could swing the long steering sweeps with precision.

Getting the array of boats ready for their plunging ride was a job that called for a man with a booming voice and a certain amount of patience. The Reverend Dobbs proved to have all the characteristics required. His voice would ring out over the tumult and shouting and when the loaded boats were, in his estimation, properly aligned, he would signal for the gates to be opened.

The waters rushed out, lightly picked up the boats, and gave them a gentle nudge down stream. But, as the volume of water increased, the pressure of the boats in the extreme rear hustled the leading boats cruelly, making the steering efforts of even the strongest and most skilled crews of slight avail.

Sometimes the leading boats would capsize, spilling their barrels of oil. Sometimes boats in the rear, driven by the savage force of the released waters, would rear and buck like unbroken colts, riding up and over smaller and slower-moving boats. Again, this often resulted in the loss of a cargo of precious oil. The fifteen mile stretch of Oil Creek between Titusville and Oil City was a lively area when the oil boats came down, hellbent and often out of control. Often the wooden flotilla met other boats laden high with empty barrels, being dragged up the creek by tired and muddy teams of horses. Collisions were frequent; men were often sadly mangled and dozens of horses were killed or maimed on such occasions.

It cost the oil producer a dollar a barrel to ship his oil in the flatboats. No guarantee was asked or given that the oil would reach the beachhead of the Allegheny River at Oil City.

As the peak of the flood reached Oil City, there would be lifted a great shout: "Pond freshet!" and the citizens all came streaming out of the bars and warehouses to watch the end of the racing fleet of oil boats. Very often

From *The Valley of Oil*, by Harry Botsford, pp. 159–162. Copyright, 1946, by Harry Botsford. New York: Hastings House, Publishers.

some of the fleet would be out of control and would end on a sandbar in the river, leaning drunkenly and spilling part of their contents.

As oil barrels were spilled, the men in the boats, more concerned in salvaging what was left of the cargo, paid scant attention to where the fugitive barrels went. More than one of the early oil field fortunes stemmed from the agility and enterprise of men who made a profitable business of salvaging the spilled barrels of oil and selling them for their own account. In passing, it may be said that this business was not looked upon with disfavor, nor was it considered in the least dishonest.

At Oil City, the barrels were reloaded on larger boats that slowly floated down the broad Allegheny River to Pittsburgh, where the oil was marketed. Several small steamers plied between Pittsburgh and Oil City; they were an essential link in the transportation system that enabled the early oil producers to carry the new mineral to a waiting market.

One job of these steamers was to bring back the crews of the oil barges, and to haul the empty barrels back to Oil City. To the clerks of these steamers was entrusted the responsibility of selling the oil, collecting the money for it, and delivering the funds to the producers who would be waiting on the wharves at Oil City. All business was conducted on an honor basis. No books were kept, no receipts were given or demanded. Yet there is no evidence in the records that any one of the steamboat clerks ever defaulted or betrayed the trust involved, and millions of dollars figured in this business.

A Pleasure Voyage from Steubenville to Pittsburgh

Our boat being fitted up with great care, and all the skill possessed by its worthy builder, we again set out on our contemplated visit, and got along finely for more than twenty miles, running at the rate of from two to three miles an hour, and passing all the Islands, and everything else we come to, without any trouble, or the application of any power save that of steam.

We all felt highly pleased with our situation and prospects, and looked with disdain on the petty keelboats as we passed them, and pitied the poor fellows who had to work their way by pulling and bushwhacking. Soon, however, an accident occurred which convinced us that after all, this is a world of disappointments. We were informed by the engineer that the force pump was broke all to pieces—that it could not be repaired, and that we could go no further without a new pump. This threw a terrible gloom over the prospects, and awakened in our minds all the unpleasant associations

From "First Steubenville Steamboat," letter to the editor, *The Olden Time,* A Monthly Publication Devoted to the Preservation of Documents and Other Authentic Information in Relation to the Early Explorations and the Settlement and Improvement of the Country around the Head of the Ohio, edited by Neville B. Craig, Vol. II (August, 1847), No. 8, pp. 370–373. Pittsburgh: 1848. Cincinnati: 1876.

connected with our former failure. We felt that we could never overcome the mortification of again returning without seeing Pittsburgh; and after a long and sullen consultation, we came to the determination that we would go ahead without a force pump—that as often as our boilers became empty, or so low as to cause danger of explosion, we would lie to shore, open an avenue in their upper sides, introduce a funnel, and by means of buckets, dip the water out of the river and fill them; and as this was considered an expedient which would require considerable labor, it was agreed that all the male passengers should assist in its accomplishment. To this agreement some of the party made serious objections, alleging that their fine clothes would become so much sullied that they could not make a genteel appearance when they should reach Pittsburgh. A large majority were, however, in favor of it, and the influence of public opinion soon compelled the minority to yield. Accordingly we all went to work, and although we felt our employment tedious, tiresome, and disagreeable, still by patience and perseverance we in this way replenished our boilers as often as they needed it, until we worked our way to the city of Pittsburgh. We were well aware before we adopted this expedient that it would be a serious undertaking. Still we were met with many difficulties after we put our plan in operation, which did not before develop themselves.

The matter of reaching water above our heads, we found to be very fatiguing, and the trickling of the drippings down our coat sleeves by no means pleasant or agreeable; besides this, almost every time we landed to fill our boilers, we got fast on bars, and to get off again generally kept us in employment while the water was boiling.

On the evening of the third day we reached what is called the *dead man's ripple,* and after filling our boilers discovered that our coal was nearly exhausted, that it would be folly to attempt to encounter such a current without a better supply of fuel, and upon inquiry learned that there was no coal bank within less than six or seven miles, nor was there any cord wood in the neighborhood to be obtained. This state of things occasioned much dissatisfaction and murmuring on the part of the passengers, and drew upon the head of our worthy Captain many curses for his want of forecast. As night was approaching, however, it was agreed upon as our only expedient that we must lay over until morning, and in the meantime procure fence rails, and prepare for the flues such quantities as would enable us to reach a coal bank some six or seven miles ahead. Accordingly we all took off our coats and went to work and cut and carried rails until a late hour in the night, that we might be able to make an early start in the morning, but being much fatigued we overslept ourselves and were quite late in getting off next day, and when we got under way, to our great disappointment and mortification, we found that with such rails as we had procured for fuel we could not overcome the current we had to encounter. We tried it again and again, but whenever we would reach a certain point in the ripples, like the Irish Captain we found ourselves advancing backwards. This perplexing predicament put us all out of humor and drew upon the head of the Captain a fresh volley of complaints and rebukes, and the pilot, who was altogether dissatisfied, began to threaten to leave the boat. The Captain, who seemed unwilling to bear the blame, alleged that the helmsman was in fault, that he kept too far from shore, and although the Captain was warned of the consequences, he compelled the helmsman to approach so near the beach that before we knew what we were about, a heavy current struck the bow of the boat and swung her with tremendous force on the bar below, leaving us almost on a dry beach.

This seemed to bring our voyage to an almost insupportable crisis. All was uproar and confusion. Some declared they would return home, while others said they would walk to Pittsburgh. The pilot and Captain got into a real jangle, while some of the passengers and crew began to hunt up their baggage, and all gave indications of abandoning the boat. At this critical and most discouraging juncture, our worthy old friend, who had quieted our disturbances on our first voyage, again interfered, and by his kind and conciliatory demeanor, and great influence, soon reconciled all parties, and effected an agreement: that the captain should procure a team, and have brought from the nearest coal bank a load of coal, and that the passengers and crew should in the meantime loosen the boat, and set her afloat again.

With this understanding we all went to work in good earnest, for by this time our fine clothes had become so much sullied that no one any longer thought it of any importance to keep his work at arm's length, and about two o'clock P.M. we succeeded in getting our boat off the bar, and as good luck would have it, about the same time our good Captain hove in sight with his load of coal.

Our prospects, which looked dark indeed in the morning, now began to brighten up, and we were all cheerful and happy in view of the prospect of again successfully prosecuting our journey. We had raised the steam pretty high, so that no time should be lost after we should get our coal aboard, and from appearances we had every reason to believe that we should be under way again in a few minutes; but unfortunately at the very point of time when our Captain had his teamster back his wagon with endgate off to the brink of a precipice immediately above the boat, someone to amuse himself, and probably for the purpose of startling his next neighbor, let a puff of steam escape from the safety valve, which frightened the poor horses, so that they snorted and ran like wild animals, scattering our coal over a ten-acre cornfield.

This threw us again into great commotion. All was noise and bustle, and a terrible hue and cry raised against "the fool" who had done the mischief. The Captain, who was of rather evenly temper, seemed to be provoked past all endurance, and when he cast his eyes over his scattered coal, declared if he could find out who had frightened the horses, he would skin him, for he had again and again forbidden anyone to meddle with that safety valve. Fortunately for the aggressor, we were never able to find out who he was.

As soon as this flurry was over, we all turned out and gathered up as much coal as took us over the ripple, and then with the aid of our rails got up to the coal bank, where we received a fresh supply.

Nothing further of much importance occurred on our way up. We had all become so well disciplined to our work, and the absolute necessity of strict attention to it that we began to move on without much flinching or murmuring. We took our time, and if anything occurred on shore, or elsewhere, that was interesting or amusing, we would stop to enjoy it. On one occasion, a wounded deer was discovered swimming the river some half mile below, when we immediately landed, and sent out a file of men on the Jolly Boat to try to capture it. The poor animal was soon overtaken, and after a terrible battle, was dragged into the boat, to all appearance dead. By this time, they were, perhaps, more than a mile below us, and found that the hardest part of the adventure was to row up again. Being elated, however, with victory, and anxious to show their booty, they rowed hard, and soon found themselves within a short distance of us. We were all paraded on deck, anxious to see the captured deer, but, to the great surprise of all, just when they were about to board us, the poor animal, having come to life again, sprung out of the boat and swam with apparently more vigor and speed than when it was first pursued, and they again found themselves some half mile down the river before they overtook it.

Thus far I have said nothing about our fare, but an effort on the part of the cook to prepare a piece of this venison for dinner brings that part of the narrative forcibly up to my recollection. Our boat had been furnished with a cooking stove, of the utility of which our cook seemed to have but little conception. At that early day but few cooking stoves were in use, and like steamboats, those that were in use were, at best, of but poor construction, and, as to ours, an error had been committed in setting it up, which drew many curses on the poor cook, for everything which came to the table was so perfumed with gas and smoke that it was with difficulty we could swallow enough of it to save us from starvation. The true cause of this difficulty remained unexplained until after we had arrived at Pittsburgh— the cook having to bear the blame and the passengers the smoke and gas. Immediately on our arrival at Pittsburgh, the builder (who resided there) was sent for, when cook and all went to work abusing him for constructing and imposing on the public with such a stove; when, almost convulsed with laughter, he explained the whole difficulty, pointing out to us a certain plate perforated with holes, which was intended to let the steam only bear upon the victuals, but which had been so misplaced as to let all the smoke and gas (instead of the steam) penetrate and perfume everything we had eaten for the then last five days. And thus ended our pleasure voyage, for the boat was found to be so much injured on her passage up that it required some eight or ten days to repair her before she could return, and the passengers, all being anxious to get back again, had to find their way home in whatever way best suited their convenience.

Odyssey of Steamboat Machinery

. . . Steamboats wore out or were blown up or snagged or burned or something, but steamboat machinery came near to being immortal. A new steamboat seldom had new machinery; as a rule, the engines were supplied from some predecessor gone halt. The engines of the *Ida Fulton* were put into the rafter *Glenmont* and, when she wore out, into the *North Star*. Away down on the Arkansas River the steamboat *Guidon* was reported to have sunk. The watchful Captain Van Sant snapped somebody down there, bought the engines, put them into the *D. A. McDonald*, then into the *Silver Wave*, then into the *Vernie Mac*. So late as 1915 there was a towboat owned at Lyons, Iowa, that had engines old enough to be retired on a pension. They were originally constructed for the *G. B. Knapp*, built about 1866. When the *Knapp* passed out they were transferred to the rafter *Cleon*. When she was no more they went to the rafter *Jennie Hayes*, then to the pile-driver *Good Luck*, next landing upon the *Arthur S.*, and thence to be transferred to something else belike after these chronicles shall be but dust.

I think the sage old grandsires of the billiard saloon were fondest of recounting the odyssey of the engines of the packet *Joe Daviess*, once the proud property of the ubiquitous Harris family, who built her. When they sold her, she ran three trips and sank. The engines were dug up and placed in the first *Reindeer*. She made three trips and sank. Then the engines were again resurrected and put into a second *Reindeer*. She made four trips and sank. Out of the wreck emerged the engines triumphant and went into a new boat called the *Colonel Clay*. She made two trips and sank. Their next adventuring was in the new steamer *Monroe*. She ran all that season, and the best judges were satisfied that the hoodoo was broken. The next season she burned. The engines were now taken out and placed in a mill at Elizabethtown, Pennsylvania, with a serene confidence that short of earthquake the mill could not sink, anyway. But it could burn, and did so the next year. The subsequent career of these machines is so far unrecorded. It would seem likely to reward the inquiring mind.

But none of these boiler biographies contains anything equaling the adventures of the mechanical remains of the old towboat *Otter*.

About 1855 there arrived at New York two Frenchmen that, not being impressed with the beauties of a dictatorship, had fallen foul of Napoleon III. After his pleasing habit, this eccentric duce had hunted them out of France and they had gone to join Victor Hugo in his exile in the Island of Jersey. It seems they found themselves inadjustable to premature burial, so they made their way via England to America. They had evidently informed themselves of the needs of the growing West whither they were steering, for they brought along with them a steam boiler and an engine. This slightly

From *A-Rafting on the Mississip'*, by Charles Edward Russell, pp. 309–312. Copyright, 1928, by Charles Edward Russell. New York and London: The Century Co.

unusual baggage they transported to Henderson, Minnesota, where they set up a grist-mill and made money.

A few years later they decided to go into the steamboat business and built the towboat *Otter*, into which they put the boiler and engine with which they had landed, taking them out of the grist-mill. For years this craft operated prosperously on the Minnesota and then was sold to Captain Jacob Hindermann, who used her in making up rafts at the rafting works at West Newton. At the close of navigation in 1879, Captain Hindermann put his boat into winter quarters, and when the ice went out in the spring it settled the case of the *Otter*, which was torn to pieces and sank.

The famous boiler went to the bottom of the river, where it lay in the mud undisturbed and forgotten for thirty-six years. Then Captain Hindermann had it fished up and presented it to the Junior Pioneer Society of New Ulm, Minnesota. On Sunday, August 26, 1926, the gift was received with appropriate ceremony and a grand parade. The old boiler was carried on a decorated wagon drawn by six gaily caparisoned horses. Upon it, as Tiberius bestrode his horse in an Appian Way triumph, rode Captain Hindermann himself, dressed in what the press described as "a marine suit," whatever that may be, with a white cap having a blue front inscribed in gold letters with "Captain." Before him marched Hoffmeister's justly celebrated Silver Cornet Band, discoursing harmony—"as that famous band only is capable of entertaining," remarks the local newspaper.

Thus in solemn state the procession marched through the streets to the public park. There were speeches and songs and the band played and a pleasant afternoon was had by all. So we are assured. Then the old boiler was put in place as a permanent feature of the park landscape. New Ulm is probably alone among cities in the adoption of this style of adorning. It is said to be a German place. Never tell me. Nothing could be more thoroughly American than this performance.

Torch Baskets

The advent of the electric searchlight has driven from the river one of the most picturesque of all the accessories to such scenes as we boys looked down upon, night after night, during the busy times of 1854 and 1855, before I myself became part and parcel of it all. The torch, by the light of which the work went on by night, was within an iron basket, about a foot in diameter and eighteen inches deep, swung loosely between the prongs of a forked iron bar or standard, which could be set in holes in the forward deck, leaning far out over the water, so as to allow live coals from the burning wood to fall into the river and not upon deck.

From *Old Times on the Upper Mississippi*, The Recollections of a Steamboat Pilot from 1854 to 1863, by George Byron Merrick, pp. 34–35. Copyright, 1909, by George Byron Merrick. Cleveland, Ohio. Reprinted by permission of The Arthur H. Clark Co.

When a landing was to be made at a woodyard or a town, the watchman filled one or perhaps two of these torch baskets with split "lightwood" or "fatwood"—Southern pine full of resinous sap, which would burn fiercely, making a bright light, illuminating the deck of the boat and the levee for hundreds of feet around. As the boat neared the landing, the pine splinters were lighted at the furnace door, the torch being carried to place and firmly fixed in its socket. Then came out the attending demon who fed the burning, smoking "jack" with more pine fatwood and from time to time with a ladle of pulverized rosin. The rosin would flare up with a fierce flame, followed by thick clouds of black smoke, the melted tar falling in drops upon the water, to float away, burning and smoking until consumed. This addition to the other sights and sounds served more than any other thing to give this night work a wild and weird setting. We boys decided, on many a night, that we would "go on the river" and feed powdered rosin and pine kindlings to torches all night long, as the coal-black and greasy but greatly envied white lamp-boy did, night after night, in front of our attic windows on the levee at Prescott. The cleaner and brighter but very commonplace electric light has driven the torch from the river; and if one is to be found at all in these degenerate days, it will be as a curiosity in some historical museum.

Steamboat Whistles and Bells

Every packet took pride in her whistle and bell. Some of the large bells weighed as much as eight hundred pounds, and great skill went into their workmanship. They were elaborately decorated and were masterpieces of the art of bell founding. This art flourished and attained a high standard, reaching its climax about 1845.

So that the bells would have a clear musical tone, a generous amount of silver was used in casting them. For this purpose silver dollars were melted, as bulk silver was not in use at this time. It was not unusual for a captain, when he desired a bell for his boat, to contribute personally five hundred silver dollars; and, in his enjoyment of the deep mellow tone this amount of silver would insure, he would consider the money well spent.

When a boat's business in port was nearly finished, the bell sounded slowly quite a number of strokes as a notice to all parties concerned that the boat was about to take her departure. Three strokes of the bell was a signal to the crew on watch to stand by their posts; the engineer replied by blowing three blasts on a small whistle to indicate that everything in his department was in order and that he was ready to leave.

About the time that bell founding reached its height the steam whistle came into use. Which boat was the first to carry a steam whistle is uncertain, but it is said that the packet *Revenue* has a right to this distinction.

From *Steamboatin' Days*, Folk Songs of the River Packet Era, by Mary Wheeler, pp. 3–5. Copyright, 1944, by Louisiana State University Press. Baton Rouge, Louisiana.

The *Revenue* was built at Pittsburgh by Captain William H. Fulton. Her first trade was in the Upper Ohio.[1] There is a story that Captain Fulton first realized the possibilities of a steam whistle for river boats when he heard a factory whistle blown by steam while he was visiting in the city of Philadelphia about a hundred years ago.

The steam whistle soon took over some of the duties of communication that had previously been associated with the bell. The great lines evolved their own call, or blast, that was used by all of their boats. This call was sounded in making a landing, but in passing another boat in the channel a universal unchanging code developed. The right of way belonged always to the descending boat, but the ascending craft was the first to announce the direction, either to the right or left, that she deemed best to take in passing. If this was satisfactory to the descending boat, the signal was repeated to signify consent. However, if the descending pilot thought this course unwise, three or more short blasts were given. After this message was acknowledged by a repetition, the descending pilot stated the direction he preferred. Consent of the other boat was again expressed by a repeating of the signal last heard. One whistle blast indicated that the right-hand direction was desired, two blasts the left.

It used to be a point of pride with people who knew and loved the language of the river to be able to recognize the approach of an important boat by the sound of her whistle or bell. Each whistle possessed a tone that could be identified, in addition to its own particular blast, and every great bell had its own individual quality.

From Trumpet to Bells

. . . There was a decided disposition in the early days of the river navigation to follow too closely the habit of the sea, and to pretend that the Mississippi was an interior ocean. The captains, for instance, having been accustomed when at sea to issue their orders through a trumpet, necessary there, to make them heard in the roar of the waves and the storm, still insisted upon using the trumpet upon the quiet waters of the Mississippi, and shouted stentoriously through the trumpet at their mates but a few feet distant, with all the worst nautical oaths and expressions. It was not until years afterwards that the simple process of giving orders by means of bells was adopted.

---

[1] The Ohio above Louisville, Kentucky, is known as the Upper Ohio; the Lower Ohio is from Louisville to Cairo, Illinois.—M.W.

From *Fifty Years on the Mississippi;* or, Gould's History of River Navigation, by E. W. Gould, p. 208. Entered . . . 1889, by E. W. Gould. . . . St. Louis: Nixon Jones Printing Co., Columbus, Ohio: Long's College Book Co. 1951.

Too Many Bells

There were a few captains on the river who seemed to have a passion for ringing bells. George B. Merrick tells of a pilot who had this bell-ringing habit. From the pilot house he would keep the engineer and his second over-busy executing his orders given in this way. On one trip the engineer got so far behind with these orders that after the steamboat had tied up to the bank at a landing it took him "seven hours and a half" to catch up with his bells.

The "Wheeling"

A curious reminder of the early rivalry between Pittsburgh and Wheeling remains. This rivalry developed into an antagonism which often had pronounced expression among boatmen of the two cities, and sometimes led to personal encounters when they mingled at popular gathering places. It is related that when the fine passenger packet, *Valley Forge,* was completed at Pittsburgh in 1842, it made a trial run to Wheeling. As an innovation, the staterooms and compartments on the boat were given the names of different cities and towns along the Ohio.

When the boat arrived at the Wheeling wharf a delegation of men of the city came on board to inspect the new craft. They were greatly pleased with the idea of naming the compartments for places, and asked the captain to be shown the one named for their city. They were escorted to the aft end of the boat and shown the little room usually having on its door the designation, "Men." Instead, in this case, across its door in gold letters was the name, "Wheeling." For a moment the visitors were stunned. Then the enormity of the insult to their city was borne in on them. Their civic pride was outraged, and with wild whoops they began ripping the offending door from its hinges.

The crew was called and the visitors were unceremoniously dumped on the wharf, whence they disappeared uptown where they soon rounded up a strong body of reinforcements. The party rushed to the waterfront, vowing they would burn the *Valley Forge.* But the lines had been cast off and the boat was safe in mid-stream on their arrival. The offending word was removed before the boat again ventured to return to the place, but to this day boatmen on the local rivers refer to the men's room as the "Wheeling."

From *Old Man River,* Upper Mississippi River Steamboating Days Stories, Tales of the Old Time Steamboats and Steamboatmen, by Charles E. Brown, p. 9. Madison,. Wisconsin: Wisconsin Folklore Society. 1940.

From *Monongahela,* The River and Its Region, by Richard T. Wiley, pp. 234–235. Copyright, 1937, by Richard T. Wiley. Butler, Pennsylvania: The Ziegler Company.

Steamboat Decoration

Steamboating had a romance and glamor never attained in any other kind of transportation. The large sidewheel passenger steamboat was beautiful. Her lines, with a graceful sheer, made her set on the water like a swan; the ornamental railings were filigree of woodwork; her smokestacks towered high above the water line and their tops were cut to represent plumes or fern leaves. From the hull to the hurricane deck the boat was painted a glistening white, with the tops of the wheelhouses a sky blue, as was the breeching around the smokestacks. The pilothouse with its ornamental crown added to the appearance of the entire structure. The dome of the pilothouse matched in color the wheelhouse. A red line near the top of the hull extended from the stem to the stern, and the skylights or ventilators over the main salon were of stained glass. The main cabin, which extended nearly the full length of the boat, was done in white and gold; the walnut or rosewood of the panels at the stateroom doors provided an agreeable contrast.

There was usually a small landscape over the stateroom doors. (It is not generally known that two of our best landscape artists, Carl Brenner and Harvey Joiner, of Louisville, got their start by doing such paintings.) Before electric lights were generally used, many boats had lard-oil lamps in crystal chandeliers. The bridal suites and the ladies' cabins were models of decoration; French plate mirrors in hand-carved and gilded frames adorned them; marble-topped tables, deeply velveted upholstered chairs and settees were provided; and a piano of the best make completed the furnishings.

The name of the boat painted on the sides of the wheelhouses was a triumph of the sign painter's art; it was frequently done in gold leaf. Sometimes immediately above the name of the boat was painted a landscape or figure. The boat's colors were beautiful. Flying from the forward flagpole, called the jackstaff, was a long flag outlined in red, white, and blue, with the name of the boat in red on white ground. About halfway up on the jackstaff was an ornament, called the night-hawk. This enabled the pilot to steer the boat by various landmarks either day or night, so that an imaginary line, drawn from the forward landmark through the night-hawk, the pilot-house, and the verge-staff to landmarks on the shore astern enabled him to keep the boat on its course day or night. Inboard on each wheelhouse was a flagstaff which flew burgees bearing the names of the cities between which the boat operated. On the flagstaff at the rear of the texas the union jack was flown and on the rear flagstaff, called the verge-staff, flew the Stars and Stripes.

It was customary for the city or the person for whom the boat was named to present a complete set of colors to the vessel. This took place upon her

From "Steamboats at Louisville and on the Ohio and Mississippi Rivers," by Arthur E. Hopkins, *The Filson Club History Quarterly*, Vol. 17 (July, 1943), No. 3, pp. 146–148. Louisville, Kentucky: The Filson Club.

first call to her home port, when a large number of citizens came aboard, bands played, speeches were made, and the public was invited to participate in the dinner aboard the boat.

Ante-bellum Riverboat Art

As a result of the predilection of owners and captains of steamboats preceding the Civil War for figureheads on their vessels, quite a substantial business in carving such adornments was built up in Cincinnati in conjunction with the fabrication of the once-familiar, but now almost obsolete, Indian cigar signs.

Some expert workmen were engaged in this work, and when their products, gilded and painted to suit the fancies of the steamboatmen, were put into place on the extreme bows of the steamers, they were considered quite an adornment. The figures represented various objects, ranging from roosters, dogs, eagles, to enormous images of Liberty and Pocahontas.

One captain, who ran on the Red River in Indian days, adopted a novel method of preventing any possible attack upon his vessel by the savages. He had made for his boat the figure of a boa constrictor, through the coils of which, wrapped about the bow, there ran a pliable steam pipe, which was attached to one of the boilers. The great head of the serpent, mouth open, forked tongue out and fangs showing, projected four feet below the bow. Going up the river, the steam would be turned into the contraption, and it would spurt out of the mouth of the wooden serpent, and, at the same time, give a fair imitation of hissing. Any bunch of hostile Kiowas or Comanches, gathered on the bank, always turned tail and fled helter-skelter when they took one look at the monstrous serpent. They called it heap bad medicine.

Then in that era also, it was customary to have pictures painted on the big paddle boxes, if the boat was a sidewheeler. Artists and near-artists had their fling at this sort of work. Some of the creations were praiseworthy, but the most of them were just a shade removed from the monstrosities of delirium tremens. One favorite picture was that of a sunburst. This gave to the artist the opportunity to utilize an abundance of florid colors, and some of the sunbursts were of very striking design and finish. The very early *Ben Franklins* had on their boxes pictures of the great philosopher, editor and statesman flying a kite, with the lightning striking a key attached to its tail. Other steamers had on their paddle boxes the pictures of pretty girls of gigantic size; others had pastoral and battle scenes. One had the picture of an elderly woman knitting socks; and, in fact, there was scarcely a sidewheel vessel that did not have adornments of the foregoing types on their boxes. However, the advent of the sternwheeler put a crimp in that peculiar

From *Thrills of the Historic Ohio River.* by Frank Y. Grayson, p. 196. Cincinnati: Cincinnati Times Star. [No date.]

industry, and even the sidewheelers discarded the practice in favor of plain lettering of the name of the steamer and the line to which it belonged. Also, the panels in the forward part of the cabin lent themselves to the painting of scenes of battle, harvesting, city life, and the like. Some of them were well executed, but the majority of the pictures were mere daubs, or a similar type to those itinerant "artists" used to paint on saloon mirrors. The more color in them, the better the captain liked them. He never failed to maneuver a favored passenger into such a position as to get for himself an eyeful of the pictures.

Trapped in the Boiler

A popular horror story on the river is the one about the fireman who was sealed up in the boilers by mistake after the periodic cleanout. This unfortunate person is supposed to have been trapped inside while the engineer pumped up the boilers, the fires were lit, steam was made, and the fireman was only missed after the boat had made a hasty departure and was bowling up the river. [Of this incident John Wallace, in *The Practical Engineer,* 1853] says: "As to the particulars, I never have heard much, as it was a rather delicate matter to say much about." However, of one man who did get shut in a boiler, Wallace gives us these details: "He was at the front end, and one of the gauge cocks happening to be out, he whistled through the gauge cock hole, and was heard by someone on the boat, who immediately gave the alarm and the man-plate was taken off and he came out. His name was John Scott, engine builder, Pittsburgh."

A Very Small Steamboat

The *Michigan,* a very small steamboat, made the first arrival at Des Moines during the season of 1856, coming in on April 16th with freight and passengers. Captain J. W. Johnson was a very clever gentleman, but a little sensitive about the size of his boat. It is reported that at Keosauqua, where he landed to leave some freight, he was visited by the villagers and took great pride in showing them his craft. Among them was a well known wag, who asked, with a look of deep concern:

From *The Monongahela,* by Richard Bissell, p. 203. Copyright, 1949, 1952, by Richard Pike Bissell. *The Rivers of America,* edited by Carl Carmer. New York and Toronto: Rinehart & Co., Inc.

From "History of Steamboating on the Des Moines River, from 1837 to 1862," by Tacitus Hussey, *Annals of Iowa,* Vol. IV (April, 1900), No. 5, 3d Series, pp. 361–362. Des Moines: Published by the Historical Department of Iowa.

"Captain Johnson, how long is your boat going to lie here?"

"About two hours," the captain replied.

"Well, now look here," said the sober-faced man, "my wife has never seen a steamboat, and she is sick in bed. Now can't you let me put your boat on my wagon, take it up to my house and show it to her? I promise to take good care of it and will be back with it in two hours."

When the Passengers Wooded Up

The enormous steamboats of the Ohio and the Mississippi require such vast supplies of fuel for their long journeys, some of which extend to weeks, that in early spring, upon the opening of the navigation, detachments of men are set on shore at convenient places, whose duty it is to cut wood, pile it up on shore, and carry it on board the boat that has engaged their services. These men, a rough and roisterous but not vicious race, lead here wretched lives, consumed by low fevers and devoured by mosquitoes, but receive enormous wages. The boats necessarily stop often to wood-up, as the term is, and tie up to such a wooding place. The passengers avail themselves of the opportunity to take a stroll on shore, to examine the snakes and vipers which are apt to accumulate beneath the huge woodpile, and to take a drink; hence, unfortunately, *to wood* has in the West become a popular euphemistic term for "to take a dram." A distinguished British nobleman, recently connected with royalty, was hence not a little puzzled when a Western member of Congress, in a moment of hilarity, invited him to leave the Minister's house, where they met at a large party, for the purpose of "wooding up."

The Revolving Woodyard

Does any one remember the *Caravan?* She was what would now be considered a slow boat; *then* [1827] she was regularly advertised as the "fast

From *Americanisms; The English of the New World*, by M. Schele De Vere, pp. 349–350. Entered . . . 1871, by Charles Scribner & Co. . . . New York. 1872.

Originally entitled "A Bully Boat and a Brag Captain."
By Sol Smith. From *Big Bear's Adventures and Travels*, Containing the Whole of the Big Bear of Arkansaw and Stray Subjects, Illustrative of Characters and Incidents in the South and Southwest, in a Series of Sixty-Eight Southern and Southwestern Sketches, including the Great Stories of "Swallowing an Oyster Alive," "Jones' Fight," "The Kalamazoo Hunt," "Purchasing a Live Lobster," "A Game at Seven Up," Etc., Etc., pp. 106–112. Entered . . . 1858, by T. B. Peterson. Philadelphia: T. B. Peterson and Brothers.
One of the oldest and assuredly one of the best correspondents the *Spirit of the Times* ever boasted of is the writer of the story which follows. "Old Sol," as he is familiarly termed, has been, in the course of his eventful life, "every thing by turns,"

running," etc. Her regular trips from New Orleans to Natchez were usually made in from six to eight days; a trip made by her in five days was considered remarkable. A voyage from New Orleans to Vicksburg and back, including stoppages, generally entitled the officers and crew to a month's wages. Whether the *Caravan* ever achieved the feat of a voyage to the Falls (Louisville), I have never learned; if she did, she must have "had a *time* of it."

It was my fate to take passage in this boat. The Captain was a good-natured, easy-going man, careful of the comfort of his passengers, and exceedingly fond of the *game of brag*.[1] We had been out a little more than five days, and we were in hopes of seeing the bluffs of Natchez on the next day. Our wood was getting low, and night coming on. The pilot on duty *above* (the other pilot held three aces at the time, and was just calling out the Captain, who "went it strong" on three kings) sent down word that the mate had reported the stock of wood reduced to half a cord. The worthy Captain excused himself to the pilot whose watch was *below,* and the two passengers who made up the party, and hurried to the deck, where he soon discovered, by the landmarks, that we were about half a mile from a wood-yard, which he said was situated "right round yonder point." "But," muttered the Captain, "I don't much like to take wood of the yellow-faced old scoundrel who owns it—he always charges a quarter of a dollar more than anyone else; however, there's no other chance." The boat was pushed to her utmost, and, in a little less than an hour, when our fuel was about giving out, we made the point, and our cables were out and fastened to trees, alongside of a good-sized wood-pile.

"Hollo, Colonel! how d'ye sell your wood *this* time?"

A yellow-faced old gentleman, with a two weeks' beard, strings over his shoulders holding up to his armpits a pair of copperas-colored linsey-woolsey pants, the legs of which reached a very little below the knee; shoes without stockings; a faded, broad-brimmed hat, which had once been black, and a pipe in his mouth—casting a glance at the empty guards of our boat, and uttering a grunt as he rose from fastening our "spring line," answered,

"Why, Capting, we must charge you *three and a quarter* THIS *time.*"

"The d——l!" replied the Captain (Captains did swear a little in those days), "what's the odd *quarter* for, I should like to know? You only charged me *three* as I went down."

"Why, Capting," drawled out the wood merchant, with a sort of leer on

---

but unlike many a "Jack of all trades" he is really "good at anything." As editor, manager, preacher, or lawyer, he has not only commanded success but deserved it. For many years he has been associated with Mr. [Noah] Ludlow in the management of the Mobile, New Orleans, and St. Louis theaters. Within a few weeks he has been admitted in practice as an attorney and counsellor at law "in all the Courts of the state of Missouri." We will only add that we wish him in *brief* lots of practice.— William T. Porter

---

[1] It must be recollected that the incidents here related took place seventeen years ago. Within the last ten years, although I have traveled on hundreds of boats, I have not seen an officer of a boat play a card.—S.S.

his yellow countenance, which clearly indicated that his wood was as good as sold, "wood's riz since you went down two weeks ago; besides, you are awar' that you very seldom stop going *down*; when you're going *up*, you're sometimes obleeged to give me a call, becaze the current's aginst you, and there's no other woodyard for nine miles ahead; and if you happen to be nearly out of fooel, why—"

"Well, well," interrupted the Captain, "we'll take a few cords, under the circumstances"—and he returned to his game of brag.

In about half an hour we felt the *Caravan* commence paddling again. Supper was over, and I retired to my upper berth, situated alongside and overlooking the brag table, where the Captain was deeply engaged, having now the *other* pilot as his principal opponent. We jogged on quietly—and seemed to be going at a good rate.

"How does that wood burn?" inquired the Captain of the mate, who was looking on at the game.

" 'Tisn't of much account, I reckon," answered the mate—"it's cotton-wood, and most of it green at that."

"Well, Thompson (three aces, again, stranger—I'll take that X and the small change, if you please—it's your deal)—Thompson, I say, we'd better take three or four cords at the next woodyard—it can't be more than six miles from here (two aces and a bragger, with the age! hand over those V's)."

The game went on and the paddles kept moving. At 11 o'clock it was reported to the Captain that we were nearing the woodyard, the light being distinctly seen by the pilot on duty.

"Head her in shore, then, and take in six cords, if it's good—see to it, Thompson, I can't very well leave the game now—it's getting right warm! This pilot's beating us all to smash."

The wooding completed, we paddled on again. The Captain seemed somewhat vexed when the mate informed him that the price was the same as at the last woodyard—*three and a quarter*; but soon again became interested in the game.

From my upper berth (there were no staterooms *then*) I could observe the movements of the players. All the contention appeared to be between the Captain and the pilots (the latter personages took it turn and turn about, steering and playing brag), *one* of them almost invariably winning, while the two passengers merely went through the ceremony of dealing, cutting, and paying up their *anties*. They were anxious to *learn the game*—and they *did* learn it. Once in a while, indeed, seeing they had two aces and a bragger, they would venture a bet of five or ten dollars, but they were always compelled to back out before the tremendous bragging of the Captain *or* pilot—or if they *did* venture to "call out" on "two bullits and a bragger," they had the mortification to find one of the officers had the same kind of a hand and were *more venerable!* Still with all these disadvantages, they continued playing—they wanted to learn the game.

At 2 o'clock the Captain asked the mate how we were getting on.

"Oh, pretty glibly, sir," replied the mate, "we can scarcely tell what headway we *are* making, for we are obliged to keep the middle of the river, and there is the shadow of a fog rising. This wood seems rather better than that we took in at old yellow-face's, but we're nearly out again, and must be looking out for more. I saw a light just ahead on the right—shall we hail?"

"Yes, yes," replied the Captain, "ring the bell and ask 'em what's the price of wood up here?—I've got you again; here's double kings."

I heard the bell and the pilot's hail: "What's *your* price for wood?"

A youthful voice on the shore answered: "Three *and* a quarter!"

"D——n it!" ejaculated the Captain, who had just lost the price of two cords to the pilot—the strangers suffering *some* at the same time. "Three and a quarter again! Are we *never* to get to a cheaper country?—Deal, sir, if you please—better luck next time." The other pilot's voice was again heard on deck—

"How much *have* you?"

"Only about ten cords, sir," was the reply of the youthful salesman.

The Captain here told Thompson to take six cords, which would last till daylight—and again turned his attention to the game.

The pilots here changed places. *When did they sleep?*

Wood taken in, the *Caravan* again took her place in the middle of the stream, paddling on as usual.

Day at length dawned. The brag party broke up, and settlements were being made, during which operation the Captain's bragging propensities were exercised in cracking up the speed of his boat, which, by his reckoning, must have made at least sixty miles, and *would* have made many more if he could have procured good wood. It appears the two passengers, in their first lesson, had incidentally lost one hundred and twenty dollars. The Captain, as he rose to see about taking in some *good* wood, which he felt sure of obtaining, now he had got above the level country, winked at his opponent, the pilot, with whom he had been on very bad terms during the progress of the game, and said, in an undertone—"Forty apiece for you and I and James [the other pilot] is not bad for one night."

I had risen, and went out with the Captain, to enjoy a view of the bluffs. There was just fog enough to prevent the vision taking in more than sixty yards—so I was disappointed in *my* expectation. We were nearing the shore for the purpose of looking for wood, the banks being invisible from the middle of the river.

"There it is!" exclaimed the Captain. "Stop here!"

Ding-ding-ding! went the big bell, and the Captain hailed:

"Hollo! the woodyard!"

"Hollo yourself!" answered a squeaking female voice, which came from a woman with a petticoat over her shoulders in place of a shawl.

"What's the price of wood?"

"I think you ought to know the price by this time," answered the old lady in the petticoat. "It's three and a qua-a-rter! And now you know it."

"Three and the d——l!" broke in the Captain. "What, have you raised on *your* wood too! I'll give you *three* and not a cent more."

"Well," replied the petticoat, "here comes the old man—*he'll* talk to you."

And, sure enough, out crept from the cottage the veritable faded hat, copperas-colored pants, yellow countenance and two weeks' beard we had seen the night before, and the same voice we had heard regulating the price of cottonwood squeaked out the following sentence, accompanied by the same leer of the same yellow countenance:

"Why, darn it all, Capting, there is but three or four cords left, and *since it's you*, I don't care if I *do* let you have it for *three—as you're a good customer!*"

After a quick glance at the landmarks around, the Captain bolted and turned in to take some rest.

The fact became apparent—the reader will probably have discovered it some time since—that *we had been wooding all night at the same wood-yard!*

Wooding Subterfuges of Crow Creek Indians

. . . The Agency Indians, as they gradually began to absorb the idea of doing a little manual labor, found out that there was money to be made by cutting wood for the boats, and at a few widely separated points they commenced doing so occasionally. This was especially the case at Crow Creek, where the ravines above the Agency were full of red cedar and cottonwood timber. The cedar would burn readily even when full of sap, and the steamboat men promptly took all of it that the Indians could pile on the river bank. But when they saw only green cottonwood corded up, they would pass it by. The dusky woodsmen soon learned that cedar was what the boats wanted, and when they had only cottonwood to offer they undertook a simple deception to aid in disposing of it. Stacking the timber with the freshly hewn ends toward the landing, they would smear these ends with vermilion face paint to make it resemble cedar, trusting that when a boat had actually stopped at the bank, she would take it away, rather than waste more time.

Another trick devised by these wily savages in the interest of trade owed its origin to the changeable nature of the Missouri's channel, which would sometimes shift across the river from the base of the bluffs where their woodpiles lay, leaving these inaccessible to boats. Not comprehending that the boatmen could have any means of knowing exactly where the channel lay, the Indians, when they saw a steamer approaching, would wade out through the shallow water in front of their wood-piles and there sit down.

From *The Conquest of the Missouri*, Being the Story of the Life and Exploits of Captain Grant Marsh, by Joseph Mills Hanson, pp. 119–120. Copyright, 1909 and 1937, by A. C. McClurg & Company; 1946, by Rinehart & Company, Inc. New York and Toronto. Murray Hill Books, Inc.

Leaving only their heads above the surface, they would beckon to the pilot to come in, thinking that he would suppose them to be standing to their necks in water deep enough to carry his boat. Captain [Grant] Marsh, soon becoming familiar with these subterfuges of the red men, always kept his wits on the alert when approaching Crow Creek.

A Vicious Circle

[In the early days] the size of a boat was determined by the number of boilers she carried, and in describing any vessel a riverman would term her "a two-boiler boat," or "four-boiler boat," without reference to her length or breadth of beam. The reason for this was that every vessel was obliged to carry as many boilers as could be crowded upon her in order to make her go at all. The waste of steam and fuel was enormous, for the practice of exhausting in the chimneys had not yet been thought of nor had that of heating the water before it went to the boilers. The big steamer *Eclipse,* Captain Sturgeon, built in the '50's, had a battery of fifteen boilers, eight large and seven small, and to keep them heated required wood by the car load. Captain Marsh tells a story, once current along the river, of the old *Nebraska,* a boat of the same class as the *Eclipse.* It is to the effect that once on a trip to New Orleans she landed at a yard and took on one hundred cords of wood. As there were no snubbing posts at the landing to tie to during the progress of the work, Captain Jolly held her up to the bank by the outside wheel, which made it necessary to keep the engines going. When the fuel was loaded and the boat ready to start, it was discovered that all the wood taken aboard had been used up in holding her to the bank!

"King of the River"

In the early years of the steamboat traffic each boat could make only one trip a season, and each journeyed only to its own company's upriver post. The annual departure from St. Louis was a momentous and gala event. There were often a hundred or more passengers bound for the Indian country on various errands. Missionaries, generals, traders, clerks, engagés, perhaps a painter and a scientist or two; delegations of Indians returning from visits to Washington or St. Louis; almost certainly a couple of gamblers, immaculate and soft-spoken, who would disembark quietly after a few days and take the next boat back to civilization with well filled pockets; buckskin-

---

Ibid., pp. 16–17.

From *The Land of the Dacotahs,* by Bruce Nelson, pp. 102–103. Copyright, 1946, by the University of Minnesota. Minneapolis: University of Minnesota Press.

clad hunters, trappers, and traders with long flowing hair; and soldiers bound for the frontier outposts.

A final drunken brawl lasting for several days was customary for the crew and the rougher element among the passengers. Then, with a salute of cannon and a rattle of musketry, the steamer cast off her lines and stood out into the river for the long summer's voyage.

Once the drinkers had recovered from their hangovers and the forecastle was cleared, the interest of all on board was occupied for several days with a contest among the crew for the championship of the boat. Butting, kicking, biting, and gouging, with no holds barred, the merry roustabouts persisted until one of them had conquered the rest, whereupon the winner was awarded a red sash and the title of "King of the River." Frequently it was an honor earned at the expense of an ear, several teeth, or even an eye. "A more bull dog affair no one need wish to see" was the opinion of an old river captain who witnessed a grudge fight between two of these river roughnecks.

A Real Kentucky Love Letter

The following is taken from the *New Orleans Picayune* as a specimen of a Kentuckian's love letter to his gal.

On board the Steam Boat R.N.O.
March 21st, 1838

Dear Ann—We are about to shove out, and I have only time to say good-bye. I want you to whip Liza for me before I come back; give her *gos*. If nothing breaks, in about three weeks, I shall be down again. It makes me mighty wrothy to think I have to go without seeing you. I'd clear my way through the biggest kind of a cane brake to see you any time. Give my respects to all the family and the gals in particular. The "Wild Bill" has got his steam up, and is fast letting go his cable. So good-bye—off we go. Don't forget your promise, for God's sake. Yours until death.

S—— J,

Greaser on board St.Bt.R——

From *The Spirit of the Times*, A Chronicle of the Turf, Agriculture, Field Sports, Literature and the Stage, edited by William T. Porter, Vol. VII (May 26, 1838), No. 15, p. 118. New York.

Making Tow

Shorty and Diamond and I trudged along the bank through the cinders and sandburs.

"Ouch! Oh, them useless burs," Shorty said, stopping to pick them off his blue random-mix socks.

About a hundred yards upstream our eight barges were tied off below the tipple [at Alton], lying there very quiet and subdued, each loaded with nearly a thousand tons of Central Illinois coal. It was up to us to get behind this dead weight and shove it 640 miles upstream [to St. Paul]. But first we had to lace our fleet together with chains, cables, and screw ratchets until all eight barges were one solid, integrated, inseparable unit.

* * * * *

I like coal. I like a beautiful big river barge piled full of it. It is black, greasy, real—it almost looks good enough to eat—but it doesn't really taste good. If it were rare, coal would make nice jewelry. After a rain the coal in the barge has a special smell. In the winter the snow settles on the symmetrical peaks, cols, *couloirs*, chimneys, slopes and crevasses, making scale-model mountain ranges in the barges. I have towed a lot of fuel oil, gasoline, and Bunker C., but there's no charm in petroleum, just a continuous sickening smell.

* * * * *

There were a couple of big 235-foot Federal barges against the bank, with our barges hanging outside them. We climbed up on the Federals and walked across the deck onto our loads. I looked over the rigging the other watch had left for us. Diamond and Shorty kicked idly at the rigging and argued. . . .

* * * * *

Joe came across the deck of the Federal.

"Here comes the Chief High Second Mate, boys," said Shorty so Joe could hear him. "Let's all get some big smiles on."

"Ain't this calm, peaceful atmosphere got you cheered up none yet? Man, you sure got them evening blues," said Joe, and he took off his cap with the star on it and ran his fingers through his streaked blond hair.

"All right, boys, here's the way she looks," he said, concentrating and looking around him at the barges. "They got 108 and 111 all jockeyed up and ready to face up to. Now they got all our rigging right here for us, must of brought the boat alongside and throwed it off. First we make the coupling here between 111 and 16. That's 112 ahead of 16, and we got to yank her out and set her in here where 30 sets. We'll let 9 that's up on the head flop around on the outside of 30, hang the both of them

---

From *A Stretch on the River*, by Richard Bissell, pp. 59–67. Copyright, 1950, by Richard P. Bissell. Boston: Little, Brown and Company. An Atlantic Monthly Press Book.

on the head, and we got her made, slick as a Rock Island whore and twice as cheap. Run them ratchets out, boys. St. Paul, here we come."

Down on the boat the Captain tossed *Real Detective* off the bridge into the river, went into the pilothouse and turned on the radio, shoved the windows back further, stuck his head out, hollered down to the Chief Engineer, who was taking the evening air leaning against the capstan: "Hey, Curly, all them deckhands are up on the tow. Turn her loose for me, will you, and we'll shove up alongside."

"Sure y'all don't want me to come up and tie your shoelace, too?" The Chief was from down in the big bends and tall timber around Wolf Creek, Ohio River, off those big tows out of Pittsburgh, and this Upper Mississippi stuff was beneath him. He was a 250-pounder with steelrim glasses, a tan company uniform, and an unlimited tonnage license on both Diesel and steam. All his conversation was complaints or sarcasm.

The Captain shoved the indicator to SLOW AHEAD, to hold the boat against the bank, while the Chief climbed up the rocks to turn her loose. Captain Sargent picked up the log book, which had LEDGER printed on the front, and wrote:

8:35 Mile 204.2 Finished taking on stores. Commence to make tow 8 loads.

"Another day," he probably said to himself, watching the Chief, who had got the line loose and was pulling it aboard with the capstan. I suppose he was wondering what his wife and the kids were doing, and whether the chickens were laying good.

Shorty and I took one side and Joe and Diamond the other, got our single wires on and were doubling up our long wires when the boat came up alongside the barges, dead slow, with the guard lights on, quiet except for the generator that was running wild as always.

The heat of the day returned as a slow breeze came up from the south, bringing with it evening scents from the street corners of St. Louis mixed with the sweet vegetable smell of the islands and Anheuser-Busch.

I took off my shirt and tossed it under the coaming.

"Let's go and get number 9 swinging, hey, Cap?" Joe hollered up into the bugs and dark. "If he'd turn that radio off maybe we could get this here mess made up before the ice comes in," he said to Diamond. "Bill, go on up on the head of 9 and stand by to turn the side line loose. All right, Jim, *let's go*," he hollered up at the Captain again.

Sargent turned off the box and settled down to work.

Rusty and Vincent, the Junior Engineer and the striker, standing on the steel plates between the big Superiors, took off their shirts and got ready to answer the indicator. The Chief strolled through the engine room, wiped his face on his handkerchief, and retreated again to the deck, where he settled on the companionway steps and said to himself, "Boy, oh boy, look at them pore foolish deckhands sweat and strain."

Making tow can be easy if you have a good mate and a crew working together, or it can be all sweat and hard feelings. Some mates get excited, start hollering at the deckhands, get things all balled up, cuss the pilot throughout the proceedings, and end up with a deckhand in the river, another one ashore to the doctor, and everybody sore. A mate that operates on this schedule can't keep his deckhands long enough for them to learn to work together, and so no improvement is ever forthcoming and life aboard, instead of being a Little Bit o' Heaven, is more on the order of getting married and going to live with ma and pa, so far as peace and harmony is concerned.

Shorty and Diamond and I had worked together long enough to know who wanted the ball for a shot without calling time out for a discussion. And Joe was a mate that made everything look easy. Some of these mates have an instinct for the hard way; it is not in them to formulate anything but roundabout, obscure plans of action which confuse the deckhands and delay the performance. None of that in Joe. He was always out in front and always using his head.

So we labored and it grew dark. Sargent helped us with the searchlight. After about forty minutes we had the barges all shuffled around and laced together with plow steel.

"Now, you bastards," Joe said, addressing the barges, "don't let me hear no more outa you until Keokuk lock."

"I believe we've got her," Diamond said.

The first time I made tow the year before I thought it would kill me. I could scarcely pick up a ratchet. Now I was strong; for the first time in my life I was really hard. . . .

"We've got her, Cap!" Joe hollered. "Let's go!"

"Where's Al? Is he back yet?" Sargent called down.

Just then a cab with the horn blowing came tearing down the road and pulled up in the weeds.

"That's him, now, I suppose," Joe hollered. "Dropping back!"

"OK, Joe," Sargent called out. "Dropping back."

We stood on the forward deck as we dropped down to face up to the tow, taking a quick smoke. Then the boat snuggled her blunt bow and tow knees against the barges and we set the face wires. Diamond and I put our backs into the winches. We were facing up. The new trip was ready to begin.

"Leave her go, Cap," Joe hollered up at the pilothouse, and the Captain gave a single toot on the whistle to Shorty, who was out on the head of the tow eight hundred feet away. And pretty soon we could hear Shorty's voice echo down the coal piles, "A-L-L G-O-N-E." We were off to the northland empire. No one saw us go, and there were no baskets of fruit or light novels from Brentano's on our bunks.

It was night and ahead of us the Mississippi River and the Illinois bluffs had disappeared. We were heading up into a black wall. Now it was up to Mr. Pilot.

"Let him sweat for a while," Diamond said.

It had been a long, long day.

Wading Pilot

The following curious story is related by the Concord *Intelligencer*, to illustrate the accuracy of the river pilots and the hard work by which they acquire their knowledge of depths and distances:

An old pilot on the Arkansas once attracted our attention by pointing out a bed of rock—where we could see nothing. We asked how he had studied the river.

"Why, sir, I waded from the Post to Fort Gibson, three summers, and I guess I took pains to touch bottom."

The distance is near six hundred miles. Think of that, reader.

His soundings were as follows: "Ankle!—half calf!—whole calf!—half knee!—knee!—half thigh!—thigh!" *Deep thigh* was as deep as he ever wished for the *Trident;* she ran from that depth down to a bare sprinkling on the bars; at a greater depth than "by the deep thigh," the order was usually given, "Head her ashore!"

The Somnambulist Pilot

. . . There used to be an excellent pilot on the river, a Mr. X., who was a somnambulist. It was said that if his mind was troubled about a bad piece of river, he was pretty sure to get up and walk in his sleep and do strange things. He was once fellow-pilot for a trip or two with George Ealer, on a great New Orleans passenger packet. During a considerable part of the first trip George was uneasy, but got over it by and by, as X. seemed content to stay in his bed when asleep. Late one night the boat was approaching Helena, Arkansas; the water was low, and the crossing above the town in a very blind and tangled condition. X. had seen the crossing since Ealer had, and as the night was particularly drizzly, sullen, and dark, Ealer was considering whether he had not better have X. called to assist in running the place, when the door opened and X. walked in. Now, on very dark nights, light is a deadly enemy to piloting; you are aware that if you stand in a lighted room, on such a night, you cannot see things in the street to any purpose; but if you put out the lights and stand in the gloom you can make out objects in the street pretty well. So,

From *The Cincinnati Miscellany*, or Antiquities of the West; and Pioneer History and General and Local Statistics, compiled from the *Western General Advertiser*, from April 1st, 1845, to April 1st, 1846, by Charles Cist, Vol. II (November, 1845), p. 192. Cincinnati: Robinson & Jones. 1846.

From *Life on the Mississippi*, by Samuel L. Clemens, pp. 97–100. Copyright, 1874 and 1875, by H. O. Houghton & Company; 1883, 1890, 1903, by Samuel L. Clemens; 1911, by Clara Gabrilowitsch. New York and London: Harper & Brothers, Publishers.

on very dark nights, pilots do not smoke; they allow no fire in the pilot-house stove, if there is a crack which can allow the least ray to escape; they order the furnace to be curtained with huge tarpaulins and the skylights to be closely blinded. Then no light whatever issues from the boat. The undefinable shape that now entered the pilot-house had Mr. X.'s voice. This said:

"Let me take her, George. I've seen this place since you have, and it is so crooked that I reckon I can run it myself easier than I could tell you how to do it."

"It is kind of you, and I swear *I* am willing. I haven't got another drop of perspiration left in me. I have been spinning around and around the wheel like a squirrel. It is so dark I can't tell which way she is swinging till she is coming around like a whirligig."

So Ealer took a seat on the bench, panting and breathless. The black phantom assumed the wheel without saying anything, steadied the waltzing steamer with a turn or two, and then stood at ease, coaxing her a little to this side and then to that, as gently and as sweetly as if the time had been noonday. When Ealer observed this marvel of steering, he wished he had not confessed! He stared, and wondered, and finally said:

"Well, I thought I knew how to steer a steamboat, but that was another mistake of mine."

X. said nothing, but went serenely on with his work. He rang for the leads; he rang to slow down the steam; he worked the boat carefully and neatly into invisible marks, then stood at the center of the wheel and peered blandly out into the blackness, fore and aft, to verify his position; as the leads shoaled more and more, he stopped the engines entirely, and the dead silence and suspense of "drifting" followed; when the shoalest water was struck, he cracked on the steam, carried her handsomely over, and then began to work her warily into the next system of shoal marks; the same patient, heedful use of leads and engines followed, the boat slipped through without touching bottom, and entered upon the third and last intricacy of the crossing; imperceptibly she moved through the gloom, crept by inches into her marks, drifted tediously till the shoalest water was cried, and then, under a tremendous head of steam, went swinging over the reef and away into deep water and safety!

Ealer let his long-pent breath pour out in a great relieving sigh, and said:

"That's the sweetest piece of piloting that was ever done on the Mississippi River! I wouldn't believe it could be done, if I hadn't seen it."

There was no reply, and he added:

"Just hold her five minutes longer, partner, and let me run down and get a cup of coffee."

A minute later Ealer was biting into a pie, down in the "texas," and comforting himself with coffee. Just then the night watchman happened in, and was about to happen out again when he noticed Ealer and exclaimed:

"Who is at the wheel, sir?"

"X."

"Dart for the pilot-house, quicker than lightning!"

The next moment both men were flying up the pilot-house companion-way, three steps at a jump! Nobody there! The great steamer was whistling down the middle of the river after her own sweet will! The watchman shot out of the place again; Ealer seized the wheel, set an engine back with power, and held his breath while the boat reluctantly swung away from a "towhead," which she was about to knock into the middle of the Gulf of Mexico!

By and by the watchman came back and said:

"Didn't that lunatic tell you he was asleep, when he first came up here?"

"No."

"Well, he was. I found him walking along on top of the railings, just as unconcerned as another man would walk a pavement; and I put him to bed; now just this minute there he was again, away astern, going through that sort of tightrope deviltry the same as before."

"Well, I think I'll stay by next time he has one of those fits. But I hope he'll have them often. You just ought to have seen him take this boat through Helena crossing. *I* never saw anything so gaudy before. And if he can do such gold-leaf, kid-glove, diamond-breastpin piloting when he is sound asleep, what *couldn't* he do if he was dead!"

Pilot Farmer

In the course of tugboat gossip, it came out that out of every five of my former friends who had quitted the river, four had chosen farming as an occupation. Of course, this was not because they were peculiarly gifted agriculturally, and thus more likely to succeed as farmers than in other industries: the reason for their choice must be traced to some other source. Doubtless they chose farming because that life is private and secluded from irruptions of undesirable strangers—like the pilot-house hermitage. And doubtless they also chose it because on a thousand nights of black storm and danger they had noted the twinkling lights of solitary farmhouses, as the boat swung by, and pictured to themselves the serenity and security and cosiness of such refuges at such times, and so had by and by come to dream of that retired and peaceful life as the one desirable thing to long for, anticipate, earn, and at last enjoy.

But I did not learn that any of these pilot-farmers had astonished anybody with their successes. Their farms do not support them; they support their farms. The pilot-farmer disappears from the river annually, about

Ibid., pp. 361–362.

the breaking of spring, and is seen no more till next frost. Then he appears again, in damaged homespun, combs the hayseed out of his hair, and takes a pilot-house berth for the winter. In this way he pays the debts which his farming has achieved during the agricultural season. So his river bondage is but half broken; he is still the river's slave the hardest half of the year.

One of these men bought a farm, but did not retire to it. He knew a trick worth two of that. He did not propose to pauperize his farm by applying his personal ignorance to working it. No, he put the farm into the hands of an agricultural expert to be worked on shares—out of every three loads of corn the expert to have two and the pilot the third. But at the end of the season the pilot received no corn. The expert explained that *his* share was not reached. The farm produced only two loads.

"Learning the River"

To secure a pilot's license one must work thirty-six months on the river as a deck-hand, which means doing almost everything that there is to be done aboard a steamboat.

In olden times when the boats went to the mountains on the Missouri, a twenty-three hundred mile trip from St. Louis to Fort Benton, Montana, a cub pilot, generally a young man, would get in touch with some first class pilot and work for nothing, paying his board and paying the pilot from two hundred fifty to five hundred dollars for a round trip to the mountains. Between 1835 and 1879 the crack mountain pilots made as much as fifteen hundred dollars per month on a trip and from seven to ten thousand dollars for an annual trip to the mountains.

At the present time a young man wanting to "learn the river" gets a deck-hand berth and a great number of our present day pilots are proud to help them secure their license this way.

I started cubbing on the steamer *Hope* on the Missouri River and finished on my father's boats. A cub pilot starts out by doing practically nothing but watch the main pilot on watch for several months. Then some day when the big shot is in a good humor and the boat is in very good water, he will say, "Take her, Buddy, and see what you can do with her."

After the cub has tried this until he can steer a boat with reasonable safety, he will learn to "run a shore" and "run a point." (There never was a cub that tried to take his first point but what he tried to turn the point too soon.)

Next the cub is allowed to land the boat at some good landing, but only

From *Steamboating*, Sixty-Five Years on Missouri's Rivers, The Historical Story of Developing the Waterway Traffic on the Rivers of the Middlewest, by Captain William L. Heckman, "Steamboat Bill," pp. 66–70. Copyright, 1950, by Burton Publishing Company. Kansas City.

on her upstream trips. If progress continues well, he will be allowed to run a shallow crossing and still later, to turn an empty boat around and make a downstream landing. (A downstream landing without turning the boat around is known as a French landing.)

Further along in the training, the cub is permitted to "flank a bend" where there is a big set in the river. Then he may run several bridges downstream. And finally, when he can land a heavily loaded boat downstream after nightfall in a close river, he is a pilot.

In learning all this, the cub will have been "cussed out" a thousand times and have learned more philosophy than he could have obtained in almost any other profession. While he is learning to handle, maneuver, and land a boat, he has to study several dozen other things.

In reading water in the Missouri, Arkansas, and Yukon rivers the waves are highest at the point of deepest water if the wind is upstream; if the wind is downstream, the waves are highest where the water is shallowest. When it is raining, all water looks alike. Such things as these make the pilot's profession a gift from the gods or at least, a gift of the sixth sense. A pilot on an uncharted river must have a remarkable memory to keep the hundreds of marks in his memory for both day and night work.

My cubbing was in the tradition of the old mountain pilots who could remember all their marks from St. Louis to Fort Benton—thousands of them. These men would take their marks on the upstream trip and run by them coming back three months later.

One of the hardest things I had to learn about the Missouri River was "running a rainbow reef." Pulling my boat over this reef at just the proper place, the "break in the reef," bothered me. Heavy, rushing boils on a crossing or a swift, shallow bend means the deepest water; slick boils like a girl with a fresh powdered face means look out for shallow water.

A crossing on the river is the place where boats cross from one side of the river to the other and as a rule these are the flattest places. Some crossings are long, some are square.

Flanking a bend or bridge means holding your boat back and letting her drift slowly through a place where the pilot is running a close place in the river or a close bridge. It is called "making it on the run."

A set in the river is where the water draws more heavily toward one shore than the other and it is in these places that a heavy boat is generally flanked.

Reading the water means telling the deep water from the shallows—a gift that is given but few men.

By marks are meant trees, rocks, houses, hills, hollows or anything that is not a man-made marker such as Government lights.

A reef on the river is a place where there may be one foot of water on the upper side and the water drops straight down at some places under the reef to as much as fifteen feet. In other words, there may be one foot of water at a particular spot in the river while three feet away from that spot will be fifteen feet of water. This has caused many drownings.

A rainbow reef starts on one side of the river and crosses clean to the other side in the shape of a rainbow. The break in the reef is the place to look for the deepest water.

A boil is a rough surface on the river caused by the water running over an uneven bottom. A break is a submerged snag that shows on the surface of the water. A sawyer is a whipping snag that sticks up out of the water and bobs around like a cork in the wind.

The different watches a pilot stands at night are called:

1. "Long watch"—supper to midnight.
2. "After watch"—midnight to four o'clock.
3. "Dog watch"—four to breakfast.

A job on the river is always known as a "berth."

The Pilot on the Prairie

In time of high water when the river overflows its banks, it is quite easy in the night for a pilot to lose his bearings. A pilot who once grounded his boat on a prairie a long way from the channel sent the following telegram to his employers: "Am out on Lone Tree Prairie. What shall I do?"

They answered, "Go farming, you landlubber."

It was quite a task to get the boat back into the channel.

Delta Pilots

Of all the callings in the Delta, the highest stands that of the pilot. To be a pilot—ah, that is a thing for you. The youth who sits on the levee and studies every vessel that passes—almost certainly he is thinking of the day when he may be out there, riding high above the world, guiding the ships to and from New Orleans. The wrinkled old man who runs from his store toward the river—he wants to call an "Eh, là-bas!" to the Capitaine, whom he has known since he was no higher than a big muskrat. And the smiling girl who is pinning a flower at the neckline of her dress and embellishing her lips—it is all for the passing of the young pilot. You think he cannot see her close enough for such preparation? Then what does he have his telescope for? And if he is a real pilot, he will be using it! To be a pilot, that *is* a thing for you.

From *Lore and Lure of the Upper Mississippi*, A Book about the River by a River Man, by Captain Frank J. Fugina, p. 62. Copyright, 1945, by Frank J. Fugina. Winona, Minnesota: Published by the author.

From *Deep Delta Country*, Harnett T. Kane, pp. 119, 125–127. Copyright, 1944, by Harnett T. Kane. *American Folkways,* edited by Erskine Caldwell. New York: Duell, Sloan & Pearce.

He is the Delta's local hero, neighbor-who-made-good, and village spender, all in one. His is a calling of pulse-quickening possibilities—danger, adventure, and the obvious opportunities it affords for monetary and social advancement. When a friend questions the actions of such an individual, another is likely to interrupt, "But he's a pilot!" That explains, and takes care of, a great deal.

For two centuries and a half, piloting has flourished as an occupation with a special color of its own. Concerning the pilots and their methods Louisianians have grown voluble, now enthusiastic, now apoplectic; and with the years the position has undergone violent change. "Where they's pilots, they's alway' something happening," the Deltans tell you. . . .

* * * * *

. . . A committee of the Louisiana legislature at one time reported that the [pilotage] arrangements at various periods had "undergone every phase of change" between a "close monopoly" on the one hand, and, on the other, a "competition stimulated by individual ambitions, even animosities—a competition pushed to extremes by rival houses." The pendulum swung. After the first rush of reform, businessmen came forward to protest that new and raging antagonisms were almost disrupting the service. In this era of what the Delta calls the "opposition pilots," men strove with fervor against each other. A yawl boat had a pilot and several helpers to row. They were often on the water for several days, scanning the horizons. With them they took food and covering against bad weather. They were tempted to further and further risks in order to win against their opponents.

The unwritten law was that the job of pilotage went to the individual who first stepped aboard the incoming vessel. Sometimes the contest was so sharp that those approaching at the same hour would halt to belabor each other with their oars. Officers of the ship would send down seamen to intervene, or perhaps they would watch the fun from the deck, and then haul aboard the conqueror. A pilot and his men had only contempt for their rivals, and at times the term "cutthroat competition" was not a metaphorical one.

The most celebrated example of such a contest came when, on a day of dark, heavy seas, two pilots reached a vessel from opposite directions at almost the same minute. The first gained slightly; it appeared that he would have the advantage. He arrived at the port side with difficulty and caught at the bobbing ship's ladder. As he did, he gave a cry of success. The second pilot heard him through the winds; he would have to act quickly or fail. Two or three seamen looked down at him. "Toss me a rope, men," he called. The rope hit the water; the second pilot took a firm hold. The ship gave a heavy roll, away from him. The first pilot, moving up the ladder on the opposite side, was delayed as the high wall careened over him, while the pull of the vessel, with the helping hands of the seamen on the rope, lifted his rival high in the air. By the time the first pilot reached the deck, the enemy was there, wet and triumphant.

The pilots formed companies, heightening the rivalries. At last one group purchased a seagoing tug, the *Jennie Wilson,* and her owners could take their pick of the trade. This seemed opposition too formidable for the others. Not long afterward a general pilots' association was formed with the *Jennie Wilson* as flagship. Put into operation in the 1870's, she stays in service today [1944]. Remodeled from time to time, new engines installed, she is said to be the oldest pilot boat in use anywhere. The tug has seen the profession undergo a further quieting process, but it is still far from drab. It continues a business that constantly flirts with danger. Only recently great vessels have been caught by contrary winds at the river mouth and sent spinning to their doom. Steamers have fought like animals trapped in a pond; and regularly the Delta women have looked on as their pilot-husbands won praise for heroism.

By general agreement the pilot remains a riproaring guy. By and large he also keeps his rank as the best-paid man in the Delta. It is part of the code that he be carefree, a quip on his tongue, a practical joke hatching in his head. (There are, to be sure, exceptions.) A crony grins and declares, "That's a pilot for true. Jus' like his Papa. Set up the drinks, the Capitaine say' a roun' for ev'body. . . ." A pilot is a fine man to have as a relative. He ought to be good for a touch on sight, for Christmas presents, christening gifts, and favors from the politicians.

Above all, he carries on as a trencherman in the grand manner. When a woman of Plaquemines tells a guest, "This is good salmon, chère, jus' like what the pilot' got at their own table," all know that it is fine food indeed. The pilot fare partakes of the Delta's French tradition, sauced and seasoned with earnestness and resource. A fire always burns in the kitchen at their stations and over it bubbles a pot of coffee. This is the blackest, the most breath-taking brew prepared in any section of Louisiana. Nonnatives, unprepared for the first mouthful, turn red in the face. Most Louisianians, after one cup, glance around for the next one.

Thus it is that if a Deltan finds a friend behaving above his means, ordering things that he cannot afford, he tells him, "Stop acting like you think you a pilot!"

"He Like Dat Landin' "

One night going up the river on the *Ten Broeck* with our fuel barge in tow and changing watch at eleven o'clock above Apple River I said to Frank LePoint who had just taken her (as pilot), "Frank, I think I see

From *A Raft Pilot's Log,* A History of the Great Rafting Industry on the Mississippi River, 1840–1915, by Walter A. Blair, pp. 145–146. Copyright, 1929. Cleveland. 1930. Reprinted by permission of The Arthur H. Clark Co.

red and green lights up there near the mouth of the Maquoketa. In this moonlight the lights don't show very well, but I think he has a raft ahead of him; guess I will wait and see who it is."

In a few minutes Frank's keen Sioux Indian eyes caught the situation and he said, "Why, that man he's tied up. Now why you s'pose anybody tie up a raf' on such a night like dis. It mus' be Brasser [Captain George Brasser]. He like dat landin'." Sure enough! When we got up closer, by four short blasts from her whistle calling for help we recognized the raftboat *Robert Dodds* of which George Brasser was master. Running in closer, I called to ask what he wanted and could see the trouble before he answered: "Ho Cap! This dam fellar wit' his tie raf' run into me since I'm landed here and I can't move my boat—he's swung in across the *Robert Dodds'* wheel. I want you to pull him out of dis." There was a big man with a bass voice moving around on the tie raft (from the Wisconsin River) whom I judged was the pilot (a "floater"), and at my suggestion he made fast to his raft the end of a good line our mate threw out to him.

Then we slowly and carefully pulled him out of his predicament and swung him well into the channel and let him go, and we proceeded up river.

Six weeks later we landed at the office in Beef Slough to get our raft assignment. The *Robert Dodds* was landed there also and when I met Captain Brasser he had a merry twinkle in his mild blue eyes. After thanking me for the little service that night six weeks ago, he said, "I have good joke to tell you on my own self. On my las' trip down my engineer says those biler [boilers] need a clean out; so I tie up in same place I was that night you see us there. Well, sir, I was woke up along 'bout midnight and when I step out my room what you tink I see? Well, my frien', there was another tie raf' in same shape like de one you pull out wit your boat dat time I hail you in.

"Yas sir, and when I see big fellar walkin' towar's my boat I see was de same pilot; so I call out, I say, my frien', ain't dis river wide enough so you can get by me sometime when I'm clear over one side? An' here's where de fun is on me. So soon I spik like dat he stop right where he was and in dat big voice he's got he say, 'Gawd-a-mighty! Are you here yit?' "

Tippling Engineer

... Blue Johnny, an engineer noted for his tippling ..., early in the morning goes to his chief and declares: "Captain, give me the orders for

From *Big River to Cross*, Mississippi Life Today, by Ben Lucien Burman, p. 24. Copyright, 1938, 1939, 1940, by Ben Lucien Burman. New York: The John Day Company.

everything you want me to do the rest of the day, 'cause I'm going to get drunk in an hour, and then I won't be able to understand 'em." Given the orders, he remembers them in his Bacchanalian depths, and executes each one with faithfulness and precision, a phenomenon which might cause a psychologist to wonder.

Towboat Talk

. . . Sometimes I got sick of listening to it all. Their conversation and phrasing seemed overripe. I could see some eager student of Americana in a homespun tie and needing the clippers up the neck taking it all down with enthusiasm in a ring-binder notebook.

* * * * *

"We had a deckhand once and he asked me to write a letter home for him. He couldn't write very good, or he couldn't write at all, one. So I got the address wrote out for him, and then I says, 'All right, buddy, what shall I say?' 'Oh,' he says, 'tell 'em we ben goin up the river and now we're goin down her.' Kind of a simple description of steamboating, ain't it?"

"That just about tells it all. We ben goin down the river, and now we're goin up her."

"That's it, ain't it?"

"That's about all."

* * * * *

"I grant you, it's purdy in a way, but you should see the Ohio over around New Amsterdam. And Wolf Creek. And Cave-in Rock. And Madison, Indiana. Boys, now that's really purdy country."

"I suppose they got a Lake Pepin over there. And a Queens Bluff. And a Sugar Loaf. And a Trempealeau, too."

"They don't need no Lake Pepin. They got Cincinnati and Louisville. They got Pittsburgh, and a lot of things you never even heard of."

"Too bad you hadda leave and come over here to no man's land."

* * * * *

"After you get through banging them dishes together in the dishpan you can start on your beds."

"Nobody down there at St. Louis tole me I hadda make no beds on this here job."

"My, that makes me sad to hear that."

"They never said nothing about no beds."

From *A Stretch on the River,* by Richard Bissell, pp. 61, 88, 89, 90, 91, 92, 93. Copyright, 1950, by Richard P. Bissell. Boston: Little, Brown and Company. An Atlantic Monthly Press Book.

"Ain't there a nice novelty to it, though? I don't suppose you got beds down in Gasconade County."

"The hell we ain't. We got three beds right in our own house."

"My, my; you must be the rich folks in town."

"We don't live in no town. We live out on the branch, right near Gilberts Bridge."

"Leave me know when you're ready, and I'll show you just one more time how to make up them beds."

"They never said nothing about beds. I got half a notion to quit."

"Get another half notion and you'll have a whole one, and you can end your travels right up around the bend."

"Aw."

* * * * *

"He beat my young brother five years old so bad the kid was in the hospital for over a month. I been hunting for that son of a bitch for twenty years, and when I find him I'll kill him even if he's on his deathbed. Don't tell me about no stepfathers."

"Well, Mush, you ain't a-going to find him out here abumming on the boats."

"I'll find him."

* * * * *

"That's what we got that ole anvil asettin in the deck room for. That's so as when you ain't got nothin practical to do you just pick her up and hold her in your arms. Then if Captain shows up he'll see you're astrainin on something and he'll be satisfied."

* * * * *

"We got to shut down the port engine for about half an hour."

"OK."

"How much you figure we're making?"

"About three point four."

"Pretty good with that mess of coal."

"Yeh, we're going up the river."

"Considerin' the shape we're in. By god, if they don't leave us go to drydock next trip down I'm walking offn her."

"Then you better start right now raising particular hell with the office. They sure want this here coal moved."

"We ain't agonna move nothin pretty soon lessn we go into drydock."

The Steamboat Captain Who Was Averse to Racing

Early in the spring of the present year, a magnificent new steamer was launched upon the Ohio River, and shortly afterward made her appearance at the Levee, opposite the flourishing city of Cincinnati. Gilt-edged covers, enveloping the captain's "respects," accompanied with invitations to "see her through," upon her first trip down the river, were forwarded to the editorial corps in that vicinity; the chalked hats were "numerous" on the occasion. It was a grand affair, this *debut* of a floating palace, which has since maintained her repute untarnished as the "crack boat," *par excellence,* upon the Western waters. Your humble servant was among the "invited guests"—and a nice time he had of it!

I found myself on board this beautiful craft in "close communion" with a score of unquestionable "beauties." The company proved to be a heterogeneous conglomeration of character—made up of editors, lawyers, auctioneers, indescribables, and "fancies"—with a sprinkling of "none-such's." There was a stray parson, too, in the crowd—but as his leisure time "between meals" was spent in trading horses, we dispensed with his "grace before meals."

We left our moorings an hour before sunset, upon a clear cold afternoon, and passed rapidly down stream for a considerable distance, without experiencing any out-of-the-way occurrence. The "sons of temperance," and the parson aforesaid, amused themselves over a smoking whisky toddy —the "boys" were relieving each other of their superfluous dimes and quarters at *euchre,* when a tall gentleman, who was "some" (when he was sober), stepped suddenly into the cabin, and imparted the information that a well-known "fast boat" had just hove in sight, at the mouth of the Kentucky river. The cards were "dropt" instanter—the punches disappeared—and the "mourners" were soon distributed in knots upon the promenade deck, to watch the progress of events.

Our "bully" boat sped away like a bird, however, and the craft behind gave us early evidence that she should offer no child's play. The "fat was in the fire" at once—a huge column of black smoke curled up in the clear atmosphere—an extra turn or two was visible upon our own boat, and away we went! A good deal of excitement existed among the party, as the rival steamer was clearly gaining upon us. A craft like ours, with such a company, and such a captain mustn't be *beaten.*

As the boat behind us fell in under our stern, and we could "count her

By "The Young 'Un," of Philadelphia (George P. Burnham).

From *A Quarter Race in Kentucky,* and Other Sketches Illustrative of Scenes, Characters, and Incidents, throughout "the Universal Yankee Nation," edited by William T. Porter, pp. 125–129. Entered . . . 1846, by Carey & Hart; 1854, by T. B. Peterson. In *Colonel Thorpe's Scenes in Arkansaw.* Philadelphia: T. B. Peterson and Brothers, 1858.

Reprinted from *The Spirit of the Times,* May 16, 1846.

passengers," a sort of impression came over us, that, by some mistake, we had got upon the wrong boat! At least, such was the expressed opinion of the parson, as he threatened to "go down stairs" and take another drink. Our captain was a noble fellow—he paced the deck quietly, with a constant eye to wind'ard; but he said nothing. A bevy of the mourners stepped up to him, with—

"What speed, cap'n?"

"Fair, gentlemen; I may say *very* fair."

"Smart craft, that, behind," ventured one.

"Very," responded the captain, calmly, as he placed his hand upon a small brass knob at the back of the pilot house. This movement was responded to by the faint jingling of a bell below, followed immediately by a rush of cinders from the smoke-pipes, and an improved action of the paddles.

"Now we move again."

"Some," was the response, and a momentary tremor pervaded the boat as she "slid along" right smartly.

But the craft in our rear moved like our shadow on the calm waters, and as we shot down the river, it seemed as if we had her "in tow," so calmly and uniformly did she follow in our wake. The excitement of the congregation upon deck had by this time become intense, and it was pretty plain that the boats must shortly part company, or "split something." The rascal behind us took advantage of a turn in the channel, and "helm a-starboard!" was clearly heard from the look-out of our rival, as she "hove off," and suddenly fell alongside us! The parson went below at once, to put his threat into execution, as we came up into the current again, "neck and neck"; and when he returned we were running a twenty-five-knot lick, the steam smack on to 49°!

"She's going—goin' go——," muttered an auctioneer to himself.

"A perfect nonsuit," remarked a lawyer.

"Beaten, but not vanquished," added a politician; and away we scudded side by side for half a mile.

"Wouldn't she bear a *leetle more?*" meekly asked the parson.

"She's doing very well," replied the captain. "Don't get excited, gentlemen; my boat is a new one—her reputation and mine is at stake. We mustn't rush her—*racing always injures a boat,* and I am averse to it"; saying which he applied his thumb and finger to the brass knob again—the bell tinkled in the distance—and our rival pilot shortly had an opportunity to examine the architecture of our rudder-post!

I was acquainted with the engineer. I stepped below (believing we should be beaten at our present speed), and entering the engine-room—

"Tim," said I, "we'll be licked—give her another turn, eh?"

"I rayther think she moves *some* as it is," said Tim.

"Yes: but the C—— is hard on us—give her a little, my boy—just for—"

"Step in here a moment," remarked Tim; "it's all 'mum,' you know—nothin to be said, eh? Quiet—there!—don't she tremble some?"

I noticed, for the first time, that our boat did labour prodigiously!

"But come round *here,*" continued Tim: *"look there!—mum's* the word you know."

I stepped out of that engine-room (Tim said afterwards that I "sprang out at one bound"; but he lied!) in a hurry. *The solder upon the connection-pipe had melted and run down over the seams in a dozen places,* from the excessive heat—a crow-bar was braced athwart the safety-valve, with a "fifty-six" upon one end—and we were shooting down the Ohio, under a head of steam "chock up" to 54 40!

My "sleeping apartment" was well aft. I entered the state-room—got over upon the *back* side of my berth—and, stuffing the corners of the pillow into my ears, endeavoured to compose myself in sleep. It was out of the question. In attempting to "right myself," I discovered that *my hair stuck out so straight it was impossible for me to get my head within six inches of the pillow!*

I tossed about till daylight, in momentary expectation of being landed in Kentucky (or somewhere else!), but we got on finely. We led our rival half an hour into Louisville; and I immediately swore upon my nightcap that I would never accept another invitation, for a pleasure trip, from a *steamboat captain who was averse to racing!*

Getting around the Steamboat Racing Ban

The racing instinct was ineradicable in these people, if they were really of the river. Owners, underwriters, and elderly opinion (at a distance) were all against it, but it persisted virtually unchecked by good counsel as by imperative orders. Let two raft boats deliver rafts and start up the river about the same time; all the underwriters between Dubuque and kingdom come could not have prevented a race. The weight on the safety-valve had *now* been riveted to the beam, so there was no shifting of it; but nobody could prevent some handy article of a substantial character being hung where it would do the most good. Strict injunctions were issued against firing up for extra steam, and they were obeyed—in form. When an engineer saw behind him the smoke of an approaching steamboat, he was faithful to his employers and never gave orders to the firemen to heat her up. He only loafed forward in a casual way and said to one of the firemen:

"Jim, do you know what boat that is coming up after us?"

"Search me," says Jim. "I don't know."

From *A-Rafting on the Mississip',* by Charles Edward Russell, pp. 279–280. Copyright, 1928, by Charles Edward Russell. New York and London: The Century Company.

"Well, neither do I," says the chief, "and the queer thing is, I don't want to know," and walks aft, whistling.

Or if the smoke was in front it would be:

"Jack, what's that boat ahead of us, up there?"

"I don't know, chief."

"Well, by Gosh, I wish I knew!"

About ten minutes later the steam had strangely risen from 150 to 165 pounds and the wheel behind was digging up the bottom of the river. No racing—that was the rule. But of course it was a fact in nature nobody would deny that one boat could travel faster than another.

The Old Lady's Lard

. . . Gone forever the era of universal racing, with all its attendant excitements—its pet steamers, high wagers, and fierce rivalry!

A good share of American human nature was exhibited by the old lady who took passage, for the first time, on a steamboat, with several barrels of lard from her Kentucky plantation for the New Orleans market. Familiar with horrible legends of explosion, collision, midnight conflagration, she was tremblingly alive to the dangers of her position. She had extorted a solemn promise from the captain that there should be no racing, which relieved her pressing anxiety. But on the second day, a rival boat came in sight, and kept gaining upon them. Their speed was increased, but still, nearer and nearer came the rival until side by side the noble steamers wrestled for victory. Quivering in every tense nerve and strong muscle with the life and will and power that man had given them, they shot madly down the stream.

The passengers crowded the deck. Every pound of steam was put on. The old lady's nerves began to thrill with the general excitement. Life was sweet and lard precious, but what was death to being beaten?

"Captain," she implored, *"can't* we go faster?"

"Not by burning wood," was the reply; "we might with oil."

At that moment the prow of the other steamer darted a few feet ahead. This was too much.

"Captain," she shrieked, "if you let that boat pass us, I'll never travel with you again. Knock open my lard barrels and fire up with *them!"*

From *Beyond the Mississippi;* from the Great River to the Great Ocean, Life and Adventure on the Prairies, Mountains, and Pacific Coast. . . , 1857–1867, by Albert D. Richardson, p. 22. Entered . . . 1867, by Albert D. Richardson. . . . Hartford, Conn.: American Publishing Company; Philadelphia, Pa., Cincinnati, Ohio, Davenport, Iowa, Atlanta, Ga.: National Publishing Company; New York: Bliss & Company.

A Race between a Steamboat and a Train

As we were getting ready to leave Cairo, a train came in from the East, bringing several hundred excursionists *en route* to Memphis. They had intended to go through in the cars, but seeing our fine boat, they sent on an agent to engage passage. Upon learning this, the conductor of the train became very much excited, and remarked that if they wanted to reach their destination in any reasonable time, they had better remain where they were. When the remark came to my ears, I replied I would agree to take them through as quick as the cars or charge them no fare.

"That's impossible," said the railroad agent.

"Not at all," confidently said I.

"You don't mean to say that your boat can run with a railroad train?" asked the agent, with amazement.

"I do," I replied.

Do you want to bet anything on that?"

"Not a cent any further than what I have already at stake, which is to put those people now coming on board in Memphis before you get there, or charge them no fare."

In a few moments all were on board, and we backed out. I requested every one to go below, at the same time telling the pilot and engineer what my agreement was with the passengers. As we straightened down opposite the lower end of the city, the cars came dashing out of the mouth of the tunnel on the Kentucky shore, and by the time we got fairly under way, the boat and train were side by side, and it was just noon. To say that there was some tall running done would be drawing it extremely mild. Several flocks of wild geese and ducks that we came suddenly upon rose from the water and endeavored to fly ahead of us, but we passed them so fast that they looked as though they were going in the opposite direction, and doubtless they thought they were, for they filled the air with their screams, and became so demoralized that they turned somersaults and performed all sorts of aerial antics. Hundreds dropped into the water, and the feathered hosts did not get sorted over and recover their equilibrium until they had made several good dives into the river.

The number of catfish and buffalo that the boat cut in two must have been frightful, as a few hours after our arrival at Memphis the water was covered with skiffs gathering up the carcasses. Some were severed crosswise, and others split from head to tail, as though prepared for broiling. Numerous hardshell turtles were picked up in halves, showing that they fared no better than the scaly tribes.

For the first two hours it was "nip" and "tuck" as to which would win; and a gentleman who witnessed us pass Osceola, and who came down

---

From *The Log of Commodore Rollingpin:* His Adventures Afloat and Ashore, by John H. Carter, pp. 123–127. Entered . . . 1874, by G. W. Carleton & Co. New York.

on the evening train, said he could distinguish nothing but two blue streaks behind us. At Randolph we were fully a length in the lead, and were gaining steadily, though the old iron horse had got down to his work handsomely. His wheels were going so fast that they were invisible, and the buzzing sound which they produced told that he was on business. All the windows in the train were bolted down, and the conductor, after giving orders to the passengers to hold on to the seats, lashed himself to one of the stove fastenings and hallooed to the engineer to "turn her loose." The inmates of those cars looked like a corps of bareback circus riders on their last round, when the clown, ringmaster, and all the supes are urging the nag up to his highest speed, for they maintained almost a horizontal position and held on entirely by their hands. But it was no use; we arrived at Memphis fully a quarter of a mile ahead, just three hours and forty-three minutes out from Cairo. Our boat came out of the contest unscathed, further than losing overboard the pilot's wig, which occurred before her wheels had made three revolutions.

During the run I remained beneath the hatches, and had no other view of what was going on than that afforded through the portholes, for it would have been certain death to have ventured on deck. The excitement among the passengers in the cabin was intense. Hundreds of thousands of dollars were offered that the *American Empire* would win, but there were no takers.

About an hour after we had landed here, a committee came on board, and after an ancient custom established over a century ago, when boats were run by steam, presented me with the "horns," which they said I was entitled to as the "Champion of the Mississippi." These are the famous antlers once worn by John W. Cannon and Thomas P. Leathers, and judging from their size—thirty-two feet between the tips—those old heroes must have been giants. I received the gift with becoming modesty, and told the committee I would endeavor to make myself equal to the situation, but I rather doubt my ability to fill the bill, for you know we are not so stout now as men were in the good old times.

Big Eating

The bell rang for the evening meal. I walked with Captain Buck [of the *Golden Eagle*, bound from St. Louis to St. Paul] to the dining room. "Eating's one of the fine things on a steamboat," he said. "I like to feed my passengers right. But seems like people don't eat the way they used to. It used to be terrible on a boat I knew that ran up in the tributaries. There was a man that was carpenter on her would eat a dozen eggs for breakfast. Eat them hard boiled in the shell, shell and all. Just put salt and

From *Big River to Cross*, Mississippi Life Today, by Ben Lucien Burman, pp. 233–234. Copyright, 1938, 1939, 1940, by Ben Lucien Burman. New York: The John Day Company.

pepper on the outside and swallow 'em whole. And the passengers were worse. Big lumberjacks from up around the head of the river. They'd eat fifteen flapjacks and three or four big steaks at a meal. The boat was crowded and they used to have two or three sittings, and the lumber-jacks'd try to come and eat a meal each time. The purser caught on to 'em though. After they'd eaten he'd mark a big X on their backs with chalk, and by the time they got it rubbed off, the meals'd be all over."

The Way to Enjoy Life

The crew and officers of one of the tinseled river steamers had been noticing something they could not explain. In one of the best cabins, nearly two months earlier, an elderly, jovial-mannered individual had taken passage at Natchez. Arriving at New Orleans, he announced that he would not get off, but remain until they reached St. Louis. At St. Louis he gave notice that he would stay on until they arrived back in New Orleans; and so it went.

The old fellow wasn't a gambler; that they knew, because they could spot the brotherhood a vessel's length away. He wasn't a thief or a murderer; he smiled along, talking, offering cigars, buying toddies, sitting around with the rest of the passengers. Still, they were disturbed by this phenomenon. Finally the captain had to do something. With several mum-bled apologies, he brought up the subject.

His guest's answer became historic: "Of course, sir, I'll tell you. It's the finest way to pleasure myself that I know. No hotel in America can equal this. The finest food—your wild game, your glazed fish, your roasts, sauces and pastry!" The gourmet purred. "My cabin—it's as finely equipped, as well decorated, as any room I've enjoyed in my life. The bar, the cabin, the promenade—nothing to match 'em, I tell you. And the company! I meet all my friends, the best people in the world. Why should I want to leave?"

The captain, pink with pride, bought the man a drink. The incident went the rounds, but the explanation brought little surprise. Everybody agreed the man was right.

From *Natchez on the Mississippi*, by Harnett T. Kane, pp. 295–296. Copyright, 1947, by Harnett T. Kane. New York: William Morrow & Company.

The Nervous Passenger

The timid old lady approached the captain of the steamboat. "Captain," she said anxiously, "they say a great many men have been drowned in this river. Is that true?"

The captain smiled reassuringly. "My dear madam," he said, "you must not believe everything you hear. I assure you I have never yet met a man who had been drowned in the Missouri River."

Steamboating Dodges

It must be borne in mind that in the early days of steamboating there were few or no regular packets running in regular trades, and leaving on regular days; going on the principle of sailing for cork and a market as ships often do, and queer tricks were often resorted to, to get a trip of freight and passengers when other boats were up for the same destination.

I have often and often known Ohio River boats [to] lie at St. Louis with steam up and all the appearances of starting in an hour—lay there five or six days, and all the time the captain and officers protesting they were going in as many hours. If some passengers were in sight, they would ring the big bell, fire up so as to throw out a column of black smoke from the chimneys, and work the wheels so as to give every indication of starting, when they had not half a cargo and had no idea of going. One noted captain, nicknamed "Ephraim Smooth," was in the habit of pulling out his watch and saying: "If you are over an hour away from the boat you will be left."

There was another dodge resorted to by some, and as they wanted to make all the show of starting by keeping up fire without the expense and waste of fuel, or from keeping firemen, one captain full of inventive genius was caught by a passenger who had been waiting three days in the delusive hope of starting, building a fire in the breeching of the chimneys, and when asked what was he doing that for, said: "They were a new kind of boilers, and had to be fired in that way."

From *The Missouri*, by Stanley Vestal, p. 47. *The Rivers of America*, edited by Hervey Allen. Copyright, 1945, by Walter Stanley Campbell. New York and Toronto: Farrar & Rinehart, Inc.

From *Fifty Years on the Mississippi;* or, Gould's History of River Navigation, by E. W. Gould, pp. 677–678. Entered . . . 1889, by E. W. Gould. . . . St. Louis: Nixon Jones Printing Co. Columbus, Ohio: Long's College Book Co. 1951.
Letter to E. W. Gould from Captain Joseph Brown, St. Louis, Mo., April, 1889.

Ruses for Smuggling Liquor up the Missouri

The annual outfit of the American Fur Company for the Upper Missouri for 1843 was sent up in the steamboat *Omega,* Captain Joseph A. Sire master and Captain Joseph La Barge pilot. The boat carried as passenger the celebrated naturalist, Audubon, who was ascending the river with a small company in the interests of his scientific pursuits. There was on board the usual amount of liquor, which was gotten safely past Fort Leavenworth. The point of greatest danger was at that time Bellevue. It happened, however, on the present occasion that the agent was absent from the post when the boat arrived and accordingly there was no inspection. Elated at this unexpected good fortune, Captain Sire lost no time in putting off the freight destined for this point and in getting on his way. He pursued his voyage until nine o'clock that evening, and doubtless felicitated himself that he was out of danger. But it appears that the agent had delegated the function of inspector during his absence to the commander of the United States troops in the vicinity. The boat left her mooring at daylight next morning, but had scarcely gotten under way when a couple of rifle shots were fired across her bow. She brought to at once and made for the shore. There they found a lieutenant in charge of a few dragoons who had come from the camp four miles distant. The young officer came on board and presented to Captain Sire a polite note from Captain Burgwin, who commanded the detachment of troops, stating that his orders required him to inspect the boat before letting her proceed.

This was like a dash of cold water on the buoyant spirits of Captain Sire and none the less so to Audubon, to whom as well as to the company the loss of the liquid portion of the cargo would have been irreparable. The naturalist had a permit from the government to carry with him a quantity of liquor for the use of himself and party, and upon showing his credentials to the young officer he was, to use his own words, "immediately settled comfortably." But in the moment of his good fortune he did not forget his companions who were not yet "settled comfortably." He understood that time was required for the crew to prepare for the approaching function, and he could at least help to secure this time by delaying inspection as long as possible. He accordingly expressed a desire to visit the camp, and the lieutenant detailed a dragoon to accompany him. The great naturalist rode four miles to camp to call upon an obscure army officer whom he knew he could see in a short time by waiting at the boat. The officer was overwhelmed at the honor of the visit, and when Audubon offered to present his credentials he politely and gallantly replied that his name was too well known throughout the United States to require any

From *The American Fur Trade of the Far West,* A History of the Pioneer Trading Posts and Early Fur Companies of the Missouri Valley and the Rocky Mountains and of the Overland Commerce with Santa Fé, by Hiram Martin Chittenden, Vol. II, pp. 678–683. Copyright, 1901, by Francis P. Harper. New York. 1902.

letters. Audubon says of the occasion: "I was on excellent and friendly terms in less time than it has taken to write this account of our meeting." Between his entertaining conversation and the shooting of some birds he contrived to detain the Captain for a good two hours before they returned to the boat.

The time had not been wasted by Captain Sire and his loyal crew. The shallow hold of the steamboat of those days was divided lengthwise into two compartments by a partition or bulkhead running the full length of the boat. A narrow-gauge tramway extended down each side of the hold its entire length, the two sides connecting with each other by a curve which passed under the hatchway in the forecastle. Small cars received the cargo let down through the hatchway and carried it to its place in the hold or brought it out again when the boat was being unloaded. A car could pass from the stern of the boat on one side of the hold around the curve in the bow and to the stern of the boat on the other side. There being no windows in the hold, everything was buried in blackness a few feet from the hatchway. Workmen were lighted in their labors by means of candles.

During the absence of Audubon the crew had loaded all the liquor upon the cars, and had run them down one side of the hold far enough from the hatchway to be entirely concealed in the darkness. They were carefully instructed in the part they had to play in the approaching comedy, and very likely were put through a preliminary rehearsal or two.

When Captain Burgwin arrived in Audubon's company he was received most hospitably and treated to a luncheon, in which was included, as a matter of course, a generous portion from the private store embraced in Audubon's "credentials." By this time the young Captain was in most excellent temper toward his hosts, and was quite disposed to forego the inspection altogether. But the virtuous Sire would not have it so. "I insisted, as it were," says the worthy navigator in his log of May 10th, "that he make the strictest possible search, but upon the condition that he would do the same with the other traders."

A proposition so eminently fair was at once agreed to by the inspector, whose mellow faculties were now in a most accommodating condition. The shrewd steamboat master, who never forgot to be sober when his company's interests were at stake, escorted the officer down the hatchway, and together they groped their way along the hold by the light of a not too brilliant candle. It may be imagined with what zeal the scrupulous Captain thrust the ineffectual flame into every nook and corner and even insisted that the inspector move a box or a bale now and then to assure himself that everything was all right.

Arrived at the foot of the hold they passed through an opening in the partition and started back on the other side. The officer was doubtless too much absorbed with the effects of his recent collation to notice the glimmer of light under the hatchway at the other end of the boat, where a miniature train with its suspicious cargo was creeping stealthily around the curve and disappearing toward the side which they had just left. The party finished their inspection and everything was found quite as it should be. With many protestations of good will the clever hosts and their delighted guest parted company and the good Captain Sire went on his way rejoicing. But woe to the luckless craft of some rival trader which should happen along with no Audubon in the cabin and no tramway in the hold!

In the year following that of the incident just related, Captain Sire and La Barge were in charge of the company's annual boat, this year the *Nimrod*. The same agent, a Mr. Miller, still held the reins of authority at Bellevue. He was an ex-Methodist minister, as zealous in suppressing the liquor traffic among the Indians as he had ever been in the regular practice of his profession. It was his boast that no liquor could pass his agency. He rummaged every boat from stem to stern, broke open the packages, overturned the piles of merchandise, and with a long, slender pointed rod pierced the bales of blankets and clothing, lest kegs of alcohol might be rolled up within. The persistent clergyman put the experienced agents of the company to their wit's ends, and it was much as ever that they succeeded in eluding his scrutiny.

The urgency of the problem, however, produced its own solution. Captain Sire had the alcohol all packed inside barrels of flour. But he knew that even this device would alone not be enough, for the energetic agent would very likely have the barrels burst open. The Captain therefore had them all marked as if consigned to Peter A. Sarpy, the company's agent at Bellevue, and they were labeled in large letters "P.A.S." The moment the nose of the boat touched the landing at Bellevue, the Captain, as was his custom, ordered the freight for that point placed on shore, and the barrels were promptly bowled out upon the bank and carried into the warehouse. The agent, never suspecting this freight, went on board, and after the most rigid search, found nothing. The boat was permitted to proceed, but contrary to its usual haste in getting on its way as soon as the loading or unloading was complete, it remained the rest of the day and gave out that it would not sail until the following morning. The extraordinary good character of the boat on this occasion and the unusually long delay in departing roused the suspicions of the agent, who stationed a man to watch the boat and to whistle if he saw anything wrong.

Everything remained quiet until some time after midnight, except that a full head of steam was kept up in the boilers. Presently there was great activity on the boat, although with an ominous silence about it all. The pilot, Captain La Barge, was quietly engineering the reloading of the barrels. He had spread tarpaulins on the deck and gang plank to deaden the noise, and the full crew of the boat were hurrying the barrels back in a most lively fashion. "What does this mean?" one of the deck hands asked of another. "We unloaded these barrels yesterday." "Why, don't you see," was the brilliant reply of another, "they're marked 'P A S'; they've got to pass."

The work was quickly over and every barrel was on board, when the agent's sleepy guard awoke to the fact that something was going on. He uttered his signal, and the agent made haste to turn out and see what was the matter. La Barge and Captain Sire, who knew full well what the whistle meant, did not linger to make explanations. Captain La Barge seized an axe and cut the line. "Get aboard, men!" he shouted. "The line has parted!" The boat instantly dropped back into the current and then stood out into the river under her own steam. She was already too far from the bank to be reached when the reverend inspector appeared and wanted to know why they were off so early. It was about 3 A.M. "Oh, the line broke," replied Captain La Barge, "and it was so near time to start that it was not worth while to tie up again."

This was a little too much for the agent, who could not understand how it happened that the boat was so thoroughly prepared for such an accident, with steam up, pilot at the wheel, crew at their places, and all at so early an hour. Next day he found that the barrels consigned to Sarpy were gone, and saw how completely he had been duped. Mortified and indignant, he reported the company to the authorities, and a long train of difficulties ensued, with ineffectual threats of canceling the company's license. Meanwhile the alcohol found its intended destination in the stomachs of the Indians, and the company reaped the enormous profit which traffic in that article always yielded.

Dancing on Sunday

Commodore Davidson, one of the biggest boat owners on the upper Mississippi, was another of the pious but strong-armed captains. No gambling or dancing or other public diversions unsanctioned by Methodists were permitted on his boats. However, Captain Laughton, commanding the commodore's *Alexander Mitchell,* was made of more earthy material and on a certain Sunday he allowed a few of his passengers to engage in the Virginia Reel. They danced until late under the brilliant chandeliers of the cabin, and then went to bed, not feeling any immediate effects of heavenly wrath upon their sin. The boat kept on going down the river. It seemed as if they were to escape punishment.

But they weren't. At three o'clock the next morning a tornado screamed its way over the land and swooped down on the *Alexander Mitchell.* Both chimneys were ripped off, the roof of the pilot house sailed upward and onward, followed by part of the hurricane deck on the port side. Trudall, the mate, was standing by the boat's bell when the twister struck. It passed

From *Mississippi Steamboatin'*, A History of Steamboating on the Mississippi and Its Tributaries, by Herbert Quick and Edward Quick, pp. 126-127. Copyright, 1926, by Henry Holt and Company. New York.

on, taking Trudall with it, blowing him a full quarter of a mile to the shore where it neatly dropped him.

"You see," said the commodore sternly, "that's what comes of dancing."

Love Boats

Over some of the sloughs and the backwaters and swamps that lead off from them there hangs a fading memory and perhaps the ghost of an odor compounded of raw whisky and cheap perfume. In their time the sloughs were part of one of the nation's frontiers. Lawless men have always flocked to the edge of things; but in a mining camp, sooner or later, there was law, even if only lynch law. It was different in the dubious backwaters of the river, for the Mississippi was itself a boundary line between states, and men—and women—whom the law would lay its hand upon needed only to cross from one bank to the other in order to escape jurisdiction.

So there came into being the floating dance hall which was also a saloon and a brothel. It might be just a pair of flatboats joined together and covered with one-story buildings, such as Charles Edward Russell saw as a boy at Davenport and which, as he recites, had "a generic name not to be repeated in print." Thieves, female harpies, and men who would do murder for a meed were aboard these floating dives. Their chosen victims were the rude raftsmen and lumbermen who at winter's end had come out of the valleys of the six great timber rivers in response to the primal urges of lust and liquor. Among the victims was an occasional town inhabitant of better social rank, of the sort that Proverbs characterizes as "a youth devoid of understanding." About the only thing to be said for the predaceous hosts and hostesses is that they used to sing "Buffalo Gals," which is a good song.

With thicker settlement, the floating resorts, also called "love boats," disappeared. They never quite came back, but there was something rather like them during prohibition, and still moonshine is made in sloughs and swampy woods behind some of the islands. Somehow stagnant water and righteous living never got along well together.

A Floating Theater

The "Chapman Family," consisting of old Mr. Chapman, William Chapman, George Chapman, Caroline Chapman, and Harry and Therese Chap-

From *Flowing South,* by Clark B. Firestone, pp. 180-181. Copyright, 1941, by Robert M. McBride & Company. New York.

From *The Theatrical Journey-Work and Anecdotal Recollections of Sol Smith,* Comedian, Attorney at Law, Etc., Etc., Comprising a Sketch of the Second Seven Years of His Professional Life, together with Sketches of Adventure in After Years, pp. 112-113. Entered . . . 1854, by T. B. Peterson. Philadelphia.

man (children) came to the west this summer [1853], opened a theater at Louisville, and afterwards established and carried into operation that singular affair, the "Floating Theater," concerning which so many anecdotes are told. The "family" were all extremely fond of fishing, and during the "waits" the actors amused themselves by "dropping a line" over the stern of the Ark. On one occasion, while playing *The Stranger* (Act IV, Scene 1) there was a long stage wait for Francis, the servant of the misanthropic Count Walbourgh.

"Francis! Francis!" called the Stranger.

No reply.

"Francis! Francis!" (A pause) "Francis!" rather angrily called the Stranger again.

A very distant voice—"Coming, sir!" (A considerable pause, during which the stranger walks up and down, à la Macready, in a great rage.) "Francis!"

Francis. (entering)—Here I am, sir.

Stranger.—Why did you not come when I called?

Francis.—Why, sir I was just hauling in one of the d——dest big cat fish you ever saw!

It was some minutes before the laughter of the audience could be restrained sufficiently to allow the play to proceed.

Showboat Calliope Lore

The feature of the showboat best known to residents of the Mississippi Valley was the calliope. There are few hamlets on a navigable river of the region which have not at some time heard Captain Bill [Menke's] boats burst into a concert of steamy melodies.

I was sitting with him at the railing of the *Goldenrod* on a quiet afternoon, when a passing towboat chanced to blow for a landing, a squat Diesel with a flat, unmusical whistle.

Captain Bill's genial face showed his disapproval. "They could use some of my old calliopes on these new boats. That was real river music, the calliope. The best ads in the world, too. You could hear 'em for eight miles."

The towboat blew another flat blast. Captain Bill winced again. "I'd have rather lost almost anything than a good calliope or a good calliope player. Not one in a hundred pianists could ever learn how to handle 'em. You needed fingers strong as a blacksmith because of the steam pressure. The best players on the river were Crazy Frank and a girl they called Louisville Lou."

From *Children of Noah*, Glimpses of Unknown America, by Ben Lucien Burman, pp. 124-126. Copyright, 1951, by Ben Lucien Burman. New York: Julian Messner, Inc.

There is a strange story of Captain Bill and a calliope. The showboat was playing in a little town on Bayou Teche, not many miles from New Orleans. A woman was in the local jail waiting to be hanged, the only one of her sex, according to reports, ever sentenced to execution in Louisiana. The showboat was at the settlement for some time, and each afternoon entertained the residents with a program of songs on the calliope. One day the condemned woman sent word to Captain Bill to say how much she enjoyed the playing, and would he please play something while she was being hung.

"I did what she asked," said Captain Bill. "Human beings are hard to figure out sometimes."

He lit a black cigar. "I remember another time we played the calliope. It was on the upper Mississippi, and we were passing the state penitentiary where they said the man that wrote the 'Prisoner's Song' was behind the bars. We played the 'Prisoner's Song' on the calliope when we passed, and people around there said it made him mighty happy. We never played it after that. The 'Prisoner's Song' and 'Home Sweet Home' are bad luck on a showboat."

He noticed my smile and grew serious. "All right. I know you think I'm foolish. But I'll tell you something that happened right in your home town of Covington. We were playing down at the foot of Russell Street there, doing wonderful business, when a new calliope player came on the boat from a circus, didn't know about showboats, and before I could stop him he played 'Home Sweet Home' all the way through. Half an hour later something went wrong with the government dam at Fernbank and all the water rushed out. We came down like an elevator, right on a snag that ripped a big hole in her bottom. It took all summer before we got her raised."

A serious problem with the calliope was keeping it repaired. Out in the open night and day, exposed to every kind of weather, the keys were always sticking and rusting, making the playing of certain notes impossible. Moreover, the whistles were easy to remove. Often some knowing tramp living on the riverbank would come aboard at an unguarded moment and carry off one of the metal tubes to a junk yard, where he would trade it for the price of a whisky.

How Captain Billy Menke Stopped a Leak
in the Showboat

"Guess I've seen some pretty funny times," said the genial Captain Billy Menke, as we sat on the deck of the *Goldenrod* at St. Louis, and

From *Big River to Cross*, Mississippi Life Today, by Ben Lucien Burman, pp. 166-167. Copyright, 1938, 1939, 1940, by Ben Lucien Burman. New York: The John Day Company.

watched a towboat pushing some oil barges up the water. "But I guess about the funniest was one night up near Pittsburgh. It was February, bitter cold, and we were just starting to go South for the season. We backed out from the wharf, when all of a sudden there was a bump, and the boat began acting mighty queer. I ran down in the hold, and I heard a terrible gurgling, and when I got my flashlight going, I saw a hole as big as a man's body right in her prow where she'd hit a piling. She was starting to sink, and I knew if I didn't do something mighty quick, in about two seconds she'd be at the bottom of the river. And then I had an idea. Maybe it was the story I read when I was in school about the Dutch boy that put his finger in the dike and saved the city. Anyway, I jumped right square into the break where the water was coming through, to plug it with my body. It was a big hole, but I was a pretty husky fellow in those days. I went through as far as my stomach, and stopped. I couldn't squeeze down any further."

Captain Billy lit one of the heavy black cigars beloved of rivermen, and smoked it cheerfully. "Well, I stayed in that water I don't know how many hours, while they tried to swing her around and beach her. It was bitter cold, and my brothers and the crew kept bringing whisky to keep me warm. I'm not much of a drinker, but I sure took it that night. It was daylight when they got her landed. But I was happy. Not a teaspoonful of water had got past me. And my brothers said I plugged that hole so tight, when they pulled me out I popped, just like the cork in a bottle of champagne."

A Note in a Bottle

During the two years that we had been out with the *Princess,* our greatest drawback had been music. Although we had had a piano aboard nearly all that time, we could never seem to get anyone to play it for any length of time at the salary we offered. The salaries pianists often asked were outrageous, but we firmly held out that six dollars a week with board and room was enough for any actor or musician. Although my sister Florence could pick out "A Hot Time in the Old Town Tonight" with one finger, it didn't seem to fit in very well with a wedding or death-bed scene.

I had often said that if ever I married, the girl would have to meet with two requirements: First, she must live along the river, and second, she must be able to play piano. Strange to say, she did both. I came to know her in the most unusual manner. It all came about on Dog Island at "Old Maid" crossing just above the mouth of the Cumberland River where we were blown in early one morning. On the head of the island, near Smith-

From *Children of Ol' Man River,* The Life and Times of a Show-Boat Trouper, by Billy Bryant, pp. 203-209. Copyright, 1936, by Lee Furman, Inc. New York.

land, Kentucky, stranded high and dry, was a large drift pile. Now to
the rivermen of our type there is nothing that affords such keen delight
as the process of foraging through a pile of drift because one can expect
to find anything from a corpse to a ten-dollar bill wrapped neatly around
a dry willow branch. After an hour or so of poking around in this one I
had salvaged a gallon of black walnuts, a cork preserver stenciled
Str. Helen White, a baby's high chair, and, away down at the bottom of
the drift, a bottle with a note in it which read:

> Into the shallow waters of the Wabash blue,
> I cast this note as a message to you,
> It comes from a lonesome girl yet in her teens,
> Who has been cast aside by the man of her dreams
> If it should drift unobserved from here to the sea,
> What difference would it make to you and to me?
>   LONESOME
>   1228 Wright Street
>   Logansport, Indiana

I carefully unfolded the damp piece of paper and slowly read its contents again. I checked the course it had taken. "Lonesome" had set the
bottle adrift at the head waters of the Wabash River and it had drifted to
Warehouse Landing, and out into the Ohio where the two rivers meet, a
few miles below Uniontown, Kentucky.

I had been too busy all my life keeping mud off the forw'd end of the
boat and stores on the aft end to entertain many love affairs. Just the
same, I was interested in the lonesome little girl who, at a low ebb, had
written the note, and I began to wonder what she was like and particularly whether she played the piano.

The next day at Cave-in Rock, Illinois, I had a tintype taken of myself
as I sucked a milk shake through a straw and enclosed the picture with
a note written on pink paper highly scented with sachet powder. This
is what I wrote:

> I am the pirate that discovered your note,
> On the head of Dog Island and that's no joke,
> But you can save your stamps for other beaus,
> If you can't play a piano, read, fake and transpose.

In spite of the impudence of my letter and [the] idiotic picture I had
enclosed, a correspondence sprang up between us that lasted for several
months during which time she never once disclosed her true identity.

That fall we went out on docks with our boats and I was so busy
scrubbing and painting that I neglected to write and completely forget her
for the time being, so I heard from her no more.

Spring came along with the usual hustle and bustle and on our opening
day, still minus a piano player, we received a telegram from an ad we
had inserted in the *Billboard* which read "At Liberty—Experienced Pianist
—Salary your limit—Can join at once without ticket, Address Joe Costello,
Grass Creek, Indiana."

"An Italian," Dad said, a note of doubt in his voice as he again read the message aloud.

"Oh, you can't tell, Sam," Mother replied. "He may not be an Italian at all."

"Don't kid yourself," I interrupted. "With a name like that, what else could he be?"

"Well, suppose he is?" Mother said. "You see what his message says. Salary your limit—Can join without ticket. Lots of good musicians are Italians, and we do need a piano player."

"You're right, Mother," Dad said. "Run up and send him a wire to join at once," he told me.

"Yes," my sister added as I went out the door, "and bring back some garlic and a bale of spaghetti."

The next day I met all the incoming trains and stopped each man that alighted with a grip, but none of them answered to the name of Costello. Tired and disgusted, I returned to the boat, where Mother came running to meet me.

"The piano player is here, and she's a dear," she exclaimed.

"She?" I cried in surprise.

"Yes, the he's a she. Her name's Josephine," she went on with a twinkling eye, "and not an Italian either but as Irish as Paddy's pig. And she's beautiful, son," she whispered.

Later, when I was introduced to her she looked at me in a peculiar way, as if she were inspecting a marked-down garment on a bargain counter, and I agreed that Mother was right. She was as pretty as a picture and there was an air of refinement about her which made me wonder whether she would ever be able to adapt herself to the crude life of the river.

She was energetic and talented and good-humored, and she soon set my doubts at rest on that point. After each meal, she would roll up her sleeves and never leave the kitchen until the last dish was dried. She scrubbed and redecorated her room all by herself as if she had settled down for the rest of her life. She was a wizard at the piano, and her marvelous playing and feminine charm often created more interest than the show. As the people left the boat each night, she would entertain them with a medley of Irish songs which she played and sang in her own delightful way. When my sister took sick, she jumped into the leading role on short notice and with complete success and also played the piano before and after the show and between the acts. The entire crew, including myself, fell madly in love with her, but she gave us all a wide berth and attended strictly to her own business.

She was an expert swimmer. One day at Vevay, Indiana, as she finished a swim, she asked me to hand her her bathrobe, from under the shelf back of the door in her room. In doing so, I accidentally upset her scrapbook, which came tumbling to the floor and lay open before me. There I saw a familiar sheet of pink writing paper and I read:

I am the pirate that discovered your note,
On the head of Dog Island and that's no joke,
But you can save your stamps for other beaus,
If you can't play a piano, read, fake, and transpose.

With my cheeks flaming with embarrassment and pleasure, I dashed out to her, the open scrapbook in my hand. A few minutes later, with my arms about her—wet bathing suit and all—she told me that she had read the ad while visiting friends at Grass Creek, and, piqued because I had not written to her, had wired us from their address.

Three weeks later I proposed to her and we were married at Christmas time in Cincinnati. Since she had been born and raised on the bank of the Wabash and was an accomplished pianist, I had fulfilled my early vows about my marriage.

The Famous Four Bryants now were five and, as time proved, were later to become six—all the additions the strange result of a note in a bottle.

Jazz Gets Started on the Riverboats

One of the most beautiful sounds in the city of New Orleans was Fate Marable playing his steam calliope about seven in the evening every night. Those calliope concerts from the riverboats *J.S.* and *Bald Eagle* started in the first couple of years after the boats started using music—around 1916 and '17, I'd say. Well, Fate would play the calliope in the evening to let the people know the boats were going to cut out on excursions. All over the river, Fate Marable had a fabulous reputation.

This is how the riverboats got music on them. Those boats had roustabouts on them, and half of those roustabouts played guitar, and nearly all sang. Well, when those boats went up the river, the roustabouts were on the lower deck and the passengers, the gamblers, et cetera, stayed up on the upper deck. But when the people on the upper deck heard the singing and playing of the roustabouts, they would come downstairs, and that gave Strekfus, the owner of the boats, the idea of putting music on the boats.

As told by Danny Barker. From *Hear Me Talkin' to Ya*, The Story of Jazz, by the Men Who Made It, edited by Nat Shapiro and Nat Hentoff, p. 75. Copyright, 1955, by Nat Shapiro and Nat Hentoff. New York and Toronto: Rinehart & Company, Inc.

Louis Armstrong on the *Dixie Belle*

My river life on [the *Dixie Belle*] (it lasted for two years) is one of my happiest memories and was very valuable to me. It all grew out of a funny accident—another of the breaks I said I have had. Kid Ory's Band had been engaged one evening to play on a truck that was to drive through the streets advertising some big dance. They were always advertising like that with trucks and bands in New Orleans. Well, we were playing a red-hot tune when another truck came along the street with another hot band. We came together at that same corner of Rampart and Perdido Streets where I had been arrested five years before and sent to the Waif's Home. Of course that meant war between the two bands and we went to it, playing our strongest. I remember I almost blew my brains through my trumpet.

A man was standing on the corner listening to the "fight." When we had finally outplayed the other band, this man walked over and said he wanted to speak with me. It was "Fate" Marable, a noted hot pianist and leader of the big band on the excursion steamer *Dixie Belle*. He said he had heard me blow and wanted me for his band. It was in November of 1919. I had been with Kid Ory at the Peter Lalas Cabaret at Iberville and Maris Streets for sixteen months. I had learned a lot from Ory and had begun to get a little reputation, in a small sort of way, as a hot trumpeter. But while I could play music, like most of the others I couldn't read it much yet—just a little. I had made my mind up I wanted to learn.

It may sound funny that I was so quick to leave Kid Ory and sign up for the boat with "Fate" Marable, as though I were just running out on Ory after the big chance he had put my way and all he had done for me. The excursion boats had a big name in those days. They played the Mississippi ports away up to St. Paul and beyond. When they went North on these trips they always had white orchestras, but for the first time it was planned that year to take a colored orchestra along on the *Dixie Belle* when she shoved off in the spring on her trip North. I guess that was because the colored orchestras that had been coming up strong in New Orleans in the last few years, like Kid Ory's, were so hot and good that they were getting a real reputation. The chance to be with that first colored jazz band to go North on the river might have turned any kid's head at nineteen. But even that wouldn't have been enough to make me leave Ory. I wanted to get away from New Orleans for another reason and that was because I was not happy there just then.

Ten months before, when I was eighteen, I got married. I had married a handsome brown-skinned girl from Algiers, Louisiana, named Daisy Parker. We two kids should never have been married. We were too young to understand what it meant. I had to be up most of the night every night, playing

From *Swing That Music,* by Louis Armstrong, pp. 35-42. Copyright, 1936, by Louis Armstrong. London, New York, Toronto: Longmans, Green and Company.

in the orchestra, and in that way I neglected her, but I was so crazy about music that I couldn't think about much else. I see now it must have gone hard with a young and pretty girl up from a small town. And was she pretty! She naturally wanted to come ahead of everything else and she had a very high temper, partly, I guess, because she was so young and inexperienced. And in that same way I was quick to resent her remarks, so, as I say, we were not happy—in fact, we were very unhappy, both of us. . . .

Ory knew all about our troubles. He had done his best to help smooth us out, but maybe nobody could have. So when he found I had the chance to go with that fine band on the river for a while, he understood it would be a good thing.

New Orleans, of course, was the hottest and gayest city on the Mississippi then, even including St. Louis, so all through the winter months, from November until April, when the weather is not so hot and New Orleans is at its highest, the excursion boats would stay right there, running dance excursions up and down the river every night and tying up in the daytime.

The steamer *Dixie Belle* was one of the biggest and best of them. She had her berth at the foot of Canal Street. The orchestra would start playing at eight o'clock while she was at the wharf, to attract people, and then she would shove out into the river at eight-thirty every night with a big crowd on board and cruise slowly around until about eleven o'clock when she would come back in. The *Dixie Belle* was fixed up inside something like a dance hall. She was a paddle wheeler, with great paddle wheels on each side, near the middle, and she had big open decks and could hold a lot of people.

So all that winter, which was the winter of 1919 and 1920, we cruised there around New Orleans and every night when we pulled in, of course I would go home to Daisy. Sometimes we were very happy, and I would hate to think of April coming, when I was to go north on the boat.

The orchestra on the *Dixie Belle* was . . . a twelve-piece orchestra and every man was a crackshot musician. "Fate" Marable had recruited them from the best bands in town, taking this man here and that one there and each one because he was a "hot" player on his own particular instrument. "Fate" was a fine swing pianist himself, and he knew that in time they would learn to play together. Now the most famous jazz orchestras of that day, as you will remember, had had no more than six or seven pieces (though some of the pure brass bands, the marching bands, had more). The old "Dixieland" had only five pieces, and so had Freddy Keppard's "Creole Band." "King" Oliver's famous "Magnolia" and Kid Ory's band had seven pieces each. So, you see, twelve pieces *was* big.

Winter passed and finally April came. The *Dixie Belle* was all cleaned out and fixed up with new paint and polish and finally the day came for us to start up the river. My mother and "Mamma Lucy" came down to see us off, but Daisy wasn't there. We had had another quarrel.

As we pulled out into the river and turned north, I began to feel funny, wishing one minute they'd left me back on the wharf and feeling keen the next moment that I was going. The sweeping of the paddle wheels got louder and louder as we got going. It seemed they had never made so much noise before—they were carrying me away from New Orleans for the first time.

In the seven months to come I was to follow the Mississippi for nearly two thousand miles, and visit many places. It was a handful of traveling, believe me, for a kid who'd always been afraid to leave home before.

We shoved away early in the morning so we could make Baton Rouge, our first stop, by night-down. It was a run of about eighty miles, upstream. A few passengers were on board, as it was to be a day trip, although the *Dixie Belle* was not meant to be a boat for regular passenger travel, but only for big excursion parties, so she was not fitted out with many state-rooms.

It was a warm spring day and the river was high with water, but not flooding. The musicians did not have much to do except laze around on the decks and watch the shores, or now and then throw a little dice or something. After a while, when we had had our last look at New Orleans, I found myself a nice corner up on the top deck right under the pilot house and settled down with my trumpet and a polishing rag. I had bought myself a fine new instrument just before starting out, but even that wasn't shiny enough for *this* trip. No, suh! So I took the rag and shined her a little and then I put her to my mouth and tried out a few blasts. She sounded strong and sweet, with a good pure tone. I swung a little tune and saw we were going to get along fine together. So then I rubbed her up some more, taking my time, until I was satisfied. Over on the left shore a great cypress swamp was passing slowly by—there must have been hundreds of miles of it, stretching away off to the west—dark and hung all over with Spanish moss. I felt very happy where I was. The sun was just warm enough, the chunking of the paddle wheels was now pleasant to hear and everything was peaceful. Pretty soon I spread the rag on the deck beside me and lay my new trumpet on it and began to think of how lucky I really was. There I was, only nineteen years old, a member of a fine band, and starting out on my first big adventure. And I had my new trumpet to take with me. I reached over and let my hand lay on it, and felt very comfortable. . . .

PART SIX

Home by the River

Introduction

In hundreds of little ways and as many big ones, the lives and fates of the people of the river country were shaped by the river. Towns founded on river banks and bends lived and died by the river's whim and the flow of travel and transportation. Floods moved towns like Shawneetown and wiped out towns like Kaskaskia. To accommodate those who decided to go on farther west, crossing and outfitting points sprang up at Westport Landing (Kansas City), Independence, St. Joseph and Council Bluffs.

In the vast rangeland west of the Missouri, in the days before the bridge was built at the present Mobridge, South Dakota, hungry cattle had to be ferried across to spring grassland on specially built boats like floating stock yards. In the fall, when the cattle were on their way to the railroad as fat beef ready for market, they were driven across pontoon bridges. Farther upstream, in Montana, herds were swum across the Missouri by cowboys called "river men," wearing life belts and riding "river horses."

Thus the river crept into the language as well as the occupational folkways of the river country. In Louisiana, according to Harnett Kane, the Acadians who moved from the Teche to the prairie continued to "naviguer" the land, to "embarquer" in their buggies and to "moor" their mounts. In the Delta the best grades of cotton were called "benders," "rivers" and "creeks," according to whether they were grown on bends of the Mississippi, tributaries, or smaller streams.

In the days before good roads and railroads, the social and economic life of farms, plantations and towns along navigable rivers was dominated by the steamboat. Farmers set their clocks by the punctual passing of boats, and sleepy little villages like Mark Twain's Hannibal were awakened from their lethargy by the magic cry of "S-t-e-a-m-boat a-comin'!" only to go back to sleep as soon as the boat was on its way again. In southern Illinois towns along the Mississippi the more pretentious houses had cupolas from which people could watch boats racing on the river. Many a steamboat bell ultimately found its way into a church steeple; for example, the bell of the Christian Church of Savannah, Missouri, was salvaged from the ill-fated sidewheeler *Saluda*, which exploded and sank near Lexington, Missouri, on April 9, 1852. In the fifties a river packet bound upstream for St. Paul, carrying asparagus seed in her cargo, struck a snag and sank when she reached Lake Pepin. Floating ashore, the seed sprouted into asparagus plants that still grow along the roads and in the fields near Bogus Creek and elsewhere, between Pepin and Stockholm.

As it became good advertising for cities along the river to sponsor steamboats named after them, so it was good business for captains to run errands and to do other favors for people along the way. A favorite story tells of the old lady who hailed and stopped a packet on its way down to New Orleans and asked to speak to the captain. "Well, cap'n," she said, producing a small bundle from under her shawl—"here's eleving eggs, and I want you to trade 'em off for me in Orleans, and git me one spool of thread, one skein of silk, and the rest in beeswax. And, cap'n, would ye be kind enough to wait a little minute? You see that old hen is on the nest now, and I want orfully to get another egg to make up the dozen."

Many a present-day Midwesterner still cherishes fond and vivid memories of his or her river childhood. "Tell about the pecans," said Lettie Gay Carson to me in a reminiscent mood, "how good the wild pecans are along the Mississippi and how much better they grow there than along the Ohio. About skating on ice till you got to where you could see it bend. About fish fries as family reunions.

"We had many relatives," she went on. "We hitched up a team of horses to the wagon and all drove to Gilgal Landing for a fish fry. Channel cat, fried in corn meal in deep, black sheet-iron skillets set on iron bars over the fire. Homemade potato chips, pickled beets, pickled peaches and sometimes watermelon. Another sport without parents supervising was to get out in canoes and go over the flood lands—in flat-bottomed canoes over the cornfields. The bay at Quincy, Illinois, was a wonderful playground. The big entertainment was the excursion boats. We'd either go up to Keokuk, forty miles north, or down to Hannibal, forty miles south. The boat would stop for the people who wanted to go to the cave a mile below Hannibal. One little girl, like Becky Thatcher, got lost in the cave. She died, so it was closed for a while.

"One day the boys and I, instead of going on the excursion boat, decided to go in one of the boys' canoes. The river was in flood and he didn't think of the half-submerged logs, the wing dams sticking out perpendicularly. We just went down the middle of the river. When we got to Hannibal we had a rather perilous experience because the whirlpools around the piers of the bridge were dangerous at that time.

"When we lived in Quincy, every night the whole family would just get up from the supper table and say, 'We'll just go out and look at the river.' "

B. A. B.

Settlers' Progress on the Mississippi

Although every European traveler who has glided down the Mississippi, at the rate of ten miles an hour, has told his tale of the squatters [settlers], yet none has given any other account of them than that they are "a sallow, sickly looking sort of miserable beings," living in swamps, and subsisting on pignuts, Indian-corn, and Bear's-flesh. It is obvious, however, that none but a person acquainted with their history, manners, and condition, can give any real information respecting them.

The individuals who become squatters, choose that sort of life of their own free will. They mostly remove from other parts of the United States, after finding that land has become too high in price, and they are persons who, having a family of strong and hardy children, are anxious to enable them to provide for themselves. They have heard from good authorities that the country extending along the great streams of the West is, of all parts of the Union, the richest in its soil, the growth of its timber, and the abundance of its game; that, besides, the Mississippi is the great road to and from all the markets in the world; and that every vessel borne by its waters affords to settlers some chance of selling their commodities, or of exchanging them for others. To these recommendations is added another, of even greater weight with persons of the above denomination, namely, the prospect of being able to settle on land, and perhaps to hold it for a number of years, without purchase, rent or tax of any kind. How many thousands of individuals in all parts of the globe would gladly try their fortune with such prospects, I leave to you, reader, to determine.

As I am not disposed too highly to color the picture which I am about to submit to your inspection, instead of pitching on individuals who have removed from our eastern boundaries, and of whom certainly there are a good number, I shall introduce to you the members of a family from Virginia, first giving you an idea of their condition in that country, previous to their migration to the west. The land which they and their ancestors have possessed for a hundred years, having been constantly forced to produce crops of one kind or another, is now completely worn out. It exhibits only a superficial layer of red clay, cut up by deep ravines, through which much of the soil has been conveyed to some more fortunate neighbor, residing in a yet rich and beautiful valley. Their strenuous efforts to render it productive have failed. They dispose of everything too cumbrous or expensive for

From *Audubon and His Journals*, by Maria R. Audubon, with Zoological and Other Notes by Elliott Coues, Vol. II, pp. 443–449. Copyright, 1897, by Charles Scribner's Sons. New York.

[In "The Squatters of the Mississippi"] Audubon employs the word squatters, which is correct enough in the sense that these people often arrived and settled before the Government had defined the matter of ownership of public lands. But [as he explains] it is not to be assumed that he means shiftless and irresponsible nomads. Donald Culross Peattie, *Audubon's America* (Boston, 1940), p. 125.

them to remove, retaining only a few horses, a servant or two, and such implements of husbandry and other articles as may be necessary on their journey, or useful when they arrive at the spot of their choice.

I think I see them at this moment harnessing their horses, and attaching them to their wagons, which are already filled with bedding, provisions, and the younger children, while on their outside are fastened spinning-wheels and looms, and a bucket filled with tar and tallow swings between the hind wheels. Several axes are secured to the bolster, and the feeding-trough of the horses contains pots, kettles, and pans. The servant, now become a driver, rides the near saddled horse, the wife is mounted on another, the worthy husband shoulders his gun, and his sons, clad in plain substantial home-spun, drive the cattle ahead, and lead the procession, followed by the hounds and other dogs. Their day's journey is short, and not agreeable; the cattle, stubborn or wild, frequently leave the road for the woods, giving the travelers much trouble; the harness of the horses here and there gives way, and needs immediate repair; a basket, which has accidentally dropped, must be gone after, for nothing that they have can be spared; the roads are bad, and now and then all hands are called to push on the wagon, or prevent it from upsetting. Yet by sunset they have proceeded perhaps twenty miles. Rather fatigued, all assemble round the fire, which has been lighted, supper is prepared, and a camp being erected, there they pass the night.

Days and weeks, nay months, of unremitting toil pass before they gain the end of their journey. They have crossed both the Carolinas, Georgia, and Alabama. They have been traveling from the beginning of May to that of September, and with heavy hearts they traverse the State of Mississippi. But now, arrived on the banks of the broad stream, they gaze in amaze-ment on the dark deep woods around them. Boats of various kinds they see gliding downwards with the current, while others slowly ascend against it. A few inquiries are made at the nearest dwelling, and assisted by the in-habitants with their boats and canoes, they at once cross the Mississippi and select their place of habitation.

The exhalations arising from the swamps and morasses around them have a powerful effect on these new settlers, but all are intent on preparing for the winter. A small patch of ground is cleared by the ax and the fire, a temporary cabin is erected, to each of the cattle is attached a jingling bell before it is let loose into the neighboring canebrake, and the horses remain about the house, where they find sufficient food at that season. The first trading-boat that stops at their landing enables them to provide themselves with some flour, fish-hooks, and ammunition, as well as other commodities. The looms are mounted, the spinning-wheels soon furnish some yarn, and in a few weeks the family throw off their ragged clothes and array them-selves in suits adapted to the climate. The father and sons meanwhile have sown turnips and other vegetables; and from some Kentucky flatboat, a supply of live poultry has been procured.

October tinges the leaves of the forest, the morning dews are heavy, the days hot, the nights chill, and the unacclimated family in a few days are attacked with ague [malaria]. The lingering disease almost prostrates their whole faculties, and one seeing them at such a period might well call them sallow and sickly. Fortunately the unhealthy season soon passes over, and the hoar-frosts make their appearance. Gradually each individual recovers strength. The largest ash-trees are felled; their trunks are cut, split, and corded in front of the building; a large fire is lighted at night on the edge of the waters, and soon a steamer calls to purchase the wood and thus add to their comforts during the winter.

The first fruit of their industry imparts new courage to them; their exertions multiply, and when spring returns, the place has a cheerful look. Venison, Bear's-flesh, Wild Turkeys, Ducks and Geese, with now and then some fish, have served to keep up their strength, and now their enlarged field is planted with corn, potatoes, and pumpkins. Their stock of cattle, too, has augmented; the steamer, which now stops there as if by preference, buys a calf or a pig, together with the whole of their wood. Their store of provisions is renewed, and brighter rays of hope enliven their spirits.

Who is he of the settlers on the Mississippi that cannot realize some profit? Truly none who is industrious. When the autumnal months return, all are better prepared to encounter the ague which then prevails. Substantial food, suitable clothing, and abundant firing, repel its attacks; and before another twelvemonth has elapsed the family is naturalized. The sons have by this time discovered a swamp covered with excellent timber, and as they have seen many great rafts of saw logs bound for the mills of New Orleans, floating past their dwelling, they resolve to try the success of a little enterprise. Their industry and prudence have already enhanced their credit. A few cross-saws are purchased, and some broad-wheeled "carry-logs" are made by themselves. Log after log is hauled to the bank of the river, and in a short time their first raft is made on the shore and loaded with cordwood. When the next freshet sets it afloat, it is secured by long grapevines or cables, until the proper time being arrived, the husband and sons embark on it, and flow down the mighty stream.

After encountering many difficulties, they arrive in safety at New Orleans, where they dispose of their stock, the money obtained for which may be said to be all profit, supply themselves with such articles as may add to their convenience or comfort, and with light hearts procure a passage on the upper deck of a steamer, at a very cheap rate on account of the benefit of their labor in taking in wood or otherwise.

And now the vessel approaches their home. See the joyous mother and daughters as they stand on the bank! A store of vegetables lies around them, a large tub of fresh milk is at their feet, and in their hands are plates filled with rolls of butter. As the steamer stops, three broad straw hats are waved from the upper deck, and soon husband and wife, brothers and sisters, are in each other's embrace. The boat carries off the provisions for which value has been left, and as the captain issues his orders for putting on the steam, the happy family enter their humble dwelling. The husband gives his bag of dollars to the wife, while the sons present some token of affection to the sisters. Surely, at such a moment, the squatters are richly repaid for all their labors.

Every successive year has increased their savings. They now possess a large stock of horses, cows, and hogs, with abundance of provisions, and domestic comfort of every kind. The daughters have been married to the sons of their neighboring squatters, and have gained sisters to themselves by the marriage of their brothers. The government secures to the family the lands on which, twenty years before, they settled in poverty and sickness. Larger buildings are erected on piles, secure from the inundations; where a single cabin once stood, a neat village is now to be seen; warehouses, stores and workshops increase the importance of the place. The squatters live respected, and in due time die regretted by all who knew them.

Thus are the vast frontiers of our country peopled, and thus does cultivation, year after year, extend over the western wilds. Time will no doubt be when the great valley of the Mississippi, still covered with primeval forests, interspersed with swamps, will smile with cornfields and orchards, while crowded cities will rise at intervals along its banks, and enlightened nations will rejoice in the bounties of Providence.

Indian Removal

We left Rising Sun, [Indiana], on Sunday the 13th of December, 1835, on board the Steam Boat *Alpha* for Florence, Alabama. The river full of ice when we left. Saturday, the 19th, found us about 100 miles up the Tennessee River. . . .

December 20, '35, we saw the wreck of the old *Rising Sun* Steam Boat converted into a house 150 miles up from the mouth of the river.

The morning of the 22nd found us at Waterloo, a town without houses at the foot of Muscle Shoals, a sorry set of steam boat men. We had to reship freight in Keels to Florence, above, which delayed us some days.

While there Beatty and Ingersoll, Govt. Agents, came in with about 511 Creek Indians to be removed to the Indian Territory up the Arkansas River to Fort Gibson. We bought two Keel boats and took the Indians aboard, a Keel boat on each side, and started on our trip. Was getting $2200 for the trip and were to stop and lay up nights for the Indians to camp out and do their cooking &c. . . .

We happened to make Memphis just in the evening and so had to land on the opposite side of the river. Next morning the party who went by land to take the ponies through were crossing the river so it was impossible to

From *The Ohio*, by R. E. Banta, pp. 295–296. Copyright, 1949, by R. E. Banta. *The Rivers of America*, edited by Hervey Allen and Carl Carmer. New York and Toronto: Rinehart & Company.

From untitled memoirs of John Hewitt Jones, in the possession of R. E. Banta.

get away for the Indians must see their ponies and would bring them into camp and make a terrible fuss over them and were very loth to part with them. Some offered to sell a nice little pony for $5 for fear they would not go through the trip.

We entered the mouth of White River and went through a cut-off into the Arkansas River on the morning of the 2nd of January 1836.

We anchored out in the river at Little Rock—the agents and the Boat having some business to transact. We had to use this precaution to keep the Indians from getting in to town and getting whisky, for when they did there was a tear round among the Indians. The women (squaws) would down a fellow and tie his legs and tie his arms and let him lay till he got sober. Little Rock was of about 1000 inhabitants, a very pretty place.

We had lost time and the agents agreed we might run some of the nights to make up. The first night, the river being very snaggy, we stove one of the Keel boats and made a terrible rumpus among the Indians, again having to lay up of nights and leave the sunken Keel boat at Lewisville. It was a very dark night, the stove Keel boat sinking fast with about 250 Indians on board, causing great confusion and such a time to get them and their baggage on the Steam Boat. The yelling of the yellow skins, big and little, old and young, was not easily forgotten. . . .

It was a fine sight to see the camping of the Indians on the trip. As soon as the Boat was tied to the shore and a plank out, the first to leave was the squaws, who gathered up their kit, which was usually tied up by the corners in a blanket in which was their tents, blankets, cook articles &c. They would throw it over their backs and let the tie come across their foreheads, resting on their backs, and in one hand take an ax and in the other and under their arm a little papoose and run ashore and up the bank.

They would chop trees and make a fire and prepare supper. I often used to walk through the camp of pleasant evenings. It looked like a little village. They parched corn in a kettle and then would pound it in a mortar or deep cut trough in a log and then boil it up and make a very fine dish which they called "sophka" and would broil their meat stuck on a stick before the fire.

This was played on the violin by a half-breed Indian (Creek) on the Steam Boat *Alpha*, which was removing them from their old home in Georgia, in the winter of 1835, to their new home in the Indian Territory:

> Alas! for them—their day is o'er—
> Their fires are out from hill and shore;
> No more for them the wild deer bounds;
> The pale man's ax rings through their woods;
> Their pleasant springs are dry.
> Their children—look! by power oppressed.
> Beyond the mountains of the west,
> Their children go—to die,
> By foes alone their death song must be sung.

We only got a few miles above Fort Smith, the water being too low, and had to give up the trip and return. We bought 25 Bbls. Pecans at Fort Smith for $5 per Bbl. and started back. We had to check up near Van Buren and stay there two weeks, when the river rose and we left and got back to Rising Sun in March, all safe.

It was not long till we sold the *Alpha*. It proved to be poor stock—my last dollar was gone—so I had to start again.

The Galesburg Boat Party

The "boat party," as it was known for years in the annals of the town, usually prefixed by some such adjective as "unfortunate" or "ill-fated," had set out in the spring of 1836 with high hopes. John C. Smith, a canal boat proprietor of Utica in a small way, was active in deliberations of the subscribers to Gale's plan from the very beginning. Able, energetic, but somewhat visionary, and more familiar with water transport than other methods of progression, he conceived the idea of emigrating to the new settlement in a canal boat by way of the Erie Canal (which he knew thoroughly), Lake Erie, the Erie and Ohio Canal, and the Ohio, Mississippi and Illinois Rivers (of which he was profoundly ignorant); some two thousand miles by water as against one thousand by land (or land and water) adopted by other emigrants.

He organized his company, and a canal boat of the packet type was bought on shares, and fitted up for the voyage. The men's cabin was used for storage of baggage and household goods, leaving only a narrow passageway to get to the bunks. The horses and wagons of the settlers were put on board, the horses to serve as motor power on the tow path. The galley was equipped for cooking, a supply of provisions laid in, and in May the boat started from New London, near Utica, for Buffalo, with Smith as captain, his wife as chief cook, and thirty-seven people on board, seventeen of them small children, one an infant.

On the comparatively quiet trip to Buffalo the passengers of this remarkable ark settled down to some sort of routine. Some were strangers to the others, but with a common purpose and sharing the same discomforts and relaxations, they become as the report says "one large family." Cooking three times a day for thirty-seven people proved too much for Mrs. Smith, and Mrs. Phelps, in spite of six children clinging to her skirts, took charge, and for a time all went smoothly. It was rather close quarters for seventeen lively youngsters, and to give the elders some respite, "Aunty Kitty," as one of the spinsters was affectionately known, organized a sort of school along what would now be known as kindergarten lines, with regular lessons, and

From *They Broke the Prairie*, by Earnest Elmo Calkins, pp. 85–91. Copyright, 1937, by Earnest Elmo Calkins. New York: Charles Scribner's Sons.

the future students of the Prairie College that was to be were thus kept quiet for some hours daily.

As may well be imagined in such a company, religious worship was more important than education, and prayer meetings were held daily. Each Saturday night the boat was tied up, and on Sunday they attended the nearest public service, or if there was none available, they organized their own in a convenient schoolhouse, and invited the neighborhood to join them.

At Buffalo passengers, goods and livestock were transferred to one of the lake steamboats bound for Cleveland; the canal boat was hitched behind. Off Ashtabula a violent storm struck them, so severe the steamboat captain thought his vessel endangered and cut the canal boat adrift. He landed the passengers at Cleveland, dumped their goods on the dock where they lay in the rain and were seriously damaged, while the party anxiously awaited news of their ark.

When the canal boat arrived, the damaged dunnage was loaded into it, the horses again put to work on the tow-path, and the party started to cross Ohio by way of the Ohio and Erie Canal, a winding and tortuous journey. They ascended the valley of the Cuyahoga, fringed with tulip, walnut and sassafras trees, with a lock every half mile, to Akron, the modern rubber tire city, whose name is Greek, meaning Elevation, now a sort of industrial acropolis. The canal passed through the center of the town by means of twelve locks. Beyond Akron it traversed a lake, with a bridge for the tow horses. Newportage marked the place where the fur traders carried their canoes from the Cuyahoga to the Tuscarawas.

The mayapple was in full bloom, kingfishers, red-headed woodpeckers and orioles perched on the alder bushes and watched the boat slide slowly by. They gazed in wonder at prehistoric mounds and barrows frequently visible from their boat. They saw corn just springing into leaf, the largest fields they had ever beheld, a foretaste of what was later to become a familiar sight in Illinois. A tourist traveling west in those days beheld the whole cycle of the development of a new country from unbroken prairie to well-tilled farm, but in reverse order, like a movie run backward.

From the high level the canal descends to the valley of the Muskingum and then cuts across to the Scioto, which it follows all the way to the Ohio. On Licking Summit it passes through a cut thirty feet deep; the tow line is lengthened, the horses looking small so high above the boat. They pass Circleville, appropriately named, for the village is surrounded by an Indian mound twelve to twenty feet high like a circular wall. Instead of the conventional public square there is a circular plaza in the center of the village, in which stands a round brick courthouse. After Chillicothe they arrive at Portsmouth where the Sciota and the canal empty into the Ohio, having negotiated fifty-three locks since Licking Summit. They find Portsmouth an inconsiderable town, with broad, unpaved streets, set high on its bank eighty feet above the river. On the trees which border the Ohio they saw curious vegetable growths which must have puzzled them, for it was their first sight of mistletoe. It had no sentimental associations for them, for these New England Christians did not celebrate Christmas.

Isaac Mills decided to leave rather than face the even worse discomforts and dangers beyond. His announcement caused the utmost consternation. He was the only member of the party with any money left. The others had sunk all they possessed in the venture. The unduly prolonged trip had exhausted their resources. Without him they could not go on, but would be left stranded, their journey half completed. Mills finally yielded to their urgings and remained with the party and defrayed its expenses, a decision that cost him his life.

The long stay in Cincinnati was for the purpose of rigging up some sort of propeller on the stern of the vessel so as to drive it upstream on the Mississippi, worked by a horse in a treadmill on board, and some such contrivance was made, not very efficient, as the sequel proved. Meanwhile the company visited the city, then a town of some 20,000 and saw its sights, which must have included the market, where rows and rows of four-horse Ohio wagons were backed to the curb, permitted to sell every sort of provender but fresh meat.

Cincinnati was then as now the pork city, and its streets were kept comparatively clean by the droves of hogs that roamed at will and ate up the garbage thrown out by the housewives. . . .

* * * * *

As the ill-fated bark moved away from the Cincinnati landing and down the Ohio, things grew worse. The river was low, the air foul with miasma, the sun scorching, and the mosquitoes ferocious. They knew as little about malaria and fever and ague as they did about navigating a river full of snags and sandbanks. Often in the middle of the day when the heat became unbearable they tied up to the shore, and the party took refuge in the shade of the trees along the bank. Every one was more or less sick. The lighter cases nursed the serious ones. It became a grim test of endurance, with no immediate escape from the evils that beset them.

The canal around the rapids at Louisville had just been completed, so they were able to get by where formerly travelers by steamboat had been transferred to another vessel. Between Louisville and the Mississippi lay the bottom lands of Egyptian Illinois with their dreary water-logged deadly towns, Shawneetown, Ft. Massac, Golconda, lawless, disorderly, and inhospitable, hardly safe for such unworldly pilgrims to stop at. In caves along the river lurked bands of pirates who robbed and murdered defenseless travelers by water.

In the Mississippi there was constant delay. Even experienced river pilots are often fooled by this treacherous stream. The propeller refused to work. Parts of it continually dropped off into the river, and Noble Phelps acquired such experience in diving that when Captain Smith lost his watch over the side, he went in and recovered that also. At St. Louis they refused an offer of $1000 for their boat; it would have been wiser to have accepted. Slowly they worked north while the sick lay in their bunks and longed for land.

At length they were forced to make the best arrangements they could for a tow, and were hauled up the Illinois as far as Copperas Creek, about twenty miles below Peoria, and forty from Log City. They had been eleven weeks on the way, and conditions were now desperate. Smith, Mills, and Lyman were seriously ill. They were all big men, men over six feet tall. Only one young man had sufficient strength to sit on a horse. He was dispatched to Log City for help.

A rescue party with teams, blankets, and whatever supplies might alleviate the sufferings of the boat load of invalids was quickly assembled. The sight that met its eyes was a sad one. Emaciated, sallow, weak, the company showed the effects of the long strain. The sick and dying were lifted into the wagons for the long, rough, jolting journey back to Log City. Captain Smith died at Knoxville. Mills and Lyman lived only a few weeks. These three were the first martyrs. They lie in Hope Cemetery which the settlers had laid out near the site of their new city. Little Moses Root died the following spring.

In a one-room cabin were installed the worst cases, thirteen in number, on beds of poles set in the walls, laced with ropes to support straw-filled ticks. Other beds were made up on the chests that held the clothing, which had to be removed whenever anything was needed. In the center of the room was a huge box stove on which all the cooking was done. In this improvised hospital in the heat of an Illinois summer the survivors slowly recovered. Compared with so lamentable an experience, the minor discomforts and discouragements of the next company, which came all the way by land in covered wagons, were the acme of luxurious travel.

General Tipton's Jack

John C. Barnes was the pioneer blacksmith in Tipton [Tennessee], north of Hatchie. His shop was on the waters of Fisher's creek. Barnes was a good citizen, though a bachelor, and had the advancement and prosperity of the settlement very much at heart. Of robust constitution, he stood six feet two in his stocking feet, broad across the chest, with shoulders and arms of a Vulcan, and was a skilful and most reliable workman with all.

The bringing into cultivation of the rich new lands [of West Tennessee] began to require more work stock than were brought in by the settlers. Barnes, wishing to contribute his share toward *increasing* the stock of the land, proposed bringing a jack into the settlement and establish his headquarters at his blacksmith shop. His proposition was approbated by the

From *Old Times in West Tennessee*, by Joseph S. Williams, pp. 67–76. Entered . . . 1873, by Joseph S. Williams. Memphis, Tenn.: W. G. Cheeney, Printer and Publisher.

neighborhood, with promises of patronage. But the grave question arose, first, as to where one could be had, and secondly, the money required to pay for one. A good jack in those days was worth from six to eight hundred dollars, which was more money than Barnes, backed by the *settlement*, could conveniently raise. My father, hearing of Barnes' enterprise, and equally anxious with the lower settlement, to begin the raising of mules, sent for him. Barnes, full of hope-giving promise, with the message he had received, was at my father's to breakfast the next morning. He and my father talked over the subject matter of his visit, which resulted in his going over to see General Tipton, residing south of the Hatchie, near Covington.

General Tipton was among the first settlers south of the Big Hatchie, in the county which bore his name. His place of dwelling was beautifully situated, four miles northeast of Covington, where he established a large plantation. He early introduced into the country the "best blooded stock." He took great interest in raising fine horses, mules and cattle, by which he became a great benefactor to the early settlers. Barnes, without delay, went over to see the General, and by an arrangement satisfactory to both parties, obtained his fine jack "Moses," and brought him over to his blacksmith shop. There being no printing offices yet in the country, Barnes repaired to old man Gaines, who taught a school in the settlement, and who wrote a fine, big hand, and got him to write off handbills, which he did, announcing, in a flowing hand, that "General Tipton's celebrated Jack, 'Moses,' fifteen and a half hands high, would keep his headquarters for the season at Barnes blacksmith shop," etc. Sticking them up, one at the school-house, one at the meeting-house, and through the settlement generally, the neighbors flocked to the blacksmith shop to see General Tipton's famous jack "Moses," and Barnes felt that his fortune would be made in one *season*. His blacksmith work, in the meantime, kept him busy during spring and early summer [and], with the *standing* profits that promised to crop out of the "celebrated Moses," he passed the summer with golden dreams of a rich harvest from his enterprise.

The Chickasaws had not yet abandoned the Big Hatchie country as their favorite hunting-ground. Bands of hunters came in every fall, hunting in the Hatchie Bottom, until they loaded their ponies with deer, bear and other skins, which they took to Bolivar, a trading post for Indian traffic. Game of every description was so plentiful that the whites paid little or no attention to their coming or going. They were proverbially polite, friendly, and wholly inoffensive. To the nearest settlers they would bring in the finest haunches of venison, fat gobblers and bear meat. They hunted for the most part for the *peltries*, curing only as many venison hams as they could conveniently pack away on their ponies.

The hunting season had opened. Barnes, however, was no hunter. He was regarded as the rising man of the settlement, and began to think it was not good to be "alone in the world." A wedding was soon talked of at Captain Childress', some six miles below in the "thick woods." Barnes was spotted as the lucky man, and the Captain's eldest daughter as the woman. She was a widow. The wedding came off, and Barnes took his bride home. Arriving at home with his loving charge, he was met with the stern reality that "Moses" had gotten out and taken himself off to the "wilderness." All hands had gone to the wedding, and none could tell how he got out or whither he had gone. It was night, and nothing could be done until morning. Barnes rose early, and his first care was to find the whereabouts of the General's jack. Finding from his tracks that he had gone in the direction of the Hatchie Bottom, he returned to breakfast. After breakfast, he, with his foreman in the shop, went in search of "Moses." Taking his track, they followed it until they came to the thick switch-cane, where they could track him no farther. Bogueing about in the cane until night came upon them, they were compelled to return, having hunted all day in vain.

A general search was made the next day, several of the neighbors joining in the hunt; but "Moses" had lost himself in the wilderness, where he could not be found. Barnes grew uneasy; he was troubled. Could he have been stolen? Hardly, for he had been tracked to the thick cane. The Chickasaws were in camp some eight miles above. None had been seen so low down, and if they had, no one thought for a moment that they were guilty of the theft. They had been coming in every hunting season, and were never known to trespass upon any one's rights. No, the Chickasaws had never been guilty of a wrong. In the meantime the winter rains set in early, overflowing all the streams. The Hatchie rose rapidly, inundating the bottom. "Moses" had not yet returned. The conclusion Barnes came to was that he had been caught in the overflow and drowned.

The winter passed, and Barnes had to report to the General the loss of his jack, acknowledging his responsibility in the premises. He promised to make good his value as soon as he was able to do so. The General, kind at heart and in sympathy with Barnes for his loss, was lenient. Barnes went to work in his shop, redoubling his energies. Newcomers were rapidly settling around him. His shop work increased. He made and sharpened all the plows for eight or ten miles around. Happening to be on the river fishing one day, as a trading boat was descending, the Captain hailed him and inquired whether any *peltries* were on sale in his neighborhood. In the meantime the boat drifted around in the eddy where he was fishing, coming up broadside to the bank. The deck, or roof, of the boat was covered with skins of all kinds. It was sunny September, and the skins were being sunned and aired. A conversation grew up, Barnes asking the Captain what kind of skins he was buying, what he was paying, and the points he was trading to and from, when the Captain remarked that he had bought a hide of an animal at Bolivar novel in the *peltry trade*. The novelty was turned over, with the hair side up, a huge hide, with head, ears, and the eye holes well stretched. No sooner was Barnes' attention called to it when he exclaimed: "By thunder! Captain, it's my jackass's skin. 'Moses,' have I found you at last? Captain, where did you come across that hide?" The Captain told him that he purchased it with other skins from Bills & McNeal, of Bolivar. Barnes then related the story of the missing jack, and the Captain, being impressed with the truth of the statement, readily turned the hide over to Barnes, who took it home and put it away for safekeeping.

The following month, October, the Chickasaws came in for their fall hunt. Barnes was on the lookout for them. They came down to the number of sixty or seventy, and camped at the mouth of Fisher's Creek, in the vicinity where "Moses" had lost himself the fall previous. They were very friendly. Barnes was favorably known to many of them. He had, on previous seasons, repaired their guns. Wholly ignorant of the grave charge awaiting them, several were soon out to the shop to have the locks of their guns fixed. Barnes had a talk with them. Learning that it was the same party that were in the bottom hunting the fall previous, he fell upon a strategy to get them out to his shop. Fixing their locks, he told them that a great "shooting-match" was going to take place at his shop next Saturday, then three days off, and invited them to come and bring all of their best shots; that they were going to shoot for the skin of a large and beautiful animal, the only one of the sort that was ever killed in the Hatchie Bottom. Delighted with the opportunity of shooting with the white man, and for such a prize skin, they left in great glee, promising to come and bring all of their best marksmen. Barnes was not long in communicating with his neighbors and arranging for the "shooting match." Saturday came. The best shots of the neighborhood, numbering thirty, had arrived. Soon the Indians came galloping up on their ponies, numbering between sixty and seventy.

The blacksmith shop was at the cross-roads, on a high, level bench of land, thickly shaded with large poplar, oak and hickory, free from undergrowth. A broad board had been charred, by holding it over a fire until it was black. The "bull's eye" was cut and pinned in the center of the "blackboard," which was nailed breast high on a large poplar, and ninety yards [were] stepped off. The Indians were to choose from among them five of their best shots, and the whites the same number. Judges were appointed to arrange the order of shooting. A silver half-dollar was cast up, "heads or tails," to decide which side would have the first shot. It was won by the red men. The judges announced everything ready for the shooting to begin. Four shots, in their order, were made, and the judges decided there was a "tie." The last round would decide. The red man squared himself to the mark, slowly bringing his rifle to his shoulder, and in breathless silence raised its long barrel until his sight covered the "bull's eye," and fired. *He drove the center.* It was the first shot that broke the cross (†). The Indians yelled with gleeful delight. The remaining shots were wide of the mark, and the Chickasaws whooped and yelled, calling for the prize skin.

Barnes was ready with it. He deliberately walked out with the hide of "Moses" rolled up under his arm, and unrolled it upon the ground, to the astonished gaze of the red men. There was the hide of the celebrated jack, "Moses," with its mouse-colored hair and black streak running down its back, its flanks and belly white as cotton, relieved by the dark rings of the neck and head, with ears sticking up, and eye-holes circled with thick tufts of short white hair, spread out on the ground. The red men pressed up close to get a sight. The winner of the prize gathered it up, to exhibit it, as well as to examine it more closely. Turning it over, he broke out with a jolly, semi-savage "Ha! ha! ha! Me kill him. Me shoot him. See my bullet hole [running his finger through the fatal hole] Ha! ha! Me sell him to Bolivar. Me get him again. Ha! ha!"

Old man Fullen—Ben Fullen, proprietor of "Fullen Ferry"—who was not in the secret of Barnes' strategy, exclaimed aloud that it was "the hide of General Tipton's jack"; he would "swear by the *flesh marks* that it was. See them eye-holes, and them rings round his big ears!"

"Hush!" said Barnes, "let me speak."

Asking them all to be quiet, he spoke, addressing himself to the Chickasaws. He explained to them the nature and uses of the animal whose hide was before them; that it belonged to a great General, who lived on the other side of the Hatchie; that ["Moses"] strayed away from his shop into the thick cane last fall, while he was absent from home; that he and his neighbors had hunted for him for weeks, and concluded that he was caught in the overflow and drowned; that he had to pay the General six hundred dollars for his loss; that he was a poor man, not able to pay that big money; that he had been good to them, fixing and repairing their old guns whenever they came to him, and never charged them much; that the Chickasaws were a brave, honorable nation; that they had never stolen anybody's property, nor trespassed upon any one's rights. The brave young man, who was the best shot and won the hide, acknowledged that he killed him. He was satisfied that he thought he was shooting some wild animal; that he felt innocent of doing harm. Yet, they were in the white man's country, where laws were made; that the laws did not have any respect to persons and ignorance was no excuse; that all were alike guilty, and they must pay him for killing the animal. If they refused, the man of the law was upon the ground, who would have them all arrested and carried to jail.

The utmost respect and attention was paid to Barnes while he was making this plain talk. The older heads of the red men gathered together in the grove, and held council in the matter. After a long talk, the young hunters having gathered around them, they dispersed, each man going to his pony. Their movements were eagerly watched and noted by the thirty good marksmen at the shop. Getting their ponies, they all came leading them up before the shop. An intelligent looking old hunter spoke:

"We sorry for killing him. We think he belong to the woods. We find him in thick cane. We think him wild. We sorry for Barn—good man, work much. We take no white man's hoss, pony, nothin' that b'longs to white man. We honest. We pay. We have ponies; that's all [motioning toward the long line of ponies held by their owners]. Take pay. We honest."

The strategy was a success. The red men had shown themselves true CHICKASAWS. Barnes told his red friends to point out the ponies they wanted to give up in payment for the jack. The old hunter who acted as spokesman said: "Take, take plenty. Red man pay white man. Let white man say." Barnes then suggested that three white men and two red men be appointed as appraisers. They were appointed, and passed upon the value of the ponies, fixing their value at seventeen dollars and a fraction as the average, turning over to Barnes thirty-five ponies in payment and full satisfaction for his jack. What became of General Tipton's jackass was satisfactorily explained.

The Chickasaws meted out a full measure of justice to our friend Barnes —six hundred dollars' worth of ponies satisfied the law. It was their first lesson—stunning lessson under the teachings of stern, written law. They would have no more of it, so they cut short their hunt, and bid a long farewell to the Big Hatchie country, their old hunting ground, and returned to their "beloved prairies," soon to be yielded up to the progress of Southern agriculture. Barnes had a public sale and sold off the ponies, distributing the illegitimate proceeds of his jack through the settlement, thereby increasing the stock of the land. My eldest brother purchased three of them; most excellent hunting ponies they were.

Baldy Parker and the Stranger up the Yazoo

The land up the Yazoo belonged to the state [of Mississippi], and the State sold it for $1.25 per acre. The fellows that got up there first weren't any too anxious to see new folks coming in and entering land. Used to try all kinds of schemes to get them out.

There were two brothers up there named Parker. One of them was a surveyor—we called him "Baldy"—and the other was lumbering, getting timber out of the cypress breaks and rafting it down. Almost all the timber used from Vicksburg to New Orleans came out of there.

One time a man came up the Yazoo to take up land and went to stop with Baldy Parker. When they sat down to dinner Baldy took some flour and sprinkled it all over his meat.

"What's that?" asked the stranger.

"Quinine," says Baldy. "Haven't you got any?"

"No," says the fellow. "What would I want it for?"

"You'll find out if you go out there in the swamps," Baldy tells him. "It's full of malaria. We eat quinine on everything."

The fellow was quiet through the rest of the meal.

Pretty soon they got up to go out, and Baldy took up a pair of stovepipes.

"What do you do with them pipes?" asks the stranger.

From *American Adventures*, A Second Trip "Abroad at Home," by Julian Street, pp. 511–512. Copyright, 1916, 1917, by P. F. Collier & Son, Inc.; 1917, by The Century Co. New York.

As told by Captain S. H. Parisot, Vicksburg, Mississippi.

"Wear 'em, of course," says Baldy. "Haven't you got any?"

"No," says the fellow. "What for?"

"Why," says Baldy, "the rattlesnakes out there will bite the legs right off of you."

With that the fellow had enough. He didn't go any farther, but turned around and took the boat down the river.

Losantiville

. . . In 1788 John Cleves Symmes, the first United States judge of the Northwest Territory, purchased from Congress a million acres of land, lying on the Ohio between the two Miami Rivers. Mathias Denman bought from him a square mile at the eastern end of the grant "on a most delightful high bank" opposite the Licking [River], and—on a cash valuation for the land, of two hundred dollars—took in with him as partners Robert Patterson and John Filson. Filson was a schoolmaster, had written the first history of Kentucky, and seems to have enjoyed much local distinction. To him was entrusted the task of inventing a name for the settlement which the company proposed to plant here. The outcome was "Losantiville," a pedagogical hash of Greek, Latin, and French: *L*, for Licking; *os*, mouth; *anti*, opposite; *ville*, city—Licking-opposite-City or City-opposite-Licking, whichever is preferred. This was in August. The Fates work quickly, for in October poor Filson was scalped by the Indians in the neighborhood of the Big Miami, before a settler had yet been enticed to Losantiville. But the survivors knew how to "boom" a town; lots were given away by lottery to intending actual settlers; and in a few months Symmes was able to write that "It populates considerably."

A few weeks previous to the planting of Losantiville, a party of men from Redstone had settled Columbia, at the mouth of the Little Miami, about where the suburb of California now is; and a few weeks later, a third colony was started by Symmes himself at North Bend, near the Big Miami, at the western extremity of his grant; and this the judge wished to make the capital of the new Northwest Territory. At first, it was a race between these three colonies. A few miles below North Bend, Fort Finney had been built in 1785–86, hence the Bend had at first the start; but a high flood dampened its prospects, the troops were withdrawn from this neighborhood to Louisville, and in the winter of 1789–90 Fort Washington was built at Losantiville by General Harmar. The neighborhood of the new fortress became, in the ensuing Indian war, the center of the district.

To Losantiville, with its fort, came Arthur St. Clair, the new governor

From *On the Storied Ohio*, An Historical Pilgrimage of a Thousand Miles in a Skiff, from Redstone to Cairo, by Reuben Gold Thwaites, pp. 179–181. Copyright, "Afloat on the Ohio," 1897; "On the Storied Ohio," 1903. Chicago: A. C. McClurg & Company.

of the Northwest Territory (January, 1790); and, making his headquarters here, laid violent hands on Filson's invention, at once changing the name to Cincinnati, in honor of the Society of the Cincinnati, of which the new official was a prominent member—"so that," Symmes sorrowfully writes, "Losantiville will become extinct. . . ."

Why North Bend Lost Out to Cincinnati

. . . In Burnet's *Notes on the Northwestern Territory*, it is related that Ensign Luce, who, at the request of Judge Symmes, was sent from Louisville to North Bend with the detachment of eighteen soldiers, for the performance of the service which Kearsey had so unceremoniously shirked, of affording protection to the Miami settlers, came without any orders as to the precise spot in the purchase at which he should permanently quarter himself; and that in the exercise of the discretion which he considered had been allowed him in that respect, he immediately displayed a most unaccountable and obstinate predilection for the station opposite the mouth of the Licking, and in despite of the remonstrances and entreaties of the Judge, left the Bend within a few days after his first appearance there, and betook himself, with his command, to the place of his choice, where he forthwith commenced the construction of a permanent military work, greatly to the chagrin and detriment of the dwellers at the Bend, who had planted themselves there in the belief that they would there be sure of the constant presence of a body of soldiers for their defense. The narrative thus proceeds:

"About that time there was a rumor prevailing in the settlement, said to have been endorsed by the Judge himself, which goes far to unravel the mystery in which the removal of the troops from the Bend was involved. It was said, and believed, that while the officer in command was looking out very leisurely for a suitable site on which to build the blockhouse, he formed an acquaintance with a beautiful, black-eyed female, who called forth his most assiduous and tender attentions. She was the wife of one of the settlers at the Bend. Her husband saw the danger to which he would be exposed if he remained where he was. He therefore resolved at once to remove to Cincinnati, and very promptly executed his resolution. As soon as the gallant commandant discovered that the object of his admiration had changed her residence, he began to think that the Bend was not an advantageous situation for a military work, and communicated that opinion to Judge Symmes, who strenuously opposed it. His reasoning, however, was not as persuasive as the sparkling eyes of the fair Dulcinea now at Cincinnati.

From *Cincinnati's Beginnings,* Missing Chapters in the Early History of the City and the Miami Purchase, Chiefly from Hitherto Unpublished Documents, by Francis W. Miller, pp. 88–90. Copyright, 1879, by Peter G. Thomson. Cincinnati. 1880.

"The result was a determination to visit that place and examine its advantages for a military post, which he communicated to the Judge, with an assurance that if on examination it did not prove to be the most eligible he would return and erect the fort at the Bend. The visit was quickly made and resulted in a conviction that the Bend could not be compared with Cincinnati as a military position. The troops were accordingly removed to that place, and the building of a blockhouse commenced. Whether this structure was on the ground on which Fort Washington was erected by Major Doughty cannot now be decided. That movement, produced by a cause whimsical and apparently trivial in itself, was attended with results of incalculable importance. It settled the question whether North Bend or Cincinnati was to be the great commercial town of the Miami country. Thus we see what unexpected results are sometimes produced by circumstances apparently trivial."

How Cairo Got the Court House from Thebes

The last county made in Illinois—I don't mean by the Legislature but by Nature, and where dirt was so short that it lies under water part of the year —is called Alexander, and used to boast two rival towns, both thoroughly Egyptian in their nomenclative association—Cairo and Thebes. Twenty years ago Thebes was the "seat of justice"; but Cairo was then beginning to entertain magnificent expectations, and her citizens wanted to have the Court House removed to their town. The contest waxed warm. The Thebans contended that Cairo was only a "daub of mud on the tail of the State," while Thebes was destined to hold the same relation to Alexander that its ancient namesake did to Egypt in the time of Menes. [See Herodotus.] But to settle the dispute the Legislature must be appealed to, and that involved the choice of a man favorable to the change. This narrowed the fight right down to a hot county canvass between the Theban and Cairoine interests.

A Cairo man conceived a scheme that was ahead of anything yet achieved by Uncle Abe's brigadiers in the way of "strategy." He wrapped a boulder in a green hide, making a perfectly round mass, to which he attached a mule; then night after night he drew the stone through sand and mud. By going on a straight line, the mule's tracks were concealed, and the track left resembled that made by a huge serpent. These tracks were mainly in the south end of the county, and caused an excitement that almost absorbed the election interest. Soon it was reported that Mrs. So and So had seen a huge snake. The wonder grew apace. Anon it was currently reported that two men had seen the great serpent five miles above

From *Lincolniana;* or The Humors of Uncle Abe, Second Joe Miller, by Andrew Adderup. Springfield, Ill., pp. 33–36. Entered . . . 1864, by J. F. Feeks. New York.

Cairo. The excitement increased. Several daring hunters followed the track, of which new ones were made every night; but the trail always led into water and was lost. Several persons missed hogs and calves, which were supposed to have gone into the capacious maw of the serpent. Finally word was given out that a great hunt was to come off in the lower part of the county, and the rendezvous was appointed. On the morning hundreds were there from all parts of the county, and dividing into squads they started to scour the country about. At night they returned from their snakeless hunt, but so anxious were the people to get rid of his snakeship that they furnished an abundance of edibles and whisky. All were in hilarious spirits, determined to renew the hunt on the following morning. By daylight the hunters were again on the tramp, and men from the lower part of the county happened to fall into the squad.

About 3 o'clock in the afternoon, a squad of Thebans hove in sight of a small village, *i.e.*, one house, a blacksmith shop and a grocery, where, seeing a large crowd assembled, they hurried up in expectation of seeing the dead monster. *But the men were voting!*

"Thunder!" cried a Theban, "this is election day, and I'll bet my bottom dollar we're sold!"

They started for the rendezvous and spread their suspicions; but so few reached their own precincts that the Cairo man was elected.

Then the joke came out; but the Thebans couldn't see the "laughing place," their rage and mortification was so intense.

Uncle Abe was a member of the Legislature when an effort was made to change the county seat of Alexander; and though he liked the joke hugely by which the Thebans had been "diddled," he saw the honesty of the thing and so voted against any change.

They Call It Egypt

The nickname "Egypt," for the southern portion of the state of Illinois, is now well over 100 years old. It has historical, geographical and agricultural significance. Moreover, the soubriquet has caught the imagination of the public both inside the state and beyond its borders. Heard in everyday conversation locally and frequently seen in print, the nickname as an oddity bids fair to rival that of other states. The term "Egypt"

By Grace Partridge Smith. From *Names* (Journal of the American Name Society), Vol. II (March. 1954), No. 1, pp. 51–54.

According to M. Schele De Vere (*Americanisms*, New York, 1871, pp. 214–215), the name "Egypt" reflects not only the natives' opinion of the "productivity of the soil" but also the outsiders' opinion of the "Egyptian darkness" (mental) prevailing there, among the "low Germans" and "poor, shiftless, and ignorant outcasts from Kentucky and Tennessee." General James Winchester bestowed the name Memphis on Fort Pickering from a similar fancied or real resemblance between the "Nile of America" and the granary of the ancient world.

has firmly entrenched itself in the regional idiom and is responsible for having added copiously to the ever-growing body of Illinoisiana.

Despite the popularity of the nickname, it is doubtful whether the majority of persons living in southern Illinois can explain its origin. To those who have had no contacts with the area, the term is a seeming misnomer. Newcomers to the section, travelers or otherwise, continually bombard those they meet with the query, "Why do you call it *Egypt*?" East and West, the reaction is the same. In a recent letter to the writer, a Yorker posed the fantastic question, "Do Egyptians *really* live in southern Illinois?" To a Vancouver oil-station attendant, the sign "Egypt, Illinois" on an incoming car was puzzling. He went straight home to consult an atlas, but later complained he couldn't find any town in Illinois by that name.

This "name on the land" represents an area that has been compared in shape to an inverted triangle, its peak resting at Illinois' tip-city, Cairo, and its base suggested by an imaginary line drawn from Vincennes, Indiana, to East St. Louis, Illinois. This boundary as an upper limit for Egypt has been generally agreed upon by specialists in the social and political history of the area. Besides, various documentary evidence supports the placement of Egypt's northern boundary.

"*Greater* Egypt" is a term frequently applied to the whole section in question, probably entering the regional vocabulary when an effort among southern Illinoisans to promote and protect business and other interests in their midst resulted in formation of a Greater Egypt Association. The combination "*Little* Egypt" is sometimes used, originally designating a group of extreme southern counties, but today the usage is frowned upon, since both the regional public and the press feel that it has connotations with the exotic Syrian dancer of World's-Fair fame of half-a-century ago. For this reason and other trifling objections, purists in Egyptian terminology refuse to accept the term.

Rather than being "contemptuously" bestowed on the area, as one writer asserts, the epithet "Egypt" as applied to southern Illinois claims respect from both history and tradition. Historians emphasize the far-sightedness of an enterprising businessman of St. Louis, Missouri, who obtained from the Territorial Legislature in 1818 an Act incorporating the City and Bank of Cairo. This pioneer financier was so impressed with conditions at the confluence of the Mississippi and Ohio Rivers that he named the new town after the Old World city in deference to the similarities between the two sites. Later, the establishment of towns given Egyptian names (Karnak, Thebes) tended to *fix* southern Illinois' regional epithet.

A traditional as well as a popular explanation of the origin of the nickname derives from economic conditions in the upper half of the state in the first quarter of the nineteenth century. In those early years, there was a famine in northern and central Illinois. During this time many heads of families were obliged to journey southward for supplies where there were abundant yields of grain. An old-timer [John G. Comegys] writes thus of these conditions:

. . . In the summer of 1824, there was not a bushel of corn to be had in central Illinois. My father settled that year in Springfield. We had to live there for a time on venison, blackberries and milk while the men were gone to Egypt to harvest and procure breadstuffs.

And another reminiscence of that early day:

Egypt—the term originated among the early settlers who were frequently obliged to come to this fertile country of southern Illinois for food as did the Israelites of old in the land of Egypt.[1]

The place-name under discussion is defined in dictionaries, gazetteers, and other sources of information. Few of these definitions give the corn story, referring rather to the influence of the christening of Cairo in spreading the use of the epithet "Egypt" for southern Illinois. Such is the gist of Stewart's definition and that of Shankle, who remarks in addition, ". . . and on account of the fact that the people of southern Illinois are dark-complexioned, thus resembling the inhabitants of Egypt." Other proposals crop up from time to time to explain the origin of the nickname. Its use is by no means confined to present-day vocabulary. It was used by Lincoln during the Third Lincoln-Douglas Debate; a "splendid horse" presented to General Grant as he was sojourning in Cairo in 1861 was christened "Egypt." Many more examples attest the popularity of this nickname.

What this name hath wrought may be appreciated by referring to some of the various ways it is used in local and regional life of the area: bricks in down-town Carbondale are frequently stamped "Egyptian." Southern Illinois University in Carbondale has played on the nickname to the full. From time to time, it has issued annuals, brochures, and the like with such titles as *The Egyptian, The Mummy-Box, Scarab, Obelisk, Sphinx,* and others with appropriate hieroglyphics and exotic designs for cover-decoration. Latest of symbolic usage is the adoption of "Saluki," Royal Dog of ancient Egypt, to indicate the prowess of Southern's athletic teams. A specimen of this breed, named "King Tut," serves as their mascot.

In business, the regional epithet is a handy term for the exploitation of corporations in the area. Examples are common in every southern Illinois town. In our midst, we have such business enterprises as Egyptian Iron Works, Egyptian Sales Agency, Pyramid Roofing and Lumber Company, Greater Egypt Association, Mail-Me-Monday of Little Egypt, and many other combinations. Chicago has its Egyptian Club and no doubt southern Illinois groups elsewhere play on the name.

In spite of the certainty that the popular epithet that has designated southern Illinois for over a century does not hark back for its origin to

[1] A correspondent (Roberson of Arnzville) in the *Chicago Journal*, February 8, 1872.—G.P.S.

activities of Egyptian colonists in the New World, it is of interest to follow a discussion of these early adventurers in America by James Rendel Harris, eminent English philologist and paleographer. This author claims that a number of states in the Middle West were exposed in pre-Columbian days to Egyptian civilization. Arkansas, Kansas, Kentucky, Missouri, and Tennessee, were, he states, originally Egyptian settlements.[2] From his arguments, he may have thought to include Illinois in the list. However this may be, in the light of these surmises, the epithet chosen for their area by southern Illinoisans appears peculiarly apt.

The Icarians of Nauvoo

. . . Soon after the Mormons departed . . . an attempt [was made] to establish a Utopia at Nauvoo. A member of this Utopian community told me its history. "We called ourselves Icarians," said he, "and the plan was to work one for all and all for one. As the words of our golden rule put it, 'From each according to his powers; to each according to his needs.' It was a beautiful idea; but you know the story of Icarus. He made himself wings and fastened them on with wax. They carried him wherever he wished to go, until one time he flew too near the sun and the wax melted. Then down he came, and we done the same thing. Our leader was Etienne Cabet, a great French lawyer, writer, and politician. He was well educated and had most rosy prospects; but he wanted to reform the world and he sacrificed everything for that. He begun with writing a novel called *A Voyage in Icarie,* describing an ideal nation. The book was a great success, and the people in France were enthusiastic over it—yes, crazy over it— and they wanted to see such an attractive state of things as was pictured in the novel realized.

"So Cabet began organizing, and soon no less than four hundred thousand persons had signed themselves his followers. Then he made the proposal to build up an actual Icaria in America, and the idea swept France like wildfire. Shortly, he had secured land in Texas, and sixty-nine men of his Paris disciples volunteered to go there. They left their families and voyaged to the new country. The land Cabet had bought they supposed was easily accessible; but it proved to be unbroken prairie, which they only reached after a terrible overland march of two hundred and fifty miles. They were loaded down with absurd and useless baggage, not one of them could speak English, and they were artisans or professional men who knew nothing of farming and pioneer life. They stayed

[2] Cf. Harris' *After-Glow Essays,* No. 7 ("A Temple in Tennessee"), London, 1935, *passim.*—G.P.S.

From *Highways and Byways of the Mississippi Valley,* written and illustrated by Clifton Johnson, pp. 195–198. Copyright, 1906, by The Macmillan Company. New York and London.

through the summer, but eighteen died of malaria, and the rest were so disheartened that they started back for France.

"They got as far as the Red River and there met a new lot of recruits, and the whole party went to New Orleans and spent the winter. A committee was sent up the Mississippi to seek a more favorable locality than the one abandoned in Texas. This committee reported enthusiastically on Nauvoo, and in March, 1849, Cabet himself with three hundred men, women, and children came here and established homes. We fixed over old buildings and put up new, and we had gardens and shops of various kinds, and after a while we built a distillery and manufactured whisky. That was against our principles, but we needed the money. Every one had something to do, and yet no one was to over-exert himself. It was Cabet's idea to make labor pleasant, and he done it; but he didn't make us prosperous, and while a great many joined, a great many left, too. The largest number we had in the colony at one time was about six hundred. Some of those who joined had the sense to get out after being with us only a short time, and seeing the scheme was not practical. Often a woman would induce her husband to leave because we had to be very economical, and she'd been used to better things. Then, again, we had everything in common, and a man who was pretty smart and knew he could make money faster'n most of the others didn't like to be pinned down to an equal share, and so he'd cut loose.

"Cabet thought we should be such a happy family and give the world such a beautiful example of working for each other that every one would flock to join. But he didn't know human nature; and though the newcomers brought money, and money was sent us by people in France, we was always hard up, and that sort of thing didn't attract the public to become Icarians. Cabet was a splendid talker, and it was delightful to listen to his Sunday lectures. He was admirable in many ways; still, there began to be a lot of disagreeing and criticising among his followers. He was a lawyer by trade, and he made so many laws an opposition sprung up that at last succeeded in outvoting him and putting in a new man as president. Then Cabet's partisans refused to work, and the new president refused to feed them, and the colony broke up in a row. That was in 1856. Cabet went down near St. Louis, and in December of that year he was found one morning frozen in his bed."

Winona and the River

The earliest explorers of the Upper Mississippi, French, English, and American, all make mention in their records of *Prairie aux Ailes,* or Prairie

From *Minnesota, A State Guide,* Compiled and Written by the Federal Writers' Project of the Works Progress Administration, pp. 263–265. Copyright and sponsored, 1938, by the Executive Council, State of Minnesota. New York: The Viking Press.

with Wings, and many landed here. Fur traders settled in the neighborhood of the Indian bands before the Black Hawk War of 1831–1832.

Aside from scrubby growths along the [Mississippi] river's banks, the
entire prairie had but a single tree. Despite this, Winona [Minnesota]
owes its beginning and its greatest prosperity to wood. The founder of
the village was Capt. Orren Smith, of the steamboat *Nominee*, that plied
between Galena and St. Paul. The ship's boilers were great consumers of
cordwood, and the captain conceived the idea of locating a townsite whose
prospective settlers might be induced to supply his fuel. The two landing
places on Wabasha's Prairie impressed him favorably, and, deciding to
secure both, he left his ship's carpenter, Erwin H. Johnson, and two
others on shore with instructions to hold the landings and to cut wood
from the opposite (Wisconsin) bank. Thus it was that Winona was born
to the clanging of a bell, the hiss of escaping steam, and the splash of
paddle wheels, at exactly 10 o'clock on the night of October 15, 1851.

*   *   *   *   *

Lumbering and wheat shipping [in the Fifties and Sixties] were closely
identified with steamboat traffic, but as early as 1823 the Winona bluffs
echoed to the shrill whistle of the *Virginia,* and before the village was
founded steamboat lines were in regular operation. From its beginnings
river traffic was vital to the existence of Winona, and when it was threatened in 1857 drastic action was inevitable. That was the year when the
unruly Mississippi tried to plow a new main channel through what is now
the bathing beach slough north of Latsch Island. Steamboats, with officers
none too friendly to the growing settlement their rival captain had founded,
began to follow the new course of the river, ignoring Winona's landings.
But the village grimly met the emergency. The county officials, in a carefully concocted scheme, voted to erect an elaborate stone courthouse.
They awarded the contract to one of their own number, who started to
get out the required stone from the Wisconsin bluffs. The first load was
piled on a huge barge and started down the river. But at the debouchure
of the new channel it met with an "unfortunate accident." The barge was
wrecked, its load of stone permanently blocked the new course of the
river, and again steamboats were forced to swing into the Winona landings. From this time until the end of the century the river was Winona's
great highway. Then steamboating declined and with it ended one of the
most vivid chapters of Winona's history.

Captain Tapper: from Ferryman to Toll Keeper

I. CAPTAIN TAPPER ADVERTISES

The citizens of St. Anthony were not content to stay on their own side of the river. The beautiful country on the west side drew sightseers and picnickers then as it does now. Besides, when the reservation had been still more restricted, boomers began to pour into the district beyond the Mississippi. In 1851 appeared this quaint advertisement in the *Express*:

ST. ANTHONY FERRY

Capt. John Tapper is prepared to convey the traveling public across the Mississippi in his unrivaled ferry-boat. The assiduity with which he transacts all business committed to his charge is sufficient to guarantee the public that all business entrusted to him will be safely and punctually attended to.

As the classic plains of All Saints (the west side) are attracting the attention of the lovers of nature and also those desirous of speculation, he would suggest to strangers the propriety of not leaving St. Anthony without visiting this world-renowned retreat.

The captain will always be in attendance at the sounding of the horn, which can at all times be found in his boat.

II. "THERE IS NO GOING BACK——"

The "classic plains" filled up so rapidly that the ferry soon proved inadequate; so the forerunner of our present steel arch bridge, a suspension bridge, the wonder of the citizens, was hung across the channel. Captain Tapper was promoted to the position of toll-keeper, and for years was the most familiar figure in the two communities. One of his remarks deserves to live forever as a motto for the Northwest. General Andrews, state forester, says that when he arrived in St. Anthony, bent on seeing the country beyond the bridge, he paid his five cents and was allowed to pass. When he wanted to return, the captain demanded toll again.

"But I paid once," said the general. "Do I have to pay to go back?"

"Young man," replied Tapper, "there is no going back in this country."

"Laughing Water" City

As early as 1850 consideration of a name for the new town to be founded on the west bank of the river had begun. The name of "Lowell" was suggested because of the manufacturing possibilities; also that of

From *The Story of Minneapolis*, by E. Dudley Parsons, pp. 28–29. Copyright, 1913, by E. Dudley Parsons. Minneapolis, Minnesota.

From *One of Our First Families and a Few Other Minnesota Essays*, by A. J. Russell, pp. 41–45. Minneapolis: Leonard H. Wells, Publisher. 1925.

"Albion," because the new settlers were mostly of English descent; "Hennepin," "Brooklyn" and "Addiesville" were mentioned and Colonel Goodhue in the *Minnesota Pioneer* by way of grim humor suggested "All Saints." The first Board of County Commissioners of Hennepin County in October of 1852 fixed upon the name of "Albion." This name was not satisfactory, and was ignored by the settlers.

The problem was in everybody's mind and feeling ran high. On November 4, 1852, Charles Hoag retired for the night and, sometime during this night of November 4–5, the name of "Minnehapolis" flashed into his mind. While considering the name of "Indianapolis" as an ideal name for an American city, he conceived the idea of combining the local "Minnehaha" with the Greek "polis" and so "Minnehapolis" was born.

When Mr. Hoag arose on that morning of November 5, 1852, he pronounced the name of "Minnehapolis" to his family, the first time that the syllables had sounded in human ears.

November 5, 1852, was the date for the appearance of the weekly paper, the *St. Anthony Express,* of which George D. Bowman was the editor. Mr. Hoag sat down after breakfast, wrote a letter to this paper and hurried across the river to secure its publication. The forms of the *Express* had been locked up when Mr. Hoag arrived at the office, but Mr. Bowman, impressed by the new name for the town, had them unlocked, the letter put in type and inserted in the page. It ran as follows:

Minnehapolis, Opposite St. Anthony, November 5, 1852.

Mr. Bowman:

We are accustomed, on this side of the river, to regard your paper as a sort of exponent of public sentiment, and as a proper medium of public expression—

My purpose, in this communication, is to suggest a remedy for the anomalous position we occupy of dwelling in the place selected by the constituted authorities of Hennepin county as the county seat; which as yet bears no name, unless the miserable misnomer, All Saints, shall be considered so thrust upon us that the unanimous determination of the inhabitants cannot throw it off— It is a name that is applicable to no more than two persons in the vicinity of the falls, and of doubtful application even to them.

The name I propose, Minnehapolis, derived from Minnehaha (laughing water) with the Greek affix, polis (a city), meaning "Laughing Water City," or "City of the Falls"—you perceive I spell it with an "h," which is silent in the pronunciation.

This name has been favorably received by many of the inhabitants to whom it has been proposed, and unless a better can be suggested it is hoped this effort to christen our place will not prove abortive as those heretofore named. I am aware that other names have been proposed, such as Lowell, Brooklyn, Addiesville, etc., but until some one is decided upon we intend to call ourselves Minnehapolis.

This was the first time the name had appeared in print. In the next issue of the *Express,* on November 12, 1852, appeared the following editorial doubtless written by Mr. Bowman:

"MINNEHAPOLIS"

When the communication proposing this name for the promising town growing up on the other side of the river was last week handed to us we were so
much engaged as to have no time to comment. The name is an excellent one,
and deserves much favor from the citizens of the Capitol of Hennepin. No other
in our opinion could be chosen that would embody to the same extent the qualities desired in a name. The "h," being silent, as our correspondent recommends,
and as custom would soon make it, it is poetical and euphonious; the nice adjustment of the Indian "Minne" with the Greek "polis" forms a beautiful compound, and, finally, it is as all names should be when it is possible, admirably
descriptive of the locality. By all means, we would say, adopt this beautiful and
exceedingly appropriate title, and do not longer suffer abroad from connection
with the meaningless and outlandish name of All Saints.

This name was received with general favor and in a meeting of the
settlers at Colonel Stevens' house the silent "h" was dropped out of the
word and the name as it appears today was agreed upon. Colonel Stevens
says of this gathering:

It will be seen by the above that the editor totally ignored, as almost every
one else did, the selection of the name by the county commissioners. In short,
from the appearance of Mr. Hoag's article of Nov. 5, the Anglo-Saxon "Albion"
was doomed. * * * It was finally settled at an accidental meeting of most all the
citizens at my house, in December, 1852. It was decided to withdraw the silent
"H" and call the place "Minneapolis."

Crossing the Missouri

"What on earth is that?" exclaimed Margaret McAuley, as we approached the ferry landing a few miles from where Omaha now stands.

"It looks for all the world like a great big white flatiron," answered
Eliza, the sister, "doesn't it, Mrs. Meeker?" But, leaving the women folks
to their similes, we drivers turned our attention more to the teams as we
encountered the roads "cut all to pieces" on account of the concentrated
travel as we neared the landing and the solid phalanx of wagons that
formed the flatiron of white ground.

We here encountered a sight indeed long to be remembered. The "flatiron of white" that Eliza had seen proved to be wagons with their tongues
pointing to the landing—a center train with other parallel trains extending
back in the rear and gradually covering a wider range the farther back

From *The Busy Life of Eighty-Five Years of Ezra Meeker,* Ventures and Adventures; Sixty-three Years of Pioneer Life in the Old Oregon Country; An Account of
the Author's Trip across the Plains with an Ox Team, 1852; Return Trip, 1906–7;
His Cruise on Puget Sound, 1853; Trip through Natchess Pass, 1854; Over the Chil-
coot Pass; Flat-boating on the Yukon, 1898, [by Ezra Meeker], pp. 26–28. Copyright,
1916, by Ezra Meeker. Seattle, Washington: Published by the Author.

from the river one would go. Several hundred wagons were thus closely interlocked, completely blocking the approach to the landing by new arrivals, whether in companies or single. All around about were camps of all kinds, from those without covering of any kind to others with comfortable tents, nearly all seemingly intent on merrymaking, while here and there were small groups engaged in devotional services. We soon ascertained these camps contained the outfits, in great part, of the wagons in line in the great white flatiron, some of whom had been there for two weeks with no apparent probability of securing an early crossing. At the turbulent river front the muddy waters of the Missouri had already swallowed up three victims, one of whom I saw go under the drift of a small island as I stood near his shrieking wife the first day we were there. Two scows were engaged in crossing the wagons and teams. In this case the stock had rushed to one side of the boat, submerged the gunwale, and precipitated the whole contents into the dangerous river. One yoke of oxen, having reached the farther shore, deliberately entered the river with a heavy yoke on and swam to the Iowa side, and were finally saved by the helping hands of the assembled emigrants.

"What shall we do?" was passed around, without answer. Tom McAuley was not yet looked upon as a leader, as was the case later. The sister Margaret, a most determined maiden lady, the oldest of the party and as resolute and grave as the bravest, said to build a boat. But of what should we build it? While this question was under consideration and a search for material made, one of our party, who had gotten across the river in search of timber, discovered a scow, almost completely buried, on the sandpit opposite the landing, "only just a small bit of railing and a corner of the boat visible." The report seemed too good to be true. The next thing to do was to find the owner, which in a search of a day we did, eleven miles down the river. "Yes, if you will stipulate to deliver the boat safely to me after crossing your five wagons and teams, you can have it," said the owner, and a bargain was closed right then and there. My! but didn't we make the sand fly that night from that boat? By morning we could begin to see the end. Then busy hands began to cut a landing on the perpendicular sandy bank on the Iowa side; others were preparing sweeps, and all was bustle and stir and one might say excitement.

By this time it had become noised around that another boat would be put on to ferry people over, and we were besieged with applications from detained emigrants. Finally, the word coming to the ears of the ferrymen, they were foolish enough to undertake to prevent us from crossing ourselves. A writ of replevin or some other process was issued, I never knew exactly what, directing the sheriff to take possession of the boat when landed, and which he attempted to do. I never before nor since attempted to resist an officer of the law, nor joined to accomplish anything by force outside the pale of the law, but when that sheriff put in an appearance, and we realized what it meant, there wasn't a man in our party that did not run for his gun to the nearby camp, and it is needless to add that we did not need to use them. As if by magic a hundred guns were in sight. The sheriff withdrew, and the crossing went peaceably on till all our wagons were safely landed. But we had another danger to face; we learned that there would be an attempt made to take the boat from us, not as against us, but as against the owner, and but for the adroit management of McAuley and my brother Oliver (who had joined us) we would have been unable to fulfill our engagements with the owner.

Pony in the Quicksand

. . . We were on the edge of a stream that ran toward the Platte River— awful muddy. Too early to camp. Must be going across. Pa was looking it over. Had Pinto.

We rushed after him to watch. No telling what we might see.

They started across. Step by step, Pinto felt his way through the water. Pa talked to him and patted his neck. Looked dangerous to me. Ma looked scared, too, and pale. I looked at Albert, and just then he yelled, "Watch OUT." He ran down to the very edge of the river.

Pa and Pinto were down! Oh, for goodness' sake! So quick!

Pinto was scared. He kicked and thrashed about like everything. Pa patted and coaxed, trying to get him up. Quicksand! Quicksand!

All of us were yelling and screaming. I couldn't tell where the most excitement was, on the bank or in the water. I looked again for Ma, but she and Aunt were running back to the wagon. Ma had her apron up to her face, crying into it. Aunt hugging her. I stood there and cried like a big baby myself, I was so scared.

It looked, though, like Pinto would come up. He was trying. But every kick put him deeper. Pa was swimming now and trying to pull him out of the muddy water by the bridle. He pulled and pulled, but Pinto was stuck. He knew it, for he quit trying.

"Let 'im go, Pat!" Uncle Mike called, "Let 'im go! He's a goner! You'll drown! Come on!"

"Come on, Mr. Quinn! Come on!" The drivers tried to make Pa hear. It seemed like an hour, but of course it wasn't.

Pa let loose of Pinto's bridle. He looked awful, out there in that muddy water. Once he went clear under. We thought he was a goner, too. But he bobbed up again, spitting and coughing. Then he got to where it wasn't so deep and started to wade.

"Pinto! Pinto!" George screamed to the pony, but Pinto didn't seem to hear. He was sinking down and down. He wasn't even trying. I had so many tears in my eyes, I couldn't see him. I wiped them out with my sleeve and looked again.

From *Though Long the Trail*, by Mabel Hobson Draper, pp. 56–58. Copyright, 1946, by Mabel Hobson Draper. New York and Toronto: Rinehart & Company, Inc.

I could see his beautiful spotted head above the water and his beautiful black eyes. He sank farther, till just his dear soft nose was out. And while the men were pulling Pa up the bank by the arms, I saw that dear soft nose go under. I couldn't even see the place through the muddy water.

We ran to Pa, sitting there on the bank, shaking like he had a chill, and breathing hard. Uncle Mike came with a big bottle of whisky. "Here! Take a swig o' this, Pat. Warm ye up."

Pa took a quick drink out of the bottle, then stood there, feeling better but awful solemn. "By gorry," he said, "we've got to get across!" He looked around at the drivers. "Any one else want to try it?"

"I'll do it!" one of the young men said. "I been lookin' it over. I think it's all right, further up."

"By golly, he's a brave one!" George said to Steve.

It was all right though. He went first, then all the wagons.

Portages

Portages are made for the purpose of getting below or above those falls which could not be passed in any other manner, also for the purpose of going from one stream to another, and sometimes they are made to shorten the distance to be traveled, by crossing points or peninsulas. It was invariably the habit of our voyagers to run a race, when they came in sight of a portage, and they did not consider it ended until their canoes were launched in the water at the farther end of the portage. The consequence of this singular custom is that making a portage is exceedingly exciting business. Two men will take the largest canoe upon their shoulders and cross the portage on a regular trot, stopping, however, to rest themselves and enjoy a pipe at the end of every thousand paces. At landing, the canoe is not allowed to touch the bottom, but you must get out into the water and unload it while yet afloat. The loads of furs or merchandise which these men sometimes carry are enormous. I have seen a man convey three hundred and fifty pounds up a steep hill two hundred feet high, and that too without once stopping to rest; and I *heard* the story that there were three voyagers in the northern wilderness who have been known, unitedly, to carry *twenty-one hundred pounds* over a portage of eight miles. In making portages it is occasionally necessary to traverse tamarack swamps, and the most horrible one in the northwest lies midway between Sandy Lake and the Saint Louis River. It is about nine miles in length and a thousand-fold more difficult to pass than the Slough of Despond, created by the

From *A Summer in the Wilderness;* Embracing a Canoe Voyage up the Mississippi and around Lake Superior, by Charles Lanman, pp. 144–145. Entered . . . 1847, by D. Appleton & Company. New York and Philadelphia.

Written at Sault Saint Marie, August, 1846.

mind of Bunyan. In crossing it, you sometimes have to wade in pure mud up to your middle; and on this route I counted the wrecks of no less than seven canoes, which had been abandoned by the over-fatigued voyagers; and I also noticed the grave of an unknown foreigner, who had died in this horrible place from the effect of a poisonous root which he had eaten. Here in this gloomy solitude had he breathed his last, with none to cool his feverish brow but a poor ignorant Indian—alone and more than a thousand leagues from his kindred and home.

The Ice Express

When steamboats replaced the pioneer river craft, townships increased and, presently, stage lines webbed the wilderness, serving the scattered communities between Lake Michigan and the Mississippi. By 1860 high Concord coaches, gilded and painted like circus wagons and drawn by four horses, were swaying over the land with names as fine as any steamboat bore: the *Prairie Queen, Star of the North,* the *Madison Maid,* the *Western Monarch.*

The coach drivers were men of the roads who could follow a faint track in the prairie grass and splash their teams across a hidden ford. They knew the bottomless places in the sloughs and where snowdrifts formed in the valleys. Young men, they wore beards that all but hid the ruddy, wind-whipped color in their faces. In uniform they were not distinguishable from any woodsman—flannel shirt, corduroy trousers tucked into high boots, a cloth cap or a battered felt; but authority was in their voices.

Winter was the favorite season for travel in that river-veined land. The Upper Mississippi froze into a smooth, hard road and sled runners slipped along it at a pace no summer wheels on its banks could match. Ahead of the Ice Express went a riverman who knew every trick of the hidden tide. Like as not, he was a Norseman: there was always something intimate and personal in the Norsemen's association with their river. He could judge the strength of the ice by the ring of iron hoofs and, mounted on his own horse, he led the express safely over the white road. As a rule, the travelers spent the night in river settlements. Sometimes they camped on the bank or in a willow clump on a snowy island, its blankness marked only by the tracks of muskrats and birds. Then presently a crackling fire threw its wavering light on a row of faces above heavy buffalo robes, and on the dark mass of the horses feeding to one side; and there were heartening food smells and songs and laughter. At dawn they would glide swiftly off again on the iron-bound runners: with the steam of horses, and their own

From *Upper Mississippi*, A Wilderness Saga, by Walter Havighurst, pp. 66–67. Copyright, 1937, by Walter Havighurst. *The Rivers of America,* editor, Constance Lindsay Skinner; assistant editor, Elizabeth L. Gilman. New York and Toronto: Farrar & Rinehart, Inc.

breaths, like small magical clouds in the crisp clearness; hearing the sleigh bells scatter in the cold air, and the high guiding cry of the pilot at the river bend.

Words and Ways in the Mississippi Valley

I may as well set down here some of the new words and phrases which I found to be the current coin of the country, and show into what queer forms the Queen's English has been twisted on the frontier. Not long after our arrival [in Jacksonville, Illinois, in 1838], a boy of my own age invited me to share with him the freedom which kind-hearted Gov. Duncan had given to range through his watermelon patch. On our way I asked if we should find many; he answered, "Thousands, lots and gobs and mortal slathers." Invited to dine, my host said as we came to the table, "Holp yuself to whatsomever ye like, for if you don't holp yuself, nobody'll holp ye to yer meals' vittels." "He's a-cavortin' on a high horse" was said of a man trying to put on style. "I'll be consarned if she's not a tarnation fine gal" would be said of a pretty young woman. "You needn't be tryin' to bullyrag and scrouge me unless you're spilin' for a fight; and if you are, I reckon you'll find me an owdacious scrouger that'll jist bodiacerously split you right open down the middle." "You onery low-down dog," answers the person thus challenged, "ye needn't try to get shet of me with all yer tomfool brag; I'll knock you into a cocked hat soon'r'n ye kin say Jack Robinson."

The hours of the day were told by the motions of the heavenly bodies— so many hours before sun-up, and so many after sun-down; and after the rising, it was one, two, three hours by sun, and so on until noon, which was always called dinnertime; and after that, three, two, and one hours by sun—and people were as accurate in numbering the hours as if they had referred to watches and clocks, and were rarely at fault even in cloudy or rainy weather. The time for beginning evening service, whether at church or other gatherings, was early candlelighting, or, as it was more popularly called, "yearly candlelightin'." An object thought to be particularly fine or handsome was called a "jewholloper"; anything ingenious and new was a "sharp contraption," and whatever smacked of fraud was a "hookensnivvey." A poor man was declared to have a mighty small chance of "truck and plunder," and a rich one to have an "orful sight of this

From *The Lance, Cross and Canoe;* The Flatboat, Rifle and Plough in the Valley of the Mississippi; The Backwoods Hunter and Settler, The Flatboatman, The Saddle-Bags Parson, The Stump Orator and Lawyer, as the Pioneers of Its Civilization; Its Great Leaders, Wit and Humor, Remarkable Extent and Wealth of Resource, Its Past Achievements and Glorious Future, by W. H. Milburn, pp. 668–669. Entered . . . 1892, by William Henry Milburn. New York and St. Louis: N. D. Thompson Publishing Company.

world's goods and filthy lucre." A common form of imprecation was "I'll be dog-oned—you be dog-oned." "Scrumptious" signified very good. "Rinctum-rhino" was hard cash, and so was "spondulics." "It is the longest pole that knocks down the persimmons" was the figure for ability or effective work. "I never cross a river till I get to it" and "I never swap jack-knives while swimming a horse over a river" were two sayings of the famous backwoods preacher, Peter Cartwright, which, adopted by Abraham Lincoln, have passed into proverbs; and, by the way, many of Mr. Lincoln's best stories and idioms were derived from the old preacher.

"Toploftical" or "stake an' rider a'rs" meant high and supercilious manner, the latter phrase derived from a new and more carefully builded fence. An adversary vanquished in the argument, it was said, "tuk water"; and a man who fled from any kind of danger "tuk to the timber," and those who went in pursuit of him were said to "smoke him out," i.e., by building a fire around him, and stifling him with the smoke. "Jee-whillikins," an exclamation of surprise or admiration.

"A bunch or string of cattle"—a herd. The "beetinest han'," that which is sure to win. "Collogan'," to unite generally for evil purposes. "Juberous" —doubtful. "To come down on him like a thousand of brick" or a "thunder gust o' woodpeckers," to overwhelm an antagonist.

The public lands, called indifferently "Government" or "Congress" lands, were laid off in tracts a mile square—640 acres—called a section; this was subdivided into a half section—320 acres—and this again into quarter sections—160 acres—and the subdivisions went on to eighty and forty acres, so that it was usual to speak of a "forty," an "eighty," or a "hundred and sixty," or "two eighties," "three forties," and the like.

A short man was said to have "a mighty small chance of legs," and a tall one to have "awful grass-tanglers." A person in difficulty was like "a little dog in tall grass." A good woman on her way from "meeting" went shouting along the road. Asked the meaning of her joy, she cried: "Oh, that blessed word the preacher said, 'met-a-physic!' Glory! religion's meat and physic both!"

The Fifth Calf

One of our party declared that in all his travels he had never met with a more inhospitable set than the settlers we had just quitted; while another related an anecdote.

He had been traveling in Ohio on a day like this—the rain came down

From *A Merry Briton in Pioneer Wisconsin*, A Contemporary Narrative Reprinted from Life in the West: Back-Wood Leaves and Prairie Flowers: Rough Sketches on the Borders of the Picturesque, the Sublime, and Ridiculous, Extracts from the Note Book of Morleigh in Search of an Estate, published in London in the year 1842, pp. 22–23. The State Historical Society of Wisconsin. 1950.

awful, and he put up his wagon and team at a large farmhouse; the folks, he said, were like the folks we had just seen, only perhaps they showed more bristles all at once, for they never asked him to sit down; nevertheless he did sit down, and watch them eating their breakfast; then saw the dinner prepared and eaten. Evening came on, and with it supper for a dozen; they spread out pans of rich milk and cream upon the table that tempted him sorely to ask for a drop of something to drink, but he refrained; and the boors and their dames began supping up the milk before him. They talked of cows and calves; one said "he had seen three calves that were reared by one cow." Another said "he had seen four that were all suckled by one cow, and became fine beasts."

"I have seen five," chimed in the hungry chasseur.

"Well, now—that beats all," exclaimed the boor. "We know very well that four calves might suck a cow at the same time; one might suck at one side, one at the other, one before, and one behind; but what did the fifth do?"

"The fifth," said the chasseur—"the fifth—why, he, great calf as he was, looked on like myself, while the others sucked up the milk." And having said thus, I bowed to the calves and hogs, and drove away in my wagon, at ten at night, not having eaten a morsel the whole day, and my horses having fared likewise in the empty barn.

Planting a Crop before Building a Fence

The Pascagoula River is in southern Mississippi. . . .

The swamps around the Pascagoula are the most dangerous in Dixie, except the Okefenokee swamps in Georgia, which form the Suwanee River.

* * * * *

They have some strange customs in the Pascagoula swamps. I was down there one day swimming in a "wash hole" with a friend. He told me a couple, very good friends of his, were having quite a bit of trouble with the neighbors.

"You see," he explained, "the fellow planted his crop before he built his fence and it caused a lot of hard feelings."

I have seen feuds fought in the South over such things as a man putting in his crop before he built a fence and then having some neighbor's stock come in and ruin the field. I told my friend I would talk to the couple and see if I could smooth things over. They were sitting on their front porch when I arrived. They asked me to "pull up a chair and set a spell."

From *Look Away!* A Dixie Notebook, by James H. Street, pp. 189–192. Copyright, 1936, by James H. Street. New York: The Viking Press.

"Much obliged," I said. "I just dropped by to talk to you. I understand you and your neighbors are having a little argument because you planted your crop before you built a fence. Now that's nothing to fall out about. You always can plant another crop. You know how it is when you don't build a fence. Neighbors might have stock that would trample your ground."

The man's face went white. The woman looked at me in a frenzy of rage. I kept on talking. The woman got up and went into the house. The man just sat there, boring a hole through me with black, snapping eyes. Then he got up and went in the house. I didn't like the way he stalked in, so I left in a hurry. I got back to my part of the state several days later and happened to tell a friend about it.

"Can you," I said, "figure a couple getting so mad just because they planted a crop before they built a fence?"

I told my friend all I had said and he laughed for ten minutes.

"My God, Jimmie," he whooped, "don't you know that in the Pascagoula swamps, planting a crop before building a fence means having a baby before you are married?"

I never went back to those swamps.

Wedding on Medicine Creek

An early marriage ceremony in Livingston County [Missouri], took place with the couple on one side of Medicine Creek and Squire Jordan on the other side. The creek was booming. The young man swam the stream and brought the squire down from his house. Then the young man swam back and took his place beside the young woman. Squire Jordan couldn't swim. He wanted to postpone the ceremony a few days until the creek went down. The young folks wouldn't have it. They joined hands and told the squire to go ahead. The questions and answers were shouted across the creek and the knot was tied. . . .

Chill Tonic

I think the hill people flocked to the lowland clearings partly for the fun of it and the hell of it, but they hoped to improve their circumstances,

From *Centennial History of Missouri (The Center State)*, One Hundred Years in the Union, 1820–1921, by Walter B. Stevens, Vol. II, pp. 677–678. Copyright, 1921, by the S. J. Clarke Publishing Co. St. Louis and Chicago.

From *From Missouri*, by Thad Snow, pp. 135–138. Copyright, 1954, by Thad Snow. Boston: Houghton Mifflin Company.

which probably they did. If they came to improve their health, they were out of luck from the start, because they were dead sure to be smitten with malaria, ague, chills and fever, or whatever you choose to call this wretched mosquito-borne malady that has afflicted the human race from the beginning, and still abides with most of mankind. I think we all ought to know about malaria, and if possible have a few chills (sometimes called "ager fits") in order to enjoy an understanding relationship with our forebears. You can't have a truly brotherly feeling for most of the human race at the moment unless you've gone blue in the face, had your teeth chatter and your bones ache with a malarial chill. Usually the chill lasts only an hour, but while you've got it you know you are dying and you don't care.

For a long time I have been wanting to pay a reverse tribute to the doctors of the Delta and to the makers and vendors of various "chill tonics" that have been fraudulently sold by the millions of bottles to ignorant lowland work people. It was at least fifty years ago that the treatment of malaria was standardized. I mean it was positively demonstrated and known to the medical profession, and to all who concocted and peddled "chill tonics," that thirty grains of quinine taken during the twelve hours before "chill time" would always stop (third-day) chills like magic. That sounds simple enough, and it is just as simple as it sounds. Hundreds of times I have filled six five-grain capsules with quinine and told poor devils who were completely down and out of malaria when and how to take them; and never once has the dose failed to stop the wretched malady immediately. For years I was a sort of "medicine man," an unfailing worker of magic. I got credit for being better and smarter than any doctor, so far as concerned the treatment of chills and fever.

* * * * *

A few days after the human victim has been bit and infected [by the anopheles mosquito] he comes up with a chill, after which he has a few hours of fever. The first chill isn't so bad, usually. That is, his bones don't ache too badly, and his teeth don't chatter. If he has his first chill, let us say, on Monday at noon, then the next one will come on Wednesday at about eleven in the morning and it will be about fifty per cent worse. The next one on Friday will be worse still. The chills will go on and on, striking every other day. The chills get harder and the fever that follows lasts longer. The poor devil loses weight, drags his feet, and his cheeks sink in and get "yaller" like a pumpkin.

Once I looked into a thousand gaunt yellow faces and talked to their owners for an hour. I'll never forget it. I think it was in 1918. I was billed to talk one Saturday afternoon to the businessmen of Malden, which was then a town right on the edge of the Little River swamp where the clearing was going strong. The town was filled with woods workers, in to get their weekly supplies. I was to talk to the businessmen, but not very many of them could leave their business on Saturday afternoon.

The big hall filled jam full of the yellow, bedraggled timber people, so after some brief remarks to the overlords of the town, I talked to and with the ague-shaken swampers. We had a swell time. Among other things I told them all about malaria and told them how to stop it cold. I told them about the proven, unfailing, standard thirty-grain treatment, then asked for a show of hands. I asked everybody that knew about it or had used it under a doctor's orders to put up his hand. Nobody had ever heard about it. Only a few had been to a doctor. They couldn't afford it. Nearly all had taken or were then taking "chill tonic."

Let me tell you about chill tonic, if I am able to do so without falling into blasphemy. It is the goddamndest stuff. Now there are two or more synthetic drugs that stop chills and fever, but then only quinine was known or used. It was and is a "specific," which is the medical term for a sure-shot cure. So the only ingredient in chill tonic that was worth a damn was the quinine. All the manufacturer of "tonic" had to do, if his idea was to stop chills, was to put enough quinine in his solution, and put proper directions for taking on his bottle. Did he do this? Not on your life! Instead, he designed his formula and directions to string out the malaria for about six weeks so that the poor devil would buy bottle after bottle till he wore the malaria out or possibly till he finally got enough to kill the malaria germs in his blood, like a "standard" dose of quinine would do in twelve hours' time.

I never met a chill tonic maker personally, which is just as well. But the druggists were in the conspiracy too. They liked to sell the tonic because there was a big profit on each bottle and the customer came back again and again, whereas quinine was a staple, honest product that sold at a more modest profit, and one sale was apt to be the last one for quite some time. Druggists were businessmen first and humanitarians second, if at all.

Doctors were perhaps not quite so bad as druggists because many more chill sufferers bought tonic than went to doctors. But I never knew a doctor to prescribe the thirty-grain, sure-shot dose, and never knew one to tell anybody about the standard treatment, which they knew perfectly well all about. However, doctors usually gave the patient enough quinine to stop his chills after the third or fourth visit. The first visits, so far as I could observe, were used by most doctors to get acquainted with the malaria-stricken patient. All the doctors and druggists that I am talking about are dead and gone long since. Those who have now taken their place, no doubt, have quite different ethical codes, and anyway, malaria, even in the Delta, is pretty much a thing of the past.

I was so naive once as to suggest to the editor of a local paper that he ought to print a piece about the standard treatment, as a matter of news or as a message of good cheer to his suffering subscribers. He flipped over the pages of the last issue of his paper and showed me five ads for chill tonic. . . .

Herb Doctor

Uncle Barney Allison . . . is known among the Negroes as "Doc," because, they will tell you, he is an herb doctor. Barney said, "Yaas'm, I doctors. Fo' a long time now, evuh since I quit the rivuh, I ain't done nothin' else but doctor. I goes out in the woods an' stays near 'bout all day. I digs down an' gits the herbs—'bout fifteen diffunt kinds of 'em. I cooks 'em down fo' medecin. I knows jes how to fix 'em. The fust man I cured was when I was 'leven year ole. I had to go all the way out to Rattle Snake Hill to git the herbs fo' him, an' when he was well he give me a new suit of clothes. The herbs don't grow 'ceptin' where they is snakes.

"You kin read in the Book 'bout the herbs. They is all numbered an' when you comes to a pizen number you mustn't tech it. The Book says they is a herb fo' evuh disease on the earth. They is a herb fo' consumption, but I ain't nevuh come acrosst it yit. They is one fo' a bad cold, but the Book says won't nobody nevuh find that root till the end of time. The drug sto' man keeps a-tryin' to cure a bad cold. I won't say he don't try, but he ain't nevuh foun' nothin'.

"No'm, nobody nevuh taught me how to doctor people. It was with me when I was born. I'm the seventh son, an' I was born with a double veil on my face. Evuh seventh son born with a veil has such a strong Power of the Sperit that they has to have a godmother to keep 'em frum dyin'. The Sperit is so strong in 'em it kills 'em, ef they ain't a godmother to take keer of 'em. My godmother had to raise me till I was seventeen year ole. Sometimes when I puts out my han' fo' a herb, a voice says to me, 'Don't tech that one.' I kin hear it, an' it comes to me jes what to do.

"Evuhthing that is happenin' in the whole worl' is in the Book. It says evuh nation goin' to be at war, an' when the las' battle is fitten the sun will be red as blood, an' at twelve o'clock in the day it will be dark as midnight. Yaas, Lawd, evuhthing the Book says is slippin' up on us. They won't evuhbody be killed. Even when the las' battle is fitten they will be some left, but the Book says we has to ride through blood up to the saddle skirts. They ain't no herb to keep people frum fightin'."

Delta Healers

Today many Deltans, white as well as Negro, go to the remède-man or remède-woman far more often than to the doctor. He or she is a per-

From *Steamboatin' Days*, Folk Songs of the River Packet Era, by Mary Wheeler, pp. 31–32. Copyright, 1944, by Louisiana State University Press. Baton Rouge.

From *Deep Delta Country*, By Harnett T. Kane, pp. 225–227. Copyright, 1944, by Harnett T. Kane. *American Folkways*, edited by Erskine Caldwell. New York: Duell, Sloan & Pearce.

son with a "gift," a power granted by the gods to heal illnesses simple or serious. He does not sit in splendor or proud self-satisfaction; he works for a living at a shrimp factory or in his garden. He knows how to do certain curing things, he tells you; he will do them for all who call. It is his duty. For his services he can ask no price. If some want to leave a little present, c'est bien.

He tries to heal by teas and other medicines, prayers and incantations. For a sprained ankle or wrist, the remède-man will draw forth a string and, whispering a standard prayer with his own modifications, will tie eleven knots. Within three days, the trouble is gone. For a baby that is having trouble in teething, he holds ready a rattlesnake's vertebra, to be hung around his neck. To "raise a fallen palate," a knot of hair at the top of the head is pulled tight, and salt and pepper is swallowed. For one who injures a hand, a tisane, or tea, of parsley roots is used; applying it, the remède-worker makes the sign of the cross.

Regularly, in most of his treatments, he employs his index finger to make cross marks upon the flesh. It "bring God into the cure." For "sun-pain," or sunstroke, great care and no little skill are required, he says. Salt is dropped into a potful of river water to the accompaniment of prayers. Then the patient is bathed in the liquid. When this has been done three times, he is saved. The remède-man gives clear evidence that the heat has left the patient's head. He places a glass of water over it, and calls the family to see. Presto! Small bubbles rise in the water. Look at that heat pouring out!

There are remède-makers and remède-makers, specialists by inclination or by the demand of their customers. Some give heat treatments, or induce vomiting. Some set bones with considerable effectiveness, or cure simple infections. They murmur messages to the world beyond; they recite the Lord's Prayer and the Catholic Hail Mary in French. Their materials are often plain folk-medicines that have been effective in many places. In serious cases they may cause death or fail to avert it. Again, they or the patient's faith may bring recovery.

Marie is recognized as a leading remède-woman of the west bank. A mulatto of copper skin and straight black hair, she is a plump, serene woman in her fifties. Her father was celebrated for curing children of spasms; he prayed and he purged them. She does much of her work with "waste-away sickness." When a child is weakly, the mother calls Marie. Marie heats a large pot of water on the stove, says her rituals over it for seven minutes, dropping in her herbs and making her signs of the cross without interruption. A few baths in it, she tells you, and the child is pink with health. In the old days she obtained her "waste-away" medicine from the swamp; now she sends to the New Orleans drugstores, and the cost is heavy. She showed me the patented mixture. "Maybe it's the wars; or maybe the docteurs, they put something to make it high for us," she thinks.

Marie has a sister who is best with "sun-pain." Marie once knew that remède "good, good," but forgot it because she did not use it frequently.

Marie, in turn, is so expert with "waste-away" that her sister brought her own child to Marie. And how does one get to be a remède-worker? Generally he is "born with the gif'," a veil over the face or another indication. Otherwise, "something happen'" when he is a child; a message is received from somewhere. Even then, a technique must be acquired from one who know remèdes. There is a certain date on which the art must be learned, St. John's Eve or Christmas. "I could recite it to you all night long," she explained as she rocked. "It would make no difference. It wouldn' do for you or for me, 'less you had the gif' and 'less it was the right time to learn."

In the earlier days, one desiring to be a remède-man prepared himself on St. John's Eve. He made a fire with green moss from the trees, and he jumped through the smoke until he fell exhausted. Then he had visions, got up, and hurried to an expert. If the latter approved his descriptions of what he had beheld, he would now be instructed. Then and today, if a remède-worker is about to die, he has a duty. He will call someone and pass on his secrets. When a remède-man falls sick, the neighbors watch for the arrival of a younger friend. At the sight of him, they know. The poor old one, he is about to leave, and he must now impart his knowledge. Well, this new little willow sapling, he won' be half the man his teacher was.

Bayou Pierre Plant Lore

There is a plant provided for every kind of ailment; we simply have to find what has always existed for us, old Con used to say. And she had found a use for every plant that grew in the swamp, the fields, or about people's houses.

The king root of all the forest is high-John-the-conqueror. It will ward off any disease that has been brought on by conjure and all witches quake when they see a bit of it in a person's hand. This magic plant is the marsh St. John's-wort, a member of the same family which in Europe has been credited with the power of preserving people against lightning. In the swamps of the South the Negroes fear to tread on this plant lest they be seized and borne away by hants. It is commonly placed under the doorsteps to prevent the nightly visitations of ghosts, witches, and nightmares. It is a cure-all for any kind of wounds, and the dew that gathers upon its leaves is excellent for strengthening the eyesight.

Sampson-snakeroot, a member of the pea family whose flower is of a

From "Fern-Seed—for Peace," by Ruth Bass, Folk-Say, A Regional Miscellany: 1930, edited by B. A. Botkin, pp. 150–154. Copyright, 1930, by B. A. Botkin: Norman, Oklahoma: University of Oklahoma Press.

purplish color and whose long, tough root is a "rattlesnake-master," holds a place in the swamp Negro's affections next to tobacco and coffee. Its roots are boiled into a powerful and invigorating tonic, and they drink it by the jugfuls. It is a sure cure for cramping and for loss of manhood. Chewing this root and spitting its juice at a person's feet will give the chewer control over that person. Always chew some Sampson-snakeroot while trading and you will get the best of the bargain. It will make a person brave, proudful, and mannish. Even chewing leaves of the plant in the presence of any one will give you a measure of control of the person. Carrying a bit of the root in one's pocket will prevent snakes from biting you.

Devil's-shoestring, a species of cross-vine that bears bright-colored, trumpet-shaped flowers, is a powerful plant that is often used in making "tricks" by conjurers. Chewed and rubbed on the hands, it will give a man control over a woman. This is also useful in drawing a good gambling hand. Plant-of-peace, a fairy-like little orchis that grows profusely in the swamp, is boiled into tea and consumed in great quantities as a protection against enemies. It also brings sweet dreams to the drinker. Besides these one finds the swamp Negro using shame-weed, or sensitive-plant, to make evil-doers ashamed and willing to give up their wicked ways. He chews heart-leaves to soften the hearts of those whom he desires to win. Toadstools wet with camphor will ward off conjuration. Mistletoe hung over the door will keep out conjurers. Queer little figures carved from the wood of mistletoe are often found on the mantel-shelves over the fireplaces or hung on the heads of beds. These and many other forest plants, Con knew and used. But not these alone; the flowers and weeds that are cultivated or discouraged about the cabins—each has some special purpose for the Negro who knows how to use it.

Blue vervain, a purplish-blue member of the verbena family, is the one flower found around the doorstep of every cabin in the Bottoms. It is planted there to attract lovers. Vervain is sometimes called herb-of-the-cross because it is said to have grown on Mount Calvary and therefore possesses every sort of miraculous power. It has great value as a love potion. It is used as a bridal token. It "hinders witches from dey will." The cultivated verbena possesses the same powers. The verbenas are very susceptible to each other's pollen; consequently all colors and mixtures are found about the cabin doors. Wherever a new shade is found growing, every black woman that passes is sure to ask for a cutting until that shade is soon blooming about every cabin door in the swampland. It is at all times most carefully tended and watered.

Prince's-feather, a tall plant with queer, deep-crimson plush flowers, is found in every yard, not only for decorative purposes but because of its efficacy in laying tricks and warding off conjuration. Mustard seed planted under the doorsteps will keep out ghosts and witches. Sprinkling collard seed around the bed will drive off bad dreams and nightmares. Red pepper, red onions, and "palma-Christian" are always found growing in the garden patches near the cabins. Red pepper is an effective charm against hoodoo. It is worn in the shoes, hung over the door, and strung across the smoky rafters inside the houses. It is used to cure chills and fevers. Red pepper is most powerful if planted by a mad person or an idiot. The woman who desires never to have a child mixes red pepper and gunpowder in tea of the red-shanks root. She puts this in a bottle and sets it away for nine days. She drinks a little of this every time the moon changes and remains childless. Red onion carried in the left hand in the presence of a conjurer will prevent him from conjuring a person. Red onion juice mixed with the tracks of a woman's left foot, then tied in red flannel and worn in the left breast pocket, will call a woman you desire to you. On the whole, red onions are lucky to have in the house. Added to the diet in generous quantities, they produce health and strength. Garlic is also effective in preventing conjuration. A bit of he-garlic carried in the pocket will ward off the evil eye and bring good luck generally.

Con also taught me that wrapping in leaves of "palma-Christian," or castor-oil plant, will not only cure chills and fever, but as poultices the leaves will relieve headache and "heatin'-spells." Waving chinaberry leaves at them will drive off unwanted animals and insects such as stray dogs, goats, flies, or mosquitoes. But never wave a chinaberry limb at a stray cat!

Even the rank-growing, evil-smelling weeds about the cabin lots all have some power. The jimson-weed with its white and pale lavender blooms is able to tell the time of day. Precisely at four o'clock in the afternoon these bell-like blossoms open up and give out their sickening too-sweet odor to attract the great sphinx moth that hovers over them, seemingly suspended by magic, so fast is the flutter of its wings. The jimson-weed never miscalculates and opens up sooner than four o'clock for fear the bees might call and gather its narcotic-like nectar to mix with their honey. Jimson-weed leaves pounded with the dried head of a snake is a powerful poison that, used in a trick, will bring blindness and even death upon the victim. Jimson-weed root, pounded with fresh pokeberry root, made into tea, and swallowed on the first night of the new moon, will prevent conjure during that moon. Dried jimson-weed leaves smoked in cigarettes will cure asthma. Blood-o'-Jesus, a common weed whose coarse, dark-red leaves cover the lots and farmyards, is a useful plant. Mix its roots with sugar, spice, and bluestone, wrap (always wrapping towards you) in red flannel and carry about. It will bring you peace and safety. Bowels-of-Christ, a kind of green salvia whose leaves turn red around the edge, is stewed in lard to make an excellent salve.

Old Con also taught me that certain trees are taboo. The black folk of the Bayou Pierre Bottoms never burn wood that pops loudly when burning. Sassafras wood pops and will cause the death of someone present when it is burned. They never burn wood of a tree that was struck by lightning. They never plant a cedar tree except in a cemetery. Plant a cedar tree in your yard and someone you love will die as soon as the tree has grown large enough to shade a grave. They never burn cobs of seed corn, or the hulls of seed beans or peas, lest the sun burn up that crop. Hulls must be thrown in the road and corn cobs must rot in the field. If you scatter peanut hulls around your door, it means that you will soon go to jail. Trees that rub together in the wind and make a creaking sound are looked upon with suspicion. Dogs and cats can see spirits, so they avoid such trees. The bark of these trees steeped in rain water and made into a sort of wine is used by conjurers to make them strong in the head. The dogwood tree is a symbol of immortality because its buds for next year's bloom appear before the leaves fall off in autumn. Dogwood root tea made from roots "dug crosswise uv de worl'" is a common bitter drink of all swamp women. Christ was hung on a cottonwood tree, that's why its leaves tremble so. Judas was hung on the redbud tree. Swamp Negroes are afraid to pass a blooming Judas or redbud tree at night. The swamp maple whose beautiful crimson flowers light the swamps in February and whose small leaves are pale underneath is believed by the swamp folk to have the power, in some mysterious way, to turn white before a storm.

Beale Street Baptism

"Come to Jesus, all yo' sinnahs. Throw down yo' dice an' pray. Somebody's allus holdin' out when I calls fo' de votes o' de sinnahs whut has been eludin' me all dis heah time. Lif' up yo' eyes, quit yo' policy writin', an' stan' on de banks o' de Jo'dan, fo' de time has come fo' yo' all t' stop dem evil ways an' be bo'n again."

The Rev. H. C. Toombs, pastor of the Progressive Colored Baptist Church, located at Pontotoc and Rayburn, observed Easter Sunday with a baptism in the Mississippi River, held yesterday afternoon at 3:30 o'clock at the foot of Beale Avenue. The majority of his congregation were assembled for the occasion on the levee. Some of them were perched on a side track that juts out from the main line of the Illinois Central Railroad. It was an occasion for prayer and rejoicing.

In the muddy water of the rising river, after a stirring sermon, delivered with the deep feeling and conviction of his position as leader of the Progressive Colored Baptist Church, Rev. Toombs and three assistants immersed four repentants, two men and two women, who professed their faith in no uncertain terms. Sincerity and enthusiasm, coupled with fervent prayer, marked the ceremony, with the voices of the congregation in full harmony, shouting the praises of the Master.

Choosing Easter Sunday as the appointed day, Rev. Toombs and his

From *Howdy Judge*, by George D. Hay, "The Solemn Old Judge," pp. 5-9. Copyright, 1926, by G. D. Hay. Nashville: Published by the McQuiddy Press.

flock were greeted by the full glare of the afternoon's sun, the warmth of which was somewhat lost when entrance was made into the stream near the Lee Line Docks, where for an hour the water and the sun were forgotten and only the occasional whistle of a passing steamer interrupted the proceedings. Steamboats came and steamboats went, but Rev. Toombs remained a veritable rock of Gibraltar, flaying his flock into submission, chastising them for sins committed and sins contemplated. The "amens" were numerous. Especially did one enthusiastic sister chime in at the most unexpected times and delay matters; but her sincerity could not for a moment be questioned, and the preacher soon became more lenient with her, and, toward the latter part of the ceremony, even went so far as to ask her advice on certain quirks and turns in the ritual, with which he for the moment lost contact.

Chanting "On Jordan's Banks We Stand," "Shine On, Eternal Day," and "The Sun Always Burns Up the Rain," the members of the Progressive Colored Baptist Church aroused fishermen who were taking advantage of the Sunday holiday for rest, and caused many Sunday strollers to stop, look, and listen.

"Dis heah country is busted up int' too many faiths," began Rev. Toombs, as he stood on the river bank, dressed in the conventional black robes of office, with large white linen collar and black cap. "Dey's only one God an' one baptism. Dey ain't no maybe 'bout it; it's de truf, ef I ever tole it in mah life. Ef I ain't right, I'se gwine question de Lawd hims'f 'bout it. Sprinklin' watah in de face an' on a man's haid ain't gwine let him th'oo de pu'ly gates when he goes t' the gahden above fo' admittance, c'ase de good Book says a man must be put clear undah de watah, lesssn't he ain't propahly baptized.

"Brethren, I don't know what yo' Bible says 'bout it, but in mah good Book it say no man's haht is true less'n he accepts de Lawd by baptism. Yo' haht mus' be true an' no lies mus'n 'scape f'm yo' lips. O' co'se folks git mad once 'n a while; da's t' be expected. Show me a man o' woman who nevah gits mad, an' I'll show you a railroad track leadin' straight to heaven. Now, ain't dat right?"

With frequent interruptions on the part of certain ardent members of Brother Toombs' congregation, whose shouts of approbation could not be quieted, nor was there any particular effort made by the preacher himself to quiet them, the sermon was allowed to progress.

"De Lawd ain't got no place fo' liahs. Yo' all mus' tell de.barefooted truth ef yo' wants to git to heaven. I ain't got no use fo' de man whut totes two faces undah his hat. I totes one, an' ef you' don't lak it, yo' don' have to. A man mus' live his religion mawnin', noon, an' night. Be whut yo' is an' no mo', an' de good Lawd will have me'cy on yo' soul. Yo' cain't live a sheep an' die a goat an' dey ain't no use yo' tryin', mah good brothahs an' sistahs.

"God means fo' yo' t' se've Him all de time. Dey's too many so-said Christians who say, 'Excuse me, God,' an' tu'n right 'roun' an' shoot craps an' play policy right smack in de back yahd o' de chu'ch. Ef I was in Washington right now, I'd tell Pres'dent Hahding I'se bo'n again. I wouldn't give a dime wid a dozen holes in it fo' a man whut ain't bo'n again. Dey's too much shoutin' gwine on in Memphis. Folks mus' act instead o' talk.

"Jesus says yo' mus' love eve'body; da's whut he says. Yo' mus' love de white man, yallah man, red man, gray man; en' ef dey's any mo' kin' o' men, yo' mus' love 'em, too, ca'se dey ain't no white an' black heavens. Jes' tell 'em Toombs loves 'em all, an' dey won't be nothin' mo' 'to it. Ef I thought God had two kinds o' heavens, I'd quit him cold right now.

"Ef religion wuz a thing money could buy, some folks would sho' have t' walk on dey bare feet. Some say niggahs don't go to heaven. We may sit in de back o' de street cahs an' trains, but we all sits togethah when we gits to heaven, ca'se dey ain't no back seats up deah.

"Live yo' lives so clean an' upright folks will tremble when dey see yo' comin' down de street. One good man kin chase a thousan' crapshootahs away.

" 'Nothah thing I must speak 'bout, an' dat is morality. Mah Bible says a man whut follows de Lawd mus' be de husban' o' one wife. It says he mus' rule his house wid a iron rod an' keep he chillums in de backgroun'.

"Some folks talkin' 'bout hahd times. Shucks, dey ain't do hahd times wid me, ca'se I loves de Lawd. Some o' yo' all is roustabouts an' po'tahs, but it don't make no diff'rence ef yo' loves de Lawd.

"Dey's one othah thing I craves, an' dat is 'bout de preachin' men. Yo' mus' have mo' respec' fo' de preachin' man. Some folks shoots craps right in front o' de preachah, an' you' all knows da's wrong. Yo' musn't tempt no preachah wid no dice, ca'se he's got a hahd enough time o' it as it is.

"Dey ain't no man gwine knock yo' down fo' tellin' de truf. Jes' throw de fat in de fire an' let's all be rejuvenated in de Lawd, while I baptises dese heah sinnahs whut's gwine rejoice wid us when dey come up.

"Farewell, yo' sinnahs, farewell. Yo' all talkin' 'bout farewell now, but wait till de wah is ovah. Does yo' all know whut I mean? When da wah is ovah an' we'se all in de gahden above!"

"He Don' Let the River Slip Anything pas' Him"

The new arrival [in the Delta] quickly learned his first lesson. There had long been a saying here that no matter what you wanted, if you kept your eyes on the Mississippi it would come to you, whether it were a baby carriage or a mate in a skiff, a casket or a crate of apples. Any spring could

From *Deep Delta Country*, by Harnett T. Kane, pp. 77–79. Copyright, 1944, by Harnett T. Kane. *American Folkways*, edited by Erskine Caldwell. New York: Duell, Sloan & Pearce.

be counted upon to wash down the makings of a house for a man who needed one—boards, stumps, sometimes a whole tree with green leaves. The river was a casual provider. A levee break above brought table tops, broken windowsills, half of a roof, and chairs. "Me, I hate to see that sight," a Delta woman once told me. "I think of the terrible day our own house was wash' out." But her husband had no time for pity. He was out snaring the wreckage.

What a man reached first was his. Simply to see it as it bobbed along— that was not enough. When a choice item appeared, a heavy trunk of cypress in some cases, eight or ten might spy it at the same time along both sides of the stream. Each would run to the water edge, give a shove to his skiff, and from then on it was the back muscles that counted. The man who got there first would put his hand on the wood, drive in his spike, and tow the prize home. Then he would go to work in his yard just behind the river bank. For miles about him stood houses erected in conformity with the river's varying burdens—boards unmatched, the front of one material, the rest of another or several others. And if the family did not mind, who were you to ask questions?

With the river also came food. Upstream, at New Orleans and elsewhere, people were always dropping or tossing away edible stuff. Workmen were careless at the wharves. Foremen gave orders to cast out cargoes for which there was no demand or which showed a trace of spoilage. As years passed, the importation of bananas from the tropics reached sizable proportions at New Orleans, and large supplies of the fruit were discarded. Much of it looked barely ripe, but by the time it reached the customers in other parts of the country, it might have rotted. Soon this produce would be moving past the Deltans.

A family that kept the Mississippi under close scrutiny was one that profited. A father told his young son, "Take the levee, and call me when you see something, you hear?" In heavy spring, when the stream poured strongly past, an endless file of Deltans were to be seen squatting at the river bank. Talking of a wise man, the neighbors said, "He don' let the river slip anything pas' him!" Here was the ultimate compliment.

When a ship anchored for repairs or overhauling, the nearest residents rowed out to make friends, and barter took place. The native had his rice, his ducks, and his fish. The ship's people had cigarettes, tinned goods, and foreign fruits. Now and then a Delta man paddled near the path of an approaching vessel and asked for gifts. One who possessed no other words of English learned the names of a commodity or two, and the effect of the word "please." Amused officers or crew members tossed out small presents and the Deltan smiled his appreciation. When the ship produced nothing, he shook his fists. All that trip for nothing; and now it was the turn of the crew to grin.

A few have told me how shrewd husbands donned their wives' sunbonnets, tied their dresses about them, and made high-pitched appeals. The scheme generally worked. One sardonic Frenchman, as soon as he received a gift under such circumstances, would stand up in his boat, lift the dress high in the air to display his full male costume beneath, and yell, "Ya-ah!"

Roustabouts and Mates

The most picturesque of all river front characters when steam-boating was at its height was the roustabout. He it was who loaded and unloaded the bales of cotton, barrels of sugar and of molasses, sacks of rice, crates of machinery and miscellaneous cargo which came to the port by river or was shipped from the port to points upriver or downstream. Steamboats had regular berths at the then slanting docks; they had, too, whistles that to the trained ear were individual, so that when a certain steamboat's whistle signaled her arrival, there was prompt assembly of roustabouts at her known berth to vie for the tickets that would be dispersed by the boat's mate if the mate were one for whom the roustabouts liked to work. The mate's practised eye ran over the assembly and quickly spotted the industrious and handed them tickets which would identify them to the paymaster after the unloading was completed. When a mate had run out of first choice men, he would scrutinize the remainder for physique and alertness and select up to the limit of the gang required for most efficient discharge of the boat's cargo.

Mates were not always the choosers. Just as they had preferences among the roustabouts, so did the roustabouts have preferences among mates. The slave drivers and toughies among them did not always find a full quota of roustabouts immediately available at the landing, unless arrivals of steamboats had been scarce and the men were in need of money.

Fish Trap

During the summer succeeding my return from St. Mary's parish, I conceived a plan of providing myself with food, which, though simple, succeeded beyond expectation. It has been followed by many others in my condition, up and down the bayou, and of such benefit has it become

From *Crayon Reproductions of Léon J. Frémaux's New Orleans Characters and Additional Sketches by Léon H. Grandjean,* [unpaged]. Copyright, 1949, by Léon H. Grandjean. [New Orleans:] Alfred F. Bayhi.

From *Twelve Years a Slave,* Narrative of Solomon Northup, A Citizen of New York, Kidnapped in Washington City in 1841, and rescued in 1853, from a Cotton Plantation Near the Red River, in Louisiana, pp. 200–203. Entered . . . 1853, by Derby and Miller. Auburn, New York.

that I am almost persuaded to look upon myself as a benefactor. That summer the worms got into the bacon. Nothing but ravenous hunger could induce us to swallow it. The weekly allowance of meal scarcely sufficed to satisfy us. It was customary with us, as it is with all in that region, where the allowance is exhausted before Sunday night, or is in such a state as to render it nauseous and disgusting, to hunt in the swamps for coon and opossum. This, however, must be done at night, after the day's work is accomplished. There are planters whose slaves, for months at a time, have no other meat than such as is obtained in this manner. No objections are made to hunting, inasmuch as it dispenses with drafts upon the smoke-house, and because every marauding coon that is killed is so much saved from the standing corn. They are hunted with dogs and clubs, slaves not being allowed the use of fire arms.

*   *   *   *   *

My cabin was within a few rods of the bayou bank, and necessity being indeed the mother of invention, I resolved upon a mode of obtaining the requisite amount of food, without the trouble of resorting nightly to the woods. This was to construct a fish trap. Having, in my mind, conceived the manner in which it could be done, the next Sunday I set about putting it into practical execution. It may be impossible for me to convey to the reader a full and correct idea of its construction, but the following will serve as a general description:

A frame between two and three feet square is made, and of a greater or less height, according to the depth of water. Boards or slats are nailed on three sides of this frame, not so closely, however, as to prevent the water circulating freely through it. A door is fitted into the fourth side, in such manner that it will slide easily up and down in the grooves cut in the two posts. A movable bottom is then so fitted that it can be raised to the top of the frame without difficulty. In the centre of the movable bottom an auger hole is bored, and into this one end of a handle or round stick is fastened on the under side so loosely that it will turn. The handle ascends from the centre of the movable bottom to the top of the frame, or as much higher as is desirable. Up and down this handle, in a great many places, are gimlet holes, through which small sticks are inserted, extending to opposite sides of the frame. So many of these small sticks are running out from the handle in all directions that a fish of any considerable dimensions cannot pass through without hitting one of them. The frame is then placed in the water and made stationary.

The trap is "set" by sliding or drawing up the door, and kept in that position by another stick, one end of which rests in a notch on the inner side, the other end in a notch made in the handle, running up from the center of the movable bottom. The trap is baited by rolling a handful of wet meal and cotton together until it becomes hard, and depositing it in the back part of the frame. A fish, swimming through the upraised door towards the bait, necessarily strikes one of the small sticks, turning the handle, which displaces the stick supporting the door; the latter falls, securing the fish within the frame. Taking hold of the top of handle, the movable bottom is then drawn up to the surface of the water, and the fish taken out.

There may have been other such traps in use before mine was constructed, but if there were I had never happened to see one. Bayou Boeuf abounds in fish of large size and excellent quality, and after this time I was very rarely in want of one for myself, or for my comrades. Thus a mine was opened—a new resource was developed, hitherto unthought of by the enslaved children of Africa, who toil and hunger along the shores of that sluggish, but prolific stream.

Shelling

. . . Now and then I saw small mussel boats moving along the Mississippi's shore or coming out of one of its tributaries. They were flat-bottomed, each with a rack over it on which were hung two iron bars with a hundred or more stout crowfoot hooks suspended by short trot-lines. Mussels lie in the mud or gravel of the river's bottom with their valves slightly open; they close them tightly when a hook enters, and are brought to the surface. So in a sense this industry goes on out of sight, seems obscure, and in fact is little remarked upon. Yet it is important, because every man who has half a dozen shirts and half a dozen suits of underwear in his bureau drawers uses at least a hundred pearl buttons a year. These were once the shells of fresh-water mussels.

The fishery is called clamming, or shelling. It is almost a monopoly of the Mississippi and its affluents. Mussel shells in the rivers draining to the Atlantic can be used only for lime stucco, poultry grit, and road metal. Those in the Mississippi Valley are worked up into buttons which have the luster of pearls.

Shelling is a profitable business. A single day's catch by a sheller on Lake Pepin netted him fifty-four dollars. In one year more than fifty million pounds of shells, with a value of more than a million dollars, were taken from the Mississippi basin and transformed into buttons and novelties with a value of about eight million dollars. Along the Iowa coast for nearly two hundred miles there are button factories, with Muscatine leading, where the industry began half a century ago. I have seen mussel shells—indeed, I had one—from which as many as a dozen button blanks had been stamped.

As a veteran riverman put it to me, the shells go to the factories, the meat—which is lightly cooked in the process of detaching the shells—goes

From *Flowing South*, by Clark B. Firestone, pp. 181–183. Copyright, 1941, by Robert M. McBride & Company. New York.

to the poultry yard and pig-pen, and any pearls are clear profit. These used to be marketed under the false name of oriental pearls but now carry their own colors. Sometimes they are found as often as one to twenty shells, sometimes as rarely as one to a hundred thousand. They are known to the trade as true pearls, baroques, slugs, and chicken feed. True fresh-water pearls are of regular form—round, oval, pear-shaped, or dewdrop—and if lustrous, translucent, and agreeably colored, command a good price. In one year, when the catch of shells in the Mississippi River and Great Lakes region brought the fishermen a million and a quarter dollars, the pearls and slugs taken were valued at nearly one-tenth of that sum.

Shrimping

The shrimping season brought each year a pleasant variety in our table menu and some excitement for us. Beginning in the late spring, it lasted four or five months. We caught the shrimp by placing shrimp boxes in the Mississippi River, out in front of our place ["Retreat Plantation," near Plaquemine, Louisiana]. These boxes were kept filled with table refuse, ham bones, or cantaloupe rinds together with a little cornmeal, which attracted quantities of shrimp into these home-made traps. Once in, the shrimp were unable to get out. We youngsters always welcomed the opportunity to go swimming in the river, while bringing these moored boxes to shore. Often the boxes would be emptied of enough shrimp to fill several tubs and wash pans. These delicious crustaceans would be made into a savory shrimp "gumbo" Aunt Josephine was noted for, or boiled and served on an immense platter—enough for everyone. Boiled river shrimp eaten cold with salt and pepper was a standard dinner entrée nearly every day in the summer. There is no greater delicacy than Mississippi River shrimp. They are smaller but the flavor is more subtle than the larger Gulf shrimp—truly a dish for an epicure.

The Blessing of the Shrimp Fleet

"Deus, qui dividens aquas ab arida. . . ."
The words echoed on this August morning over the softly agitated waves where the two bayous converged. God, who had separated sea from

From *Plantation Life on the Mississippi*, by William Edwards Clement, in collaboration with Stuart Omer Landry, p. 8. Copyright, 1952, by William Edwards Clement. New Orleans: Pelican Publishing Company.

From *The Bayous of Louisiana*, by Harnett T. Kane, pp. 81–85. Copyright, 1943, by Harnett T. Kane. New York: The Hampton Publishing Co., distributed by William Morrow & Company.

land, was being asked once again to grant favor to those who follow the water. Two thousand years earlier, the first Christians sought by ceremonial to invoke safety and good fortune for the ships that they sent across the Mediterranean. Centuries later, off the Normandy and Brittany coasts, French peasant-fishermen knelt while their priests intoned the same words. In coastal Louisiana, with rites that have changed little through the years, the Church of Rome was bestowing its blessing on the shrimp fleet.

We had risen before dawn, the Boudreaux and I, and everybody had helped stow things into the family lugger, the *Jeune Fille.* Yesterday, Papa Boudreaux and the boys had put the last touches on the shining vessel, after days of scouring and painting it with white and green. Like all the Boudreaux neighbors, we had our line of small colored flags flying in the breeze, nets newly tarred, and all the family arranged on deck, in chairs from the kitchen, or otherwise disposed beneath the canvas, so that we would not be boiled red as crawfish in the sun. The girls were in crisp blue taffeta. Papa had on his best starched khaki pants, and Maman and Grand'mère wore their stiff black bonnets. For an hour now we had moved along lakes and inlets and other waters, crowding among hundreds of others on the same route, waving bonjour as we went.

"Comment ça va?"

"Pas much . . ." Maman shrugged to her friend.

"Allo, Allo! . . ." All the Héberts were calling to us from an adjoining boat.

"A goo-ood year, you say, Martin? . . . Aye, the baby!"

Jean-Jacques, starting to roll toward the edge of the deck, was caught before he went far, and Maman turned to lecture the two sisters. But by this time we were at the landing, and Maman had to store up her feeling. Others, four thousand or so of them, had arrived, and Mass had started. From the place we chose we could see and hear everything. Under the oak at the edge of the shore the mothers' society of the congregation had set up a white altar, with flowers from the woods. Dwarfed by the girth of the great tree was a miniature organ, connected to a sound truck. On other days the oak-lined spread of green was a picnic-ground; now it became a cathedral, the arched branches forming the groins. The crowd, seated on the grounds, half in shadow, half in sunlight, turned to the Archbishop in his golden cope and tall miter, a resplendent figure against an unwonted background, the darting silver of the water, the green and lavender of the hyacinths, the slow movement of an occasional boat.

Incense floated up about the dripping gray moss, and the sound of the altar bell rang out. Automatically all who had stayed on their boats dropped to their knees with the others on shore. The prelate, next taking up his sermon, recalled that the disciples of Christ were drawn from the fishermen of Galilee. Through the night, at the Lake, they cast in vain. Then He told them to try once more, and lo! the nets came heavily loaded. . . . Now there would be days when you, too, would cast your nets without success. . . . Be not discouraged; His all-seeing eye will be on you. And in the storm, when your boat tosses like a thin leaf, hold firm. . . .

Papa Boudreaux was a solemn man that day. From the beginning of my visit with the family, a week earlier, he had told me of the hard and perilous days ahead. This and that man, as careful as he, had never been seen after a trip. A slip off a wet deck, a sudden sickness so far out. . . . Maman, perspiring in a dress that was too tight, had also lost her usual jollity; she held firmly to the baby in her arms and her lips moved. Who knew whose man would be next? Grand'mère, who had described how three of hers—her husband and those two boys—had not returned, now looked toward her son. On how many more occasions would she herself be on the lugger? Seventy-eight years is a long time.

The organ notes reached a climax; the Mass ended. The greatest moments were to come. A rush to the boats. Those who had stayed on the water gesticulated to the others to row back in a hurry, while some stepped, not without permission, across the closely packed vessels that stretched far out. Chanting the Litany of the Saints, the Archbishop, his assistants, and the altar boys were moving across the grass to the bank and to the vessel that awaited there. For the rest of the year this was an oyster barge; today, newly whitened, a small cross at its top, it was transformed. Slowly it moved toward a central position, and on the two hundred or so luggers, hearts began to beat faster.

Most of the others looked toward us, and nudged and pointed. For Papa Boudreaux had been chosen this year for the supreme honor; his hull would be the first to be touched by the sanctified water. (Two men had a fist fight in the previous week before the selection was made.) My friend Boudreaux, at the wheel, was peering now for the signal. It came, and the murmur of the crowd grew louder for a moment, and then ended. Mon Dieu! Maman put her hand to her mouth; the motor would not start. We sat frozen. The eldest boy, the forthright Jules, said, "Jesus! . . . what a time—" and Maman hushed him. Everybody prayed. Ah, there it was; the lugger slipped forward. As we approached the Archbishop, all dropped to their knees, heads lowered. The prelate dipped his gold aspergillum into the container of holy water and lifted it high. As the boat passed, the drops fell on the scrubbed deck, on the nets, on the shoulders of the nearest ones. The baby was intrigued by the sparkling spots, and dipped her finger wonderingly into one of them. Maman pulled her back; and we were on our way.

Ours was also the first boat in the procession that formed. The others took place behind us as each was blessed, and we moved up the long waterway, crowds watching and waving: the *Sea Dream*, the *Normandie*, the *Barbara Coast*, the *Little Hot Dog*, the *God Bless America*, the *Madame of Q.* . . . The water march over, we returned to the oak grove, where the proprietor had the party ready.

Today was more than a religious occasion; it was the great social day of the bayous. On both sides were long boards resting on wooden supports, with newspapers covering the tables thus formed. Men hobbled out of the kitchen with tall buckets, pungent, steaming, early shrimp by the unlimited pounds. "Shrimp for all," read the sign, and that was literally true. Enough shrimp was emptied over the newspapers, to be shelled and eaten at the participants' will, for the rest of the day and for the night as well. Shrimp for lunch, shrimp for dinner; and for many, including the Boudreaux and me, there had been shrimp for breakfast too. (Fried with potatoes, they start a day surprisingly well, though I wonder what the dietitians would say about it.)

During a lull in the day's events, the dancing and the games, I was taken to the cooking room by the proprietor. It was a lesson in mass production—and an introduction to the inferno. In the center was a former sugar-house kettle, supported by a brick base into which piles of wood were being thrust. The holder was filled to the brim with the shellfish, coral-hued in their cooked state. From them rose billows of smoke, peppery and aromatic. Five helpers stirred, dumped, removed, and kept the fire going, and they seemed entirely unaffected by the heat; but I had to leave after a moment of it. The owner told of the day's schedule in figures that sounded astronomical; gallons, hampers, pounds of red and green pepper, salt, onions, lemons, bay leaf, cloves. He did not tell everything; he had to keep the secret of his mixture. People came from all around on Saturday for his sea food, he explained. They got all they wanted, as many plates as each could consume, and free, to go with what they bought for drinks. Above my sneezing, the effect of the condiments, I heard him say, as he smiled: "It is not an expenditure. It is an investment."

The Trappers of Louisiana

For the average American, Louisiana means sugar plantations, cottonfields, Negroes, or a section of the U.S.A. where Huey Long once held seignorial sway. Outside of the fur merchants and some zoologists and members of various Conservation Department staffs, few are aware of the fact that the southern part of Louisiana ranks alongside of Siberia as one of the world's chief fur preserves.

Most people have engraved vividly in their minds the exciting exploits of the Hudson Bay region and the Northwest, when millions of dollars of furs passed through the frontier post of St. Louis, and how the great Astor fortune was founded. But although the highest priced pelts, such

From *American Earth*, The Biography of a Nation, by Carleton Beals, pp. 319–320, 321–326. Copyright, 1939, by Carleton Beals. Philadelphia, New York and Toronto: J. B. Lippincott Company.

as the precious silver fox, are found only in the far north, the beaver, which for a long time constituted the pillar of the fur trade in America, was trapped all the way from frigid Hudson Bay to the tropical sections of Mexico; for decades the tropics and subtropics have held important places in the fur industry. Today the beaver's place has largely been taken by the humble muskrat, the valuable copyu rat, or nutria, as it is known in the fur trade, and other important fur-bearing animals. The best habitat of these is the tropical or sub-tropical regions of North and South America. Because of the innumerable muskrats, the millions of grass-covered acres of semi-marshlands give Louisiana the distinction of being the greatest fur-producing commonwealth in the Union.

Parts of the swampy soil are literally honeycombed with burrows branching into underground tunnels—these lead to the banks and levees where the muskrats have built their houses out of cat-tails, bulrushes and other abundant grasses. Peaty humus and eatable sedge, the herbivorous muskrat's main foods, also abound in the Louisiana marshlands.

Thus the muskrats are the mainstay of the pelt wealth. In the grassy coastal marshlands of the southern part of the state—principally in the parishes (counties) of Terrebonne, Lafourche, St. Mary, Cameron—the animal has found conditions ideal for shelter, food, and mating. The richest lands are supposed to be on Delacroix Island in St. Bernard Parish, but Houma, in Terrebonne Parish, sets itself up proudly as the fur capital of the United States—a brisk little city with shrimp, oyster and fish-packing industries, in addition to its activities as an outfitting center for trappers.

* * * * *

Fur trapping in Louisiana is, like most imperial undertakings, a story of several centuries of adventure, hardship, and sudden wealth. It goes back to the glamorous days of the *voyageurs de bois,* the fur-trading forefathers who blazed a trail through the wilderness from northern Canada down to the mouth of the Mississippi, and from the Ohio westward across the Rockies. The first notable French fur trader, Iberville, who settled at Biloxi, Mississippi, outfitted *voyageurs* to compete with the English, all through the western country.

Following Iberville, Louis XIV granted seignorial jurisdiction over the region to Antoine Crozat, a Paris merchant. Crozat drove such harsh bargains with the natives and French colonists that the fur trade languished. Next came John Law with his *La Compagnie des Indies,* a great New World trading monopoly, including furs. But even after Law's swollen bubble burst, New Orleans remained an important fur center. Despite Indian wars and conflicts with the English, it was estimated in 1745 that 1600 Frenchmen in the colony were engaged in the fur trade. The pelts stored at New Orleans that year were valued at 9,621 livres.

The trappers faced their dangers in the wilderness with a prayer on their lips to Saint Anne—the patron of the *voyageurs*—to protect them from wolves and hostile Indians. The friendlier Indians were given powder and rum in exchange for pelts.

Much of this trade was with the upper Mississippi, but experienced trappers soon settled in the lower regions, first in Mississippi, then in St. Bernard and Plaquemines parishes. When the colony was temporarily turned over to Spain, the Spanish settlers, especially Canary Islanders, promptly planted themselves on the Delacroix Isle and adjacent high ground and carried on the trade. A vast area was soon inhabited by "free" and "company" fur traders, many of whom were trappers.

Free and company traders alike carried off and raped Indian girls and cheated the Indians on every hand. A typical case: for 1,000 crowns' of fine beaver skins, some natives were given a small amount of gunpowder and told that it was a magic variety which, when planted, would produce as much powder as they might want! In those freebooting days, foolhardiness, braggadocio, lies, intrigues, theft and murder were the order of the day.

After the colony was turned over to the United States in 1803, and American settlers drifted in, fur trading more or less remained in the hands of the original French and Spanish descendants and the Cajuns. They roamed freely over the large expanse of trapping lands.

Thus Louisiana fur trapping involves the thrilling record of the conquest of a frontier, a story of cunning, violence and death. Today it is the story of the passing of one of the last frontiers in America, the ending of individual initiative, the rise of large companies, the establishment of a great monopoly—this, too, with violence and death.

* * * * *

Just as his fathers had done before him, the trapper built his own shack among the marsh grasses where he stayed during the trapping season, accompanied by whatever sons were old enough to carry a few traps on their backs. He built his own pirogue—the light dugout hewed and burned from the solid trunk of a cypress—which he used to paddle over the stretches of open water on the daily visits to the traps. His wife and daughters, those brief prosperous days, were able to live in their cozy cottage on the mainland and made only an occasional necessary trip out to the shack.

The average trapper is a rough man, roughly clad, simple, hospitable, honest, often illiterate. His hands are horny and scarred from his harsh toil and the saline marsh water where he sets his traps and works. The trappers are a wiry breed, "like braided whip-cord and rawhide." Though some are occasionally caught poaching during off-season or on the wrong lands, otherwise they are honest. A Conservation Commission official told me he had had no record of robbery among them for fourteen years.

By the middle of November the Cajun and other native trappers are prepared for their arduous labors. If they are not working for a company, by that date they have prepared their camp, a crazy plank shanty not much more impressive than the pile of mud and branches where the muskrats themselves nest. Occasionally, instead of such a hut, the trapper converts a raft into a houseboat for the two and a half or three months of the open season. The shacks are built on the driest ground possible, though often the bayous and streams rise and flood through them. Frequently the trapper and his family live ankle deep in water for days at a time. In the shack's interior, sometimes plastered with a few pictures cut out from popular magazines, are a short-length woodstove, sometimes a kerosene or gasoline lamp, barrels for packing the furs, a cot or two, steel traps and wire stretchers. The diet consists of salt meat, flour, canned meat and vegetables. The coffee is dripped "black as a darky's heel, hotter than the hinges of hell, stronger than Arkansas religion." Red beans and rice complete the bill of fare. It is a rough frontier diet with plenty of calories, palatable after dawn-to-dark labor in the marshes.

On the first legal day he is up before daybreak and as the first light flickers over the marshes, he dons his rubber hip boots and sets out, bent half double under the load of a hundred and fifty steel traps, so heavy that most mortals could not carry them across the street, let alone thread the treacherous swamps.

Here and there bunches of tall reeds thrust up, or the rousseau cane, commonly called "rozo," which serves as a hint to the trapper of the haunt of the muskrats. He follows the trail of the animal and at convenient intervals in the vicinity of the nest of small clumps of dried marsh and twigs he sets out his traps.

The latest type of trap has two jaws, the first to catch the animal's foot, the second, more powerful, whips over to crush. Formerly the trapper found paws in the trap, and many rats escaped mutilated; now they are held and mercifully killed almost instantaneously.

No bait is used, and much depends upon the skill with which a trap is placed and set. To anchor it, the trapper plunges a staff into the matted prairie vegetation; this also serves as a marker.

The following morning the grilling hard work begins in earnest. Up again before dawn, the trapper takes a swig of hot coffee, ties a lunch to his belt and is off. Clear cold days bring the muskrats out best. "Ha! Zee first rat musque!" he cries. The jaws of the trap are pried open, the animal extricated, and the trap reset.

The careful trapper carries his catch back to camp to be skinned and treated. Those less ethical skin their rats on the spot and grind the carcasses into the swamp under the heel of their boots—to gather maggots and spread disease among the healthy live animals. The one who properly returns with the dead animal, at most can carry a hundred.

Long after dark, the trapper returns home, throws down his catch, hurriedly eats his steaming supper; then, by the light of the flickering kerosene lamp, the whole family skins the animals. A swift slash by the tail, a two-handed grasp of muscular fingers, a swift jerk, and the skin comes off over the head like a nightshirt. Every shred of fat or flesh must be carefully scraped off by dull knives so as not to injure the pelt. The skins are then stretched on steel frames, a U-shaped piece of very stiff wire.

Though it is late at night before the trapper can turn in, he rises the next day at the same early hour to repeat the process. It is a grueling labor which lasts without a single break for the seventy-five or ninety days of the season. Some seasons there are frequent freezes. There have been times when the ice did not thaw for a week. And while the winter is the most healthful part of the year, even so the trapper and his family are exposed to malaria, typhoid, pneumonia, pernicious anaemia, hookworm, and other dire diseases.

In the town of a popular muskrat district, boats and huts line the banks of the bayous, as in a Venetian slum. The huts are on stilts because of the frequent flooding, often set among great live oaks festooned with gray Spanish moss. A few, if the soil is good, have tiny gardens; perhaps a pig or two roots in the mud of a tiny pen. Down the water lane, in the few places where the output is not yet controlled by the large companies, come the fur buyers in launches. They bring the day's news from civilization or from other bayous; they haggle over the prices and the grading of the furs.

* * * * *

On the way north, where most of the skins are sent to be tanned, the muskrat pelt passes through the hands and warehouses of from five to seven commission men, each of whom adds a percentage to the cost.

Formerly the bulk of the skins was shipped to Europe to be finished, then returned to New York. With the War, new chemical, dyeing and tanning industries developed in this country, and large establishments sprang up, mostly in New York.

More recently efforts have been made, by such new companies as the Delacroix Corporation, to shift the finishing process to New Orleans. It is argued that there is no justification for shipping out the raw hides when work could be given to thousands near the scene of trapping operations. But most of the output each year still goes to northern fur centers.

After the season is over, the trapper brings the returns of his "take" home. When debts are paid, clothes and other necessities purchased for the family, plans are made to improve the house. But even before these things, the trappers in the various villages get together and hold a *fête* in some empty storeroom to celebrate the end of the season and the men's return. There, amid a mad jargon of French, Spanish and English, occasionally with a dash of Italian or perhaps Portuguese, they sing and dance, drink and eat plentifully, court, discuss plans for the young folks' education, recount experiences undergone during the season in the swamps, kid each other about the new-fangled thermos bottle or swanky-looking leather jacket one of them has bought the day before at Old Martín's or José's general store.

Pirogue Maker

The pirogue, a beautifully modeled, "one piece" boat, was carved from the red heartwood of an immense cypress log. Such logs are almost impossible to find these days. So are most of the men who could take a seasoned log and within a few days, if time was pressing, make from it a boat of such perfect dimensions and proportions that when in use it seemed a part of its surroundings.

I once watched one such pirogue made; carved from a 36-inch log. Just fourteen actual working hours, within two consecutive days, were used by Andre Bourg, famous worker in wood from Terrebonne Parish, in making that boat. Neither calipers nor measuring rule was used; just an axe, a foot adz, hand adz and plane were his tools, but two long curving strips of wood, probably used for a century by him and his ancestors, gave him the lines that determined the overall shape and sheer of the little craft.

I sat beside Andre as he made that pirogue, watched and photographed it at various stages and have it yet, still in perfect condition, for a pirogue is a lifetime boat when properly cared for. Too, I gained from Andre much of philosophy.

"Hit's easy to mek a pirogue from a fine log lak dis," he told me. "Yo' mus' jus' chop away the wood yo' don' need and tha's de pirogue. Hit was h'inside dat log all de time."

Pirogue Races

. . . The annual pirogue race on Bayou Barataria is immensely popular. It attracts throngs, not only from the Cajun country, but also from New Orleans and neighboring towns. Each year hundreds of people line the marshes along the three-and-one-quarter-mile course to watch the stirring contest.

A pirogue is a frail shell of a boat, hewn out of a single log, averaging thirteen feet in length and twenty-two inches in width. They are indispensable in the swamps and along the bayous and coastal marshes, being the only practical means of transportation. While their frailty makes them difficult to handle, these Cajuns skim over the water at amazing speeds,

From "Louisiana," by Arthur Van Pelt, in *Wildfowling in the Mississippi Flyway,* edited by Eugene V. Connett, pp. 327–328. Copyright, 1949, by D. Van Nostrand Company, Inc. New York, Toronto, and London.

From *Gumbo Ya-Ya,* A Collection of Louisiana Folk Tales, Compiled by Lyle Saxon, State Director, Edward Dreyer, Assistant State Director, Robert Tallant, Special Writer, p. 199. Material Gathered by Workers of the Works Progress Administration, Louisiana Writers' Project. Copyright, 1945, by the Louisiana Library Commission, Essae M. Culver, Executive Secretary. Boston: Houghton Mifflin Company.

the boats often loaded with shrimp and crabs. Children often use them in traveling to and from school.

So great is Cajun skill that the races are thrilling sights. In 1940 Adam Billiot won the race for the fourth consecutive year, establishing a new record of thirty-five minutes and twenty seconds for the four-mile course. Billiot was only a youth of twenty at the time, but for years the highest praise anyone of the bayou folk can give another, has been, "That man, he paddle like a Billiot, yes!" In 1940 a "Nawthun Yankee" entered the pirogue race for the first time. This caused much consternation. If this "Nawthuner" won, the humiliation of the Cajuns would be without precedent. They managed very well, however. The "Nawthuner" came in *last*. Pirogues are for Cajuns.

Creole New Year's

Among the Creoles the day of days was not Christmas. On December 25 the family went to church and enjoyed a quiet period with its immediate members. The occasion for true holiday joy was the coming of the new year. While a Christmas tree was unheard of, a tree always appeared for the latter event—*l'arbre du jour de l'an,* not a fir but a cypress dragged from the swamp. It went undecorated; the Creoles of all generations would make up for any lack by the sparkle of their eyes and spirits. In the early morning, before light had come over the levee top, the children were awake. Nurses, hard pressed to keep them in control, whispered warnings. If they misbehaved and were punished on New Year's Day, they would be bad and also spanked on every day to follow.

By seven o'clock the young were running down the steps. New Year's stockings were ready for them, filled as they had hoped; other gifts were piled at the base of the New Year's tree. Greetings, kisses, handing about of presents—and then the expected interruption. From outside came a rumble; the Negroes had arrived for their part of the occasion. From dawn to dusk the blacks would in theory be free to enjoy the day as they wished. Gaily dressed, faces shining, they approached the house—hobbling old women, stout men from the field, Negroes of all hues from blue-black to cream. They waited a moment, hesitant; the habits of bondage held them back.

"Bonne année!"

Valcour Aime [whose plantation lay about a mile and a half south of Donaldsonville, Louisiana], said it. Maman said it, and the children. A dark man stepped forward, his wife and then their children. Behind them the rest swarmed, smiling shyly, guffawing, grinning. A woman in-

From *Plantation Parade,* The Grand Manner in Louisiana, by Harnett T. Kane, pp. 37–40. Copyright, 1945, by Harnett T. Kane. New York: William Morrow and Company.

quired about the young girls. What, not awake yet? They must be gotten up. It was all a kind of ritual. Upstairs ran the women, knocking at each doorway and rushing in to cry, "Bonne année!" As they did so, they bowed deep. The girl in bed must also bow. They asked about her health, she about theirs. Then New Year's wishes: Might the year bring her health, wealth, a good husband and a young one. (Or rich, anyway, some one snickered.) Good-bys, and the women raced down to the rear court. Here a second tree was in place for the Negroes. Several head of cattle had been killed and divided into packages with gifts attached. All looked to one side; as scheduled, a giant figure rounded the corner, a black Santa Claus in red and white, his face if not his identity well concealed. The crowd fell back in mock terror.

"Who's 'at?"

"Papa Noël, me!"

"Who Papa Noël?"

The banter went on until the mask dropped, or another accident took place; and then every one pretended high-pitched amazement at the discovery of Santa's identity. Santa reached over to take his little Térèse in his arms; he and Monsieur Aime now started the main business of the day—the distribution of the presents. "Testut!" Testut came up for the meat and a suit of clothes. Behind him moved Marie, his wife; for her a dress and a neckerchief. Then Jacques and his wife Honorée. She had become a mother again during the year, and she received two dresses. (Holiday generosity and incentives could be combined.) Pots, pans, flour, a red hat—the gift-giving went on. The last slave bowed, and a call reached them. Breakfast, she was ready.

The slaves hurried to the tables in the court, while the Aimes retired to their breakfast. At both repasts the rule was known: Eat well, because if you have a thin meal on New Year's Day, you will be hungry every morning till the next. Today the slaves knew bounty—grits, thick loaves of French bread, fried oysters and shrimp, eggs, gravies, milk and butter. They ate deep and they asked questions of one another. You think white folk' eat 'at way ev'y day, Antoine? It a wonder they don' buss apart, right in front of theyself!

The meal over, the slaves lined up and the whites gathered to watch. Valcour Aime recognized in the dance a method of relieving some of the tensions of a race in servitude. Weekly he permitted the field workers to relax with their rhythmical steps, remembered from the old country or evolved in the new. Their instruments were horns, drums, fiddles with one string; they danced alone, or in groups, or as a pair in wild performances on which the rest gazed with avid interest. They sang songs whose meanings the Aimes did not quite guess, but which stirred all with their weird sadness. The tempo changed to dances of joy, of physical delight in living, the pleasure of man in woman. On it went for an hour and more. As spirits flagged, Monsieur Aime stepped forward with Gabi and the others. He made a brief speech, and the crowd returned to the quarters.

By this time from neighboring homes and parishes more members of the Famille Aime were arriving. They were led to the parlor where a heavy fire was no less warming than the wishes of Papa Valcour. Monsieur Aime stood at the door, his Joséphine at his side. Drinks were ready, brandies, whiskies, eggnogs, and the favorite sweet cordial of the women, anisette. (Her husband assured everybody that his Clarice could never stand more than three glasses of the mixture.) New Year's Day continued without letup. About dusk the house servants announced a meal, not heavy but select: pheasant, quail, snipe, salads, fruit, and holiday cake. The last caller drained the small cup of black coffee without which he could hardly have made his adieux. Papa Valcour, Maman, and Gabi bowed as the final carriages rolled through the iron gates toward the levee. In the Negro quarters fires glowed beneath the trees, and a dull hum went on. The New Year had begun well for those who lived in these "Gardens of Versailles."

Alligator Killing

Some years since, a gentleman in the southern part of Louisiana, "opening a plantation," found, after most of the forest had been cleared off, that in the center of his land was a boggy piece of low soil covering nearly twenty acres. This place was singularly infested with alligators. Among the first victims that fell a prey to their rapacity were a number of hogs and fine poultry; next followed most of a pack of fine deer hounds. It may easily be imagined that the last outrage was not passed over with indifference. The leisure time of every day was devoted to their extermination, until the cold of winter rendered them torpid and buried them up in the mud. The following summer, as is naturally the case, the swamp, from the heat of the sun, contracted in its dimensions; a number of artificial ditches drained off the water, and left the alligators little else to live in than mud, about the consistency of good mortar; still the alligators clung, with singular tenacity, to their native homesteads as if perfectly conscious that the coming fall would bring them rain. While thus exposed, a general attack was planned, carried into execution, and nearly every alligator of any size was destroyed. It was a fearful and disgusting sight to see them rolling about in the thick mud, striking their immense jaws together in the agony of death. Dreadful to relate, the stench of these decaying bodies in the hot sun produced an unthought-of evil. Teams of oxen were used in vain to haul them away; the progress of corruption under

From *The Mysteries of the Backwoods;* or, Sketches of the Southwest: Including Character, Scenery, and Rural Sports, by T. B. Thorpe, pp. 141–144. Entered . . . 1845, by Carey & Hart. Philadelphia. 1846.

the sun of a tropical climate made the attempt fruitless. On the very edge of the swamp, with nothing exposed but the head, lay a huge monster, evidently sixteen or eighteen feet long; he had been wounded in the melée, and made incapable of moving, and the heat had actually baked the earth around his body as firmly as if embedded in cement. It was a cruel and singular exhibition to see so much power and destruction so helpless. We amused ourselves in throwing things into his great cavernous mouth, which he would grind up between his teeth. Seizing a large oak rail, we attempted to run it down his throat, but it was impossible; for he held it for a moment as firmly as if it had been the bow of a ship, then with his jaws crushed and ground it to fine splinters. The old fellow, however, had his revenge; the dead alligators were found more destructive than the living ones, and the plantation for a season had to be abandoned.

In shooting the alligator, the bullet must hit just in front of the fore legs, where the skin in most vulnerable; it seldom penetrates in other parts of the body. Certainty of aim, therefore, tells in alligator shooting as it does in everything else connected with sporting. Generally, the alligator, when wounded, retreats to some obscure place; but if wounded in a bayou, where the banks are steep and not affording any hiding places, he makes considerable amusement in his convolutions in the water and in his efforts to avoid the pain of his smarting wound. In shooting, the instant you fire, the reptile disappears, and you are for a few moments unable to learn the extent of injury you have inflicted. An excellent shot, that sent the load with almost unerring certainty through the eye, was made at a huge alligator and, as usual, he disappeared, but almost instantly rose again, spouting water from his nose, not unlike a whale. A second ball, shot in his tail, sent him down again, but he instantly rose and spouted; this singular conduct prompted a bit of provocation, in the way of a plentiful sprinkling of bits of wood, rattled against his hide. The alligator lashed himself into a fury; the blood started from his mouth; he beat the water with his tail until he covered himself with spray, but never sunk without instantly rising again. In the course of the day he died and floated ashore; and, on examination, it was found that the little valve nature has provided the reptile with, to close over its nostrils when under water, had been cut off by the first shot, and thus compelled him to stay on the top of the water to keep from being drowned. We have heard of many since who have tried thus to wound them, and although they have been hit in the nose, yet they have been so crippled as to sink and die.

The alligator is particularly destructive on pigs and dogs, when they inhabit places near plantations; and if you wish to shoot them, you can never fail to draw them on the surface of the water if you will make a dog yell or pig squeal; and that too, in places where you may have been fishing all day, without suspecting their presence. Herodotus mentions the catching of crocodiles in the Nile by baiting a hook with flesh, and then attracting the reptile towards it by making a hog squeal. The ancient Egyptian manner of killing the crocodile is different from that of the present day, as powder and ball have changed the manner of destruction; but the fondness for pigs in the crocodile and alligator, after more than two thousand years, remains the same.

Arrow Fishing

There are several kinds of fish that attract the attention of the arrow fishermen. Two kinds only are professedly pursued, the "carp" and the "buffalo." Several others, however, are attacked for the mere purpose of amusement, among which we may mention a species of perch and the most extraordinary of all fish, the "gar."

* * * * *

. . . These terrible destroyers of fish [the gar], have no true representatives in the sea; they seem to be peculiar to waters tributary to the Mississippi. There are two kinds of them, alike in office, but distinct in species. . . . They are, when grown to their full size, twelve or fifteen feet in length, voracious monsters to look at, so well made for strength, so perfectly protected from assault, so capable of inflicting injury. The smaller kind, growing not larger than six feet, have a body that somewhat resembles in form the pike, covered by what look more like large flat heads of wrought iron than scales, which it is impossible to remove without cutting them out, they are so deeply imbedded in the flesh. The jaws of this monster form about one-fourth of its whole length; they are shaped like the bill of a goose, armed in the interior with triple rows of teeth, as sharp and well set as those of a saw. But the terror is the "alligator gar," a monster that seems to combine all the most destructive powers of the shark and the reptile. The alligator gar grows to the enormous length of fifteen feet; its head resembles the alligator's; within its wide-extended jaws glisten innumerable rows of teeth, running down into its very throat in solid columns. Blind in its instinct to destroy, and singularly tenacious of life, it seems to prey with untiring energy, and with an appetite that is increased by gratification. Such are the fish that are made victims of the mere sport of the arrow fisherman.

The implements of the arrow fisherman are a strong bow, five or six feet long, made of black locust or cedar (the latter being preferred), an arrow of ash, three feet long, pointed with an iron spear of peculiar construction. The spear is eight inches long; one end has a socket, in which is fitted *loosely* the wooden shaft; the other end is a flattened point; back of this point there is inserted the barb, which shuts into the iron as it enters an object, but will open if attempted to be drawn out. The whole of this iron-work weighs three ounces. A cord is attached to the spear,

Ibid., pp. 36–41, 44–45.

fifteen or twenty feet long, about the size of a crow quill, by which is held the fish when struck.

Of the water craft used in arrow fishing, much might be said, as it introduces the common Indian canoe, or, as it is familiarly termed, the "dugout," which is nothing more than a trunk of a tree, shaped according to the humor or taste of its artificer, and hollowed out. . . . The arrow fisher prefers a canoe with very little rake, quite flat on the bottom, and not more than fifteen feet long, so as to be turned quick. Place in this simple craft the simpler paddle, lay beside it the arrow, the bow, the cord, and you have the whole outfit of the arrow fisherman.

In arrow fishing, two persons only are employed; each one has his work designated—the "paddler" and "bowman." Before the start is made, a perfect understanding is had, so that their movements are governed by signs. The delicate canoe is pushed into the lake, its occuptants scarcely breathe to get it balanced, the paddler is seated in its bottom, near its center, where he remains, governing the canoe in all its motions, without *ever taking the paddle from the water*. The fisherman stands at the bow; around the wrist of his left hand is fastened, by a loose loop, the cord attached to the arrow, which cord is wound around the forefinger of the same hand, so that when paying off, it will do so easily. In the same hand is, of course, held the bow. In the right is carried the arrow, and by its significant pointing, the paddler [is given] directions for the movements of the canoe. The craft glides along, scarcely making a ripple; a "feed" is discovered, over which the canoe stops; the bowman draws his arrow to the head; the game, disturbed, is seen in the clear water rising slowly and perpendicularly, but otherwise perfectly motionless; the arrow speeds its way; in an instant the shaft shoots into the air and floats quietly away, while the wounded fish, carrying the spear in its body, endeavors to escape. The "pull" is managed so as to come directly from the bow of the canoe; it lasts but for a moment before the transfixed fish is seen, fins playing, and full of agonizing life, dancing on the top of the water, and in another instant more lies dead at the bottom of the canoe. The shaft is then gone after, picked up, and thrust into the spear; the cord is again adjusted, and the canoe moves towards the merry makers of those swift ascending bubbles, so brightly displaying themselves on the edge of that deep shade cast by yonder evergreen oak.

* * * * *

The crumbling character of the alluvial banks that line our southern streams, the quantity of fallen timber, the amount of "snags" and "sawyers," and the great plentifulness of game make the beautiful art of angling, as pursued in England, impossible. The veriest tyro . . . with his rough line and coarser hook *can catch fish*. . . . The joined rod, the scientific reel, cannot be used; the thick hanging bough, the rank grass, the sunken log, the far reaching *melumbrium*, the ever still water, make these delicate appliances useless. Arrow fishing only, of all the angling in the interior streams of the southwest, comparatively speaking, claims the title of an *art,* as it is pursued with a skill and a thorough knowledge that tell only with the experienced, and to the novice is an impossibility.

* * * * *

The origin of arrow fishing we know not; the country where it is pursued is comparatively of recent settlement; scarce three generations have passed away within its boundaries. We asked the oldest piscator that lived in the vicinity of these "dry lakes" for information, and he told us that it was "Old Uncle Zac," and gave us his history in a brief and pathetic manner, concluding his reminiscenes of the great departed as follows:

"Uncle Zac never know'd nothing 'bout flies, or tickling trout, but it took him to tell the difference 'twixt a yarth-worm, a grub, or the young of a wasp's nest; in fact, he know'd fishes amazin', and bein' natur-ally a hunter, he went to shooten 'em with a bow and arrer, to keep up yearly times in his history, when he tuck Inguns and yerther varmints in the same way."

Shanty-Boat Justice

All shanty-boat folks are not orn'ry. Some really try to abide by rules and regulations which saner but less happy men have written as a chart for good behavior. There was the case of the shanty-boat lad over in Mississippi.

Three river boatmen had been robbing his fish traps and even had gone so far as to pour lime in the boy's favorite fishing creek. A lime fisherman is the "low-downdest cuss in the world." The lime makes the fish come to the surface for air.

Aunt Mattie used to say:

"Anybody who will lime a fish hole will steal a nickel off a dead man's eye and kick him 'cause it ain't a quarter."

The shanty-boat boy took his grievance to the law but got no satisfaction. He told a deputy sheriff he would take the officer to the culprits, but the officer dodged the assignment. The lad asked for a commission so he could right the wrong in a legal manner. The high sheriff said he would make the accuser a deputy and give him warrants for arrest of the thieves.

"But," the sheriff cautioned, "you must serve these warrants on the three men."

The boy 'lowed he would.

From *Look Away!* A Dixie Notebook, by James H. Street, pp. 86–87. Copyright, 1936, by James H. Street. New York: The Viking Press.

The next day he brought three bodies in a wheelbarrow to the sheriff. The lad said quietly: "I served the warrants like you told me."

The warrants were stuck under the bills of the caps of the three dead men.

How the News Traveled in Bayou Lafourche

. . . One day a farmer told me the story of the day the news of the First World War armistice reached Lafourche, back in 1918. Octave, up at the northern end, received a telegram. He had a cousin, way down at the other limit, who would want to hear this news, yes. Octave started toward his car, when Arsène, his neighbor, stuck his head out of the window to ask what was the matter. Octave told him, "La guerre est finie!" Arsène ran to his other window and called the word to Gustave, next door. Gustave gulped and ran to his other window. Before the hour was past the news had gone from house to house; and when Octave, chugging as fast as he could, reached his destination at the lower line, his cousin came out and cried: "Octave, you have heard? La guerre est finie!" . . .

The Last of the Darbys

On all my trips to the Teche district, I had wanted a chance to study the old Darby house near New Iberia, but until very recently, for one reason or another, I had to be content with photographing it and listening to the colorful legends about it. The stories chiefly concerned the present master, M. François Darby, a very old gentleman who has long been a recluse and an object of awe in the neighborhood. I give the tale as I have it from the innkeeper, but I also heard several variant versions which substantiate the main points.

François is the grandson of the builder of the house, François St. Mar Darby, an Englishman of good birth, who received the land from his father, who got it by an original grant from the Spanish. The first François married Felicité de St. Armond, a beautiful French lady of an important family. He built Darby to please her French taste. The Darbys grew wealthy and maintained houses also in New Orleans and at Paris,

From *The Bayous of Louisiana*, by Harnett T. Kane, p. 144. Copyright, 1943, by Harnett T. Kane. New York: The Hampton Publishing Co., distributed by William Morrow & Company.

From *White Pillars*, Early Life and Architecture of the Lower Mississippi Valley Country, by J. Frazer Smith, pp. 159–160. Copyright, 1941, by Wm. Helburn, Inc. New York.

where they stayed most of the year. The present François Darby, third of the name, was educated in Paris, together with a brother and sister, and presented to society in New Orleans just as the War broke out. The end of the conflict left them poor and they retired, unwed, to their last possession, the home on the Teche. Unwilling to mingle with the simpler folk of the neighborhood, they withdrew to themselves and became poorer and bitterer as the years passed. They even came to quarrel with each other (so the legend insists), each living to himself in the house; for months refusing to speak one to the other, conversing by means of notes, or singing to a favorite tune such messages as "Y-o-u-r c-o-w-s a-r-e i-n m-y m-e-a-d-o-w a-n-d y-o-u w-i-l-l b-e r-e-s-p-o-n-s-i-b-l-e f-o-r a-n-y d-a-m-a-g-e." The sister was the first to die. Her favorite mode of torment was to threaten to will her part of the property to first one and then the other brother—as the mood struck her. (When after her death the will was opened, it was only a blank piece of paper.) Octave, the younger brother, reduced to selling milk, further offended his brother when at long last he made friends with the townfolk, even to the point of drinking with them in the beer-parlors. He died many years ago, at sixty-five. And so François was left in the decaying house, the last of the Darbys.

A short time ago when I was passing through New Iberia from New Orleans, I was told that old François had recently died. A filling station owner told me that the old Darby house was fast going to pieces; part of the roof and rear walls were already gone, and the storm of the night before had probably about finished it up. I hurried out to the edge of town and up the narrow, winding, moss-covered lane; and sure enough the front wall, the roof, the gallery, and two sides were all that were left standing. Through a door off its hinges I could see the blue sky. It was only a stage setting; but I started sketching to save what I could.

The entourage seemed to be in place. The oaks were as majestic as when the house was in its prime, although their moss draped low as if at half-mast. No sign of life about substantiated the rumors I had heard in New Orleans that François had "passed on." I sketched a while, then made some camera shots. The place had atmosphere; indeed, it was positively dramatic. I kept picturing the three ageing Darbys here and there as they went reluctantly about their bitter tasks. The old framework scenery swayed and squeaked in the wind as if it might well fall in a heap. I grabbed my pad to invade the interior for plans to make a restoration in case such a collapse should take place before I could get away.

The ground floor was all of brick with scant traces of brick floor under the gallery. Only a few of the brick columns remained, and those minus all their stucco; on the garden side they were completely gone, with nothing but a little pile of red "bats" to mark the places. The doors and windows had lost their glass and their once graceful blinds were half gone, half flapping in the breeze. As the plan developed on my pad, I made my way to the second floor to explore the main rooms. I was three careful steps up the flight of the gallery stairs which literally hung on one carriage, when I looked up and saw a large wooden molasses bucket on the way down. Before I could move, the head of a little gray-bearded man with keen black eyes and a bush of gray hair was in full view, staring me squarely in the face. From behind his big bucket he began to question me in rapid French. Then it came in English: "What's your name? What do you want here? What's that you have in your hand?"

I held my ground, probably too puzzled to move, but to my amazement, after I replied humbly to his queries, he put out his hand in greeting. "My name is François Darby, and this is my house. Make yourself at home."

He could not do too much for me. He led the way back up the stairs, insisting that I walk immediately behind him, both of us on that one little peg which held the last contact of the upper carriage to the second floor beam. Once he had gained the second floor gallery, he pulled back a shutter and bowed me into his room, the only one left with any part of a full roof over it. His father's father had built the place, he informed me, and he himself was now ninety-three.

In this room were an old, broken mahogany bed without head or foot pieces, a chest, one chair, and a long box in front of the fireplace, in which burned a slow fire. All of the other rooms were empty except for a few French books in one corner cupboard. It seemed impossible for anyone to live in such a place; but proudly he offered no word of apology, and seemingly missed none of the grandeur he had seen half a century ago. I found so much of broken beauty that I also forgot that the roof and some of the walls were missing.

Town on the River

Along the western banks of the Mississippi are little towns that have been made and broken by the river. Many are quaint, old-fashioned villages hugging the banks of the river and sheltered by high bluffs from the cold winds that often sweep across the outlying prairies. Quiet and serene, they give the impression of being quite content with their situation, with never a dream of expanding inland. They have an air of permanence, these old river towns. Other settlements may be tentative communities of transient pioneers, but the present inhabitants of the little river towns are the grandchildren of the founders. Facing the river, they seem to belong to it, having no desire to climb the bluffs and live on the prairie beyond. Uneven sidewalks of flagstones, abandoned sawmills, warehouses gauntly fronting the river and slowly sinking into decay, the faint

From "River Towns," by Marie E. Meyer, *The Palimpsest,* Vol. VII (December, 1926), No. 12, pp. 381–386. Copyright, 1926, by the State Historical Society of Iowa. Iowa City.

trace of a boat yard, an old boat landing now overgrown with weeds and willows—are all mute evidences of a past that was part of the great river. Drowsing away, living much in the past, these towns seem to be awaiting the whistle of the long-silent raft-boat which will arouse them to activity once more.

Rambling old houses of nondescript architecture line the streets that parallel the river or cling to the steep hillsides of the diagonal coulee. Since lumber was cheap, only the best material was used in the mansions of a generation ago, and the rafts yielded their choicest logs for the homes of the river men. Doors with transoms above, and kitchens finished like a steamboat cabin are eloquent reminders of the owner's occupation. Occasionally the pilot house or the cabin of an old boat was the beginning of a comfortable residence of later days.

These are not typical country towns, for the farmer and the river man had very little in common. The farmers came to trade and sell their produce, but they were really outsiders, on-lookers at the various activities that filled the lives of the river folk. A certain dash, an air of sophistication and worldly experience born of many trips to New Orleans and St. Louis distinguished the dwellers of these towns from their rural neighbors.

The river man was a type. Just as the sea captain was devoted to his ship, so was the river man devoted to the river and its traditions. An aristocracy of the river was the natural product of the golden age on the Mississippi. The names of captains, pilots, and lumbermen were known from New Orleans to St. Paul. Sons followed in their father's wake, and, learning river lore from childhood, they often served apprenticeships as "cub" pilots under men who had been associates of Mark Twain.

Transportation of both freight and passengers was made by boat. As late as 1900, several towns in Scott County boasted no railroad connections with the outside world. A "hack" made daily trips of fifteen or more miles from Le Claire to Davenport during the winter months, and steamboats served in the open season. The mail, carried by rail to Illinois towns opposite, was ferried across to the Iowa shore. And crossing the Mississippi in an open boat when the ice breaks up in the spring is no enviable task.

After the ice went out in the spring, every able-bodied man was ready to "go on" a boat, and he stayed until the "fleet" laid up in October or November. (Today it may be only a government boat engaged in surveying, dredging, or marking the river.) With their season's earnings captains, pilots, deck hands and stokers all settled down to a comfortable and idle winter. Of course, it can be truthfully said that many of these families who enjoyed beefsteak in the fall probably ate liver in the spring. But merchants were lenient in advancing credit, so why bother about bills? No river man of the old school found employment elsewhere when off the river, for he knew no other trade or business.

Saloons, gambling rooms, billiard parlors, dances, and other social activities provided entertainment and recreation during the long winter months. Show boats . . . visited these river towns regularly. Just as the circus band drew small boys to the tent, so did the calliope draw them to the river bank. The saloon flourished above all other places of business, drink being the greatest weakness of the river man. A town of about two thousand inhabitants at one time boasted of thirteen saloons! Tying up for the night at a town was the signal for a celebration, and probably more than one member of the crew needed assistance in returning to the boat. No wonder the notoriously tough river towns were the object of many revivals and prayer meetings!

The typical river man was a genial fellow, liberal with his money, which went more easily than it came. He was not much worried about the future for he assumed that the river would always provide a living. So it is that few river men died rich and many in their old age depended solely upon the small pension granted by former employers.

How the heart of the merchant in river towns was gladdened in those old days when a steamboat whistled and a boat put out to shore or when a landing was made! No wonder he slept above his store, for boats came and went by night as well as by day. Once, while looking through some papers in my father's desk, I found an old order for supplies to be ready when the boat passed Le Claire. It contained thirty-six items, including canned goods, fresh fruits and vegetables, hams, toothpicks, soap, molasses, and brooms. A footnote attached, stating that only goods of the best quality would be accepted, was proof that the crews were well fed and that packets spread a bounteous table for the passengers.

River cooks were noted for their skill, and many favorite dishes among the housewives in river towns today were originally prepared on the steamers. With a great abundance of everything, the packet cooks found no difficulty in creating dishes that would tempt the traveler. Three or four kinds of meat, innumerable vegetables, both hot and cold bread, fruits, and pastries were included in each meal. Indeed, I have very pleasant childhood memories of stolen visits to a boat whose cook was a favorite of all children, and never did we leave empty-handed. Amusing stories are often related about these cooks—of he who carried salt in one vest pocket and pepper in the other pocket, and of the one who annually cast a pan of biscuits into the water in memory of all river cooks who were dead.

Since life was centered about the river, it is only natural that the arrival and departure of a boat was more or less of an event to the children. Many youngsters learned to read by spelling out the names of favorite boats, and such fascinating names they were—*Phil Sheridan, Red Wing, Northwestern, Le Claire Belle, Eclipse, Diamond Jo, North Star, Saturn*—all symbolical of romance and adventure. . . .

PART SEVEN
"Too Thick to Drink and Too Thin to Plow"

Introduction

To frontier humor and fantasy the life of the river country brought a whole new crop of anecdotes and yarns relating the true and not-so-true, new and not-so-new, experiences of the rugged individualists who ran the boats and the "characters" who traveled on them. If these stories were not always as true as they seemed, even when based on actual happenings, that is because actual happenings always stimulate the yarn-spinner's imagination to improve on the facts. And if these stories were not always as new as they seemed, it is because, like Hiram Chittenden's pilot story-teller, the narrator is passing on as his own adventures the "accumulated stories of many years, but as new to the tenderfoot as if told for the first time." The folk story-teller also has a way of making a story seem like his own even when it happened to someone else, as if he, a silent partner in the action, were also a partner of providence and the yarn were gospel.

A typical specimen of a river story-teller revising a traditional yarn in the light of his own experience is the story of the flatboat caught in the Pot, which Donald Davidson, in *The Tennessee* asks the retired mate, S. L. Massengale, if he knows. "Oh, yes, he knew that story, but it wasn't a flatboat, it was a raft, a log raft. And it really happened, it happened to a cousin of his named Brown. They used to run logs in those days down the river to South Pittsburgh. Didn't try to haul 'em overland, but run 'em down the river. And his cousin Brown, that night, they got caught in the eddy of the Pot. It made a back-current, 'a whirl about as long as from here to yan side of the river.' And they saw the folks in the cabin fiddlin' and dancin', and then another cabin with fiddlin' and dancin,' and then another, and another. But it was the same cabin all the time." [1]

Some tall tales are not so funny as they might be because they do not steer close enough to fact and hold a straight course but, like the raft caught in the Pot or the boat that wooded all night at the same woodyard, they keep going in circles. In trying to improve on fact, the narrator may pile it on a little too thick, straining not so much the credulity as the patience of the audience. Mark Twain, who was a master of "thickening" the plot as well as timing, lets us into his secret when in *Life on the Mississippi* he has the mate interrupt the tough yarns of a fellow-passenger with the cold, inexorably repeated warning: "Wait—you are getting that too strong; cut it down, cut it down—you get a leetle too much costumery onto your statements: always dress a fact in tights, never in an ulster."

---

[1] Another version, by David Hunter Strother ("Porte Crayon"), is given in *A Treasury of Southern Folklore* (1949), pp. 429–430.

The steamboat was a boon not only to the social and economic life of the river country but also to its story-telling. For piloting a steamboat calls for the kind of memory and imagination, in knowing the shape of the river and getting the boat into shape, that are the prerequisites of the skilful spinner of yarns. Since stories are most at home on a journey, a leisurely steamboat passage on a meandering river provides a congenial setting for recalling and swapping experiences and yarns. And in the collection of odd sticks and odd traits that the steamboat attracted both among its passengers and crew—oldtimers, greenhorns, sharpers, suckers, Easterners, Westerners, natives, foreigners—we have as rich and revealing a body of odd experiences for anecdotes and yarns—tight scrapes, narrow escapes, feuds, frauds, pranks and tricks—as can be found anywhere on the frontier.

B. A. B.

Swapping Horses in Mid-Stream

An Indiana man was traveling down the Ohio in a steamer, with a mare and a two-year-old colt, when by a sudden careen of the boat all three were tilted into the river. The Indiana man, as he rose puffing and blowing above water, caught hold of the tail of the colt, not having a doubt that the natural instinct of the animal would take him ashore. The old mare took a direct line for the shore; but the frightened colt swam lustily down the current with the owner. "Let go the colt and hang on the old mare," shouted some of his friends. "Pooh, pooh!" exclaimed the Indiana man, spouting the water from his mouth, and shaking his head like a Newfoundland dog; "it's mighty fine, you telling me to leave go the colt; but to a man that can't swim, this ain't exactly the time for changing horses!"

Too Much Pepper

Commodore William F. Davidson of the old White Collar Line of Mississippi River steamboats was a very pious man. It was his custom

From *The American Joe Miller;* A Collection of Yankee Wit and Humor, compiled by Robert Kempt, p. 201. London: Adams and Francis. 1865.

From *Old Man River,* Upper Mississippi River Steamboating Days Stories, Tales of the Old Time Steamboats and Steamboatmen, [by Charles E. Brown], p. 5. Madison, Wisconsin: Charles E. Brown, Wisconsin Folklore Society. 1940.

to assemble the members of his crew on deck on Sunday mornings and to there hold a prayer meeting. On such occasions he always offered the prayer himself. One of these prayers he once concluded, according to a river tale, with the following words:

"And, Oh Lord, bless the poor. Give to every poor family a Barrel of Pork—a Barrel of Flour—a Barrel of Sugar—a Barrel of Salt—a Barrel of Pepper." Then, hesitating for a moment, he added: "Oh, h——l no—that's too much Pepper!"

Steamboat *versus* Railroad Travel

It is a question whether this steamboating is a more dangerous mode of travel than others. It had a sort of settlement the other day, at least in the mind of one of the Negroes, who exclaimed:

"If yer blowed up on the railroad, thar you is; but, good Lord, if yer blowed up on a steamboat, whar is yer?"

Why a Steamboat Is Called "She"

The question is often asked why we use the feminine pronoun in speaking of a boat. Why always say she? I've heard many reasons given:

Because it takes a smart man to manage her.

Because no two of them act alike.

Because they need a little touching up with paint now and then to look right.

Because her title is not complete without a "husband." (Until recent years every American vessel's *Annual License* had to have some one named in it as "Ships-husband" or "Managing-owner.")

Because she moves with such grace and quiet dignity.

Occasionally some one builds a freak so homely and awkward looking that we all refer to it as "it." No one uses the feminine in speaking of it.

From "Down the Mississippi," by George Ward Nichols, *Harper's New Monthly Magazine,* Vol. XLI (November, 1870), No. CCXLVI, p. 843. New York: Harper & Brothers, Publishers.

From *A Raft Pilot's Log,* A History of the Great Rafting Industry on the Upper Mississippi 1840–1915, by Walter A. Blair, p. 16. Copyright, 1929. Cleveland. 1930. Reprinted by permission of The Arthur H. Clark Co.

A Horse of a Steamboat

The following specimen of the Western superlative is said to be from the mouth of a Kentucky steamboat captain. While dilating, in a strain of exuberant commendation, on the excellence of his craft, he says: "She trots off like a horse—all boiler—full pressure—it's hard work to hold her in at the wharfs and landings. I could run her up a cataract. She draws eight inches of water—goes at three knots a minute—and jumps all the snags and sand-banks."

Catfish Tow

The people loved jokes about the [Illinois] river. A Peoria paper printed a long fish story of which the hero was a cook on the steamship *Peoria*. He used as bait a hog that had died on board, attaching the whole carcass to the stern cable by means of a meat hook. This unusual line was inadvertently left all night in the water. The passengers awoke the next day to find the boat being carried, stern foremost, downstream in spite of the engine. The cause was, of course, that an enormous catfish had swallowed the bait and was now hurrying home, towing the steamship behind him. Captain Keese, being used to such emergencies, got out his rifle and shot the catfish.

The editor seemed to feel it necessary to add at the end of this account the parenthetical notation: "(a hoax)."

"Arkansas Snipe"

"You're off now. Good bye! Take care of yourself, and give those bears particular fits!" sung out Dory, as the plank of the steamboat on which we were bound down the Mississippi was drawn in, and we left our friend Marion—one night last winter—on the wharf boat at Napoleon, Arkansas.

We should have left him in pitch darkness had it not been for the pitch-

From *The American Joe Miller,* p. 93. Entered . . . 1853, by H. Long & Brother. Philadelphia: T. B. Peterson.

From *The Illinois,* by James Gray, pp. 246–247. Copyright, 1940, by James Gray. *The Rivers of America,* edited by Stephen Vincent Benét and Carl Carmer. New York and Toronto: Farrar and Rinehart, Inc.

From *The Grey-Bay Mare and Other Humorous Sketches,* by Henry P. Leland, pp. 54–57. Entered . . . 1856, by J. B. Lippincott & Co. Philadelphia.

pine lights which shed a halo of glory around his head, and the tail of his Newfoundland dog. They were bound up the Arkansas River on a bear hunt. A more whole-souled man, a finer dog, never walked—although a Scotch terrier *is* a better dog for bears; and as we left him behind, there was a sense of something lost.

In order to find composure and fill up the vacuum, we adjourned to the Exchange or Social Hall of the steamboat to take a "snifter." On entering this favored region, we were at once made aware of the fact that the Rackensackians at Napoleon considered a fair "Exchange" no robbery; on payment of our Roland of a Marion they had given us an Oliver of an Arkansian. He was a beauty. Straight as a hickory sapling, and fully as tough, he seemed to be just the stuff that red-eye whisky barrel hoops are made of—water-proof at that. He was already a firm friend of the bar-keeper, having taken two drinks inside of ninety seconds, and as he still wore a thirsty look in his left eye, we at once asked him to take another.

"Stran-ger," said he, "count me in thar!"

So we did, and after drinks all round, we settled about the stove with segars. Conversation soon fell on bear-hunting, deer-hunting, and finally was closing up with a description of a mighty big coon hunt, wherein our friend, the Rackensackian, had performed prodigies of valor in the way of putting whisky *hors du combat,* or out of harm's way—cut down an untold number of cottonwood or pecan trees, and pitched into a liveoak till he made dead wood of it; and finally killed on that one hundred crows, whose united weight he judged to be well on to a ton! After this we knew the man, but Dory, in whose locks the hayseed still gleamed, was moved, in turn, to tell his tale of hunting, and dwelt long and hotly on a certain snipe shooting excursion where each gunner bagged his four dozen birds. He drew it strong, being away from home, and went on sawing away how the snipe rose and fell, until the Rackensackian man woke up with the question:

"What ar' snipe?"

"Snipe," said Dory, "are the best game that flies. The kind I mean are called English or Wilson's snipe, and are splendid! Long legs, long bills, dusky hue—"

"Stran-ger, stop thar! I've seen the critters; know 'em like an old boot," interrupted the Rackensackian. "I've been down in the Lewsianny swamps —I have! Do you raally eat them 'ar critters on North!"

"Certainly we do," said Dory, "but you said you had seen them down in the Louisiana swamps. They winter there, I expect."

"Winter and summer both. Thar 'ar a few, I should think, in Arkansaw! Two of my boys was down choppin' wood for the steamer t'other day; and them 'ar snipe sung so loud they come back again at night and said thar war a camp-meetin' goin' on down river."

"Sung?" inquired Dory. "That is singular. At the North, as they rise, I have heard them utter a low whistle, but never knew they sung before!"

"Sing!" said the Rackensackian, "they sing so they make my ha'ar stand on eend. You raally shoot them 'ar critters on to the North? Stranger, if you'll only come up to my plantation and shoot off the crop thar, I'll give you the best horse you can pick out, and throw in a Negro to take keer of him."

"Where do you live?" asked Dory. "If I am ever up your way, you'll have to owe me a horse and a Negro."

"Wal, stranger, I live at Powder Horn P'int, on Meto Creek, 'bout thirty miles from Napoleon, and cuss me if the man that shoots off them 'ar birds for me don't be my eternal friend—he will! Look hyar, the infernal things pitched into my youngest child arter it was born, so that its head swelled up as big as a punkin."

"Pitched into your child! Swelled head! Big as a pumpkin! Did snipe do this?" asked Dory, in great hopes of having discovered something new.

"Wal, they did! Leastwise, what you call snipe. We call 'em mus-kee-ters!"

Grand tableau. Curtain descends to slow music of toddy-sticks, broken ice, and the song of an *Arkansas Snipe!*

Mules *versus* Mosquitoes

Mosquitoes is bad this year. . . . Was up at Jake Powers' farm yesterday up by Two Mile and the skeeters was so bad I seen his mules kick some flint stones laying there to make a spark and start a smudge fire in the grass, and then they stood in the smoke. Was all right, I guess, till a bad wind got to blowing, and Jake got scared the fire'd catch the house. So he brought water from the river and put it out. The mules was mighty sore.

Bears in the Delta

Even the bears of the Mississippi backwoods found the pickings good in the Delta. One night when we had played till dawn for a well-known planter, we were suddenly called to the back steps to see a bear gathering roasting ears in the corn field. When the crafty old creature had filled his arms, he went to the hog pen and commenced tossing the ears to the porkers. But the bear was not fattening hogs for the planter's table, not by a long sight. While the hogs ate, the big animal lumbered over the low fence, batted down the fattest and juiciest one he could lay his paws on, and calmly threw his

From *Children of Noah*, Glimpses of Unknown America, by Ben Lucien Burman, p. 89. Copyright, 1951, by Ben Lucien Burman. New York: Julian Messner, Inc.
As told by Tooter Bill, Mississippi River shanty-boat man.

From *Father of the Blues*, An Autobiography by W. C. Handy, edited by Arna Bontemps, pp. 83–84. Copyright, 1941, by W. C. Handy. New York: The Macmillan Company.

kill over the fence. He had climbed back and started off with his meat on his shoulder when the planter plugged him.

On our way home that day one of the musicians told us a story that was gaining currency in the Delta. Every one knew that President Theodore Roosevelt had just recently come to Bobo, about ten miles south of Clarksdale [Mississippi], for the purpose of bagging some of these Mississippi bears himself. It was not so generally known, however, that a member of the President's party had sought to borrow the bear hounds of a man who lived down the bayou. The emissary was politeness itself, and he made a point of conveying to the owner of the hounds that it was President Roosevelt himself who wished to hunt with his dogs. The old Negro assured the young man that what he said was all well and good but added, "I don't give a damn if Booker T. Washington wants them, he can't get my dogs less'n I comes along. On'erstand?" The story went on to conclude that the President accepted the services of the old man in the hunt and—P.S.—he got the hounds.

On the same hunt President Roosevelt was quoted by highly enthusiastic home town folks as saying, "I'm not here as the President, but as a bear hunter, and all hunters—black and white—will mess from the same pot."

Still another legend that followed that bear hunt had the President amazed at the number of bears rounded up by the hounds of the old man from down the bayou. The Negro thereupon assured his President that this was not exceptional. His hounds always gave as good an account of themselves. As the bears came into sight, he made another observation. He had never shot a bear in his life.

"You haven't? Well, how do you kill them?" the President asked.

"Well, suh, I'll tell you," the old fellow replied. "When the hounds corner the bear, I jes steps up quick and sticks the bear with a knife."

He was said to have made a successful demonstration later.

The Hunting Dog of the Tombigbee Bottoms

Well, one time there was a fellow down in Monroe County, [Mississippi], and he had a dog that pure loved to hunt. He'd hunt possums, squirrels, coons, and even a fox now and then, but the man who owned him didn't have time to go out every time the hound wanted to hunt.

But sometimes when he had taken the dog hunting they had flagged down Erbie Lee's train in the Tombigbee bottoms between Amory and Fulton; they'd ride a piece until they came to where they wanted to hunt, and they'd ask the engineer to let them off. Then they'd hunt until they heard the

From *The Greenhouse*, Cuttings from Another Year's Crop in the *Commercial Appeal*, by Paul Flowers, Vol. XI (December, 1954), p. 20. Memphis, Tennessee.

As told by J. Frank Chambers of Booneville, Mississippi.

train whistle on its trip back, so the man would flag it again for the ride back to town.

Well, the dog learned that the train would stop on flag signal, so when his master couldn't go hunting, the dog would go down to the railroad and get on the track right in front of the engine and wag his tail hard as he could, and the engineer would stop for him, give him a ride, and let him off in the Tombigbee bottoms. So the dog would go on and catch a coon or a possum or a rabbit and come back to wait until the train came along again. Then he'd flag it with his tail, climb aboard, and ride on home.

Tail-less Possums

Jack Frost has reigned lord paramount in the neighborhood of Salt River, Missouri. He has "rowed up" that famous stream and curtailed the proportions of the possums that fructify on its banks. The *Salt River Journal* states, on the authority of an old hunter, that all the possums seen in that section of the country during the past winter were tail-less. Their tenancies in tails have been docked by the Frost King. No longer do they like Othello "their round, unvarnished tails deliver" to the grasp of the trapper. No more —like the moon in Addison's superb hymn—do they "take up their wondrous tails." They are no tale bearers. It is insinuated by a western contemporary that not alone stress of weather but scarcity of food has been the cause of the cutting short of these nether adornments of the Salt River possums. They have eaten their tails to the very stumps for no other earthly purpose than that of keeping their souls and bodies together. It is told of the beaver that when sorely pressed by the hunters he will bite off his tail, and leave it in the hands of his pursuers, thinking justly that it is better to escape without a tail than to be caught tail and all, and boiled down into the substance of a short napped hat. The possums of Salt River have been actuated by a similar motive. They live on the banks of a famous stream—explored hitherto only by our Whig friends.

A Snake for Company in the Woods

. . . In my route southward, I rowed down the river past the curious old town of Plaquemine, and by four o'clock in the afternoon commenced to

From *The Spirit of the Times*, A Chronicle of the Turf, Agriculture, Field Sports, Literature and the Stage, edited by William T. Porter, Vol. VI (May 14, 1836), No. 13, p. 99. New York.

From *Four Months in a Sneak-Box*, A Boat Voyage of 2600 Miles down the Ohio and Mississippi Rivers, and along the Gulf of Mexico, by Nathaniel H. Bishop, pp. 178–181. Copyright, 1879, by Nathaniel H. Bishop. Boston: Lee and Shepard, Publishers.

search for an island or creek where a good camping-ground for Sunday might
be found. The buildings of White Castle Plantation soon arose on the right
bank, and as I approached the little cooperage shop of the large estate,
which was near the water, a kindly hail came from the master cooper and
his assistant. Acceding to their desire "to look at the boat," I let the two
men drag her ashore, and while they examined the craft, I studied the
representatives of two very different types of laboring men. One was from
Madison, Indiana; the other belonged to the poor white class of the South.
We built a fire near the boat, and passed half the night in conversation.

These men gave me much valuable information about Louisiana. The
Southern cooper had lived much among the bayous and swamps of that
region of the state subjected to overflow. He was an original character, and
never so happy as when living a Robinson Crusoe life in the woods. His
favorite expression seemed to be "Oh, shucks!" and his yarns were so inter-
larded with this exclamation that in giving one of his stories I must ask the
reader to imagine that expressive utterance about every other word. Affectionately hugging his knee, and generously expectorating as he made a transfer of his quid from one side of his mouth to the other, he said:

"A fellow don't always want company in the woods. If you have a
pardner, he ort to be jes like yourself, or you'll be sartin to fall out. I was
riving out shingles and coopers' stock once with a pardner, and times got
mighty hard, so we turned fisherman. There was some piles standing in
Plaquemine Bayou, and the drift stuff collected round them and made a
sort of little island. Me and Bill Bates went to work and rived out some
lengths of cypress, and built a snug shanty on top of the piles. As it wasn't
real estate we was on, nobody couldn't drive us off; so we fished for the
Plaquemine folks.

"By-and-by a king-snake swimmed over to our island, and tuck up his
abode in a hole in a log. The cuss got kind of affectionate, and after a while
crawled right into our hut to catch flies and other varmin. At last he got so
tame he'd let me scratch his back. Then he tuck to our moss bed, and used
up a considerable portion of his time there. Bill Bates hadn't the manners
of a hog, and he kept a-droppin' hints to me, every few days, that he'd 'drap
into that snake some night and squeeze the life out of him.' This made me
mad, and I nat'rally tuck the snake's part, particularly as he would gobble
up and crush the neck of every water-snake that cum ashore on our island.
One thing led to another, till Bill Bates swore he'd kill my snake. Sez I to
him, 'Billum' (I always called him Billum when I meant bizness), 'ef you
hurt a hair of the head of my snake, I'll hop on to you.' That settled our
pardnership. Bill Bates knowed what I meant, and he gathered up his traps
and skedaddled."

The Efficiency of the Cincinnati Packers

One native son, from over in the neighborhood of the Licking hills, started the yarn about the efficiency of the Cincinnati packers. "Speaking of sausage," said this humorous neighbor, "those connecting links between hog and dog almost remind me of an affecting incident that occurred some years ago at a brisk village below the mouth of Deer Creek on the Ohio called Cincinnati. An ancient maiden friend of ours was taking a stroll on the outskirts of town one pleasant summer morning, accompanied by a favorite black poodle dog—her only protector. Walking leisurely along the flowery banks of Deer Creek, her cheek fanned by 'gentle zephyrs laden with sweet perfume,' she at length came to the residence of a fat and furious looking old German, which, it was hinted, had been the scene of many an inhuman butchery. At the front corner of the house she noticed a fresh pork hanging at the end of a large copper pipe which seemed to communicate with the interior of the house. Her poodle made a jump at the treasure, but no sooner had he reached the spot than he was caught under the ear by a steel hook and suddenly disappeared from the sight of his doting mistress. She, poor soul, horror-stricken by the mysterious disappearance, rushed frantically into the house in search of him. But alas! Like Distaffiana, she might have well exclaimed, 'Oh wretched maide—O miserable fate! I've just arrived in time to be too late!'

"For by the time she reached the back part of the premises, all that remained of her ill-fated poodle was a blue ribbon which she had tied around his neck, seventy-five links of fresh sausage, and a beautiful black woolly muff."

Old Al, the River King

On certain late afternoons, say the Negro roustabouts, when the sun is sinking toward the horizon, and the water becomes a mysterious purple, there will rise up before a steamboat a glistening alligator of a vastness beyond description, carrying in one of his scaly paws a great pipe of tobacco, and bearing on his enormous head a shiny golden crown.

For a moment this bizarre creature will remain before the vessel, surveying the river and the sandbars and the cypress swamps beyond, then will flap his tail lazily, and disappear beneath the surface, to sink back into the

From "Kentucky Yarns and Yarn Spinners," by T. D. Clark, *The Cincinnati Times-Star*, Centennial Edition, Vol. 101 (April 25, 1940), No. 100, "Business, Industry, Kentucky Section," p. 6. Cincinnati, Ohio.

From *Big River to Cross*, Mississippi Life Today, by Ben Lucien Burman, pp. 21-22. Copyright, 1938, 1939, 1940, by Ben Lucien Burman. New York: The John Day Company.

mud of the bottom from which he arose. And the roustabouts aboard the steamboat will shudder, and will touch their good luck charms, or if churchly Negroes, will breath a prayer; for they have seen Old Al, the River King.

At another time, in the cotton season, when the Negroes have been toiling without ceasing as the vessel moves from plantation to plantation, picking up at each landing a new mountain of cotton bales, the chance traveler will see a Negro furtively drop some tobacco over the railing into the yellow water. The Negro is not wasting his tobacco; this is a ritual of sacrifice, to induce Old Al, the monarch, to smoke the kingly pipe he is always carrying. For when Old Al smokes his pipe there comes a thick fog as the fumes rise through the water; the boat can no longer travel, and the roustabout may rest.

Cigarette-Smoking, Fire-Eating Frogs

The study of unnatural natural history is as intense among the roustabouts of the *Willow* as on any other Mississippi steamboat, perhaps more so because of the vessel's governmental and thus educational character. I chanced to witness one extraordinary demonstration. The solemn Hominy declared one evening that a frog would smoke a cigarette, and when the white members of the crew grew ribald, hurried ashore, and returned bearing a frog in his long black fingers. Borrowing a cigarette from one of the spectators, he lit it carefully and inserted the other end into the frog's thin mouth. The frog seemed to stare at this unexpected gift in surprise a moment, then settled down to a long smoke with all the apparent luxurious enjoyment of an old soldier for weeks deprived of his tobacco. Suddenly it gave a gulp, and before any of the astonished spectators could prevent, swallowed the half consumed cigarette, with the end still glowing redly like a beacon on the shore. It seemed to suffer no ill effects from the unusual diet, for several of the crew kept anxious watch over the little animal in a soap box transformed into the observation ward of a hospital. But it continued sprightly and agile as ever, hopping gaily over the decks whenever it was released from confinement, until at last, satisfied, its nurses let it go merrily bounding up the bank again.

"Them frogs 'll smoke a cigarette every time," Hominy remarked gravely as he watched it disappear in the crackling brush. "I've had a big bullfrog pretty near pull a cigarette out of my hand plenty of times. And talk about 'em eating fire. I used to live on a plantation down near Greenville where there was a heap of frogs. And when I'd go out to empty the ashes from the stove, frogs 'd come from everywhere and jump up and git all the red-hot coals from the pan before they hit the ground. It's 'cause a frog was born inside a fire. That there's wrote in the Bible."

Ibid., pp. 133–134.

Turkeys Lifting a Boat off a Sandbar

The *Gordon C. Greene* of Cincinnati is another packet rich in river lore. Over a glass of the Vichy constantly before him, Captain Tom, the vessel's master, quietly talked of his famous mate Bill Cropper. "Bill was sure a great one," he declared. "Nothing ever came up, storm, flood, or general destruction, that Bill wasn't ready to meet it head on. Once up near Marietta, Ohio, the boat got stuck on a sandbar. We tried everything to work her off, walking sticks to jump her, hoses to wash out the mud, everything a riverman ever heard of. But nothing did a bit of good and it looked like we were going to have to be stuck there till next high water. But then Bill got mad, and when Bill got mad things happened. The lower deck was loaded with turkeys we were taking to market. Bill took all the turkeys out of their coops, and got the carpenter to fasten staples over their feet. A couple of minutes later he ordered the rousters to take stations around the deck, and gave them all towels and aprons and any kind of rag he could lay his hands on. Then he blew a whistle and the rousters all started waving the cloths over their heads and yelling 'Shoo! Shoo!' And the turkeys flew up and lifted the boat right over into deep water. Bill was always a great help to a steamboat."

The Mule and the Whistle

Back in those years of famous packets, every owner insisted on a distinctly different whistle for his boat. That was necessary in more ways than one. Shippers and others residing along the river identified boats by their whistles. A new packet must carry on this distinction and must have a different whistle. They had 'em, too.

Even the big towboats had whistles as distinct as the packets when it came to identification of the boats named. Some were musical, others loud and coarse, while a few were just whistles.

Sometimes work animals became acquainted with a steamboat whistle. That was the case with a mule owned by a farmer named Barnett, who cultivated his big cornfields along the Ohio River near Scuffletown, Kentucky.

In those days there was a very neat little sternwheel packet operated from Owensboro to Evansville named *Two States*. She left Owensboro about 10 in the morning and usually passed Scuffletown around 11:30. Approaching the place her pilot sounded the whistle for a hail or to land.

The mule learned to recognize the *Two States* whistle and it knew it was

Ibid., pp. 190–191.

From "In the Pilothouse," by Joe Curtis, The Memphis (Tennessee) *Commercial Appeal*, May 17, 1946, p. 24.

turning out time for noon. If it was halfway of the field, it threw up its head and answered the whistle in regular mule fashion. It stopped and could not be forced to budge until unhitched from the single plow and started toward the barn for a noon meal of corn or oats.

The *E. Jenkins*

Aubrey Haynes is Marine Superintendent of the Mississippi Valley Barge Line. He is a big, bluff fellow, kind and generous, and in love with the Western rivers and their history. I met Aubrey at Vicksburg, while I was waiting for the towboat *Indiana* to come up from Natchez. As we sat there on the deck, we talked about steamboats. The *Indiana* is one of the Mississippi Valley Barge Line's towboats, and Aubrey was allowing me the trip. I wanted to see the Mississippi and the Ohio in order to learn more about Mike Fink, the old keelboatman, who had poled and bushwhacked and cordelled and warped his way up and down the rivers from around 1790 until 1820 or so.

Well, Aubrey and I talked awhile, and then, seeing that the *Indiana* was not even in sight, he said, "Let's go up to my dad's house and talk with him. He's a retired pilot, and he can tell you a lot." And then, as we left the dock, Aubrey asked me, "You ever hear of the *E. Jenkins?*"

"No," I replied.

"Big boat," Aubrey told me. "She was the biggest steamboat ever known in the world. She was the pride of all the roustabouts. They used to tell stories about her. They constructed that boat entirely out of imagination, and they told stories about her. There was no boat like the *E. Jenkins!*"

Cap'm Aubrey Haynes, Sr., lived in a house up on a hill, and when I got out of the car, he came down to greet me. Somehow, he seemed too active to be a retired Mississippi pilot, and there was in him the same generosity and kindliness I had found in his son, but now, those same qualities were sweetened by age. There was no bitterness in him at all.

It was a fine house, comfortably furnished, and on the walls were pictures of old steamboats. So we sat there in the living-room and talked about steamboats. And after a while, Aubrey, Jr., asked his father, "You remember the *E. Jenkins*, don't you?"

And Captain Haynes said yes.

Now it is difficult to talk of the Haynes family by calling each Haynes Cap'm, for all four of them, father and three sons, are steamboat captains. Bob is captain and pilot on the *Indiana*, and Nat is captain and pilot on the *Ohio*. Aubrey, Jr., was once a pilot on the immortal *Kate Adams*.

Aubrey Haynes, Sr. had been on any number of steamboats, although I cannot recall the names of any of them. There is no telling how many boats

By Julian Lee Rayford, Mobile, Alabama. 1947.

an old-time steamboat man might have worked on, for, on another trip many months later on the Ohio River, I heard of Shoofly Wright, who, in the course of his career, was pilot on close to 200 boats, and worked on 210. Of course, Shoofly was an exception, but it just goes to show you.

"The *E. Jenkins*," Aubrey Haynes, Sr., said. "Sure! When her roustabouts went out there and sang the leadline, it sounded like the most wonderful kind of church music you ever heard in all your life. Just like a choir in a church! And her whistle was just like a cally-ope inviting everyone to the circus." Neither his son nor I interrupted him, and he went on. "The old folks say that the *E. Jenkins*, when she went by, the people used to stand out there on the riverbank and watch her from Easter Sunday to high noon on Decoration Day. Yes, sir, she was the biggest steamboat the world ever did see!"

"How big was she?" Aubrey, Jr., asked his father.

"Oh, the *Jenkins*? She was thirty miles long. They had to put hinges on her every half a mile or so, so she could make the turns in the River. She sure was the Bull o' the Woods, all right. Course, I don't see how she could've been a bull, because a boat—you always call it a she or a her, anyhow; but that's what they used to call her, the Bull o' the Woods!"

"I can agree with that," Aubrey, Jr., assented, offering cigarettes to his father and me. "The *E. Jenkins* was a stern-wheeler, and they had to send all the way to California and get whole redwood trees to make the wheel-arms for her wheel, because each wheel-arm was over three hundred feet long. I can't tell how high that wheel was, but they say it took from spring to autumn for it to make just one revolution. Why, Lord! that wheel on the *Sprague,* they could have used that in the alarm clock on the *E. Jenkins!*

"I'll tell you how big it was," he continued. "That wheel splashed the water up so high—well, you know where the flow of water comes up against the stern? They had big nets that they spread out up there to catch the fish. That wheel scooped up every fish in the river, just as nice as you please, and threw 'em into that system of nets up there on the stern. And they had a fish cannery right up by the nets. I tell you, that fried catfish in cans was mighty nice."

"You haven't told him the main thing yet," Aubrey Haynes, Sr., put in.

"What's that?" his son asked.

"Why, about the searchlights on the *E. Jenkins*! They were so powerful you could see the Capitol in Baton Rouge from Natchez on the darkest night."

"That's right! Absolutely right!" Aubrey, Jr., agreed. "One night the *E. Jenkins* was at Cairo, and a man said to the pilot, 'I wonder what old Amos McFishface (whatever his name was) is doing up there in St. Louis, tonight.' Well, the pilot flashed that big searchlight up toward St. Louis, and there was Amos McFishface! They could see him just as plain as day! He was leaning against that old stone house that Manuel Lisa built on the bluff. That was some searchlight, all right!"

After that, there might have been a lull, but Cap'm Haynes, Sr., urged his son, "How 'bout the trains, Aubrey?"

"Oh, yes!" Aubrey, Jr., answered. "The roustabouts used to say there was a passenger train and a freight train on the *E. Jenkins*, and they kept a regular schedule every day. They ran over a track on the guards around the boat. Those trains went without any trouble at all until they came to one of the hinges. The hardest hinge to get over was the big one out in the middle of the pasture that was planted amidships. Both trains had trouble getting over those hinges because those hinges were big!"

All I could do from then on was sit there in amazement as the story grew. It was the first time I had ever seen a folk legend become such a reality, as the Hayneses developed it.

Aubrey, Sr., put in softly, "Cap'm on the *E. Jenkins* was a strange man. Some o' the roustabouts said he rode a bicycle, and others said he rode a white horse around the boat. They even said he was a ghost, that he might pop up any minute."

"And that mate," Aubrey, Jr., took it up, "he sure was mean! He was so mean that the roustabouts hated him, and one time here at Vicksburg they got so mad at him, they hollered him off the boat. Said they wouldn't work for him. They stood out there on the bank, and they hollered him off, and he come off, too. But you know what he did? Man, he was sure slick! He went and hid himself in a big ol' trunk, and the trunk was carried aboard the *E. Jenkins*. And when the boat was out in the middle o' the river and headed up to Helena, he come out o' that trunk, and wasn't he mad, though! Had a big black-snake whip in his hand, and he said he was the mate, and they'd put him off the *E. Jenkins*, would they! He'd show 'em!

"I bet they never tried to put that mate off the *E. Jenkins* again! He said he came back because anybody who ever worked on the *E. Jenkins* loved her too much to leave her. But he was so mean I bet you no other steamboat would have hired even his shadow!"

"How was the food on the *E. Jenkins*?" I inquired.

"The food!" Aubrey, Jr., cried. "Man, the food was so good you can't describe it. The commonest, lowest-paid roustabout on the *E. Jenkins* got chicken and watermelon at every meal! And a pilot wouldn't eat unless he had champagne for breakfast! That was a wonderful boat. Any roustabout would tell you that. It was the roustabouts who told the stories about her. Isn't that right, Dad?"

"That's right. Ask any roustabout between New Orleans and Cairo, and clean on up to St. Louis, and he could always tell you something about the *E. Jenkins*."

Cap'm Haynes, Jr., was going on with enthusiasm now. He said, "They had elevators up to the forty-second deck, and on the thirty-ninth deck they had the grand double-rush ballroom. Every pendant of glass in the chandeliers of that room was tipped with a fourteen-carat diamond. All you had to do was light one candle in that ballroom and all those diamonds blazed up like a bonfire! And they say that out on the hurricane deck it was wonderful, too. Young fellows walking around with their sweethearts under the magnolias."

"Magnolias on the hurricane deck?" I wondered.

"Why, of course!" Aubrey, Jr., retorted. "They had coal mines in the *Jim Johnson,* didn't they? It was just as easy to have magnolias on the *E. Jenkins!* I tell you, the people who built that *Jim Johnson* must have been purely utilitarian. Nothing utilitarian about the *E. Jenkins*—everything there was beautiful. Magnificent oil paintings on the door to every cabin."

I smiled as I said, "It's a pity we can't have a boat like that on the Mississippi now."

There was silence a moment, and then I said, "She certainly was a big boat—"

Aubrey Haynes, Jr., told me, "Yes, sir, she was the Bull o' the Woods! They had a one-mile race track around one of the smokestacks, and they had a baseball park on top of the pilot house—"

The *Jim Johnson*

Yes, I first came to Boonville [Missouri] with the *Jim Johnson* on one of its last trips up. I was a member of the crew stationed on the bow, and I got off here in the spring and boarded the stern end of the boat when it came by in the fall. I got to like Boonville so much during that first summer that I came back here to live when the *Jim Johnson* finally tied up for good.

Yes, that's what I said. It was a big boat. It took all summer for it to pass Boonville and the waves rolled for three days after it had gone by.

The smokestack of the *Jim Johnson,* I'm telling you, was so tall we killed the fire in the fall and in the spring the smoke was still coming out. When we came up the river we made so much smoke the chickens went to roost, thinking it was night.

Navigation of the Missouri and Mississippi Rivers was difficult, to be

From the Rural Life edition of the *Boonville* (Missouri) *Advertiser,* July 21, 1939. Reprinted in *The Missouri Historical Review,* Vol. XXXIV (July, 1940), No. 4, pp. 581–582. Columbia, Missouri.

. . . [Wilbur] Haley, who in his youth worked side by side with river pilots and engineers and deck hands who knew every sandbar from the Upper Missouri to the Gulf and every bit of history connected with each, vouches for the veracity of this story. He got it straight, and can tell you many amazing things about this steamboat extraordinary and its awful captain who weighed 750 pounds and had but one eye, and that in the middle of his forehead—truly a man capable of commanding a boat like the *Jim Johnson.* . . .

Haley knows that if you find a resident of Boonville or Franklin, or any other river town, who was ancient enough . . . most likely this ancient river man would tell you a story that went like this.—Editor, *Boonville Advertiser.*

sure, but the *Jim Johnson* had rubber joints to enable it to make the bends in the rivers of this size.

What did we haul on the *Jim Johnson*? Oh, everything, but it was a combination freighter and pleasure boat. We made most of our money off the excursion trade. We had regular tourist camps on board for passengers who wanted to spend the season with us.

Our guests never lacked entertainment or something to do. A baseball diamond was laid out on the roof, and for lovers of the turf sport we had horse racing around the base of the smokestack. . . .

It took an enormous crew to run the *Jim Johnson*. Once we came up the river short of help and hired the entire male population of Boonville.

When trying to cut down expenses one month, we put a proposition to the clerk not to dot the i's or cross the t's on the pay checks. He did this and saved a barrel of ink.

It was quite a task to feed the crew, but we grew most of our own food. One season of my work on her was spent in the turnip patch on the head end of the bitts.

I'll never forget how disgusted I was the night one of the boys left the fence down and an old sow got in and ate a hole in my nicest turnip and gave birth to 300 pigs inside. No, that was not necessarily my largest turnip, but it was my nicest one.

The *Jim Johnson's* kitchen was pretty well organized. When we had eggs for breakfast they used a steamshovel to scoop out the shells. The chef employed eight peg-legged men with tin cans tied on their pegs to walk on dough and cut the biscuits out. . . .

Once, up by Arrow Rock, where there was an extra-deep hole, a bunch of us decided to go fishing. We had heard there was a big fish in that deep hole, and we were set on catching him.

We used a three-inch cable for line and the *Jim Johnson's* extra anchor for the hook, baiting with a team of yearling mules. We went up stream about a mile and heaved 'er in, tying the loose end about a large oak tree on a small island.

While we were sitting around swapping yarns, we noticed the oak tree was waving back and forth, so we knew we had a bite.

Using a huge windlass, we managed to get the fish's head out of water, but the river dropped so fast the boat grounded. It was getting dark, so we pushed him back in and decided to wait until morning to work out a way to land him.

Next morning when we went back up the river the tree and the island were gone. We found the island about five miles below Boonville, where it had lodged on a riffle, and the tree pulled out.

We never did learn the length of the fish, but he measured an estimated 16 feet between the eyes.

How long ago did the *Jim Johnson* operate? Well, sir, I worked on her for several seasons, but I just can't recollect the years. We never had any calendars on the boat because it didn't make any difference what time we arrived at any place.

We had a system of keeping time, though. In order that the crew might know when pay-day came around, we painted one paddle on the wheel white. It came up once a month.

You're right, boy, the old days on the river are gone forever. The *Jim Johnson* was a great boat, sir, a great boat. . . .

The Green Passenger Who Wanted to Be a Captain

To some of our readers the following incidents may appear a little too strange to be true—bordering somewhat upon fiction, or at least, our account of it a little exaggerated; but we assure you the whole affair actually occurred on a steamboat. We will call no names, but give the boat the title of *Tobacco Plant* for the present occasion.

It is known to those who "have travelled" that generally there are persons travelling on board a steamboat who may be termed "green," and although at home they appear to possess good common sense, yet when they go aboard a steamboat, there are so many strange sights, curious machinery, &c., they appear to be so much out of their element that (to those on board who are daily accustomed to everything pertaining to a boat) they make themselves very foolish and troublesome. They are generally very inquisitive—ask ten thousand questions, and become extremely annoying, especially to the officers of the boat, and sometimes the strangest kind of answers are given to the different questions propounded, as the following scene will show:

The steamer *Tobacco Plant* was on her downward passage on the Missouri River. She landed at one of the towns, where several passengers came on board, among them a stout athletic man, who observed as he came on board:

"Wal, I've got on one er these swimming allegators at last. I've hearn tell a good deal about these critters, and seen 'em running, but this is the first one I ever travelled on."

This speech and the manner it was spoken created a little curiosity among the crew and passengers, and everyone appeared anxious to explain to him the different curiosities of the boat. At last the customer thought he would like to command a boat—yes, he believed he "would make a first rate Captain," and some mischievous wag told him that the *Clerk* was anxious to employ a commander, the one then commanding not suiting. Upon this intelligence the stranger forthwith accosted the Clerk:

"I'm told you want a Captain, sir, and as I have nothing perticlar to do, I reckon I'd as soon be a Captain as anything else."

The Clerk, perceiving the game, followed suit, and answered as follows:

From *Southern and South-Western Sketches,* Fun, Sentiment and Adventure, edited by a Gentleman of Richmond, pp. 145–150. Richmond: J. W. Randolph. N.d. [1855.]

"Yes, sir, I want a Captain. I am about to discharge the one I now have —he don't suit me; and if you and I can agree, as you have applied before anybody else, you shall have the situation—'first come, first serve.'"

"Wal, now," said the stranger, "I'm not much acquainted with a steamboat, but take me on land, and I am *thar*—I've seen a good deal of the world—have been to Kentucky several times, and once to New Orlans, but I always went by land. But I suppose being a Captain is like everything else—requires bravery, attention, and a good understanding of *human natur*. Now, I've seen a good deal of the world and men—I *driv* stage wunst, and was a long time overseer on Col. Wheaton's plantation, but, Mr. Clerk, you must tell me a little about what a Captain has tu du. I want to know my duty thoroughly 'fore I commence, you know."

"Yes," said the Clerk, "you must understand your duties well. The first thing a Captain—that is, *my* Captain—must do is, in the morning to see that the beds are well made, the berths well swept, and then call the roll of all the stewards, deck hands and servants, in order to see if any have been killed, or thrown overboard during the night, or if any are sick. Then he must consult me about breakfast and dinner—that is, if I am up and shaved —and if we have chickens or turkeys in the coop, to count them and see that they are well fed, and see that every man on board does his duty and never, when in port, allow the chambermaid to go onshore without first leaving a lock of her hair, which must be deposited in the iron safe."

The stranger listened to this yarn with the greatest attention, believing it all gospel truth, and promised most sacredly strictly to comply with the rules.

It was not long before all on board, officers, passengers, and deck hands, were in the secret, and all played well their parts. Every hour the poor would-be Captain grew more impatient to take command, and if he saw the Captain of the boat idle, or doing what appeared to *him* a little out of the way, he was sure to report the same to the Clerk, and urge his immediate discharge. The Clerk would apparently get in a great rage, curse the negligent Captain, and threaten to discharge him the moment he arrived in St. Louis.

"Why, Mr. Clerk," said the stranger, "I seen that lazy, good-for-nothing Captain of your'n sittin' up thar on the *roof* of the boat, laughin' and talkin' with that tother man in the glass box, turnin' a wheel, and when I told him that his time was short, and that if he didn't look sharp he'd run on a log, and the boat would be tipped over—he told me to 'go to the devil.'"

"He did!" said the Clerk. "Well, if that's the way he conducts himself— if that's the way he insults his is-to-be successor—and if that's the way he neglects his duty, zounds! I'll have him put ashore instantly—the scoundrel."

Soon after this, the boat "rounded to" for wood, and, as usual, the Captain went on shore to see if everything was right. The stranger watched him close, and seeing that he did not assist the hands in "toting" the

wood on the boat, thought it was great negligence; and, to show the Clerk
that he would not be negligent in his duty, off with his coat and commenced "lugging" in the fuel in good earnest. This of course created a
great laugh, which enraged the hero to distraction—he cursed the Captain, the mate, and all hands. The Clerk, of course, kept out of sight, and
when the boat was again under way, the faithful candidate for the captaincy took particular pains to relate the whole proceedings to his supposed employer, urging at the same time the immediate discharge of that
"rascally Captain."

The Clerk, perceiving the poor man was getting highly excited, and that
if the joke went much further that serious consequences might ensue,
thought he would continue the game with the passengers, and accordingly
with as grave a face as possible, said to his *afflicted* friend:

"Well, Captain [by this time everybody on board called the poor devil
'Captain'], I can see but one way for you to manage now: you must call
the passengers together, state to them your cause, and then request them
to sign a petition recommending you to the captaincy of the *Tobacco
Plant;* don't be afraid now—take a bold stand and demand your right."

"Wal," said the stranger, "I reckon that it is the best course; but how
shall I get them together?"

"O, tell the steward to ring the dinner bell."

"Steward! steward! you black rascal, ring the bell, and call the passengers together. Capt. —— wishes to consult them on important business,"
vociferated the stranger in a very commanding tone.

"Hush up, old Snoodlepup," replied the steward, in a significant tone.

"What, you scoundrel, do you know who you are talking to; you scoundrel. I'll let you know who I am"; and collaring the steward, was about
to flog the rascal when the mate came up, and a general battle ensued,
in which the poor "Captain" got a bloody nose, [a] black eye, and his
coat nearly torn off from his back. The Clerk made it convenient to step
up about this time.

"Why, Captain, is it possible that I see you fighting? Have you so soon
lost sight of the dignity of your station? What will the passengers think?"
said the Clerk in a very solemn tone.

During this controversy, most of the passengers assembled, and all were
making anxious inquiries if "Capt. —— was injured?"

The word was now whispered about for passengers to be seated, when
all obeyed, when the Clerk informed *the* Captain that it was expected that
he would then give the passengers a true history of his genealogy and of
his life, and to be particular in stating all he knew about Fulton, steamboats, and steam saw mills, &c., and then ask them to sign a petition recommending him to the responsible station of master of the *Tobacco Plant.*
Accordingly, he mounted a chair and commenced his speech, and although
the passengers interrupted him by asking foolish questions, and would
break out in a roar of laughter, &c., still the infatuated Captain continued,
supposing the passengers were pleased with his remarks. After having re-

peated the tale some half a dozen times, the Clerk, getting tired of the harangue, whispered to him, "You have said enough now—the passengers expect you to treat them, and then they will sign your petition." So elated was he that he called for wine, and soon ran up a big bill, and the passengers had a glorious time of it. It was not long before the Captain got quite merry—in fact, dead drunk, and he was taken to his berth, where he lay till the next morning, when the Clerk waited upon the Captain, and apparently very sorry at the unfortunate affair, addressed him thus:

"Captain, are you aware of your behaviour last night? You were drunk, sir, yes sir, beastly drunk—and it becomes my painful duty to inform you that I can't have a drunken Captain on my boat. Good morning, sir."

At this intelligence, the stranger, much chagrined—begged, apologized, and even cried—but all to no purpose—his prospects were blasted forever.

By this time the boat had nearly reached St. Louis, and one of the passengers, out of kindness to the stranger, went to him, and told him the whole secret—the game that had been played upon him, and advised him to go into his berth, and there remain till after the boat landed, and then leave the boat with all convenient dispatch.

Barnum on the Mississippi

. . . One of [Barnum's] adventures on the Mississippi [told by him], not contained in his published autobiography, always seemed to me as Yankee as any of those he has related. He was on his way up the river from New Orleans, where he had been to spend the winter in some speculation. Some of the sporting gentlemen who make their home on the river engaged him in the favorite betting game of poker, a bluff or brag game in which the skill consists in managing so as to have the best cards or in boldly betting on the worst. It was hard, I think, to beat the great showman in either, but luck was against him, and he was dead broke.

He landed at a small town in Mississippi, where he found the chances of winning money at play very small, in consequence of a revival of religion that was going forward. But P. T. had more than one string to his bow. Not long before this time he had been a preacher—as it happened, a Universalist. He announced his profession, and obtained a place to preach, but found his creed anything but popular. The Southerners are orthodox in their religious notions, and like strong doctrine. The revival was attracting crowds to the Presbyterian Meeting-house. Something had to be done, and the exhibitor of dwarfs and prima donnas was equal to the occasion. He dismissed his small and indifferent congregation, walked over to the Presbyterian meeting, and announced to the astonished and de-

From *Forty Years of American Life*, by T. L. Nichols, pp. 64–65. London: Longmans, Green & Co., 1874.

lighted assembly that he had been converted from his errors. There was great rejoicing; he was invited to preach, was rewarded with a good collection, resumed his voyage, and had good luck at poker all the way to St. Louis.

The Dandy Frightening the Squatter

About thirteen years ago, when the now flourishing young city of Hannibal [Missouri], on the Mississippi River, was but a "woodyard," surrounded by a few huts belonging to some hardy "squatters," and such a thing as a steamboat was considered quite a sight, the following incident occurred:

A tall, brawny woodsman stood leaning against a tree which stood upon the bank of the river, gazing at some approaching object, which our readers would easily have discovered to be a steamboat.

From *The Literary Apprenticeship of Mark Twain,* with Selections from His Apprentice Writing, by Edgar Marquess Branch, pp. 217–218. Copyright, 1950, by the University of Illinois Press. Urbana.

That Sam Clemens made early use of this [tall talk] tradition is shown by his first piece [written at the age of seventeen], "The Dandy Frightening the Squatter," which employs a theme and plot long familiar to Southwestern humor. An analogue of this tale had appeared in the Bloomington *Herald,* a paper both Orion and Sam Clemens knew, and Sam's version was published May 1, 1852, in the Boston *Carpet-Bag,* a weekly that featured native humor and which was sometimes quoted in the Hannibal *Journal* [of Orion Clemens].

"The Dandy Frightening the Squatter" is a humorous anecdote, a species of the tall tale. It was simply supposed to raise a laugh. The story may have begun, like other tall tales, as a person-to-person report of an actual incident, but its theme was a standby in contemporary comic writing. Possibly Sam Clemens had set in type Fred L. Ballard's story, "Doing a Dandy," published in the *Missouri Courier,* June 27, 1850. Also he must have known a tale that appeared in Orion's *Journal* almost a year after "The Dandy" was published. The *Journal* story related the discomfiture, at the hands of the rustic Jonathan, of "a Boston exquisite, reeking with hair-oil and cologne." The plot of Sam Clemens' tale, too, had been used at least once before. The "Dandy" therefore is unmistakably imitative: either Sam's reading or the oral tradition provided his model, and the writing bears few marks of direct observation. Wide experience and technical skill had to come before he could achieve individuality within the tradition.

For him to be imitative was also to be native. His story relates the undoing of an eastern fop who, like Sam five years later, was showing off on board a steamboat. . . . Thus Sam Clemens selected one of the most western of all western themes for his first story—a theme implied in the ironical inversion of the title. The squatter trounces the dandy; the West turns the tables on the East. The West, indeed, was aggressively aware of sectional cleavages. Harsh criticism by travelers from England and the East had made westerners resent even the slightest implication of superiority by outsiders.—E.M.B., *ibid.,* pp. 7–9.

For additional analogues and analysis, see Franklin J. Meine, *Mark Twain's First Story* (Iowa City, 1952). Mr. Meine discovered the story in 1927.

About half an hour elapsed, and the boat was moored, and the hands busily engaged in taking on wood.

Now among the many passengers on this boat, both male and female, was a spruce young dandy, with a killing moustache, etc., who seemed bent on making an impression upon the hearts of the young ladies on board, and to do this, he thought he must perform some heroic deed. Observing our squatter friend, he imagined this to be a fine opportunity to bring himself into notice; so, stepping into the cabin, he said:

"Ladies, if you wish to enjoy a good laugh, step out on the guards. I intend to frighten that gentleman into fits who stands on the bank."

The ladies complied with the request, and our dandy drew from his bosom a formidable looking bowie-knife, and thrust it into his belt; then, taking a large horse-pistol in each hand, he seemed satisfied that all was right. Thus equipped, he strode on shore with an air which seemed to say —"The hopes of a nation depend on me." Marching up to the woodsman, he exclaimed:

"Found you at last, have I? You are the very man I've been looking for these three weeks! Say your prayers!" he continued, presenting his pistols, "you'll make a capital barn door, and I shall drill the key-hole myself!"

The squatter calmly surveyed him a moment, and then, drawing back a step, he planted his huge fist directly between the eyes of his astonished antagonist, who, in a moment, was floundering in the turbid waters of the Mississippi.

Every passenger on the boat had by this time collected on the guards, and the shout that now went up from the crowd speedily restored the crestfallen hero to his senses, and, as he was sneaking off towards the boat, was thus accosted by his conqueror:

"I say, yeou, next time yeou come around drillin' key-holes, don't forget yer old acquaintances!"

The ladies unanimously voted the knife and pistols to the victor.

Free Passage to Memphis

Well, the first river story I ever wrote was right here in Memphis. I was working on this paper—the *Commercial Appeal*, and I was doing the Federal Building. I found out that they had a lot of old records stored away that went back before the Civil War—of steamboats and other matters. I went to digging in there and wrote a story about the Civil War, Memphis, and the river. (They had a law that when a boat came in it had to register and gives the names of the crew and the list of passengers and prominent people. All that had to be listed with the port of entry here.)

As told by Joe Curtis to B. A. Botkin, Memphis, Tennessee, May 19, 1955.

The president of the Commercial Publishing Company at that time was W. J. Crawford. He had fought through the war in the Confederate army, enlisted at Vicksburg, in a company there. He always liked, in the summertime, to take a big black cigar and stand out in front of the Court Square. There's an alley that runs from Front Street to Main Street, and it is called the Whisky Chute. One time they had fourteen saloons in there. That was where the steamboat men used to come and get drunk. I wrote my river story, and Mr. C. P. J. Mooney, the editor, liked it and gave me a byline.

That day, coming down through the Chute and crossing Main Street in front of Court Square to cut off a little distance, Mr. Crawford said: "Curtis, that was a damn good story you had there, the river story."

"Did you like it?"

"Yes, it brought back my Confederate days when I had just got out of the Confederate army in Vicksburg. All I had was my pants and coat and shirt and 75 cents in my pocket. I decided to go to Memphis, and the only way I could get there was to find some tender-hearted captain to let me work my way up. I went down to the river. There was a boat there en route from New Orleans to Cincinnati. So I went on board the boat. The captain was standing on the lower deck, watching the freight come down the levee to go on the boat. I asked him for free transportation from Vicksburg to Memphis. He said, 'No, goddam it, no! I've been hauling you tramps up the river and I've gotten tired of it. I won't take you unless you have the money.' Well, I went off ashore. He had gotten up to the hurricane deck and he hollered, 'Young man, come back.' He says, 'Was you really in the Confederate army? The reason I ask this is I've been so imposed upon.' Then he wanted to see my official discharge from the army service. I took it out of my pocket and showed it to him, and he read it and he said, 'Come on upstairs with me.' He took me to the clerk's office and he said to the clerk, 'Give this young man free passage, meals and berth from Vicksburg to Memphis.' And it wasn't long till I was in the firm of Mallory and Crawford, cotton factors, and we shipped a good many bales in the season and every bale that we shipped North or South went on that damn Yankee's boat."

The Way the Captain Figured It

"They used to tell a pretty good story on old Captain Sam Fluffer," broke out the man at the wheel, after coming on watch the next day, "though I can't vouch for its truth, for I always found old Sam to be a pretty square man. It is like this: You see, Captain Fluffer had just

From *The Man at the Wheel*, by John Henton Carter (Commodore Rollingpin), pp. 45–47. Copyright, 1898, by John Henton Carter. St. Louis: E. B. Carver.

brought out a new Red River boat, and she was lying at the New Orleans landing, waiting for the season to open. There were already enough boats in the trade, and more than enough, but the old man said that was no fault of his. He wanted some of the business, too, and if somebody had to suffer he couldn't help it; business was business. But it so happened that wages just then were up pretty high, and as he didn't want to take the chances of losing money, he was in a quandary what to do. At last an idea strikes him and he put up his sign to leave. The men on the levee, seeing the boat was going out, went on board and wanted to ship. They kept tackling him for a job, and wanted to know what he was paying.

" 'Well,' said the old man, who was sitting on the boiler deck and taking things easy, 'I don't know; I always want to do what's right; there's nothing small about me. How would it do to give the crew one-third of what the boat makes?'

"The boys got together and consulted. The pilots and engineers thought one-third was pretty good, and soon the rest of the crew decided to take their chances, too, so they sets in and made the trip. When the boat got back to port, and the cotton was all out, the decks scrubbed and everything put in its place, and the crew was all dressed up ready to go ashore and have some fun as soon as they got their money, the old man, noticing them standing around the office, said: 'Well, boys, as the trip is over, I guess we'd better now settle up.' So he goes to work figuring and thinking for a while, and then turned to the crew and said, 'I'm might sorry for you, boys, might sorry for you, but the fact is, there isn't anything coming to you.'

" 'Nothing coming to us!' said one of the men. 'How's that? Didn't the boat make any money?'

" 'Yes,' said Captain Fluffer, 'she made some money; there's no denying that, because figures won't lie; but you see, boys, *she only made my two-thirds!*' "

"Think I'm Lost"

I was steersman on the famous modern packet, *Kate Adams*, and we were going downstream at a fast clip on a very dark night. There was a rail across the middle of the pilot house, and passengers were allowed to come up and observe the pilot at work. But they had to keep back of the rail. Joe McGwin was the pilot that watch, and he was more or less a practical joker. Gus Phillips, the master of the *Kate Adams*, was standing right beside Joe.

Well, all the government navigation lights were out, and Joe said to the Cap'm, "Think I'm lost, Cap'm, think I'm lost."

As told by Aubrey Haynes, Jr., to Julian Lee Rayford, at Vicksburg, Mississippi, May 3, 1946. From the notebooks of Julian Lee Rayford, Mobile, Alabama.

Now the Cap'm knew Joe had made that remark for the benefit of the passengers, and he wanted to keep the joke going, so he said he hoped Joe was not lost, because if he went around behind one of those islands ahead, there were so many snags and reefs that he had heard of several boats went that way and were never heard of any more.

A young Memphis lawyer with his family aboard said, "Are you sure you don't know where you are?"

Joe didn't want to offend the passenger, and he did want to carry on the joke, and he said it was against the law to talk to the pilot when he was busy.

That made the lawyer become alarmed, and he demanded that the Cap'm do something immediately. He wanted to get off at the next landing, even if he had to take an ox-cart back to Memphis.

Cap'm told him, "You needn't worry. This pilot knows his business. Joe, show 'em you know your business!"

Joe knew that right under a little gap in the timberline, against the sky, was a wood pile at Pushmataha Point. He arranged his searchlight by hand control so that it would show the wood pile exactly. He said to the lawyer, "When I turn my light on, you'll see seven cords o' wood, just to show you I know what I'm doing!" And with that he clicked the light on, and the beam of light hit on the wood pile.

Lawyer said, "That's all right. I believe you know what you're doing, but you've taken ten years off my life. And I still don't believe there are seven cords o' wood in that pile!"

Years later, that lawyer became a judge in Memphis, and Joe was picked up for speeding and brought before that judge. Both men had good memories, and they both remembered that night on the packet.

The judge asked Joe, "Do you believe in an eye for an eye and a tooth for a tooth?"

And Joe said, "If you're referring to that ten years I took off your life, hell, no!"

Hard Trader

. . . "Tar" Johnson had a bad day at trading once upon a time. They're famous for hard trades over in the headwaters of the Hatchie River [which flows into the Mississippi and separates Tipton from Lauderdale counties, Tennessee].

"Tar" Johnson got his name because he made tar out of pine sap and sold it for such necessities of life as he couldn't produce in the clearing;

From *The Greenhouse*, Cuttings from Another Year's Crop in the *Commercial Appeal*, by Paul Flowers, Vol. X (December 1, 1953), p. 9. Memphis, Tennessee.

[As] Dr. Wick Anderson, who is a sort of Ambroise Paré of Prentiss County and self-styled kingfish of the Tippah Hills, says.—P.F.

things like short sweetening and snuff, Arbuckle's coffee, white flour and saleratus. He drove a yoke of oxen to a durgen, which was the name for logwagons back then.

Well, Mr. Johnson loaded up a few barrels of tar on the durgen and gee-hawed the oxen over to a community store, to trade for staples, but the tar market was glutted that season (this was before controls and subsidies and all that) and the merchant didn't want to do business. But "Tar" Johnson was in the shorts, and didn't dare go back home without makins for bread.

"Tell you what I'll do," said "Tar" Johnson to the merchant, "you take my tar, and out of half of what you give for it, I'll take the staple stuff I need. Then out of the other half I'll just take in trade anything you want to get rid of."

The free enterpriser thought that over for a while and agreed. So when "Tar" Johnson prodded up his oxen to go home, he had coffee, flour, sugar, saleratus, and snuff, and two gross of grindstones that had been piled up in the merchant's barn for eighteen years.

The Commission Merchant's Bill

. . . On the Mississinewa, a gentleman had fitted up a [flat] boat and loaded it with a cargo of venison, hams, honey, corn, dried fruits, furs, pelts, etc., and started it down the river consigned to a commission merchant at Attica, on the Wabash canal. He expected the load to bring enough to pay for 160 acres of land which he expected to enter when he received the money for his cargo. He waited and waited to hear from the commission merchant, and as no news came he wrote the merchant to know if the goods were sold, and if not, why not. After he had waited until his patience was nearly exhausted, he received word that the goods were sold and the following bill, the merchant informed him, would be deducted for his trouble:

Storage	$ 25.00
Drayage	20.00
Boatage	30.00
Shrinkage	15.00
Commissionage	40.00
Total	$130.00

This left the shipper about sixty dollars for his load. He sat down and sent the merchant the following reply: "You d——d infernal villain, put in stealage and keep it all."

From "Randolph County," by Sam Ginger, in *Reminiscences of Adams, Jay and Randolph Counties* [Indiana], p. 303. [No author, publisher, place, or date.]

The Gravy Train

. . . Occasionally [on Beale Street], when a lucky gambler wins all the money and breaks up the game, everybody in the house forms a line behind him and follows him all over town until he has spent all his winnings. If he walks, they walk behind him; if he gets a car, they climb into taxis and follow him; if he boards a street car, they crowd in to its capacity and even hang on the outside. This kind of gratuitous following is known on Beale Street as the "gravy train."

One night, a smart gambler who had broken up the game gave his gravy train the runaround until all but one member of it had dropped out exhausted. The survivor, after following him until one o'clock in the morning, walked up to him and said:

"Brother, if you ain't gwine tuh spend nuthin', nor gwine tuh give me nuthin', I'se gwine ax you tuh please give me carfare tuh go back whar I started."

The Wife-Trader

I was traveling by fishboat one day toward Cocodra, when a lanky fellow passenger in tar-stained brown overalls and a battered Western hat that gave him the appearance of a sheriff on the Pecos, an individual known as Dollar Joe, began to expound on the niceties of the Mississippi dweller's code.

"When you're a fisherman, first thing you got to learn is to let everybody live way he wants," remarked Dollar Joe, cutting off a generous slice from a plug of tobacco. "Ain't your business what he's doing, unless he crosses up his neighbors. I'll show you what I mean."

He chewed meditatively a moment. "Guess you heard about that fellow down here owned a couple of mighty good hunting dogs, and he'd sell 'em to some man that was going away. Like you know, the dogs was trained to come right back, and then he'd sell 'em all over. We didn't do nothing to that fellow. We figured that was kind of like horse trading."

He spat with perfect accuracy at a passing turtle. "Well, a while ago a fellow come here with his wife on a shantyboat, from somewheres up in Missouri. And he done the same thing like the fellow with the dogs, only he done it with his wife. She was a pretty woman, good cook, too,

From *Beale Street,* Where the Blues Began, by George W. Lee, pp. 77–78. Copyright, 1934, by George W. Lee. New York: Robert O. Ballou.

From *Children of Noah,* Glimpses of Unknown America, by Ben Lucien Burman, pp. 27–28. Copyright, 1951, by Ben Lucien Burman. New York: Julian Messner, Inc.

and every new fisherman that come in here didn't know nothing, the Missouri fellow'd trade his wife to him for his nets and his shanty-boat. The woman'd stay with the new man a couple of weeks, and then say she was mad at him, and go back to her husband. Well, we talked it over. And we figured that fellow was sure crossing up his neighbors. We got ways of fixing people like that on the river. One night when they was asleep, we cut the lines tying their shantyboat to the shore, and just let 'em drift down the river. On the river you don't need no judge or no sheriff. Cutting a line's best kind of law there is anywhere. Too bad, ain't it, you can't cut the lines of people you want to get rid of in a town?"

"Stuck Good"

The Cajun is shrewd and often clever at outwitting the "foreigners" trespassing in his bayou land. Apparently his motives are mixed, on the one hand the fun of proving himself smarter than the city stranger, on the other the opportunity of financial gain.

Two New Orleans men drove through a Louisiana storm toward Vacherie, Louisiana. Lightning flashed, thunder roared, rain came down in glittering sheets. Suddenly the automobile groaned and sank axle-deep in a mudhole. To make matters worse, the storm abated within a few minutes, the clouds vanished, and a mockingly cheery sun beamed down on the wet world. Just at that time a team of animals appeared, a horse and a mule, harnessed for pulling. And on the back of the mule rode a Negro, and on the back of the horse straddled a Cajun.

The white man dismounted and approached the driver of the car.

"Hello!" he said brightly. "I am Paul Auzot [pronounced O-zoo]. Me, I live on farm up way a little bit. This here is Étienne."

The Negro grinned. Paul Auzot examined the wheels of the car.

"Uh huh," he mumbled. "Uh huh. You is stuck good, yes. If you had sense to pull over 'bout two inches you would not be in here. But there is worse hole farther on, so maybe it is just as good you get in this one. 'Course you is city fellow and you don't know damn thing anyway."

"Listen, Mr. O-zoo," said the city fellow, "how about letting up on the sermon and pulling us out of here?"

Mr. O-zoo looked at Étienne. "Leesten him," he chuckled. "He don't like to talk, no. M'sieu, if you was talk a little 'fore you come out here you would not be in there, and you would have save five dollar she gon'

From *Gumbo Ya-Ya*, A Collection of Louisiana Folk Tales, compiled by Lyle Saxon, State Director, Edward Dreyer, Assistant State Director, Robert Tallant, Special Writer, Material Gathered by Workers of the Works Progress Administration, Louisiana Writers' Project, pp. 204–206. Sponsored and copyright, 1945, by the Louisiana State Library Commission, Essae M. Culver, Executive Secretary. Boston: Houghton Mifflin Company.

cost you to get out, hein? If you was talk a little and first ask about this road you would be smart, yes."

The driver tried to be hard-boiled. "Look here," he said. "That's enough. All I want you to do is to get me out of this mudhole. And, by the way," he added suspiciously, "there's something very peculiar about the way you and your friend there came along here all harnessed up."

Auzot laughed. "Is nothing funny, m'sieu. Is business, yes. And it cost you five dollar."

"That's too much," the driver snorted.

"Five dollar is what I charge," said the Cajun. "You want me and Étienne take a little ride? Is another car stuck farther down this same road."

"No, no," groaned the victim. "Get to work. Just shut up!"

"Hokay! Hokay!" The Cajun turned to Étienne. "Now, Étienne, first we hitch car and pull her to bridge, hein? Then we is turn on bridge till nose she points to Vacherie."

An elaborate procedure followed. Auzot mounted the horse, and Étienne, to its occupants' amazement, straddled the hood of the automobile, holding fast to the harness. With much wheezing and chugging, the car pulled out of the mudhole and slowly began to approach the bridge. Suddenly, there was a loud "Ouch!" from Étienne and he seemed unable to keep his seat.

Paul turned and laughed at him. "Well, of all damn fools you is wors' *borique* in whole world!" he chuckled. "If you ain't got more sense than to sit your gogo on hot engine you ought to get burned good, yes."

Étienne jumped off and walked the rest of the way.

At the bridge, Paul accepted the five dollars from the driver. "I do good job, hein?" he asked proudly. "You see, me, I got one horse and one mule for team. I keep mule to pull and horse for his brains. *Adieu, monsieur*. We see you again sometime, hein?"

"Look here," asked the driver. "Is that your land there?"

"Yes, monsieur, on that side of bridge," Paul admitted.

"Is that road yours?"

"Yes, monsieur," Paul again admitted. But by this time both he and Étienne were mounted on their steeds.

"And this road I'm going to use," asked the motorist, with a final sigh, "does it belong to you too?"

"Oh, no, monsieur," answered Paul cheerfully. "That road she belong to Joe Serpas. And you don't need to worry about nothin' like holes in his road. That Joe Serpas he ain't got sense enough to see that his road got holes. He ain't smart like me, no. *Adieu, monsieur!*"

Gene Shepard's Hodag

. . . Gene Shepard was a Wisconsin man, and a riverman; he was born at Fort Howard at the mouth of the Fox, and he spent most of his life on or near the rivers, dying at last at the Pines, his beautiful home at the confluence of the Pelican and Wisconsin rivers. He was a lettered man, a born naturalist and raconteur. It was Shepard who took up the Paul Bunyan legends to augment and embellish them. And it was Shepard who brought the hodag to life.

Late in the last decade of the last century, Gene Shepard came out of the north woods and announced that he had discovered a prehistoric monster, and, after great effort and incalculable danger, had ensnared it. It would soon be put on exhibition, he promised, and, true to his promise, so it was. It was indeed fearsome to look upon: a bovine creature, with six large spines on the ridge of its back, two blinking eyes, and a wide, toothy mouth, which, with its large eyes, the ridged back and long, thick saurian tail gave it a ferocious appearance. Shepard exhibited it that year at county fairs at Wausau and Antigo, keeping it in a dimly lit tent, where each time it moved it emitted unearthly groans, its eyes leered, its nostrils blew forth flames. Shepard's pleasant conceit spread from one end of the country to another, and on the heels of the publicity won by the hodag came eastern writers and scientists, including a representative of the Smithsonian Institution, to examine Gene Shepard's monster, about which he had been having a lot of fun, lecturing with great gravity on the habits of the beast, habits which were peculiar, to put it mildly. "It will eat nothing but white bulldogs, and then only on Sundays. . . . It never lies down, but just leans up against the trunks of trees, and at such times, it can only be captured by cutting deeply into the trunks of its favorite trees."

The coming of a scientific expedition finally forced Shepard to admit that the hodag was nothing more than a hoax; its body had been expertly shaped by a wood carver; he had fashioned the spines along its back from bull's horns, and the hodag's eyebrows from bear's claws, while the claws on its paws were nothing more than steel spikes. The hoax had been carefully covered with oxhides to serve as the hodag's skin, and Shepard had brought Rhinelander and the valley of the Wisconsin into the news in such a way as to bring to the area thousands of curious tourists, even going so far as to circulate picture postcards of the hodag in black and white and in color, and, moreover, of a party of friends assembled, armed with axes and pitchforks, to hunt hodags!

The hodag came to an untimely end in a fire at Ballard Lake a few years later. It was not the only one of Gene Shepard's hoaxes and prac-

From *The Wisconsin,* River of a Thousand Isles, by August Derleth, pp. 207–210. Copyright, 1942, by August Derleth. *The Rivers of America,* edited by Stephen Vincent Benét and Carl Carmer. New York and Toronto: Farrar & Rinehart, Inc.

tical jokes; but it was certainly the most famous. Before Shepard had finished with his hoax, he had circulated a thrilling story of its capture— how he had blocked the entrance to its cave with rocks, and then chloro- formed it by means of a sponge attached to a long pole, how he had then tied it securely and brought it to Rhinelander. Subsequently, Shepard claimed to have captured a female hodag with "thirteen eggs"; all of these, he maintained, hatched out, and he was on the verge of training the hodag's young for exhibition of the creatures when he was forced to reveal the hodag as a hoax.

In his book, *The Hodag*, Luke Kearney enters into the spirit of Shep- ard's hoax and tells a slightly different version of the capture of the pre- historic beast:

How to capture the hodag was a real man-sized job, and none realized it more fully than the heroic Mr. Shepard. He ordered a crew of men to dig a large pit, several miles from the point where he had first sighted the animal. This huge excavation, which was fifty feet in diameter and thirty feet deep, was covered with poles thrown across the opening. The trap was successfully hidden by limbs and grass, laid carefully across the poles. . . . Because the hodag relished beef on the hoof more than any other food, the ox was to serve mankind in a new way for scientific futurity. The hero led the ox through the dense forest until he came in sight of the monster. Then came a growl so deep, loud and sepulchral that it fairly shook the earth, causing a vibration so great that it started a great shower of leaves and limbs from the giant trees. The ox became frantic, but his brave leader steered him along the blazed trail with greater force than before. On they went, toward the pit, while traveling towards them was the hodag, bent upon capturing his prey! Though the beasts' powerful legs were short, he covered the ground with unbelievable swiftness, tearing out trees and the heavy growth of underbrush and leaving in his wake great gashes in the earth itself. At intervals one could hear an indescribable growl, and with each breath, the beast emitted an odor that baffled description! Finally, only one hundred yards separated the great animal from his prey, then forty, and then twenty yards. At the crucial moment, one could hear the rasping teeth of the pursuing beast coming together as he opened and closed his ugly jaws. . . . The leader directed the ox in such a manner that he avoided the pit, but the impetus of the great hodag carried him forward over the mass of branches and grass, which covered the trap. In he crashed, emitting a roar that could be heard for miles, as he struggled to extricate himself. Friendly hands led the hero away, and the ox, with tongue hanging from his mouth, was rewarded with a good bed and plenty to eat that night.[1]

---

[1] Luke Shore Kearney [Luke Sylvester Kearney], *The Hodag and Other Tales* of the Logging Camps (Wausau, Wisconsin, 1928), pp. 14–16.

The Trapper's Pipe

As late as 1857 the American Fur company was quite a power in the northwest country; in former days it had been almost absolute. Its headquarters were in St. Louis, Missouri, and it had forts and trading posts on the upper Missouri, while its employes wandered up and down the river, to and fro, from St. Louis to the mountains, at that time. Through Nebraska many of these old employes had settled on the banks of the river; some were ferrymen, some had little farms, and some kept store, or still hunted and trapped for a living.

These employes were of two entirely distinct classes; one, the superior, or governing class, had charge of the trading posts, made trips into the Indian country for furs, and handled a great deal of property, besides being law-givers and rulers as far as their posts or domain went. The other class were mere workmen; they cordelled the flatboats up the river, did camp work, or hunted and trapped with the Indians for the company. Among the former class were two men who were very intimately connected with the early history of Nebraska. I allude to Peter A. Sarpy and Clement Lambert. Sarpy was generally known; a county is named after him, and he lived at Bellevue, its county seat, for years. Of Lambert . . . not so much is known, and yet he was an important figure in a very important transaction in an early day. In 1857 both Lambert and Sarpy were keeping little trading posts at Decatur, Nebraska, on the southern boundary of the Omaha Indian reservation.

*   *   *   *   *

In the summer of 1857 two of the French employes, . . . of the working class, started from a fort on the headquarters of the Missouri river in a canoe, to come down to St. Louis to draw their money for three years' trapping, etc., to have a good time, and return to the mountains for another two or three years' toil.

One morning they camped on a little island just above the mouth of Wood Creek, near the town of Decatur, in Burt county, this state. After cooking their frugal breakfast they put their traps in the canoe and traveled off, one Frenchman in the bow, and the other in the stern, paddling and steering the canoe.

There was another peculiarity of these men; they always wore the same clothes summer and winter, and generally a fur cap of some untrimmed native skin. In the broiling sun of July this cap was there, and in the middle of December just the same. One of these Frenchmen, however, thought he would make an innovation upon that custom, and while laying off at Sioux City he went up town and bought him a cheap, broad-

From "Some Frenchmen of Early Days on the Missouri River," by Hon. J. A. MacMurphy, of Omaha, in *Transactions and Reports of the Nebraska State Historical Society*, Vol. V, pp. 43–48. Lincoln, Nebraska: Lincoln Printing Co., Printers. 1893.

brimmed straw hat. On this summer morning as they paddled out from the island, the canoe ran under some willows, the broad-brimmed hat flopped in the wind, caught on the willows, the man with the paddle threw up his hands to save the hat, the canoe made a bobble, and over they went. One Frenchman scrambled out to shore, the other was never seen again.

As we were sitting round our man-cooked, home-made breakfast that morning, in rushed this dishevelled and saturated Frenchman and in voluble St. Louis patois, poured his story into his countrymen's ears.

When I could get round to the English of it, this is the way he told it:

"Yas, we pull out from de leetle ile. I was in de bow, just goin' to lite my pipe, Paul, he was steer canoe. Paul's hat, he ketch on bush, Paul throw hees hand up—over we go—and den I los' my pipe."

"And what became of Paul?" was asked.

"Paul! oh, Paul, he was drown, and all the pape' in hees pocket for our mon' in St. Louis—and I los' my pipe."

Twenty times that day did he tell that story, as one after another dropped in, and always wound up with—"den I los' my pipe."

"And where was Paul?" each one would ask, and the same answer— "Oh, Paul was drown—and I los' my pipe."

* * * * *

. . . At that time pipes of the red sandstone of Minnesota, of Indian make, handsomely carved and ornamented, were very valuable. The place where this pipe stone was found belonged to the Sioux, and our Indians, Omahas and Pawnees, could not get these pipes, except through them, and an outsider hardly at all. An Indian frequently gave a pony for a pipe, or other traps valued at even a hundred dollars were traded for one of these pipes, especially if it had been blessed, as you may say, by a great medicine man of the tribe. Such a pipe, with its cabalistic symbols, tassels, brass-tacked and carved wooden handle, was almost unpurchasable from the lucky owner. In fact, some Indians or Frenchmen would quicker trade a squaw off than such a pipe. So you see the Frenchman's loss was considerable, and no chance to procure another [pipe] probable.

Irishman on a Keelboat

There were two methods of cordelling a [keel] boat up the stream. Sometimes one end of a long rope was carried on ahead and fastened to some object in the river or on shore, and the crew then stood in the bow and propelled the boat by pulling on the rope. The usual method, however, was for the crew to walk along the shore and pull the boat after them as canal mules do.

From *Stories of Missouri*, by John R. Musick, pp. 88–89. Copyright, 1897, by American Book Company. New York, Cincinnati, Chicago.

There is an amusing story told of an Irishman working his passage up the Mississippi in a keelboat. He was at Ste. Genevieve, and wanted to go to St. Louis. Learning that a boat was going up the river to that place, he asked the captain if he might work his passage.

"Certainly," said the captain, who stood in the bow of the boat with a long pole in his hand.

The Irishman took his carpetbag aboard. When all were ready to start, he joined the crew on shore and, seizing the rope, assisted in pulling the craft upstream. After two or three miles of such navigation he said: "Faith, if it wasn't for the name of riding, I'd about as soon walk."

Big Olaf and the Buzz Saw

. . . The volume of lumber grew steadily down the Mississippi. Every river led to rich tracts of pine and the stream itself was the road to market. By 1850 developments were growing in all the great Wisconsin pineries, and sawmill towns were springing up on the six great lumber rivers—the Wisconsin, Black, Red Cedar, St. Croix, Chippewa, and Wolf.

In the sawmills changes came quickly to meet the growing trade in finished lumber. The rotary saw replaced the crude "muley" saw and cut twenty times as much lumber in a day's shift. Promptly millmen learned how ruthless that whirling blade could be, and in time the familiar warning passed into common speech: "Don't monkey with the buzz saw."

With the rotary saw spitting its spray of sawdust and the multiple blades snarling through great logs, a mill crew was never far from danger. Every mill town had its men with mutilated hands. Over and over they told the story of big Olaf's explaining to the foreman how he had just lost a finger. The foreman thought the saws were guarded, but Olaf demonstrated how it had happened: "Vell, Ae tak da boord dis vay wit' dis hand an' dis vay wit' da oder. Ae move da boord op to da machine lak dat, an da first ting Ae know—*YUMPIN YIMINY, DAR GOES ANODER VON!*"

Axel Tornbom's Horse

Veterinary come to fix op my sick horse. Ven hae came hae vant funnel to pour stuff in horse's face. Ae got notting lak dat but dinner

From *Upper Mississippi*, A Wilderness Saga, by Walter Havighurst, p. 157. Copyright, 1937, by Walter Havighurst. *The Rivers of America,* editor, Constance Lindsay Skinner; assistant editor, Elizabeth L. Gilman. New York & Toronto: Farrar & Rinehart, Inc.

Ibid., p. 66.

horn, but hae say dat's fine. Hae steck leetle end in horse's mouth an pour med'cine in. Purty soon det horse act crassy en yump aroun' en hae snort en ven hae snort hae blow da horn vat got stuck in horse's neck. Avery time hae snort da horn go toot en scare him. Vay op da road hae go, snortin' en tootin'. Ven hae get to draw bridge, da man tenk boat ban tootin', open da bridge en in go dar horse an hae drownded.

Ole's Whisky Cache

One of the lumberjacks preparing for a winter in the woods began checking over his needs. Finding that he had overlooked one very important article, he visited his favorite drinking place and ordered a quart bottle and a half-gallon jug of good whisky.

While on the train on his way to camp, he opened the quart bottle and passed it around to all his fellow jacks, but never once did he mention that he had a reserve of a half-gallon jug in his "turkey." When he reached camp late that evening, he stealthily buried his jug alongside a large pine stump. There it was to remain until mid-winter, when it would be brought out for his treat to the men who were remaining at work during the holidays.

Christmas eve came, and upon returning to camp from his day's work, he went out to the stump where lay buried his jug of Christmas cheer. He carefully dug away the frozen ground covering the jug, but, as he picked it up, it fell apart. Hurried examination proved that the contents of the jug had frozen and cracked the jug. His holiday cheer had vanished into the earth.

Well, here was one angry Swede. Instead of remaining in camp at work during the holidays, he took the first train for town. Landing there with blood in his eye, he immediately set out for the saloon where he had purchased his jug of whisky. Arriving there, he began berating the bartender for having sold him whisky that would freeze. The barkeep, visualizing a good beating, hurriedly started to do a little fast talking.

"Hey, hey, there, Ole, don't get so tough—I made a mistake, that's all!"

"Mistake," screamed Ole, *"mistake!"*

"Yah, mistake," the bar-keep sputtered. "You see, Ole, I sold you summer whisky accidentally, that's all. I didn't know that you were not going to drink it until winter!"

From *Logs on the Menominee,* The History of the Menominee River Boom Company, by Fred C. Burke, pp. 75–76. Copyright, 1946, by Fred C. Burke. Marinette, Wisconsin.

The Drunk at the Pump

. . . [A] jack . . . had brought his pay from a hard winter's work into town and immediately proceeded to forget the lonesomeness of the forest lands by staging an extended spree. After two or three days of roistering, he awoke during the wee hours one morning with a terrific thirst. Finding himself back in his hotel room, and realizing that it was too late to get into a saloon for a "freshener," his thoughts somewhat reluctantly turned toward water to quench the internal fire.

Stumbling down the stairway and out into the dark yard in front of the hotel, he groped for the pump. After several minutes of earnest labor with the pump handle had brought no results, and not knowing that this particular pump needed to be primed, he stood back and sadly addressed the pump, saying, "I don't blame you a bit, Mister Pump—when I have money I never come near you—it's only when the saloon is closed or I am broke that I even think of you!"

A Preacher and a Gray Mare

. . . The Grand Chain . . . is a chain of sunken rocks admirably arranged to capture and kill steamboats on bad nights. A good many steamboat corpses lie buried there, out of sight; among the rest my first friend, the *Paul Jones;* she knocked her bottom out, and went down like a pot, so the historian told me—Uncle Mumford. He said she had a gray mare aboard, and a preacher. To me, this sufficiently accounted for the disaster; as it did, of course, to Mumford, who added:

"But there are many ignorant people who would scoff at such a matter, and call it superstition. But you will always notice that they are people who have never traveled with a gray mare and a preacher. I went down the river in such company. We grounded at Bloody Island; we grounded at Hanging Dog; we grounded just below this same Commerce; we jolted Beaver Dam Rock; we hit one of the worst breaks in the 'Graveyard' behind Goose Island; we had a roustabout killed in a fight; we burst a boiler; broke a shaft; collapsed a flue; and went into Cairo with nine feet of water in the hold—may have been more, may have been less. I remember it as if it were yesterday. The men lost their heads with terror. They painted the mare blue, in sight of town, and threw the preacher overboard, or we should not have arrived at all. The preacher was fished out and

Ibid., p. 77.

From *Life on the Mississippi,* by Samuel L. Clemens, pp. 201–202. Copyright, 1874 and 1875, by H. O. Houghton & Company; 1883, 1899, 1903, by Samuel L. Clemens; 1911, by Clara Gabrilowitsch. New York and London: Harper & Brothers, Publishers.

saved. He acknowledged, himself, that he had been to blame. I remember it all, as if it were yesterday."

That this combination—of preacher and gray mare—should breed calamity seems strange, and at first glance unbelievable; but the fact is fortified by so much unassailable proof that to doubt is to dishonor reason. I myself remember a case where a captain was warned by numerous friends against taking a gray mare and a preacher with him, but persisted in his purpose in spite of all that could be said; and the same day—it may have been the next, and some say it was, though I think it was the same day—he got drunk and fell down the hatchway and was borne to his home a corpse. This is literally true.

PART EIGHT

History into Legend

Introduction

The legend of the Mississippi begins with its history and its history begins with its name, which is a legend in itself—history into legend. "I was asking for something savage and luxuriant," writes Whitman in *An American Primer*, "and behold here are the legendary names. . . . What is the fitness—What the strange charm of aboriginal names? . . . They all fit. Mississippi!—the word winds with chutes—it rolls a stream three thousand miles long." The phrase "savage and luxuriant" expresses in terms of contrast the "strange charm" and legendary character of the river and the country through which it winds and rolls. In *Description of Banvard's Panorama of the Mississippi River* (1847), the author concludes as follows the traveler's impressions, upon descending the Mississippi for the first time in a steamboat, of the contrast between the wilderness and the invention that brought a luxuriant civilization to it:

A contrast is . . . strongly forced upon the mind, of the highest improvement and the latest pre-eminent invention of art with the most lonely aspect of a grand but desolate nature—the most striking and complete assemblage of splendor and comfort, the cheerfulness of a floating hotel, which carries, perhaps, hundreds of guests, with a wild and uninhabited forest, it may be an hundred miles in width, the abode only of bears, owls, and noxious animals.

But scale and magnitude are not enough in themselves to account for the appeal of the Mississippi to the folk imagination. The gigantic moving panorama of the river is the setting for the human drama of men against the river—epic figures pitting their strength and craft against the might and perversity of the Titan. They add conflict to contrast.

According to the Nebraska poet, John G. Neihardt, in *The River and I* —and this is quite in line with the opinion that the Mississippi should be called the Missourissippi—it is not the "convenient boundary line" of the Mississippi but the "eternal fighting man," the Missouri, that is the "river of an unwritten epic." The reason may well be that the "Missouriad" of the fur trade called for men who were a match for the mountains as well as for the rivers—men like Ashley and Henry, Harvey and Mackenzie, Hugh Glass and John Colter. Here too belongs Mike Fink, who in 1822 joined Ashley's men and was killed in a scrimmage at Fort Henry—shot by Talbott in revenge for Fink's murder of Carpenter in the shooting of the whisky cup.[1] And here belongs Sacajawea, the "Bird Woman," who risked her life and her baby's to save the journal of Clark when one of the canoes of the Lewis and Clark expedition upset.

To most of us, heroes have a way of becoming mere names, but to their

[1] See *A Treasury of American Folklore* (1944), pp. 47–50.

successors on the river they are often a real presence. As Louis Armstrong tells us, in *Swing That Music,* when the *Dixie Belle* was approaching Jackson Island, the captain called him over to see it. "This is Mark Twain's country," he said. "He was a very great man. I never pass this part of the river without feeling that his spirit rests over it." But to Louis Armstrong the island "in the dark, looked just the same as a hundred other islands we had passed in the river . . . since we left New Orleans."

When we read of this captain's experience or hear rivermen say that an old steamboatman turns into a white mule when he dies, or that the goats of the Anchor Line will travel only on its boats, staying on board only as long as they are well treated, we understand what Dr. Hewitt L. Ballowe means when he says, regarding the headless zombie of Batture du Diable: "Everything is crystal clear if you give rein to your imagination."

B. A. B.

The Mississippi Bubble

. . . In 1716, when the Duke of Orleans, as Regent of France, found himself at the head of the government, the financial situation of France had become desperate. The public debt was immense; it was a legacy bequeathed by the military glory of Louis the XIVth and the other pompous vanities of his long reign. The consequence was that the load of taxation was overwhelming, merely to pay the interest of this debt, without any hope of diminishing the capital. All the sources of industry were dried up. . . .

It was at this time, when the wisest heads in France were not able to see their way through the embarrassments of the treasury, that John Law came forward with his panacea. It was to liquidate the debt of the state, to increase its revenue, to diminish taxation; and all these prodigies were to be suddenly produced by the easiest process in the world—the creation of a bank by which fictitious capital, quite as good as any real one, would be produced at will. . . .

* * * * *

Law now began to develop the stupendous projects he had so long meditated. The success of his private bank had gained him so much credit that

From *History of Louisiana, The French Domination,* by Charles Gayarré, Vol. I, pp. 199–202, 206–215, 221–231. Entered . . . 1854, by Charles Gayarré. New York: William J. Widdleton, Publisher. 1867.

the Regent was induced to change its character, and to make it a royal institution . . . in December, 1718. . . .

. . . The charter of the Mississippi Company had been registered by the parliament of Paris on the 6th of September, 1717. The capital of the company was one hundred millions of livres, to be furnished by the stock-holders and to be divided into shares of five hundred livres. . . . To entice subscribers, their shares were made payable in a depreciated paper currency, called *"billets d'état,"* or state bonds, which, however, in the hands of subscribers, were taken at par or full value, although their depreciation amounted to between sixty and seventy per cent. This was such a tempting bait that it was greedily gulped down by the public, and the subscription was soon more than filled up. By this operation of taking the depreciated paper currency of the state in payment of subscriptions, the company became the creditor of the state for a sum of one hundred millions of livres, on which interest was to be paid at the rate of four per cent.

* * * * *

Law was appointed director-general of the Mississippi Company, as he had been of the Royal Bank, and both institutions were merged into one another. . . .

. . . He gave another proof of his wonderful legerdemain by purloining from the French government a still more extraordinary grant than the preceding ones—which was the exclusive privilege of trading to the East Indies, China, and the South Seas, together with all the possessions and effects of the China and India companies, now dissolved, upon condition of liquidating all just claims upon them. It was then that the Company of the West, or Mississippi Company, dropped its original name to take up that of the Company of the Indies, with the privilege of creating additional shares to the amount of twenty-five millions, payable in coin.

* * * * *

Through this curious process of complex annexation and assimilation, John Law had succeeded in erecting the most stupendous financial fabric that has ever been presented to the world. In one company, and through it in one man, was vested nothing less than the whole privileges, effects and possessions of the foreign trade companies of France, the great farms of the kingdom, the mint, the general receipt of the king's revenues, and the management and property of a royal bank, with an immense capital! Thus one man, an obscure foreign adventurer [a bankrupt, an adulterer, a murderer, and an exiled outlaw, who had escaped from prison in England and fled to the continent at the age of twenty-three], through his creature, the company, had condensed into one lump, which his hands encircled, all the trade, taxes, and revenues of one of the most powerful kingdoms of Europe, and through the Royal Bank he might, according to his will, increase to any amount the circulating medium of that country!

. . . The desire to become stockholder in a company which promised to realize the fable of the hen with the golden eggs was fevered into frenzy. There was a general rush of greedy subscribers, far exceeding the number wanted, and in their struggles to be ranked among the privileged ones whose claims were to be admitted, the greatest interest was exerted, and every stratagem put in practice.

At the same time, the press was teeming with publications on the Mississippi, or the Colony of Louisiana, and France was flooded with pamphlets describing that newly-discovered country and the advantages which it offered to emigrants. The luxuriant imagination of prolific writers was taxed, to clothe Louisiana with all the perfections they could invent. It was more than the old Eden, so long lost to mankind. There the picturesque was happily blended with the fertile, and abundance smiled on rocky mountains as on the alluvial plains of the valleys. The climate was such that all the vegetable productions of the globe existed, or could be introduced with success in that favored land. To scratch the soil would call forth the spontaneous growth of the richest harvests of every kind. All the fruits ever known were to be gathered in profusion from the forests, all the year round, and the most luscious peaches, pears, apples, and other like nutritious delicacies, dropping from their parent boughs, were piled up in heaps under cool shades and on the velvet banks of bubbling streams. There dust and mud were equally excluded, as the ground was lined in all seasons with a thick carpet of flowers, endless in variety, and perfuming the air with their sweet breath. The finest breed of all domestic or useful animals was there to be found in all the primitive vigor and gentleness of their antediluvian perfection. The poor peasant, who, during a long life in France, had never dreamed of eating meat, would there feed on nothing less than wild ducks, venison, pheasants, snipes, and woodcocks. The birds kept up a never-ceasing concert, which would have shamed the opera singing of Paris. The rivers and lakes were stocked with fish, so abundant that they would suffice to nourish millions of men, and so delicate that no king ever had any such on his table.

The seasons were so slightly marked that the country might be said to be blessed with a perpetual spring. None but gentle winds fluttered over this paradise, to fan and keep forever blooming its virgin beauties, and in their gamboling flight through boundless prairies and forests, they produced the effect of Eolian harps, lulling enchanted nature to sleep with heavenly music. The sky was brighter, the sun more gorgeous, the moon more chastely serene and pure, and the nights more lovely than anywhere else. Heaven itself seemed to bend down upon earth in conjugal dalliance and to environ it with circumambient love. There, it is true, it could not be said to have been positively ascertained that the fountain of eternal youth had been discovered, but it was beyond doubt that there was in the atmosphere a peculiar element which preserved from putrefaction; and the human body, being impregnated with it, was so little worn out by the action of its organs that it could keep itself in existence almost indefinitely; and the Indians were known to retain the appearance of youth even after having attained five or six hundred years. Those very Indians had conceived such an attachment for the white men, whom they considered as gods, that they would not allow them to labor, and insisted on performing themselves all the work that might be necessary for the comfort of their pale-faced brethren. It was profanation in their eyes not to minister to all the wants of their idolized guests.

More enticing than all that was the pretended discovery of inexhaustible mines of gold and silver, which, however, it would not be necessary to work by the usual tedious process, because the whole surface of the country was strewed with lumps of gold, and when the waters of the lakes and rivers were filtered, particularly the thick water of the Mississippi, it yielded an invaluable deposit of gold. As to silver, it was so common that it would become of no value, and would have to be used in the shape of square stones, to pave the public roads. The fields were covered with an indigenous plant which was gifted with the most singular property. The dew which gathered within the perfumed cup of its flowers would, in the course of a single night, be converted into a solid diamond; and the soft texture of the flowers, bursting open and dropping down under the weight of its contents, would leave the precious gem resting on the stem in unrobed splendor, and reflecting back the rays of the morning sun. What is written on California in our days would appear tame when compared to the publications on Louisiana in 1719; and the far-famed and extravagant description of the banks of the Mississippi given at a later period by Chateaubriand would, at the time I speak of, have been hooted at as doing injustice to the merits of the new possession France had acquired.

When the extreme gullibility of mankind, as demonstrated by the occurrences of every day, is taken into consideration, what I here relate will not appear exaggerated or incredible. Be it as it may, these descriptions were believed in France and from the towering palace to the humblest shed in the kingdom, nothing else was talked of but Louisiana and its wonders. The national debt was to be paid instantaneously with the Louisiana gold, France was to purchase or to conquer the rest of the world, and every Frenchman was to be a wealthy lord. There never had been a word invested with such magical charms as the name of Louisiana. It produced delirium in every brain; to Louisiana every one wished to go, as now to California, and some of the most unimproved parts of that colony were actually sold for 30,000 livres the square league, which, considering the difference in value in metallic currency between that time and the present, makes that sum almost equal to twenty thousand dollars at the present day.

Who could describe with sufficient graphic fidelity the intense avidity with which the shares of the Company of the Indies were hunted up? All ranks were seized with the same frantic infatuation. To be a stockholder was to be reputed rich, and the poorest beggar, when he exhibited the proof that by some windfall or other he had become the owner of one single share, rose at once to the importance of a wealthy man and could command the largest credit. There was a general struggle to raise money, for the purpose of speculating in the stocks of the marvelous company, which was to convert everything it touched into gold. Every kind of property was offered for sale and made payable in stocks. Castellated domains which had been for centuries the proudly cherished possessions of the same families were bartered away for a mess of financial porridge, and more than one representative of a knightly house doffed off the warm lining that had been bequeathed to him by his ancestors, to dress himself, like a bedlamite, in the worthless rags of unsubstantial paper. Such rapid mutations in real estate the world had never seen before! Lands, palaces, edifices of every sort were rapidly shifted from hand to hand, like balls in a tennis-court. It was truly a curious sight to behold a whole chivalrous nation turned into a confused multitude of swindling, brawling, clamorous, frantic stock-jobbers. Holy cardinals, archbishops, bishops, with but too many of their clergy, forgetting their sacred character, were seen to launch their barks on the dead sea of perdition to which they were tempted, and eagerly to throw the fisherman's net into those troubled waters of speculation which were lashed into fury by the demon of avarice. Princes of the royal blood became hawkers of stocks; haughty peers of the realm rushed on the Rialto, and, Shylock-like, exulted in bartering and trafficking in bonds. Statesmen, magistrates, warriors, assuming the functions of pedlers, were seen wandering about the streets and public places, offering to buy and to sell stocks, shares, or actions. Nothing else was talked of; the former usual topics of conversation stood still. Not only women, but ladies of the highest rank forgot the occupations of their sex, to rush into the vortex of speculation, and but too many among them sold everything, not excepting their honor, to become stockholders.

The company having promised an annual dividend of 200 livres on every share of 500 livres, which, it must be remembered, had been originally paid for in depreciated *billets d'état*, or state bonds, making the interest to be received on every share still more enormous, the delirium soon culminated to its highest point. Everything foreign to the great Mississippi scheme was completely forgotten. The people seemed to have but one pursuit, but one object in life; mechanics dropped their tools, tradesmen closed their shops; there was but one profession, one employment, one occupation, for persons of all ranks—that of speculating in stocks; and the most moderate, the few who abstained from joining the wild-goose chase, were so intensely absorbed by the contemplation of the spectacle which was offered to their bewildered gaze that they took no concern in anything else. Quincampoix Street, where the offices of the company were kept, was literally blocked up by the crowd which the fury of speculation and the passion for sudden wealth attracted to that spot, and persons were frequently crushed or stifled to death. "Mississippi!—Who wants any Mississippi?" was bawled out in every lane and by-lane, and every nook and corner of Paris echoed with the word "Mississippi!"

Immense fortunes were lost or acquired in a few weeks. By stockjob-
bing, obscure individuals were suddenly raised from the sewers of poverty
to the gilded rooms of princely splendor. Most amusing anecdotes might
be told of persons thus stumbling by chance into affluence; and heart-
rending stories might be related of such as, from the possession of every
luxury, were precipitated into the depths of absolute destitution; while
those who had become spontaneously rich, being made giddy with their
unexpected acquisitions, launched into such profusions and follies that
their return to poverty was as rapid as their accession to wealth, through
which it might be said they had only passed with the velocity of steam
locomotion. He who could write in all its details the history of the Mississippi bubble, so fatal in its short-lived duration, would give the world
the most instructive composition, made up of the most amusing, ludicrous,
monstrous, and horrible elements that were ever jumbled together.

The distribution of property underwent more than one grotesque change.
The tenants of the parlor or saloon went up to the garret, and the natives
of the garret tumbled down into the saloon. Footmen changed places with
their masters, and the outside of carriages happened to become the inside.
Law's coachman made such a large fortune that he set up an equipage
of his own. Cookmaids and waiting-women appeared at the opera, bediz-
ened in finery like the Queen of Sheba. A baker's son, who used to carry
his fathers' loaves in a basket to his customers, was, by a sudden turn of
the wheel of fortune, enabled to purchase plate to the amount of four
hundred thousand livres, which he sent to his wife, with the recommendation of having it properly set out for supper, and with the strict injunction
of putting in the largest and finest dish his favorite stew of onions and
hog's feet. The Marquis d'Oyse, of the family of the Dukes of Villars
Brancas, signed a contract of marriage, although he was at the time
thirty-three years of age, with the daughter, three years old, of a man
named André, who had won millions at the Mississippi lottery. The conditions of the marriage were that it should take place when the girl should
reach her twelfth year, and that in the meantime the marquis was to
receive three hundred thousand livres in cash, twenty thousand livres every
year until the day of the wedding, when several million would be paid
to the husband by the father of the bride. All these meteors, who were
thus blazing in their newly-acquired splendor, were called "Mississip-
pians," on account of the source of their fortune.

*   *   *   *   *

It must not be supposed that Law had carried on all his projects so far
without encountering incessant opposition. Among his adversaries the parliament of Paris had been the most redoubtable, and that powerful body
had been always on the watch to seize a favorable opportunity to crush
Law and his system. That opportunity was soon to present itself. Undermined by the intrigues of his other colleagues in the ministry, carried
away by the innate imperfections of his system farther than he had in-

tended, terrified at the mighty evolutions of the tremendous engine he had set to work and could no longer control or stop, the victim of a combination of envy, apprehension, ignorance and avarice, which interfered with his designs, and made him pay too dear for protection or assistance, Law felt that the moment of his fall was approaching, and saw with terror the threatening oscillations of the overgrown fabric he had reared. He tried to conceal his embarrassments, by inducing the company to declare that they had such a command of funds as to be able to propose lending any sum on proper security at two per cent. But in vain did they put on this show of confidence in their own resources—the smiling mask deceived nobody. There were symptoms which too plainly denoted approaching dissolution and death. Among these dark spots was the number of bank notes which had been manufactured and which, on the 1st of May, 1720, exceeded 2600 millions of livres, while the whole specie in the kingdom amounted only to 1300 millions.

Then happened what has been frequently seen since: the superabundance of paper money produced a scarcity of specie. It became evident to the most obtuse that these bank notes had no representative, and that sooner or later they would be no more than worthless rags. As soon as that discovery was made, every one hastened to convert his shares or bank notes into gold or silver, and to realize the fortune he had acquired. . . .

The alarm of the public mind became such that it was thought necessary to equalize the proportion between the bank notes and the coin; and on the 21st of May, 1720, an edict was issued which, in violation of the pledge of the state and of the most solemn stipulations, and as a beginning of bankruptcy, reduced the value of the company's bank notes to one half, and cut down the shares from 10,000 and even 20,000, which was their highest ascent, to 5,000 livres. The effect of this edict was instantaneous and overwhelming. At once, all confidence was lost in the bank notes; generally consternation prevailed; and no one would have given twenty cents in hard coin for millions in blank paper. There was a rush on the bank for payment, and one will easily form a conception of the fury, despair, and distress of the people when he is informed that on the stopping of payment by the bank there was paper in circulation amounting to 2,235,085,590 livres. The whole of it was suddenly reduced to zero.

In the whole of France there was but one howl of malediction, and guards had to be given to Law, who had become an object of popular abhorrence. Even the life of the Regent himself was put in jeopardy, and it became necessary to station troops in different parts of Paris, where seditious and inflammatory libels had been pasted up and circulated, to increase the confusion and tumultuous disorder which reigned everywhere. It was apparent that France had been transformed into a volcano, from which the slightest cause would have produced an eruption.

With regard to Louisiana, there had been also a great revolution in the public estimate of her merits. She was no longer described as a land of promise but as a terrestrial representation of Pandemonium. The whole country was nothing else, it was said, but a vile compound of marshes, lagoons, swamps, bayous, fens, bogs, endless prairies, inextricable and gloomy forests, peopled with every monster of the natural and of the mythological world. The Mississippi rolled onward a muddy and thick substance which hardly deserved the name of water and which was alive with every insect and every reptile. Enormous trunks, branches, and fragments of trees were swept down by the velocity of the current, and in such quantity as almost to bridge over the bed of the river, and they prevented communication from one bank to the other, by crushing every bark or canoe that attempted the passage. At one epoch of the year, the whole country was overflowed by that mighty river, and then all the natives betook themselves to the tops of trees, where they roosted and lived like monkeys, and jumped from tree to tree in search of food, or they retired to artificial hills of shells, piled up by preceding generations, where they starved, or fed as they could by fishing excursions.

In many of its parts, the country was nothing but a thin coat, one foot thick, of alluvial soil, kept together on the surface of the water by the intermingled teguments of bind-weeds and the roots of other plants, so that if one walked on this crust he made it, by the pressure of the weight of his body, heave up around him in imitation of the waves of the sea, and great was the danger of sinking through this weak texture. Tempting looking fruits and berries invited the taste, it is true, but they were all poisonous. Such portion of the colony as was not the production of the Mississippi, and therefore a mere deposit of mud, was the creation of the sea and consisted in heaps of sand. Hence it was evident that the country was neither fit for the purposes of commerce nor for those of agriculture, and could not be destined by the Creator for the habitation of civilized man. The sun was so intensely hot that at noon it could strike a man dead as if with a pistol shot; it was called a stroke of the sun. Its fiery breath drew from the bogs, fens, and marshes the most pestilential vapors, engendering disease and death. The climate was so damp that in less than a week a bar of iron would be coated over with rust and eaten up by its corroding tooth. The four seasons of the year would meet in one single day, and a shivering morning was not unfrequently succeeded by a sultry evening. The ear was by day and by night assailed by the howls of wolves and by the croakings of frogs so big that they swallowed children and could bellow as loud as bulls. Sleep, sweet sleep, nature's balmy restorer, was disturbed, if not altogether made impossible, by the buzz and sting of myriads of mosquitoes, which thickened the atmosphere and incorporated themselves with the very air which the lungs inhaled.

In such a country the European race of men rapidly degenerated, and in less than three generations was reduced from the best-proportioned size to the dwarfish dimensions of misshapen pigmies. As soon as the emigrant landed, he was seized with disease, and if he recovered, the rosy hue of health had forever fled from his cheeks; his wrinkled and sallow skin hung loosely on his bones, from which the flesh had almost entirely departed; his system could never be braced up again; and he dragged on a miserable, sickly existence, which fortunately was not of long duration. In such a climate, old age was entirely unknown, and the statistical average of life did not exceed ten years. There man lost the energies both of his body and mind, and through the enervating and baleful influence of the atmosphere soon became stultified into an indolent idiot. Even the brutish creation did not escape the inflictions to which humanity was subject, and experienced the same rapid transformation. Thus, in a short time, horses were reduced to the size of sheep, cattle to that of rabbits, hogs gradually shrunk up so as to be no bigger than rats, and fowls dwindled into the diminished proportions of sparrows. As to the natives, they were cannibals, who possessed all the malignity and magical arts of demons, and waged incessant war against the emigrants, whose flesh they devoured with peculiar relish. This delineation of the features of Louisiana was very different from those of the first portrait, so many copies of which had been industriously circulated through France. It had been Hyperion; now it was a Satyr.

It is easy to conceive the startling effects produced on the mind of a people already in a paroxysm of consternation by such malicious misrepresentations, which the enemies of Law took care to scatter far and wide. Thus, the tide of emigration which was pouring onward rolled back, and the prospect of establishing a powerful colony in Louisiana, which, at first, had appeared so feasible and loomed out to the imagination of the speculator in such vivid colors and with such fair proportions, was nipped in the bud, and was looked upon as an impossibility. Under the exaggerated and gloomy apprehensions of the moment, no actual tender of money, and no promises of future reward could have tempted anybody to embark for Louisiana. So universal was the terror inspired by the name of Mississippi that (it is a well-known fact) it became even a bugbear to the nursery, and that for half a century after the explosion of Law's great Mississippi scheme, when French children were unruly and unmanageable, and when all threats had proved ineffectual, the mother would, in the last resort, lift up her finger impressively and in a whispering tone, as if afraid of speaking too loud of something so horrible, would say with a shudder and with pale lips to her rebellious progeny: "Hush! or I will send you to the Mississippi!" . . .

However, the Western or Mississippi Company having contracted the obligation to colonize Louisiana and to transport thither, within a fixed time, a certain number of emigrants, found itself under the necessity, in order to comply with the terms of its contract, to have recourse to the most iniquitous and unlawful means. As it was indispensable that there should be emigration—when it ceased to be voluntary, it was necessary that it should be forced. Thus violence was resorted to, and throughout France agents were dispatched to kidnap all vagrants, beggars, gipsies, or people of the like description, and women of bad repute. Unfortunately, the power given by the government to these agents of the company was abused in the most infamous manner. It became in their hands an engine of peculation, oppression, and corruption. It is incredible what a number of respectable people of both sexes were put, through bribery, in the hands of these satellites of an arbitrary government, to gratify private malice and the dark passions or interested views of men in power. A purse of gold slipped into the hand, and a whisper in the ear went a great way to get rid of obnoxious persons, and many a fearful tale of revenge, of hatred, or of cupidity might be told of persons who were unsuspectedly seized and carried away to the banks of the Mississippi before their voices could be heard when crying for justice or for protection. . . .

Guarded by a merciless soldiery, they, on the way to seaports, crowded in the public roads of France like droves of cattle, and as they were hardly furnished with means of subsistence or with clothing by their heartless conductors, who speculated on the food and other supplies with which they were bound to provide their prisoners, they died in large numbers, and their unburied corpses, rotting above ground, struck with terror the inhabitants of the districts through which the woebegone caravan had passed. At night, they were locked up in barns, when any could be found, and if not, they were forced, the better to prevent escape, to lie down in heaps at the bottoms of ditches and holes, and sentinels were put round to watch over them. Hunger and cold pinched the miserable creatures, and their haggard looks, emaciated bodies, and loud wailings carried desolation everywhere. . . .

Law was considered as the author of all these cruelties and misfortunes, and he became still more odious to the people. The parliament of Paris thought that the moment was come at last to pounce upon Law; and to gratify their long-cherished resentment, he was summoned to appear in person before that high tribunal to answer for his misdeeds and for his violations of the laws of the kingdom. On his refusal or neglect to do so, the parliament ordered him arrested, and had determined, on his being brought to the palace where they sat, to close their doors; and in order to prevent the expected interference of the Regent, their intention was to try summarily the hated foreigner and to hang him in their courtyard. . . . Aware of this plan, Law left his residence and fled to the Regent's palace, which was the only place where he felt himself secure against the pursuit of his enemies. There he cast himself at the feet of his august protector and bathed his hands in tears. . . .

The Regent gave to Law assurance of his protection and vouched for his life; but this was all he could do. He had to bow to the force of public opinion and to bend to the storm which menaced even his royal person. It was evident that Law could no longer stay in France. . . .

In October, 1721 [after residing in Brussels and Bavaria and traveling elsewhere on the Continent], he returned to England, and at first was received with distinction by persons of high rank. . . . As soon as it was ascertained that he was poor, it followed of course that he was nobody and no longer to be countenanced or noticed.

In 1722, John Law turned his back upon England for the last time and, returning to the Continent, retired to Venice, where he lived in obscurity and where he died on the 21st of March, 1729, in a state of indigence and in the fifty-eighth year of his age. . . .

"Up Salt River"

Through most of America's political history, defeated parties and candidates have been taking rides up Salt River. A typical reference is found in the autobiography of David Crockett, Tennessee coonskin-cap politician, in his account of a visit to New York during the Jackson administration. At a Whig banquet there, a Georgia orator "made a speech that fairly made the tumblers hop; he rode the Tories up and over Salt River." In all old-time election jollifications there was a boat on wheels, which was fabled to carry the defeated up a stream of oblivion. The fable was current in speeches, editorials, and headlines, and its strong pictorial quality appealed to cartoonists. The usual drawing showed a lonely river flowing among dead trees draped with Spanish moss, on which buzzards sat watching a boat's crew, with the sunset on their haggard and dejected countenances. Sometimes the artist lightened the sketch by making the crew ragged but joyous, as all true adventurers are even when the game goes against them.

Though few have known or thought about it, there is a real river underlying the legend, just as there is a real Arcadia under the Arcady of the poets, and a real Bohemia under the realm of dreaming, passionate artists. What only steamboatmen, farmers, and the Roarers of vanished yesterdays seem to have thought worth doing, I have done. I have gone up Salt River, far enough to savor its quality. The mental picture I have of it seems to fit the legend. There is that about the lower stretches of the little Kentucky waterway which suggests the words of Isaiah: "The screech owl shall rest there. . . . There shall the great owl make her nest. . . . There shall the vultures also be gathered."

* * * * *

Salt River is a fresh-water stream. It gets its name from the fact that, very early in the history of Kentucky, salt was made upon its banks. Salt springs, in the Old West at least, are usually found by the sides of rivers; in this case they were near Shepherdsville, twenty-eight miles above the river's mouth. Here, an early account says, "the fires of an hundred salt furnaces gleamed through the forest." Writing in 1796, the geographer Jedidiah Morse records that their output supplied Kentucky and Cumberland, and was "exported to the Illinois country."

From *Sycamore Shores*, by Clark B. Firestone, pp. 125, 127, 128–129, 131–132. Copyright, 1936, by Clark B. Firestone. New York: Robert M. McBride & Company.

The river rises near Danville, flows north through Bluegrass and west through Pennyroyal, Kentucky, and reaches the Ohio twenty-six miles below Louisville. Nearly a hundred and fifty miles long, it serves a significant region and does its bit to make the map of Kentucky. Danville, beside its springs, was an ancient state capital. With its tributary, Rolling Fork, it forms the boundary lines of four Kentucky counties.

Harrodsburg, best known of the communities upon Salt, is the oldest town in Kentucky, oldest place of English settlement west of the Alleghenies. *Nick of the Woods*, by Robert Montgomery Bird, best novel of Western life before *Uncle Tom's Cabin*, launches its story upon the same stream. If the novel averages at least a fight to a chapter, so does the history of Salt River, as long as the northern bank of the Ohio was known as the Indian Shore. Savage raids were incessant, many of them into the region of the salt licks, rendezvous of wild beasts and wild and half-wild men. They may be called salt wars; ancient Germany knew such. One engagement of the first rank took place beside the waters of Salt; but this was in the Civil War and on a tributary, forty thousand men under Buell and Bragg fighting a bloody and indecisive battle at Perryville in 1862.

On the water of Salt is Catholic Kentucky, settled in the long ago from tidewater Maryland. There also is the Lincoln country. On the thin red soils near Hodgenville, Thomas Lincoln farmed for a while, and there the accepted story is that Abraham was born.

* * * * *

There is more to explain about the stream than the fact that the journeys of the defeated were supposed to be upon it. "Pride goeth before destruction and an haughty spirit before a fall." Salt River became a parable of the one as well as the other. Colossal metaphor, provocative language tempered by boisterous humor, Homeric boasting and posturing—these were the marks of the Salt River Roarers of early American tradition. The picture their tirades present is of a rude frontiersman, who has been communing with corn liquor, standing on a stump and proclaiming his own terrors to a sniggering crowd. At the end he flaps his arms like a barnyard fowl, leaps in air, cracks his heels together, and emits a prolonged "cock-a-doodle-doo!"

* * * * *

Whence the double fable of political disaster and of rodomontade? Authorities and would-be authorities concern themselves only with one side of it—the Ride of Defeat. The explanation accepted in Europe is that Salt River is not navigable, nor very boatable. Other statements are that refractory slaves used to be punished by hiring them out to row keelboats up the river; that the salt-boilers upon it were rough characters; that river pirates infested it; that after Kentucky summer elections, candidates, victor and vanquished alike, went up Salt River for a rest as far as Harrodsburg springs. The story accepted in Kentucky, and repeated to me by state officials, is that when Henry Clay was candidate for President in 1832, he engaged a Jackson Democrat to row him up the Ohio to Louisville, where he was to speak. The boatman rowed him up Salt River instead, and he did not reach his destination until the day after election, when he learned of his own defeat. An intriguing picture, but one too full of geographic and logical improbabilities to credit.

As one who has traveled upon it, I must dismiss any theory based on the assumption that Salt River, because of shoals and snags and tortuous ways, is difficult for rowboats. It is not. It flows nearly due north and then nearly due west. Windings not delineated on the maps it has, as all rivers have; but these are not troublesome. As Thomas Jefferson notes: "Salt River is at all times navigable for loaded batteaux seventy or eighty miles. It is eighty yards wide at its mouth, and keeps that width to its forks, twenty-five miles above." The channel is so deep that whenever there is a good stage of water on the Ohio, the biggest steamboats can enter Salt and ascend it a dozen miles to Pitt's Point, where Rolling Fork joins it. Thirty feet of water in the Ohio acts as a sort of dam for Salt, throwing it into pool. With its flow thus husbanded, you can row up Salt River as easily as down. In an account of a battle with Indians in 1788, I find the statement that "the current was entirely deadened by back water from the Ohio to a place near the licks called Mud Garrison"—nearly a thirty-mile stretch.

Salt River has known the steamboat, even though no whistle now wakes the echoes of its shores. A regular line of packets operating out of Louisville served it. From old copies of the *Waterways Journal* I learn that in 1898 the *Scioto* and the *Raymond* were carrying merchandise up the river and bringing down hay, livestock, poultry, fruit, and vegetables. These packets were a hundred feet long and thirty feet wide, and drew three and a half feet of water.

Sucker, Puke, and Badger

I [1]

. . . Col. James Johnson of Kentucky had gone [to Galena] with a party of miners in 1824, and had opened a lead mine about one mile above the present town. His great success drew others there in 1825; and in 1826 and 1827 hundreds and thousands of persons from Illinois and Missouri went to the Galena country to work the lead mines. It was estimated that the number of miners in the mining country in 1827 was six or seven thousand. The Illinoisans ran up the Mississippi River in steamboats in the spring season, worked the lead mines during warm weather,

[1] From *A History of Illinois, from Its Commencement as a State in 1818 to 1847*, by Gov. Thomas Ford, edited by Milo Milton Quaife, Vol. I, pp. 85–87. Chicago: The Lakeside Press, R. R. Donnelley & Sons Co. Christmas, 1945.

and then ran down the river again to their homes in the fall season; thus establishing, as was supposed, a similitude between their migratory habits and those of the fishy tribe called "Suckers." For which reason the Illinoisans were called "Suckers," a name which has stuck to them ever since.

There is another account of the origin of the nickname "Suckers," as applied to the people of Illinois. It is said that the south part of the State was originally settled by the poorer class of people from the slave States, where the tobacco plant was extensively cultivated. They were such as were not able to own slaves in a slave State, and came to Illinois to get away from the imperious domination of their wealthy neighbors. The tobacco plant has many sprouts from the roots and main stem, which if not stripped off suck up its nutriment and destroy the staple. These sprouts are called "suckers," and are as carefully stripped off from the plant and thrown away as is the tobacco worm itself. These poor emigrants from the slave States were jeeringly and derisively called "suckers," because they were asserted to be a burthen upon the people of wealth; and when they removed to Illinois they were supposed to have stripped themselves off from the parent stem and gone away to perish like the "sucker" of the tobacco plant. This name was given to the Illinoisans at the Galena mines by the Missourians. Analogies always abound with those who desire to be sarcastic; so the Illinoisans by way of retaliation called the Missourians "Pukes." It had been observed that the lower lead mines in Missouri had sent up to the Galena country whole hordes of uncouth ruffians, from which it was inferred that Missouri had taken a "Puke" and had vomited forth to the upper lead mines all her worst population. From thenceforth the Missourians were regularly called "Pukes"; and by these names of "Suckers" and "Pukes" the Illinoisans and Missourians are likely to be called, among the vulgar, forever.

II [2]

As usual with folklore the story here presented of the origin of the popular nicknames for Missourians and Illinoisans defies definite documentation. To complete the recital, it should be added that the term "Badger" as applied to residents of Wisconsin is claimed to have originated at the same time as "Puke" and "Sucker." The "Suckers" were those miners who came up to the mines in the spring and returned down river (or overland) to winter in the older settlements. Those who "holed up" for the winter in the mining country were called "Badgers."

Another story of the origin of the name "Sucker" was once related by Stephen A. Douglas to a group of fellow-congressmen. He described with appropriate detail the sufferings of George Rogers Clark's men when, invading the French Illinois in 1778, they were lost in the immense prairies and in danger of dying of heat and thirst. Just at eventide they emerged upon the bank of the Kaskaskia River and saw on the opposite bank the

[2] Milo Milton Quaife, *ibid.*, p. 87–88n.

townsmen of Kaskaskia seated on their porches, imbibing through straws
a cool and delectable liquid. The sight overwhelmed the suffering Virginians, who with one accord charged across the stream shouting, "Surrender, you Suckers, surrender!" Thus was the mint julep, the invention
of the settlers of the French Illinois, first made known to Virginians; and
the inventors and their descendants have ever since gone by the name the
thirsty invaders shouted at them across the waters of the Kaskaskia in
the summer of 1778.

Pike, Poker, and Piker

It was before we left St. Louis that I received a letter inviting us to
visit in the town of Louisiana, Missouri. I quote a portion of it:

Louisiana is in Pike county, a county famous for its big red apples, miles of
rock roads, fine old estates, Rhine scenery, capons, rare old country hams, and
poker. Pike County means more to Missouri than Missouri does to Pike.
   Do you remember "Jim Bludso of the *Prairie Belle*"?

> He weren't no saint—them engineers
> Is pretty much all alike—
> One wife in Natchez-under-the-Hill
> And another one here in Pike.

We can show you the "willer bank on the right," where Bludso ran the *Prairie
Belle* aground and made good with his life his old promise:

> I'll hold her nozzle agin the bank
> Till the last galoot's ashore. . . .

* * * * *

. . . Pike . . . is indeed a great county. And the fact that it was originally settled by Virginians, Kentuckians, and Carolinians still stamps it
strongly with the qualities of the South. . . .

* * * * *

In the old days Pike County embraced many of the other present
counties, and, running all the way from the Mississippi to the Missouri
River, was as large as a good-sized state. Pike has colonized more Western
country than any other county in Missouri; . . . "The West used to be
full of Pike County men who had pushed out there with their guns and
bottles."

* * * * *

From *Abroad at Home*, American Ramblings, Observations, and Adventures of
Julian Street, pp. 253–254, 268, 271. Copyright, 1914, by P. F. Collier & Son, Inc.,
and the Century Co. New York.

Another interesting item relates to the origin of the slang term "piker," which, whatever it may have meant originally, is used today to designate a timid, close-fisted gambler, a "tightwad," or "short sport."

When one inquires as to the origin of this term, Pike County, Missouri, begins to remember that there is another Pike County—Pike County, Illinois, just across the river, which, incidentally, is I think the "Pike" referred to in John Hay's poem.

A gentleman in Clarksville explained the origin of the term "piker" to me thus:

In the early days men from Pike County, Missouri, and Pike County, Illinois, went all through the West. They were all good men. In fact, they were such a fine lot that when any crooks would want to represent themselves as honest men they would say they were from Pike. As a result of this all the bad men in the West claimed to be from our section, and in that way Pike got a bad name. So when the Westerners suspected a man of being crooked, they'd say: "Look out for him; he's a Piker."

In St. Louis I was given another version. There I was told that long ago men would come down from Pike to gamble. They loved cards, but oftentimes hadn't enough money to play a big game. So, it was said, the term "Piker" came to indicate more or less the type it indicates today.

"Bayou" and the "Bayou People"

. . . The good Southern word *bayou* . . . has about as many pronunciations as it has users. The most concise of the pronunciations I have heard is *buy*, a pronunciation once used in my presence by a Baptist preacher who announced that he intended to go to *Bilerbatry*, from which I gathered that his intention was to go to a little place near Mobile, named Bayou Labatre. A scholar who has looked into the pronunciation of *bayou* had decided in favor of "buy-u" and I am quite willing, when Congress passes the necessary legislation forcing all of us to use the same pronunciation, to drop my *bay-u* and content myself forever afterwards with *buy-u*.

The origin of this word was for a long time uncertain. Scholars were inclined to derive it from the French word *boyau*, meaning an intestine or gut. It took considerable stretching of the imagination for them to explain how this somewhat unpleasant meaning of the French word suggested such a body of water as *bayou* denotes. William Darby, an American geographer at the beginning of the nineteenth century, recorded his belief that *bayou* is derived from the Spanish word *bahia* or *baya* meaning "bay," but this derivation has so little to commend it that it has not been heard of for a long time.

From *Some Sources of Southernisms*, by M. M. Mathews, pp. 81–84. Copyright, 1948, by the University of Alabama Press. University, Alabama.

A little more than fifty years ago [in the *Nation* for November 15, 1894, p. 361] Prof. W. S. Wyman, an excellent scholar well versed in the languages used by the Indians who formerly occupied Alabama, solved very neatly and conclusively the problem of the origin of *bayou*. From his researches into the early history of the French occupancy of this southern country, particularly Louisiana, Professor Wyman found that one of the first Indian tribes in the Louisiana area that the French encountered were the Bayogoula Indians, a small tribe of Muskhogean stock, who by war and pestilence had disappeared entirely by 1721. Their name in their own language, *Báyuk-ókla*, "bayou people," shows similarity with other Choctaw names, as Pascagoula (from Choctaw *Pask-okla*, bread people); Pensacola (*Pansh-okla*, the hairy people); Apalachicola (*Apelach-okla*, the helping people, allies). . . .

Professor Wyman was not only able to identify our word *bayou* in the name of these Bayogoula Indians, but he also found more direct evidence that the word is from the language of the Choctaw Indians. In accounts written by Frenchmen who were in the Louisiana area at an early time he found the term, written in the French *bayouc* and *bayouque*, occurring over and over again. The earliest of these accounts was one written by a ship-carpenter who accompanied D'Iberville to Louisiana in 1699. In his account there occurs a passage which translated reads as follows: "Five leagues further and keeping always to the left on the lake [i.e., Pontchartrain] one finds a stagnant stream which the Indians call bayou."

Professor Wyman's article pointed out clearly that the Choctaw *bayuk*, meaning "a small sluggish stream," is the source of our term which is now common all over the country. This article also called attention to the occurrence in such names as *Pascagoula, Pensacola, Apalachicola*, of the same Choctaw Indian element *okla* meaning people that occurs in the state name of *Oklahoma*, which is the Choctaw way of saying "red people." Professor Wyman also pointed out that the Choctaw word *bayuk*, having passed through the alembic of French pronunciation and writing, accounts for such names among us as *Boguechito, Boguefalala, Boguelisa*. In these there is clearly seen the old Choctaw word *bayuk*, meaning "a small stream."

The "Beautiful" Ohio

The first brave English adventurers who looked with eager eyes upon the great river of the Middle West learned that its Indian name was represented by the letters *Oyo*, and it has since been known as the Ohio River. The French, who came in advance of the English, translated the

From *The Ohio River*, A Course of Empire, by Archer Butler Hulbert, pp. 2–4. Copyright, 1906, by G. P. Putnam's Sons. New York and London.

Indian name, we are told, and called the Ohio *La Belle Rivière*, the "beautiful river."

We have, however, other testimony concerning the name that cannot well be overlooked. It is that of the two experienced and well-educated Moravian missionaries, Heckewelder and Zeisberger, who came into the trans-Allegheny country long before the end of the eighteenth century. Upon such a subject as the meaning of Ohio, one might easily hold these men to be final authorities. John Heckewelder affirms that *Oyo* never could have been correctly translated "beautiful"; Zeisberger adds that in the Onondaga dialect of the Iroquois tongue there was a word *oyoneri* which meant "beautiful" but only in the adverbial sense—something that was done "beautifully," or, as we say, done "well." Mr. Heckewelder, knowing that it was commonly understood that the French had translated *Oyo* when they gave the name La Belle Rivière to the Ohio, took occasion to study the matter carefully. He found that in the Miami language *O'hui* or *Ohi*, as prefixes, meant "very"; for instance, *Ohiopeek* meant "very white"; *Ohiopeekhanne* meant the "white foaming river."

> The Ohio River [he writes], being in many places wide and deep, and so gentle that for many miles, in some places, no current is perceivable, the least wind blowing up the river covers the surface with what the people of that country call "white caps"; and I have myself witnessed that for days together, this has been the case, caused by southwesterly winds (which, by the way, are the prevailing winds in that country) so that we, navigating the canoes, durst not venture to proceed, as these white caps would have filled and sunk our canoes in an instant. Now, in such cases, when the river could not be navigated with canoes, nor even crossed with this kind of craft—when the whole surface of the water presented white foaming swells, the Indians would, as the case was at the time, say *"juh Ohiopiechen, Ohiopeek, Ohiopeekhanne";* and when they supposed the water very deep, they would say *"Kitschi, Ohiopeekhanne,"* which means "verily this is a deep white river."

For one, I like the interpretation of "Ohio" as given by these old missionaries—the "River of Many White Caps." True, there is a splendid, sweeping beauty in the Ohio, but throughout a large portion of its course the land lies low on either bank, and those who have feasted their eyes on the picturesque Hudson, or on the dashing beauty of the Saguenay, have been heard to call in question the judgment of the French who named the Ohio La Belle Rivière. But it must be remembered that the French first saw the upper waters of the Ohio, which we now know as the glittering Allegheny. *La Belle Rivière* included the Ohio and the Allegheny; it was not until the English had reached the Ohio, about the middle of the eighteenth century, that it came to be said that the Allegheny and Monongahela formed the Ohio at Pittsburgh. To one acquainted with the roaring Allegheny, dancing down through the New York and Pennsylvania hills, and who can see how clear the waters ran in the dense green of the ancient forests—to such a one it is not difficult to see why the French called it La Belle Rivière.

"Great Waters"

First of the Europeans who surely saw the [Mississippi] river were De Soto and his men in 1541. De Soto gave it no name that we know of, for he was not a man who cared about naming. He seems rather to have been content with the old name Espiritu Santo, and his men called it most often simply Río Grande, "big river." When his scribes, however, inquired its name of the Indians, they found that it had many. This was only to be expected, for there were many tribes living near such a long river, and they spoke different languages. Also, like other Indians, they may have had a name for every bend and reach. So the scribes wrote down that it was called variously Chucagua, Tamalisieu, Nilco, and Mico, and that at its mouth it was called simply The River. We know also that it has been called Okachitto, Olsimochitto, Namosi-sipu, Sassagoula, and Culata.

But far to the north in the land of lakes and wild rice lived the tribes who spoke the widespread Algonquian language—Chippewas, Miamis, Outagamis, Illinois, and many others. Along the edge of their country flowed a branch of the river, and though there it was much smaller, yet it was still the largest stream that those northern tribes had seen. They differed a little in their speech; some said Kitchi-zibi, and some Mis-sipi, and others Misisipi. Whatever they said, the meaning was plain, for among their commonest words was that meaning "big," and in differing forms it still stands, not only in Mississippi, Michigan and Massachusetts, but also probably in Missouri. Moreover, *sipi* was plainly "river," and it also may be found in Chesapeake. This then was the word that the French heard, variously sounded as they passed from tribe to tribe.

Yet there was no just reason why this name as said by these northern tribes should have displaced all the others, and even caused the smaller branch of the river to be held the chief one. This came about more by accident. For, when Jolliet and Marquette first approached the river, they had as guides two Miamis. Then, as they passed farther and farther down the river, they thought of it as having still the same name, though the Indians living there might not have recognized the words. Even when they passed the mouth of the great muddy Pekitanoui, they considered that to be only a tributary, not stopping to think that it might be longer than the branch called Mississippi, and in some other ways too a greater river. So, because the explorers first voyaged *down* the river, the northern name spread along it clear to the mouth. But if the explorers had come from the south, they would naturally have called the river by some southern name. When they reached the forking, they might have taken either to be the main river. Or, the lower stream and each of the upper branches might

From *Names on the Land,* A Historical Account of Place-Naming in the United States, by George R. Stewart, pp. 93–95, 278. Copyright, 1945, by George R. Stewart. New York: Random House.

have been known and named separately by overland travelers before their joining was learned. Then, as has happened with other rivers, there might have been a different name for each of the three, and men would have said that the lower river was "formed by the union" of the two upper branches.

Even after it was well known, the name Mississippi did not certainly establish itself for some time. Jolliet had called it Buade; and Marquette, Conception. Frontenac and La Salle tried to make it Colbert. A few years later, others called it Louisiane, and St. Louis. But perhaps because they could not agree, finally they all used the Indian name that came from the far north.

When the English approached the river, they called it sometimes Malabanchia. This was a Choctaw name, "place of foreign speech," and was used because of the French living upon it. But in the end the English also said Mississippi.

* * * * *

The romantics . . . desired names with a suggestion of poetry. The simple primitive descriptives supplied almost nothing of this, but such people generally know next to nothing of Indian languages, and so suffered little restraint. Mississippi, "big river," was a simple Indian name, but a Frenchman's false translation "vieux Père des Rivières," led to millions of American school-children being taught the falsehood that Mississippi meant "Father of Waters." It was a falsehood not only about a single name, but about Indians in general—for such a figure of speech would hardly have been used for a river.

"Big Muddy" or "Big Canoe"

. . . The idea of "muddy water" as a meaning for "Missouri" has been so persistent that an inquiry into its origin is justified. . . .

So far as is known, Marquette, the famous French explorer, was the first to record a name for the Missouri River. In describing his voyage down the Mississippi River in 1673, Marquette wrote, "We descend, following the course of the river, toward another called Pekitanoui, which empties into the Mississippi, coming from the Northwest." The fact that Marquette used the word "called" seems to indicate that the name "Pekitanoui" was in vogue among the Indians. We must bear in mind, however, that he was writing an Indian word in letters of the French language. Marquette, himself, did not include a definition, but John G. Shea, who edited Marquette's narrative, explained in a footnote that "Pekitanoui" meant "muddy water." Perhaps, then, Marquette was responsible only for

From "The Word 'Missouri,'" *The Missouri Historical Review,* Vol. XXXIV (October, 1939), No. 1, pp. 87–92. Columbia, Missouri: The State Historical Society of Missouri.

recording the name "Pekitanoui" and not for any definition of the name.

Marquette prepared a map of the Mississippi country which he auto-graphed and this autograph map is reproduced in Shea's *Discovery and Exploration of the Mississippi Valley* (1852 edition). On this map is found the Pekitanoui River and on the river is an Indian village to which the name "8eMess8rit" is given. It has been explained that the figure "8" in French refers to the syllable "ou" or to some variation of "ou." Thevenot published Marquette's journal in 1681 and a map published by Thevenot, purporting to be Marquette's original map, uses the term "Ou-Missouri" to designate the village for which Marquette used the term "8eMess8rit." The village has been definitely identified as a village of the Missouri Indians, who are known to have lived in the locality assigned by Mar-quette.

In 1687 Joutel and Father Douay, in company with the remnants of La Salle's party, ascended the Mississippi after the death of La Salle. Both Joutel and Father Douay left accounts of their experiences. Joutel wrote that on September 1, 1687, the group "pass'd by the Mouth of a River call'd *Missouris,* whose water is always thick, and to which our Indians did not forget to offer sacrifice." Like Marquette, Joutel made no attempt at definition and he indicates also that "Missouris" was a name used by the Indians. His explanation that the water was "always thick" is the only approach he makes toward "muddy water." Father Douay, describing the same occasion, wrote of the "famous river of the Massourites or Osages," and explained that the Osage Indians had numer-ous villages on a river of their name which emptied into the river of the Massourites, "to which the maps have also extended the name of Osages." Douay thus distinguished between the Missouri and Osage Rivers, and, more important still, he was giving the river the name of the Indians who resided along its banks.

Father St. Cosme did the same when he made a voyage down the Mississippi in 1699 and mentioned the great river of the "Missouris." In 1712, Father Marest wrote a letter in which he said: "Seven leagues be-low the mouth of the Illinois River is found a large river called the *Missouri*—or more commonly Pekitanoui; that is to say, 'muddy water,'—which empties into the Mississippi on the West side; it is extremely rapid, and it discolors the beautiful water of the Mississippi, which flows from this point to the sea."

The accounts of Joutel, Douay, St. Cosme, and Marest seem to be responsible for the application of the name "Missouri" to the river "Peki-tanoui." Shea says that "Pekitanoui" was used to denote the river until Marest began to use "Missouri" in 1712. The evidence presented here, however, shows that certain forms of the word "Missouri" had been ap-plied to the river before 1712 and that Douay expressly attached to the river the name of the Indians living along the banks of the river. Cer-tainly the name "Pekitanoui" ceased to be used and the name "Missouri" came to be applied not only to the river but to the area about it and ultimately to the Territory and State. To Marest seems to belong the credit for using the word "Missouri" as we know it and for defining "Pekitanoui" as "muddy water," though he does not explain the authorship of the definition.

The fact that "muddy water" so aptly described the Missouri River made it easy for the definition of "Pekitanoui" to be ascribed to Missouri. The easy, simple explanation was accepted and Missouri historians only occasionally departed from the prevailing idea of "muddy water," if they gave any attention at all to the meaning of the word "Missouri." . . .

An examination of *The Missouri River and Its Utmost Source,* by J. V. Brower, published in 1897, shows the existence of a few varied opinions with regard to the meaning of Missouri. Brower stated that the word "Missouri" originally meant "Living on the Mouth of the Waters." Among the numerous theories was the idea of an interpreter at the Sac and Fox agency that the word "Pekitanoui" meant "Missourian," and the suggestion that the word "Missouri" belonged to the Sioux language. None of the explanations offered by Brower seem to have become current.

In 1897, the same year that Brower published his book, William F. Switzler advocated a new theory well supported with evidence. This theory, which had first appeared in the Brooklyn *Eagle,* was first expressed in Missouri by Switzler in an editorial in the Boonville (Missouri) *Democrat* on October 22, 1897:

Missouri does not and never did properly mean "muddy water," but "Wooden Canoe." It belongs to the Illinois dialect of the Algonquin Indian language, the language which was generally spoken (as maintained by many historians) by the various aboriginal tribes which inhabited the country between the Mississippi River and Delaware Bay. Discussing this subject, some years ago, the Brooklyn *Eagle* maintained that it is not very difficult to gather support for the definition and derivation of the word "Missouri." Among the Indians of Maine a boat or canoe was called "A-ma-Sui." With the Narragansetts it was "me-shu-e," with the Delawares it was "Ma-sho-la"; with the Miamis about Lake Michigan it was "Mis-so-la"; with the Illinois tribe it was "Wic-wes-Missouri," for a birch bark canoe, and "We-Mis-sure" for a wooden canoe or canoe fashioned from a log of wood. The name Missouris or Missouri was originally applied by the Indians of the Lake Michigan region to the tribe of Indians living west of the Mississippi and along the shores of the muddy river—the Missouri. The term meant the "wooden canoe people," or "the people who use wooden canoes." The Lake Michigan Indians used birch-bark canoes, as did Marquette and Joliet in their descent of the Wisconsin to the "Conception" [the name Marquette gave the Mississippi], while the Indians on the Muddy River used canoes dug out of logs because the birch-bark canoes were too frail for the navigation of that turbulent stream. . . .

Although Switzler's explanation was quoted several times immediately following its first appearance, the theory did not become popular and seemed buried in the files of the Boonville *Democrat* and a few other newspapers.

*   *   *   *   *

In 1923, a copy of the Boonville *Democrat* of October 22, 1897, containing Switzler's explanation, was sent by the State Historical Society of Missouri to Dr. J. Walter Fewkes, then chief of the Bureau of American Ethnology of the Smithsonian Institution. Fewkes' reply modified Switzler's definition slightly. . . .

. . . It errs in saying that the name signifies "wooden" canoe or "log" canoe. Marquette applied it to a village and not to the river. The form used on his map is 8eMess8rit. The part of the name that signifies "canoe" is -8r-, usually transcribed from this French spelling by -our. . . . It is just possible that the final -i-t is a shortened form of the common Algonquin word for village *o-tan*. . . . The initial 8e is pronounced, and the qualifying stem is -mess-, meaning "large, great." The whole would then signify "the town of the large canoes." . . .

"Itasca"

Whence came the beautiful name Itasca? That is a question which has kept historians in a quandary for several generations. At the time neither Schoolcraft, nor Allen, nor Houghton, nor Boutwell [who accompanied Schoolcraft on the expedition that discovered the source of the Mississippi in 1832] seem to have given a satisfactory explanation of the origin and use of this name. In 1853 Mrs. Mary H. Eastman published the *American Aboriginal Portfolio* in which she recounts that Itasca was the daughter of Manabozho, the Spirit God of the Chippewa, whose falling tears formed the lake. Mrs. Eastman declared that Schoolcraft had received the story from his Chippewa guide and had told it to her. Schoolcraft a little later confirmed this theory when he himself wrote a poem on the lovely Itasca which was included in his *Summary Narrative* of the expeditions of 1820 and 1832 published in 1855. In the same book, however, he states that Ozawindib had given the Indian name for the lake as Omushkös, which was the Chippewa name for elk.

In 1872 new light was shed on the origin of the name by Reverend William T. Boutwell. Replying to an inquiry as to the origin of the word Itasca, Boutwell declared that while paddling slowly westward across Lake Superior, Schoolcraft had turned to him and said: " 'I would like to give a name to Elk Lake that will be significant or expressive, as the *head* or *true source* of the Mississi[ppi]. Can you give me any word in Latin or Greek that will convey the idea?' I replied, 'No one word will express the idea—the nearest I can come to it is Veritus Caput—or if you prefer the noun Veritas—you may coin something that will meet your wishes.' In less than five minutes he replied, 'I have got the thing'—handing me a slip of paper on which was the word *Itasca*. . . . It was

From *Steamboating on the Upper Mississippi*, the Water Way to Iowa, Some River History, by William J. Petersen, pp. 17–21. Copyright, 1937, by the State Historical Society of Iowa. Iowa City.

then & there & in just this manner the word, the name *Itasca* was coined. The Ojibwas invariably called the lake Omushkos Sagaeigun [Elk Lake]."

Thus, at the suggestion of Boutwell, the name Itasca was coined by Schoolcraft, by taking from the expression *veritas caput* the last four letters (*itas*) of the word *veritas* and combining them with the first two letters (*ca*) of the word *caput*—which gives the new word Itasca. It may be added that the fanciful creation of new words or names by dividing two familiar words and combining the parts as in the case of Itasca was not uncommon in the period of the Schoolcraft explorations.

Although the Boutwell explanation of the name Itasca was generally accepted in the years that followed, some writers still clung to the Chippewa legend. And there were others who believed that the word might have been derived from the Ojibway words *ia* (to be), *totosh* (the female breast, implying origin), and *ka* (terminal sub-inflection), the whole, *ia-totosh-ka*, signifying a *fount*. This explanation was actually accepted in the 1882 edition of Webster's Dictionary. Students of the Dakota Indians also pointed to a possible origin from the language of that nation.

. . . A contemporary verification of Boutwell's *Veritas Caput* by a member of the expedition may now be presented. It comes from Schoolcraft himself! Leaving Lake Itasca on July 13, 1832, the day of the discovery, Schoolcraft hastened down the Mississippi, arriving at Fort Snelling eleven days later. On the following day (July 25, 1832) he wrote a letter to Dr. Addison Philleo, editor of a Galena newspaper, describing the expedition to the true source of the Mississippi River. The concluding paragraphs of Schoolcraft's letter furnish all the evidence needed to substantiate the Boutwell explanation:

The Mississippi [above Cass Lake], expands into several lakes, the largest of which is called lac Traverse. A few miles above this it forms into a south west and north west branch. We ascended the latter [*sic*] through a number of lakes to its source in a small creek. From thence we made a portage of 6 miles, with our canoes, into La Biche or Itasca Lake (from a derivation of the expression *veritas caput*) which is the true source of this celebrated stream, being at the same time its most western and northern head. This lake is about 7 miles long, having somewhat the shape of the letter Y. It has clear water and pleasant woody shores. It has a single island, upon which I landed, caused some trees to be felled, and hoisted the national flag. I left this flag flying, and proceeded down the N.W. or main fork. A descent of about 180 miles brought us back to our party at Red Cedar, at Cape [or Cass] lake.[1]

---

[1] The Schoolcraft letter of July 25, 1832, as first published in the August 22, 1832, issue of *The Galenian* and later copied in the December 1, 1832, issue of *Niles' Register*, was discovered in November, 1936, by Dr. William J. Petersen, Research Associate in the State Historical Society of Iowa.

The True Story of Evangeline

Emmeline Labiche, petiots, was an orphan whose parents had died when she was quite a child. I had taken her to my home, and had raised her as my own daughter. How sweet-tempered, how loving she was! She had grown to womanhood with all the attractions of her sex, and, although not a beauty in the sense usually given to that word, she was looked upon as the handsomest girl of St. Gabriel. Her soft, transparent hazel eyes mirrored her pure thoughts; her dark brown hair waved in graceful undulations on her intelligent forehead, and fell in ringlets on her shoulders; her bewitching smile, her slender, symmetrical shape, all contributed to make her a most attractive picture of maiden loveliness.

Emmeline, who had just completed her sixteenth year, was on the eve of marrying a most deserving, laborious and well-to-do young man of St. Gabriel, Louis Arceneaux. Their mutual love dated from their earliest years, and all agreed that Providence willed their union as man and wife, she the fairest young maiden, he the most deserving youth of St. Gabriel.

Their bans had been published in the village church, the nuptial day was fixed, and their long love-dream was about to be realized, when the barbarous scattering of our colony took place.

Our oppressors had driven us to the seashore, where their ships rode at anchor, when Louis, resisting, was brutally wounded by them. Emmeline had witnessed the whole scene. Her lover was carried on board of one of the ships, the anchor was weighed, and a stiff breeze soon drove the vessel out of sight. Emmeline, tearless and speechless, stood fixed to the spot, motionless as a statue, and when the white sail vanished in the distance, she uttered a wild, piercing shriek and fell fainting to the ground.

When she came to, she clasped me in her arms, and in an agony of grief, she sobbed piteously. "Mother, mother," she said, in broken words, "he is gone; they have killed him; what will become of me?"

I soothed her grief with endearing words until she wept freely. Gradually its violence subsided, but the sadness of her countenance betokened the sorrow that preyed on her heart, never to be contaminated by her love for another one.

Thus she lived in our midst, always sweet tempered, but with such sadness depicted in her countenance, and with smiles so sorrowful, that we had come to look upon her as not of this earth, but rather as our guardian angel, and this is why we called her no longer Emmeline, but Evangeline, or God's little angel.

From *Acadian Reminiscences,* With the True Story of Evangeline, by Felix Voorhies, pp. 81–90. Copyright, 1907, by Felix Voorhies. New Iberia, Louisiana: Frank J. Dauterive, Publisher.

As remembered by the author from his grandmother's telling.

For the present-day "Evangeline Country" and the Longfellow poem in relation to the Voorhies version, see Harnett T. Kane, *The Bayous of Louisiana* (New York, 1944), pp. 256–264.

The sequel of her story is not gay, petiots, and my poor old heart breaks, whenever I recall the misery of her fate. . . . I will now tell you what became of poor Emmeline. . . .

Emmeline, petiots, had been exiled to Maryland with me. She was, as I have told you, my adopted child. She dwelt with me, and she followed me in my long pilgrimage from Maryland to Louisiana. I shall not relate to you now the many dangers that beset us on our journey, and the many obstacles we had to overcome to reach Louisiana; this would be anticipating what remains for me to tell you. When we reached the Teche country, at the Poste Des Attakapas, we found there the whole population congregated to welcome us. As we went ashore, Emmeline walked by my side, but seemed not to admire the beautiful landscape that unfolded itself to our gaze. Alas! it was of no moment to her whether she strolled on the poetical banks of the Teche, or rambled in the picturesque sites of Maryland. She lived in the past, and her soul was absorbed in the mournful regret of that past. For her, the universe had lost the prestige of its beauties, of its freshness, of its splendors. The radiance of her dreams was dimmed, and she breathed in an atmosphere of darkness and of desolation.

She walked beside me with a measured step. All at once, she grasped my hand, and, as if fascinated by some vision, she stood rooted to the spot. Her very heart's blood suffused her cheeks, and with the silvery tones of a voice vibrating with joy: "Mother! Mother!" she cried out, "it is he! It is Louis!" pointing to the tall figure of a man reclining under a large oak tree.

That man was Louis Arceneaux.

With the rapidity of lightning, she flew to his side, and in an ecstacy of joy: "Louis, Louis," said she, "I am your Emmeline, your long lost Emmeline! Have you forgotten me?"

Louis turned ashy pale and hung down his head, without uttering a word.

"Louis," said she, painfully impressed by her lover's silence and coldness, "why do you turn away from me? I am still your Emmeline, your betrothed, and I have kept pure and unsullied my plighted faith to you. Not a word of welcome, Louis?" she said, as the tears started to her eyes. "Tell me, do tell me that you love me still, and that the joy of meeting me has overcome you, and stifled your utterance."

Louis Arceneaux, with quivering lips and tremulous voice, answered: "Emmeline, speak not so kindly to me, for I am unworthy of you. I can love you no longer; I have pledged my faith to another. Tear from your heart the remembrance of the past, and forgive me," and with quick step, he walked away, and was soon lost to view in the forest.

Poor Emmeline stood trembling like an aspen leaf. I took her hand; it was icy cold. A deathly pallor had overspread her countenance, and her eyes had a vacant stare.

"Emmeline, my dear girl, come," said I, and she followed me like a child. I clasped her in my arms. "Emmeline, my dear child, be comforted; there may yet be happiness in store for you."

"Emmeline, Emmeline," she muttered in an undertone, as if to recall that name, "who is Emmeline?" Then looking in my face with fearful shining eyes that made me shudder, she said in a strange, unnatural voice: "Who are you?" and turned away from me. Her mind was unhinged; this last shock had been too much for her broken heart; she was hopelessly insane.

How strange it is, petiots, that beings, pure and celestial like Emmeline, should be the sport of fate, and be thus exposed to the shafts of adversity. Is it true, then, that the beloved of God are always visited by sore trials? Was it that Emmeline was too ethereal a being for this world, and that God would have her in his sweet paradise? It does not belong to us, petiots, to solve this mystery and to scrutinize the decrees of Providence; we have only to bow submissive to his will.

Emmeline never recovered her reason, and a deep melancholy settled upon her. Her beautiful countenance was fitfully lightened by a sad smile which made her all the fairer. She never recognized anyone but me, and nestling in my arms like a spoiled child, she would give me the most endearing names. As sweet and as amiable as ever, every one pitied and loved her.

When poor, crazed Emmeline strolled upon the banks of the Teche, plucking the wild flowers that strewed her pathway, and singing in soft tones some Acadian song, those that met her wondered why so fair and gentle a being should have been visited with God's wrath.

She spoke of Acadia and of Louis in such loving words that no one could listen to her without shedding tears. She fancied herself still the girl of sixteen years, on the eve of marrying the chosen one of her heart, whom she loved with such constancy and devotion, and imagining that her marriage bells tolled from the village church tower, her countenance would brighten, and her frame trembled with ecstatic joy. And then, in a sudden transition from joy to despair, convulsively gasping, struggling for utterance, and pointing her finger at some invisible object, in shrill and piercing accents she would cry out: "Mother, mother, he is gone; they have killed him; what will become of me?" And uttering a wild, unnatural shriek, she would fall senseless in my arms.

Sinking at last under the ravages of her mental disease, she expired in my arms without a struggle, and with an angelic smile on her lips.

She now sleeps in her quiet grave, shadowed by the tall oak tree near the little church at the Poste Des Attakapas, and her grave has been kept green and flower-strewn as long as your grandmother has been able to visit it. Ah! petiots, how sad was the fate of poor Emmeline, Evangeline, God's little angel.

A Vicksburger's Account of Life during the Siege

It got to be Sunday all the time. Seven Sundays in the week—to us, anyway. We hadn't anything to do, and time hung heavy. Seven Sundays, and all of them broken up at one time or another, in the day or in the night, by a few hours of the awful storm of fire and thunder and iron. At first we used to shin for the holes a good deal faster than we did afterward. The first time I forgot the children, and Maria fetched them both along. When she was all safe in the cave she fainted. Two or three weeks afterward, when she was running for the holes, one morning, through a shell-shower, a big shell burst near her and covered her all over with dirt, and a piece of iron carried away her game-bag of false hair from the back of her head. Well, she stopped to get that game-bag before she shoved along again! Was getting used to things already, you see. We all got so that we could tell a good deal about shells; and after that we didn't always go under shelter if it was a light shower. Us men would loaf around and talk; and a man would say, "There she goes!" and name the kind of shell it was from the sound of it, and go on talking—if there wasn't any danger from it. If a shell was bursting close over us, we stopped talking and stood still; uncomfortable, yes, but is wasn't safe to move. When it let go, we went on talking again, if nobody was hurt—maybe saying, "That was a ripper!" or some such commonplace comment before we resumed; or, maybe, we would see a shell poising itself away high in the air overhead. In that case, every fellow just whipped out a sudden "See you again, gents!" and shoved. Often and often I saw gangs of ladies promenading the streets, looking as cheerful as you please, and keeping an eye canted up watching the shells; and I've seen them stop still when they were uncertain about what a shell was going to do, and wait and make certain and after that they sa'ntered along again, or lit out for shelter, according to the verdict. Streets in some towns have a litter of pieces of paper and odds and ends of one sort or another lying around. Ours hadn't; they had *iron* litter. Sometimes a man would gather up all the iron fragments and unbursted shells in his neighborhood, and pile them into a kind of monument in his front yard—a ton of it, sometimes. No glass left; glass couldn't stand such a bombardment; it was all shivered out. Windows of the houses vacant—looked like eyeholes in a skull. *Whole* panes were as scarce as news.

We had church Sundays. Not many there, along at first; but by and

From *Life on the Mississippi,* by Samuel L. Clemens, pp. 280–282. Copyright, 1874 and 1875, by H. O. Houghton & Company; 1883, 1890, 1903, by Samuel L. Clemens; 1911, by Clara Gabrilowitsch. New York and London: Harper & Brothers, Publishers.

Years ago I talked with a couple of the Vicksburg non-combatants—a man and his wife. Left to tell their story in their own way, those people told it without fire, almost without interest. . . . What the man said was to this effect.—S.L.C., *ibid.,* pp. 279–280.

by pretty good turnouts. I've seen service stop a minute, and everybody sit quiet—no voice heard, pretty funeral-like then—and all the more so on account of the awful boom and crash going on outside and overhead; and pretty soon, when a body could be heard, service would go on again. Organs and church music mixed up with a bombardment is a powerful queer combination—along at first. Coming out of church, one morning, we had an accident—the only one that happened around me on a Sunday. I was just having a hearty hand-shake with a friend I hadn't seen for a while, and saying, "Drop into our cave to-night, after bombardment; we've got hold of a pint of prime wh——" Whisky, I was going to say, you know, but a shell interrupted. A chunk of it cut the man's arm off, and left it dangling in my hand. And do you know the thing that is going to stick the longest in my memory, and outlast everything else, little and big, I reckon, is the mean thought I had then? It was, "The whisky is *saved*." And yet, don't you know, it was kind of excusable; because it was as scarce as diamonds, and we had only just that little, never had another taste during the siege.

Sometimes the caves were desperately crowded, and always hot and close. Sometimes a cave had twenty or twenty-five people packed into it; no turning room for anybody; air so foul, sometimes, you couldn't have made a candle burn in it. A child was born in one of those caves one night. Think of that; why, it was like having it born in a trunk.

Twice we had sixteen people in our cave; and a number of times we had a dozen. Pretty suffocating in there. We always had eight; eight belonged there. Hunger and misery and sickness and fright and sorrow, and I don't know what all, got so loaded into them that none of them were ever rightly their old selves after the siege. They all died but three of us within a couple of years. One night a shell burst in front of the hole and caved it in and stopped it up. It was lively times, for a while, digging out. Some of us came near smothering. After that we made two openings— ought to have thought of it at first.

Mule meat? No, we only got down to that the last day or two. Of course it was good; anything is good when you are starving.

When Smallpox Was the Cargo

In the month of June, 1837, the American Fur Company's steamboat *St. Peters* came upstream on her annual voyage, laden with a cargo such as the Indian country had never seen. Aboard her were several cases of smallpox.

These cases could have been isolated, but the company officials were negligent. The Indians insisted on boarding the boat, because they knew

From *Land of the Dacotahs*, by Bruce Nelson, pp. 108–109. Copyright, 1946, by the University of Minnesota. Minneapolis: University of Minnesota Press.

she carried goods for them, and at Fort Clark a Mandan Indian made away with a blanket infected with the dread smallpox virus. Farther up-river at Fort Union an attempt was made to keep the Indians at a distance; but the red men, knowing of old the ways of government officials, feared they were to be defrauded of their goods and refused to scatter over the prairie as they were advised. Next, the commander of a company fort, one Jacob Halsey, decided to vaccinate the assembled Indians and "have it all over in time for the Fall trade."

It did not occur to this amateur practitioner that it might be dangerous to inoculate the previously unexposed Indians with material taken directly from the cases aboard the steamboat. Picture, then, his innocent surprise when twenty-seven squaws out of thirty he had "vaccinated" fell ill with particularly malignant and fatal forms of the disease. Possessing no racial immunity to smallpox, they succumbed to the disease sometimes within twenty-four hours. The infected survivors fled in every direction from the fort. Terror-stricken and unaware that quarantine or isolation was the only hope for the remaining Indians, they carried the disease far and wide to yet uninfected tribes and villages.

When in late summer the epidemic had run its course, seventeen thousand Indians had perished among the tribes of the upper [Missouri] valley: Blackfeet, Assiniboins, Mandans, Arikaras, Crows, and Sioux. The villages of the friendly Mandans were reduced to thirty families. The Sioux, who were more hostile and so more widely scattered, suffered least of the northern plains tribes.

An eyewitness to this terrible disaster reported: "The atmosphere, for miles, is poisoned by the stench of the hundreds of carcasses unburied. The women and children are wandering in groups without food, or howling over the dead. The men are flying in every direction. The proud, warlike, and noble-looking Blackfeet are no more. Their deserted lodges are seen on every hill. No sound but the raven's croak and the wolf's howl breaks the solemn stillness. The scene of desolation is appalling beyond the power of imagination to conceive."

Large numbers of Indians, believing the disease to be a visitation of the evil spirits upon them for their sins, drowned their wives and children and then plunged into the river themselves. A grimly human touch was recorded by another observer: "Many of the handsome Arickarees, who had recovered, seeing the disfiguration of their features, committed suicide, some by throwing themselves from rocks, others by stabbing and shooting. The prairie has become a graveyard; its wild flowers bloom over the sepulchres of Indians."

This decimation of the northern tribes struck the fur trade a ruinous blow; for it left few fur gatherers among the Indians to carry on the far-flung trapping and hunting activities the trade entailed. More effectively than by force of arms, the Indians' power was broken—for purposes of war as well as peaceful commerce—and the way was further opened for an increase in the white man's penetration of the river's upper reaches.

Bronze John

On July 18, 1878, the *John Porter* loosened its cables and slowly chugged out of New Orleans and up the Mississippi River. One of the finest tow boats on the river, it was pushing a chain of 18 barges towards Pittsburgh, 2,200 miles away. It carried a crew of 35 men, with John Bickerstaff as captain. The *John Porter* had not gone very far when one of the firemen became sick. His skin turned yellow, he hiccuped a great deal, and finally he threw up a black vomit that had an unbearable stench. Two others soon were like him. At Vicksburg the sick men were taken ashore, and the voyage was resumed.

The sickness continued to spread, however. A man would turn yellow and start retching that black stuff; they would leave him at the next town and go on up the "Massassip." Presently another poor devil would come down. The *John Porter* had to pull up at many a town before it finally reached Cairo, and bucked the broad, winding Ohio. Terror squeezed the hearts of the boatmen. "Yellow Jack!" whispered some. "It's Bronze John!" others said. And these tough, iron-muscled men were afraid.

The *John Porter,* stern wheel revolving, kept on pushing its way up the Ohio. Crew members continued to turn ghastly yellow and get that awful look in their eyes. But now the stricken boat did not turn shoreward and make for a town quay. News of its pestilence had gone ahead to all the towns and villages lining the Ohio; and armed men stood by the river banks, ready to shoot any of the crew who tried to land. Dozens of towns declared themselves quarantined against the *John Porter.* Grimly she pushed on, bearing her cargo of delirious men and abominable stench.

At Cincinnati, which was also quarantined against her, two young doctors boarded the death ship and stayed as the *John Porter* continued its fateful voyage. Doctors Carr and Slough did what they could. They labored heroically to lighten the sufferings of the victims. But there was little they could do. In those days the cause of yellow fever was not known, and there was no cure.

On Saturday, August 17, at 8 P.M., the *John Porter* halted a mile below Gallipolis. The authorities were notified, and a committee came, put the boat under quarantine, and gave what aid it could to the ten fever victims on board. Captain Bickerstaff was one of them. The crew was told the boat would have to be moved away from the town. Next morning it started, but the cylinder packing gave way and the boat came to a stop. Repairs were soon made, and it chugged upstream once more. The *John*

From *Gallipolis,* Being an Account of the French Five Hundred and of the Town they Established on La Belle Rivière, compiled by Workers of the Writers' Program of the Work Projects Administration in the State of Ohio, pp. 33–35. Sponsored by the Federal Commission and the Local Committee for the Gallipolis Sesquicentennial Celebration. Copyright, 1940. Columbus: The Ohio State Archaeological and Historical Society.

Porter had not gone far when a rocker arm snapped, and the boat drifted back to a point near the town. A local foundry was immediately put in blast, and by midnight, Sunday, a new shaft was ready. Several of the crew died during the night. On Monday morning the rest of the crew declared they would go no farther.

Captain Porter, one of the boat's owners, telegraphed $1,000 for their relief and ordered a new captain to take over. As soon as they were paid, the crew deserted, leaving only the doctors, the mate, and the stricken ones on the boat. Guarded during the day by a watchman on the river bank, and at night by Captain John Case, the boat lay here for some days. The people crowded the shore line to stare at it. Two men from the town went out to the boat and with tar, sulphur, and lime daubed it from prow to stern. The boat was declared free of taint, and out of curiosity a number of townsmen boarded the craft to see what it looked like.

A few days later Shephard Sheldon and James T. Myers, the men who had "disinfected" the boat, were dead. In many houses in Gallipolis lay other victims, who turned yellow, vomited the black stuff, and usually died in a little while. Terror raced through the town. Hundreds fled to other places before the quarantine kept them in their homes. Great fires of coal tar burned day and night at the corners of the main streets, but by now the streets were deserted. The schools closed, and business places shut their doors. People huddled inside their houses and were afraid to go near one another.

And day after day people in this house and that turned yellow, then black, and quickly died. "Bronze John" played no favorites; he crept past fires and through walls and struck. Of every three persons stricken, two died and the third mysteriously recovered. Men went at night to the houses of death and spread tar, sulphur, and lime wherever they could, while other men carted the black bodies to the cemetery and dumped them into hastily dug trenches. There was no time for building coffins or saying prayers. Men were paid as much as $100 for burying a corpse. For six weeks the terror raged. More than 50 townspeople came down with the dread disease; of these, 35 died.

The frosts came in mid-September and the plague ebbed away. No further cases were recorded. On September 13 the river rose and pushed loose the *John Porter*, anchored below the town, and all its barges. Some men on board the steamer managed to secure the boat, but the barges drifted downstream. A new crew was made up, supplies were taken on, and a short time later crowds again lined the river bank to watch the *John Porter* take off. This time they were silent. None ventured to visit the boat that had brought so much tragedy to the town.

The Year of Marvels

Many things combined to make the year 1811 the *annus mirabilis* of the West. During the earlier months, the waters of many of the great rivers overflowed their banks to a vast extent, and the whole country was in many parts covered from bluff to bluff. Unprecedented sickness followed. A spirit of change and a restlessness seemed to pervade the very inhabitants of the forest. A countless multitude of squirrels, obeying some great and universal impulse which none can know but the Spirit that gave them being, left their reckless and gamboling life and their ancient places of retreat in the north and were seen pressing forward by tens of thousands in a deep and sober phalanx to the south. No obstacles seemed to check this extraordinary and concerted movement: the word had been given to go forth, and they obeyed it, though multitudes perished in the broad Ohio, which lay in their path. The splendid comet of that year long continued to shed its twilight over the forests, and, as the autumn drew to a close, the whole Valley of the Mississippi, from the Missouri to the Gulf, was shaken to its center by continued earthquakes. It was at this very epoch, in which so many natural phenomena were combining to spread wonder and awe, that man, too, in the exercise of that power with which his Creator has endowed him, was making his first essay in that region of an art, the natural course and further perfection of which were destined to bring about yet greater changes than those effected by the flood and the earthquake; and at the same time that the latter were agitating the surface, the very first steamboat [Nicholas J. Roosevelt's *New Orleans*] was seen descending the great rivers, and the awe-struck Indians on the banks beheld the Pinelore [1] flying through the turbid waters.

The Great Shake

In the year 1809, in the thirteenth year of my age, my father with his family emigrated from the State of Kentucky to the southeastern corner

From *The Rambler in North America, MDCCCXXXII–MDCCCXXXIII*, by Charles Joseph Latrobe, Vol. I, p. 86. New York: Published by Harper & Brothers. 1835.

[1] The Choctaw name for the steamboat, literally "fire-canoe."—C.J.L.

From *The Earthquake of 1811 at New Madrid and along the Mississippi Valley*, together with Other Tales, by Capt. Chas. Ross, pp. 3–8. Entered . . . 1847, by George Conclin. Cincinnati.

Among those who lived on the borders of the Mississippi Valley, in the latter part of the year 1811, there are few, if any, who do not recollect the tremendous earthquake that shook not only the whole of this great valley but also the vast mountains that partly surround it. The origin or cause of this earthquake is supposed to be

of the State of Missouri, and located on the bank of the Mississippi, in the village of the Little Prairie. The inhabitants of that pleasant little village were all French, except my father's family (the most of them were from Canada) and scarcely any of them could speak a word of English. However, there was no difficulty in getting acquainted with them, and we soon became, like the rest of the villagers, all of one family. Now, to point out the former location of the village of Little Prairie would be almost impossible; but it appears to me that the bank of the river where the village stood has washed away near three quarters of a mile back, and the bank on the other side has made near the same distance towards where the village once stood; so that the happy scenes of my boyish days are extinct. The chief employment of the French people consisted in raising cattle, hunting, fishing, and trapping. In hunting, my soul delighted from my childhood, and, being a Kentuckian, I was wedded to my rifle by nature. I soon imagined myself a favorite in the village, learned a little of the French language, and made a bosom friend of one Jean Baptiste Zebon. Baptiste was a man of about twenty-two; he knew the ranges of the deer and bear, and was expert with the rifle. He was also a famous trapper, which sport, at that day, was lucrative, for beaver and otter were plenty; and often for two weeks at a time, Baptiste and myself were out on hunting and trapping excursions, alone by ourselves, without creating the least uneasiness amongst the villagers at home. The last trapping expedition we had, by me will never be for-

oxine matter under the bed of the St. Francis River, some thirty or forty miles from the Mississippi, west of Madrid; and its materials, it appears, are not yet exhausted, as scarcely a year passes but that several shocks are felt in the neighborhood of Madrid from these explosions.

The following narrative I obtained from an old and very respectable friend of mine, now living, near the scene of its action. I will give it, as near as I can recollect, in his own words.

* * * * *

To the skeptical reader, I will remark that the trapping ground on which my friend and Baptiste were encamped during that memorable earthquake (I distinctly recollect it, I felt it here in Cincinnati) is in the western congressional district of Tennessee, and not far from the Ohio River. This is the district that Col. Crockett represented in Congress. The neighborhood of the once little lake is now called "The Shakes." The earthquake put a mark on that place which time only will eradicate. It was one of Crockett's private hunting grounds, and I have often heard the Colonel tell of his bear-hunting down in the "Shakes." The lake, which evidently was once the bed of the main river, is now as high and dry a piece of ground as there is anywhere in the vicinity, and is now a beautiful prairie. The earthquake also created a fall in the river near New Madrid, of about eight feet, that lasted several days before the current washed it level. The Island No. 10 was split in two, the middle of it sunk, and the main channel ran through the gap for many years. The Island No. 32, if we are to judge from the largest trees being roots up and tops down, was completely capsized. The main channel, for a long time, ran through this forest; the roots still being visible, and out of water at a low stage, until the government snag boats, under the superintendence of Captain Shreaves, removed them. I could give many similar incidents of the effects of this earthquake, but the room in this book is limited.— C.R., Cincinnati, August 27, 1846, *ibid.*, pp. 3, 8.

gotten. Forget it—no! Its recollections, were I to live till I was as old as Methuselah, I would carry to my grave.

Up to this time we never had felt an earthquake; and were comparatively happy. We had been told by an Indian that about ten miles from the opposite bank of the river, in Tennessee, there was a lake of some considerable magnitude. This would be a new trapping ground to us, and Baptiste and myself were not long in making up our minds on trying our luck in Tennessee. Accordingly, about the 24th of December, 1811, we shouldered our rifles and our traps and bid adieu to our friends, all except my father, who accompanied us across the river for the purpose of bringing back the canoe. When the old man had bade us good-bye, we took up our line of march as directed, due east, until about two o'clock P.M., when we struck upon the margin of the little lake, and after reconnoitering it some hour or two, we found it was on the west bank, of a crescent form, about half a mile wide, and something like three miles long. While surveying the lake, I shot a large buck that had come to water; near that spot we selected a place for a tent, and whilst Baptiste barked the trees and built the tent, I was engaged in taking care of the venison, taking off the skin and saddles and jerking the meat. This employment consumed the remainder of the day. Our hard day's travel through the heavy canebrakes had given us an appetite for our suppers, and after toasting our feet and roasting our fresh meat over the fire, and eating for about an hour, we wrapped ourselves in our blankets for a snooze. It was some time before I could sleep. It was natural—my anticipations were great, my fortune was made on the banks of our new discovered little lake, and my castle was built high in the air several times before I could get asleep. Next morning, we were up before the sun, and eat breakfast. This little lake had evidently been, some day or other, a part of the river, and it was as full of beaver and otter as any lake I had ever seen, crawling about its banks, and swimming like flocks of geese in the water until nine o'clock in the morning.

But to my story. The most of this day was consumed in setting traps for the night, and when night came we eat our suppers and went to sleep, and slept soundly until about four o'clock in the morning, when we were awakened by a noise like distant thunder, and a trembling of the earth, which brought us both to our feet. The dash of the water against the bank of the lake, and rattling of the limbs in the tree-tops—now and then the falling of a dry branch in the water or near us on the ground—all these things first led me to believe there was a storm approaching. But no. There was not a breath of air stirring. What was it? was the inquiry. It soon became still. My friend said, "May be, he is de shake of de earth—may be de whirlwind!" An earthquake I feared it was, and the mention of it ran through my soul with terror. Now imagine my feelings. But a boy, scarce fifteen years old, ten miles from a human being, except my friend, and a dark night. Baptiste said, "We will be down again, it was nothing but the whirlwind." I knew he was only trying to pacify me, and to please him, I turned in again; but there was no sleep for either of us.

The thoughts of being in a wilderness among wild beasts, and the terrors of the earthquake, ran in my head for near an hour, and I really thought it never would be day. At length, against my companion's will, I got up and built a fire, and day began to dawn. My mind soon began to freshen on our traps, and when about to rouse Baptiste, came the next shock. It was awful! Like the other—first, a noise in the west like heavy thunder, then the earth came rolling towards us, like a wave on the ocean, in long seas, not less than fifteen feet high. The tops of the largest sycamores bending as if they were coming to the ground—again, one rises as it were to re-instate, and bending the other way, it breaks in twain and comes to the ground with a tremendous crash. Now the scene became awful in the extreme. Trees were falling in every direction—some torn up by their roots, others breaking off above ground, and limbs and branches of all sizes flying about us, and the earth opening, as it were to receive us, in gaps sometimes fifteen feet wide—then it would close with the wave. The water of our little lake was fast emptying itself in these openings, and as they would close it would spout high in the air— and soon, as far as I could see, with the alternate wave of the earth and water of the lake, there was a crashing of timber and spouting of water. At one time I would be splashing about in the water, and then holding a tree top, until the shake began to subside, when I espied a spot of ground above water, and in attempting to reach it I got into a crevice, where I lost bottom, but being somewhat amphibious, I at length reached the place. The earth now became quieter; but my thoughts were that the world was at an end, and this time and place was selected by me to offer up a supplication to my God. With fervency I dropped on my knees, raised up my eyes and hands towards heaven, when my friend bawled out, at the top of his voice, "Stop! What for you speak to de God now? Why you no speak to de God three months? Come back. Take care de b-r-a-n-c-h!" The earth and lake becoming still quieter, my friend commenced a lecture. We were both yet alive and unhurt, and thinking the earth was everywhere destroyed, excepting the spot where we stood, says Baptiste, "If de God kill all de rest, and leave us, me no want to stay. And if de God kill us and leave all de rest, he not de God me take him for." My friend seemed much braver than myself; but I more than once, during the worst of the shake, saw him raise his eyes towards heaven, and say, "Sacré bon Dieu! Senior!" then bawl out, "Take care of de b-r-a-n-c-h!"

The shock had now subsided, and everything had become still. The day had fairly dawned, and the change of the scenery was visible. The whole forest seemed as if an awful hurricane had completely destroyed it. The soft alluvial earth was opened in many rents of great depth, in which our little lake had completely lost itself. What was to be done, was the next question. Shall we seek our home—or have we a home? Our camp was completely demolished, one of our guns and all our meat and ammunition, flint, punk, steel and blankets lost in a deep crevice, and our bodies wet and cold. Something must be done, or we will freeze. So without much deliberation we bent our course westward, and after climbing over the tops of trees, and scrambling around cracks in the earth so wide that we could not leap over them, through mud and canebrakes, now worse than ever, until near sundown, we reached the bank of the Mississippi immediately opposite our once loved village.

Hungry as we were, not having eat a particle since the night before, our hearts leaped with joy. But my friend's countenance changed, as we were seated on a log surveying the opposite side of the river—he turned pale as death. The cause was too soon visible. No smoke arose from the chimneys of our habitations, and not a single human being could be seen. A solitary cow lowed as she stood alone, deserted by her thousand companions, and all else seemed desolate. Fatigued and hungry, we wandered up and down the shore, gazing on the other side for the appearance of some human being until dark night. None approached. Our clothes were not yet thoroughly dried, and a cold night approaching, we were chilled and hungry; we had no means of lighting a fire, and again death seemed to stare us in the face. Shall we lie down and freeze, or stand up till we famish for want of food? It was of but little difference which. However, one gleam of hope yet remained. If we lived until the next morning's sun, contrive to build a raft of floating logs, and with sticks paddle across the river. To do this it would be necessary to build our raft a mile further up the river, so that we could make the landing on the other side. On this we resolved, and as we were compelled to keep ourselves in motion to keep awake and from freezing, we were on the spot a dozen times before day.

That was the longest night I ever experienced. The last shock of the earth the morning previous seemed to me to keep the ground vibrating half an hour, but I suppose the whole time did not consume more than four minutes. But the night ensuing seemed as if it were three months long. Still imagining some awful change of the world, my friend several times remarked, "There [will] be no day!" But the day did come and, with the little strength we had left, we set ourselves to work; but I should judge it was near noon before the raft was in readiness; and when in the act of shoving it out in the stream, a man made his appearance on the river bank, at the village. Baptiste hailed—we were too far—he did not hear him. We left the raft, and ran down the shore nearly opposite to him and hailed again. The man seemed to notice us—but without answering he ran from us as if the wolves were after him. A man had been in sight—a canoe was under the bank near him—but he was gone! The raft was now our only alternative. Here again we were disappointed. The raft, as poor a makeshift as it was, had gone adrift. We were both too much exhausted to swim in the cold water after it, and all hope from it was inevitably lost. We walked to another drift pile, but were too weak even to attempt another raft, and we sat ourselves down with our eyes towards the village.

"When in de tar," said my friend, "and got plenty money, then me got plenty friend. Sacré! when me in de tar, with de larguin, then me want no plenty friend. Me want de friend now. Me want him bring de canoe."

During this conversation, I picked up a honey-suckle, had split it apart, and was about to devour it. Baptiste halloed at me, knocked it out of my hands, saying, "What for you want to die and leave me by myself!"

He thought that it was poison, and that I wanted to destroy myself. But a man again appeared, we hailed him at the top of our voices; he answered, descended the river bank, launched the canoe, and came over for us. It was my father. He informed us that on account of the shake, the inhabitants had all left the village and encamped some two miles back in the prairie, and that the village was a mass of ruins—that some two hours before, they had selected one of their Frenchmen to repair to the village, and report its condition—that he had returned at full jump, out of breadth, and the first words they got out of him were that he had seen a ghost or the devil on the opposite side of the river. This information reminded my father of us, and he accordingly came in search of us. The village, sure enough, was all in a heap of ruins, but there had been no lives lost. We made ourselves comparatively comfortable in our camps for a few days until everything was in readiness for a grand march. Often did I endeavor to give a history of my frightful adventures to my friends, but was as often interrupted by their story of the earthquake, so that I could scarcely get in a word edgeways. We all kept company as far as New Madrid; here my father with his family took leave of the French people, crossed the river at the Iron Banks, and once more in Kentucky, we settled down for the winter. From New Madrid, the French proceeded northward to St. Louis, and the greater part of them went back to Canada. Our stock of cattle was very large, and the most of them were left behind at the Little Prairie. They fared as well through the winter without us as if we had been with them, as the prairie grass was high, and there was plenty of cane.

I left my father in the spring, and returned to the Little Prairie, and found the stock in good order; and being the natural heir to the Little Prairie, I have made it my home ever since. I afterwards met Jean Baptiste Zebon, in the latter part of the last war, above St. Louis. He was in the army. On meeting, we both wept with joy. Our time together was short; but he promised faithfully, when his time of service had expired, he would join me at the Little Prairie. I have never heard a whimper of him since.

The Legend of Reelfoot Lake

'Way back when this here country was full of Indians, seems there was an old buck lived with his tribe at the foot of those three-hundred-foot bluffs you can see over there on the east side of the lake. He was the big wheel in his tribe, all right enough, and his tribe was happy and contented in these rich bottom lands that border the Mississippi. But the old boy was sad just the same. Seems as if his only son had been born with a twisted foot—sort of a clubfoot. When the boy walked or ran he had an odd rolling gait, so the Indians called him Reelfoot.

Well sir, the boy overcame his tough handicap, made himself a mighty hunter, pulled off deeds that no other Indian would tackle, won the respect of every man in the tribe. When the old chief died, Reelfoot took over the job. Did right well at it, too. The tribe prospered. But young Reelfoot wasn't happy—not by a long shot! On account of that doggone foot of his, none of the Chickasaw maidens would have anything to do with him. His wigwam was cold and silent—and he had to board out.

In those days, just like now, the grass always looked greener on the other side of the fence. Reelfoot allowed that he'd shop for a wife down south. He gathered up a good-sized bunch of the toughest warriors in his tribe—and a cutthroat crew they were, too. He told 'em to behave themselves, at least until he gave the word—and hit the trail to the south.

At last this peaceful-looking war party got into the Choctaw territory, where Reelfoot heard of a princess said to be slicker 'n a button, with good looks, a neat hand with turtle egg omelets, and a quiet tongue. She was the only daughter of Copiah, chief of the Choctaws. Reelfoot and his boys put on their best bibs and tuckers to call on the old chief. Just a sociable call, mind you. Gave the old boy pearls and rare skins, just to show him Reelfoot's heart was in the right place and to impress on him that Reelfoot was a sure-enough big shot, not some Johnny-come-lately.

Copiah seemed to be pretty well impressed, so Reelfoot mentioned, casual like, that he wondered who that pretty squaw was over in the corner. Copiah said she was his daughter. Reelfoot intimated that if Copiah twisted his arm a mite and gave him plenty of wampum to go with her, he just might take the little girl off the old chief's hands. Copiah wasn't interested.

Reelfoot 'lowed he might not have to have his arm twisted, might even

From tourists' souvenir map of Reelfoot Lake, compliments of Tiptonville, Tennessee, Lions Club. Courtesy of Dr. S. Charles Kendeigh, Department of Zoology, University of Illinois, Champaign-Urbana, Illinois.

For an eye-witness account of the earthquake and the formation of Reelfoot Lake, see letter of Eliza Bryan, New Madrid, Missouri, March 22, 1816, in *The Life, Travels, Labors, and Writings of Lorenzo Dow* (New York, 1857), pp. 242–244.

forget the dowry. He'd just marry the girl to do Copiah a favor. Copiah
still wasn't interested.

Reelfoot got down to brass tacks. He was a big chief. He had plenty
this, plenty that, plenty other. He wanted to marry the girl, would see
that she had everything her little heart desired. How about it? Copiah
got mad. Said he wasn't fixin' to let his daughter marry some whipper-
snapper he'd never heard of—and go off where he might never see her
again. And besides that, he didn't want a son-in-law with a club foot.

That last remark got under Reelfoot's skin, and he hinted that he
might take the girl home with him, anyhow, and knock her old man in
the head in the bargain if he made any more cracks like that. Copiah got
uneasy, because the hard-looking crew Reelfoot had brought with him
looked like they might take considerable pleasure in doing a job like that.

It was Copiah's next move, so he called out his high Sachem—his
chief medicine man—complete with rattles, snakeskins, human bones and
all. The medicine man grunted, moaned, beat his head on the ground a
couple of times, and declared that the Great Spirit had just spoken to
him. The Great Spirit says (he said) that there's an Indian name of
Reelfoot looking for trouble. Going to find it, too, if he doesn't behave
himself. It's against tribal law for an Indian to steal his wife from another tribe, and if Reelfoot disobeys, look out. The Great Spirit will do
away with Reelfoot and all his people.

Well, sir, Chief Reelfoot didn't scare very easy. He and his men went
off, but the more he thought about it the more he was convinced that
the medicine man was just running a bluff on him. Late that night, Reelfoot and his bucks doubled back, slipped into Copiah's village, slit the
throats of a couple of dogs that looked like they wanted to bark, and
snatched the princess off so quietly that not a man in the village stopped
snoring.

The trip home was uneventful. Reelfoot and his men had no trouble
dodging Copiah and other pursuers, and Reelfoot was more and more
convinced that the medicine man was just putting on an act—he hoped!

Messengers were sent ahead, and when Reelfoot and his war party
swaggered in home with the princess, the big feed was ready. That was
a real day of rejoicing. At last Reelfoot had a wife—and a real princess
at that. While the deer and the fat coons and the haunches of bear meat
smoked and sizzled over the fires, the members of the tribe who could
stop drooling long enough started the music. The tom-toms began to sing
and the kettledrums began to roll and the people began to chant.

But with them the wind began to sing, too. Thunder began to roll,
and then the earth rolled with it. It was an earthquake, but one such
as had never been felt before. The big cypress trees popped like twigs,
and fell crashing to the ground. Then, from the sky, the miserable Indians
heard a voice. "Reelfoot!" said the voice, "you have disobeyed! I warned
you—now I punish you!"

Yep, it was the Great Spirit—and mad! He stamped a foot and the ground sank for miles around. He called to the Mississippi River, and the Father of Waters heard him and ran upstream for forty-eight hours to cover Reelfoot's hunting grounds.

When the Great Spirit's anger and the storm quieted down, there was a huge body of sparkling blue water, lapping softly over Reelfoot, his princess, and his people. And that, young feller, is what the old-timers tell. Me, I dunno!

Legends of Crow Wing

[Crow Wing, Minnesota] is beautifully situated on the east side of the Mississippi, directly at the mouth of the river known by that name. . . .

Crow Wing is not only one of the most delightfully located nooks in the world, but it is rich in historical and legendary associations. A famous battle was once fought here, between the Chippeways and Sioux. A party of the latter had gone up Crow Wing River for the purpose of destroying a certain Chippeway village. They found it inhabited only by women and children, every one of whom they murdered in cold blood, and consumed their wigwams. It so happened that the Chippeway warriors had been expecting an attack, and had consequently stationed themselves in deep holes on a high bank of the river at Crow Wing, intending to fall upon the Sioux party on their way up the river. But they were most sadly disappointed. While watching for their enemies, they were suddenly startled by a triumphant shout that floated *down* the stream. In perfect agony they looked, when lo! the very party that they were after came into full view, shouting with delight and tossing up the scalps which they had taken. Many a Chippeway brave recognized the glossy locks of his wife or child and knew his gloomiest anticipations to be true. They remained in ambush for a few minutes longer, and when the enemy came within reach of their arrows, every single one of them was killed, while their canoes, plunder and bodies were suffered to float down the stream unmolested; and the pall of night rested upon the hills, the glens, the waveless river, and the Chippeway camp.

Among the many legends associated with Crow Wing is one about a white Panther, whose home was here when the world was young. That Panther was the Prophet of a certain Chippeway tribe, and had power to speak the Chippeway language. A young brave was anxious to revenge the death of a brother, and had sought the oracle to learn the success of his intended expedition. The Panther told him that he must not go,

From *A Summer in the Wilderness;* Embracing a Canoe Voyage up the Mississippi and around Lake Superior, by Charles Lanman, pp. 68–70. Entered . . . 1847, by D. Appleton & Company. New York and Philadelphia.
Written at Crow Wing, July, 1846.

but wait until a more propitious season. But the young man headed his party, and went; and every one of his followers was killed—himself escaping by the merest chance. Thinking that the Panther had caused this calamity, he stole upon this creature and slaughtered it, in the darkness of midnight. The dying words of the oracle were: "Cruel and unhappy warrior, I doom thee to walk the earth forever, a starving and undying skeleton." And it is said that this specter man, whenever the moon is tinged with red, or the aurora borealis floods the sky with purple, may be seen flitting in perfect solitude along the banks of the Mississippi.

The Legend of Starved Rock

Starved Rock is the unpoetical name of a singular spot on the Illinois River about sixty miles east of this place [Rock Island] and eight miles south of Ottawa. It is a rocky bluff, rising from the margin of the stream to the height of more than a hundred feet, and is only separated from the mainland by a narrow chasm. Its length might probably measure two hundred and fifty feet. Its sides are perpendicular, and there is only one point where it can be ascended, and that is by a narrow stair-like path. It is covered with many a cone-like evergreen and, in summer, encircled by luxurious grape and ivy vines and clusters of richly colored flowers. It is undoubtedly the most conspicuous and beautiful pictorial feature of the sluggish and lonely Illinois, and is associated with the final extinction of the Illinois tribe of Indians. The legend, which I listened to from the lips of a venerable Indian trader, is as follows.

Many years ago, the whole region lying between Lake Michigan and the Mississippi was the home and dominion of the Illinois Indians. For them alone did the buffalo and antelope range over its broad prairies; for them did the finest of rivers roll their waters into the lap of Mexico, and bear upon their bosoms the birchen canoe, as they sought to capture the wild waterfowl; and for them alone did the dense forests, crowding upon these streams, shelter their unnumbered denizens.

In every direction might be seen the smoke of Indian wigwams curling upwards to mingle with the sunset clouds, which told them tales of the spirit land.

Years passed on, and they continued to be at ease in their possessions. But the white man from the far east, with the miseries which have ever accompanied him in his march of usurpation, began to wander into the wilderness, and trouble to the poor red man was the inevitable consequence. The baneful "fire water," which was the gift of civilization, created dissensions among the savage tribes, until in process of time, and

---

Ibid., pp. 26–29.
Written at Rock Island, July, 1846.

on account of purely imaginary evils, the Pottawattomies from Michigan determined to make war upon the Indians of Illinois. Fortune, or rather destiny, smiled upon the oppressors, and the identical rock in question was the spot that witnessed the extinction of an aboriginal race.

It was the close of a long siege of cruel warfare, and the afternoon of a day in the delightful Indian summer. The sunshine threw a mellow haze upon the prairies, and tinged the multitudinous flowers with deepest gold; while, in the shadow of the forest islands, the doe and her fawn reposed in perfect quietness, lulled into a temporary slumber by the hum of the grasshopper and wild bee. The wilderness world wore the aspect of a perfect sabbath. But now, in the twinkling of an eye, the delightful solitude was broken by the shrill whoop and dreadful struggle of bloody conflict upon the prairies and in the woods. All over the country were seen the dead bodies of the ill-fated Illinois, when it was ordered by Providence that the concluding skirmish between the hostile parties should take place in the vicinity of Starved Rock.

The Pottawattomies numbered near three hundred warriors, while the Illinois tribe was reduced to about one hundred, who were mostly aged chiefs and youthful heroes—the more desperate fighters having already perished, and the women and children of the tribe having already been massacred and consumed in their wigwams. The battle was most desperate between the unequal parties.

The Illinois were about to give up all for lost, when, in their frenzy, they gave a defying shout, and retreated to the rocky bluff. From this, it was an easy matter to keep back their enemies, but alas! from that moment they were to endure unthought of suffering, to the delight of their baffled yet victorious enemies.

And now to describe in words the scene that followed and was prolonged for several days were utterly impossible. Those stout-hearted Indians, in whom a nation was about to become extinct, chose to die upon their strange fortress, by starvation and thirst, rather than surrender themselves to the scalping-knife of their exterminators. And, with a few exceptions, this was the manner in which they did perish. Now and then, indeed, a desperate man would lower himself, hoping thereby to escape, but a tomahawk would cleave his brain before he touched the ground or water.

Day followed day, and those helpless captives sat in silence, and gazed imploringly upon their broad beautiful lands, while hunger was gnawing into their very vitals. Night followed night, and they looked upon the silent stars, and beyond, to the home of the Great Spirit, but they murmured not at his decree. And if they slept, in their dreams they once more played with their little children, or held converse with their wives, and roamed the woods and prairies in perfect freedom. When morning dawned, it was but the harbinger of another day of agony; but when the evening hour came, a smile would sometimes brighten up a haggard countenance, for the poor, unhappy soul, through the eye of an obscure faith, had caught a glimpse of the spirit land. Day followed day, and the last lingering hope was utterly abandoned. Their destiny was sealed, and no change for good could possibly take place, for the human blood-hounds who watched their prey were utterly without mercy. The feeble, white-haired chief crept into a thicket and there breathed his last. The recently strong-bodied warrior, uttering a protracted but feeble yell of exultation, hurled his tomahawk upon some fiend below, and then yielded himself up to the pains of his condition. The lithe form of the soft-eyed youth parted with its strength, and was compelled to totter, fall upon the earth and die. Ten weary, weary days passed on, and the strongest man and last of his race was numbered with the dead—and a glorious banquet was presented to the eagle and the raven.

The Great Fish Who Is Called a Sandbar

A party of warriors were winding their way homeward along the bank of a muddy river after a successful invasion of the country of their enemies. Their war paint and dancing eagle plumes gleamed in the last rays of the setting sun. Toward the right of the party walked a couple of stalwart braves. There was a tenderness in their manner to each other that at once revealed a close comradeship, since the love of two men who have faced danger together often surpasses their love for women.

They had been on the warpath for many days and nights, and now over forty-eight hours had passed since their last morsel of food had been consumed. So it was with much pleasure that Chaske, one of the two friends, caught a large pike in the river.

Chaske quickly prepared the fish for his friend, Hepan, who was weaker than he. But after it had been prepared in perfect Indian style Hepan refused to eat it. In vain Chaske urged, hoping to overcome his friend's

From *More Santee-Sioux Indian Legends,* Nebraska Folklore Pamphlets, Reproduced from Material Gathered for a Book on the State, Issued Irregularly by the Nebraska Writers' Project, J. Harris Gable, State Supervisor, Robert E. Carlson, Editor, Prepared in Cooperation with the State Superintendent of Public Instruction, No. 23 (October, 1939), pp. 8–9. Lincoln, Nebraska.

. . . Taken from the files of the *Word Carrier,* a missionary paper published by the Santee Mission School, at Santee, Nebraska. They appeared between the years of 1883 and 1887, when the paper had a circulation of less than 300 copies.

* * *

The missionaries and Indian students who translated these legends for the *Word Carrier* made very little attempt to attain a smooth, literary style. Consequently considerable editing has been necessary, although every attempt has been made to retain the simple, childlike style of the Santee-Sioux.

Like most Indian legends, these have lost much of their atmosphere and picturesqueness in translation and in print; since they were originally composed for narration around an evening campfire, where, silhouetted in front of an unbroken sky in a windswept plains country, the Indian story-teller dramatized the exciting parts of the legends.—R.E.C.

reluctance to share his meal. At length, being unable to resist the plead-
ings of Chaske, Hepan said: "My friend, I do as you urge because you
love me; but if I eat the pike, don't become weary of bringing me water
from the river during the night." So, with this understanding, the two
joyfully partook of the fish. But the meal was scarcely over before Hepan
said: "Chaske, bring me some water." Chaske joyfully brought his friend
water, since he was happy to do any service for him. But soon the large
pailful was empty and his friend was still panting for water.

Chaske, in an attempt to allay his friend's painful thirst, made frequent trips to the river. But the thirst, instead of becoming quenched,
became more and more intense; and as the night wore on the flagging
energy of Chaske suggested an easier and surer method of quenching his
friend's unaccountable thirst. It was to move him to the bank of the
stream where he could drink his fill. Upon proposing it, his friend agreed
to the idea but at the same time exclaimed: "My friend, you have un-
done me." So Chaske carefully helped Hepan to the river's edge and
then left him, to snatch an hour's rest before the dawn came.

Chaske had scarcely dozed off before the voice of his friend awoke
him with the words: "Behold me." When Chaske reached him, the upper
half of his body had turned into a pike. In distress and anguish, Chaske
upbraided himself for bringing about his friend's misfortune by taking
him to the river's edge, but it was too late to help now; the fish part
was already submerged in the river, and the remainder of his body was
following fast until the last vestige of a man had disappeared, having
been replaced by a great pike that stretched across the mouth of the
river. As time sped on, the sand washed upon it until to casual observers
it looked like an ordinary sandbar.

Many canoes, during the years that followed, were wrecked on the big
fish. These accidents kept on occurring until one day an Indian maiden,
who had been Hepan's beloved, came slowly down the stream in a birch
bark canoe that was loaded with beaded moccasins and all kinds of
maiden handiwork, which she dropped into the water for her lost lover.
The large fish, as a token of acceptance, did the one thing it could do:
submerged itself under the water.

The paleface, who now use the Missouri, call the great fish a sandbar
because their river boats are sometimes left stranded on top of it. Only
we, the Indians, know it is a great fish who was once a man.

The Legend of Standing Rock

This story of Standing Rock [on the west bank of the Missouri in
North Dakota] is a legend of the Arikaras, who once had their villages

From *Prairie Smoke,* by Melvin R. Gilmore (Pahok), pp. 13–16. Copyright, 1929,
by Columbia University Press. New York.

along the Missouri River between the Grand River and the Cannon Ball River. Afterwards, being harassed by hostile incursions of the Dakotas, they abandoned this country to their enemies and moved farther up the Missouri River, joining themselves in alliance with the Mandans.

There was once a young girl in the Arikara tribe who was beautiful and amiable and not given to heedless, chattering, idle amusement. She was thoughtful and earnest, and was conversant with the ways of all the living creatures—the birds and the small mammals and the trees and shrubs and flowers of the woodlands and the prairies. She was in the habit of going to walk by herself to visit and commune with all these living creatures. She understood them better than most people did, and they all were her friends.

When she became of marriageable age she had many suitors, for she was beautiful and lovely in disposition. But to the young men who wooed her she answered, "I do not find it in my heart to marry any one. I am at home with the bird people, the four-footed people of the woods and prairies, the people of the flower nations and the trees. I love to work in the cornfields in summer, and the sacred squash blossoms are my dear companions."

Finally, her grandmother reasoned with her and told her that it was her duty to marry and to rear children to maintain the strength of the tribe. Because of filial duty she finally said, when her grandmother continued to urge her to marry a certain young man of estimable worth who desired her for his wife, "Well, grandmother, I will obey you, but I tell you that good will not come of it. I am not as others are, and Mother Nature did not intend me for marriage."

So she was married and went to the house already prepared for her by her husband. But three days later she came back to her mother's house, appearing sad and downcast. She sat down without speaking. Finally her grandmother said, "What is it, my child? Is he not kind to you?" The girl answered, "Oh, he is not unkind. He treated me well." And with that she sped away into the forest. Her grandmother followed her after a little while, thinking that out among her beloved trees and plants she might open her heart and tell what was the trouble. And this she did, explaining all the trouble to her grandmother. And she concluded her talk with her grandmother with these words: "And so you see, grandmother, it is as I said when you urged me to marry. I was not intended for marriage, and now my heart is so sad. I should not have married. My spirit is not suited to the bounds of ordinary human living, and my husband is not to be blamed. He is honorable and kind. But I must go away and be with the children of nature." So her grandmother left her there where she was sitting by a clump of chokeberries, having her sewing kit with her and her little dog by her side.

She did not return home that night, and so the next morning young men were sent to search for her. At last she was found sitting upon a hill out on the prairie, and she was turned to stone from her feet to her waist. The young men hastened back to the village and reported to the officers who had sent them out.

Then the people were summoned by the herald, and they all went out to the place where the young woman was. Now they found she had become stone as far up as her breasts.

Then the priests opened the sacred bundle and took the sacred pipe, which they filled and lighted, and they presented it to her lips, so that thus she and they in turn smoking from the same pipe might be put in communion and accord with the spirit. But she refused the pipe and said, "Though I refuse the pipe, it is not from disloyalty or because of unwillingness to be at one with my people; but I am different by nature. And you shall know my good will towards my people and my love and remembrance of them always, for whoever places by this stone in summer time a wild flower, or in winter time a twig of a living tree, or any such token of living, wonderful Nature at any time, shall be glad in his heart, and shall have his desire to be in communion with the heart of Nature." And as she said these words she turned completely into stone, and her little dog, sitting at her feet and leaning close against her, was also turned into stone with her. And this stone is still to be seen, and is revered by the people. It is from this stone that the country around Fort Yates, North Dakota, is called Standing Rock.

Legends of the Falls of St. Anthony

Associated with the Falls of St. Anthony is the following Indian legend. A Chippeway woman, the daughter of a chief, and the wife of a warrior, had been cruelly treated by her faithless husband. She was not beautiful, but young and proud, and the mother of a lovely daughter-child. Goaded to the quick by repeated wrongs, she finally resolved to release herself from every trouble, and her child from evil friends, by departing for the Spirit Land, and the Falls were to be the gateway to that promised heaven. It was an Indian summer evening, and nature was hushed into a deep repose. The mother and her child were alone in their wigwam, within sight and hearing of the Falls, and the father was absent on a hunting expedition. The mother kissed and caressed her darling, and then dressed it with all the ornaments in her possession, while from her own person she rejected every article of clothing which she had received from her husband, and arrayed herself in richer garments which she had made with her own hands. She then obtained a full-blown lily, and crushing its petals and breaking its stem, she placed it on a mat in the centre of

From *A Summer in the Wilderness;* Embracing a Canoe Voyage up the Mississippi and around Lake Superior, by Charles Lanman, pp. 62–63. Entered . . . 1847, by D. Appleton & Company. New York and Philadelphia.
Written at the mouth of Saint Peter's, July, 1846.

her lodge, as a memorial of her wrongs. All things being ready, she seized the child, hastened to the river, launched her frail canoe, and in a moment more was floating on the treacherous stream. According to a universal Indian custom, she sang a wild death-song,—for a moment her canoe trembled on the brow of the watery precipice, and in an instant more the mother and child were for ever lost in the foam below.

Winona

The most romantic legend . . . associated with the Mississippi Horicon [Lake Pepin] is the story of Winona. She was the daughter of a chief, and lived about one hundred years ago. She was exceedingly beautiful and universally beloved. Her father had promised her hand to a favorite warrior, but her heart had been pledged to another, not less brave, but more noble and youthful. For many months she would not listen to the wishes of her father; but his sterner nature was roused, and he vowed that she *must* marry the object of *his* choice. Weeks passed on, and she knew that she must yield. Nightly did she meet her accepted lover, but always talked to him of the Spirit Land, as if she had been a queen of that fantastic realm. The marriage night had been appointed, and the chief had proclaimed a feast. To all outward appearance a change suddenly came over the daughter's mind, and she smiled and talked, like one about to be made a happy bride. Among the delicacies that were to be eaten on the occasion was a certain berry that was found in great perfection upon a certain hill or bluff. It was a pleasant summer afternoon, and all the female friends of Winona, accompanied by herself, were picking the desired berries.

Carelessly did they all wander up the hillside, while an occasional laugh would ring upon the air; but Winona was only seen to smile, for (though those loving friends knew it not) her heart was darkened by many a strange shadow. Carelessly did the berry-gatherers wander on; when all at once a low melancholy song fell upon their ears, and lo! upon the very edge of a beetling precipice stood the form of the much loved Winona.

Her song was death-like, and when her companions were intuitively convinced of the contemplated deed, they were stupefied with horror. Winona motioned them to keep back, while her song increased until it became a perfect wail. The burthen of it was,

> "Farewell, sisters:—
> I am going to the Spirit Land;
> My warrior will come after me,
> And we shall be blessed."

Ibid., pp. 48–50.
Written at Lake Pepin, July, 1846.

One moment more, and Winona, the pride of all the Indian villages on Lake Pepin, was deeply buried in its clear cold bosom. And this is the story that hallows the loftiest peak of this lake. I obtained it, as here related, from one of her kindred, and I believe it to be true. As to Winona's warrior, it is said that he lived for many years a hermit, and finally died a madman. So runneth many a song of life.

Gunboat Gold

Clarendon is on the White River, perhaps seventy-five miles up from its juncture with the Arkansas. It has a population of about two thousand now and I suspect it was considerably less than a thousand in 1864.

Word was circulated in Clarendon one day that a Union gunboat was on its way up the river with a safe full of gold to pay the troops stationed upstream. So the patriotic Clarendon citizens wheeled out an old cannon that had been abandoned in some retreat, loaded it up to the muzzle, and pushed the cannon up on the levee, commanding the river at the downstream bend. They piled brush in front of the gun to hide their operations. Then they waited.

Presently the gunboat hove in sight, splashing slowly against the considerable current. She swung in toward the right bank to take advantage of an eddy, swung in toward Clarendon and the hidden gun. The Clarendon men waited until they knew they could not miss their target and then let drive at the gunboat's water line.

It was a direct hit. A gaping hole was torn in the boat's side and she immediately listed to starboard and began to settle. But as she sank, the gunboat made Clarendon pay for her death. She raked the town with volley after volley from her cannon.

When I was a boy my father had a sawmill on the banks of the White River at Clarendon. At low-water stage the rusted smokestack of the sunken Federal gunboat still was visible. No one ever had made an attempt to raise her and salvage the cargo.

It was taken as a matter of fact in Clarendon that the safe still was aboard at the bottom of the river and that the safe held several thousand dollars in gold.

My brother Glen once tried to initiate a project to recover that safe when he found he could rent a diver's suit in Memphis. He took the matter up with several young fellows around town, fellows who ordinarily were ready for a fight or a frolic or anything else that offered entertainment, night or day. But Glen found everyone singularly apathetic to this proposal.

From *The Arkansas*, by Clyde Brion Davis, pp. 277–279. Copyright, 1940, by Clyde Brion Davis. *The Rivers of America*, edited by Stephen Vincent Benét and Carl Carmer. New York and Toronto: Farrar & Rinehart, Inc.

Yes, they reckoned there was a lot of gold down there in the gunboat. They reckoned there was more gold than they could make in several years' hard work. It wasn't that the gold still was technically the property of the United States even after passage of half a century. No, it wasn't that. They just didn't want to mess with that old gunboat.

You see, quite a passel of Yankees had gone down with that old boat. The Yankee skeletons would be down there still, guarding that safe of Yankee gold. The Clarendon young men hadn't lost anything down there with those Yankee skeletons. And they wanted no truck with *any* skeletons at the bottom of the White River.

So, as far as I know, the Yankee gold is still there—if, indeed, there ever *was* a safe of gold aboard the Yankee gunboat.

The Lost Gold of Tonty

An old French and Indian legend relates that Tonty possessed a large hoard of gold, and fearing that it would fall into the hands of the Canadian Governor who dismissed him, and thus aroused Tonty's hatred, the disgraced Frenchman buried this treasure on or about Starved Rock. It would have been too bulky and too conspicuous to attempt carrying on the new adventures he was determined to find.

Many years later, at the hour of his death, Tonty revealed the hiding place to the priest who held the crucifix for him. This priest kept the secret in hope of finding the hoard, but shortly after Tonty's death was drowned when a canoe he was paddling upset. The story, telling of the gold, had been circulated, but as the hiding place remained a mystery sealed by death, the only results were a number of wildgoose chases.

As long afterwards as forty-seven years some Frenchmen from Peoria made up a party, including Father Buche and Captain De Frond, this party instituting a search for the lost gold. They unearthed a cache of Indian trinkets and trading relics, but the gold itself was not discovered. During their hunt the party honeycombed the top of Starved Rock, these holes remaining visible up to a very recent date.

Father Buche left in manuscript form the following interesting account of the search:

We had spent five days in digging pit-holes on the summit of Le Rocher, and found a large quantity of articles which were intended for Indian trade, but [of] the precious metal—the object of our search—we found none. On the last day of our stay we dug a hole close to the old earthwork, and continued working until it was quite dark, when the devil appeared to us in the form of a huge

From *Starved Rock through the Centuries*, by John B. McDonnell and Lloyd E. Reeve, pp. 63–65. Copyright, 1927, by John B. McDonnell and Lloyd E. Reeve. Champaign, Illinois: The Service Press.

bear. On seeing this monster we dropped our tools and hurried down from the rock, put our camp kit in the canoe, and started down the river.

Evidence of the great spread of this story, and the remarkable credence placed in it may be seen in the fact that Indians as far distant as western Kansas heard of and conducted a search for the treasure. A group of Pottawattomies from this locality came east on a hunt for the treasure, but mistaking Buffalo Rock, due to false information and like appearance, for Starved Rock, wasted their time searching several miles east of the probable concealment of the gold. After much digging they, too, abandoned the search.

So the tale of Tonty's gold is set down as one of many legends. If the gold existed, it probably still remains in its original cache, perhaps on the very summit of Starved Rock, and mayhap with the passing of each year is closely trodden upon by thousands of unsuspecting feet. It may be there today—who knows?

The Treasure of the Devil's Punch Bowl

On the northern outskirts of Natchez on the Mississippi is a strange geographical phenomenon known as the Devil's Punch Bowl. It is a gigantic semi-circular depression in a bluff near the Mississippi River said to have been caused by a huge meteorite that fell on the bluff in prehistoric times. The pit covers several acres and resembles the crater of a long extinct volcano. This hole is credited with having been the rendezvous of various bands of pirates in days past, including the outlaw king, John A. Murrell. But what is remembered most is the fact that it was used as a banking place for ill-gotten treasures.

Strange accounts of scientific phenomena have brought anxious seekers from afar with picks and shovels. For instance, captains of ships passing by this point report that their compasses are greatly disturbed; sometimes they spin completely around. Some authorities say that this is because of an immense amount of iron that was sunk into the earth by the falling meteorite. Others, remembering the old tales of outlaw days, say that the instruments' antics are due to the presence in the crater of great pots containing gold and silver coins.

Legend has it that the great pirate, Sir Henry Morgan, first visited the place and stored a loot there nearly a hundred and fifty years before the time of Murrell, and writers have pointed out the place as one of Lafitte's banks. Many other outlaws in time made this haven their residence and secreting place. That one band of outlaws might have found the loots of

From *Reverend Devil*, A Biography of John A. Murrell, by Ross Phares, pp. 247–248. Copyright, 1941, by Ross Phares. New Orleans: Pelican Publishing Company.

their predecessors and carried them away seems not to appeal to the logic of the treasure seeker.

It is not likely that Murrell spent much time at the Bowl. That place was a retreat for river pirates who preyed upon the river traffic. After Morgan, there were never any great loots on the stream to be taken as was the case on the Gulf in the heyday of the Spanish conquests. Immigrants and traders from upstream formed the bulk of the traffic. . . .

De Soto's Casket

[During the 1937 flood at Memphis] it was Refugee S. A. Denison . . . who came to town with the most startling possession of all. He came rumbling across Harahan Bridge in an old truck loaded with a steel casket!

When Red Cross workers had recovered sufficiently from the shock to ask him what was the big idea—what he had in that casket—he let them have another wallop.

"Why, that's old Hernando De Soto."

Here's the story back of that strange announcement.

Refugee Denison, a now-and-then employee of the government's river engineering depot, lived in the swampland near West Memphis, Arkansas. Near by was an Indian mound on the bank of the river, and one hot day of the previous summer Mr. Denison's dog, Fluffy, had started scratching into the mound, trying to make a cool place in which to take a nap. She unearthed a part of a steel casket, and when Mr. Denison discovered it he unearthed more of it.

Near by was a rather rough, outdoor dance platform and beer stand, patronized by those who seek entertainment in out-of-the-way places. One night a small group of customers started discussing the old steel casket over their beer, and one member of the group said he'd bet that was De Soto in that coffin.

"De Soto died on the bank of the river along here somewhere," he said.

His friends weren't inclined to argue. Why, sure! Sure that was old Hernando De Soto. And let's drink one to the old boy.

That gave Mr. Denison an idea. He left the casket in its original position, but he excavated around it. Then he erected a canvas fence and started charging a dime admission, warning all hesitant prospective customers that after he proved conclusively that it was De Soto, there would be a substantial hike in prices. Through the glass window in the lid of the casket a part of the skeleton could be seen.

He did well. At all hours of the night folks from Memphis drove down

From *Memphis Bragabouts*, Characters I Have Met, by Eldon Roark, pp. 102–105. Copyright, 1945, by McGraw-Hill Book Company. New York and London: Whittlesey House.

the lonely swamp trail to drink beer and do a little dancing to juke-box music and to see De Soto and discuss history and archaeology.

Some skeptical customers wanted to know how De Soto happened to have a steel casket with him. Surely he hadn't lugged a thing like that on his long tortuous expedition from Florida, had he?

But the question didn't stump Mr. Denison. Some touring professor—Mr. Denison didn't remember the name—who had stopped to study the remains had assured him that it probably was De Soto. Yes, De Soto had carried not one steel casket but a couple, for just such an emergency as that which finally overtook him. He was a far-sighted man, De Soto was.

One Mississippi farmer was so impressed with Mr. Denison's rare possession and business that he offered to trade him his small farm for it, but Mr. Denison was then dreaming of big money from "De Soto's farewell tour of America," and refused.

Anyway, when the flood waters came rolling toward the mound, Mr. Denison didn't lose any time deciding what he should load into the truck. He grabbed De Soto. To hell with everything else.

The Red Cross put Mr. Denison and his casket in a vacant store building down in an industrial section of the city, along with a group of other refugees, and Mr. Denison stayed right there with De Soto—slept beside him—for he wasn't taking any chances on something's happening to old Hernando.

No attempt was made to revive the swamp beer business after the flood waters receded; for customers couldn't go through a sea of mud, and Mr. Denison had to find a new place in which to exhibit his historical skeleton. Besides, he was ready for a shot at bigger money.

So he rented space in a vacant building on South Main Street here in Memphis and opened up. "See the discovery of the century! See Hernando De Soto himself—in person!"

And then Mr. Denison made another amazing discovery. He found that the people bustling by on a busy city street weren't nearly so interested in history and archeology—in culture and the finer things of life—as those who sat and laughed and drank beer in eerie swamp shadows on an Indian mound at midnight. The venture was a complete bust.

De Soto was finally placed in storage, and there he slept several years, with his room rent mounting all the time. And then, because of that and because during his expansion program, Mr. Denison had taken in a business partner, De Soto's rest was disturbed by a lawsuit. As a result, title to the old fellow passed to some Northern exhibitor, and I think De Soto was taken on tour. I haven't any idea where he is today. Probably he has retired to his well-earned rest.

The Zombi of Bayou Teche

Long ago when the lions, the elephants, the tigers, and all this kind of vermin, lived on the banks of the Grand Lac, there was a woman who lived with her daughter on the banks of Bayou Teche. Her daughter had a lover who came to see her every day, but the mother did not wish any one to come to see her daughter, because she was afraid that some one would marry her and take her very far away where she would not be able to see her any more.

One day the neighbors would tell the old woman: "We have seen your daughter with a lion in the wood behind the house," or, another day they would tell her: "How is it that your daughter walks about with a tiger without the tiger eating her?" Other persons would say: "But your daughter is not one of God's creatures,[1] and I saw her in the wood with a wild cat."

The mother, at last, asked her daughter if it was the truth that was being said. The daughter, naturally, said that it was a lie, but the mother began to watch her and she saw that it was the truth, that her daughter was in the habit of associating with the wild beasts, without their doing her any harm. Then she said to herself: "They must be tame beasts, for my daughter feeds them without their doing her any harm, and she does not want to tell me so because she is afraid that I will prevent her from seeing them."

The mother was glad to see the kind heart of her daughter, and, as she had some supper remaining, she went out to feed the beasts. She went to a lion which ran after her, and which would have eaten her up, if she had not closed her gate. After that the old woman could not put her foot out of her house without a beast coming to run after her.

The poor old woman was half crazy, she was so much afraid, and she did not know what to do. One day she saw a little bird which told her that the animals would continue to be good to her daughter and bad to her, if she did not let her daughter marry the young man whom she loved. You may imagine that, in order to make the wild beasts go away, she said yes, and there was a grand wedding, where I danced a great deal, although I was only two years old, and now I am more than one hundred years old.

But how angry the mother was when she heard it was her son-in-law who changed himself into good beasts for her daughter and into bad

As told in the Creole dialect by Edmée Dorsin, St. Mary Parish, Louisiana. From "Four Louisiana Folk-Tales," by Alcée Fortier, *The Journal of American Folk-Lore,* Vol. XIX (April-June, 1906), No. LXXIII, pp. 125–126. Copyright, 1906, by The American Folk-Lore Society. Boston and New York: Houghton, Mifflin and Company.

[1] An insane girl.—A.F.

beasts for her. But she was so much afraid of him that she did not dare to say anything. Fortunately that man is now dead, and he was the last zombi [wizard] around here.

The Zombi of Batture du Diable

On the charts of the River pilots it is Devil Flats, but the natives call it Batture du Diable. A vagary of the great Mississippi shoaled the water there with a heavy deposit of silt, and grounded the ships of unwary up-stream navigators who ventured in to escape the swift outside current.

No one knew how the Zombi first came to choose the Batture as a walking place. It was refreshing there under the luxuriant willows, and it was a nice promenade along the top of the levee from his grave below the Old Fort. He chose the most interesting part of the day to commence this: at nightfall, when smoke curled from the chimneys of the houses in preparation of supper, when the men streamed in from the fields, and cattle from the marsh to the smudges that had been lighted for their comfort, and when the greediest of the chickens lingered to pick a few more grains before going to roost. The Zombi was a pathetic figure, pausing to turn the head that he carried under an arm so that the eyes would enjoy the peaceful scene.

From the beginning there was perfect understanding between him and the people on that side of the River. He passed up at the close of day; later, when they were in bed, he passed down again. The ones on the west bank, however, had a sickening fear of him. This didn't bother the old folks, but seriously inconvenienced the young men who went courting over there, where desirable girls lived, girls with well-off papas who had provided them with comfortable *dots*. But, then, he was not an ordinary whatever-you-might-want-to-call-him. Old-timers, who had been in places where such things are common, said that he was a zombi, and the younger people accepted this ruling.

A classic zombi, such as may be seen on certain islands in the Caribbean, is a person who has died, and whose soul has gone on beyond. A voodoo bocor [1] recalled the body from death and the grave to work as a slave, or to go on and on in subtle, sinister punishment or revenge.

The people of that part of the parish knew so much because a sublimated version of the vile cult remained among them from other and unhappy days. Even now it exists in a still more attenuated form. But it will pass with the years, as such things do.

From *Creole Folk Tales,* Stories of the Louisiana Marsh Country, by Hewitt L. Ballowe, pp. 82–85. Copyright, 1948, by Louisiana State University Press, Baton Rouge.
[1] Priest.

In a heartbreaking odyssey, torn from their homes, scattered to the four winds, some shiploads of Acadians had been dumped upon the beaches of the black islands. There they had remained in unspeakable wretchedness, scorned and despised by the natives, until, in little groups, they trickled as if through a homing instinct into Louisiana. They fanned out into the marsh, where nature gave bountifully. In this more favorable environment they discarded the viler aspects of a cult in which they had become steeped, but retained with childish naïveté what would be of service to them in warding off unseen terrors that lurked around them, the diseases and hurts where there was no help at hand, the deviltries of mean-hearted people.

They could appreciate how wonderful the Zombi of the Batture was. What magic, the old folks used to say, what power, that could make a zombi out of a man who had his head cut off. The people of today don't know anything about that, but they marvel at the flesh staying on his bones a hundred years and at the soldier's uniform that is as bright as the day he put it on.

The Zombi had been a British soldier. When the flower of the British army waded through the marsh to attack New Orleans, and Jackson's men mowed them down at Chalmette until the survivors fled in wild disorder, a British fleet started up the River to co-operate. It never arrived, although history makes scant mention of the two little forts that held them off for five days until the ships gave up the attempt to pass. Instead, they buried their dead on the bank and stole away to sea again.

It is known that there were several companies of free men of color in the defense of the forts. Many of these men had come from the fruit islands; also, many of the English soldiers had seen service down there. Everything is crystal clear if you give rein to your imagination. What horrible crime had called for so terrible a retribution? The prince of *sorciers* had inflicted it, and hadn't bothered to return the head, severed by a chain shot, to its shoulders. The time when that happened wasn't yesterday. A weary expiation!

A zombi is flesh and blood; flesh, at least. This one is real. Remy, in drunken braggadocio, walked up and offered his bottle. The Zombi hauled off with his disengaged arm and gave him a *soufflet* [2] on the side of his jaw that left a print of fingers which persisted for weeks.

Revenants [3] and *esprits* [4] have shadowy shape but no substance. There are many theories as to how to lay them. If one offers a pinch of salt to a zombi, and it is accepted, the wretched thing goes back to eternal rest in the grave. More than one person has asked why, *pour l'amour du bon Dieu*, none has been offered in this case. The questioner receives a pitying stare. Who, in his or her good senses, would get that close? . . .

[2] Slap.
[3] Ghosts.
[4] Spirits.

The Piasa

I. In the Descriptions by French Explorers [1]

. . . Marquette says (see his *Discoveries of the Mississippi*, published in Paris in 1681):

We here met from time to time numberless fish which struck so violently against our canoes that at first we took them to be large trees which threatened to upset us. . . . As we were descending the river we saw high rocks with hideous monsters painted on them and upon which the bravest Indian dare not look. They are as large as a calf, with head and horns like a goat, their eyes are red, beard like a tiger's and a face like a man's. Their tails are so long that they pass over their bodies and between their legs, under their bodies, ending like a fish's tail. They are painted red, green, and black, and so well drawn that I could not believe they were drawn by the Indians, and for what purpose they were drawn seems to me a mystery.

Again he says:

Passing the mouth of the Illinois we soon fell into the shadow of a tall promontory, and with great astonishment beheld the representations of two monsters painted on its lofty limestone front. Each of these frightful figures had the face of a man, the horns of a deer, the beard of a tiger, and the tail of a fish, so long that it passed around the body, over the head and between the legs. It was an object of Indian worship, and greatly impressed me with the necessity of substituting for this monstrous idolatry the true God.

Father Hennepin, another early explorer of the wilds of the West, [who] published a small volume in 1698 entitled, *A New Discovery of a Vast Country in America,* which he dedicated to William III, King of Great Britain, says, pages 168 to 170:

This made our voyage the more easie, for our men landed several times to kill some Fowl and other Game with which the Banks of the Mischasipi are plentifully stocked; however, before we came to the River Illinois we discovered Messorites who came down along the River, but as they had no Pyrogues with them we crossed to the other side, and to avoid any surprise during the night we made no fire and thereby the Savages could not discover whereabouts we were, for doubtless they would have murthered us, thinking we were their enemies.

I had quite forgot to relate that the Illinois had told us that towards the Cape which I have called in my map St. Anthony, near the nation of the Messorites, there were some Tritons and other Sea Monsters painted which the boldest Men durst not look upon, there being some Inchantment in their face. I thought this was a story, but when we came near the place they had mentioned we saw instead of these Monsters a Horse and some other Beasts painted upon the Rock with Red Colors by the Savages. The Illinois had told us likewise that the rock on which these dreadful Monsters stood was so steep that no man could climb up to it, but had we not been afraid of the Savages more than of the

[1] From *The Piasa,* or, The Devil among the Indians, by Hon. P. A. Armstrong, pp. 9–12. Morris, Illinois: E. B. Fletcher. 1887.

Monsters we had certainly got up to them. There is a common Tradition among the people that a great number of Miamis were drowned in that place, being pursued by the Savages of Matsegamie, and since that time the Savages going by the Rock use to smoak and offer Tobacco to these Beasts to appease, as they say, the Manitou, that is, in the language of the Algonquins and Accadians, an Evil Spirit, which the Iroquois call Okton, but the Name is the only thing they know of him. While I was at Quebec I understood M. Jolliet had been upon the Mischasipi and obliged to return without going down the River because of the Monsters I have spoken of who had frighted him, as also because he was afraid to be taken by the Spaniards, and having an opportunity to know the truth of that Storey from M. Jolliet himself, with whom I had often traveled upon the River St. Lawrence, I asked him whether he had been as far as the Arkansas. That Gentleman answered me that the Outtaouats had often spoken to him of these Monsters, but that he had never gone further than the Hurons and the Outtaouats, with whom he had remained to exchange our companie's Commodities with their Furs. He added that the Savages had told him that it was not safe to go down the River because of the Spaniards. But notwithstanding this Report I have found nowhere upon the River any mark as crosses and the like that could persuade me that the Spaniards had been there, and the Savages inhabiting the Mischasipi would not have expressed such admiration as they did when they saw us if they had seen Europeans before. . . .

* * * * *

Two immensely large petroglyphs of a monster—or more properly speaking, monsters, for they do not appear to have been alike, though substantially so . . . were found, first incised or cut upon a layer of bluish gray sandstone overlying a bed of limestone on the north bank of the Mississippi, immediately where the Illinois State Prison was built at Alton, Illinois, which were quite distinct when that locality was first settled by the white people, and traces of their outlines remained until the rock whereon they were delineated was quarried by the convicts of the penitentiary as late as about the year 1856. From the mouth of the Illinois River at Grafton to Alton, Illinois, a distance of twenty miles, the Mississippi River runs from west to east, and its north bank or Illinois side is a high bluff, the highest point being the eastern end. This bluff is but a continuous perpendicular strata of limestone, ranging from forty to fifty feet high, with a layer of bluish gray fine grit sandstone, about twenty feet deep, lying on the top or over the limestone, and upon this sandstone, at an elevation of some eighty feet above the base of this ledge of rocks and the river's surface, these monsters were incised and afterwards painted. They were about of equal size and measured thirty feet in length by twelve feet in height. From their hideous shape and size they were a mortal terror to all the Indian nations of the then northwest. Each nation had one or more traditions connected therewith, some calling them *The Piasa*, others called them *The Piusa*. In painting these monsters but three colors were used—red, emblematic of war and vengeance; black, symbolic of death and despair; and green, expressive of hope and triumph over death in the land of dreams, beneath, beyond the evening star, where they located their happy hunting grounds.

II. In the Illini Tradition [2]

. . . The tradition of the Piasa [writes Prof. John Russell, of Jersey County, Illinois [3]] is still current among all the tribes of the Upper Mississippi, and those who have inhabited the valley of the Illinois, and is briefly this:

Many thousand moons before the arrival of the pale-faces, when the great Magalonyx and Mastodon, whose bones are now dug up, were still living in the land of the green prairies, there existed a bird of such dimensions that he could easily carry off in his talons a full grown deer. Having obtained a taste of human flesh, from that time he would prey upon nothing else. He was artful as he was powerful, and would dart suddenly and unexpectedly upon an Indian, bear him off into one of the caves of the bluff and devour him. Hundreds of warriors attempted for years to destroy him, but without success. Whole villages were nearly depopulated, and consternation spread through all the tribes of the Illini. At length Ouatogo [Waw-to'-go], a chief whose fame extended even beyond the Great Lakes, separating himself from the rest of his tribe, fasted in solitude for the space of the whole moon and prayed to the Great Spirit, the Master of Life, that he would protect his children from the Piasa. On the last night of his fast the Great Spirit appeared to Ouatogo in a dream, and directed him to select twenty of his warriors, each armed with a bow and poisoned arrow, and conceal them in a designated spot. Near the place of their concealment another warrior was to stand in open view as a victim for the Piasa, which they must shoot the instant that he pounced upon his prey. When the chief awoke the next morning he thanked the Great Spirit, and returning to his tribe, told them the dream. The warriors were quickly selected and placed in ambush as directed. Ouatogo offered himself as the victim. He was willing to die for his tribe. Placing himself in open view of the bluff, he soon saw the Piasa perched on the cliff, eyeing his prey. Ouatogo drew up his manly form to its utmost height; planting his feet firmly upon the earth, he began to chant the death song of an Indian warrior. A moment after, the Piasa arose into the air and swift as the thunderbolt darted down upon the chief. Scarcely had he reached his victim when every bow was sprung and every arrow sent to the feather into his body. The Piasa uttered a wild, fearful scream that resounded far over the opposite side of the river, and expired. Ouatogo was safe. Not an arrow, not even the talons of the bird had touched him. The Master of Life, in admiration of the generous deed of Ouatogo, had held over him an invisible shield. In memory of this event the image of the Piasa was engraven on the face of the bluff.

III. In the Miami Tradition [4]

Many thousand moons before the coming of the white man, in the caves of the Piasa bluffs lived two monsters with wings of an eagle, only much

[2] *Ibid.,* pp. 29–30.

[3] *The Evangelical Magazine and Gospel Advocate,* Utica, New York, July, 1848, reprinted in *Mumford's Magazine,* Chicago, 1887.

[4] From "The Significance of the Piasa," by Clara Kern Bayliss, *Transactions of the Illinois State Historical Society for the Year 1908,* Ninth Annual Meeting of the Society, Springfield, Ill., January 30–31, 1908, pp. 115–116. Publication Number Thirteen of the Illinois State Library. Springfield. 1909.

larger, and with claws of an alligator. . . . They spent the greater part of their time resting and dozing on the rocks or flying over the country. The voice of one was like the roaring of a buffalo bull; of the other, like the scream of a panther. They swooped down and carried off young deer and elk, which they bore to their cavern home to devour at their leisure. But they never molested the Indians until one morning when the Miamis and Mestchegamis met in battle array in the Piasa canyon to do each other to death. In the midst of the carnage, just when the Mestchegamis were wavering and about to fly, these two horrible monsters came flying down the canyon uttering bellowings and shrieks, while the flapping of their wings roared on like so many thunder claps. Passing close over the heads of the combatants, each picked up a Miami chieftain and bore him, struggling, aloft, leaving the tribe terrified and demoralized.

The Mestchegamis, thinking the Great Spirit had sent the monsters to aid them against their enemies, gave a great war whoop and renewed the battle, which now became a rout and a massacre. The Miamis fled across the country and dared not stop until they had crossed the Wabash River.

Long after, when they had helped to nearly exterminate the Mestchegamis at Starved Rock, they visited the scene of their ancient defeat, and there on the rocks were the petroglyphs of the monsters.

PART NINE

Where the Blues Begin

Introduction

For travelers on the river boats the singing of Negro rousters—deckhands and stevedores—was one of the most picturesque and entertaining features of the romance of the rivers. For the boatmen themselves, as for sailors and voyageurs, boat songs were, like any other work songs, "an incentive to steadier and better labor." In the case of "Sam Marshall's Song," a Negro fireman was paid extra wages to sing to attract custom at the landings. Besides possessing a voice of "rare sweetness and power," as George Byron Merrick tells us in *Old Times on the Upper Mississippi*, "Sam was a born *improvisatore*." And as he stood on the capstanhead, with his chorus gathered about him, he would line out his improvised stanzas praising the "speed and elegance of this particular boat, the suavity and skill of its captain, the dexterity of its pilot, the manfulness of its mate, and the loveliness of Chloe, its black chambermaid."

In slavery days, as we read in *Slave Songs of the United States* (1867), boat songs were a carry-over from shouts or religious dances (parodied in the "walk-around" of the minstrel shows), the same songs being used for rowing as for shouting. The explanation is that the words didn't much matter, the main thing being the rhythm and especially (as H. E. Krehbiel notes) the "peculiarly propulsive rhythmical snap, or catch, which has several times been described as the basis of 'ragtime.'" It was this snap that made almost any words adaptable to rowing and to roustabouting, from the repeated vocables "O-hi-o," chanted by one keelboatman to the others pushing on the poles (a chant which John Habermehl curiously assumes to be the origin of the name of the river), to the chanted directions of roustabout hollers or the declarative statements of levee hollers.

It is easy to see how simple instructions spoken by a mate or driver can become the basis of a chant. For example, the mate heard by J. T. Trowbridge during wooding-up, iterating with horrible crescendo, "Get along, *get along!* Out o' the way 'th that wood! *out o' the way,* OUT O' THE WAY! OUT O' THE WAY! Git on, GIT ON, GIT ON!" Or the straw boss calling to Negroes unloading fertilizer from "Mistuh Pickens' boat," as reported by Richard Amerson of Livingston, Alabama, to John A. Lomax:

> Go git yo' sack!
> Whoa back, buddy, whoa back!
> I gotta coat here to fit yo' back!

The stevedore's jerky trot or waddling run across the gangplank, with as much side as forward motion, became known as "coonjining," and from the movement the word came to be applied to the jingles sung by the workers. In *John Henry*, Roark Bradford humorously relates the word

556

"coonjine" (of unknown origin) to the driver's commands, "Hey . . . jine dat step. Roll yo' cotton, but jine dat tread!" "Jine it, you coon, jine it! Grab your cotton and jine dat step!" It is possible that the word is related to *counjai* or *counjaille,* the name of an Antillean dance, and through it to *Koundjo,* an African dance with drums (in the West Indies, *Candio* or *Candjo*).

But whatever the origins of Negro roustabout and levee hollers, their idiom passed naturally into the dance rhythms of minstrel songs and the earthy moans and hollers of the blues. As bookkeeper for his brother Dunning's Cincinnati firm of Irwin & Foster, steamboat agents and commission merchants, Stephen Foster had an opportunity to hear levee songs and "water music" of the kind reported by Lafcadio Hearn in the Cincinnati *Commercial* and echoed in Foster's *"Glendy Burk":*

> Ho! for Lou'siana!
> I'm bound to leabe dis town;
> I'll take my duds and tote 'em on my back
> When de *Glendy Burk* comes down.

"Negroes sang about everything," as W. C. Handy learned in the Mississippi Delta from (among others) the roustabouts who came to Clarksdale in the evenings and on days-off from the river eighteen miles away. And into their river songs the singers put everything from their admiration for boats that raced or burned to their troubles with bosses, bullies and women.

During the 1937 flood "rivergees" at the Memphis fairgrounds sang the "High-Water Blues":

> Down at the Fairgrounds on my knees,
> Prayin' to the Lord to give me ease—
> Lord, Lord, I got them high-water blues!

And when Boss Ed Crump turned up in high-topped boots they quipped:

> Oh, the river's up and cotton's down,
> Mister Ed Crump, he runs this town.

In December, 1954, at the age of 81, blind and ill, W. C. Handy returned to Memphis, where he and the blues began, to appear at the sixteenth annual Blues Bowl Game at Melrose Stadium. Earlier in the day he led a parade of high-school bands and marching Elks from Court Square down Main and to Handy Park on Beale. There, disregarding his doctor's orders, he "drew from beneath his overcoat his golden trumpet. And then he blew one last time the silver notes." One last time, the doctors and the newsmen may have thought. But not so Handy. "I'll be back next year," he said, "and for many more years to come."

B. A. B.

The Story of "On the Banks of the Wabash"

... "On the Banks of the Wabash" ... came eventually to be adopted by [my brother Paul Dresser's] native State as its State song, and in that region streets and a town were named after him. In an almost unintentional and unthinking way I had a hand in that, and it has always cheered me to think that I had, although I have never had the least talent for musical composition or song versification. It was one of those delightful summer Sunday mornings (1896, I believe), when I was still connected with his firm as editor of the little monthly they were issuing, and he and myself living with my sister E——, that we had gone over to his office to do a little work. I had a number of current magazines I wished to examine; he was always wishing to compose something, to express that ebullient and emotional soul of his in some way.

"What do you suppose would make a good song these days?" he asked in an idle, meditative mood, sitting at the piano and thrumming while I at a nearby table was looking over my papers. "Why don't you give me an idea for one once in a while, sport? You ought to be able to suggest something."

"Me?" I inquired, almost contemptuously, I suppose. I could be very lofty at times in regard to his work, much as I admired him—vain and yet more or less dependent snip that I was. "I can't write those things. Why don't you write something about a State or a river? Look at 'My Old Kentucky Home,' 'Dixie,' 'Old Black Joe'—why don't you do something like that, something that suggests a part of America? People like that. Take Indiana—what's the matter with it—the Wabash River? It's as good as any other river, and you were 'raised' beside it."

I have to smile even now as I recall the apparent zest or feeling with which all at once he seized on this. It seemed to appeal to him immensely. "That's not a bad idea," he agreed, "but how would you go about it? Why don't you write the words and let me put the music to them? We'll do it together!"

"But I can't," I replied. "I don't know how to do those things. You write it. I'll help—maybe."

After a little urging—I think the fineness of the morning had as much to do with it as anything—I took a piece of paper and after meditating a while scribbled in the most tentative manner imaginable the first verse and chorus of that song almost as it was published. I think one or two lines were too long or didn't rhyme, but eventually either he or I hammered them into shape, but before that I rather shamefacedly turned them over to him, for somehow I was convinced that this work was not

From "My Brother Paul," in *Twelve Men,* by Theodore Dreiser, pp. 99–102. Copyright, 1919, by Boni & Liveright, Inc.; 1926, by Theodore Dreiser. New York.

for me and that I was rather loftily and cynically attempting what my good brother would do in all faith and feeling.

He read it, insisted that it was fine, and that I should do a second verse, something with a story in it, a girl perhaps—a task which I solemnly rejected.

"No, you put it in. It's yours. I'm through."

Some time later, disagreeing with the firm as to the conduct of the magazine, I left—really was forced out—which raised a little feeling on my part; not on his, I am sure, for I was very difficult to deal with.

Time passed and I heard nothing. I had been able to succeed in a somewhat different realm, that of the magazine contributor, and although I thought a great deal of my brother, I paid very little attention to him or his affairs, being much more concerned with my own. One spring night, however, the following year, as I was lying in my bed trying to sleep, I heard a quartette of boys in the distance approaching along the street in which I had my room. I could not make out the words at first but the melody at once attracted my attention. It was plaintive and compelling. I listened, attracted, satisfied that it was some new popular success that had "caught on." As they drew near my window I heard the words "On the Banks of the Wabash" most mellifluously harmonized.

I jumped up. They were my words! It was Paul's song! He had another "hit" then—"On the Banks of the Wabash," and they were singing it in the streets already! I leaned out of the window and listened as they approached, the whole song being sung in the still street, as it were, for my benefit. The night was so warm, delicious. A full moon was overhead. I was young, lonely, wistful. It brought back so much of my already spent youth that I was ready to cry—for joy principally. In three more months it was everywhere, in the papers, on the stage, on the street-organs, played by orchestras, bands, whistled and sung in the streets. . . .

The Battle of New Orleans

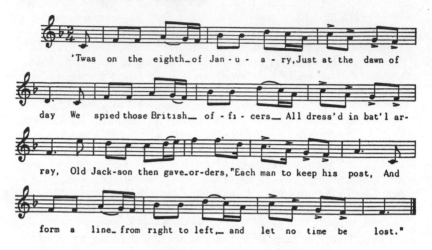

'Twas on the eighth of Jan-u-a-ry, Just at the dawn of day We spied those British of-fi-cers All dress'd in bat'l ar-ray, Old Jack-son then gave or-ders, "Each man to keep his post, And form a line from right to left, and let no time be lost."

With rockets and with bombshells, like comets we let fly;
Like lions they advanced [on] us, the fate of war to try.
Large streams of fiery vengeance upon them we let pour
While many a brave commander lay withering in his gore.

Thrice they marched up to the charge, and thrice they gave the ground;
We fought them full three hours, then bugle horns did sound.
Great heaps of human pyramids lay strewn before our eyes;
We blew the horns and rang the bells to drown their dying cries.

Come all you British noblemen, and listen unto me;
Our frontiersmen has proved to you America is free.
But tell your royal master when you return back home
That out of thirty thousand men but few of you returned.

From " 'The Battle of New Orleans,' " by Paul G. Brewster, *Southern Folklore Quarterly,* Vol. I (September, 1937), No. 3, pp. 25–27. Gainesville, Florida: The University of Florida in Cooperation with the Southeastern Folklore Society.

The contributor, Mr. Martin G. Fowler, of Petersburg [Indiana], wrote to me on May 12, 1935: "I have an Old Song, as unique as any you may receive . . . 'Battle of New Orleans,' *composed and sung, by the soldiers who fought the battle,* Jan. 8th, 1815. Was sung at home over one hundred years ago, by thousand American volunteer soldiers, but I don't think it was ever printed in book, not even in newspapers. My Grand-father, Thomas Fowler, who was a captain under General Andrew Jackson, and fought in that great Battle, come home and years afterwards sung the song to his children and grand-children. I learned the song orally from my father [Abner N. Fowler] and coppied it down—words and music . . . when very young."
—P.G.B

El-a-noy

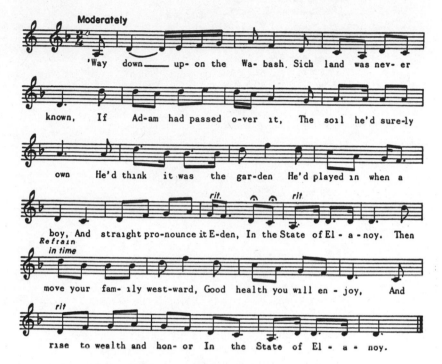

'Way down up-on the Wa-bash. Sich land was nev-er known, If Ad-am had passed o-ver it, The soil he'd sure-ly own He'd think it was the gar-den He'd played in when a boy, And straight pro-nounce it E-den, In the State of El - a - noy. Then move your fam- ily west-ward, Good health you will en - joy, And rise to wealth and hon- or In the State of El - a - noy.

'Twas here the Queen of Sheba came
  With Solomon of old,
With an assload of spices,
  Pomegranates and fine gold;
And when she saw this lovely land,
  Her heart was filled with joy,
Straightway she said, "I'd like to be
  A Queen in El-a-noy."

She's bounded by the Wabash,
  The Ohio and the Lakes,
She's crawfish in the swampy lands,
  The milk-sick and the shakes;

From *The American Songbag*, by Carl Sandburg, pp. 162–163. Copyright, 1927, by Harcourt, Brace & Company, Inc. New York.

John D. Black, a Chicago attorney-at-law, lived on the Ohio River as a boy and heard his father sing "El-a-noy." Shawnee Ferry was a crossing point for many who had come by the Ohio River route or on Wilderness Road through Cumberland Gap, headed for Illinois. The fourth verse is probably a later addition thrown in by some joker who felt challenged by the preceding verses.—C.S.

But these are slight diversions
  And take not from the joy
Of living in this garden land,
  The State of El-a-noy.

Away up in the northward,
  Right on the border line,
A great commercial city,
  Chicago, you will find.
Her men are all like Abelard,
  Her women like Heloise [rhymes with "boys"];
All honest, virtuous people,
  For they live in El-a-noy.

Last chorus:

  Then move your fam'ly westward,
    Bring all your girls and boys,
  And cross at Shawnee Ferry
    To the State of El-a-noy.

We'll Hunt the Buffalo!

Moderato

1. Come all you brisk young fellows, who have a mind to roam Unto some for-eign coun-try, a long way from home, Unto some for-eign coun-try a-long with me to go, And we'll
set-tle on the banks of the love-ly O-hi-o.

Chorus
Slower   Lively
Sweet and sha-dy groves' Thro' the wild woods we'll wan-der and we'll
hunt the Buf-fa-lo, And we'll hunt the Buf-fa-lo, Thro' the
wild woods we'll wan-der, and we'll hunt the Buf-fa-lo.

Come, all ye pretty fair maids, and spin us some yarn
To make us some nice clothing, to keep ourselves warm;
For you can knit and sew, my loves, while we do reap and mow,
When we settle on the banks of the lovely Ohio.

There are fishes in the river just fitted for our use;
There's tall and lofty sugar cane that yields us some juice;
There is all kind of game, my boys, beside the buck and doe,
When we settle on the banks of the lovely Ohio.

From *Songs of Yesterday*, A Song Anthology of American Life, by Philip D. Jordan and Lillian Kessler, pp. 305–307. Copyright, 1941, by Philip D. Jordan and Lillian Kessler, Garden City, New York: Doubleday, Doran & Co., Inc.
Words by F. M. Arranged by A. Reiff.
For Oklahoma play-party versions, see "Shoot the Buffalo," B. A. Botkin, *The American Play-Party Song* (Lincoln, Nebraska, 1937), pp. 308–312.

If ever those wild Indians do unto us come nigh,
We will all unite together, lads, to conquer or to die;
We will march into their tents, boys, and strike the deadly blow,
When we settle on the banks of the lovely Ohio.

Down the River

I [1]

PLAY-PARTY VERSION

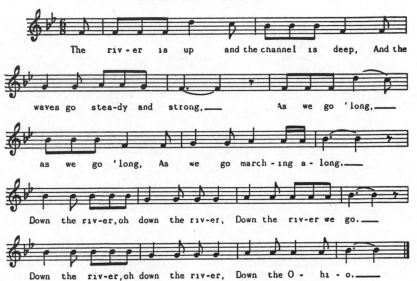

The riv-er is up and the channel is deep, And the
waves go stea-dy and strong,— As we go 'long,—
as we go 'long, As we go march-ing a-long.—
Down the riv-er, oh down the riv-er, Down the riv-er we go.—
Down the riv-er, oh down the riv-er, Down the O - hi - o.—

Longways dance for three or more couples.

All form in two lines, boys in one and girls in the other, with partners facing. The first boy and the last girl walk to the center, swing, retire, and then swing the player next on his (or her) partner's left. Repeat until the first boy has swung all of the girls and the last girl all of the boys. Both return to their original positions. The first couple meet and promenade down the center, taking position at the bottom of their respective lines.

Repeat from the beginning and continue repeating until all of the players are in their original relative positions.

---

[1] From *The Play-Party in Indiana*, A Collection of Folk-Songs and Games with Descriptive Introduction and Correlating Notes, by Leah Jackson Wolford, pp. 40–41. Indiana Historical Collections (Vol. 3). Copyright, 1916, by the Indiana Historical Commission. Indianapolis.

Tune from A. W. Mason, Columbus, Indiana. Words from R. W. Stone, Jay County, and game from John Underwood, Brown Township.

II [2]

ORIGINAL VERSION

Oh! the river is up and the channel is deep,
  And the wind blows steady and strong.
Let the splash of your oars the measure keep,
  As we row the old boat along.
Oh! the water is bright, and flashing like gold,
  In the ray of the morning sun.
And old Dinah's away up out of the cold,
  A-getting the hoe-cake done.
Oh! the river is up and the channel is deep,
  And the wind blows steady and strong.
Let the splash of your oars the measure keep
  As we row the old boat along.

Chorus:

  Down the river, down the river,
    Down the Ohio;
  Down the river, down the river,
    Down the Ohio.

Oh! the master is proud of the old broad-horn,
  For it brings him plenty of tin.
Oh! the crew they are darkies, the cargo is corn,
  And the money comes tumbling in.
There is plenty on board for the darkies to eat,
  And there's something to drink and to smoke,
There's the banjo, the bones, and the tambourine—
  There's the song, and the comical joke.
Oh! the river is up, etc.

[2] American Broadside Collection, New York Public Library, Music Division. A. W. Auner, Song Publisher and Printer. Philadelphia, Pennsylvania.

De Boatman Dance

De boatman dance, de boatman sing, De boatman up to
eb'-ry ting; And when de boat-man get on shore,
He spends his cash and works for__ more. Dance, de boat-man,
dance, O dance, de boat-man, dance, O dance all night. 'till
broad day light, And go home wid de gals in de morn-ing.
Hi ho, de Boatman row, Floating down de rib-er on de O-hi-o.
Hi ho, de Boatman row, Floating down de rib-er on de O-hi-o.

De boatman is a thrifty man,
Da is none can do as de boatman can;
I neber see a pretty girl in all my life
But dat she be some boatman's wife.
Dance, etc.

[De oyster boat should keep to de shore,
De fishin' smack should venture more.
De schooner sails before de wind,
De steamboat leaves a streak behind.

By Daniel Decatur Emmett.
From *Minstrel Songs, Old and New*, A Collection of World-Wide, Famous Minstrel and Plantation Songs, Including the Most Popular of the Celebrated Foster Melodies, Arranged with Piano-Forte Accompaniment, pp. 146–147. Entered . . . 1851, by Firth, Pond & Co. Copyright, 1879, by Mrs. S. C. Foster and Mrs. Marion Foster Welch; 1882, by Oliver Ditson & Co. Boston.
As sung by the Ethiopian Serenaders.

I went on board de odder day
To see what de boatman had to say;
An' dar I let my passion loose,
An' dey cram me in de calaboose.

I've come dis time, I'll come no more,
Let me loose, I'll go ashore;
For dey whole hoss, an' dey a bully crew
Wid a hoosier mate an' a captain too.] [1]

When you go to de boatman's ball,
Dance wid my wife or not at all;
Sky-blue jacket an' tarpaulin hat,
Look out, my boys, for de nine tail cat.

When de boatman blows his horn,
Look out, old man, your hog is gone;
He steal my sheep, he cotch my shoat,
Den put 'em in bag and tote 'em to boat.

Push Boat

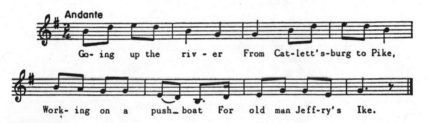

Going up the river From Catlett's-burg to Pike,
Working on a push boat For old man Jeffry's Ike.

---

[1] *Heart Songs* (New York, 1909), pp. 76–77.

From *Ballad Makin' in the Mountains of Kentucky,* by Jean Thomas, with Music Arranged by Walter Kob, pp. 35–38. Copyright, 1939, by Henry Holt and Company, Inc. New York.

. . . The Big Sandy River, a stream in the northeastern part of Kentucky, . . . is formed by small tributaries and eventually flows into the Ohio at Catlettsburg, Boyd County.

Collected on George's Creek from the singing of Little Robin, "Old Robin's push-boat ditty" belonged to Lady Elisabeth's grandfather Robin, who "plied the waters of the Big Sandy many a year before steamboats came into this country. . . . 'It was a mighty task,' observed Lady Elisabeth, 'for men to steer the boat with a long pole fashioned like a paddle, pushing against the bank to keep their craft in the stream. Full of danger, it was—when there was a master tide. But the Preston race never feared the waters, no matter how they raged. . . . You noticed in this ditty the name of "Jeffy" . . . that stands for Thomas Jefferson Preston, who in his lifetime owned and run a push boat on the Big Sandy River. That was the only way then to take sorghum and ginseng and such to swap in the settlement. "Jeffy" was the father of Ike Preston, my near kin, and the settlement he made mention of, Catlettsburg, is a nigh piece from where the Big Sandy jines the Ohio River. And Buffalo, that's the name of the creek that helps swell the Sandy. . . .' "—J.T., *ibid.,* pp. 35, 37–38.

Working on a push boat
    For fifty cents a day;
Buy my girl a brand-new dress
    And throw the rest away.

Working on a push boat,
    Water's mighty slack;
Taking sorghum 'lasses down
    And bringing sugar back.

Pushing mighty hard, boys,
    Sandbar's in the way;
Working like a son-of-a-gun
    For mighty scanty pay.

Going down Big Sandy
    With Pete and Lazy Sam;
When I get to Catlettsburg,
    I'll buy myself a dram.

Going down the river,
    I live in Buffalo;
Lordy, lordy, Cynthie Jane,
    Don't I hate to go.

I wish I had a nickel,
    I wish I had a dime;
I'd spend it all on Cynthie Jane
    And dress her mighty fine.

The weather's mighty hot, boys,
    Blisters on my feet;
Working on my push boat
    To buy my bread and meat.

Working on a push boat,
    Working in the rain;
When I get to Catlettsburg,
    Good-bye, Cynthie Jane!

Levee Camp Holler

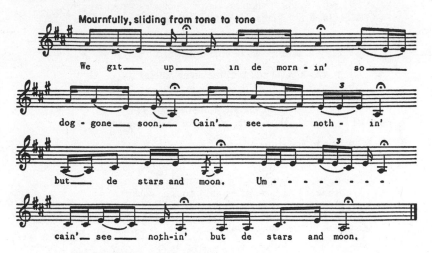

Mournfully, sliding from tone to tone

We git___ up___ in de morn - in' so___ dog - gone___ soon,___ Cain'___ see___ noth - in' but___ de stars and moon. Um - - - - - - - cain'___ see ___ noth-in' but de stars and moon.

> I looked all over de whole corral,
> An' I couldn' fin' a mule wid his shoulder well,
>> Um-m, etc.

> Runnin' all aroun' de whole corral, Lawdy-Lawdy-Lawd,
> Tryin' to git de harness on Queen an' Sal.

> Way down on de river an' I couldn' see,
> Couldn' hear nothin', Lawdy-Lawd, but "Whoa-haw-gee."

> "Cap'n, cap'n, ol' Nell is sick."
> "God damn ol' Nell, put de harness on Dick."

> My name is Ron, I wuks in de san', oh my Lawd,
> I'd ruther be a nigger dan a po'-white man.

> Cap'n, cap'n, what's de matter wid you?
> Ef you got any Battle-Ax, please, suh, give me a chew.

> Oh, Lawd, dat been my woman cry, oh Lawd,
> Go away, Eadie, quit worryin' my min'.

> Lawd, a brown-skin woman wear my watch an' chain,
> But a jet-black woman, um-m Lawd, cain' call my name.

From *American Ballads and Folk Songs,* collected and compiled by John A. Lomax and Alan Lomax, pp. 49–52. Copyright, 1934, by The Macmillan Company. New York.

This song is the workday of a Negro behind a team of mules. Wherever the scrapers pile up dirt on the levees of the Southern rivers, this song rises from the dust and heat. It voices the daylong reflections, the recurrent experiences and conflicts of the Negro mule-skinner. . . . The air was recorded from the singing of a prisoner at Angola, Louisiana. The words come from levee camps in the far South—J.A.L. and A.L.

Lawd, a brown-skin woman get anything I got,
But a jet-black woman cain' come in my back yard.

Heared a mighty rumblin' down 'bout the water trough,
Mus' been de skinner whoppin' hell out de walkin' boss.

Cap'n got a 44 an' he try to play bad,
Take it dis mornin' ef he make me mad.

Cap'n, cap'n, will you sen' me some water?
Ain' had none since dis long mornin'.

Lawd, de cap'n call me an' I answered, "Suh."
"Ef you ain' gonna work, what you come here fuh?"

This time, this time another year,
I may be rollin', but it won' be here.

Cap'n, cap'n, doncha think it's mighty hard?
Work me all day on 'lasses an' lard, oh, Lawd.

I ask de cap'n what time o' day.
He look at me, an' he walk away.

I'd ruther be a nigger an' plow ol' Beck
Dan a white hillbilly wid a long red neck.

I got a clock in my stomach an' a watch in my head.
I'm a-gettin' superstitious 'bout my hog an' bread.

I look at de sun an' de sun look high.
I look down on de boss man an' he look so sly.

"Boss man, boss man, cain' you gimme my time?"
An' de boss man say, "One day behin'."

"Boss man, boss man, cain' you gimme one dime?"
An' de boss man say, "One dime behin'."

Ask Cap'n George did his money come,
Said, "De river too foggy, de boat won' run."

Well, if I had my weight in lime,
I'd whip my cap'n till he wen' stone blin'.

He don' like whisky, but he jes drink a can.
Oh, I'd ruther be a nigger dan a po'-white man.

You cain' do me like you did po' Shine.
Take Shine's money, but you cain' take mine.

Cap'n, cap'n, you mus' be cross,
Six o'clock in hell 'fo' you knock off.

Roustabout Holler

Chanting:

> *Now boys, we're on the steamer* Natchez,
> *And we got to load this here cotton and cottonseed here*
> *Before anybody can shut his eyes like he's asleep;*
> *So we might just as well tear around,*
> *Get us a gobo apiece.*
> *Let's go on and load this stuff, what do you say?*
> *We're up here and got it to do.*
> *Where you at there, you old nub-fingered nappy?*
> *Let's hear from you, blow your horn, let's load some cotton.*

Oh-h-h-h,
Wake up, sleepy, and tell your dream,
I want to make you acquainted with two blue seams.[1]

Oh-h-h-h,
Midnight was my cry, 'fo' day was my creep,
I got a pretty little gal in big New Orleans, lives on Perdido Street.

Oh-h-h-h,
If yo' shoulder bone gits so' this time,
Git you a little sody an' turpentine.

Oh-h-h-h,
I left my home in '84,
And I ain't never been dere no more.

Oh-h-h-h,
I know my sweetie goin' open the do'
As soon as she hear the *Natchez* blow.

From *Our Singing Country*, A Second Volume of American Ballads and Folk Songs, collected and compiled by John A. Lomax and Alan Lomax; Ruth Crawford Seeger, Music Editor, pp. 350–351. Copyright, 1941, by John A. Lomax. New York: The Macmillan Company.

Sung by Henry Truvillion, Newton, Texas, 1939. AAFS Record No. 2658.

[1] Sacks of cottonseed had two blue stripes running from bottom to top.—J.A.L. and A.L.

Oh-h-h-h,
The *Natchez* up the bayou an' she done broke down,
She got her head toward Memphis, but she's New Orleans boun'.

Oh-h-h-h,
Did you hear Daniel in the lion den?
Lord, have mercy, hear me now.

Oh-h-h-h,
Po' roustabout don't have no home,
Here today and tomorrow gone.

Oh-h-h-h,
'Fo' day was my cry, midnight was my creep,
I got a sweet little gal in big New Orleans, I does all I can to please.

Oh-h-h-h,
Catch this here sack, boys, and leave it go,
Take her down the river further, 'cause they ain't no mo'.

Mississippi Sounding Call

From *Folk Music of the United States*, from the Collections of the Archive of American Folk Song, Album 8, *Negro Work Songs and Calls*, edited by B. A. Botkin. Record No. 36B3. Washington, D.C.: Folklore Section, Library of Congress. 1943.

Called by Joe Shores at Greenville, Mississippi, 1939. Recorded by Herbert Halpert. Transcribed by Herbert Haufrecht.

At the time of this recording Joe Shores, age 52, was pilot on the night run of the *A. C. Jaynes*, a ferryboat plying between Greenville, Mississippi, and Arkansas City, Arkansas.

Quarter less four: 22½ feet; half twain: 15 feet; quarter twain: 13½ feet; mark twain: 12 feet, or 2 fathoms; quarter less twain: 10½ feet.—B.A.B.

When it is necessary to know the depth of the water at any point in the river, the test or sounding is made by dropping a 33-foot rope, to the end of which is fastened a pipe filled with lead. The pipe is about one and a half inches in diameter and twelve inches in length. A few inches of heavy chain are put into the pipe, and around this melted lead is poured. The weight of a lead is between six and ten pounds. The rope is fastened to a link of the chain that is allowed to extend past the length

Quarter less four,
Half twain,
Quarter twain,
Mark twain,

Quarter less twain,
Nine and a half feet,
Nine feet,
Eight and a half feet.

---

of the pipe. The length of the lead line is marked at four feet by a piece of white flannel woven into the rope, at six feet by a piece of leather, at nine feet by a piece of red cloth; at Mark Twain there is a piece of leather split into two thongs, at Mark Three, a piece of leather in three thongs, and at Mark Four there is a single leather strip with a round hole. These signals are recognized by the leadsman as the rope slips through his hands in the darkness.

The soundings are called out as the line drops. A depth less than Quarter Less Twain is given in feet. After Mark Four is reached the measurement is usually given as No Bottom.

There are two methods of taking soundings. If the length of the pipe at the end of the rope rests in a horizontal position on the ground of the river bed, the measurement is known as Laying Lead. If only the end of the pipe is allowed to touch the bottom, the measurement is Standing Lead.

The report of the leadsman must reach the pilot quite a distance away. On large boats the messages are sometimes relayed by a man stationed between the leadsman and the pilothouse. The Negroes call this "passin' the word." In order to make themselves understood, often through wind and rain, the measurements are sung in a sustained chant, and each leadsman evolves his own tune and rhythm that he associates with the various depths.

One old Negro who used to take soundings or "heave the lead" on the Ohio gave this explanation of the prolonged tones. "You hold it out so the man who is passin' the word kin hear it mo' bettuh than if you cuts it off short."

The leadsmen realize the importance of their task. They enjoy the knowledge that their reports can cause such concern to the captain and the pilot. A Negro leadsman once said to the captain, "I laks you better than I do the pilot. I always gives you mo' watuh then I do him."

No leadsman would ever confess to the crime of "Dry Leadin'," or reporting a depth not carefully measured. But it was probably on a night in winter that this song was first sung—a night so cold that it was not pleasant to draw up the line dripping with icy water:

Captain, captain, don't you think I'm sly?
Goin' to do my leadin' an' keep my lead line dry.

When a pilot "calls for the lead," he gives the command with a signal from the whistle or bell. Soundings are taken from either side of the boat, and when necessary from both sides. One signal from the pilothouse sends a leadsman to the starboard side, two signals to the larboard. The same signals from the pilothouse recall the leadsman from his post. The Negroes say: "He blows you on, an' you has to stay out there till he blows you off."

Soundings are taken at the discretion of the pilot, when making a crossing, going through seldom used chutes, or at any time when there is doubt regarding the depth of the water. When a leadsman is at work the pilot expects to be informed of the depth of the channel about every hundred feet.

Throughout the leadsman's chanting, pilots listen hopefully for "No Bottom." To them this is the leadsman's sweetest song. When a boat can be kept in deep water the danger of going aground is avoided.—Mary Wheeler, *Steamboatin' Days* (Baton Rouge, 1944), pp. 59–61.

John Gilbert

You see that boat a-com - in', She's com-in' roun' the ben', An' when she gits in, She'll be load-ed down a-gin.

Chorus

John Gil-bert is the boat, Di De Oh,— Di De Oh,— John Gil-bert is the boat, Di De Oh,— Run-nin' in the Cin-cin-nat-i trade.

Lee P. Kahn was the head clerk,
    Captain Duncan was the captain,
Billy Evit was the head mate,
    Runnin' in the Cincinati trade.

She hauled peanuts an' cotton,
    An' she hauled so many
When she got to Johnsonville,
    Her work would just begin.

She hauled so many peanuts
    Her men run from her.
They went out in the wildernesss,
    An' they never come back no mo'.

From *Steamboatin' Days*, Folk Songs of the River Packet Era, by Mary Wheeler, pp. 43–46. Copyright, 1944, by Louisiana State University Press. Baton Rouge, Louisiana.

The *John Gilbert* ran from Cincinati to Florence, Alabama. She was built in Pittsburgh, Pennsylvania, in 1881, and was named for Captain John Gilbert, of Evansville, Indiana, president of the Ohio and Tennessee River Packet Company.

A certain section through which this boat passed was known for its trade in peanuts. The *John Gilbert* was loaded with this product by the thousand pounds and the vessel was nicknamed by the rousters "The Peanut John." It is said that on one trip the *John Gilbert* carried the largest cargo of peanuts ever received in Cincinnati. All available space on the main deck, boiler deck, and hurricane deck was used to store the cargo. Two thousand sacks of peanuts were taken on at Brit's Landing, over five thousand more up the Tennessee at Sycamore, and another load at Johnsonville—M.W.

She hauled so many peanuts
  The rousters run from her.
They couldn't git nobody to load her
  But the free labors.[1]

They put her to Florence, Alabama,
  Runnin' in the St. Louis trade,
An' when she got to Chester
  She broke half in two.

I'm Wukin' My Way Back Home

Stanza

Tim-ber don't git too heav-y fo' me, An' sacks too heav-y to stack, All that__ I crave__ fo' man - y a long day,__ Is yo' lov-in' when I__ git back.

Chorus

I'm__ wuk - in' my way__ back home, I'm__ wuk-in' my way__ back home, I'm__ wukin' my way__ back home, Ba - by, I'm wuk-in' my way__ back home.

Oh, fireman, keep her rollin' fo' me,
Let's make it to Memphis, Tennessee,
Fo' my back is gittin' tired,
An' my shoulder is gittin' sore.

---

[1] Men not regularly employed on the boat, or men taken on from the shore for an emergency.—M.W.
  Ibid., pp. 13–14.

Down in the Mississippi to the Gulf uv Mexico,
Down below Natchez,
But ef the boat keep steppin'
I'll be seein' you soon.

Now Paducah's layin' roun' the ben',
Now Paducah's layin' roun' the ben',
Captain, don't whistle, jes ring yo' bell,
Fo' my woman'll be standin' right there.

Alberta, Let Yo' Hair Hang Low

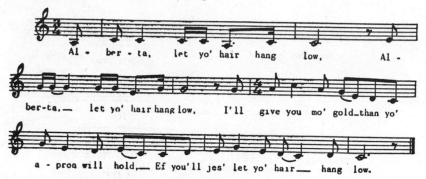

Alberta, what's on yo' mind?
Alberta, what's on yo' mind?
You keep me worried, you keep me bothered, all the time.
Alberta, what's on yo' mind?

Alberta, don't you treat me unkind,
Alberta, don't you treat me unkind,
'Cause I'm worried, 'cause I'm bothered, all the time.
Alberta, don't you treat me unkind.

Ibid., pp. 86–87.

On the Banks of the Ohio

Sentimentally

1. I asked my love to take a walk, Just to be a-lone with me, And as we walked we'd have a talk, A-bout our wed-ding day to be.

Refrain

Oh, dar-ling, say that you'll be mine, In no one's arms I will you find Down be-side dark wa-ters flow On the banks of the O-hi-o. 2. I asked your o.

I asked your mother for you, dear,
    And she said you were too young.
Only say that you'll be mine,
    Happiness in my home you'll find.

I drew a knife across her breast,
    In my arms she dearly pressed,
Crying, "Oh, please don't murder me,
    For I am unprepared to die."

I took her by her pale white hand,
    Led her to the river brink;
There I threw her in to drown,
    Stood and watched her float down.

Going home between twelve and one,
    Thinking of the deed I'd done,
I killed the only girl I loved
    Because she would not marry me.

From *Songs of the Rivers of America,* edited by Carl Carmer, music arranged by Dr. Albert Sirmay, p. 168. Copyright, 1942, by Farrar & Rinehart, Inc. New York and Toronto.

The Banks of the Little Eau Pleine

The__ sun in the west was. de-clin-ing_____ And__ ting-ing the tree-tops with red._____ My__ wan-der-ing feet bore me on-ward,_____ Not__ car-ing_____ whith-er they led._____ I hap-pened to see a young school-ma'am.__ ___ She mourned in a sor-row-ful strain,_____ She mourned for a jol-ly young rafts-man_____ On the banks of the Lit-tle Eau Pleine._____

Saying, "Alas, my dear Johnny has left me,
I'm afraid I shall see him no more.

By Shan T. Boy.

From *Ballads and Songs of the Shanty-Boy,* collected and edited by Franz Rickaby, pp. 25–29. Copyright, 1926, by Harvard University Press. Cambridge.

This ballad, widely current in Wisconsin, Michigan, and Minnesota, is interesting as being one of those whose origin and authorship are definitely known. The author [is] Mr. W. N. ("Billy") Allen. . . . The song is compounded wholly of imagination except for the character of Ross Gamble, who was a well-known pilot on the Wisconsin River at the time the verses were composed. Mr. Allen placed the time of composition "somewhere in the 70's." He was living at Wausau, Wisconsin at that time.

For [the tune] *Erin's Green Shore,* see Cox, *Folk-Songs of the South,* No. 181.

The Little Eau Pleine is a small tributary of the Wisconsin River, lying entirely within Marathon County, Wisconsin.

The ballad is often known as "Johnny Murphy."—F.R., *ibid.,* pp. 196–198.

Only five of the thirteen stanzas are given here, sacrificing the humor to the pathos.

He's down on the lower Wisconsin,
   He's pulling a fifty-foot oar.[1]
He went off on a fleet with Ross Gamble
   And has left me in sorrow and pain;
And 'tis over two months since he started
   From the banks of the Little Eau Pleine."

I stepped up beside this young school-ma'am,
   And thus unto her I did say,
"Why is it you're mourning so sadly,
   While all nature is smiling and gay?"
She said, "It is for a young raftsman
   For whom I so sadly complain.
He has left me alone here to wander
   On the banks of the Little Eau Pleine."

* * * *

"If John Murphy's the name of your raftsman,
   I used to know him very well.
But sad is the tale I must tell you:
   Your Johnny was drowned in the Dells.
They buried him 'neath a scrub Norway,
   You will never behold him again.
No stone marks the spot where your raftsman
   Sleeps far from the Little Eau Pleine."

* * * *

"My curses attend you, Wisconsin!
   May your rapids and falls cease to roar.
May every tow-head and sand-bar
   Be as dry as a log schoolhouse floor.
May the willows upon all your islands
   Lie down like a field of ripe grain,
For taking my jolly young raftsman
   Away from the Little Eau Pleine."

* * *

---

[1] A reference to the long oars or sweeps, operated by several men, used in propelling, or more especially for guiding, rafts of logs or lumber on the large rivers.
—F.R.

Cribisse! Cribisse! (Crawfish! Crawfish!)

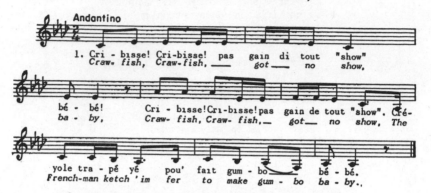

2. Quand to lève les matins, to trouve mo "gone," bébé.
   Quand to lève les matins, to trouve mo "gone,"
   Mo fou mo "camp" coté cribisse "hole," bébé.

3. Créyole, créyole, qui gain jiste neuf jou', bébé,
   Créyole, créyole, qui gain jiste neuf jou',
   Li cassé sos bras dans trou cribisse, bébé.

4. Cribisse, cribisse, pas peu' "six-mule team," bébé,
   Cribisse, cribisse, pas peu' "six-mule team,"
   Mé li parti galpé quand li wa créyole, bébé.

5. Gardez tout 'lontour lit créyole, bébé,
   Gardez tout 'lontour lit créyole,
   To pas wa arien que pasé têtes cribisse, bébé.

2. Get up in the morning, you find me gone, baby,
   Get up in the morning, you find me gone,
   I'm on my way to the crawfish pond, baby.

3. Frenchman, Frenchman, only nine days old, baby,
   Frenchman, Frenchman, only nine days old,
   Broke his arm in a crawfish hole, baby.

4. Crawfish ain't skeered of a six-mule team, baby,
   Crawfish ain't skeered of a six-mule team,
   But run from a Frenchman time he see 'im, baby.

5. Look all round a Frenchman's bed, baby,
   Look round a Frenchman's bed,
   You don' find nothin' but crawfish heads, baby.

From *Louisiana French Folk Songs*, by Irène Thérèse Whitfield, pp. 137–138. Copyright, 1939, by Louisiana State University Press. Baton Rouge, Louisiana.

The song "Cribisse! Cribisse!" is used to satirize the Frenchman in return for all the derision he has made of the *nèg' 'méricain*. It is sung in English as well as in French.—I.T.W.

Voyageur Songs

I. LA SAUVAGESSE (THE GIRL OF THE WILDS)

1. Je suis du bord de l'O- hi - o. J'ai le cou- ra- ge pour no - bles - se. Ma joie est d'être à mon ca - not, De le gui- der a- vec a- dresse. Ma vie est la ch sse et la pêche. En - fin, je suis la Sau- va - gesse.

Chorus

Tou ra- ta- tou ra- ta-tou- ra, Tou ra- ta- tou ra- ta- tou- ra J'ai le cou - ra-ge pour no-blesse et ma prou- es- se. J'ai le cou- ra- ge pour no - blesse et ma prou - es - se.

Je suis du bord de l'Ohio.	I am from the banks of the Ohio.
J'ai le courage pour noblesse.	I have a heart for great deeds.
Ma joie est d'être à mon canot,	My joy is to be in my canoe,
De le guider avec adresse.	To guide it skilfully.
Ma vie est la chasse et la pêche.	My life is to hunt and to fish.
Enfin, je suis le Sauvagesse,	In fine, I am the girl of the wilds,

From "Voyageur Songs of the Missouri," by Marius Barbeau, *Bulletin of the Missouri Historical Society,* Vol. X (April, 1954), No. 3, pp. 339–340, 345, 349–350. Copyright, 1954, by Missouri Historical Society. St. Louis.

A substantial body of come-all-ye's, which the voyageurs chanted in deep earnest, often with tears, consisted of tragic recollections and experiences of the canoemen in their adventurous lives. . . . A semi-lettered jongleur composed the song of *La Sauvagesse.*—M.B.

Collected in Montreal by E.-Z. Massicotte in 1919 from Ephrem Terreault, who had learned it from his mother, at St. Remi de Napierville, in 1870.

English translations by Mrs. Max W. Myer.

Chorus:

Tou ratatou ratatoura,
(*Twice*)
J'ai le courage pour noblesse
et ma prouesse. (*Twice*)

Mon père s'appelait Ritou,
Ma mère était une sorcière,
Ils vécurent toujours bons époux,
Moururent enfants de la lumière,
Inspirés du grand Manitou.
Ils m'ont nommée la Marinière,
Tou ratatou, etc.

Quand la tempête éclate fort,
Que le vent fait siffler ma voile.

Qu'il m'est doux de quitter le bord,
Pour m'adventurer en nacelle.
La foudre fait un tendre écho,
L'éclair qui brille m'est salutaire,
Tou ratatou, etc.

Chorus:

Tou ratatou ratatoura,
(*Twice*)
I have a heart for great deeds
and gallant exploits. (*Twice*)

My father's name was Ritou,
My mother was a witch,
They lived a happy pair,
Died as children of light,
Inspired by the great Manitou.
They named me the water girl,
Tou ratatou, etc.

When the tempest blows mightily,
So that the wind makes my sails
whistle,
How I love to quit the shore,
To venture forth in my bark.
The thunder is a gentle echo,
The brilliant lightning does me good,
Tou ratatou, etc.

II. Le Voyage (The Voyage)

Ah! c'est un mariage
Que d'épouser le voyage.

Oh! it's like a marriage
If to voyage you pledge yourself.

Je plains qui s'y engage
Sans y être invite.
Leve tot, couche tard,
Il faut subir son sort,
S'exposer à la mort.

I pity him who binds himself
Without having been urged.
Rise early, turn in late,
He must endure his fate,
Expose himself to death.

Dans le cours du voyage,
Exposé aux naufrages;
Le corps trempe dans l'eau,
Eveillé par les oiseaux;
Nous n'avons de repos
Ni le jour ni la nuit.
N'y a que de l'ennui.

During the course of our roving,
Shipwrecks we are chancing;
Our bodies by water soaked,
By the birds we'll be awakened;
By slumber all forsaken
Both by day and night.
For us there is no delight.

Dans le cours du voyage,
Exposé aux orages;
Préoccupés du temps,
Battu de tous les vents.
Ah! je vous dis, mes frèr's,
Personne, sur la terr',
Endure tant de misèr'.

During the course of our roving
Thunderstorms we're risking;
By the weather we are worried,
By all the winds we're flurried.
My brothers, hear me tell,
No one, outside of hell,
In such misery does dwell.

Dans le cours du voyage,
Il faut bien du courage.
Vaut mieux être habitant;
On a moins de tourment.
L'habitant sèm' du grain;
Dort du soir au matin.
Sa femme en a bien soin.

During the course of our roving,
Courage we'll needs be showing.
I'd rather be a settler,
He has a life that's better.
The settler sows the corn;
Sleeps from eve to morn.
His good wife watches o'er him.

Ah! c'est un mariage
Que d'épouser le voyage.
Moi, j'attends la journé',
Jour de mon arrivé'.
Jamais plus je n'irai
Dans ces pays damnés,
Pour tant m'y ennuyer.

Oh! It's like a marriage
If to voyage you pledge yourself.
The day that I attend
Is the day of my journey's end.
No more my way I'll wend
To infernal lands condemned,
Where 'neath heavy troubles I bend.

La Guillannée

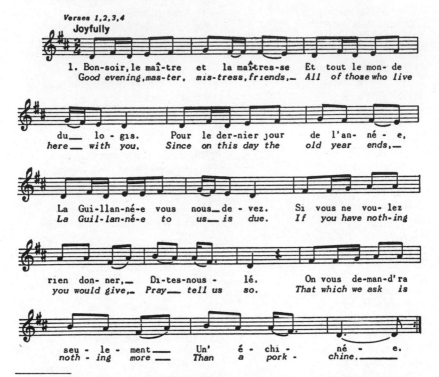

Verses 1,2,3,4
Joyfully

1. Bon-soir, le maî-tre   et   la maî-tres-se   Et tout le mon- de
Good evening, mas-ter,   mis-tress, friends,_   All of those who live

du__ lo - gis.   Pour le der-nier jour   de l'an- né - e,
here__ with you,   Since on this day the   old year ends,—

La Gui-llan-né-e vous   nous__de - vez.   Si vous ne vou- lez
La Guil-lan-né-e to   us__ is due.   If you have noth- ing

rien don- ner,__   Di-tes-nous -   lé.   On vous de-man-d'ra
you would give,__   Pray__ tell us   so.   That which we ask is

seu- le - ment__   Un' é - chi -   né - e.
noth - ing more __   Than a pork -   chine.___

From *Folk Songs of Old Vincennes,* French Texts Collected by Anna C. O'Flynn and Joseph Médard Carrière; English Versions by Frederic Burget and Libushka Bartusek; Introduction and Notes by Joseph Médard Carrière; Melodies Collected and Harmonized by Cecelia Ray Berry, pp. 10–13. Copyright, 1946, by H. T. Fitz-Simons Co. Chicago, Illinois.

This used to be the most widely known of all songs among the French-speaking population of the Northwest. The name *Guillannée* is to be explained as an abbreviation of *gui de l'année, gui de la nouvelle année,* New Year's mistletoe. The history of this song takes us back to pagan times, when the Druids would cut the mistletoe at the winter solstice and present it to their followers as something sacred. At an early date, the Church transformed this pagan custom and gave it a Christian character by associating it with a collection for the poor. For generations, in the French communities of Indiana, Illinois, and Missouri, on New Year's Eve a group of men and youths wearing masks spent most of the night going from house to house. When they entered a home, they struck the tune of the lively carol, *La Guillannée,* then they danced, told stories, and teased the young ladies. In the meantime, the mistress of the house passed cakes and drinks around and put her donation for the poor in a basket or a sack which the masqueraders carried along with them for that purpose. This quaint custom has survived to this very day in a modified form in Prairie du Rocher, Illinois, and Sainte Genevieve, Missouri. In certain Canadian localities like Ottawa, Ontario, the *Guillannée* celebration is still held every New Year's Eve by the Society of Saint Vincent de Paul for the benefit of the poor.—J.M.C.

5. C'sont ses a-mours qui la ré-vei-llent Et qui l'em-pê-chent
Wak-ened is she when-e'er love stirs,— Sleep,gen-tle sleep,is

de— dor-mir, Dan-sons, dan-sons la Gui-llan-né-e, Dan-
put— to flight.Dance on, dance on la Guil-lan-né-e, Dance

sons, dan-sons la Gui-llan-né-e, La Gui-llan-né-e, la
on, dance on la Guil-lan-né-e, La Guil-lan-né-e, la

Gui-llan-né-e, Dan-sons, dan-sons la Gui-llan-né-e.
Guil-lan-né-e, Dance on, dance on la Guil-lan-né-e.
Adieu:

Nous sa-lu-ons la com-pa-gni-e Et la pri-
Now we sa-lute all those as-sem-bled, Beg their in-

ons d'nous ex-cu-ser. Si l'on a fait quel-que fo-
dul-gence, if ac-cused Of hav-ing jest-ed as they

li-e, C'é-tait pour se dé-sen-nu-yer.
trem-bled, We ask that we may be ex-cused.

2. Un' échinée n'est pas grand'chose;
   Ce n'est que dix pieds de long.
   Et nous en f'rons une fricassée
   De quatre-vingt-dix pieds de long.
   Si vous ne voulez rien donner,
   Dites-nous-lé.
   On vous demand'ra seulement
   La fille aînée.

   'Tis but a trifle we implore.
   Ten feet of pork-chine's all we pray;
   Of it we'll have no less, no more
   Than ninety feet of fricassée.
   If you have nothing you would give,
   Pray, tell us so.
   That which we ask is nothing more
   Than your daughter fine.

3. On y fera faire bonne chère,
   On y fera chauffer les pieds.

   On y fera faire bonne chère,
   On y fera chauffer les pieds.

   Quand on fut au milieu du bois,
   On fut à l'ombre;
   J'ai entendu chanter l'coucou
   Et la colombe.

   Let us amuse her, we implore,
   We'll warm her feet, pray don't de-
   cline.
   Let us amuse her, we implore,
   We'll warm her feet, pray don't de-
   cline.
   While in the cool and fragrant grove,
   There in the shade,
   I heard the cuckoo and the dove,
   Cooing in the glade.

4. Ô rossignol du vert bocage,
   Ambassadeur des amoureux,
   Allez donc dire à ma maîtresse
   Que j'ai toujours le coeur joyeux.
   La fille qui n'a pas d'amant,
     Comment vit-elle?
   Elle ne dort ni jour ni nuit,
     Mais toujours veille.

5. C'sont ses amours qui la réveillent
   Et qui l'empêchent de dormir.

Refrain:

   Dansons, dansons la Guillannée,
   Dansons, dansons la Guillannée;
   La Guillannée, la Guillannée,
   Dansons, dansons la Guillannée.

Adieu:

   Nous saluons la compagnie
   Et la prions d'nous excuser.
   Si l'on a fait quelque folie,
   C'est pour se désennuyer.

O, nightingale of verdant grove,
Envoy of lovers ev'rywhere,
Go tell my pretty lady-love
That joy is in my heart fore'er.
As for the maid who has no love,
  How can she live?
Slumber she knows not, day or night.
  Wakefulness is hers.

Wakened is she whene'er love stirs,
Sleep, gentle sleep is put to flight.

Refrain:

Dance on, dance on la Guillannée,
Dance on, dance on la Guillannée,
La Guillannée, la Guillannée,
Dance on, dance on la Guillannée.

Adieu:

Now we salute all those assembled,
Beg their indulgence if accused
Of having jested as they trembled,
We ask that we may be excused.

Rhyme of Old Steamboats

The *Fred Wyerhaeuser* and the *Frontenac*,
The *F. C. A. Denckmann* and the *Bella Mac*,
The *Menomenee* and *Louisville*,
The *R. J. Wheeler* and *Jessie Bill*,
The *Robert Semple* and the *Golden Gate*,
The *C. J. Caffery* and the *Sucker State*.

The *Charlotte Boeckler* and the *Silver Wave*,
The *John H. Douglas* and *J. K. Graves*,
The *Isaac Staples* and the *Helen Mar*,
The *Henrietta* and the *North Star*,
The *David Bronson* and *Nettie Durant*,
The *Kit Carson* and *J. W. Van Sant*.

From *A-Rafting on the Mississip'*, by Charles Edward Russell, pp. 345–346. Copyright, 1928, by Charles Edward Russell. New York and London: The Century Company.

Home-made poetry once popular on the Mississippi. The author of this compilation . . . is unknown. It seems to have been circulated by recitation, after the manner of true folklore, but finally got into print. In 1927 it was resurrected by Mr. F. X. Ralphe, of Hastings, Minnesota, who found it among old papers and sent it to the Burlington *Post*. Old rivermen recognized it as a once popular ballad of nomenclature. All the names are of steamboats once well known on the river and most of them raft boats.—C.E.R.

The *Chauncey Lamb* and the *Evansville*,
The *Blue Lodge* and the *Minnie Will*,
The *Saturn* and the *Satellite*,
The *Le Claire Belle* and the *Silas Wright*,
The *Artemas Lamb* and the *Pauline*,
The *Douglas Boardman* and *Kate Keen*.

The *I. E. Staples* and the *Mark Bradley*,
The *J. G. Chapman* and the *Julia Hadley*,
The *Mollie Whitmore* and *C. K. Peck*,
The *Robert Dodds* and *Borealis Rex*,
The *Pete Kerns* and the *Wild Boy*,
The *Lilly Turner* and the *St. Croix*.

The *A. T. Jenks* and *Bart Linehan*,
The *C. W. Cowles* and *Brother Jonathan*,
The *Pete Wilson* and *Anna Girdon*,
The *Inverness* and the *L. W. Barden*,
The *Nellie Thomas* and the *Enterprise*,
The *Park Painter* and *Hiram Price*.

The *Dan Hines* and the *City of Winona*,
The *Helen Schulenburg* and *Natrona*,
The *Flying Eagle* and the *Moline*,
The *E. Ruthledge* and *Josephine*,
The *Taber* and the *Irene D.*,
The *D. A. McDonald* and *Jessie B.*

The *Gardie Eastman* and the *Vernie Swain*,
The *James Malbon* and the *L. W. Crane*,
The *Sam Atlee* and the *William White*,
The *Lumberman* and the *Penn Wright*,
The *Stillwater* and the *Volunteer*,
The *James Fisk Jr.* and the *Reindeer*.

The *Thistle* and the *Mountain Bell*,
The *Little Eagle* and the *Gazelle*,
The *Mollie Mohler* and the *James Means*,
The *Silver Crescent* and the *Muscatine*,
The *Jim Watson* and the *Last Chance*,
The *Kate Waters* and the *Ed. Durant*,

The *Dan Thayer* and the *Flora Clark*,
The *Robert Ross* and the *J. G. Park*,
The *Eclipse* and *J. W. Mills*,
The *J. S. Keator* and the *J. J. Hill*,
The *Lady Grace* and the *Abner Gile*,
The *Johnnie Schmoker* and the *Georgie Lysle*,
The *Lafayette Lamb* and the *Clyde*,
The *B. Hershey* and the *Time and Tide*.

Cincinnati Levee Life and Songs

Along the river-banks on either side of the [Cincinnati] levee slope, where the brown water year after year climbs up to the ruined sidewalks, and pours into the warehouse cellars, and paints their grimy walls with streaks of water-weed green, may be studied a most curious and interesting phase of life—the life of a community within a community—a society of wanderers who have haunts but not homes, and who are only connected with the static society surrounding them by the common bond of State and municipal law. It is a very primitive kind of life; its lights and shadows are alike characterized by a half savage simplicity; its happiness or misery is almost purely animal; its pleasures are wholly of the hour, neither enhanced or lessened by anticipations of the morrow. It is always pitiful rather than shocking; and it is not without some little charm of its own—the charm of a thoughtless existence, whose virtues are all original, and whose vices are for the most part foreign to it. A great portion of this levee life haunts also the subterranean hovels and ancient frame buildings of the district lying east of Broadway to Culvert Street, between Sixth and Seventh Streets. But on a cool spring evening, when the levee is bathed in moonlight, and the torch-basket lights dance redly upon the water, and the clear air vibrates, to the sonorous music of the deep-toned steam-whistle, and the sound of wild banjo-thrumming floats out through the open doors of the levee dance-houses, then it is perhaps that one can best observe the peculiarities of this grotesquely picturesque roustabout life.

Probably less than one-third of the stevedores and longshoremen employed in our river traffic are white; but the calling now really belongs by right to the Negroes, who are by far the best roustabouts and are unrivaled as firemen. The white stevedores are generally tramps, willing to work only through fear of the workhouse; or sometimes laborers unable to obtain other employment, and glad to earn money for the time being at any employment. . . . "Before Freedom," as the colored folks say, white laborers performed most of the roustabout labor on the steamboats; the Negroes are now gradually monopolizing the calling, chiefly by reason of their peculiar fitness for it. Generally speaking, they are the best porters in the world; and in the cotton States, it is not uncommon, we are told, to see Negro levee hands for a wager carry five-hundred-pound cotton-bales on their backs to the wharf boat. River men today are recognizing the superior value of Negro labor in steamboat traffic, and the colored roustabouts are now better treated, probably, than they have been since the war. Under the present laws, too, they are better protected. It used at one time to be a common thing for some ruffianly mate to ship sixty or

From *An American Miscellany*, by Lafcadio Hearn, Articles and Stories Now First Collected by Albert Mordell, Vol. I, pp. 147–160. Copyright, 1924, by Dodd, Mead and Company, Inc. New York.
The [Cincinnati, Ohio] *Commercial*, March 17, 1876.

seventy stevedores, and, after the boat had taken in all her freight, to hand the poor fellows their money and land them at some small town, or even in the woods, hundreds of miles from their home. This can be done no longer with legal impunity.

Roustabout life in the truest sense is, then, the life of the colored population of the Rows, and, partly, of Bucktown—blacks and mulattoes from all parts of the States, but chiefly from Kentucky and Eastern Virginia, where most of them appear to have toiled on the plantations before Freedom; and echoes of the old plantation life still live in their songs and their pastimes. You may hear old Kentucky slave songs chanted nightly on the steamboats, in that wild, half-melancholy key peculiar to the natural music of the African race; and you may see the old slave dances nightly performed to the air of some ancient Virginia reel in the dance houses of Sausage Row, or the "ball rooms" of Bucktown. There is an intense uniqueness about all this pariah existence; its boundaries are most definitely fixed; its enjoyments are wholly sensual, and many of them are marked by peculiarities of a strictly local character. Many of their songs, which have never appeared in print, treat of levee life in Cincinnati, of all the popular steamboats running on the "Muddy Water," and of the favorite roustabout haunts on the river bank and in Bucktown. . . . Of these the following song, "Number Ninety-Nine," was at one time immensely popular with the steamboatmen. The original resort referred to was situated on Sixth and Culvert Street, where Kirk's building now [1876] stands. We present the song with some necessary emendations:

> You may talk about yer railroads,
> > Yer steamboats and can-*el*.
> If 't hadn't been for Liza Jane,
> > There wouldn't bin no hell.
>
> *Chorus:*
>
> > Oh, ain't I gone, gone, gone,
> > Oh, ain't I gone, gone, gone,
> > Oh, ain't I gone, gone, gone,
> > > Way down de ribber road.
>
> Whar do you get yer whisky?
> > Whar do you get yer rum?
> I got it down in Bucktown,
> > At Number Ninety-nine.
>
> I went down to Bucktown,
> > Nebber was dar before,
> Great big niggah knocked me down,
> > But Katy barred the door.
>
> She hugged me, she kissed me,
> > She told me not to cry;
> She said I wuz de sweetest thing
> > Dat eber libbed or died.

*   *   *   *   *

> Yonder goes the *Wildwood,*
>   She's loaded to de guards,
> But yonder comes de *Fleetwood,*
>   An' she's the boat for me.

The words, "Way down to Rockingham," are sometimes substituted in the chorus, for "Way down de ribber road."

One of the most popular roustabout songs now sung on the Ohio is the following. The air is low, and melancholy, and when sung in unison by the colored crew of a vessel leaving or approaching port, has a strange, sad sweetness about it which is very pleasing. The twofold character of poor Molly, at once good and bad, is somewhat typical of the stevedore's sweetheart.

> Molly was a good gal and a bad gal, too,
>   Oh, Molly, row, gal.
> Molly was a good gal and a bad gal, too,
>   Oh, Molly, row, gal.
>
> I'll row dis boat and I'll row no more,
>   Row, Molly, row, gal.
> I'll row dis boat and I'll go on shore,
>   Row, Molly, row, gal.
>
> Captain on the biler deck a-heaving of the lead,
>   Oh, Molly, row, gal.
> Calling to the pilot to give "Turn ahead,"
>   Row, Molly, row, gal.

Here is another to a slow and sweet air. The chorus, when well sung, is extremely pretty:

> *Chorus:*
> Shawneetown is burnin' down,
>   Who tole you so?
> Shawneetown is burnin' down,
>   Who tole you so?
>
> Cythie, my darlin' gal,
>   Who tole you so?
> Cythie, my darlin' gal,
>   How do you know?
>
> How the h——l d'ye 'spect me to hold her,
>   Way down below?
> I've got no skin on either shoulder,
>   Who tole you so?
>
> De houses dey is all on fire,
>   Way down below.
> De houses dey is all on fire,
>   Who tole you so?

My ole missus tole me so,
 Way down below.
An' I b'lieve what ole missus says,
 Way down below.

The most melancholy of all these plaintive airs is that to which the song "Let her go by" is commonly sung. It is generally sung on leaving port, and sometimes with an affecting pathos inspired of the hour, while the sweethearts of the singers watch the vessel gliding down stream.

I'm going away to New Orleans!
 Good-by, my lover, good-by!
I'm going away to New Orleans!
 Good-by, my lover, good-by!
  Oh, let her go by!

She's on her way to New Orleans!
 Good-by, my lover, good-by!
She bound to pass the *Robert E. Lee,*
 Good-by, my lover, good-by!
  Oh, let her go by!

I'll make dis trip and I'll make no more!
 Good-by, my lover, good-by!
I'll roll dese barrels, I'll roll no more!
 Good-by, my lover, good-by!
  Oh, let her go by!

An' if you are not true to me,
 Farewell, my lover, farewell!
An' if you arc not true to me,
 Farewell, my lover, farewell!
  Oh, let her go by!

The next we give is of a somewhat livelier description. It has, we believe, been printed in a somewhat different form in certain song books. We give it as it was sung to us in a Broadway saloon:

I come down the mountain,
 An' she come down the lane,
An' all that I could say to her
 Was, Good-by, 'Liza Jane.

Chorus:

Farewell, 'Liza Jane!
Farewell, 'Liza Jane!
Don't throw yourself away, for I
Am coming back again.

I got up on a house-top,
 An' give my horn a blow;
Thought I heerd Miss Dinah say,
 "Yonder comes your beau."

> Ef I'd a few more boards,
>   To build my chimney higher,
> I'd keep aroun' the country gals,
>   Chunkin' up the fire.

The following are fragments of rather lengthy chants, the words being almost similar in both, but the choruses and airs being very different. The air of the first is sonorous and regularly slow, like a sailor's chant when heaving anchor; the air of the next is quick and lively.

> *Belle-a-Lee's* got no time,
>   Oh, Belle! oh, Belle!
> *Robert E. Lee's* got railroad time,
>   Oh, Belle! oh, Belle!
>
> Wish I was in Mobile Bay,
>   Oh, Belle! oh, Belle!
> Rollin' cotton by de day,
>   Oh, Belle! oh, Belle!

> I wish I was in Mobile Bay,
> Rollin' cotton by de day,
>   Stow'n' sugar in de hull below,
>   Below, belo-ow,
>   Stow'n' sugar in de hull below!

> De *Natchez* is a new boat; she's just in her prime,
> Beats any oder boat on de New Orleans line.
>   Stow'n' sugar in de hull below, &c.

> Engineer, t'rough de trumpet, gives de firemen news,
> Couldn't make steam for de fire in de flues.
>   Stow'n' sugar in de hull below, &c.

> Cap'n on de biler deck, a scratchin' of his head,
> Hollers to de deck hand to heave de larbo'rd lead.
>   Stow'n' sugar in de hull below, &c.

Perhaps the prettiest of all these songs is "The Wandering Steamboatman," which, like many other roustabout songs, rather frankly illustrates the somewhat loose morality of the calling:

> I am a wandering steamboatman,
>   And far away from home;
> I fell in love with a pretty gal,
>   And she in love with me.
>
> She took me to her parlor
>   And cooled me with her fan;
> She whispered in her mother's ear:
>   "I love the steamboatman."

The mother entreats her daughter not to become engaged to the steve-dore. "You know," she says, "that he is a steamboatman, and has a wife in New Orleans." But the steamboatman replies, with great nonchalance:

> If I've a wife at New Orleans;
> I'm neither tied nor bound;
> And I'll forsake my New Orleans wife
> If you'll be truly mine.

Another very curious and decidedly immoral song is popular with the loose women of the "Row." We can only give one stanza:

> I hev a roustabout for my man—
> Livin' with a white man for a sham,
>> Oh, leave me alone,
>> Leave me alone,
> I'd like you much better if you'd leave me alone.

But the most famous song in vogue among the roustabouts is "Limber Jim," or "Shiloh." Very few know it all by heart, which is not wonderful when we consider that it requires something like twenty minutes to sing "Limber Jim" from beginning to end. . . . The air is wonderfully quick and lively, and the chorus is quite exciting. The leading singer sings the whole song, excepting the chorus, *Shiloh*, which dissyllable is generally chanted by twenty or thirty voices of abysmal depth at the same time with a sound like the roar of twenty Chinese gongs struck with tremendous force and precision. A great part of "Limber Jim" is very profane, and some of it not quite fit to print. We can give only about one-tenth part of it. The chorus is frequently accompanied with that wonderfully rapid slapping of thighs and hips known as "patting Juba."

> Nigger an' a white man playing seven-up,
> White man played an ace; an' nigger feared to take it up,
> White man played ace an' nigger played a nine,
> White man died, an' nigger went blind.
>
>> Limber Jim,
>> [All.] Shiloh!
>> Talk it agin,
>> [All.] Shiloh!
>> Walk back in love,
>> [All.] Shiloh!
>> You turtle-dove,
>> [All.] Shiloh!
>
> Went down the ribber, couldn't get across;
> Hopped on a rebel louse; thought 'twas a hoss,
> Oh, lor', gals, 't aint no lie,
> Lice in Camp Chase big enough to cry,—

Bridle up a˚rat, sir; saddle up a cat,
Please han' me down my Leghorn hat,
Went to see widow; widow warn't home;
Saw to her daughter—she gave me honeycomb.

Jay-bird sittin' on a swinging limb,
Winked at me an' I winked at him.
Up with a rock an' struck him on the shin,
G——d d——n yer soul, don't wink again.

Some folks says that a rebel can't steal,
I found twenty in my corn-fiel',
Sich pullin' of shucks an' tearin' of corn!—
Nebber saw the like since I was born.

John Morgan come to Danville and cut a mighty dash,
Las' time I saw him, he was under whip an' lash;
'Long come a rebel at a sweepin' pace,
Whar 're ye goin', Mr. Rebel? "I'm goin' to Camp Chase."

Way beyond de sun and de moon,
White gal tole me I were too soon.
White gal tole me I come too soon,
An' nigger gal called me an old d—d fool.

Eighteen pennies hidden in a fence,
Cynthiana gals ain't got no sense;
Every time they go from home
Comb thar heads wid an ole jaw bone.

Had a little wife an' didn' inten' to keep her;
Showed her a flatboat an' sent her down de ribber;
Head like a fodder-shock, mouf like a shovel,
Put yerself wid yaller gal, put yerself in trubble.

I went down to Dinah's house, Dinah was in bed,
Hoisted de window an' poked out her head;
T'rowed, an' I hit her in de eyeball,—bim;
"Walk back, Mr. Nigger; don't do dat again."

Gambling man in de railroad line,
Saved my ace an' played my nine;
If you want to know my name,
My name's High-low-jack-in-the-game.

> Limber Jim,
>   Shiloh!
> Talk it again,
>   Shiloh!
> You dancing girl,
>   Shiloh!
> Sure's you're born,
>   Shiloh!

Grease my heel with butter in the fat,
I can talk to Limber Jim better'n dat.

> Limber Jim,
>> Shiloh!
> Limber Jim,
>> Shiloh!
> Walk back in love,
>> Shiloh!
> My turtle dove,
>> Shiloh!

[Patting Juba]
> And you can't go yonder,
>> Limber Jim!
> And you can't go yonder,
>> Limber Jim!
> And you can't go-oo-o!

Duncan and Brady

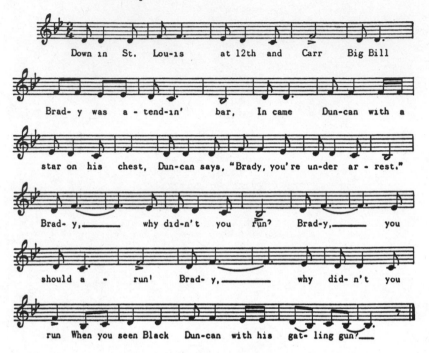

Down in St. Lou-is at 12th and Carr Big Bill
Brad- y was a - tend-in' bar, In came Dun-can with a
star on his chest, Dun-can says, "Brady, you're un-der ar - rest."
Brad- y,_____ why did-n't you run? Brad-y,_____ you
should a - run! Brad- y,_____ why did- n't you
run When you seen Black Dun-can with his gat- ling gun?___

> Duncan and his brother were playing pool
> When Brady came in acting like a fool;
> He shot him once, he shot him twice,
> Saying, "I don't make my living by shooting dice!"

From *The American Songbag*, by Carl Sandburg, pp. 198–199. Copyright, 1927, by Harcourt, Brace and Company, Inc. New York.

A Nebraska-born woman, now practising law in Chicago, gives us one verse and a tune from St. Louis. . . . Geraldine Smith . . . heard it from Omaha railroad men. . . . Then from the R. W. Gordon Collection we have text B.—C.S.

There was hardship and want in the St. Louis of 1893. There was also crime and depravity. The Cleveland panic had done its work among Negroes; they were leaving the South in endless streams, and St. Louis was drawing more than its share of the migrants. The overcrowding which resulted produced intolerable conditions. Sitting space in pool halls became a real luxury. Thousands of vagrants slept on the cobblestones of the levee. Police brutality reached a point seldom equaled. Officers of the law carried night sticks a yard long and learned to hurl them at the feet of fleeing migrants in such a way as to trip them up when they tried to run. . . . Out of their brushes with the law grew such popular songs as "Brady, He's Dead and Gone" and "Looking for the Bully."—Arna Bontemps and Jack Conroy, *They Seek a City* (Garden City, N. Y., 1945), pp. 89–90.

Chorus:

>Brady, won't come no more!
>Brady, won't come no more!
>Brady, won't come no more!
>For Duncan shot Brady with a forty-four!

"Brady, Brady, don't you know you done wrong
To come in my house when my game was going on?
I told you half a dozen times before,
And now you lie dead on my barroom floor!"

Brady went to hell lookin' mighty curious,
The devil says, "Where you from?" "East St. Louis."
"Well, pull off your coat and step this way,
For I've been expecting you every day!"

When the girls heard Brady was dead
They went up home and put on red,
And came down town singin' this song—
"Brady's struttin' in hell with his Stetson on!"

Last chorus:

>"Brady, where you at?
>Brady, where you at?
>Brady, where you at?
>Struttin' in hell with his Stetson hat!"

Alabama Bound

1. Oh, de boats on de rib-ber ___ turn roun' an' roun' ___ An' all de wo-men on de Eas' shore yell "Al - a - bam- a boun'!" You want to be lak me. You want to be lak me, Ah got a gal in Birm- in'- ham town, An' one in Ten - nes - see.

Oh, de boat's up de ribber,
    An' de tide's gone down;
Believe to mah soul dat
    She's Alabama boun'.

"Where was you, sweet Mama,
    When de boat went down?"
"On de deck, baby, yellin',
    'Alabama boun'!' "

Got a train in Cairo
    Forty coaches long.
All I want dat train to do
    Is fetch mah gal along.

Doctuh Cook's in town,
    Doctuh Cook's in town.
He foun' de No'th Pole so doggone cold
    He's Alabama boun'.

From *Songs of American Folks,* by Satis N. Coleman and Adolph Bregman, pp. 62–63. Copyright, 1942, by The John Day Company, Inc. New York.
As sung by Tom Gregory of Georgia.

How "St. Louis Blues" Was Born

It occurred to me that I could perhaps make more headway in [the] direction [of a popular hit] without the questionable help of my four lively and robust youngsters at home, all bent on using my legs for teeter-boards. The noisy rumpus warmed the heart but it put a crimp in my work. I could feel the blues coming on, and I didn't want to be distracted, so I packed my grip and made my getaway.

I rented a room in the Beale Street section and went to work. Outside, the lights flickered. Chitterling joints were as crowded as the more fashionable resorts like the Iroquois. Piano thumpers tickled the ivories in the saloons to attract customers, furnishing a theme for the prayers at Beale Street Baptist Church and Avery Chapel (Methodist). Scores of powerfully built roustabouts from river boats sauntered along the pavement, elbowing fashionable browns in beautiful gowns. Pimps in boxback coats and undented Stetsons came out to get a breath of early evening air and to welcome the young night. The poolhall crowd grew livelier than they had been during the day. All that contributed to the color and spell of Beale Street mingled outside, but I neither saw nor heard it that night. I had a song to write.

My first decision was that my new song would be another blues, true to the soil and in the tradition of "Memphis Blues." Ragtime, I had decided, was passing out. But this number would go beyond its predecessor and break new ground. I would begin with a down-home ditty fit to go with twanging banjos and yellow shoes. Songs of this sort could become tremendous hits sometimes. On the levee at St. Louis I had heard "Looking for the Bully" sung by the roustabouts, which later was adopted and nationally popularized by May Irwin. I had watched the joy-spreaders rarin' to go when it was played by the bands on the *Gray Eagle,* or the *Spread Eagle.* I wanted such a success, but I was determined that my song would have an important difference. The emotions that it expressed were going to be real. Moreover, it was going to be cut to the native blues pattern.

A flood of memories filled my mind. First, there was the picture I had of myself, broke, unshaven, wanting even a decent meal, and standing before the lighted saloon in St. Louis without a shirt under my frayed coat. There was also from that same period a curious and dramatic little fragment that till now had seemed to have little or no importance. While occupied with my own miseries during that sojourn, I had seen a woman whose pain seemed even greater. She had tried to take the edge off her grief by heavy drinking, but it hadn't worked. Stumbling along the poorly

From *Father of the Blues,* An Autobiography, by W. C. Handy, edited by Arna Bontemps, pp. 118–123. Copyright, 1941, by W. C. Handy. New York: The Macmillan Company. 1942.

lighted street, she muttered as she walked, "Ma man's got a heart like a rock cast in de sea."

The expression interested me, and I stopped another woman to inquire what she meant. She replied, "Lawd, man, it's hard and gone so far from her she can't reach it." Her language was the same down-home medium that conveyed the laughable woe of lamp-blacked lovers in hundreds of frothy songs, but her plight was much too real to provoke much laughter. My song was taking shape. I had now settled upon the mood.

Another recollection pressed in upon me. It was the memory of that odd gent who called figures for the Kentucky breakdown—the one who everlastingly pitched his tones in the key of *G* and moaned the calls like a presiding elder preaching at a revival meeting. Ah, there was my key— I'd do the song in *G*.

Well, that was the beginning. I was definitely on my way. But when I got started, I found that many other considerations also went into the composition. Ragtime had usually sacrificed melody for an exhilarating syncopation. My aim would be to combine ragtime syncopation with a real melody in the spiritual tradition. There was something from the tango that I wanted too. The dancers at Dixie Park had convinced me that there was something racial in their response to this rhythm, and I had used it in a disguised form in the "Memphis Blues." Indeed, the very word "tango," as I now know, was derived from the African "tangana," and signified this same tom-tom beat. This would figure in my introduction, as well as in the middle strain.

In the lyric I decided to use Negro phraseology and dialect. I felt then, as I feel now, that this often implies more than well-chosen English can briefly express. My plot centered around the wail of a lovesick woman for her lost man, but in the telling of it I resorted to the humorous spirit of the bygone coon songs. I used the folk blues' three-line stanza that created the twelve-measure strain.

The primitive Southern Negro as he sang was sure to bear down on the third and seventh tones of the scale, slurring between major and minor. Whether in the cotton fields of the Delta or on the levee up St. Louis way, it was always the same. Till then, however, I had never heard this slur used by a more sophisticated Negro, or by any white man. I had tried to convey this effect in "Memphis Blues" by introducing flat thirds and sevenths (now called "blue notes") into my song, although its prevailing key was the major; and I carried this device into my new melody as well. I also struck upon the idea of using the dominant seventh as the opening chord of the verse. This was a distinct departure, but as it turned out, it touched the spot.

In the folk blues the singer fills up occasional gaps with words like "Oh, lawdy" or "Oh, baby" and the like. This meant that in writing a melody to be sung in the blues manner one would have to provide gaps or waits. In my composition I decided to embellish the piano and orchestra score at these points. This kind of business is called a "break"; entire books of different "breaks" for a single song can be found on the music counters today, and the breaks become a fertile source of the orchestral improvisation which became the essence of jazz. In the chorus I used plagal chords to give spiritual effects in the harmony. Altogether, I aimed to use all that is characteristic of the Negro from Africa to Alabama. By the time I had done all this heavy thinking and remembering, I figured it was time to get something down on paper, so I wrote, "I hate to see de even' sun go down." And if you ever had to sleep on the cobbles down by the river in St. Louis, you'll understand that complaint.

St. Louis had come into the composition in more ways than one before the sun peeped through my window. So when the song was completed, I dedicated the new piece to Mr. Russell Gardner, the St. Louis man who had liked "Jogo Blues," and I proudly christened it the "St. Louis Blues." The same day on Pee Wee's cigar stand I orchestrated the number and jotted down scores for the men of my band.

The song was off my chest, and secretly I was pleased with it, but I could scarcely wait for the public verdict. Blurry-eyed from loss of sleep, I went with the band to the evening's engagement on the Alaskan Roof.

The one-step, maxixe and other dances had been done to the tempo of "Memphis Blues," which the Vernon Castles slowed up to introduce their original dance, the fox-trot. When "St. Louis Blues" was written the tango was the vogue. I tricked the dancers by arranging a tango introduction, breaking abruptly then into a low-down blues. My eyes swept the floor anxiously, then suddenly I saw the lightning strike. The dancers seemed electrified. Something within them came suddenly to life. An instinct that wanted so much to live, to fling its arms and to spread joy, took them by the heels. By this I was convinced that my new song was accepted.

When the evening was over, the band piled into cabs and followed me home to celebrate the birth of the new blues. But Maggie, arms akimbo and rolling pin poised, was waiting for Jiggs at the door. I had been away from home twenty four hours, burning up worlds of energy to produce a song, but maybe I should have stated where I was going and what I intended to do. Failing to make that clear, I presume, the fault was mine. But it's an awkward thing to announce in advance your intention of composing a song hit between midnight and dawn. The talk more naturally follows the act, and that is what ultimately happened in my case.

The men of the band got a big kick out of my domestic drama. But after all, heads are made to be lumped in this funny-paper world—aren't they?

A criticism leveled at the "St. Louis Blues" by the trombonist of our band was that it needed a vamp, a vamp in the prevailing manner, to allow more time for the singer.

"Never. Never!" I exploded.

But the next day a pause mark was placed over the final note in the introduction in order to favor the singer with the required delay, and with that "St. Louis Blues" was completed, born in an age of vamps, September, 1914, without a vamp. Two years had elapsed since I first published "Memphis Blues," five years since I played this first jazz composition using Osborne and the tenor sax that moaned like "a sinner on revival day." Well, they say that life begins at forty—I wouldn't know—but I was forty the year "St. Louis Blues" was composed, and ever since then my life has, in one sense at least, revolved around that composition.

Index of Authors,[1] Titles, and First Lines of Songs

[1] Including names of singers and other informants and persons who recorded them.

Index of Subjects, Names and Places